Culture, Ethnicity, and Justice in the South

Culture, Ethnicity, and Justice in the South

The Southern Anthropological Society, 1968–1971

Southern Anthropological Society

THE UNIVERSITY OF ALABAMA PRESS
Tuscaloosa

Note on this Edition: The page numbers from the original Proceedings are shown in addition to the new page numbers in the running feet for this edition.

Library of Congress Cataloging-in-Publication Data

Culture, ethnicity, and justice in the South : the Southern Anthropological Society, 1968-1971 / Southern Anthropological Society.
    p. cm.
  Reprint of the first five titles in the series: Southern Anthropological Society proceedings.
  Includes index.
  ISBN 0-8173-1448-2 (cloth : alk. paper) —
  ISBN 0-8173-5173-6 (pbk. : alk. paper)
  1. Ethnology—Southern States. 2. Folklore—Southern States. 3. Southern States—Social life and customs. 4. Southern Anthropological Society—History. I. Southern Anthropological Society. II. Southern Anthropological Society proceedings.
  GN560.S68C85 2005
  306'.0975—dc22   2004013042

Southern Anthropological Society Proceedings No. 1 (1968), *No. 2* (1968), *No. 3* (1969), *No. 4* (1971), *and No. 5* (1971) originally designed, typeset, and distributed by the University of Georgia Press for the Southern Anthropological Society. The design and typography of the original volumes are used by permission of the University of Georgia Press.

Contents

Introduction

Miles Richardson

AS A SENIOR member of the Southern Anthropological Society, I'm sure the younger scholars would forgive me if I began with something like, "It seems only yesterday that anthropologists from the far corners of the region came together in Atlanta in 1968 to usher in a new era for the South." As a matter of fact it was a long time ago, back to the Archaic at least, maybe even the Paleoindian era, getting close to a half century in any case. At that time, the South had a coterie of nationally prominent scholars, such as John Honigmann, John Gulick, Solon Kimball, and Arden King. Archaeologists, feasting on the WPA's bounty of shovel hands, had pioneered the penetration of the Old South: Charles Fairbanks of Florida, Hale Smith of Florida State, David DeJarnette of Alabama, Robert Wauchope of Tulane, William Haag of Louisiana State, and Art Kelly of the University of Georgia, to name a few. But in the 1960s— the golden age of grants and expansion—an influx of recent Ph.D. recipients, several from the region's fledgling doctoral programs, joined their betters: Charles Hudson from North Carolina, Miles Richardson from Tulane, and soon the first graduates from the new program at Georgia, Carole Hill and John Peterson. Also new were people such as Malcolm Webb and Michael Olien, who ventured into the region from programs at Michigan and Oregon. Counting both the established and the freshly scrubbed but excluding the sociologists with whom we met, we numbered eighty-seven, not a lot from the perspective of today's abundance, but enough to produce the first Proceedings.

A major figure in the production of the first Proceedings—as well as the next ten or so—was Charles Hudson. He negotiated a most favorable publication agreement with the University of Georgia Press, became the series editor, and played a prominent role in bringing people together at the key symposium.

The first Proceedings devotes itself to a field just crystallizing as a separate subject of specialization, medical anthropology. Among the papers are surveys of the newly emerging field, analyses of contemporary mental health conditions, and several examinations of folk practices. One of the latter—

close to my heart, if not my mouth—is "pica," or more generally, *geophagy*. A fieldworker hasn't really arrived until the moment when he or she can ask, "Do people around here eat dirt?"

On the agenda of this first Proceeding, and in the very formation of SAS, is the theme of justice, implicit for some, more vocal for others, but constant and strong in all. Anthropology's concern for the human species emerged early as a commitment to set the record straight. Setting straight a record that ideologues (if not demagogues) had twisted almost at will to suit the powers that be, required the application of anthropological research to the region's languages, cultures, archaeologies, and human compositions, which SAS did from its very beginning.

For the organizational meeting, we met jointly with the Southern sociologists. Then for the next meeting, we abandoned the sociologists and met on our own. Some had vaguely mentioned pooling efforts with the well-established Southeastern Archaeological Conference, which met in the fall. But no one, especially the archaeologists, appeared particularly anxious for such a union. In addition, by staying with a spring meeting, we were hopeful that the southern sunshine would tempt our northern colleagues to leave the ice and snow and contribute their voices to ours in articulating critical themes of the day. Sure enough, Elizabeth Eddy, chair of the key symposium, persuaded Conrad Arensberg from New York City and Han Buechler from Syracuse to join the southern contingent in pursuit of another emergent specialty, urban anthropology. Arensberg rose to the occasion, as he always did, with a panoramic, cross-cultural view of the urban, and John Gulick closed the volume with a succinct discussion of research strategies for a discipline committed to the small and the intimate.

For the third meeting, Arden King asked Stephen Tyler and me to organize a program to be held in New Orleans. I had the responsibility of putting the program together, while Steve, who was at Tulane at the time and was still this side of postmodernism, understandably, became chair of the key symposium and editor of the resulting Proceedings. In the freshness of our Ph.D.'s, Steve and I wanted to expose the foundations of the field, so we settled on the theme of concepts and assumptions in contemporary anthropology. The Tulane environment encouraged us to bring together members of all four major fields, so Francis Johnston from UT at Austin sought commonality in human behavior, culture, and biology, while William Haag of LSU exposed the presuppositions of archaeologists. In the absence of a linguist, Jan Brukman of the University of Illinois acknowledged the role of the linguist paradigm in the development of the then "new ethnography," one of several "news" that "flowered" in the 1960s. Our greatest success, however, came through implementing the "southern strategy" of warm weather garnished by the delights of New Orleans to persuade Eric Wolf, then at Michigan, to kick off the key symposium with a wonderful lacing together of American anthropologists and American society.

The 1970 meeting in Athens was a banner year, producing not just one

Proceeding but two. Proceeding Four, organized and edited by J. Kenneth Morland from Randolph-Macon Women's College at Lynchburg, demonstrates that the South, a regional subculture to be sure, was not all that "Solid"—that is, White, Evangelical, and Democrat—as so many stereotypically assumed. A series of compact papers range over the landscape from Tennessee to Louisiana and bring forth black divines, gypsies, mountain kin, plain folk, Native Americans, and of course, the 1960s epithet, "hippies." Subjects likewise addressed include drinking, hunting, shouting, and dying. To Morland's credit, not one mint julep, not one verandah, and not one Southern "gentleman" grace the work. "Being relevant," Morland explains in his introduction, "characterized the period's most ardent desire," and this volume spoke directly to that desire. As did the next one.

Red, White, and Black contains the papers of the key symposium organized by the ever-dedicated Charles Hudson. The subtitle declares the volume to be about Indians in the Old South, and in order to address these people, the authors divide themselves into two parts, each with a commentator. Part I concerns itself with the time of European contact. Led off by a geographer, who promotes the use of early maps as a means of recovering southeastern Native American landscapes, a physical anthropologist, a linguist (from that great "Southern" metropolis, Berkeley, California), and a historical archaeologist follow with comprehensive assessments of each subject during the critical period that saw the birth of the "Old" South. In his overview of the chapters, Charles Fairbanks of Florida applauds the chapters as the "first general synthesis in many years" and then marvels at the spate of recent publication of documents and new editions of classic studies generated by the expansionist 1960s.

Part II began with a historical review of the antebellum elite's mixed attitude toward the native inhabitants and the slaves who replaced them. Even as they pushed Native Americans westward, the elite talked, albeit sporadically, of the nobility of the vanishing Indian, while the best they could say about African Americans was, "We treat our Negras well." Another historian ponders the case of the non-plantation whites in the early Old South. Two factors, he concludes, kept them tied to the mythology of Southern egalitarianism: the availability of land once the Native Americans were "removed," which allowed at least a few onto the road to elite status, and the presence of a stigmatized underclass, which "glorified" their whiteness. In the following chapter, an anthropologist pursues the similar theme of divide and rule, but between the Indians and African Americans. Considering the presence of the French and Spanish, along with the two minorities, there were many antagonisms for the English to stir up and promote to their benefit, which they did quite successfully. In the next chapter, an anthropologist argues that the very label, "Old South," reduces the region to the planter-slave stereotype and blinds us to the position of Native Americans in the composition of Southern society. Historian, Charles Crowe of Georgia, concludes Part II with a well-fashioned comment that underscores the different positions of Native Americans and African Americans in Southern mythology. It is as if the Europeans stripped African American slaves of any admirable trait and applied those to Native Americans, *after* the Indians were "removed."

And so ended the fifth Proceeding of the Southern Anthropological Society. Like its predecessors, it brought attention to the emergence of anthropologists in a region long shunned by the established doctoral programs in the Northeast, Midwest, and on the West Coast. Southern anthropologists, either *in* or *of* the South, in Carole Hill's terms, showed to a critical, revolutionary, flower-loving, civil-rights promoting generation just how relevant anthropology was to the goals of that generation. Today, the younger set and us crotchety Archaics must continue to proclaim that anthropologists, here in a region of such tragic dimensions and in a country so skewed off course from the 1960s, work for justice through a four-field documentation of the human endeavor.

Proceedings No. 1.
Essays on Medical Anthropology

Edited by Thomas Weaver

SOUTHERN ANTHROPOLOGICAL SOCIETY

Founded 1966

ESSAYS ON MEDICAL ANTHROPOLOGY

Table of Contents

PREFACE

This publication is the first of a projected series to be issued annually by the Southern Anthropological Society. The Society, hereafter cited as SAS, is the youngest of the regional anthropology societies, yet its publication program is the most ambitious. An explanation of how this came about follows.

SAS was born in New Orleans on April 8, 1966. Meeting jointly with the Southern Sociological Society, 42 of the anthropologists present came together for an organizational meeting. The officers elected were charged with arranging for a 1967 spring meeting and with drawing up a constitution. In the months that followed, SAS officers fulfilled their stated duties and went one step beyond in drawing preliminary plans for publication of certain papers to be presented at the 1967 meeting.

The second annual meeting of SAS, again in conjunction with the Southern Sociological Society, was held in Atlanta, Georgia on March 30-April 1, 1967. Some 87 anthropologists registered, and a diversified program of papers was well attended. Thomas Weaver and Ralph Patrick organized two sessions on medical anthropology since this was the area that the officers had selected for publication provided that SAS members approved.

The 1967 business meeting was scheduled so that the adoption of a constitution came up first. Next, officers were elected according to provisions in the constitution. Thirdly, a plan for the annual publication of Proceedings was approved as a means of implementing the primary purpose of SAS. This is stated in the SAS constitution as "the promotion of anthropology in the southern United States."

The system envisaged for future SAS Proceedings is essentially the same as that which gave rise to this volume. Each year SAS officers will pick a theme or subject to stress at the next annual meeting. Normally, two or more programs will be built around this theme from invited papers. An editor, chosen by SAS officers, will select the articles to be published from the invited papers. The chosen editor will normally be the program chairman or chairman of the "theme" sessions.

SAS will include volunteered papers on a variety of subjects at its annual meetings. Their very variety, however, prevents them from becoming a unified volume. Unity is essential if for no other reason than increasing the saleability of Proceedings. SAS membership is too small to warrant printing for its members alone.

The goals of Proceedings are admittedly pragmatic. It is designed to promote anthropology in the South. It is intended to increase attendance at SAS meetings and thus get Southern anthropologists to work together for their common good. It has an implicit message to anthropologists in other areas that anthropology in the South is now moving into the

v

discipline's mainstream. It is even hoped that budding anthropologists will no longer exclude our area from job consideration. It may surprise some people that there are enough anthropologists in the South to organize a society, let alone sponsor a publication program.

Behind the goals must lie a consistent philosophy for our editors. Already stated is the necessity of a unified publication. In addition, a high standard of quality must be maintained. This starts with the invited papers and continues through necessary revisions and time-consuming editorial work. Both Charles Hudson, proceedings editor, and Thomas Weaver, editor of this volume, have had the difficult task of setting up the initial model. It seems obvious to me that they have already established a high level for future editors to maintain.

SAS is indebted to the University of Georgia Press and its director, Ralph Stephens, for bringing out this volume. The University of Georgia Press will also print subsequent numbers of the series.

The University of Georgia Department of Sociology and Anthropology has in effect been a joint sponsor of these Proceedings. The Department has furnished typing services, materials, and, most importantly, has provided us with our proceedings editor, Charles Hudson.

Frank J. Essene
President, SAS

MEDICAL ANTHROPOLOGY:
TRENDS IN RESEARCH AND MEDICAL EDUCATION

Thomas Weaver
University of Pittsburgh

Introduction

A complete delineation of the field of medical anthropology, even considering its relative youthfulness, would require more time and space than is presently available. Earlier summaries have been written by Caudill (1953) and Polgar (1962). The purpose of this paper, less comprehensive by comparison, is to provide a brief contextual framework for understanding contributions in this field.

Medical anthropology is that branch of applied anthropology which deals with various aspects of health and disease and hence, strictly speaking, although primarily the contribution of anthropologists, it must also include those contributions from non-anthropologists which relate cultural, cross-cultural, comparative, or ethnic material to medicine.

It may be useful to distinguish, as Straus (1957) has done for sociology, between the anthropology of medicine and anthropology in medicine. In this sense anthropology in medicine includes the applied or more directly related contributions made by anthropologists involved in research, teaching, administration, and consulting in medical and public health settings. Anthropology of medicine would then encompass basic or background anthropological contributions to the understanding of sociocultural factors in health and disease which result from research by anthropologists who are usually outside of a formal medical setting.

There are many factors which have led behavioral scientists to do research on medically related problems and to become associated with medical and public health schools in teaching, research, and other activities. Some of these factors derive from broad scale social changes and from changes in the medical profession itself. These include the enormous growth of voluntary health insurance programs (Health Insurance Council 1965); governmental activity in social legislation (Coggeshall 1965); and the increased investment of private philanthropic foundations (Rusk 1967). These trends have resulted in an explosion in medical knowledge and technology, in greater construction of health facilities than before, and in experimentation in new health and medical programs. A greatly expanded and improved communications media together with a continued high level of public education has resulted in greater public knowledge and sophistication in medical matters.

Changes and trends in medicine include increasing specialization,

1

the continued low production of physicians by medical schools, the movement of medical care away from the home to the office and then to the hospital, an interest in international medicine and in the medical economics
of developing countries, and a concern for multiple disease causation,
epidemiology, and psychosomatic medicine.

The total effect of these changes has been a depersonalization
of medicine, a greatly increased demand for services and for application
of the latest medical knowledge, an increased criticism of the physician,
a greater number of successful malpractice suits, increased costs of medical care and medical education, fragmentation of communication between
the doctor and his patient, and the segmented treatment of the patient by
many different specialists.

As the physician and medical educator has become more concerned
with the increasing complexity of these problems and the growing health
needs of the nation, he has gradually turned to the behavioral sciences for
help in obtaining that useful information about social and cultural factors
of human life which lies beyond the scope of the biological sciences.

Anthropological Research

Long before their research was offered to or requested by the field
of medicine, representatives of all subdisciplines of anthropology were
concerned with the collection of data pertaining to health and disease.
Physical anthropologists have long been associated with teaching anatomy
in medical schools. Anthropological linguists are involved in kinesic
studies and research in communication and illness behavior. Archaeologists
and physical anthropologists have long been interested in the diseases
of palaeoanthropic man. The subdiscipline most concerned with medical
subjects, however, has been social and cultural anthropology.

Perhaps a special mention of physical anthropology is necessary
because of its neglect in other discussions of medical anthropology. Washburn (1951) has described the new directions away from a science of measurement to one concerned with heredity and process which physical anthropology
has taken as a result of the influence of genetics and a greater concern with
functional anatomy. Along with this has gone a willingness to accept
techniques which have been developed in connection with medical technology (Cobb 1956). This shift has provided many new and interesting contributions to genetics, anatomy, and medicine (Pollitzer 1963).

Examples of the use of physical anthropological data in medicine
are too numerous to attempt a detailed listing. Some of these include the
work of physical anthropologists working with archaeologists in the field
of paleopathology (Kerley and Bass 1967) and the correlation of sickle cell
anemia with malaria and the development of agriculture (Wisenfeld 1967;
Livingstone 1958). Other examples of the uses of physical and cultural

2

anthropology in medicine are summarized by Alland (1966).

Present trends indicate a continued close linkage between physical anthropology and medicine in education and research. Some have predicted, for example, that eventually all classes in anatomy given in schools of medicine will be taught by physical anthropologists. However, a good case for the opposite point of view could be made based on the knowledge that anthropology is not producing the physical anthropologists needed to fill the requirements of departments of anthropology.

The research contributions from social and cultural anthropology have been more extensive than those from other anthropological subdisciplines. One of the best early assessments of the field has been provided by Caudill (1953). Contributions are reviewed under the following headings: (1) primitive medicine in nonliterate societies; (2) the organization and practice of medicine in contemporary western society; (3) psychosomatic medicine, social medicine, and multiple stress in disease; and (4) types of disorders. It is not necessary to review again the contributions of anthropologists in these various categories; it is worthwhile mentioning, however, that some of the pioneer background studies are quite early, at least as early as contributions from other behavioral sciences.[1] Rivers (1924), for example, discussed the relations between medicine, magic, and religion, and Clements (1932) provided an early analysis of five basic concepts of disease. In the intervening years there have been many other contributions to the understanding of the cultural background of illness and health. It is interesting to note that many of the early direct contributions to the field have been by non-anthropologists. Ackerknecht (1942), a physician, has contributed many items in the area of primitive medicine. Even today there is much greater activity on the part of other behavioral scientists, particularly medical sociologists, than of anthropologists in producing direct contributions. In this connection it should be indicated that less than 30 percent of the 182 items in Caudill's (1953) bibliography can be identified as anthropological and that many of these are of a background nature.

Social anthropology has at least two dependency links to medical sociology in its applied research interests in medicine. Both are based on priority of appearance of sociology in the field. The first is that medical anthropology is guided to a certain extent by the types of problems it investigates in this area and the techniques it utilizes. The second has to do with the nature of the society within which medical anthropology is practiced. Traditionally anthropologists work in aboriginal and peasant societies, but the majority of organizations in which anthropologists work as medical anthropologists are located in urban and complex society settings. Moreover, the administrators and executives who decide on whether or not to hire anthropologists are generally concerned with the problems of complex societies and not with those of primitive peoples.

3

A more recent discussion of anthropological research which is medically related has been provided by Polgar (1962). Polgar has classified studies by social scientists in the field of health into four broad areas: (1) the dynamics of health status involving pre-existing conditions pertaining to the client, such as types of disorders or ecology of health and disease; (2) popular health culture, including descriptions of values, attitudes, and practices regarding health; (3) health personnel and health action, consisting of studies relating to the values, notions and behaviors of professional health actors, their training and careers, their place in the larger society, the social organization of the settings in which they work, and data about health action and the client in a particular kind of setting; and (4) studies of the role of the social scientist in the medical setting.

Anthropology in Medical Education

There are far fewer anthropologists involved in teaching in medical and public health schools than the numbers who have contributed to research, although their numbers have been steadily increasing over the past fifteen to twenty years. With this increase in numbers has gone an increase in curricular hours and in types of courses and topics devoted to anthropology and behavioral science. This has called for a modification of behavioral science teaching techniques and for an accommodation of materials to fit the objectives of medical education.

The arrival of the behavioral scientist in the medical and public health schools is relatively recent. One survey (New and May 1965) indicates that prior to 1956, there were only 20 behavioral scientists employed as educators in 15 schools, most of which were medical schools.[2] Between 1956 and 1961, 72 were hired in 31 schools, and between 1962 and 1964, 126 were employed in 21 schools, for a total of 218 behavioral scientists teaching in 67 schools, of whom 24 are anthropologists. The total survey also indicated that there were 353 other social scientists involved in research and administration or other services (clinical psychology) in medical and public health schools in the U.S. and Canada.

There have been several experiments in developing separate departments of behavioral science within schools of medicine. Most notable are those at Kentucky and Temple, with plans for such departments at the new medical school at Hershey, Pennsylvania and elsewhere. However, behavioral scientists are most frequently associated with departments of psychiatry within schools of medicine, either individually or in divisions or subdepartments. Therefore it is not surprising that the development of behavioral science has often been closely linked with the development of psychiatry. Webster (n.d.) has identified four trends in this connection which have affected behavioral science and psychiatry, namely (1) an increase in the total number of hours alloted to the two fields in the total

4

curriculum, (2) a shift in curriculum hours alloted from the clinical to the preclinical years, (3) an increase in interdepartmental and elective time and teaching, and (4) bolder experimentation in curriculum planning. With regard to time allowed for teaching, Webster found that the average number of psychiatry and behavioral science curriculum hours in 93 schools has increased from less than 26 hours in 1914 to 92 hours in 1940, 202 hours in 1951, and 362 hours in 1966.

The goal of the medical anthropologist as a teacher in schools of medicine and public health is to demonstrate the cultural, social, and environmental factors which impinge on the health situation. Sometimes these are negative factors, and it becomes the anthropologist's duty to demonstrate this and to provide insights into how these barriers can be overcome. Paul (1956) has indicated four contributions which can be made by the anthropologist-teacher. These are that social science concepts must be conveyed in a palatable manner, that the anthropologist must instill in the student a respect for cultural differences and at the same time convey that culture is more than a collection of customs. The fourth contribution has to do with making the public health- or physician-practitioner realize that he, too, has cultural values and preconceptions which may possibly impede his technical effectiveness.

The type of anthropological material presented in medical and public health settings has been reflected in the types of courses offered, the concepts and illustrative case materials presented, and these have often been restricted by the overall objectives of the parent department and school and by the number and qualifications of faculty available.

Titles of courses in which anthropologists are most frequently involved include those which consider one or more of the following areas: Human Behavior, Human Growth and Development, Communication and Interviewing, Health and Society, Epidemiology, The Human Community, and Human Ecology. Aside from the obvious subject of sociocultural differences or cross-cultural comparison in health and illness, the anthropologist is often called upon for presentations on one or more of the following topics: functionalism; biological and social evolution; cross-cultural patterns of child rearing; culture and personality; social adaptation to stress and the environment; cultural attitudes toward death; the concept of role; community structure and health behavior; religion and medicine; and ethnocentrism and cultural relativity.

In dealing with these topics, however, it is probably wise to remember Devereux's emphasis on the importance of the concept "culture".

> ...regardless of the variety of cultures, the "experience of having a culture" is a universal trait, and man functions as a "creator, creature, manipulator and transmitter of culture"

5

everywhere and in the same way... (Devereux 1956, paraphrasing Simmons 1942).

The provision of an understanding of _culture_ and not _cultures_ is the real contribution which the anthropologist can make. As Devereux has so aptly stated with regard to psychiatry, but equally applicable to other medical fields:

> The anthropologist cannot make a real contribution to psychiatry if he simply acquires the jargon of that science, and is content for the rest just to "trot out" his little ethnographic museum of esoteric curios. He can make a real contribution to psychiatry only if he remains an anthropologist, a student of culture, defined as a patterned way of experiencing both extra-social and social reality (Devereux 1956:47).

Once the course and its content has been selected, the type of material presented depends on the availability of a particular kind of scientist, on his special interests, and on departmental size. The total number of faculty also affects the content of course materials; schools with small faculties and relatively few course hours available tend to be less comprehensive, whereas those schools with larger and more varied behavioral science faculties are more comprehensive in their approach and have as a goal the synthesis of behavioral science and medicine.[3]

Problems and Prospects

The arrival of the anthropologist in a new field and academic setting has not been without problems. These problems have involved difficulties in accommodating his materials and teaching methods to medical curriculum requirements, in resolving methodological and conceptual differences between himself and the medical field, in adjusting to a different social and academic environment, and in compensating for the inadequate development of his own science.

The following discussion of some of the problems inherent in the addition of social scientists to medical school faculties is based in part on a listing of questions by Thurnblad and McCurdy (1967). One of the points they raise has to do with the philosophical isolation of the behavioral scientist from the medical faculty. This is undoubtedly based on the basically natural science and utilitarian case study approach which forms the background of the physician as contrasted to the primarily liberal art and humanistic approach inculcated as a background for the anthropologist. One may also add that not only is there a philosophical gap, but also one

6

of social status as well. The anthropologist, as a part of the basic science
rather than the clinical science faculty, and a late arrival at that, is almost always at the bottom of the status heirarchy in a medical setting.
This status gap is buttressed by the fact that medical schools do not always offer him senior positions, tenure, and salaries comparable with
physician faculty members. In addition he is also involved in the status
gap between physician and non-physician which transcends the medical
setting. The medical society is, generally speaking, closed to outsiders,
possibly for professional reasons, but the behavioral scientist is often
less integrated in the social than in the academic life.

His contacts with other social scientists may become limited because of his total, although peripheral, involvement in the medical setting.
For this reason it is always wise to encourage the anthropologist to continue his basic anthropological research interests along with his medical
interests and to associate with other anthropologists by providing a joint
appointment in a university department of anthropology or sociology. This
will also assure that he remains an anthropologist and does not become a
pseudo-physician, for it is only as an anthropologist that he has anything
to offer to medicine.

Physicians and students alike find it difficult to understand the
utility of the anthropological contribution to the education of the physician.
The anthropologist must repeatedly justify his importance in the face of
this utilitarian attitude. Physicians often believe that the social scientist is not prepared in his graduate training to teach medical students.
The reason for this may be that the behavioral scientist does not always
have sufficient curricular time available to adequately develop his topic,
so that he is frequently forced to present small bits of anthropological
data in lecture form. Because of his maturity, the medical student prefers seminar and small group discussion learning as opposed to lecture
preparations. He resists lectures even when they involve material which
he believes is more directly linked to becoming a physician, so it is understandable when he dislikes lectures which are believed not to be directly related to this objective. These not only involve lectures in the behavioral sciences, but also those in chemistry, biochemistry, anatomy, physiology, and psychiatry. Since the behavioral scientist occupies a lower status
position it is easier for the student to criticize and resist materials involving anthropology and behavioral science.

Not all of these problems are solely related to the medical setting
or environment. Undoubtedly there are many which may be attributed to the
state of knowledge, level of accomplishment, and ability and willingness
of anthropology as a field to provide the necessary kind of information and
education required by medicine.

If the physician is reluctant to accept the behavioral scientist on
an equal status plane, the behavioral scientist, too, and particularly the

7

anthropologist, has been reluctant to assume a dependent role in the medical setting. This reluctance is reflected in several ways, among them the small number of anthropologists who are interested in applied and medical anthropology, and their reluctance, once they have accepted employment in such a setting, to be labeled "medical" anthropologists. This is also reflected in the anthropologist's reluctance to assume the cloak of change agent. Mead (1956) has referred to this as anthropological conservatism and explains the anthropologist's position against changing cultures as deriving from his interest in studying whole cultures and his fear that they will disappear before he can record everything needed to answer questions for future scientists. The anthropologist is sometimes also reluctant to pioneer new methods and techniques. Part of his conservatism may be attributed to his felt responsibility for all forseeable effects of any changes to which he contributes his specialized skills. On the other hand, he is reluctant to introduce any change which will "contaminate his laboratory specimen" as part of his self-image as a "pure scientist".

It may well be that anthropology and the other behavioral and social sciences are not yet sufficiently prepared in terms of theoretical development to provide the type of action-oriented knowledge required by medicine. Merton (1964) has stated that it is an error to compare the present state of development of sociology (and the other behavioral sciences as well) to the ability of physics, medicine, and other natural sciences to solve contemporary problems in their fields. He feels that it is an error to appraise social science, once and for all, on the basis of its present capacity to solve the large and urgent problems of society. Social science, like all civilization, is continually in the process of development and there is no providential dispensation providing that, at any given moment, science must be adequate to the entire array of problems confronting men at that moment.

> ...it is as though the status and promise of medicine in the seventeenth century had been forever judged by its ability to produce, then and there, a preventive or cure for cardiac diseases. Suppose that the problem had been widely acknowledged to be urgent - look at the growing rate of death from coronary thrombosis! - and it might well have been that the very importance of the problem would have obscured the entirely independent question of the adequacy of the medical science of 1600 (or 1800 or 1900) for solving that particular problem. Yet it is precisely this illogic which lies behind so much of practical demands currently made of sociology (and the other social sciences). Because war and exploitation and poverty and discrimination and psychological insecurity are plaguing

8

men in modern society, social science, if it is worth its
salt, must provide solutions for each and all of them. It
is possible, of course, that social scientists are as well
equipped to solve these urgent problems in 1955 as were
Harvey or Sydenham to identify, study and cure coronary
thrombosis in 1655 (Merton 1964:7-8).

This, of course, does not mean that because anthropology has not devised
all of the techniques of coping with the specialized problems of working
in a medical setting that it does not have the powers of development along
these lines.

NOTES

1. For other contributions see bibliographies by Polgar (1962), Simmons
(1963), and Pearsall (1963). The first is recommended for its analysis of
the field and the third for the large number of items it contains (over
3,000).

2. Permission for quotation granted by Dr. Peter New, Tufts University,
School of Medicine. Of course, Dr. New is dealing with educators in
the figures he uses. On the other hand, Straus (1957) lists 110 persons
in 1956 who identify themselves as medical sociologists who are not
necessarily linked with medical or public health facilities.

3. For more detailed discussion of behavioral science course content in
medical school curricula see Straus (1963, 1965) and Thurnblad and McCurdy
(1967).

REFERENCES

Alland, Alexander, Jr.
    1966   Medical Anthropology and the Study of Biological and
                Cultural Adaptation. American Anthropologist 68:40-51.
Caudill, William
    1950   Applied Anthropology in Medicine. In Anthropology To-
                Day, A. L. Kroeber, ed. (Chicago: University of Chicago
                Press), pp. 771-806.
Clements, Forrest E.
    1932   Primitive Concepts of Disease. University of California
                Publications In Archaeology and Ethnology 32:185-252.

9

Cobb, W. Montague
  1956 The Relationship of Physical Anthropology to Medicine.
       In <u>Some Uses of Anthropology: Theoretical and Applied</u>,
       Joseph B. Casagrande and Thomas Gladwin, eds.
       (Washington, D.C.: The Anthropological Society of
       Washington), pp. 83-93.

Coggeshall, Lowell T.
  1965 <u>Planning for Medical Progress Through Education</u>
       (Evanston, Illinois: Association of American Medical
       Colleges).

Devereux, George
  1956 Normal and Abnormal: The Key Problem of Psychiatric
       Anthropology. In <u>Some Uses of Anthropology:</u>
       <u>Theoretical and Applied</u>, Joseph B. Casagrande and Thomas
       Gladwin, eds. (Brooklyn: Theo. Gaus' Sons, Inc.).

Health Insurance Council
  1965 <u>A Quarter Century of Progress in Financing Health Care</u>
       (New York: Health Insurance Council).

Hrdlička, A.
  1919 <u>Physical Anthropology: Its Scope and Aims: Its History</u>
       <u>and Present Status in the United States</u> (Philadelphia:
       Wistar Institute).

Kerley, Ellis R. and William M. Bass
  1967 Paleopathology: Meeting Ground for Many Disciplines.
       <u>Science</u> 157 (3789) : 638-644.

Livingstone, R.
  1958 Anthropological Implications of Sickle Cell Gene
       Distribution in West Africa. <u>American Anthropologist</u>
       60:533-562.

Mead, Margaret
  1956 Applied Anthropology, 1955. In <u>Some Uses of Anthropology</u>:
       <u>Theoretical and Applied</u>, Joseph B. Casagrande and Thomas
       Gladwin, eds. (Brooklyn: Theo. Gaus' Sons, Inc.).

Merton, Robert K.
  1964 <u>Social Theory and Social Structure</u> (New York: Free Press
       of Glencoe.).

New, Peter Kong-ming and J. Thomas May
  1965 Report on Teaching of Social Sciences in Medical and
       Public Health Schools. Presented at the Business Meeting
       of the Medical Sociology Section, American Sociological
       Association, Chicago, Illinois, August 30, 1965.

Paul, Benjamin
  1956 Anthropology and Public Health. In <u>Some Uses of</u>
       <u>Anthropology: Theoretical and Applied</u>, Joseph B. Casagrande
       and Thomas Gladwin, eds. (Brooklyn: Theo. Gaus' Sons, Inc.).

10

Pearsall, Marion
1963   Medical Behavioral Science: A Selected Bibliography of
            Cultural Anthropology, Social Psychology and Sociology
            in Medicine (Lexington: University of Kentucky Press).
Polgar, Steven
1962   Health and Human Behavior: Areas of Interest Common
            to the Social and Medical Sciences. Current Anthropology
            3:159-205.
Pollitzer, William S.
1963   Hemoglobins, Haptoglobins and Transferrins in Man.
            American Anthropologist 65:1295-1313.
Rivers, W. H. R.
1924   Medicine, Magic and Religion (New York: Harcourt,
            Brace and Company).
Rusk, Howard A.
1967   Demand for Doctors: Medical School Graduates Described
            as Insufficient to Meet Rise in Needs. (New York Times:
            October 15, 1967).
Simmons, Leo W.
1942   Sun Chief (New Haven: Yale University Press).
Simmons, Ozzie G.
1963   Social Research in Health and Medicine: A Bibliography.
            In Handbook of Medical Sociology, Howard E. Freeman,
            Sol Levine and Leo G. Reeder, eds. (Englewood Cliffs,
            New Jersey: Prentice-Hall, Inc.), pp. 493-581.
Straus, Robert
1957   The Nature and Status of Medical Sociology. American
            Sociological Review 22:200-204.
1963   A Role for Behavioral Science in a University Medical
            Center, The Annals of the American Academy of Political
            and Social Science 340.00 108
1965   Behavioral Science in the Medical Curriculum. The
            Annals of the New York Academy of Science 128:599-606.
Thurnblad, Robert J. and R. Layton McCurdy
1967   Human Behavior and the Student Physician. Journal of
            Medical Education 42:158-162.
Washburn, Sherwood L.
1951   The New Physical Anthropology. Transactions of the
            New York Academy of Sciences, Series II. Vol. 13, No. 7,
            pp. 298-304.

11

Webster, Thomas G.
    n.d.   Psychiatry and Behavioral Science Curriculum Hours
                in U.S. Schools of Medicine and Osteopathy. Mimeograph
                Report. (Now published in The Journal of Medical Education
                42:687-696, 1967).
Wisenfeld, Stephen L.
    1967   Sickle Cell Trait in Human Biological and Cultural Evolution.
                Science 157(3793):1134-1140.

12

ROUSSEAU AND THE DISAPPEARANCE OF SWADDLING
AMONG WESTERN EUROPEANS

Charles Hudson and Helen Phillips
The University of Georgia

"Swaddling" refers to the custom of tightly wrapping the trunk and limbs of infants in cloth or some other material. Virtually all Western European peoples are familiar with the word "swaddle" or with a similar word such as German windeln, French emmailoter, Spanish fajar, or Italian fasciare. However, other than historically minded anthropologists and physicians, relatively few people know what "swaddle" in the anthropological sense refers to. On the basis of a very informal survey, we found that about fifty per cent of the people interviewed had no idea what the word means, while the rest believed it refers to a kind of cloth, usually rags or bits of cloth, or to a soft, enfolding cloth. Thus, "swaddling" is a linguistic oddity--a word known to all, but conveying to most an erroneous meaning or no meaning whatever.

The reason for this oddity is, of course, that the word occurs in the Bible, and particularly in the passage in the Nativity which is read and enacted every Christmas: "And she brought forth her first born son, and wrapped him in swaddling clothes, and laid him in a manger" (Luke 2:7). Translators of the Bible into Western European languages had no trouble with the word for swaddling because the custom was practiced in similar form throughout Western Europe. Later, the custom was abandoned, and as a consequence we have the anomaly of a well-known word that has an erroneous meaning or no meaning at all.

The custom of swaddling invites our attention for two reasons. The first is that the custom has an extraordinarily wide distribution in time and space. We should examine with great care both the practices and the rationales attached to such an ubiquitous custom. The second reason is that the custom has apparently been abandoned only by Western Europeans and by peoples who have been influenced by Western European pediatrics. We should not only examine the rationales for practicing the custom, but also the reasons for its abandonment.

For convenience, we will divide the explanatory rationales for swaddling into two categories: instrumental and expressive (Beattie 1964:202-217). Apparently, all people who practice the custom offer both kinds of explanation. An instrumental explanation is one that accords with our own sense of cause and effect or usefulness. For example, many people who practice swaddling say that it protects the infant from the elements and from certain kinds of injury, such as insect bites. Also, they often say that it makes the infant easier to handle (Phillips 1967). These are instrumental explanations which we immediately understand. In contrast, expressive

13

explanations claim that swaddling does something for the child on grounds that we consider unacceptable. For example, many people say that swaddling makes children strong, or that it causes them to develop in aesthetically pleasing ways, or that it causes them to develop into humans as opposed to animals (Phillips 1967).

Distribution of Swaddling

Swaddling was generally practiced in the New World in association with the cradle board. Basically, the cradle board is a rigid frame made of reeds, basketry, or boards to which the swaddled infant is secured shortly after birth, and on which he remains generally until the onset of walking. Strapped to the cradle board, the infant lies in an extended position, his arms next to his sides, for almost the entire day, being removed periodically for cleaning. The infant is protected by the rigidity of the frame which distributes to the entire body any shock resulting from being knocked about or dropped. Similarly, the head of the infant is often protected by an encircling hoop attached near the top of the cradle board. By draping a cloth over the hoop the child is protected from dust, insects, and direct rays from the sun.

Early European travelers and explorers documented the use of the cradle board among virtually all the native peoples of North and South America (Mason 1889). Although their descriptions of cradle boards themselves are often satisfactory, little or no mention was made of the cultural practices or of the values and beliefs associated with them. Instead, reflecting their own beliefs and customs, they usually limited themselves to a commentary on the cruelty of the practice (Mason 1889).

Our best information on beliefs and values associated with the cradle board comes from the Navahos, many of whom continue to use cradle boards today. In addition to various instrumental explanations, the Navahos say that the use of the cradle board causes the infant to grow straight and strong. They attach considerable sentiment to them. For example, a Navaho man or woman will point proudly to a cradle board hanging in their parent's hogan, saying "that is the cradle on which I was reared." This value is symbolically expressed in the story the Navahos tell of the first cradle's creation. It was made for the Hero Twins, the sons of one of the principal Navaho divinities, Changing Woman. The earth gave the bottom boards; the hoop was made from a rainbow; the foot-rests were of sunbeams; the side loops were of sheet lightning and the lacings of zigzag lightning (Kluckhohn 1947:52). All of these are important symbols in traditional Navaho arts and oral traditions.

In addition to the widespread practice of swaddling in the New World, the custom was practiced throughout the Old World with the exception of Africa south of the Sahara, Oceania, and parts of the Middle East and Asia. Its use by the ancient Hebrews is evidenced in both the Old and New Testaments,

14

but some evidence suggests that it was not practiced by the Egyptians (Abt and Garrison 1965:12). Later evidence of its use by Semitic speaking peoples occurs in the writings of Avicenna at the beginning of the first millenium A.D. (Gruner 1939:364), and its practice in some areas continues into the present era (Grandquist 1947:100). Some documentation exists for the practice of the custom in India and China (Dingwall 1931:88-92,99), and Japan (Lipton 1965:524-25), but its distribution is somewhat spotty and of unknown time depth. Additional research may show that its distribution in Asia is greater than our present evidence indicates. Further north, both in Europe and in Asia, the custom appears to have been universal. The oldest historical reference to swaddling we have been able to discover is in the "Hymn to Delian Apollo," a Greek hymn which is thought to have been composed between the eighth and sixth centuries B.C. (Evelyn-White 1936: 333). The oldest direct archaeological evidence comes from the Basketmakers of the Southwestern United States at around the beginning of the Christian era (McGregor 1941:212-213). However, this wide distribution suggests that the custom is much older--10,000 years or more--and that it was invented in Eurasia during the upper Paleolithic era.

As we have seen, in Western Europe the custom of swaddling goes back to the beginning of recorded history. In classical Greece, infants were swaddled and placed in a "shoe-shaped two-handled basket," in a "basket woven of twigs for winnowing corn" (Metter 1947:693), and in other kinds of restraining devices (Abt and Garrison 1965:34).[1] The physicians of both classical Greece and Rome advocated swaddling as a means of pressing the limbs and body of the infant into good shape (Still 1965:32; Ruhrah 1925:5). The notion that an infant would become deformed if it were not swaddled continued throughout the Middle Ages (Still 1965:32,264; Ruhrah 1925:34,73; Dingwall 1931:57). Other reasons given for swaddling during the Middle Ages were that it thickened and protected the infant's skin, and that it rested the infant after the ordeal of birth. In addition, they recognized that it provided warmth and protection in handling. As late as 1668 the Frenchman Francois Mauriceau advocated swaddling in a popular book, saying, "He must be thus swaddled to give his little body a straight figure, which is most decent and convenient for a Man and to accustom him to keep upon the feet, for else he would go upon all fours, as other Animals do (Mauriceau in Still 1965:264)."

The custom apparently was first questioned in Europe in the sixteenth century when some physicians warned against the improper use of swaddling (Ruhrah 1925:203). Nonetheless, they felt some support was necessary for the newly born infant and advocated its continued use. The custom was first seriously attacked by English and French intellectuals of the eighteenth century when they wrote about the misery, overheating, weight, and dirtiness of swaddling; they argued that people should allow nature to take its course without the "idle aids" of human ingenuity (Still 1965:379-80). Their greatest

15

complaint was that swaddling, especially very tight swaddling, did not allow the freedom, the liberty, which they felt was necessary. The French physician Leroy noted that swaddling often produced head deformation (Cf. Boas 1940:69,74). Other French physicians argued that swaddling violated a fundamental law of nature--liberty (Dingwall 1931:60).

Abandonment of swaddling seems to have begun earliest in England, and somewhat later in France and the United States. The task of documenting this gradual abandonment is difficult because the custom lingered among the lower strata of society far longer than among the upper strata. The Englishman Alexander Buchan wrote in 1808 that the custom had been abandoned within the memory of persons still living (Still 1965:422). However, other evidence shows that the custom continued to be practiced by some people in England several decades later. In 1826 an American physician asked that "the cruel practice . . . be forever laid aside (Dewees 1826:69)." In 1881, Oswald, another American, spoke against swaddling, saying that it should be used under no circumstances (1881:145). The "barrow-coat," which is described as being a "part of the old swaddling clothes" was used in America as late as 1892 (Earle 1903:310-311). Swaddling was in general usage by French peasants in 1853. In 1869 and again in 1870, Gueniot called attention to the new-born of France, "tied and bound round with swaddling clothes like a sausage" and laced tightly in a cradle. French physicians were concerned about the custom as late as 1892 (Dingwall 1931:55-56).

To summarize, Europeans voiced cautions about swaddling in the sixteenth and seventeenth centuries; English and French intellectuals in the eighteenth century argued that the custom should not be practiced; and the custom was generally but probably not completely abandoned by English and French speaking peoples by the end of the nineteenth century. The custom is still practiced in some sectors of society in Scandinavia, particularly among the Lapps, and by a few people in Mediterranean countries such as Italy (de Kok 1935:10-11), Albania, Armenia, (Coon 1950:172), and Greece (Friedl 1963:78). Although the official policy in Russia is that swaddling is old-fashioned and should be eschewed, many Russians still practice it (Gorer and Rickman 1950). They say that swaddling prevents self-inflicted harm, causes the infant to grow straight and strong, and allows the infant to sleep better (Mead 1954:400).

Abandonment

Considering the extraordinary age and provenience of swaddling, and the tenacity of the custom even in countries where its use was discouraged, we would do well to carefully examine the reasons for its abandonment by opponents in Western Europe. We find these arguments expressed in Jean Jacques Rousseau's _Emile_. We do not argue that Rousseau singlehandedly caused the custom to fall into disuse, though his ideas about childrearing

16

and education enjoyed wide circulation and influence; we have chosen him because he voices with articulateness and clarity ideas which were already in the air.

Rousseau had three main objections to swaddling. First, and to him most important, swaddling was unnatural. Unlike the noble savages, whose infants he presumed were left free to enjoy unfettered movement, swaddling imposed on the child the unnatural chains of civilized society.[2] Second, Rousseau believed that swaddling had deleterious emotional effects. The constriction of swaddling interfered with the infant's blood circulation, causing it to cry and become irritable by interfering with natural sleep. Third, Rousseau objected that swaddling prevented the child from stretching his limbs and growing strong (1901:10-11). As we shall presently see, the first of Rousseau's objections can be interpreted in quite a different way, and the other two objections are either false or can be seriously doubted.

Others have argued that swaddling, far from being unnatural, is a natural half-way house between the enclosed world of the womb and the freedom of the post-natal world. This point was made by the Greek physician Galen, in the second century A.D. (Lipton 1965:522-523). A more recent scientist, Clyde Kluckhohn, makes a similar point. Describing the cradle board customs of the Navaho, Kluckhohn notes that like the womb, the cradle board is a restricted environment, where support is always present, and where changes resulting from movement or from temperature fluctuations are minimized in their effects (1947:65-66).

Similarly, Wayne Dennis, who observed both Navaho and Hopi child rearing, points out that the restriction to which the child is subjected during the last months of intrauterine existence is even greater than the restriction of swaddling, although there are differences between the position in which the child is held in utero and in swaddling. In utero the infant is squeezed into a flexed position; the extremities are bent, and the arms ordinarily folded upon the chest. In contrast, when the infant is swaddled, or on a cradle board, the trunk is extended. The legs are stretched out, and the arms, which are held at the sides, are bound so that the elbow may bend only slightly. Dennis concluded that a totally unrestricted condition--the one with which Western Europeans are familiar--constitutes a contrast with prenatal conditions as great or greater than the swaddled condition (Dennis 1940:95-96).

Rousseau is not the last person to argue that swaddling causes frustration, and that this, in turn, leads to undesirable short-term emotional effects. The psychologist Watson, in a classic experimental demonstration of the frustration-aggression hypothesis, restrained an infant, observed subsequent crying and anger, and concluded that rage is an innate response to the unconditioned stimulus of movement restraint (1917:166-167). However, subsequent research by Levy suggests that Watson's restraint involved the use of forcible, probably painful pressure (1944:622, 669-70). More

17

recent research has been conducted by Lipton, Steinschneider, and Richmond; in carefully controlled experiments, these investigators found that swaddling significantly reduces excitability and increases sleep (1965:538).

Rousseau's last objection, that the swaddled infant cannot stretch his limbs and develop strength as well as an unswaddled child, is contradicted by recent evidence. The Navaho, as we have already seen, believe that the cradle board causes infants to grow straight and strong. They say that children who are not reared on the cradle board, who lie on sheepskins and roll about, develop into weak, sickly children (Kluckhohn 1947:55-6). The Russians likewise insist that swaddling develops the child's strength (Mead 1945:400). Wayne Dennis in his influential experimental study of the development of motor skills among Hopi children found confirmation for this claim. He found that infants who were swaddled exhibited the same motor activities in the same sequence as those who were not swaddled. Furthermore, he found that the infants who were swaddled actually walked two days earlier than unswaddled infants, although this difference is not statistically significant (1940:82).

Obviously, since strength is a precondition for motor skills, and since strength can only be acquired through exercise, the infants reared on cradle boards must have undergone some form of exercise. In a recent paper, Hudson has hypothesized that the use of the cradle board, and probably swaddling as well, induces isometric exercise (1966). Briefly, exercise may take two forms: isometric and isotonic. In isotonic exercise, the more familiar of the two, muscular movement occurs, whereas in isometric exercise the muscles are strained but not moved. Although a controversy has arisen over whether isometric exercise is superior to isotonic exercise, it is clear that isometric exercise can increase strength. Thus, merely by straining against his binding for short periods of time each day, the swaddled infant increases his strength isometrically. Hudson has also suggested that this form of exercise may be more suited to infants than unrestricted isotonic exercise. While isotonic exercise presupposes motor skills involving relatively precise bodily movements which are absent in newly born infants, isometric swaddling assumes no motor skills whatever.[3]

Conclusions

We have seen that swaddling, once universal among Western Europeans, has so throughly fallen into disuse the word no longer conveys any meaning to most people. Most American mothers, and many pediatricians as well, feel that our way of rearing infants is both "natural" and "scientific." However, the abandonment of swaddling among Western Europeans is not a chapter in the history of science, it is a chapter in the history of ideas. Swaddling began to go out of style at the very time the notion of progress and the Romantic movement began influencing European intellectuals, particularly

18

in England and France. Europeans ceased the practice of swaddling not because it was unscientific, but because of notions about man's natural freedom. Swaddling violates some of our basic values today perhaps even more strongly than when the custom was first questioned. American mothers are horrified when confronted with this custom (Bruch 1952:166). Our feeling is that physical restraint is so categorically wrong that it should not even be allowed in punishment; even when confronted with restraining psychotic patients from harming themselves, we prefer to do it with tranquilizers rather than with physical restraint.

Our purpose here has not, of course, been to advocate the readoption of the custom of swaddling. We have tried to establish why Western Europeans abandoned the custom, and in so doing we have suggested that the scientific grounds in favor of swaddling are perhaps as compelling as the scientific grounds for not swaddling. We have seen that in Western Europe, as elsewhere, child care practices are of such fundamental cultural importance they are underlaid with powerful social values (Phillips 1967:54-62). Although as we pointed out earlier, our information on beliefs and values associated with swaddling are at best inadequate, we are relatively assured that mothers in cultures practicing swaddling are horrified with our custom of allowing our infants to wallow helplessly in unrestricted and, from their point of view, harmful freedom. It must, to them, seem grossly unnatural, and perhaps inhuman.

NOTES

1. The verbal descriptions of these devices used in ancient and mediaeval Europe suggest that they were quite similar to the cradle boards of the New World.

2. The irony of this is that the majority of Rousseau's "natural" men practiced swaddling, which he regarded as "unnatural"; but several anthropologists, who have actually observed these "natural" men, feel that swaddling is perhaps more "natural" than the custom advocated by Rousseau and practiced by ourselves.

3. The Greeks in the time of Plato believed that restraint (or swaddling) plus some kind of gentle motion, as in being carried, increased strength.

> At Athens we find not only boys but sometimes old
> men rearing birds and training such creatures to fight one
> another. But they are far from thinking that the training
> they give them by exciting. . . . provides sufficient exer-
> cise; in addition to this, each man takes up his bird and

19

keeps it tucked away in his fist, if it is small, or under
his arm, if it is large, and in this way they walk many
a long mile in order to improve the condition, not of
their own bodies, but of these creatures. . . . shall
we. . . lay down a law that the pregnant woman shall
walk, and that the child, while still soft, shall be
moulded like wax, and be kept in swaddling clothes till
it is two years old (Plato, Vol. II. 1926:7-9)?

In addition, they apparently felt that this was a natural continuation
of pre-natal exercise (Ibid.).

REFERENCES

Abt, Arthur F. and Fielding H. Garrison
  1965   History of Pediatrics (Philadelphia: W. B. Saunders
       Company).

Beattie, John
  1964   Other Cultures: Aims, Methods and Achievements in
       Social Anthropology (New York: The Free Press of
       Glencoe).

Boas, Franz
  1940   Race, Language and Culture (New York: The Macmillan
       Company).

Bruch, Hilde
  1952   Don't Be Afraid of Your Child (New York· Farrar, Strauss,
       Young).

Coon, Carleton
  1950   The Mountains of Giants. Papers of the Peabody Museum
       of American Archaeology and Ethnology, 23:1-105.

Dewees, W. P.
  1826   A Treatise on the Physical and Medical Treatment of
       Children (Philadelphia: Lea and Blanchard).

Dennis, W. and M. B. Dennis
  1940   The Effect of Cradling Practices upon the Onset of Walking
       of Hopi Children. Journal of Genetic Psychology 56:77-86.

de Kok, Winifred
  1935·   Guiding Your Child through the Formative Years (New York:
       Emerson Books, Inc.).

Dingwall, Eric John
  1931   Artificial Cranial Deformation (London: John Bale, Sons,
       and Danielsson, Ltd.).

Earle, Alice Morse
  1903   Two Centuries of Costume in America (New York: The
       Macmillan Company).

20

Evelyn-White, Hugh G.
>1966   Hesiod, the Homeric Hymns and Homerica (Cambridge: Harvard University Press).

Friedl, Ernestine
>1963   Vasilika, a Village in Modern Greece (New York: Holt, Rinehart, and Winston).

Gorer, Geoffrey and John Rickman
>1950   The People of Great Russia (New York: Chanticleer Press).

Grandquist, Hilma
>1947   Birth and Childhood Among the Arabs, Studies in a Muhammadon Village in Palestine (Helsinfors: Soderstrom and Company, Forlagsaktiebolag).

Gruner, O. Cameron
>1930   A Treatise on the Canon of Medicine of Avicenna (London: Luzac and Company).

Hudson, Charles
>1966   Isometric Advantages of the Cradle Board: a Hypothesis. American Anthropologist 68:470-4.

Kluckhohn, Clyde
>1947   Some Aspects of Navaho Infancy and Early Childhood. Psychoanalysis and the Social Sciences 1:37-86.

Levy, David M.
>1944   On the Problem of Movement Restraint. American Journal of Orthopsychiatry 14:644-71

Lipton, Earle L., Alfred Steinschneider, and Julius B. Richmond
>1965   Swaddling, a Child Care Practice: Historical, Cultural, and Experimental Observation. Pediatrics 35:supplement.

McGregor, John C.
>1941   Southwestern Archaeology (New York: John Wiley & Sons).

Mason, Otis T.
>1889   Cradles of American Aborigines. Report of the United States National Museum for 1887.

Mead, Margaret
>1954   The Swaddling Hypothesis: Its Reception. American Anthropologist 56:395-409.

Mettler, C. C.
>1947   History of Medicine (Philadelphia: The Blakiston Company).

Oswald, Felix L.
>1881   Physical Education. The Popular Science Monthly 19:145-155.

Phillips, Helen
>1967   Swaddling and Cradle Boards: Physical Restraint as an Infant-Care Practice (University of Georgia, unpublished Honors Thesis).

21

Plato
    1926   Laws, translated by R. G. Bury, 2 vols. (Cambridge: Harvard University Press).

Rousseau, Jean Jacques
    1901   Emile (New York: D. Appleton and Company).

Ruhrah, John
    1925   Pediatrics of the Past (New York: Paul B. Hoeber, Inc.).

Still, G. F.
    1965   The History of Pediatrics (London: Dawsons of Pall Mall).

Watson, J. B. and J. J. B. Morgan
    1917   Emotional Reactions and Psychological Experimentation. American Journal of Psychology 18:163-174.

22

ANTHROPOLOGICAL THEORY AND THE PSYCHOLOGICAL FUNCTION OF BELIEF IN WITCHCRAFT [1]

Hazel Hitson Weidman
University of Alabama Medical Center
University of Hawaii (1967-68)

John G. Kennedy has recently written that "...the special characteristics of witchcraft make it a particularly meaningful demonstration of the need for the integration of explicit psychological theory with sociological analysis" (1966:1-2). I am in accord with this view; however, I would distinguish between belief in witchcraft on the one hand and the carrying of such belief into action on the other. These very different aspects of the problem seem to require separate analyses. Certainly, their consequences for social system functioning may be quite divergent.

Furthermore, because anthropological and psychiatric theory have fairly well-developed bridges between them, I would plead for a better integration of these two theoretical systems specifically. In this paper I shall be concerned with belief in witchcraft, not witchcraft activity. I shall also be attempting to synthesize something of anthropological and psychiatric understandings of belief in witchcraft. It is my hope that this paper will be a small beginning in the direction of a general theory of behavior.

The Anthropological View

We are particularly fortunate in having a recent review of the anthropological literature on witchcraft. Walker has summarized the general position of anthropological theory today (1966). In his view witchcraft has six main functions. Using Kluckhohn's distinction, he sees three of these as adjustive and three as adaptive. The three adjustive functions are the instructive, the explanatory, and the emotionally ameliorative; while the three adaptive functions are the unifying, the socially controlling, and the governing.

The closest we come in this formulation to integrating explicit psychiatric theory with anthropological analysis is in the recognition that belief in witchcraft is emotionally ameliorative. This is so, because it "...facilitates the dissolution of pent-up emotions in a socially harmless way" (Walker 1966:2). This view, now generally held, appears to be a direct reflection of the work of Clyde Kluckhohn (1944), although Hallowell before him (1940) and others since have also viewed such beliefs as providing socially acceptable outlets for aggression.

I believe, however, that one facet of Kluckhohn's position has been neglected. Since his classic work on Navaho witchcraft appeared in 1944,

23

the major emphasis in discussing the psychologically ameliorative function of witchcraft has been upon the discharge of energy. True, Kluckhohn's thesis was that, given the amount and kind of aggression which existed in Navaho society, some forms of relief must exist. True, also, Kluckhohn felt that when other forms of release are inadequate, and when the witchcraft patterns are historically available, witchcraft belief is a highly adjustive way of releasing not only generalized tension but also those tensions specific to Navaho social structure (1944:106). Nevertheless, in discussing witchcraft as an important dynamic of behavior he stated that "...I have tried to emphasize that it was not so much pure hostility as ambivalence (my italics) which was the central dynamic factor" (1944:127).

The attempt to cope with the anxiety attendant upon ambivalence represents a far more fundamental process than that of simply defining and expressing that anxiety. There is more involved than simply channelling, expressing, or displacing aggression. Kluckhohn seems to have recognized this, for it is implicit in much that he said. He was not, however, articulate in this respect. Despite his grasp of psychiatric principles and his awareness of trends in psychiatry (1956) he did not have the benefit of ego psychology, of recent psychoanalytic theory, nor of current work in transcultural psychiatry. He could not, in 1944, have handled the problem very differently.

This leaves the anthropological position regarding the psychological function of belief in witchcraft with an outdated energy-discharge theory. The central dynamic factor with which Kluckhohn was concerned, ambivalence, still seems crucial but needs now to be reconsidered in the light of current psychiatric theory with its stress on ego functioning. We need to consider, for example, in what way belief in witchcraft may serve the purposes of ego integration other than by a simple release of tension.

The Psychiatric View

We have no statement in psychiatry comparable to Walker's in anthropology regarding belief in witchcraft. However, some of the more recent literature on the psychodynamics of such beliefs are indicative of current trends in this theoretical area.

Very recently Galvin and Ludwig have examined the hypothesis of Ernest Jones (1959) that "...belief in and susceptibility to witchcraft result from the guilt associated with forbidden incestuous wishes" (Transcultural Psychiatric Research 1966:64). Despite one classic case in a Spanish-American family which supports Jones' position (1961), they review a series of other cases which do not substantiate his view (1965). They retain his hypothesis as worthy of further investigation, nevertheless.

Jacquel and Morel, on the other hand, working with French peasants from Orne Province, describe four cases of belief in witchcraft, three of

24

which involve more than one person. They associate paranoidal systems
with the climate of belief in witchcraft and write that "...it would seem
that the climate of belief in witchcraft is such that paranoid delusions can
relatively easily be expressed by patients and be accepted and eventually
identified with by intimates" (1965:40).

More cross-culturally oriented psychiatrists are taking a different
approach. Parin in Mali and Collomb in Senegal, for example, deal with
much broader principles of personality dynamics. Like Evans-Pritchard
(1937) and many anthropologists who followed his lead, these psychiatrists,
too, specifically state that African tribal people think logically, empirically, and in abstract terms. These authors recognize the importance of
witchcraft beliefs in the African's relationship to the environment, but
they recognize, also, that reality perception is ordinarily successfully accomplished. Nevertheless, argue Parin and Collomb independently, their
ego-structures are weak. Id impulses enter the ego freely, and denial,
projection, and massive regression are their main ego defense mechanisms
(Wintrob and Wittkower 1966). The implications for situations of stress
are as follows:

> If an individual or group of individuals have access to
> mental processes which are usually hidden, and if
> they project their objectionable impulses as well as
> their rudimentary superego into the outer world, then it
> becomes understandable that their differentiation between
> self and non-self, and between inside and outside be-
> comes blurred, and that reality perception becomes dis-
> torted (Wintrob and Wittkower 1966:151).

On the basis of this report of their findings, I suspect that Parin
and Collomb would include Jones' "incestuous wishes" as only one kind of
objectionable impulse which might enter the ego and have to be dealt with
by means of denial and projection. In fact, according to the work of all
the psychiatrists mentioned above, the link between witchcraft beliefs and
psychodynamic functioning seems to center on weakness of the ego and on
the processes of denial and projection.

Wintrob and Wittkower suggest that Parin and Collomb's findings
provide clues for answering such questions as, "Why do magic beliefs,
frightening in quality, prevail in African society, and why are obviously
erroneous beliefs not corrected by reality testing?" (1966:151). They
describe something of the psychodynamic process whereby the distinction
between self and non-self may become blurred, but they do not outline in
detail the specific defense mechanisms which underlie Parin and Collomb's
clues regarding the perseverance of belief in witchcraft. They do say that

25

feelings of guilt are <u>un</u>common and that persecutory ideas expressed in culturally shared beliefs <u>are</u> common. It would seem to follow from this that the reason the erroneous beliefs of magic and witchcraft are not corrected by reality testing is that they represent projective processes in themselves. The anthropological explanation, of course, first advanced by Evans-Pritchard in 1937, is that the belief system itself is a closed one, logically airtight, with no possibilities for change.

By way of summarizing, my interpretation of what is implied in the work of these transcultural psychiatrists is that, under stress, denial and projection as major defense mechanisms, may be psychologically integrative for a weak ego-structure. On the other hand, because prolonged reliance upon projection weakens the boundaries between self and non-self, continued stress and increased reliance upon projective processes may eventually lead to the development of hallucinations or of a delusion. Massive regression under stress may, apparently, have similar consequences.

Collomb's observations are relevant here. He writes as follows:

> Culturally speaking, delusional states are not patho-
> logical...Hallucinations are even fostered by native
> myths, so that the frontiers between subjectivity and
> objectivity are blurred by culture. It is therefore easy
> for an individual overwrought by a traumatic situation
> to slip temporarily into hallucinations which have
> beneficial functions in many ways similar to those of
> a dream. Such hallucinations do not really disintegrate
> the patient's psyche, but rather integrate it (1965:33).

Collomb's precise meaning is not entirely clear. Certainly, Yap and Wittkower are two psychiatrists who would disagree with him that hallucinations and delusional states are not pathological (Yap 1966; Wittkower and Dubreuil 1966). The cultural response to such phenomena, however, is a different matter. It may well be that it is the self-regulating cultural processes which accompany hallucinatory and delusional states, rather than these behaviors themselves, which help reintegrate the patient's psyche. Paul has described such processes associated with emotional withdrawal in Guatemala (1956). Irrespective of Collomb's intent regarding the nature of hallucinations and delusional states, his view of the cultural "myths" which foster the tendency toward such behavior are highly pertinent.

He seems to imply that hallucinations and delusional states represent projective processes developed to different degrees. Most importantly, he suggests that the same projective processes which may eventuate in hallucinations or delusions may utilize cultural beliefs, such as those of witchcraft, presumably, in effective defense of the ego. If this is so, it seems crucial to know something more about delusional formation and its development

26

within the psyche.

Carr defines a delusion as "...an unalterable conviction maintained about a disordered perception, which remains untouched and uncorrected by what is represented by others as reality and 'common sense'" (1963: 197). Carr was writing in generic terms, but this, in essence, seems to be something of what is involved in belief in witchcraft from the vantage point of a scientific tradition.

Carr suggests that in order for a delusion to develop, there must first be a disordered relationship between perceptual experience and reality testing. Such disordering, he says, is possible only when perceptual organization does not permit absolute certainty of interpretation. This is part of the developmental process and occurs in the early years. He postulates, therefore, that the pathological process leading to delusional formation begins in early development with the specific events of having others deny the validity of a perception experienced by the child to be real and true (1963:198). Carr's hypothesis seems to provide one of the means whereby we might come to a new understanding of the psychodynamics of belief in witchcraft.

Following his lead, I would extend Collomb's remarks about the process whereby culture blurs the frontiers between subjectivity and objectivity. The particular device whereby such fluidity in ego functioning is achieved might be described as a culturally-driven wedge between reality sense and reality testing. I believe that the elements of a pathological process which may eventually blur the distinctions between self and nonself, inside and outside, must be found here. It is my opinion that cultural processes which accomplish this cleavage simultaneously insure the development of a weak ego-structure, a reliance upon denial and projection in defense of the ego, and a tendency toward transitory delusional states as a consequence of massive regression under acute stress. If I am correct in this, the problem facing us is to explain just how cultural processes accomplish such a cleavage and to indicate its significance for the psychological function of belief in witchcraft.

Toward a Synthesis of Anthropological and Psychiatric Views

Let us look at the cultural side of the problem first. In a previous paper, utilizing data from field research in Burma, I attempted to describe some of the pervasive factors in Burmese culture which might cause children and adults to doubt their own sense perceptions. These included social structural features, parental attitudes toward children, socialization practices, and language usage. The patterning along these dimensions was related to a concept of self as inadequate and a world view which required a great deal of defensive maneuvering to protect the self from harm and to

27

maintain self-esteem. I tried to show the manner in which social ambiguity, attendant upon such cultural patterns and psychological processes, contributed toward perceptual ambiguity in the individual and to a beginning disorder between reality sense and reality testing at the level of psychodynamic functioning (Weidman 1966).

I will not repeat that argument here. I believe, however, that we cannot fully understand the psychological function of belief in witchcraft until we understand the processes involved in attempts to resolve this kind of disordered relationship within the structure of the ego. For present purposes it will be important to focus upon the problem of social ambiguity and its relationship to psychological ambivalence. I think they are inextricably linked and, furthermore, that they may be centrally implicated in a potential disturbance between reality sense and reality testing, which seems to require for resolution a reliance upon beliefs such as those of witchcraft or sorcery.

Often, in speaking of the dysfunctions of belief in witchcraft, anthropologists will describe the tremendously disruptive effects of feelings of suspicion, fear, and hatred among those living in the same village. Winter, for example, speaks of the anxiety created by this belief as being heightened by the uncertainty which surrounds the identity of the witches (1963:283-284).

Psychiatrists, too, sometimes view the beliefs, themselves, as causal agents in a disruptive sequence. Wintrob and Wittkower, for example, write that, "Analogous to M. J. Field's observations in Ghana the magic beliefs of the Liberian tribal peoples create (my italics) an atmosphere of all-round fear and suspicion which permeates the whole society" (1966:11). I would argue that all-round fear and suspicion permeate the whole society, not as a consequence of magic beliefs, but because such fear and suspicion are inseparable from a definition of human nature as basically evil and a view of man as unpredictable and potentially harmful. This view of man is widespread and frequently unconcealed. Evans-Pritchard comments, for example, that, "The Zande himself is the first to declare that 'the Azande are an evil people, they are uncharitable to one another'" (1937:101). Beattie (1963), Gray (1963), and La Fontaine (1963) have argued similarly and view witchcraft beliefs, as I do, as one expression of these premises.

There now seems to be sufficient evidence for us to assume that the disruptive forces of doubt, suspicion, fear, and anxiety are present in most peasant societies, regardless of whether or not witchcraft beliefs prevail. Foster, in particular, is explicit about this (1960:174-178). If such a view is, indeed, correct, we are faced with the larger problem of why this is so and how one handles aggression, generally, within such a cultural context.

Let us take the broadest view possible and assume, for example, that culture is adaptive for the human species (at least to this point in time) and that the group is necessary for survival of the individual. Add to this a

28

definition of man as basically evil, as unpredictable and potentially harmful, and we have all of the ingredients for the necessary suppression of aggression within the group. Members of "other" groups under these conditions are almost inevitably defined as strangers and, therefore, enemies. This means that one's survival is largely dependent upon his own small community in a hostile world. When there are great potentialities for harm from individuals within one's own group as well, it is all the more imperative to prevent the disruptive effects of directly expressed aggression in the small community. At the group level of analysis the members' means of survival may ultimately be threatened. At the individual level, the direct expression of aggression may mean the possibility of ostracism, abandonment, and, ultimately, death.

Since it is, apparently, impossible for an individual to participate in group life without experiencing frustration, we must assume that the impulse to engage in prohibited indulgent or aggressive acts is more widespread than the actual transgression of norms by indulgence or aggression. When cultural values of friendliness, cooperation, generosity, and amiability sanction the suppression of aggression in the social personality at the same time evil intent is assumed for the basic personality, we may reasonably expect concealed feelings of anger, envy, jealousy, resentment, etc. This means that many social situations become ambiguous situations, with patterns of strain structured differently in diverse societies.

Under such circumstances individuals tend to relate in a double-edged way. Negative feelings are present. They cannot be entirely hidden nor brought entirely into the open. It is both dangerous to express negative feelings and to perceive them, because, ultimately, harm may come to the self as a consequence of bad feeling and its ramifications; but feel them one does and perceive them one does.

When ambiguity is a characteristic of many interpersonal relationships, people relate to each other on two levels at once. They attempt to protect themselves from the uncertainties of situations by phrasing their conversations so that no one really knows for sure what is intended. Not only do their words generally permit two possible interpretations by themselves and by others; so, too, does their behavior. This seems to be a partly unconscious process, so that people themselves may be unaware of the two-sidedness of their own motivations and their own behavior. Consequently, it is important always to be alert to the actual meanings or intentions of others, even though in actuality one can never really know. One can never know directly, for when accusations are made or questions are raised, it is imperative that the accused self be protected from the dangers of the moment by the denial of any harmful intent. No anthropologist has described such characteristics of interpersonal exchanges more successfully than has Evans-Pritchard for the Azande (1963:204-228).

Because of the ambiguity inherent in so many situations people are unwilling to act upon their convictions. They may believe they perceive a

29

situation clearly, but then they begin to doubt. An individual may actually not have intended harm. He may actually have meant no offense. But then, again, he may very well have intended both. One never knows, and one is afraid to act until one is sure. The implication is clear. "Reality" in such interpersonal relationships is built upon shifting sands, and there is no way to test what is so and what is not so. With this kind of ambiguity in social situations, anxiety, doubt, and distrust must become an integral part of the whole social process. Ambivalence, as the dynamic factor with which Kluckhohn (1944) was concerned, becomes in this formulation the psychological counterpart to social ambiguity. A sense of powerlessness may be the concomitant of such social processes, for in many situations there are no clear-cut "handles" to grasp, to respond to, and to act upon. If one is unable to master this degree of uncertainty, he may be caught in what I believe constitutes a beginning disorder in the relationship between reality sense and reality testing.

If this is so, what does it mean psychodynamically? It means that the very experiencing of reality is at stake, for, as Weisman points out, more than sense perception is required for the feeling of reality.

> ...the reality of an object depends not only on its
> emotional ties, but upon verification. In order to
> compel lasting belief, the process that we call
> reality sense and reality testing must fuse in vivid
> uncontradicted sensory experience (1958:234).

"Reality" in interpersonal relationships such as those described above may be: a) two things at once; b) it may be the first and not the second, or c) it may be the second and not the first. One never really knows, and in the face of shifting positions required by the perceived dangers of the moment, attempts at corroboration are frequently thwarted. There is no way to establish the true nature of such an interpersonal experience through reality testing. This, I submit, represents the beginning of the kind of disordered relationship between perceptual experience and ordinary corrective influences which Carr (1963) sees as being essential to the development of a delusion.

There are discrepancies between the beliefs people derive from what they sense as reality and the knowledge they obtain from attempts to test reality. Since the discrepancies relate to such intangibles as motivations and intentions, they can be resolved only by the kind of conviction which witchcraft or similar beliefs allow.

Such conviction apparently comes after the experiencing of some disturbing feeling or some disruptive event. This is what Evans-Pritchard (1937) reported and is probably what Beattie meant when he described sorcery accusations as entirely post hoc constructions (1963:36). Think for a

30

Weidman, Hazel Hitson
    1966   Cultural Values, Concept of Self, and Projection: The Burma Case. Paper presented at the conference on Mental Health in Asia and the Pacific, held at the East-West Center, Honolulu, Hawaii, March 28-April 1.

Weisman, Avery D.
    1958   Reality Sense and Reality Testing. Behavioral Science III:228-261.

Winter, E. H.
    1963   The Enemy Within: Amba Witchcraft and Sociological Theory. In Witchcraft and Sorcery in East Africa, John Middleton and E. H. Winter, eds. (London: Routledge and Kegan Paul)., pp. 277-299.

Wintrob, R. and E. D. Wittkower
    1966   Magic and Witchcraft in Liberia: Their Psychiatric Implications. Paper presented at the Association for the Advancement of Psychotherapy Meeting, Atlantic City, New Jersey, May 8th. Mimeograph, 14pp. Abstracted in Transcultural Psychiatric Research III, October, pp. 149-152.

Wittkower, E. D. and G. Dubreuil
    1966   Cultural Factors in Mental Illness. Paper presented at the Symposium on the Study of Personality: An Interdisciplinary Appraisal, held at Rice University, Houston, Texas, November 4-5.

Yap, P. M.
    1966   The Culture-Bound Reactive Psychoses. Paper presented at the conference on Mental Health in Asia and the Pacific, held at the East-West Center, Honolulu, Hawaii, March 28-April 1.

35

THE PUBLIC HEALTH NURSE AS A MENTAL HEALTH RESOURCE[1]

Dorothea C. Leighton, M.D. and Nora F. Cline, R.N.
University of North Carolina

Introduction

In 1966 we undertook a small study to quantify the mental health aspect of the work of public health nurses and to specify some of its dimensions. Of particular interest to us were the nurses' own definitions of these problems, their preparation for working with them, and their feeling of adequacy in the area of mental health work. This paper reports findings involving 106 public health nurses who were working in Health Departments in North Carolina and who collaborated with the authors to furnish data about themselves, about five randomly selected patients from their caseloads, and about their caseloads in general. The long range goal was to devise in-service mental health training programs for public health nurses on the basis of our findings.

The origin of the ideas behind the study lies in several years' experience by one of us (Cline) as a practicing public health nurse, and her subsequent years in schools of public health as an educator in mental health and public health, helping public health nurses and others to recognize and work with emotional problems that occur in patients, families and communities. Public health nurses working in community health programs spend varying amounts of time visiting families in their homes. They may have been called there for any one of a long list of reasons ranging from a need for bedside nursing to that of providing health information and guidance for a prenatal patient, a growing child, a family crisis. Once in the home, they may discover problems that challenge their ability to work with the person and situation for which their help was requested. They have the opportunity to play an important role in prevention and early detection of illness of many kinds, including mental and emotional illness. In many communities they are the principal health workers in the lives of many of the families, and are both in the position and under the necessity to provide what help they can with any emotional or behavioral problems family members may have.

Characteristically, family situations with which the public health nurse works involve illness, tension, death, injury, and grief. There are also problems which generate and grow out of deprivation, inadequacy, conflict, anxiety, dependence, and hostility. Some are related to change in the community, in society, and in the family structure itself. In addition to acting as a catalyst by which interaction between patient-in-need and helping agency is stimulated, she is called upon increasingly to participate in the treatment and rehabilitation of mental hospital patients when they

36

are discharged to the community.

Working as she does in the home, the public health nurse lacks the support of the structured hospital environment and of professional colleagues immediately available for help in making decisions and coping with family crises. She may, herself, experience anxiety in varying degrees in relation to a patient's aggressive behavior, to a patient's rejection of her, to the intensity of a relationship, to her uncertainty that she is doing the "right" thing, or to her inability to translate her theoretical knowledge into constructive behavior for on-the-spot action. With this background, we proceed to assess the problems and needs for mental health education by public health nurses in North Carolina.

Method

The State of North Carolina comprises four geographic subdivisions which have different demographic and cultural characteristics (see map). Although we did not expect that the public health nurses would show different characteristics on this basis, we assumed that their patients might do so, and so took the areas into account in drawing our sample. In addition, we included the proportion of white/non-white in the design. Using four public health nurses as the sampling unit, we also tapped the population density factor, since the nurse population is roughly in proportion to general population. Thus the less densely populated counties would have only one unit (or less), while the counties with large cities would provide multiple units.

By random means within the geographic-demographic limitations described, we drew the names of 124 nurses who were working in 24 Health Departments, which represented 30 counties (some counties having a joint health department with one or more neighbors). All the nurses were visited either in their own health department or at meetings where those from several counties came together for our convenience. Questionnaires were distributed and explained, and each nurse was requested to complete the work as soon as she could. In some cases returns were very rapid, in others work responsibilities led to considerable time lapse (2-3 months) between instruction-giving and receipt of the completed papers.

The nurses were asked to bring to the meeting a list or card file of their caseloads. We supervised the selection of the five cases for each nurse, using a table of random numbers or else a random start and every Nth case. Because many of the files or lists were kept by families rather than by individuals, each selected family was discussed and a suitable adult designated from whom the nurse would gather information with questionnaire IV (see appendix).

The nurse had two short forms to fill out about herself, questionnaires I and II. Questionnaire I requested information regarding her education and

37

experience; questionnaire II was a set of open-ended questions covering mental health complaints by patients, additional mental health problems observed by the nurse, her opinion regarding her adequacy in working with such problems, her sources of help, her estimate of the time she spends on this aspect of her practice, how effective she considers herself to be in this area, and what additional knowledge she needs. The nurse also filled out questionnaires III and IV for the five sample patients. Questionnaire III sought detailed demographic and sociocultural facts about the families in the sample. It also requested a list of all the diagnosed or observed mental health problems exhibited by family members. Questionnaire IV is a set of 20 psychological screening questions which the nurse asked each of her five subjects and which are used to achieve an estimate of the subject's "mental health level." More will be said about questionnaire IV when the patient findings are discussed.

Findings

The Nurses. Completed papers were received from 106 of the 124 nurses (85%). The nurses had an average age of 39.5 years, ranging from 22 to 61. Eighty-nine percent had graduated from three-year diploma schools; the balance had received a baccalaureate degree from four-year schools. Twenty-two percent had received some formal training in public health work, the rest only short courses in in-service training. The average number of years spent in professional nursing was 16.4, of which 9.5 had been in public health nursing. Approximately 90% had done all of their public health nursing in North Carolina.

As for mental health training, 57% had had "some courses." Of these, 24% had had three months or more of psychiatric affiliation; 16% a one-week orientation session at a state mental hospital; the rest had short courses, workshops and instructions from nurse consultants. In spite of this amount of training, only seven nurses considered themselves adequately prepared to cope with the emotional problems of their patients. Thirty-seven percent gave qualified responses and 47% said frankly that they did not have sufficient training.

The responses to the questions about what kind of "mental health complaints" their patients had, and what additional kinds of "mental health problems" the nurse noticed, afforded an opportunity to learn what the nurses classified in this broad area of behavior. They averaged 7 responses to the two questions, with a total of almost 300 different symptoms or behavior items. These ranged from psychiatric diagnostic terms on the part of a few nurses to such items as "worry about inability to pay drug bills," "moral laxity," and "unwillingness to assume responsibility for behavior of children."

A graduate student, in consultation with two psychiatrists, categorized

38

the 300 items under five headings:

  1. "Neurotic"--anxiety, depression, tension, psychosomatic, personality instability and insecurity as well as personality disorganization. A few symptoms which might indicate psychosis, such as hallucinations, were also put in this category.
  2. "Social deprivation"--retardation, dependency, immaturity, inactivity, difficulty concentrating and paying attention, aimlessness, worry about financial problems. These were separated from Group 1 because they seemed more indicative of a reaction to poverty than spontaneous neurotic manifestations.
  3. "Behavior problems"--acting out, aggressive behavior, hostility and anger, legal offenses, alcoholism, drug abuse, and associated problems.
  4. "Chronic illness and disability"--symptoms associated with senility, physical disability, or impairment, chronic disease and associated psychological and emotional reactions.
  5. "Interpersonal family problems"--between spouses, parent-child, between siblings, or with relatives and friends.

By far the most frequent patient complaint reported was "nerves" or "nervousness," followed in frequency by family problems and financial worries. Although most of the additional patient disorders noted also fell in the "neurotic" category, "depression" was frequently specified by the nurse rather than generalized "nervousness." Additional problems ranked second and third by the nurses were aspects of social deprivation (other than financial) and behavior problems.

In spite of the statement reported above that only 7 of the 106 nurses considered themselves adequately prepared for mental health work with their patients, 63% reported that they had been able to achieve "some improvement" in their patients' problems. They attributed this to their interpersonal skills, their interest in the patient, their willingness to listen to problems, and to their non-judgmental attitude. Many of them mentioned seeking help of some kind with reference to patient problems from such resources as family doctors, nurse and health department colleagues, school personnel, ministers, welfare department personnel, Alcoholics Anonymous, and mental health clinics. In the more rural counties the resources were usually very limited, while in or near large cities they were much more plentiful. Some utilized these same kinds of resources as places to refer the patient. There was little evidence that the nurses tended

39

to disregard mental health problems and much evidence that they did what they could on a common sense basis to improve the life circumstances of their patients, whether or not they considered themselves adequately trained to handle "mental health problems."

Many nurses found it difficult to estimate how much extra time they spent on the mental health problems of their patients. A few said "maybe three-quarters of an hour per visit." Others guessed "about 15 minutes." Still others said they could not differentiate time spent in this way from time spent on physical illness and other demands.

The Patients. The demographic and sociocultural data regarding the patient group was gathered in questionnaire III by the usual type of question used in surveys. The nurses were requested to either fill it in from their records and their personal knowledge of the family or to ask the questions at the same time they asked the screening questions designed to assess the patient's mental health status.

A word or two is in order, however, about the screening questions in questionnaire IV since these are not in such general use. We utilized twenty screening questions derived from the Stirling County Study of psychiatric disorder and sociocultural environment (Dorothea Leighton 1963). In that study, they formed a part of a quite elaborate procedure for estimating the psychiatric status of members of a general population, and were accompanied by a check list of common adult diseases, doctors' comments, and hospital records. When scored independently, it was found that the score of the screening questions tended to parallel quite closely the evaluation of each record made by two or more psychiatrists. Originally there were more than 20 questions--75 initially, and 24 in the first Stirling County survey. The original set was tested for reliability and validity before being incorporated into the Stirling County questionnaire (Dorothea Leighton 1963:200-233, Appendix E).

The impossibility of using the full-scale Stirling County method very widely, due to its complexity, led to the selection of 20 of the original questions to form a short scale which could be used under many different circumstances to obtain a reading on "mental health status" or "psychiatric status" or "stress" or "emotional disorder" as related to whatever else the researcher was particularly interested in. The questions, which are reproduced in an Appendix at the end of this paper, are limited to enquiries about physiological symptoms which commonly occur as a reaction to stress. Due to the circumstance that they are merely reports by the subject of his symptoms as he sees them, the set has been called the Health Opinion Survey, or HOS for short.

When one talks about results with the HOS, it is a temptation to call it a mental health score or a stress score, and evidence tends to indicate that this is a justifiable implication. In any new population group, however, it is safer to speak of it only as the HOS score, and to let the reader interpret

40

it according to his own prejudices. In order to have a control group at the "sick" end of the continuum, we undertook a study of hospitalized patients in North Carolina, after completing the current study, which will be reported in due course.

Both the HOS standardization group and the Stirling County study comprised a population of rural and small town eastern Canadians, showing a socioeconomic range from well-to-do to poverty-stricken. It seemed likely that the population in North Carolina would understand and respond equally well to the questions without particular difficulty.

In a recent North Carolina study the HOS differentiated quite clearly a group of University students who had sought psychiatric advice from the students in two classes in introductory psychology, and both of these groups from a class of students at the School of Public Health (Matthews 1966). This small study has not been published as yet, nor has the short 20-question form of the HOS. It was used in Nigerian villages as part of the Stirling County method (Alexander Leighton 1963) and it has been used in an extensive study relating stress to culture change in Peruvian villages (Kellert 1966). While it is quite probable that another set of similar questions would accomplish the same purpose as the HOS, much is to be gained for the advance of our understanding of the interplay of sociocultural factors and personality reaction by using a standard set of questions under varying circumstances. No other set that we are aware of has had as much additional related work done which appears to confirm its validity.

In addition to providing standard questions, there are also standard answers--either Yes/No, or Often/Sometimes/Never. The "sick" answer receives a score of 3, the "well" answer a score of 1, and the intermediate answer (or no answer) a score of 2. Thus, the range of score is 20 - 60, with lower scores (in the 20's) usually associated with good "adjustment" and higher scores with evidence of "psychiatric disorder." It registers psychoneurotic and psychophysiologic types of symptoms and is useless for other varieties of psychiatric reactions except insofar as they are accompanied by such symptoms. Since the great bulk of people suffering mild psychiatric disorder, associated with all sorts of environmental strains, exhibit principally these two kinds of symptoms, the HOS picks up most (though not all) such people. The prevalence of various major diagnostic categories of symptoms found in the Stirling County population may be seen in Table 3.

Let us see now what the nurses' patients showed. The 106 nurses were able to complete the forms on 514 patients. Of these, 86% were women, the reasons for which run as follows: the larger proportion of women reflects the nurse's usual contacts, influenced very likely by the fact that her working hours coincide with the working hours of the fathers. It was not possible for the nurses to spend extra time on this research; they simply worked it into their regular programs, visiting the sample families for their

41

usual purposes. In discussing each family to select a suitable adult member, we asked the nurse to interview the father if this was feasible. The high percentage of women which resulted, in spite of this effort to include more men, underlines this aspect of public health nursing practice.

Table 1 shows other demographic features, comparing the sample with figures from the 1960 U.S. census of the counties which were in the sample, insofar as the census categories matched the ones of this study.

One sees that our sample contained a much larger proportion of Negroes than is shown in the census (40% instead of 24%). This is doubtless related to the figures for income, which show that nearly 70% of the sample had less than $3000 income as opposed to 48% at this level in the census, and that a larger proportion of Negroes than whites in the sample are at the lowest income levels.

By age (from 25 years up) there is a nearly perfect match between the sample and the census.

By geographic areas the sample is fairly representative overall. There is a smaller proportion from the Piedmont than the census shows and a larger proportion from the Coastal Plain. The increased proportion of Negroes in the sample is most striking in the figures for the Coastal Plain and Tidewater areas. While it is well known that the Mountain region is part of the Appalachian area of the nation, for which special aid programs have been set up, it is less widely realized that the Coastal Plain-Tidewater strip, from Washington south to Florida, is in similar economic straits and is in process of becoming the aim of similar aid programs. Most of the industrial development of the state is located in the Piedmont region. The relative shortage in Piedmont subjects as compared to Coastal Plain subjects probably represents a disproportion between nurses and population, or else some error in the sampling technique.

By education the figures show only a slight difference between grades finished by whites and Negroes, especially in the upper levels of education. Unfortunately the census figures are divided differently and cannot be directly compared. Women receive considerably more education than men--only 24% of the men have had high school or higher education, compared to 49% of the women.

In summary, as compared to the 1960 U.S. census, our sample of patients showed that public health nurses work with: (1) an over-representation of Negroes, (2) an over-representation of women, and (3) an over-representation of low income families. In addition, their white patients tend to have a little more education than Negroes, and women have considerably more education than men.

<u>HOS Results</u>

In Table 2 we see that with a possible range of score from 20 to 60,

42

and with low score usually correlated with other evidence of low stress,
the patient group had a mean score of 33.3 with a standard deviation of
7.75. Compared to these figures, the study of University students (quoted
above) obtained a mean value of 33.5 for those who consulted a psychiatrist, 28.3 for the psychology classes, and 28.1 for graduate students in
the School of Public Health. It seems safe to say, then, that the mean HOS
for the nurses' patients is rather high.

Mean scores by race and sex show the white men highest (36.6),
Negro men next (34.7), white women third (34.0), and Negro women lowest (30.7). Mean scores by age show a rise in score with age for all
race/sex groups. The overall mean score for whites is 34.6, for Negroes
31.5. An analysis of these findings, using four age groups within each
race/sex group indicates that age makes a significant difference in the
HOS score, and so does the race/sex factor. In addition, the interaction
of age with race/sex also produces significant differences. The respective
F ratios are: Age, 30.1; Race/Sex, 54.5; and the Interaction, 12.5.

The findings for men and women are the opposite of the sex ratio
found in the Stirling County study, where women appeared to be "sicker"
than men. Exceptions were seen in one Stirling community where men were
"sicker" and in three rural slums where the sexes were about the same. The
Nigerian study showed the men "sicker." The conclusion in these studies
was that the sex showing the "sicker" score was the sex under greater
pressure of some kind. In the present study it seems likely that the higher scores for the men in both races is related to the rather recent change
from an agricultural to an industrial economy which, so far, has affected
the men more profoundly than the women.

That Negroes as a group score lower than whites probably indicates
that, in spite of the difficulty of their position, with regard both to race and
to economics, there are some supports in their life situation which compensate them to some degree. That the Negro women have the lowest scores
of all may mean that the supports are working well and that the changes of
industrialization have not impinged upon them as yet.

By geographic areas, Mountain whites have the lowest mean score
for whites (31.8 men, 32.6 women). The Piedmont is highest for white
women (34.3) and second highest for white men (35.6). Highest mean score
of all occurs for men in the Tidewater area (38.8). Other scores for whites
are very close to 33.0. For Negroes there is very little difference in HOS
score by geographic regions. Negro women show a slightly higher score
in the Piedmont than elsewhere, and Negro men a slightly lower score in the
same area.

These geographic differences can be taken to reinforce the suggested
explanations with regard to race and sex as follows: low scores for whites
in the Mountains perhaps means that, although poor, the people are living
in a stable cultural situation to which they have adapted themselves over

43

the generations. It is worth noting that women there score a little higher than men, and are possibly less content with their lot. The Piedmont is the state's area of maximum industrialization, which appears to affect adversely both white men and women and even Negro women. The contrary effect on Negro men may indicate that, for them, industrialization has been an advantage, but the difference in score is so slight that it may not mean anything.

The peak score for white men in the Tidewater region cannot be explained easily, but may well be related to findings reported of higher mortality rates in the Coastal Plain-Tidewater regions than in the other two regions of the state in 1950 (Hamilton 1955), as well as to the declaration of this area as being in need of special aid. There have also been recent rumors of high suicide rates in this area, and high mental hospital admissions, but no substantial data have come to hand beyond the mortality data quoted. Since the high score in this study results from only 6 white male respondents, it can only be regarded as suggestive.

For both races, HOS score is highest at incomes below $3000 and diminishes as income level rises. The difference is not great but is consistent. This trend is in perfect agreement with most work done on the relationship between mental health and socioeconomic status. In an article reviewing "over 25 attempts to count untreated cases of psychological disorder in community populations," Dohrenwend (1965) notes that "14 of the 18 studies which present data on the relationship with social class yielded the highest rate of judged psychopathology in the lowest economic stratum." The reason for the relationship is almost surely not limited to small income, but includes all the social and personal deprivations associated with low income in our society. The smallness of the differences in HOS score in this study is very likely due to the smallness in range of income size.

The relationship of HOS score to years of education differs between the races: whites tend to have lower scores with increasing education; Negroes show the same tendency through grade 12, following which there is a steep increase in HOS score. The same effect as seen in the Negroes was found in one group in the Stirling County study, where it appeared that "too much" education had no outlet or application and led, perhaps, to frustration. It seems possible that the same explanation may apply to the highly educated Negro in North Carolina.

Discussion

The final question is, how do these findings relate to what the nurses had to say, and even more importantly, what is their implication for further mental health training for the nurses? We can say that the patient group as a whole has an elevated mean score, slightly higher than a mean

44

score of a group of University students who had sought psychiatric help. This does not indicate that the patient group should be rushed to psychiatrists or mental hospitals for the most part, but it suggests that the nurses have had much opportunity to observe neurotic and psychosomatic symptoms and behavior (and probably many other types as well).

The variation in mean score in different geographic areas, and in other subdivisions of the patient group provides some opportunity for setting priorities. If, for example, the in-service training program cannot be set in action in all parts of the state at once, the Piedmont would be the place of choice to initiate it for that is where three of the four race/sex groups show the highest HOS scores. The nurses in the Mountain region could wait until later, for their patients show less evidence of reactions to stress.

Further implications include the need for detailed social studies of the Piedmont and the Coast-Plain-Tidewater areas to determine what aspects of life are raising particular problems for people there which cause the study sample to show elevated reactions to stress.

The plan for the in-service education of the public health nurses is being developed jointly by psychiatrists of the State Department of Mental Health, nurse consultants from the State Board of Health, and the authors (Department of Mental Health, School of Public Health). Personnel from the two State departments, regionally based, are well placed to work with the psychiatric hospital and community clinic facilities available for any required clinical teaching. Case material from the nurses' caseloads will serve as the basis for group analysis of patient and family behavior, communication skills, interpersonal relationships, social and cultural aspects of family and community living, and the processes of interaction and intervention.

An effort will be made to give priority to the topics for instruction recommended by the nurses in the study: prevention of behavioral disorder, theories of causation of mental illness, and supervised practice in counseling discharged mental hospital patients and their families.

The strength of the plan, like the possibility of doing this study, is in the collaboration of relevant groups, in this case the public health nurses, the State Department of Mental Health, the State Board of Health, and the academic resources of the School of Public Health. The absence of any of these parties would greatly weaken or entirely destroy the rich possibilities inherent in the joint plan. The greatest gains can be expected to result from pooling resources in a combined effort to improve the mental health of citizens.

NOTES

1. We wish to acknowledge with thanks the many helpful suggestions

45

provided by Mrs. Shirley Smoyak, Graduate School of Nursing, Rutgers University.

REFERENCES

Dohrenwend, Bruce P. and Barbara Snell Dohrenwend
    1965   The Problem of Validity in Field Studies of Psychological Disorder. The Journal of Abnormal Psychology 70: 52-69.

Hamilton, C. Horace
    1955   Ecological and Social Factors in Mortality Variation. Eugenics Quarterly 2:212-223.

Kellert, Stephen and Lawrence K. Williams, William F. Whyte
    1966   Cultural Change and Stress in Rural Peru, a Preliminary Report. Mimeographed (Ithaca, New York: NYS School of Industrial and Labor Relations).

Leighton, Alexander and T. A. Lambo, Charles C. Hughes, Dorothea Leighton, Jane M. Murphy, David B. Macklin
    1963   Psychiatric Disorder Among the Yoruba (Ithaca, New York: Cornell University Press).

Leighton, Dorothea C. and John S. Harding, David B. Macklin, Allister M. Macmillan, Alexander H. Leighton
    1963   The Character of Danger (New York: Basic Books).

Matthews, Margie R.
    1966   A Preliminary Descriptive Study of HOS Responses in College Students, and an Attempt at Validation. Mimeographed (M.P.H. Thesis, Department of Epidemiology, University of North Carolina, Chapel Hill).

46

TABLE 1

Demographic Characteristics of the Patient Sample, compared to 1960 U.S. Census for the same counties.

	Patient Sample			1960 Census		
By Race						
White	57.6%			76.0%		
Negro	40.1%			24.0%		

By Age (% of adults 25 years of age or older)

25-44	52%			53%		
45-64	32%			35%		
65+	16%			12%		

By Geographic Areas

	Total	White	Negro	Total	White	Negro
Mountains	5.5%	100%	0%	3.4%	93.3%	6.7%
Piedmont	63.8%	66%	34%	74.6%	79.7%	20.3%
Coastal Plain	19.0%	30%	70%	11.6%	57.6%	42.4%
Tidewater	11.4%	43%	57%	10.4%	66.2%	33.8%

By Income Level (family income)

	Total	White	Negro	Total		
Less than $3000	69.4%	65.4%	75.4%	47.7%		
$3-5,000	19.0%	21.1%	16.1%	(over $10,000 -		
Over $5000	7.0%	8.6%	4.7%	4.8%)		
Unspecified	4.4%	4.9%	3.8%			

By Education

Grades completed	Total	White	Negro	Grade Total	
0-3	9%	6%	12%	0-5	18.8%
4-8	46%	50%	43%		
9-12	42%	41%	42%	10+	34.3%
Over 12	3%	3%	3%		

	All Men	All Women
0-3	25%	7%
4-8	50%	43%
9-12	23%	45%
Over 12	1%	4%

Total

	White		Negro		Total	
	Men	Women	Men	Women	Men	Women
	72	231	38	173	110	404
	303		211		514	

47

TABLE 2

HOS Scores of the Nurses' Patients - MEAN HOS Scores by Selected Variables.

By Race, Sex, Age **

	WHITES			NEGROES	
Age	Male	Female		Male	Female
25	29.5	31.0		30.7	29.8
25-44	32.4	32.8		32.6	30.3
45-64	38.2	35.6		36.2	30.2
65+	38.1	38.1		36.1	33.0
TOTAL	36.6	34.0		34.7	30.7

By Geographic Area

	Whites		Negroes	
	Male	Female	Male	Female
Mountains	31.8	32.6	--	--
Piedmont	35.6	34.3	34.6	31.9
Coastal Plain	33.2	33.1	35.1	29.1
Tidewater	38.8	33.4	35.1	29.9

By Income Level

	Whites	Negroes
Less than $3000	35.5	32.0
$3-5000	33.5	30.7
Over $5000	33.4	29.8

By Years of Education

	0-3	4-8	9-12	college
Whites				
Male	43.2	37.1	31.4	--
Female	29.7	35.6	32.5	30.1
Negroes				
Male	36.2	35.7	30.0	45.0 (1 case)
Female	34.0	30.4	29.2	37.0

**Differences significant at least at the 1% level.

48

TABLE 3

Percent of Stirling County Population Showing Various
Major Categories of Psychiatric Symptoms

Category	Percent*
Psychosis	1-2
Brain Syndrome	2-4
Mental Deficiency	7
Personality disorder	6-8
Sociopathic behavior	5-12
Psychoneurotic	45-65
Psychophysiologic	65-72

*The categories are not mutually exclusive. The range indicates sex differences in prevalence. Taken from Tho Character of Danger, Figs. 5 and 6.

49

APPENDIX

Questionnaire IV

Twenty Questions to Assess the Patient's Health

Instructions:

These questions have been used in many studies to determine the level of people's health. In order to be able to compare different groups of people, it is important that they should always be asked in exactly the same way.

It is also important that you should insist as much as possible that the person who is being questioned makes the choice of the answer. If he says to question 2. "Well, once or twice, maybe." make him decide, if you can, whether the answer ought to be "sometimes" or "never."

If you cannot get him to choose, write down exactly what is said and then you make a choice. In the sample given, Never would be a good choice, but the way he said it might make you think that he really meant "Once in a while" (which should be marked Sometimes) instead of really just "once or twice." Just make the most sensible choice you can.

Questions:		Circle answer	(For Office use)
1. Do you have any physical or health problems		Yes	3
at the present?		No	1
2. Do your hands tremble often enough to bother you?	Often		3
	Sometimes		2
	Never		1
3. Are you ever troubled by your hands or feet		Often	3
sweating so that they feel damp and clammy?		Sometimes	2
		Never	1

50

4. Have you ever been bothered by your heart beating hard?

Often 3

Sometimes 2

Never 1

5. Do you tend to feel tired in the mornings?

Often 3

Sometimes 2

Never 1

6. Do you have any trouble getting to sleep or staying asleep?

Often 3

Sometimes 2

Never 1

7. How often are you bothered by having an upset stomach?

Often 3

Sometimes 2

Never 1

8. Are you ever bothered by nightmares (dreams that frighten you)?

Often 3

Sometimes 2

Never 1

9. Have you ever been troubled by "cold sweats?"

Often 3

Sometimes 2

Never 1

10. Do you feel that you are bothered by all sorts (different kinds) of ailments in different parts of your body?

Often 3

Sometimes 2

Never 1

51

11. Do you smoke? Often 3

Sometimes 2

Never 1

12. Do you ever have loss of appetite? Often 3

Sometimes 2

Never 1

13. Has any ill health affected the amount of work Often 3

(or housework) that you do? Sometimes 2

Never 1

14. Do you ever feel weak all over? Often 3

Sometimes 2

Never 1

15. Do you ever have spells of dizziness? Often 3

Sometimes 2

Never 1

16. Do you tend to lose weight when you worry? Often 3

Sometimes 2

Never 1

17. Have you ever been bothered by shortness of Often 3

breath when you were not exerting yourself? Sometimes 2

Never 1

52

18. For the most part, do you feel healthy enough to carry out the things that you would like to do?

Often	1
Sometimes	2
Never	3

19. Do you feel in good spirits?

Most of the time	1
Sometimes	2
Very few times	3

20. Do you sometimes wonder if anything is worthwhile any more?

Often	3
Sometimes	2
Never	1

For the Interviewer:

Do you consider this a satisfactory interview?   YES   NO

Any special Notes:

53

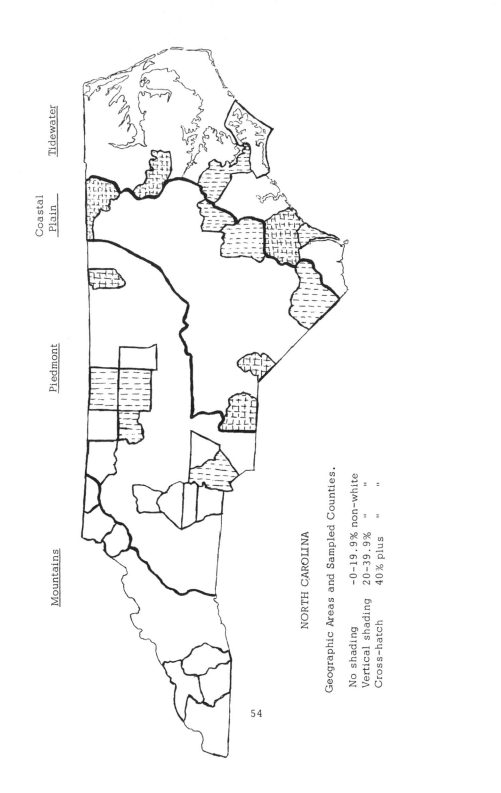

Mountains   Piedmont   Coastal Plain   Tidewater

NORTH CAROLINA

Geographic Areas and Sampled Counties.

No shading   -0-19.9% non-white
Vertical shading   20-39.9%   "   "
Cross-hatch   40% plus   "   "

54

MEDICAL ANTHROPOLOGY AT THE UNIVERSITY OF NORTH CAROLINA:
A PRELIMINARY NOTE

Peter Goethals and Berton H. Kaplan
University of North Carolina

This note reviews the experience of the University of North Carolina
Medical Anthropology Program along three dimensions: (1) epidemiology's
challenge to anthropology, (2) the opportunity for synthesis of anthropological and epidemiological method, and (3) the development of academic
norms and mechanisms to realize our program opportunities.

Epidemiology: The Challenge

The Medical Anthropology Program at the University of North Carolina,
established two years ago to provide an epidemiological training sector within the anthropology Ph.D. curriculum, has already begun to experience
certain growing pains which, even if only summarily discussed here, may
be of interest and value to those contemplating similar programs elsewhere.
Even at the risk of seeming to ignore Steven Polgar's apposite injunction of
1962 to cease and desist from cluttering our journals with yet more discussion
of "the role of the social scientist" in health programs and research, this
paper may best be launched by equating "conceptual problems" with the
role expectations of the professional anthropologist--allowing to begin with,
of course, that the anthropology field tends to attract a temperamentally
distinct group of practitioners and further allowing that, through its data and
concepts, the field reinforces certain common attitudes toward the study
of man.

One such problem lies in the continuing role expectation that, as
an earmark of his proper matriculation to full professional status, the anthropologist must conduct his first fieldwork among a suitably "exotic" people.
Even today this expectation generally implies a relatively long-term, definitely personal involvement in field research as the sine qua non of professional competence--and is, of course, tacitly linked as such to the
ethnographic tradition of studying the total culture of a particular community
using the local language as one's prime vehicle of access. While fieldwork--
and first fieldwork in particular--remains an essential didactic ingredient
in the training of every anthropologist, if it is undertaken in order to collect broad spectrum ethnographic data of prospective, but unconceptualized,
"functional" or historical interest, and if it is also implicitly regarded as
a rite of academic passage, it may appear distinctly incompatible with the
general research predilection of the epidemiologist--i.e. the closely
focused, methodologically succinct, somewhat depersonalized, and more
survey-oriented research. This apparent incompatibility can, it is clear,

55

inhibit the prospective (pre-Ph.D.) anthropologist from committing himself unreservedly to the research strategy and goals of the epidemiologist. There may, of course, also be the additional problem of how respectably "exotic" must be the trainee anthropologist's first fieldwork locale. Suffice it to say on this tender score that our Department of Anthropology has modified its expectations sufficiently to support medical anthropological research by one current degree candidate in the southern U.S.A. and prospectively by yet another into undergraduate "health culture" on the campus.

Another related problem stems from the anthropologist's heavy reliance upon various functional "modes" of social and cultural analysis-- that is, his marked tendency to view behaviour in terms of its total cultural context without necessarily delimiting the scope or subtlety of that context by means of any explicit, rigorous observational and interpretative methodology. This appears to reflect the idealistic framework which he brings (by virtue of temperament, or the implicitly inculcated values of his training, or both) to his work--namely the prevalent assumption that any really substantive understanding of behavioral patterns, whether "medical" or otherwise, simultaneously requires the widest contextual comprehension (often in terms of "related traits") plus all but perhaps the deepest personal knowledge of representative individuals within the group being studied. It need hardly be added that such combined breadth and depth in the understanding of any culture would, even with good fortune, require the better part of a lifetime to achieve; in fact, it has only begun to be approached in recent years under the stimulus of such work as Oscar Lewis' restudy of Tepoztlan (1951) and Fred Eggan's 1954 paper urging controlled and diachronic comparisons in social anthropology. All too often, the anthropologist still finds himself unable to collect sufficiently extended and telling data even about a restricted institution or cultural topic in which to root his functional analysis firmly at either the overt behavioral or psychological levels. As a result he may feel compelled either to publish an admittedly truncated analysis or to oversimplify his conclusions in terms of a currently fashionable ethnographic approach.

Frake's well known 1961 paper on disease diagnosis among the Subanun seems to exemplify this second resort: while asserting (on the basis of a componential analysis of a list of Subanun skin disease terms) that the entire "disease world" of these people, like their plant world, divides ideally[1] and exhaustively "into a set of mutually exclusive categories," he also specifically allows both for the judgement of spirit mediums and for the layman's "role playing strategies" in the Subanun diagnostic process. Yet nowhere does he even tentatively attempt to evaluate the effect of these critically important dynamics of disease diagnosis; neither does he appear to suggest the extent to which the diagnosis and treatment of skin diseases--a disease group certainly of focal importance among many neighboring tropical peoples of southeast Asia--may actually be

56

atypically structured concerns within the gamut of behaviour through which the Subanun relates to his "disease world." Hence, partly because Frake's field data were not initially collected to test this specific analytic scheme, his paper--like those of many other medically interested anthropologists--represents what John Cassel (1962) has called the "not additive" contribution to our published knowledge of human "health behaviour." Had his original field inquiry actually been shaped by a componential hypothesis, the resultant analysis would probably have proved not only more "additive" but also more compatible with current epidemiological research emphases. Yet, rigorous, hypothesis-structured field study by anthropologists (especially by those ethnologists conducting their first field work) has more frequently been the exception than the rule; given the diffuse nature of the "functional" theory which even now underlies much ethnological inquiry, it is hardly surprising that the results--as in this case--have usually been only partial and retrospective analyses.

Apart from functional analysis where he may increasingly match interests with the epidemiologist, the medical anthropology trainee is somewhat less likely to find diachronic and developmental study of health behavior of primary interest among the epidemiologists. Further, his anthropological training in ethnohistorical materials and techniques may act to discourage him from seeking a new synthesis of epidemiological method in his own field research, a point which remains to be determined as our program progresses. Yet, however compelling the ethnologist's interest in working out the historic interaction of such apparently paired medical traditions as, for example, Vedic and village therapy in India or the "hot" and "cold" dietary categories of Malaya and Latin America, he will quickly realize the necessity for repeated research visits and, of course, for utilizing whatever written records may be available. Ackerknecht's paper on malaria along the pioneer American frontier (1945) and Hudson's more recent study of association between human settlement shifts and the evolutionary spread of the yaws-syphilis-endemic-syphilis triad (1965) are two outstanding examples of ethnohistorical medicine-- both the contributions of physician-scholars. While the anthropologist is more likely to attempt historical reconstructions of more complex health phenomena (such as the diffusion of dietary categories), hopefully he will be more stimulated than discouraged in his historical interests by such exemplary synthesis of classical epidemiology with anthropological findings.

If we have chosen darkly to emphasize certain conceptual difficulties, actual and potential, for the medical anthropology student, a more extended discussion might describe several others--but, by way of healthy counterbalance, we might also indicate the contributions of John Cassel in giving the Department of Epidemiology here its productive social science orientation, its stimulating research atmosphere and, in cooperation with

57

anthropology,[2] developing this entire program. A "smooth integration"
of the anthropological and epidemiological frames of research reference
at the University of North Carolina--whatever that could mean--may never
prove either possible or desirable. Academic cleavage between anthropology and epidemiology will continue if only in terms of the additional,
idiosyncratic difficulties experienced by individual program trainees--
such as, for example, aversion to the alleged "manipulative ethics" of
the "medical establishment," reluctance (and perhaps inability) to utilize
statistical research methods, and difficulty with the concept of adaptation
(engendered in no small measure by its great breadth of reference in recent
anthropological literature). However, Charles Erasmus' (1967) recent
trenchant summary of the method and motives of anthropological inquiry
may augur a renewed initiative among many anthropologists towards dis-
solving the communications barriers separating them from scientists in
adjacent fields. The University of North Carolina Medical Anthropology
Program already represents achievement as well as further potential in what
one hopes will be a continuing trend in such scientific discourse.

Anthropological Opportunities in Epidemiology

Alland has made an interesting and important contribution to the
field of medical anthropology in a recent article (1966). In addition he has
stimulated other ideas for examining the major links between medically
oriented research and anthropological theory. Therefore, the following
observations are additional dimensions to Alland's article in which a
major focus is given to the use of medical anthropology as a link between
physical and cultural anthropology.
Alland calls for a greater synthesis between anthropology and
medicine. With regard to this point, specifically, epidemiology should
provoke a renewed interest in a socio-environmental laboratory. Probably
the most exhaustive ongoing socio-environmental laboratory that has been
developed in the social sciences is that of Alexander Leighton (1959) and
associates in Stirling County, Nova Scotia. Several ideas have been
raised which point to the necessity for such an experience. It seems
that an actual community diagnosis, as suggested by McGavran (1958)
would be of extreme importance in building a better communicative relationship between medicine and anthropology. George Rosen (1964) has also
pointed out that educating the public about environmental health problems
is one of the most neglected areas of public health. Lawrence E. Hinkle
(1964) has indicated that the future physician must know a great deal more
about the patient's environment than he presently does. So we can see that
the works of Rosen, McGavran, and Hinkle all raise the question of how
to go about developing a community diagnosis laboratory which would
better serve the modern problems of medical care and the understanding

58

of disease processes. One way of meeting this challenge would be to develop a community environmental laboratory which focuses on such questions as (1) the patterning of health and illness in a community, (2) the safety features of the physical and biological environment, (3) the nature of stress-producing and stress-reducing systems available to the group, (4) the prevailing modes of adaptation, (5) the patterning of medical referral, response, and attitudes toward health practices within a community, (6) the response to specially designed health programs, (7) the organizational effectiveness of the health professions, and (8) the current state of knowledge of the social, cultural, and emotional life of the client systems. In such a setting, a wide range of contributions from anthropology are obvious, namely the approach and methodology for studying human adaptation.

With this set of orienting but not exhaustive questions, it would be possible to develop an ongoing research program in the above areas while at the same time contributing to the solution of these problems: on the one hand, we could make contributions to developing a link between environmental understanding and medical practice, and, on the other, to provide public health with greater professional visibility.

By being thrust into a clinical context, anthropologists may find great use for the traditional medical research process: medical culture uses a triadic approach to understanding diseases. Hypotheses are often developed from clinical contexts and then studied experimentally or epidemiologically. This, of course, does not rule out new questions being raised through epidemiological investigations which are then examined clinically and experimentally. Likewise, new insights can be gained from experiments which are then examined further through epidemiological and clinical methods. Therefore, medical research can provide the anthropologist with a context to examine the contributions of anthropology to all three of these related processes of study.

There are many ways in which an anthropologist can provide the medical profession with conceptual tools for relating cultural patterns to patient responses: by contributing to an understanding of the cultural factors in etiology, by highlighting the nature of the social organization of healing systems, and by illuminating the communications processes of the diagnostic process. With regard to the latter point, we can utilize the developing field of the ethnography of communication as a way of enlarging the medical students' ability to elicit and evaluate diagnostically meaningful information, to get at the "truth" through the screening of cultural perceptions.

Alland proposes a framework for linking anthropology and medicine, and we applaud the examination of biological and cultural evolution as one way of doing it. Yet another fruitful and by no means exhaustive framework for relating anthropology to medicine would be through further examination

59

of the framework of hypotheses proposed by Alexander Leighton in his book, My Name is Legion.

It is very well to talk about adaptation, but we think that we need to begin to sharpen our conceptual tools as to the nature of a noxious or benign social system. In so doing, anthropology can make a very considerable contribution to the understanding of disease etiology. It is the more precise classification and mapping of the types of strains which we think holds great promise.

Program Goals and Mechanisms

We have noted the theoretic concerns and the opportunities available in the dialogue between anthropology and epidemiology. We now turn to a description of the program devised at the University of North Carolina to utilize the strengths of the two fields in training medical anthropologists.

One of our purposes is to examine how the conceptual and methodological tools of epidemiology and anthropology can jointly provide a better understanding of health problems while simultaneously helping to solve the classical questions of both fields. It is our hope that the main questions, the central interests, the key issues in both fields will be more imaginatively examined because of the convergence of two academic traditions with a mutual interest in the problems and processes of human adaptation.

A second goal is to provide the student with a programmed series of increasingly complex educational experiences that require correspondingly greater degrees of imagination and independence of inquiry.

Encompassed within the problem of defining the adaptive process are a number of specific interests which organize our program, e.g., the cultural and social factors in the etiology of disease, the social and cultural variables involved in the response of health practices and programs, social psychiatry, the population explosion, and the consequences of health innovations.

In the interests of providing a professionally useful program, and one which is especially congruent with the purposes of an evolving field of medical anthropology, we have decided to integrate the minor program in epidemiology fully into the basic anthropology curriculum. We are oriented towards developing a family of course areas for the development of competence in depth around a program focused on medical anthropology. Although the program goals are broad, the student can work out specific concrete interests such as family and health, socialization, social psychiatry, methodology, population, etc.

With the above goals in mind we are in the process of continuing to evolve a number of program mechanisms which will help us meet our intentions.

Cross-departmental exposure. For example, we arranged a series

60

of seminars for medical anthropology students during which the various
members of the Department of Epidemiology faculty familiarized the students
with ongoing faculty research. Such a device has permitted us to expose
the anthropology student to the social system of epidemiology.

We have established sub-area specializations such as population,
social psychiatry and their relationship to epidemiology as devices for
developing competence areas.

An informal luncheon-type seminar has been established which will
provide the students with a rallying point of identification with the medical anthropology program. We hope that such an informal setting will
provide an opportunity for students to talk about their research problems and
to hear local and outside speakers in areas related to medical anthropology. A very important consideration will be the provision of an opportunity for students to talk about their research at whatever point they are in
the research process, and thereby share with each other the realities of
thinking through an imaginative project.

As a concrete way of introducing the medical anthropology student
to medical culture, an opportunity has been created which will permit
him to participate in a human ecology course for first year medical students. This is a course in which the medical student examines the contributions which the various behavioral sciences make to an understanding
of disease etiology and treatment. This then gives our anthropology
students a chance to see the medical culture in action. We hope in this
setting to provide the students with an opportunity to assess and begin
to use the clinical contributions of anthropology to medicine, always
hoping to draw on the most classical questions and findings of anthropology.

As another concrete way of introducing the medical anthropology
student to medical culture, the opportunity has been created for the student
to participate in psychiatric and medical clinics, especially the diagnostic
rounds. In addition, there will be epidemiological field research site
visits.

In conclusion, the Medical Anthropology Program at the University of North Carolina, now in its second year, has developed jointly
within the fields (and Departments) of Epidemiology and Anthropology.
Designed to confer an anthropology degree (Ph.D.) based upon dissertation research in "health behaviour," the program aims inter alia to illustrate how the concepts and research methodology of both fields can jointly
extend our knowledge of such behaviour while simultaneously probing the
classical problems particular to each. A flexible administrative policy
has generally minimized the problems of structuring the trainees' academic
curricula and several lines of cross disciplinary training are beginning to
emerge as individual trainees express particular combinations of needs
and interests. Yet while certain recent statements (such as Alexander

61

Alland's 1966 article in the American Anthropologist) have seemed especially valuable in further defining the objectives of this new "field," the anthropologists' traditionally expected approach to data collection and analysis perhaps tends to inhibit his fullest participation in epidemiologically framed research. Certain pedagogical and conceptual issues raised by this possible tendency have been discussed.

NOTES

1. There appears to be ambiguity in Frake's use of this key term here; an extended discussion of the medically relevant theoretical significance of this analysis should also consider several other recent papers on "componential analysis."

2. In particular, Professors John Honigmann, Richard Lieban, and Ralph Patrick, of the Departments of Anthropology and Epidemiology.

REFERENCES

Ackerknecht, E.
   1945   Malaria in the Upper Mississippi Valley, 1760-1900. Bulletin of the History of Medicine, Supplement No. 4.

Alland, Alexander
   1966   Medical Anthropology in the Study of Biological and Cultural Adaptation. American Anthropologist 68:40-51.

Cassel, John
   1962   "Comment" in Polgar (1962).

Eggan, Fred
   1954   Social Anthropology and the Method of Controlled Comparisons. American Anthropologist 56:743-763.

Erasmus, Charles
   1967   Obviating the Functions of Functionalism. Social Forces 45:319-328.

Frake, C. O.
   1961   The Diagnosis of Disease among the Subanun of Mindanao. American Anthropologist 63:113-132.

Hinkle, Lawrence E.
   1964   The Doctor, His Patient and the Environment. Man, His Environment and Health, supplement to the American Journal of Public Health 54:11-17.

Hudson, E. H.
   1965   Treponematosis and Man's Social Evolution. American Anthropologist 67:885-902.

62

Leighton, Alexander H.
    1959   My Name is Legion (New York: Basic Books).
Lewis, Oscar
    1951   Life in a Mexican Village: Tepoztlan Restudied
                (Urbana, Illinois: University of Illinois Press).
McGavran, Edward G.
    1958   The Scientific Diagnosis and Treatment of the
                Community as the Patient. Public Health News (New
                Jersey Department of Health) 38:61-68.
Polgar, Steven
    1962   Health and Human Behavior. Current Anthropology
                3:159-205.
Rosen, George
    1954   Human Health, Community Life and the Rediscovery
                of the Environment. Man, His Environment and Health,
                supplement to the American Journal of Public Health
                54:1-6.

63

A FUNCTIONAL ANALYSIS OF
SOUTHERN FOLK BELIEFS CONCERNING BIRTH [1]

Alice H. Murphree
University of Florida

Introduction

Childbirth is universally recognized as one crisis period in the
life cycle, for all peoples acknowledge the mystery of life and the presence
of a new individual in the society and most, if not all, peoples feel this
crisis period to be dangerous either for the mother or child or through them
for the group (cf. van Gennep 1960; Gluckman 1962). Although some
cultures stress conception or gestation, and others emphasize delivery or
the postpartum period as the dangerous time, the various phases of the
birth process are accorded a relatively high degree of interest and emphasis
in folk tradition.

As Saunders and Hewes point out, health beliefs and practices in
our culture demonstrate many overlappings between folk and scientific
medicine (Saunders and Hewes 1953) and the same is true for our southern
sub-culture, although the use of folk medicine and scientific medical sophistication are somewhat inversely related, i.e., the greater the degree of scientific sophistication the less dependence there is on the practice of folk
medicine. Thus, in the South, while not as widely acknowledged perhaps
as in other cultures, folk beliefs persist in the rural tradition either con-
temporaneously with or as substitutes for scientific medicine. Rural residents are aware that scientific medicine denies clinical credence to "old
timey" remedies, and are consequently somewhat reluctant to admit knowledge, much less practice, of such beliefs; however, birth lore is among
the acceptable, and often dominant, discussion topics for married females,
both white and Negro.

Birth practices and beliefs are valid indices not only of attitudes
toward birth, but often toward health and life itself. When we consider
the emerging patterns of such beliefs and practices in the context of rites
of passage, it is pertinent to refer to Van Gennep. He contends that birth
rites are more than just rites of passage: ". . . these ceremonies have their
individual purposes . . . birth ceremonies include protection and divination
rites . . ." (Van Gennep 1960:11,12). He further stresses that illness
and birth, and other such rites are periods of movement, of separation from
and re-entry into the group. There is little question that the rural southern
woman experiences this sense of movement and the very real changes in
her self-image and sex roles, nor is there doubt that birth beliefs and
practices could be the basis for intensive analysis of the structural dynamics
and function of rural social organization. However, such an endeavor

64

would be far beyond the scope of this limited paper; instead, because the concept appears both apt and valid, the primary framework here will stem from a concern for the expressive and instrumental aspects of these beliefs and practices (Beattie 1964:217).

Much folk medicine qualifies as, or at least suggests, the classic homeopathic magic of Frazer's "law of similarity" or the contagious magic of his "law of contact" (Frazer 1960:12). In one of the more contemporary analyses of magic, we find the following concerning its definition and function:

> All men strive to control their social and physical environments and to determine, or at least to have prior knowledge of, their own lives. Through manipulation, explanation, and prediction, the operations of magic, witchcraft, and divination work toward this vital human end (Lessa and Vogt 1958:245).

Further, the following differentiation is made between religion and magic:

> Religion is supplicative: by ritual it conciliates personal powers in order to request their favors. Magic is manipulative; it acts ritually upon impersonal powers in order automatically to make use of them. Magic is a formula or set of formulas . . . (op. cit.).

Frazer's laws obviously apply, but Lessa and Vogt's functional and Beattie's symbolic or expressive frames of reference will place these particular beliefs and practices more accurately in the life ways of this subculture. The endeavor represented in this paper perhaps will also serve to add to our understanding of folk beliefs in general. Such other health attitudes as the mechanistic interpretation of physiology will also be discussed. This mechanistic interpretation apparently stems from a perception of psysiology in a direct cause and effect relationship--analogous to the presentation of physiology in television advertising for patent medicines. For instance, the nervous system is thought to be like an electrical system and the condition of the "coating on the nerves" determines the presence or absence, and degree, of "nervousness" for any given individual. The following section outlines the cultural situation. The birth lore reported here will be grouped into four sequential divisions of conception, gestation and abortion, delivery, and postpartum.

The Situation

The folk beliefs and practices presented in this paper were collected

65

in one of the smaller rural counties in North Florida. "Waters" County
(a pseudonym to protect the privacy of the residents) is one of the 25 to
26 counties which, early in this century, were the center of the state's
economic, political, and social growth. These counties have experienced
lack of economic growth (if not recession), out-migration of population, a
diminishing political influence, and the concomitant social and cultural
results of such phenomena, all of which contrasts sharply with other areas
of the state which are experiencing a rapidly expanding technological and
agricultural economy, plus tremendous population growth stemming from
both in-migration and a rising birth rate (U.S. Census of Population 1960).

In relation to most other rural peoples, particularly in the South,
the residents of this county are not unique in their problems or solutions,
and their attitudes and practices are representative of other comparable
rural groups. Although, appropriately, it may be thought of as part of the
southern perimeter of Appalachia, "Waters" County differs in two significant
ways from some other areas of the South. First, because it was never
within the southern plantation institution, and as a result of the depressed
economy and the out-migration of population, the current ratio of whites
to Negroes is approximately ten to one. Secondly, due in part to its agricultural marginality, this area was among those most recently settled
and retains a frontier-like essence; many of the older residents are children of the original homesteaders. Despite these variations, the material
to be discussed falls well within the cultural patterns of similar rural
southern areas and southern sub-culture generally.

"Waters" County has neither doctor nor hospital, and the nearest
orthodox medical care, other than Public Health Services, is approximately
20 to 35 miles away. One study (Murphree 1965b) showed a lack of orthodox preventive medical practices and that when illness occurred, a
common tendency was to try various alternative methods of treatment prior to seeking professional medical attention, and sometimes in its stead.[2] Such
self-treatment practices range along a continuum including "T.V." medicine
(my term for self diagnosis and treatment based on television commercials),
"what the druggist fixes up," patent medicines, and folk medicine.

Rural residents know that the value of folk medicine is minimized,
if not discredited, by orthodox medicine; and when both subjects are included in the same context, respondents may be sufficiently uncomfortable
to deny much of their folk medicine or folk belief knowledge. In a study
of self-treatment practices (Murphree 1966) 11% of the sample admitted
current, but infrequent, use of folk medicine practices, but 70% acknowledged its use in the past and 27% were able to supply at least one detailed
folk prescription. These figures have greater significance when we consider
the age of a residual population resulting from out-migration. Also, because such an aged population generally would be past the child-bearing
years, birth lore was probably much more frequently discussed in the past

66

than it is now. However, field experiences have shown that interviews focusing solely on folk medicine and couched in nonthreatening terms are highly productive of specific esoteric information. Key informants in the area of folk medicine and birth beliefs, including one "retired" and two practicing midwives, were readily identified and contacted. None of these individuals was reluctant to discuss "old timey remedies"; rather, problems most often arose in terminating interviews.

Conception

Some of the folk beliefs reported here reflect the wide concern of rural southern people of both sexes with libido. Such common statements by females as, "I lost my zip by stirring around too soon after the baby came," or "I ain't the same since I had everything took out," referring to hysterectomy, have their counterpart in the recommendation to males that Sting Nettle (Cnidosculus stimulosus) root tea will give him "courage" (Murphree 1965a). The two female statements explain a loss of sexual drive or less specifically act to validate their "puniness" (weakness)-- an attribute of the ideal female role--and combine with the mechanistic interpretation of physiology; but the male remedy is difficult to assess. It is widely known that physical contact with that particular plant produces severe and unpleasant tactile stimulation; however, the informants' usual explanation about this and other folk remedies refers only to its efficacy for many generations, which is clearly an empirical rationale. This or any of the other plant remedies present problems in analysis, in that without knowledge of the actual pharmaceutic properties, we tend to judge that use is based on magical manipulation. On the other hand, some plant remedies do have counterparts in orthodox medicine, for instance, tea from cherry tree bark prescribed for coughs has much in common with many commercial cough syrup prescriptions, the bases of which are cherry extract.

Another of the concerns focused on the sex act, or the consequences of it, is the possibility of contracting "bad blood" (venereal disease). Two folk remedies to "clear the blood" are teas, one combining Queens Delight (Stillingia sylvatica) and Prickly Ash (Xanthoxylum clava-herculis) plants and the other combining Queens Delight and Virginia Snake plant (Aristolochia serpentaria) (Murphree 1965a:182). Both remedies are among the few in this collection for which precise recipe and dosage instructions (shown below) were supplied, suggesting that "bad blood" is considered a most serious illness (at least by the male informant who supplied them).

> For a "small batch" the number of roots that can be encircled by the thumb and forefinger are gathered, washed, and pared. The roots are placed in a cooking vessel,

67

covered with water, brought to a boil, and allowed to
diminish in volume until the proper consistency is
achieved: the "color of coffee" is one criterion. The
teas are strained and sweetened with either sugar or
cane syrup and taken one tablespoonful three times a
day. With the Prickly Ash tea, it is suggested that a
"little drop of tar" from a pine tree be taken "about
once a week" during treatment in order to "keep the
kidneys clear."

Related birth beliefs and practices express a complex interrelationship of three factors. First is the belief that the sex of the child can be
determined at conception, and second is simply that male offspring are
highly desirable, at least among whites. Factors one and two are expressed
in the belief that if, during intercourse, the man carries a leather string
in his pocket, "it will bring a boy."[3]

The third factor presumes a strong homeopathic bond between the
sex of the infant and the direction right or left of the perpendicular midline
of the mother's body: to the left for girls and to the right for boys. One
informant succinctly stated all three factors in avowing that the side to
which the female turns following intercourse will determine the sex of the
infant. Whichever magical function this belief performs, and in certain
circumstances it may be any of the three, more pertinent, perhaps, is
consideration of Hertz' dichotomy of the sacred and the profane (Hertz
1960), or desirability vs. undesirability. The tenets of nineteenth century
Protestantism, expressed in most areas of rural southern living, and strongly
reflected in matters of health, expressed the superiority of males and the
moral frailty of women. This well may be an explanation for the left side
being female; it is really thought of as less desirable or even profane.
Further, we "know" that the right side, based on handedness, is the
stronger, and certainly in a rural sub-culture (as elsewhere) strength is
a masculine attribute; conversely, the ideal female sex role includes pass-
ivity, weakness, emotionality, and implicitly or symbolically, leftsideness.

Gestation and Abortion

With reference, now, to the gestation period, in the event that
the above ritual practices were either unknown or neglected during conception, the "right or left" formula may still be applied to ascertain the sex of
the infant. One such divinatory folk belief states that the predominant
direction of fetal movement indicates the sex of the infant, and another involves observing with which foot the pregnant female crosses a threshold
or begins to climb stairs.

During the gestation period, also, a phenomenon is said to occur

68

equal in interest to the curiosity surrounding the sex of the infant. This phenomenon, believed to be extremely common, results in "marking the baby," and is clearly a magical explanation. Always caused by some action or emotion of the mother, this belief seems an expression of the widespread rural conviction that "the sins of the parents are visited on the children." A birthmark on the infant is attributed to the mother's "craving" a particular food, being frightened or surprised by some animal or incident, or behaving in some unusual fashion. Some "marks" result from the mother's "craving" and eating a particular food, and others are believed to result when the mother resists or is unable to satisfy the craving; incidentally, the husband is occasionally, but not always, involved in satisfying the craving, in which case he is considered to be indulging her. For instance, one woman reported being unable to refrain from eating some of a particularly tempting crop on her "grape harbor" (a widespread folk phrase for grape arbor), and the baby was born with a "purplish mark like a bunch of grapes" on his side that "he carried 'til he died." This may imply that she was weak and could not resist the temptation and that the "mark" was punishment for and disclosure of her frailty. Another woman said she "marked her baby" because she saw a neighbor's freshly killed pork and "wanted fresh hog meat so bad I could taste it" (gluttony?) but was too polite to ask for it. Using van Gennep's classification of rites (van Gennep 1960:9) both instances would be dynamistic, contagious, and direct, with the first positive and the second negative. Relative to a mother's behavior, a negative example would be the saying, "Climb a ladder and the baby will be born with a bald spot." Ladder climbing would be considered unseemly and masculine for a woman--and baldness _is_ a masculine trait. Sometimes this same belief holds that an older child's disposition, dietary preference, or allergies are caused by prenatal "marking," i.e. "Billie Mae (an eleven year-old daughter) is scared of being around folks 'cause I got to be that way whilst I was carrying her," or "Watermelon has always made him sick on his stomach because I ate too much of it when I was pregnant."

Also pertinent to the gestation period are the practices and remedies used to terminate unwanted pregnancy, referred to by one informant as "teenage trouble." The generally accepted abortifacients such as jumping off a wagon, shed, or porch, and the less common one of stepping over a rail fence, seem more to reflect the mechanistic interpretation of biologic function than to express manipulation, but may also be expressions of something akin to "unseemly actions produce unnatural results." Using "a tablespoon of black gunpowder (ingested in a glass of water) to make a woman abort" suggests homeopathic manipulation with reliance on the explosive or expellent property of the gunpowder. Another reported practice is to "carry three whole nutmegs in your pocket and eat a little piece every day until the nutmeg is gone." This particular remedy, analogous to plant remedies, is probably well fixed in folk tradition. Nutmeg is one of the oldest known

69

spices and has a long history in herbal pharmaceutics in the New World. Kreig has this to say: "The widespread, dangerous, and false belief that nutmeg possesses abortifacient properties has caused serious poisoning and fatty degeneration of the liver in its victims" (1964:97-100).

A miscarriage, whether spontaneous or induced, may result in suffering for the mother from a condition known as "poisoned blood" (septicemia from incomplete delivery of fetal tissues). A traditional southern rural folk remedy to clear this "blood poison" is a heated poultice made from Red Oak (Quercus Falcata) bark tea and corn meal which is placed on the abdomen.

Birth

An interesting folk belief concerning the delivery phase of the birth process is that "the baby comes at the same time it is got."[4] In other words, folklore makes a positive correlation between the hour of conception, actually coitus, and the hour of birth. This seems to function as a rather fatalistic magical explanation for extended periods of labor, i.e., if delivery does not occur at the time of "getting" in one 24 hour period, it will not (or cannot) occur for another 24 hour period. However, the symbolism is unclear.

A well-known popular notion, sometimes applied in the comparison of rural and urban cultures, holds that "primitive" women bear their young with more facility than women of complex societies. In this rural folk collection, ten of the twelve items relating to delivery refer either to the difficulty or to the danger of childbirth, indicating a great concern about this phase of the life cycle and suggesting that the notion indicated above may be erroneous. Three kinds of tea were recommended as "good to keep the labor coming" or to hasten delivery. The first, made from the Low Bush Myrtle (Myrica cerefera) plant (Murphree 1965a), is as traditional as other plant remedies and, again the magical implications are obscure. The second tea, made from black pepper may be considered efficacious because the sneezing paroxysm's expulsive qualities suggest the results desired to expel the fetus, or because black pepper is believed to stimulate circulation and to "get the muscles to working." Either rationale demonstrates the mechanistic interpretation of physiology and strongly suggests magical homeopathic manipulation. The third tea, made of dirt dauber's nests, although highly recommended by a midwife, was unexplained, and a personal familiarity with these tubular, mud nests, affixed by the insect to eaves and walls of buildings, offers no assistance whatsoever. Coca-Cola was reported as useful during labor in two complementary ways: "Drinking a Coke will bring on the baby, if it is time, or ease off the pain if the time's not right." No magic seems involved in the Coke remedy; however Coca-Cola may well be considered to possess medicinal properties. Cokes are

70

"known" to contain "dope" and sometimes this soft drink is actually called
"a dope" rather than "a Coke." This is probably a cultural remnant from
the nineteenth century; witness an advertisement of the 1880's, "Coca-
Cola, The Ideal Brain Tonic, Delightful Beverage, Specific for Headache,
Relieves Exhaustion."[5] A distinct manipulative application of the law of
similarity is evident in the practice of utilizing a sharp instrument to "cut
the labor pains." A knife, razor, scissors, or ax is placed on or under
the bed, preferably without the patient's knowledge and allowed to remain
until delivery is completed. This practice is also reported from Kentucky
(Thompson 1959), and one of the Floridian informants maintained that "It
works just as good in the hospital as at home." While there are fewer home
deliveries than even fifteen years ago, this seems an excellent example
of the tenacity of folk belief and the ease with which it transports to the
orthodox medical situation.

Albeit, as far as was reported, there is nothing as exotic as the
true couvade in rural southern culture, there are indications that at least
the symbolic presence of the male is deliberately incorporated into the
birth process. It is unknown whether this is an inclusion of males into a
stress situation by the females, or an intrusion into the all important life-
producing female domain by the males. Fathers have been known to suffer
"morning sickness" and labor pains and it has been suggested that this may
be a "sympathy" phenomenon, i.e., when one of two individuals in a close
social relationship suffers, the other mirrors some of the same symptoms.
Thus the father could be manifesting his interest in, and bond with, his
wife and family, but he might also manifest shame of such weak, "womanly"
behavior. Manipulative homeopathic or contagious magic is strongly indicated in folk beliefs concerning males and delivery. Either the physical
presence of the father or some article of his clothing is often utilized to
precipitate birth.[6] One rural southern informant said, "If the father comes
into the room and puts his hand on her stomach, it helps the pain." An
excellent example of magic is the belief that "when the old man's black hat
is put over the birth place, it brings the baby quick"; and sometimes, during difficult labor, the father's hat is worn by the mother or his shirt is
placed across her abdomen. The overt magical transmission of male strength
to the female in labor, plus the notion of his symbolic presence, may be
widely recognized in folk lore, for although specific or cross cultural references were not sought, similar practices are known to occur within the
Brahman caste in India.[7]

Still another belief bearing on the father's relationship, in this
instance directly to the child, concerns the child "who never knew its
father." This particular belief states that the infant born after its father's
death is endowed with the power to see into the future and/or perform "conjures." No explanation was given for this but it is, perhaps, implied that
the father's spirit bestows the power on the child. Perhaps, because power

71

is related to uniqueness, this expresses the extreme "unnaturalness" of a child not only out-living the father but of the father dying even before the child's birth. Or perhaps such a peculiar child needs special powers to help protect him in his father's absence.

Should excessive bleeding occur during or after delivery, it is very likely that one of several commonly known verbal formulas for "stopping blood" would be used. One widely known practice (Campbell 1946, Randolph 1931, Norris 1958-59, Brewster 1939) involves the repeating of Ezekial 16:6:

> And when I passed by thee, and saw thee polluted in
> thine own blood, I said unto thee when thou wast in
> thy blood, Live: yea, I said unto thee when thou wast
> in thy blood, Live.

This should be performed by someone who "has their mind on the Lord." In addition, there is at least one other less commonly known verbal formula:

> Stand blood, don't spread, over our land, God the Father,
> God the Sun (sic), and the Holy Ghost ask it in the name
> of our Lord Savior, Jesus Christ. Amen. [8]

This is conceded to be a "conjure" and must be performed by one who has "the power." Both formulas incorporate obvious passages from the sacred religious writings of the people who use them; one, the more esoteric, uses the most sacred phrase in Christianity. Referring to the previously quoted passage from Lessa and Vogt (1958:245), a personal power is being supplicated and a favor is requested, all of which indicates that religious feelings, prominent in the sphere of health in the rural South, and religion itself merges into the area of magical belief, particularly in periods of stress. [9]

Another folk practice pertaining to delivery also has a strongly manipulative magical component with a protective element. In the event of a stillbirth, this belief states that subsequent stillbirths for that particular woman can be prevented by placing the infant corpse face down in the coffin before burial. The rationale, if known, could not be supplied by the informant, but one might conjecture that mobility of the dead infant's spirit is involved as is the suggestion that unnatural events involving death require inverse procedures.

Post Partum

After a successful delivery, the umbilical cord may be used to

72

prognosticate the number of future deliveries the mother can expect. A midwife reported validating her belief by quoting an old country doctor, that "the number of knots or bumps on the cord (counted before cutting) will tell how many babies there will be." Because both physicians and midwives are intimately familiar with the convolutional characteristic of umbilical cords, for them at least, this belief patently presupposes that all women who have had one child will have more. This overlap between folk and orthodox medicine may well express another cultural remnant, i.e., large families had high economic value in rural areas.

The delivery phase of the birth process can be considered terminated with the disposal of the placenta, membranes, and cord. All reported disposal methods are excellent examples of protective contagious magic with the implication that either mother or child may be harmed through the afterbirth. One midwife said she always burned the afterbirth, either in the fireplace or in the yard, making sure nothing remained. Because "salt keeps down infection," one midwife routinely "salted the placenta and buried it very deep or buried it in the salty dirt floor of the smoke house." Both the burning and the burying methods were also cited as protection from molestation by animals, but the belief in magical bonds is clear.

In addition to noting that the post partum period is the first opportunity for ascertaining whether the infant has been "marked" and for validating prophecies as to sex, we find that the three major concerns are excessive bleeding, "afterbirth pain," and "risin's" or abscesses of the breast.[10] Excessive bleeding would be treated by the same means as during delivery while observing such precautions as that cited by a midwife against the use of aspirin for afterbirth pain, because "aspirin thins the blood and causes more flow." Here, again, is an expression of the mechanistic conceptualization of physiology.

As for afterbirth pains, although it is believed that "you have a day and a night of afterbirth pains for every child you already got," it is also believed that these pains can be shortened or completely eliminated. One method, seemingly more empirical than magical, involved administering a "good big drink of whisky" or even a sufficient quantity to "get her drunk" as the best treatment for postpartum discomfort and fatigue. Other, perhaps more singular folk treatments, include utilization of a sharp instrument, believed as effective for afterbirth pains as for "cutting" labor pains. Also, several informants affirmed that "the old man's britches" hung on the bed post or placed across the foot of the bed would remove the possibility of afterbirth pains for the traditional nine-day confinement. Both measures are apparently the same type of reasoning as their counterparts discussed in the section on delivery. Again we have the manipulative, sympathetic magic of the sharp instruments and the magical article of the husband's clothing, symbolizing his presence.

73

The widespread concern with breast "risin's" is reflected in one informant's statement that "I just bore that pain and birthed them and then my breasts riz", implying that women's lot may be excessively painful. Many of the same remedies may be used here as for boils or "risin's" under other conditions, although these presented refer specifically to abscesses of the breast. A poultice made from axle grease was reported as good to cure a particular "risin'" and to prevent future occurrences. Another is to drink a cup of fresh milk in which the "shot from a buckshot" have been allowed to stand for one hour. Both were highly recommended but somewhat obscure, although the milk in the second seems significant. A tentative explanation is that this is imitative milk from which lumps, i.e. buckshot, have been removed is drunk to remove lumps from the breast.

A final and particularly potent cure or "conjure" involves gaining the "power to scatter (smooth away) risin's" by smothering a mole in one's hands. The significance of the mole is unclear unless we hypothesize that "risin's" are similar to mole burrows in that both are sub-surface formations. It is noteworthy that in this belief the power accrues to a man, particularly as it concerns abscesses of the breast, always associated with childbirth. The informant proudly reported that her husband had this "power" and that men "from all over the country" brought their wives to him to cure. Is this another incorporation of the male into the predominantly female sphere of activity?

Conclusion

Several folk beliefs and practices concerning birth have been presented and, where possible, their expressive functions within rural southern culture have been commented upon. Certainly, some of the basic values relative to male and female sex roles have emerged, as has the implication that these are based on stereotypic nineteenth century Protestant beliefs. There is the apparent deliberate incorporation of the male into what is usually thought to be an exclusively female sphere: pregnancy and birth, which may again express the feeling that anything so vital to the individual and the group as birth cannot, or should not, exclude men. Tied with this are the values of sacredness and profanity in the right-left dichotomy; and there is also the belief in the natural and the supernatural in an inverse relationship. Areas of overlap between folk and orthodox medicine have been illustrated with the suggested usefulness of the concept "folk-orthodox" for this phenomenon.

The folk remedies that are unexplained other than in terms of tradition may also be subsumed under Beattie's second reason for belief in magic: ". . . it may provide a way of coping with situations of misfortune or danger with which there are no other means of dealing" (1964:207). It should be noted here that attitudes are mundane concerning remedies

74

involving specific ingredients as compared to the awe for those involving "conjures" or someone "having the power" -- another expression of the natural-supernatural dichotomy.

The omission of identification of racial source for this folklore is purposeful, simply because, thus far, there seems to be little differentiation. Most of these, and other extant conjures, were supplied and practiced by whites and may or may not be specifically known by Negroes; some beliefs were reported by both races, and some by Negroes. This tends to support, and is a partial basis for, the contention (a personal one) that, at the lowest socioeconomic level, cultural differences between the races become narrower. Further research in this and many of the other areas suggested in this paper would add much to our knowledge of contemporary American culture. It should be noted also that folk beliefs exist for all stages and activities of life and, whether placebos or not, they express and are deeply rooted in cultural tradition.

NOTES

1. This is an expanded version of the paper presented at the Second Annual Southern Anthropological Society meeting in Atlanta, Georgia, March 30, 1967. Sincere appreciation is extended to Drs. Thomas Weaver and Charles Hudson for their interest and highly valuable suggestions in the revision. The beliefs and remedies were collected in the course of research during two years, supported in part by funds from National Institutes of Health, grant numbers FR 5362-04 and 05.

2. Regular family periodic examinations by physicians were reported for 7% of the base families. In 14%, only adults had regular check-ups and 79% of the families saw a physician only when there was a specific complaint. Most respondents felt the problem of cost of medical attention and the distance to acquire it were deterrents. The few who reported seeking prompt attention for illness seemed almost apologetic and said, "I'm funny about that" or "We're bad to run to the doctor." The term "bad to" connotes both frequency and deviation from the usual.

3. This implies that rural men are either fully dressed (the pocket would be in the trousers) or partially dressed (it would be a shirt pocket) during intercourse, which is not unexpected as nudity is considered sinful. It is not known at present whether this is done with intent, indicating magical manipulation, or if it is a post factum explanation, but the former seems more logical as the latter would be too great a test of memory. The informant offered no explanation concerning why this would "work."

4. This was also reported via personal communication from a woman who

75

formerly lived in Pennsylvania, indicating its widespread occurrence.

5. Advertising on a clock, now in the possession of personal friends, and formerly in a store near Knoxville, Tennessee.

6. It should be noted that customarily fathers have been permitted in hospital "labor rooms" and, in some more modern hospitals, are currently allowed to accompany the mother to the "delivery room."

7. The source for this was a personal communication from a female member of the Brahman caste.

8. This is an accurate transcription of the handwritten formula the female informant permitted me to copy. Customarily such "conjures" cannot be transmitted to one of the same sex, nor to a family member; neither can they be discussed, lest they lose their potency or the "conjurer" lose his or her power.

9. Certainly, such prevalent rural "faith healing" religious sects as the Church of God and the Assembly of God demonstrate the merging of religion and magic into magico-religious belief systems.

10. A "risin" is any painful boil, infected mass of tissue, or abscess visible on the surface of the body. In this case, it is mastitis, and it is apparently felt to be a fairly common complaint.

REFERENCES

Beattie, John
 1964 Other Cultures (New York: The Free Press of Glencoe).
Brewster, Paul G.
 1939 Folk Cures and Preventatives. Southern Folklore Quarterly III:33-43.
Campbell, Marie
 1946 Folks Do Get Born (New York: Rinehart & Company).
Currier, Richard L.
 1966 The Hot-Cold Syndrome and Symbolic Balance in Mexican and Spanish-American Folk Medicine. Ethnology 5:251-263.
Durkheim, Emile
 1954 The Elementary Forms of the Religious Life, Joseph Ward Swain, trans. (Glencoe, Ill.: The Free Press).

76

Foster, George M.
    1953   Relationships Between Spanish and Spanish-American
                Folk Medicine. _Journal of American Folklore_ 66:201-217.
Frazer, J. G.
    1960   _The Golden Bough_, abridged edition (New York: The
                Macmillan Company).
Gluckman, Max, ed.
    1962   _Essays on The Ritual of Social Relations_ (New York:
                Humanities Press, Inc.).
Hertz, Robert
    1960   _Death and The Right Hand_, R. Needham and C. Needham,
                trans. (Glencoe: The Free Press).
Kreig, Margaret B.
    1964   _Green Medicine_ (New York: Rand McNally & Company).
Lessa, William A. and Evon Z. Vogt
    1958   _Reader in Comparative Religion_ (White Plains, New York:
                Row, Peterson and Company).
Murphree, Alice H.
    1965a   Folk Medicine in Florida: Remedies Using Plants. _The
                Florida Anthropologist_ Vol. XVIII, No. 3, Part 1: 175-185.
    1965b   _The Health Resources and Practices of a Rural County_.
                A mimeographed report. Behavioral Sciences Division,
                Dept. of Psychiatry, College of Medicine, University of
                Florida.
    1966   _Self Treatment Practices in a Rural County_. A mimeographed
                report. Behavioral Sciences Division, Dept. of Psychiatry,
                College of Medicine, University of Florida.
Norris, Ruby R.
    1958-59   Folk Medicine in Cumberland County. _Kentucky Folklore
                Record_ 4-5: 101-110.
Randolph, Vance
    1931   _The Ozarks_ (New York: The Vanguard Press).
Saunders, Lyle and Gordon W. Hewes
    1953   Folk Medicine and Medical Practice. _Journal of Medical
                Education_ 28: 43-46.
Thompson, Lawrence S.
    1959   A Vanishing Science. _Kentucky Folklore Record_ 3: 95-104.
United States Census of Population
    1960
van Gennep, Arnold
    1960   _The Rites of Passage_, Monika B. Vizedom and Gabrielle
                L. Caffee, trans. (Chicago, Illinois: The University of
                Chicago Press).

77

DOCTOR MEDICINE AND BUSH MEDICINE IN KAUKIRA, HONDURAS[1]

John G. Peck
University of North Carolina

Introduction

This paper will describe some diagnostic features of two medical systems as they are practiced by the Miskito Indians in Kaukira, Honduras. One system will be termed "doctor medicine" and will refer to health-related behavior associated with the medical clinic in Kaukira run by the Moravian Church Mission. The other system will be called by its local term, "bush medicine" and will refer to the health-related behavior associated with the local native health practitioner, or sukya. Utilizing Glick's (1967) model for the analysis of diagnostic systems in terms of evidence, process and cause, complaint categories used by doctor medicine and bush medicine will be described and some suggestions will be offered to explain why bush medicine continues to operate as a viable system in the presence of a well-accepted modern medical facility.[2]

Glick (1967:34) indicates that medical systems may be distinguished from each other on the basis of the criteria of underlying diagnosis. Diagnosis involves not only the determination that an illness is present, but also ideas about causation. The dimensions along which diagnosis can be made are three in number: evidence, process and cause. Evidence is "whatever is taken as empirical indication of the existence of an illness,...what our physicians call 'signs and symptoms'" (1967:35). Process is defined by Glick as "what is actually happening to produce evidence of illness", and is equivalent to what we study as pathology. Glick's category of cause may be treated in terms of an instrumental cause, i.e., what has been done to the patient or what is used, as an efficient cause, i.e., who or what has done it to the patient; and as a final or ultimate cause, i.e., an attempt to answer the question, "why did this happen to me at this time?" The final or ultimate cause involves the patient's unique socio-cultural identity as a significant dimension in disease diagnosis and treatment behavior, rather than seeing the patient as a relatively neutral host to a pathogen, uninvolved in the process of illness. It is Glick's suggestion that "in contrast to Western medical thought, the most important fact about an illness in most medical systems is not the underlying pathological process but the underlying cause" (1967:35). In the following sections of this paper we will attempt to categorize the ways in which the two systems, doctor medicine and bush medicine, treat the three dimensions involved in diagnosing illness, i.e., evidence, process and cause.

The Miskito Indians are a Chibchan-speaking group who inhabit

78

the tropical coastal plain along the Atlantic Coast of Honduras and Nicaragua from the Rio Tinto to the Rio Punta Gorda. Together with the Sumu Indians who live further inland, they comprise the main population of the territory generally referred to as the Miskito Coast.

The village of Kaukira is located on the southern side of a narrow neck of land between the Caribbean Sea and the Caratasca Lagoon. The neck of land, at this point, is about half a mile wide and rarely more than five to ten feet above sea level. The lagoon water, while technically "fresh," is dark brown in color and fairly brackish. However, it is used by the Indians for cooking, washing, and waste disposal. The village is approximately six miles long and is rarely more than two houses wide. It is traversed by one main road or footpath. There are approximately 960 people living in about 180 structures in the village, all but a few of the buildings being used as residences.

The people of Kaukira are nominally Christian. There is a Moravian church, three native ministers, and the Mission which houses the Director of Missions for the northeast section of Honduras. There is also a house which is used by the Catholic priest, who makes periodic visits to the village from his station on the Patuka River some seventy-five miles away. The Moravian Church of the United States established a mission in Kaukira in 1932 and, with the exception of two or three periods of less than a year's duration, has been actively engaged in work with the Miskito Indians in the area since that time. In addition to the facilities at Kaukira, they maintain over a dozen local churches with Miskito ministers, a school and seminary, and a Medical Mission. They also periodically bring in specialists in various fields from the U. S., including such specialists as a dentist, carpenters, and recently an agricultural specialist who is working on improved crops for the whole Miskito Coast area. They have also supported linguistic research in the area in the past. The emphasis of the church's missionary work is on the general improvement of the standard of living of the Miskito Indians, as well as conversion to the Christian faith. In addition, the Moravian Church operates the local clinic in Kaukira.

In the past, malaria was endemic to the area, but in the last six years this disease has been considerably controlled as a result of the extensive spraying of the whole area by the World Health Organization, and the continued efforts of the various malarial control agencies of the Honduran and Nicaraguan governments.[3] A number of other parasites continue to plague the population, however, including red bugs, ticks, cockroaches, chiggers, sandflies, as well as screw worms, hook worms, tape worms, pin worms and whip worms (Pijoan 1946:157-83).

The Clinic

The clinic is a zinc-roofed structure of about 25 feet by 40 feet,

79

with a large porch attached. Inside are two examining rooms and a waiting room, as well as a storage area for medicine. It is located adjacent to the Mission house, but separated from it by a fence. There is a boat landing nearby. Patients come with their families, and it is not unusual to see 30 to 35 people gathered around outside of the clinic in the morning, talking and resting while they wait their turns.

The clinic at the Mission has been operating more or less continually for the last fifteen years. The wife of the missionary, a registered nurse, opened it when she and her husband came to Kaukira in 1948. She ran it until approximately 1959, when she and her husband were transferred to another mission station. From 1959 to 1966, the clinic was in operation only periodically. Additional medical treatment is available from a government clinic in Puerto Lempira, some 14 miles away by canoe.[4] Since June of 1966, the Mission has again been running the clinic on a six-day a week basis, processing 60 to 100 patients a day.

The missionary's wife might well be described as a happy pragmatist. She was an Army nurse during the Second World War, and in coping with the problems in Kaukira she does what she can, recognizing that in large measure what she cannot do will not get done. The clinic runs from about eight o'clock in the morning until sometime in the afternoon, after which she makes "house calls" to those in the village who are too sick to come to the clinic. Medical services are given to all who request them regardless of religious beliefs, and no direct pressure is applied on the patients to convert them to Christianity. When a patient has no money, medicines are either given free or the patient or a member of his family is given an opportunity to work around the Mission to earn the money. When medical problems beyond her scope arise, the nurse is able to consult by short-wave radio with the Moravian doctor at Ahuas, and in the event of serious emergency, to fly a doctor in or a patient out through the Missionary Air Force facilities. A short and very rugged landing field is situated behind the Mission.

The majority of conditions treated at the clinic can be subdivided into three groups, depending on the relative emphasis placed on evidence, process or cause. The first group includes those conditions endemic to the area and so widespread among patients who come to the clinic that diagnosis and treatment is virtually automatic and evidence is assumed to be present. Included here are such conditions as worms and malnutrition. Worms are both intestinal and of the liver-fluke variety. Infestation is almost universal, as is reinfestation. "Deworming" is a standard treatment for all children, and most adults. Malnutrition was reported by the nurse to be a form of vitamin B-C complex deficiency due to the total lack of green, leafy vegetables in the diet of the area. It is also probable that there is protein deficiency among the pre-school children, since milk is absent from their diet and the amount of animal protein is limited and

80

seasonal in its availability.[5] This deficiency, however, was not mentioned by the nurse.

The second category of conditions may be distinguished as being diagnosed on the basis of _evidence_, usually the verbal report of the patient, but under conditions in which _process_, i.e., the pathological agent, is assumed. Included here are such conditions as fevers, skin rashes, stomach ills, tumors and hypertension. _Fevers_ are probably related to malarial cases from the past. They are widespread, chronic, and normally treated with antibiotics. Diagnosis is based on the verbal report by the patient or an elevated temperature as an indicator of the presence of a pathogen. _Skin rashes_ are widespread among children, especially in some of the outlying areas. While the nurse could not give a specific pathogen for the rashes, she did indicate that they may be caused by swimming in polluted water, or otherwise associated with unsanitary conditions. Treatment is by topical application of medicines such as Gentian Violet. This, because of its bright blue color, produces a rather striking symbol of illness. _Stomach ills_ are common among all age groups, and again the pathogenic agent is nonspecific, but assumed to be associated with unsanitary conditions of the water supply from the Lagoon or in the foods eaten by the patients. Treatment is usually by the administration of a cathartic or an anti-diarrheal medicine, depending on the symptom pattern. _Tumors_ are referred to the Government hospital in Tegucigalpa for surgical removal if there is money to send the patient. Otherwise little is done in the way of treatment. _Hypertension_ is treated with tranquilizers. The nurse commented that many of the patients' difficulties seem to be psychosomatic in origin, and tranquilizers seemed to offer significant relief. They were used in cases in which the symptoms were mild, non-specific, and did not indicate a clearly defined pathogenic agent.

The third category of conditions treated at the clinic is distinguished by the greater emphasis placed on _cause_, both instrumental and efficient. Included here are such conditions as tuberculosis, gonorrhea, pregnancy, traumatic injuries and preventive medical intervention. _Tuberculosis_ appears to be prevalent in the population, and usually involves the respiratory tract rather than bone or other systems. It attacks people of all ages, but is especially common among women of child-bearing age. There seems to be some localization of the disease in certain villages. Again, its incidence seems to be associated with unsanitary conditions and with the contaminated water supply. Specific treatment techniques were not secured, other than a mention that severe cases were sent to a sanatorium and that the most difficult aspect of treatment seemed to be getting the patients to come to the clinic. There is some conception of the contagious nature of the disease among the people, and advanced cases of tuberculosis tend to isolate themselves by sitting at some distance from non-infected people, and by living in a designated house when coming to the village for treatment

81

at the clinic. Gonorrhea is a very widespread disease in this population.
Gonorrhea of the eyes is common in small children. Diagnosis is made
by examination rather than laboratory procedure, and treatment is by
penicillin.

Pregnancy and childbirth becomes a problem for the clinic only in
the event of some sort of difficulty indicated in the delivery. The normal
pattern for childbirth is for the woman to deliver at home, with the help
of her female relatives. In the case of prolonged labor or other obvious
difficulty, however, the woman is brought to the clinic for the nurse to
assist in the birth. The nurse remarked on the unusual number of foot
and hand presentations she had witnessed in the village. Emergency
treatment of traumatic injury represents a large portion of the clinic's
business. Cuts, infected wounds, broken bones and infected teeth are
treated. Dental problems are almost universally treated by extraction of
the tooth and administration of antibiotics. Preventive medicine is almost
entirely limited to the administration of vaccinations against small-pox
and periodic epidemics of childhood diseases. Vaccination programs
seemed to be well accepted, especially if there was evidence of the
ravages of the disease in surrounding communities.

Bush Medicine

The second, and older, system of medical behavior in the village is
bush medicine. Bush medicine is perhaps best thought of as a way of coping with life-problems of a number of different sorts, among which problems
of maintaining health loom large. No sharp distinction seems to be drawn
between life problems caused by what we think of as a pathogenic agent
and those caused by such things as good or bad fortune, friends or enemies,
"accident" or natural forces.

There are two sukyas or native medical practitioners in the village
of Kaukira. While most sukyas were reported by Conzemius (1932:162) to
have been men, there have been no male sukyas in Kaukira for the last
fifteen years. I interviewed one of the sukyas through an interpreter, and
information reported here is based upon that interview. The interview was
tape-recorded and a check of the tapes, made by a Miskito-speaker, indicated that by and large questions and answers were successfully translated
with a minimum of distortion.[6]

The sukya's power of curing is not hereditary, but is acquired. Her
children have no greater probability of being sukya than anyone else in
the village. As a child she had been sickly and weak. Soon after she was
married, she fell very ill, and during her illness the spirits came to her and
told her how to get well.[7] When she got well, they continued to appear
in her sleep, making her feel "weak." Apparently, other spirits come
around her, too, but these are the primary ones with whom she works. She

82

has tried to rid herself of the spirits, because she used to be Christian and would like to be again, but the spirits will not leave her alone. She hopes that when she gets old, they will leave her and she can again become Christian, and attend the Mission services.[8]

When asked about other sukya, she told of "Old Man Flores," an old man with a beard down to his waist, who lives about forty miles down the coast. He is a prophet rather than a sukya, and has an alwani mahbra, or ancient stone celt, a very powerful kind of magic charm. She also told of a head sukya, or Okuli who lived a long, long time ago. When he became old, he and his wife walked into the sea and disappeared, and no trace was ever found of them. She also talked of some invisible spirits or untadukya who were around the village. There had been a silk-cotton wood spirit, too, a sisin, but it was now dead, apparently killed by her spirits. She does not consult or meet with other sukya in the village, although she did say that her spirits could and sometimes did consult with either Old Man Flores or his spirits.

In consulting a sukya, the patient or a member of the patient's family comes to the sukya's house. I was told that sometimes the sukya can tell what it is that the patient comes for, even before the patient asks for help; at other times all that is necessary is for the patient to say two or three words for her to know what his problem is.

Having discussed his problem with the sukya, the patient pays her fifty centavos and goes on about his business, returning the next morning for her advice. During the night, while she is asleep, the sukya's spirits come to her and she asks them to find out what is causing the patient's problem and what can be done about it. In the morning, when the patient returns, she explains to him exactly what his trouble is, who or what is causing it, why, and what can be done about it. If it is a case of illness or misfortune which has not yet befallen the patient, she offers prescriptions for avoiding it. Her prescriptions usually involve eating special herbs and avoiding particular foods. If the herb is not one commonly known to the patient, the sukya secures it for him from the "bush," or uncultivated land surrounding the village.[9]

The sukya reported that her "patient load" averaged about two people per day. It was my impression, however, that in all probability it ran considerably higher than this. When I arrived for the interview there were perhaps fifteen adults around the house, which was an unusually large number except in the case of cooperative work projects. Also, the pathway to the house was larger and more used than most.

The conditions treated by the sukya are diagnosed primarily in terms of efficient and final causes. Almost no emphasis is placed on process. Evidence as an attribute of her diagnostic system is optional. There are some conditions which are either observable or presented verbally and other conditions, such as "future illness," in which evidence is not manifest.

83

Conditions which include evidence as part of the diagnosis include yumu, lasa diseases, toothache, and infant illnesses. Yumu is an abdominal nonspecific illness, i.e., a "stomach ache." It can be caused by many things, including "bad water in the stomach," other bad foods in the stomach, and "fear put there by spirits who make you feel afraid." She treats it by bush herbs, and/or by having her spirits chase away the spirits that are causing it. Lasa disease is a general category of nonspecific malaises caused by lasa, the "devil." The sukya can see lasa-caused disease from far away and her spirits can chase lasa away to cure a person. Toothache is caused by a "worm" in the tooth and is treated with herbs from the bush. The spirits tell her which herbs to use. No further information was given. The sukya is often consulted about sick infants.[10] She tells if the infant will get better, and advises the parents whether or not to take the child for treatment to the clinic. If it is determined that the child will die, treatment is not sought.

Conditions which the sukya treats in which evidence is not a necessary part of the diagnosis include aubia, "bad luck" and illnesses which have not yet occurred. Aubia is an invisible "bush-man" who bothers hunters. Her spirits will chase him away if she is asked before the hunt. She cannot help fishermen in the same way, even though one of her most powerful spirits is a "sea spirit." The sukya can foretell bad luck before it occurs, so that you can take countermeasures to avoid it. Also, her spirits will warn her, if asked about a future illness before it actually manifests itself, so that the patient can take preventive measures.

Snake bites are not treated by the sukya. Bush snake-bite medicine is fairly widely known. In fact, the knowledge can be purchased from people who know the specific herbs to use for specific kinds of snakes.

Summary and Conclusions

It has been shown that the identification and treatment of impaired health states by the clinic relies primarily on assumptions made about the process involved in the impairment, with less emphasis placed on what has here been termed cause. The patient, and the patient's socio-cultural identity are looked at as being relatively neutral with respect to the presence of the impaired health state or the treatment process. Rather than asking what has been done to the patient, doctor medicine asks what is going on within the patient.

Bush medicine, on the other hand, relies primarily upon cause for determining the identification and treatment of an impaired health state. Comparatively little emphasis is placed on evidence, and process is of almost no concern.

It remains to be explained, however, why the two systems continue to coexist. One possibility is that they treat different illnesses, or

84

different kinds of illnesses. There is at least a possibility that this is the case.[11] A different explanation for their continued coexistence lies in the kinds of diagnostic criteria which they use, in the sense that they provide the patient with quite different explanations for his condition. Explanations supplied by the clinic yield relatively high symptom amelioration in most cases, but relatively low causal understanding on the part of the patient. Bush medicine, on the other hand, yields a relatively high degree of understanding on the part of the patient about why he is sick, but less likelihood of there being a substantial reduction of pathogen-caused symptoms.

A large part of the disease and disability load that the population of Kaukira carries is of a chronic but non-disabling sort. Included here are such things as worms, malnutrition, fevers, stomach ills, tuberculosis, and gonorrhea, in terms of clinic-treated disorders; and yumu, lasa, aubia, "bad luck" and "future illnesses" in terms of sukya-treated disorders. One of the common features of all of these disorders is that there is no really effective or permanent "cure," given the conditions existing in Kaukira. It is under this circumstance that final causes are sought.

NOTES

1. Field research upon which this paper is based was done in Kaukira, Honduras during December of 1966 and was made possible by grants from the Department of Anthropology, University of North Carolina at Chapel Hill, and Salem College, Winston-Salem, North Carolina. Because of the extremely short duration of the research trip, conclusions must be seen at best as tentative.

2. The alternative question could also be asked: "How does doctor medicine continue to operate as a viable system in the presence of a well-accepted bush medical system?"

3. The Servicio Nacional de Erradicacion de la Malaria (SNEM) control center in Kaukira stated that only two cases of confirmed malaria had been reported for their district in the past two years.

4. The Government clinic at Puerto Lempira limits its patient load to approximately twenty patients per day, according to the missionaries.

5. Fish, while readily available, are not liked by the Miskito, and do not form a major part of the diet in this area.

6. The author expresses his gratitude to Dr. Mary Helms of Wayne State

85

University for her effort in checking taped materials.

7. She had two spirits who supplied her with her knowledge: _Writi_, who was a land spirit, and _Lewa_, who was a sea spirit. Of the _Lewa_, Conzemius says:

> The mermaid or water nymph is an evil water animal,
> which occasionally causes snags and strong ripples
> where the water otherwise is very smooth. It drives
> the fish away so that the Indians cannot catch any-
> thing, and it incites the alligator to attack the canoes
> and upset them. It also assumes the shape of a beauti-
> ful woman and walks on land to entice the young men
> down to the waterside, when suddenly it pushes its vic-
> tim into the water and devours it. Its head is that of a
> human being, but the body resembles that of a fish.
> This monster is also said to inhabit the sea, where it
> occasions waterspouts and hurricanes (1932:167).

8. These last remarks may well be the _sukya's_ response to problems of ambiguity over my identity. During my stay in the village, people at first identified me as a member of the Mission staff, and later as possibly an FBI agent. In either case, a "hedge" on her part would seem a reasonable thing.

9. Hence the term, "bush medicine."

10. This material was elicited in response to a question concerning _smaya kaikaya_, or buried poison around the village reported to cause illness in infants and small children.

11. Aside from the obvious possibility that bush medicine may be treating psychosomatic illnesses while the clinic may be treating infectious diseases, there is the possibility that the distinction between the two systems of medicine may be made on the basis of the origin of the illness state. In this case, bush medicine might be conceptualized as treating conditions caused by microbiota, indigenous to the individual, while the clinic treats primarily microbiota normally not found in the individual's microbiota. See René Dubos (1965), especially chapter V, for a discussion of this point.

86

REFERENCES

Conzemius, Eduard
    1932   Ethnographical Survey of the Miskito and Sumu Indians
of Honduras and Nicaragua. Smithsonian Institution,
Bureau of American Ethnology, Bul. 106.

Dubos, Rene
    1965   Man Adapting (New Haven, Conn.: Yale University
Press).

Glick, Leonard B.
    1967   Medicine as an Ethnographic Category: The Gimi of
the New Guinea Highlands. Ethnology 6:31-56.

Pijoan, Michel
    1946   The Health and Customs of the Miskito Indians of
Northern Nicaragua: interrelations in a medical program.
America Indigena 6:157-83.

87

PICA: A STUDY IN MEDICAL AND ANTHROPOLOGICAL EXPLANATION

Gianna Hochstein
University of North Carolina

A physician may be oriented either to the individual or to the group. If group-oriented, then he finds himself in the company of both epidemiologist and anthropologist. Unlike clinical medicine, anthropology by its nature is not concerned primarily with pathology. Anthropology has been saved from this by our unwillingness to decide just what the socially good and the socially pathological are. The advantage in such a non-judgmental position is that nothing has been excluded from the observational field.

To illustrate this divergency of anthropology from medicine, the old mystery of pica is illuminating and instructive to medical anthropologists. Since early times the question of pica has interested travellers and historians; in modern times internists, nutritionists, psychiatrists, soil chemists and anthropologists have become involved in understanding its various manifestations. The purpose of this paper is not to review the literature on pica (which has been done extensively by Laufer in 1933 and Cooper in 1957) but rather to reexamine an old issue in the framework of medical anthropology. Pica has been found in association with children of toddler age, with pregnant women, and with all manner of persons faced with food shortages. The global distribution of geophagy and its occurrence among persons of different social classes requires more than one explanatory hypothesis. What follows is a delineation of explanations held by experts from several fields, along with several of my own. These latter hypotheses are intended as heuristic efforts to utilize information now available from many disciplines toward the development of a syncretic approach to medico-cultural phenomena.

The Problem of Definition and Distribution

As early as the Middle Ages two notions were distinguished. The word "pica" was used to describe a condition in which a person craved inedible substances while "malacia" was reserved for the cravings of pregnant women. As Pliny wrote: "Praecipiunt in malacia praegnanthus." Or roughly, "We knew she was pregnant since she was nauseated and begging for pickles." One European authority reported that a common test for pregnancy prescribed mashed watermelon mixed with human milk; if the woman who ate this became nauseated, she was adjudged pregnant.

Pica comes from the Latin name for the magpie, whose appetite was presumed to be omnivorous. A broad definition of pica in the modern sense is simply "the practice of ingesting unusual substances." This is, in effect, the definition used by most anthropologists. However, the

88

predominant medical definition of pica implies pathology: "the perverted craving of substances unfit for food." The best known craving is for earth or clay, and is thereby called geophagia or geophagy, meaning "earth-eating." In the South it is simply called "dirt-eating."

Is pica a disease or a custom? The answer is that it can be either or both. What begins as a relatively harmless custom may assume the proportions of a mental disease or have severe physiological repercussions. The very serious consequences of pica fall into three categories: First, the intentional swallowing of a substance or object which remains in the stomach or intestine may have to be removed surgically. The commonest examples are stones and other objects ingested by small children. Second, the ingestion, usually by children but sometimes by psychotics, of paint containing lead. Lead-poisoning may be fatal. And third, the prolonged eating of clay or earth has been known in early times and rarely in recent clinical history to result in a condition known as cachexia africana, the African depravity. This disease entity has recently been identified as hypokalemia, a potassium deficiency disease. In former times it was regarded as inevitably fatal (Craigin 1811).

Because of the association of geophagy with such pathologies as these, the anthropologist Laufer, reviewing the literature in 1933, advised his fellow anthropologists to leave the pathological manifestations of geophagy to others. The new discipline of medical anthropology provides a rebuttal to this archaic view by maintaining that the disease is integral to the explanation of the custom.

The curious custom of eating earth has a long history and a wide distribution.[1] Pliny reports that chalk was added to spelt porridge to whiten it, while Galen, writing in the second century A.D., describes the use of clay as a medicine for stomach disorders. In China at an early date earth and clay were eaten to supplement inadequate food supplies. Kaolin appears in our modern pharmacopoeia for the same use--as an absorbent--as did clay in Greek and Roman times. However, the continuous and heavy resort to clay and earth eating is not reported in the literature until the eighteenth century. Whether the observer regards the practice as deleterious seems to determine the prevalence of reports of the condition.

Not only is the distribution of earth-eating vast and scattered, but so is the manner of handling clay and the types preferred. In India, the eating of clay became so refined that figurines made only to be eaten were sold in the bazaars. In Spain, more typical pottery shapes were customary; a woman could eat her plate rather than eat from it. In Bolivia a yellow clay is preferred; in Brazil the red type. In parts of Europe a white chalk was considered best, as was the case in China (Laufer 1933). Analysis of these ingested earths shows that some contain iron (the red ones) or copper, while others contain nothing of known nutritional value. Some

89

have a special odor or taste which the users cite as its attraction. The consistency of some is porous, others are decidely argillaceous. A search for the common denominator reveals only that all are non-organic earths.

The distribution of geophagy among ethnic groups is extensive. The mention of geophagy to any anthropologist invariably elicits a personal observation of its occurrence in the field. However, from the extensive occurrence of geophagy, it should not be inferred that all or most members of any group are habituated. Perhaps the highest incidence of clay- and dirt-eating has been found in the southern United States among adult Negro females.

There are two theories explaining how the latter group came to practice geophagy. One holds that it was derived from the Indians, who were observed eating clay in eighteenth-century Georgia and Carolina. The custom was also noted among whites in these same regions as late as 1857. The other theory postulates that the custom was brought over in slave ships from Africa. These two explanations are not necessarily mutually exclusive.

Why the practice died out among whites and persisted among the Negro population of the South has usually been answered in terms of the poorer nutrition of Negroes. Although Negroes share poverty and malnutrition with the rest of the lower strata in the South, there are some well-known cleavages in the cultural patternings of white and Negro.

The theme of women and geophagy runs through the literature and is especially linked with pregnancy. Sometimes the habit is acquired in the pubescent years, but more often the practice does not become a habit until pregnancy. Of those who indulge heavily during pregnancy, some "recover" with the birth of the child, while others continue the practice at a reduced rate.

All data on school-age children with pica antedate school desegregation in the South and deal with Negro children (Dickins 1942). The literature on pre-schoolers describes both white and Negro children with pica at the clinical level of symptom presentation. These children of both sexes range in age from one to six years. At about age six the symptoms tend to disappear. Psychopathology is inferred when the habit persists past this age. Social pathology has not been found to characterize the environments of these children (Cooper 1957).

Six Hypotheses

The questions asked about pica vary according to whether it is regarded as a disease or a custom. If the disease theory is held, it may either be viewed as a mental condition (Laufer 1933) or as a physical craving which manifests itself in self-damage (Carpenter 1845). If, on the other hand, pica is regarded as a custom, then the explanation for

90

its origins and perpetuation is sought among factors in the social and psychological life.

After several decades of critical observation, a peculiar turn of events has taken place. Those anthropologists who observed the phenomenon in the field have found no satisfactory social or cultural explanations for pica.[2] Rather, noting its association with hookworm, with pregnancy, with women in general, they decided that the explanation was physiological. More recently, nutritionists and other health workers, originally committed to a nutritional hypothesis, have attributed pica in children to a "complex of psychological and cultural factors" (Dill 1957).

Each of the following hypotheses about pica has a different degree of plausibility and amount of evidence, and each stems from a rather different scientific context.

I. A Psychological Explanation. The first hypothesis is a psychological explanation because pica and malacia are seen as responses to felt or imagined needs which have no physiological basis. The story is a familiar one. A woman wants to be treated during pregnancy and menstruation for imagined pain and discomfort. Failing special treatment and attention, she substitutes the gratification of eating substances. The story of the pica child is not basically different: he is expressing a psychological need, not real "belly hunger."

Even with the end of pregnancy or the arrival at a new phase of life at age six, the habit may persevere. As in the case of smoking, the Freudian theory of the oral personality is invoked to account for this oral fixation.

II. Anthropological Hypothesis. Strangely enough, the cultural hypothesis is probably the least developed. It has two aspects, one of origin and the other of persistence. Thus: The traditional role of women as gardeners and potters acquainted them with the advantages of clay and earth eating. Hence the custom contributed to the maintenance of the identity of the female community.

The traditional pattern among Southern Negroes has the mother taking her daughters to the clay pit to obtain the best clay, digging it out, transporting it home, perhaps baking it, eating it somewhat at whim but usually following meals. When mother or daughter becomes pregnant, more clay is recommended and usually desired.

Interviews which I conducted recently among lower class Negro mothers in North Carolina present a changing picture. The family clay pit is increasingly rare; clay is mined almost anywhere near at hand. Initiation to clay-eating may occur in the process of childhood exploration or at the hands of a girl-friend, although clay-eating itself is infrequent among the younger women.

But pica--defined broadly to include starch and flour eating--has a high incidence. To judge from a small sample of women it is a standard

91

custom. In a group of thirteen, a fourth had at one time eaten clay, half had favored starch, and another fourth favored flour. Only two denied interest in any of these substances. None was unaware of the practice, nor was it regarded as strange. Some expressed a slight repugnance for "dirt." One subject who was accustomed to one box of starch a day at the time of the interview, reported having a five-box-a-day habit during pregnancy.

    III. <u>Sensory Hypothesis</u>. The third hypothesis is the most obvious of all. It is the belly ache theory. I have chosen the word "belly" deliberately because it encompasses so much anatomy: the bowels, the intestines, the stomach, even the esophagus, and, of course, the uterus. The kind of belly ache which makes a person eat something is of a particular sort; it is caused by motility in the abdominal region (Wolf 1965).

    The most common cause of such an ache is simple hunger. Several other explanations are clearly indicated, though--worms, menstrual cramps, and the more indefinable movements of the uterus which occur in pregnancy. The uterus, lacking many nerve endings of its own, refers its contractions to the stomach or the intestine. This referred sensation, if strong enough, is called a belly ache. When its function is known, it may be called, for example, "labor pains."

    The nausea which occurs in the early months of pregnancy represents a complication imposed on simple cramping. The delicate balance between rejection of what is put in the stomach and the "satisfaction" or suppression of the motility is often remedied with soda crackers in middle class circles. One author explains it thus: "Undoubtedly sensitivity to rapid changes in gonatotrophin levels...produces the phenomenon to some extent, and we know that factors other than the psyche may be at work, for a few patients begin to vomit even before the first menstrual period is missed" (Dill 1957). More modern remedies for the nausea of pregnancy are sedatives and the amphetamines, the mechanism of action being the suppression of the sensation of turbulence in the belly (Goodman 1965).

    Hunger is a simpler matter than uterine cramping. We know from observation of stomachs through gastric fistulas that it consists of a spasm which begins in the intestine and moves through the stomach to the lower esophagus (Wolf 1965). It is satisfied by the passage of a substance from the stomach into the intestine.

    One solution to increased motility of an unknown cause in the abdominal region is its mechanical suppression by an inert substance which will not move too rapidly through the gastro-intestinal system. Clay is admirably suited for this purpose, in the same way it suppresses the agitation of intestinal worms and the turbulence of dysentery. Fluoroscopic examination reveals that the clay boluses of chronic clay eaters occur in the intestine rather than in the stomach (Mengal 1964).

    IV. <u>Nutritional Need Explanation</u>. Not surprisingly, the hypothesis

92

of nutritional need has generally been espoused by nutritionists (Cooper 1957). Clay contains substances needed by the body for food. Even where food is available there may be a lack of iron (or some other mineral) which can be obtained from eating clay. Unfortunately, although some clays contain iron and other needed minerals, others which are craved do not supply nutritional needs. It has also been duly noted in the literature that animals will go to great lengths to obtain minerals which their diets lack (Foster 1927). Why not people as well?

The answer is only a partial one. Although clays may contain needed minerals such as iron, potassium and copper, the human digestive system is not ordinarily able to make use of them. In fact, geophagy has the opposite effect--at least with respect to iron. Evidence from laboratory experiments (Hochstein 1967) on the iron-absorptive properties of substances commonly used in pica indicates that clay contained in the intestine absorbs all free iron with which it comes into contact. Thus, not only is the iron of the clay not released into the nutritional system, but any iron from foods is prevented from being digested. Thus a clay-eater who feels that he needs iron and seeks out ferrous clay will be doubly frustrated since that clay will not yield up its iron but will bind whatever iron is contained in the food he eats.

Persons who have the starch habit are less likely to become anemic since the starch does not trap iron from other foods. However, anyone who consumes five boxes of starch per day will have little opportunity to eat iron-rich foods.

V. The Microbiological Hypothesis. In the exposition of how all of these substances quiet abdominal sensations such as hunger, pain, or cramps, I left out of consideration the reasons why one might eat clay, for example, even when he or she felt nothing. Habit which has been rewarding is no doubt a part of the story. But another possibility which belongs to the realm of preventive folk medicine has been suggested by recent research into the properties of clays and earths.

Clay in vitro or in the intestine maintains the environment at a pH favorable to the growth of flora which counteract disease-producing microorganisms (Stotsky 1966). For example, living in a worm-infested area, a man may eat clay and got worms from eating it. He may then eat clay and feel better when the intestinal spasms are quieted by the absorption of free-flowing gastric juices. His eating may continue, even at a given moment when he feels nothing because the presence of clay is a form of supportive or custodial medicine.

VI. Physiological Hypothesis. This last explanation is addressed to the shared characteristics of clay, starch, and flour. Pica is a response to a condition of buccal disorder in the mouth which occurs in varying degrees during pregnancy and at other points in life. Buccal disorders may be disturbances of salivation in either extreme, that is, too much or

93

not enough salivation.

In pregnancy, the hormonal stimulation of the glands which secrete mucosa often disturb other mucosal glands. The most extreme of these disturbances is called ptyalism, in which a patient may salivate as much as ten quarts a day, compared to a normal four pints. Ptyalism is fortunately rare. Far more common is the disorder known as "pregnant nose," in which a rhinitis begins with pregnancy and abruptly ends with the birth of the baby.

Notions about the virtues of clay and starch concern several sensations: taste, smell, and feel. Clay is often said to have a sour smell. When one puts a starch ball in the mouth, as one respondent says, "it gets all slippery feeling." This is true for clay and flour as well. Subjects also speak of a prickly sensation, tackiness, and so forth (Dickins 1942). "Fluffy," another respondent said. If one thinks these people are being obscure or evasive, one should try to explain the virtues of a cigarette's taste to a non-smoker.

In the same way, it is difficult for the individual to explain why she wants a pickle (I can suggest that it draws up the skin of the mouth) or a piece of watermelon (it acts as a thirst quencher and yet fills the stomach longer than a liquid). Any of the strange cravings of pregnancy can be viewed in terms of a unique set of physiological conditions. Whether or not the woman is conscious of the many changes in her body is irrelevant if her needs change, as indeed they must.

Conclusion

An adequate explanation of a phenomenon such as pica cannot be found within the theoretical framework of any one discipline. Neither purely cultural explanations nor purely physiological explanations account for all cases. It should not be expected either that in any one instance there be only one "cause." Having progressed beyond the unicausal view of disease, we can now also view human behavior in a multicausal framework. When we ask a complex question like "Why do people eat dirt?" the answers are diverse as well as multiple: because it makes them feel better, because it increases identification with other females, because the act of mouthing is gratificatory, or even because people intuitively crave the iron contained in clay.

No one of these answers alone is satisfactory because they are operant at different levels of meaning. The most naive explanation, such as "I like it" may be as productive and important as an explanation in terms of social solidarity. The combination of a perceived gratification and an inferred solidarity in the presence of any of several possible physiological even s makes for a complex but quite believable explanation of the anomaly of   ca.

94

I have attempted to demonstrate the advantages of an uncommitted holism brought to bear on data and attitudes drawn principally from medicine, physiology, anthropology and psychology. The anthropological commitment to synthesis and explanation does not require intervention. Intervention is, however, the obligation of the physician and the social reformer. When, as occurs more and more often today, anthropologists become social innovators, they share the obligation with the physician to examine the consequences of their intervention. It remains to be seen whether medicine and anthropology can agree on these general goals.

NOTES

1. I have relied heavily on Laufer (1933) for the anthropological examples which follow.

2. Among anthropologists only Gillin (1944) has attempted to view pica as more than a physiological response, and his extension is psychological rather than sociological.

REFERENCES

Carpenter, W. M.
    1845   Observations on the Cachexia Africana, or Dirt-eating in the Negro Race. New Orleans Medical and Surgical Journal 1845:146-168.

Cooper, Marcia
    1957   Pica: A Survey of the Historical Literature as Well as Reports from the Fields of Veterinary Medicine and Anthropology, the Present Study of Pica in Young Children, and a Discussion of Its Pediatric and Psychological Implications (Springfield, Illinois: Thomas).

Craigin, F. W.
    1811   Practical Rules for the Management and Medical Treatment of Slaves in the Sugar Plantations by a Practical Planter (London).

Dickins, D. and R. N. Ford
    1942   Geophagy (Dirt-eating) among Mississippi Negro School Children. American Sociological Review 59.

Dill, Leslie V.
    1957   Modern Perinatal Care (New York: Appleton Century Crofts).

Foster, J. W.
    1927   Pica. Kenya and East African Medical Journal. June: 68-76.

95

Gillin, John P.
  1944   Custom and Range of Human Response. <u>Character</u>
           <u>and Personality</u> 13:101–134.

Goodman, L. S. and A. Gilman, eds.
  1965   <u>The Pharmacological Basis of Therapeutics</u> (New York:
           MacMillan).

Gutelius, M. F.
  1963   Treatment of Pica with a Vitamin and Mineral Supplement.
           <u>American Journal of Clinical Nutrition</u> 12:388–393.

Guttmacher, Alan F.
  1956   <u>Pregnancy and Birth</u>. New American Library (New York:
           Viking Press).

Hochstein, Gianna and Paul Hochstein
  1967   The Iron-binding Properties of Organic Substances.
           Unpublished Research.

Horney, Karen
  1967   <u>Feminine Psychology</u> (New York: W. W. Norton).

Laufer, Berthold
  1933   <u>Geophagy</u>. Field Museum of Natural History Publication
           #280, Anthropological Series XVIII:2.

Mengel, Charles E. <u>et al</u>
  1964   Geophagia with Iron Deficiency and Hypokalemia
           (Cachexia Africana). <u>Archives of Internal Medicine</u>
           114:470–474.

Stotsky, G.
  1966   Influence of Clay Minerals on Microorganisms. <u>Canadian</u>
           <u>Journal of Microbiology</u> 12:547–563.

Wolf, Stewart
  1965   <u>The Stomach</u> (New York: Oxford University Press).

THE CONTRIBUTORS

Nora F. Cline -- a public health nurse and an associate professor in the Department of Mental Health, School of Public Health, University of North Carolina. She is primarily interested in community public health and mental health programs.

Peter Goethals, Ph.D. -- an associate professor in the Department of Anthropology at the University of North Carolina. His interests are in the ethnology of Southeast Asia, the anthropology of law, and medical anthropology.

Gianna Hochstein -- a graduate student working in the medical anthropology doctoral program at the University of North Carolina. Previously an English major at Grinnell College, her main interests are now in population control and medical anthropology.

Charles Hudson, Ph.D. -- an assistant professor of anthropology in the Department of Sociology and Anthropology at the University of Georgia. His theoretical and areal interests are comparative belief systems, ethnohistory and the Southeastern United States.

Berton H. Kaplan, Ph.D. -- an associate professor of epidemiology and mental health in the School of Public Health at the University of North Carolina. He also holds an appointment as Research Associate Professor in the Institute for Research in Social Science. His primary interests are in medical anthropology, social structure and personality, and the sociology of law.

Dorothea C. Leighton, M.D. -- a psychiatrist with longstanding interests in anthropology and medicine and a professor in the Department of Mental Health, School of Public Health of the University of North Carolina. She is best known to anthropologists for books on the Navaho co-authored with Clyde Kluckhohn.

Alice Murphree, M.A. -- an Assistant in Psychiatry (Anthropology) in the J. Hillis Miller Health Center at the University of Florida. Her research interests are in rural communication, folk medicine, medical student sub-culture, and mental health.

John G. Peck, M.A. -- a graduate student in the Department of Anthropology at the University of North Carolina. His main interests are in culture and personality and community mental health.

97

Helen Phillips -- a graduate student trainee in the medical anthropology doctoral program at the University of North Carolina. As an honors undergraduate student at the University of Georgia she did research on infant restraint.

Thomas Weaver, Ph.D. -- an assistant professor and Maurice Falk Senior Faculty Fellow in the Departments of Anthropology and Psychiatry at the University of Pittsburgh. His interests are social structure, culture change, medical anthropology, field techniques and Latin America.

Hazel Hitson Weidman, Ph.D. -- an assistant professor of social anthropology in the Department of Psychiatry at the University of Alabama Medical Center in Birmingham. During 1967-68 she is an associate research fellow at the Social Science Research Institute, University of Hawaii. Her primary interests are in medical and psychiatric anthropology; her geographic areas are Southeast Asia and the Caribbean.

98

Proceedings No. 2.
Urban Anthropology
Research Perspectives and Strategies

Edited by Elizabeth M. Eddy

SOUTHERN ANTHROPOLOGICAL SOCIETY

Founded 1966

URBAN ANTHROPOLOGY:
RESEARCH PERSPECTIVES AND STRATEGIES

Table of Contents

The Southern Anthropological Society is pleased to publish this collection of papers on urban anthropology, the second number in a series of annual Proceedings. This comes at a critical time in the history of anthropology and at a significant time in the history of the world. Although anthropology has never been limited to the study of primitive societies, the study of primitive societies has given anthropology its peculiar character, its methodology and perspective. Every anthropologist is acutely aware of the crisis in his field of study because in some parts of the world primitive societies are extinct or are becoming extinct where they once flourished, and in many other parts of the world access to them is difficult or impossible. We cannot fail to be saddened by their demise and inaccessibility, but we can be heartened in the knowledge that we have learned a great deal about simpler societies since anthropology began as a formal discipline, and we can use this knowledge to help us understand more complex social institutions, such as the city. As Durkheim pointed out, it is difficult to understand one thing without knowing two things. It is difficult or impossible to understand our cities without comparing them to other kinds of communities, such as villages, or even more appropriately, as the papers in this volume indicate, cities in other cultures.

Thus, at the very time when the number of anthropologists is increasing rapidly, the traditional objects of our study are decreasing with comparable rapidity; this accounts for some of the necessity for anthropologists to do urban research. But there is another kind of necessity for urban research in anthropology. As some of the contributors to this volume argue, anthropology has been accused of having an almost grotesquely primitive or rural image of man, and this at a time when both industrial and industrializing societies suffer almost insoluble urban problems caused by people moving into (and out of) the city. Without relinquishing our primary concern with primitives and peasants, anthropologists must of necessity round out their picture of man by becoming more knowledgeable about city people. Again, it is difficult to understand one thing without knowing two things, and the value of any contribution anthropologists might make to the understanding of urban problems is enhanced at this time in the history of the world when men are moving to and from the city in unprecedented numbers, and nowhere more recklessly than in the United States.

We have chosen to continue the procedures adopted in the first number of this series, Essays on Medical Anthropology. This volume is a part of a series, but it is a self-contained entity, composed of papers by specialists, pulled together by the hand of a single editor. The only innovation is that we have determined to bring out this volume in the same year in which the papers were presented and, moreover, as soon after presentation as possible.

All the papers in this volume were presented at the third annual SAS meeting in Gainesville, Florida in the Spring of 1968. Months prior to the meeting, a Program Committee consisting of William E. Carter, program chair-

v

man, and his associates, Solon T. Kimball and Carol Taylor, began laying plans for a program that would focus on urban anthropology. The Program Committee persuaded Elizabeth M. Eddy to chair a symposium on "Urbanization and Anthropology" and Richard N. Adams to chair a symposium on "Anthropology and Latin American Urbanization." In addition, John Honigmann agreed to be chairman of a session comprised of volunteered papers on the theme of "Urban and Rural: Continuities and Conflicts." Without the efforts of the Program Committee and the chairmen of the two symposia and the session of voluntary papers, this volume could not have been prepared.

We are grateful to the authors of the papers in this volume for their cooperation in submitting preliminary versions of their papers at the time of the meeting, and for their continued cooperation in meeting deadlines for the submission of revised versions; without this cooperation, our rather strenuous publication timetable could not have been met. A further acknowledgement is due to William E. Carter, who served as second reader for some of the papers on urban anthropology presented at the meeting and assisted the editor in making a final selection of papers to be included in this volume.

Many others helped sustain all that went into the preparation of this Proceedings. Nancy Stephenson attended faithfully and efficiently to the correspondence with authors and to other secretarial details. Helen Corpeno was on hand at the symposia to help with many problems. Gloria Cochran did her usual efficient, accurate job of typing the final photo-ready manuscript. We are again grateful to the Department of Sociology and Anthropology of the University of Georgia for giving material support to the preparation of this series.

Charles Hudson
SAS Editor

URBAN ANTHROPOLOGY: AN INTRODUCTORY NOTE

Elizabeth M. Eddy
The University of Florida

In recent years anthropologists have been increasingly concerned about the relevance and relationship of their discipline to urban studies. This volume reflects this growing interest among anthropologists and provides an indication of some of the perspectives and insights that anthropology can bring to an understanding of urban phenomena.

The papers which follow were presented as part of two symposia and one voluntary session of contributed papers which were organized in connection with the Annual Meeting of the Southern Anthropological Society in Gainesville, Florida, in February 1968. The theme of this Annual Meeting was Urban Anthropology. This fact, together with the papers selected for publication in these official Proceedings of the Meeting, offer tangible evidence of the emergence of urban anthropology as a basic interest of contemporary anthropologists.

The first paper by Conrad M. Arensberg sets the keynote for the volume. Drawing on his extensive knowledge of urban studies undertaken by anthropologists and other social scientists, the author carefully delineates the distinctively anthropological contribution to the study of cities in contrast to that made by other sister disciplines. He indicates the empirical distortions that occur when anthropologists undertaking urban studies lose sight of their holistic perspective and fail to see cities as objects of study in themselves and to establish a basis for crosscultural comparisons.

In the second paper, Charles H. Fairbanks turns to a discussion of the relevance of archeology to urban studies. There is first the contribution of salvage archeology which provides man with knowledge about his early urban development. Secondly there are the more systematic contributions of archeology to basic theory about the origins of cities, the rise of industrial cities, and the destruction by urban man of his environment.

If anthropologists are to undertake urban studies in their own societies or elsewhere, they must overcome certain biases and anxieties. H.W. Hutchinson gives attention to some of these in the third paper. He warns against the anti-urban ethos commonly found in many scientific and lay writings about the city and argues that anthropologists have much to offer to the study of cities and urban problems if they examine them within the context of social and cultural forces and overcome their timidity about studying cities.

The fourth paper by Anthony Leeds gives serious attention to the content of anthropological ethnographies of cities. The author is sharply critical of the traditional emphasis of field work which has been done in cities. In the past the focus has tended to be on social phenomena which are not restricted to the city or on a selected segment of the society which, even if it is an urban

1

phenomenon, is often treated without adequate attention being given to the complex and interrelated social entities of which it is a part. To illustrate his main points, Leeds draws upon his study of <u>favelas</u> in Rio de Janeiro.

The need to view urbanism in its wider cultural context is also emphasized by Hans C. Buechler in the fifth paper. He reports a study of the reorganization of counties in the Bolivian Highlands and presents an analysis of his data in terms of rural-urban networks and hierarchies. He argues against the definition of urban and rural areas as discrete entities and points out the value of dynamic structural models which allow rural-urban connections to be examined within organizational processes.

Like the other authors in this volume, Brian M. du Toit is also concerned with the way in which urban anthropology must approach its subject matter. In the sixth paper he reports his own findings and those of others in African urban studies and argues for theoretical models which recognize fields of social interaction and take into account situational variations.

The special contribution that anthropologists can make to an understanding of social class in urban settings is illustrated by Emilio Willems in the seventh paper. The author points out that in order to understand the process of acculturation in Latin American cities, one must examine the rapidly changing urban environment, the relationship of cities to their surrounding countrysides, the disintegration of traditional urban structures, and the role of the mass media in the urbanization of folk cultures.

The eighth paper by Michael D. Olien turns to a study of the city of Puerto Limón in Costa Rica. Viewing the city as existing in a complex context, Olien examines some of these complexities in detail and gives attention to intracommunity relations, urban-rural relations, urban-national relations, and urban-international relations.

Finally, the concluding comments by John Gulick assess the present state of urban anthropology, especially as reflected in the papers in this volume. They also provide a forward look into needed strategies on the part of those anthropologists who will increasingly devote their research skills to the problem of understanding urban phenomena.

2

THE URBAN IN CROSSCULTURAL PERSPECTIVE

Conrad M. Arensberg
Columbia University

There is a great readiness today to fashion an urban anthropology. A start has been made on an anthropological treatment of problems and phenomena to be found in urban settings. Yet there is little clarity in defining the field or in making precise, or even plausible, the relevance of anthropology to urban studies. This volume will undoubtedly clarify the mission and potential of an urban anthropology, particularly as the archeological and evolutionary interests of the science are concerned. I wish to attempt some clarification of the place of an urban anthropology within cultural and social anthropology. I hope to make a little more precise the role of urban studies there.

The attempt will necessarily involve some effort to distinguish anthropology's contribution to the understanding of the nature, dynamics, and varieties of urbanization from those of neighboring or sister social sciences: sociology, economics, geography, history and the history of architecture. I will not attempt a complete specification of their respective provinces -- a futile task. Instead I will merely address myself to the contribution of the distinctively comparative and empirical methods of anthropology. I will try to say something about the comparative understanding of cities that anthropology seems to offer and leave for others any review of the work already done by anthropologists within newly swelling, or within already formed, cities. Indeed it is not anthropology within cities that is new and that makes the rubric "urban anthropology" sound novel. Community studies of American cities, for example Yankee City, Middletown, and Deep South, were done a generation ago, when social anthropology was first tried on modern industrial life. The now two-decade old kinship studies by the students of Firth in East London show us that British anthropologists have not confined their researches on urban conditions to new African towns, a fact underlined by the new summary volume, Communities in Britain, by Frankenberg (1966). What will occupy me is, rather, the effort to look at cities as wholes; to see them as objects of study in themselves is an effort necessary, to some degree at least, for crosscultural perspective on city-located cultural data and problems.

It is necessary to remember that the special skill of anthropology is comparison and that comparison is worldwide and evolutionary as well as crosscultural. It is a skill founded on an empirical determination of the varieties and forms of human behavior, established across the gamut of varying human societies of all kinds and sizes. It is founded as well on a recognition and classification of the forms of human settlement and of the

3

units of human social organization. The settlements called cities are at best only one class of these, to be distinguished empirically and comparatively from the others. Cities provide a demographic field for human interaction, a cultural environment for human behavior, and a form or forms of social organization, as well as an arena for economic and political activity. But then so do all other human communities.

If the city is to be a useful and recognizable rubric of crosscultural description and analysis, it must be understood crossculturally against a typology of the range of the varieties of its occurrence. It must be defined empirically. Our knowledge of its forms and functions in its characters as demographic field, cultural environment, social organization, and arena of specialization or integration must not rest on derivative or a priori assumptions.

The matter is important because there are a great many confusions extant. The present working definitions of the city are nearly all inherited. We have received them, in our present anthropology, either from other disciplines or from the European past. Many of the received definitions are as yet untested. With them we still assume our own urban conditions to be general, or inevitable, as once we assumed family or economic institutions to have a necessary and universal form much like our own. Many of our working definitions confuse function and form, for example insisting that centralization of decision-making makes cities or that urban agglomeration is itself such centralization of functions. What is needed, clearly, is an establishment of the historical and crosscultural range of urban or allegedly urban phenomena and a correction of gross correlations by the specification of cultural variation.

One of the offending definitional concepts is the term "urban society" so often in use today. It is used as if there were one kind of society, or one social and cultural experience common to cities, as analog of the terms "tribal society" or "peasant society." The term begs the question. It also abuses the evidence. We do not know that there is in the city a social form so uniform as to make a common experience everywhere cities seem to be reported. We know, indeed, that in some societies cities are part-cultures, while peasants or nomads are the other parts. Either the term legitimately refers to a special field of human action limited to the city, or it wrongly implies that some societies are wholly urban. If the latter, our own society is the only one even likely to have abandoned the rural-urban contrast and to have elected urbanity for everyone. Yet our own can be equally rightly called suburban or post-urban or, in Kenneth Boulding's telling phrase, "postcivilized." Nor is it crossculturally or evolutionarily meaningful to indulge in automatic equations, as is so often done today outside anthropology. (We, too, often fail to resist the contagion.) It is not proper to equate urbanization with industrialization, modernization, or, as is sometimes done, with technological advance, westernization, or increasing complexity of the division of labor. Commingled as these separate trends are in modern civilization, it remains to be seen whether their commingling is always either an inseparability or necessarily urban. It is also not sure whether these trends always lead into urban, or indeed any similar, cultural and

4

social organizational outcomes in the societies they acculturate or transform. The commingling of these trends today is less a characteristic of all cities than it is a dynamic of our particular present world order.

It seems clear that we in anthropology are going to run into difficulty if we take over such borrowed concepts as "urban society" uncritically. If such borrowed definitions turn us away from our own forte of empirical exploration and comparison, we will be in danger of making our contribution to the discussion of current urban problems and trends unrealizable. Let me therefore go over some of the phenomenal elements of the current definitions of the urban and put them in crosscultural perspective. Let me relate them to the attested experience of cities in various cultures and in various world regions and times of history and take cognizance of the range of variety in the character and juxtaposition of the phenomena the definitions made use of.

If one turns to Murdock and the Human Relations Area File, one sees that he arranges the societies reported in the ethnographies of cultural anthropology in a scale ranking them according to the size of the largest community of each. The scale gives a rough evolutionary ranking of societies from those of hunters and gatherers -- people who have nothing bigger than bands -- up to the metropolitans, the "megalopolitans" of today, to use Gottman's word. Enshrined in the scale, of course, is the notion that the city is a large and dense population aggregate. Anthropology has much experience to report on large and dense populations, in common with sociology, ethology, and biology. But not all dense populations are cities.

Next, there is much heard today of the culture of poverty. By historical coincidence confined perhaps to the last century, large and dense populations are often poor ones. But cities often are or were once rich. Poverty is not by any means only urban. Poverty is, of course, often enough connected with dense population, but not necessarily always so.

Massed, dense population is thus our subject, but massed densities are not cities. Anthropology has a legitimate interest, of course, in the cultural control of density. The ethologists have established the physiological effects of congestion in their discovery of the "sink" (decay) of behavior among overcrowded animals. The same decay seems rampant in our cities. Yet we know from our studies of India, or other river plain and delta lands, or from studies of islands like those of Micronesia, that the problems of crowding in lands both large and small are not necessarily only urban. There are many occasions of human crowding: ceremonies, pilgrimages, migrations, traffic jams, and the routs, defeats, and refugee camps of war. There is good reporting on the collective behaviors of mobs and the miseries of temporary crowding. But probably we mean by the city, instead, a permanently crowded population.

In that case, the city is well accounted a near universal response to a near universal condition of animal and human life, a specialized cultural adaptation made by man for the management of durably large and crowded populations. Yet differences in the sizes of urbanized populations and in the forms of city plans and functions show the city to be more a class of such adaptations than a unitary thing in itself. Both as settlement patterns

5

and as nodal concentrations of the functions of society, cities differ very markedly from civilization to civilization in history. Size ranges from the several thousand people for a county seat in Brazil, noted by Harris (1956) to have all the points of ethos, function, and behavior (including domination of a rural hinterland) usually called urban, up to the million-numbered metropolitan cities of the modern world. These latter indeed are so widely spread and so uniform as very large units of modern population organization, remarks the demographer Kingsley Davis, as to suggest comparisons in biological experience no longer with the mammalian world, but instead mirroring for the first time the insect world.

If concentration of functions makes cities, however, beyond permanent densities, then, too, insect-like agglomeration of population does not necessarily mean nodal centering of functions for serviced hinterlands. Hives of insects do not have subordinate villages. Nodal centering of functions may make the city in some civilizations, but it, too, is a variable phenomenon. Functions, thus, differ in their centeredness. It is a truism that federal capitals, as in the USA, Brazil, and Australia, are often today removed, by design, from commercial and communications capitals. Palace cities, port cities, and temple cities in other civilizations were often similarly separated. European and Medieval boroughs were chartered islands of free artisan and trader population divorced from feudal and ecclesiastical centers of military, agricultural, and religious power.

Our implicit definition of the city as a gathering in of the top commands of the diverse organs of control in society has derived, I feel, from Middle Eastern and Chinese civilizations and from recent European national, commercial, and industrial examples. It needs extensive reexamination. All in all, then, the city varies greatly in form as well as in size from culture to culture. The relative forms the cultural control mechanisms have attained in the human management of crowding, or in the societal achievement of nodal organization, or the centralizing encephalization of functions need careful and empirical restatement. The awareness that the form of the city differs from culture to culture must be the first step.

Let me show how a failure to attend to the variation of form in cities gets one into trouble. In his book on the early Harappan civilization of the Indus Valley, Stuart Piggott (1945), the British archaeologist experienced in the prehistory of Europe and the Near East, was much impressed with the size and the uniformity of such sites as the classic Mohenjo-daro. They represent, he infers, a civilization of urban form, with cities, writing, walls, a specialized structure looking like either a grain store or a great water "tank" (reservoir), though the absence of a central palace, temple, or fortress was disturbing. What intrigued him particularly were long rows of houses all alike and lined up on regular streets. In the ancient Near East there are no such lines of houses, and the city form of Harappan civilization was admittedly puzzling.

Piggott solved the puzzle easily enough. The Indus city could only be a late, quickly degenerated local variant of the Mesopotamian and Near Eastern city. The uniformity of city form, the existence of similar settlements

6

of long lines of like houses on their straight streets, discovered in excavations over a thousand miles apart on the Indus plains, could only represent the standardization of a centralized, monolithic, and thus monotonous empire. Early India must have had a quick and degenerate inclusion in the city and state evolutions of civilization in the Near East. The streets of houses could only be laborers' hovels.

Alas, all this is a tissue of inference, if not prejudice. It assumes a single form of the city -- the Near Eastern -- and a single cause of cultural uniformity, the imposed conformities of state power. Could Piggott have been thinking of the depressing rowhouses for laborers the London County Council erects?

If Piggott had only looked at the modern villages of the present province of Sind, the region where ancient Mohenjo-daro once stood, he might have another answer to his puzzle. The same rows of houses line similar streets today. If he had consulted the ethnographers of India or the geographers and cultural anthropologists who record present-day and historical settlement patterns, he might have learned that line villages of uniform houses on straight "castestreets," sometimes with an arch of boughs or a common gate of brushwood, is the basic form of the community throughout all of Dravidian Hindu South India, shared as well by the tribals, both Dravidian and Munda, round to Orissa and to the Santals of Bihar and Bengal. It is a settlement pattern just as much of the village as of the city, and indeed, like other city forms of other civilizations, common to both city and village, however defined.

He could have learned that this is specifically <u>not</u> the settlement pattern in Hindu villages or historical cities of either the North Indian plain nor of the Iranian and Near Eastern worlds. There, in both city and village, we find the Haufendorf settlement or the compacted clump of houses standing wall to wall, divided into quarters and laced with mazes of alleys from a common central square or city gate. There, the familiar walled "nucleated settlement," the "stone city" of the Near East, is indeed standard and throws both city and village into a common form. Yet the forms are not that either of Mohenjo-daro or of non-Aryan India.

He might have learned that both archeologically and ethnologically there is a case for a distinctive Indian tradition discernible in city and village alike. He might have read his colleague the British anthropologist David Pocock (1960). Pocock sums up the evidence of village and tribal studies of India to confirm the historian in the matter and to assert that it is false to presuppose a dichotomy between rural and urban sociology in India. Pocock indeed says quite specifically, "It would appear impossible to recognize the 'orthogenetic' character of India's cities and villages and at the same time to think of comparing them separately with their 'equivalents' elsewhere. The sociology of India's urban and rural population may <u>not</u> be divided between urban and rural sociologies" (1960).

The difference of city form between civilizations and the commonality of form between village and city in the same civilization is not a new fact, though it can yield new theory. It now has been noted from time to time by

7

anthropologists and human geographers. In the main, however, the ethno-centricity of sociological concepts, reinforced by the prevalence of ideal and functional definitions in social science, has masked empirical realities and delayed the emergence of genuinely crosscultural and formal typologies not only in our treating human settlements like these but in many other things. The invention of a class of what Lévi-Strauss called "mechanical models" for variable cultural phenomena, that is, formal and typological rather than statistical models, seems to have to be made separatim for each successive rubric of cultural data that anthropology comes to treat and to explain. It is clearly not enough, any more than in other sciences, to erect dichotomies or polarities such as patrilineal vs. matrilineal kinship systems, Gemeinschaft vs. Gesellschaft societies, etc. Such primitive first step contrast pairs for cities have already appeared. It will be useful to review some of them here, remembering all the while that the identification of the forms of the community and of the city the world's cultures display, share, or fail to share, is an empirical task that has not yet been performed. Such initial two-term classi-fications are at best heuristic perceptions of the ends of the ranges of real variation. In summing up the results of anthropological community studies, Kimball and I (1965) and others have attempted empirical typology and identification of Anglo-American communities, both rural and urban, using formal criteria and Wagley and Harris (1955) among others have attempted similar classifications in less formal and more culture-itemizing terms of Latin American communities. For cities, the job has just barely begun.

Thus the human geographers have long distinguished, very usefully, the "stone city" of the form the Near Eastern city takes -- which we have already specified -- from the "green city." In the Near East as in China and parts of Europe, especially where the open-field system occurs, the nucle-ated village -- like the city -- is also walled or enclosed; the village is a compact clump of houses, ringed by empty, unfenced gardens and fields, set about a square or central plaza. Often nothing grows in the compact settlement of houses, alleys, and squares within the wall, with a common gate, or single common outside threshing-ground, and the separation of dwellings from empty fields and wastelands is clear and unequivocal. The city, as noted, has the same form, with central square, a common wall, distinct outworks, and an open expanse of fields and lands about it, empty till a village is reached or another city looms (perhaps on a tell) on the horizon. Von Grunebaum indeed suggests that in the Hellenistic and Moslem cities, the ideal urban form was a combination of these compacted, centered villages, eventually generalized, if only symbolically, in the plan of the Chinese city and the Imperial Forbidden City, heart of China's empire.

This ideal form of the "stone city" was a great rectangle of four wards, each functionally still a homogeneous village, each complete with temple, bath, and alleys, each an urban seat of an ethnic group or millet of the hinterland, and the whole arranged north, south, east, and west along four transverse streets leading from the great gates of the common wall, set at each midpoint of the four quarters of the compass, inward to the common center: the great plaza, great mosque, or great palace. The great rectangle

8

of central palace, four walls, four gates, and local quarters and bazaars of each quarter along the streets, seems to have gone, symbolically, at least, even further, to give the pattern for the sacred Buddhist "world-mountain" (Mount Meru), and the general South Asian symbolism of imperial unification of the world exemplified both in the empire of the earth and in the plan of the mystic world of heaven. Such is the classic stone city and its many diffusions and etherealizations of its urban form in the civilizations of history. In ethnographies, Horace Miner's Timbuctoo (1953) is a perfect example, even though the ethnic groups of the wards, except the Arab one, are African.

But it is not the only form of the city. Ideal type of both the Platonist sociologists and the Eurasian mystics, the stone city differs altogether from the green city of Yucatan, or South India, or West Africa south of the Sudan, or old Japan. In the green city, the temple or palace at the heart of the congestion of houses and at the convergence of roads through the dispersed homesteads or hamlets of the countryside is empty, in that only functionaries live there. There is no neat separation of residences and fields. In milpa, garden, orchard, or grove, the peasants often live on or near their own plots; they are merely more and more thickly settled as one moves inward to the center. Whether walled or not, the city is green in that crops grow round and between the houses up to the very wall of the temple precinct. The city is a node of religious or civic organization all right, but in its form it is a mere high concentration of homesteads. It is not primarily a segregation of urban or stone things from agrarian or green things.

Once again, then, city and rural communities have a common form. Dispersed, unnucleated settlement patterns make for communities of hamlets, rancherias, or neighborhoods, very commonly reported by anthropologists all over the world, wherein by no means all tribesmen and peasants live in nucleated villages. The cultures of these non-villager people, just as does that of the classic Near-Easterners, also display cities and rural communities with a common form. But the form is different.

What seems to obscure the social science perception of the variable forms of the city, and of the varieties of settlement pattern common to city and rural community alike, is not merely the unfamiliarity of the cities of diverse civilizations to anthropologists and the unfamiliarity of tribal and peasant villages to urban sociologists. Equally obscuring is the hold (perhaps unconscious) of unilinear concepts of social and cultural evolution. Thus the green city must be a simpler stage of the stone city, and any other proffered classification, especially if it is two-fold, must represent a mere succession of stages of urban growth all leading to the ideal city which is always both an ever larger permanently massed population and an ever more nodal concentration of functions of society.

Even the brilliant reordering of urban sociology provided by Sjoberg's The Preindustrial City implies that before the industrialization of today's world all the preindustrial cities of all the world's regions were somehow alike. Yet his preindustrial cities, with their massing of the elite within the city and of the peasants in the countryside, are merely the stone cities of the Near East, China, and Latin America all over again. The "urban ethos"

9

he reports once more reflects the city that concentrates and segregates the functions of administration and information of a high literate culture as these are performed by a "prebendary bureaucracy" (as Max Weber called a mandarinate), that is, by the literati. His "preindustrial city" once more centralizes the organs of a literati-ruled imperial state and relegates the countryside to country bumpkins and food-producing helots. In its early forms, in Oriental empires, including Muscovy, it left the village some local defenses and autonomies, subject to taxfarming, to corvees, and to collective liabilities. In its last forms before industrialization (still extant) in the absolutist states such as Portugal, Naples, or the Latin-American dictatorships, it penetrated and dissolved the villages and arrogated their last customary and corporate local powers, leaving only the "amoral familism" and the underground rebellions or conspiracies of the peasant millenial movements, "la violencia," and the Mafia, so well reported by such observers as Banfield (1958), Hobsbawm (1959), and Barzini (1965).

Sjoberg's "preindustrial city," thus, is indeed an historically, regionally identifiable form of the city (and the state). It is an important, fateful one -- one indeed showing much cultural variation, a long evolution, and a final orthogenetic and distinctive overgrowth. In this it is like many another social form in cultural history. But it is not the only form of the city. It provides an indispensable key to our understanding of the classical social structures of the Mediterranean, Mideastern, and Chinese worlds. But it does not so easily explain other civilizations. For other worlds, which Sjoberg does not report, we must seek out other more appropriate theories of city form, other distributions and concentrations of societal functions, other distributions of social classes than the mandarins and the peasants.

Let us turn again, then, to these other civilizations. Let us look for other forms of the city (and the state). Turn again to India, to Ethiopia, to West Africa, to Japan, to Hinayana Buddhist South East Asia, Java, to Yucatan, even to feudal Europe, all civilizations where either there were green cities or where Wittfogel's "hydraulic empires" are hard to prove. One finds it very difficult in these regions either to argue for the urban concentration of the literate elite or even the administrative forces of royal government. In the Japanese case, as in the Nayar Kingdoms of the Malabar Coast, if there were cities at all besides the capital built round the palace, they were a few ports of foreign trade and the castle towns huddled under the walls of the dai-myō (the great lords). Yet the Japanese capital of Old Yedo (Tōkyō) under the Tokugawa shogunate was more populous in the sixteenth century than any city in Europe. The literary elite were gathered not in these towns, not even in the capital, but in monasteries and shrine centers set apart up and down the land. Commercial, governmental, and religious centers -- ports, palaces, and temples -- remained separate. They were "empty cities" in the way that the green cities of Yucatan are argued to have been -- places of only occasional assemblage or pilgrimage, empty but for compradores, or courtiers, or priests respectively. They filled up to a bursting congestion of people only at the peak of their yearly ceremonial rounds.

Up and down Indian Latin America we are taught the same lesson. The

10

pre-Spanish city form still persists, despite the in-gathering reducciones, the setting up of pueblos, and the long history of the Spanish imposition of municipal form -- with proper town houses, proper municipal palace, and central cathedral on the great square -- brought from Europe and the classical Roman world. From Ruth Bunzel's Chichicastenango in Guatemala to Harry Tschopik's Chucuita in Bolivia the Indians (not the Ladinos) keep the cities "empty," living dispersed in their ranchos, barrios, and ayllus of the country-side, pouring into the city and the cathedral square only for the great fiestas, the Dionysian climaxes of the year.

It is clear, then, that both the form and the functions we have been accustomed to call urban vary widely from culture to culture and civilization to civilization. The market place, literate communication, ceremonial and religious assemblage, and government need not be permanently centered in a shared single place. Such centering is variable and may take various forms. Neither in the city nor in the constituent villages of a culture need these things be nucleated. Some sort of network of overlapping or rotating human assemblages may be an equally adaptative decision-making device, like the sings of the Navajo or the synods of Presbyterians. Not all churches have diocesan, episcopal form. Similarly not all societies need be city centered.

The empirical task of cultural comparison, therefore, means separating out the institutions and specifying their different lacings or integration with-out assuming them to take nucleated, urban form. How they are deployed in the constituent communities of a society or how they are gathered into centers to be labelled either urban or something else is an inductive question of best range and best fit of crosscultural data. For example, is the royal capital of Dahomey a city? The question is real; much hinges in anthropology on our understanding of native sub-Saharan African "urbanism," a touchstone of civilization, like literacy.

The recent publication of Karl Polanyi's magisterial summation of the archival evidence of the economics and statecraft of Dahomey and the Slave Trade (1966) clarifies our picture of the West African kingdoms and their form of the city. Each community of the countryside had its dispersed joint-family fields and compounds of the families of the resident segments of the sibs of the people, its common connecting paths and its wastelands, its cyclical market open to all comers ready to buy with the king's cowry currency, its communal youthful dogpwe as work-gang and militia, its village hunt, and its local guild if it had a part-time non-farming specialty. Similar dispersed family compounds and fields of the officers of the community housed the headman, the market administrator, the huntmaster, and the militia chief; and the people went to them in turn at their respective calls. Equally dis-persed were the shrines of the polytheistic cults. These rose and fell as their power to grant favors or protections waxed and waned for the people, related or not, who elected to seek them out. These shrines were the original founders' houses of influential, expanding sibs, growing from village to village with prosperity and successive family divisions. A founder's place could grow into an ancestral shrine, tended by the senior headman of the sib, swelled into the temple of a cult drawing devotees from the surrounding

11

countryside.

These were the main institutions of the culture dispersed and ranked across the land. Only when they were assembled in one place, in common hegemony and superordination over the other shrines, villages, households, markets, hunts, and militias did a state emerge, a kingdom grow up for a time, and a centralized administration and redistributive economic system arise. The royal or palace city of West Africa, at least to judge it from the detailed evidence of Polanyi's <u>Dahomey</u>, seems to have been an emergent combination of military power, economic redistribution, and polytheistic ancestor cult. When these organs of West African society combined, a kingship emerged to dominate other clans, cults, and villages, and a city emerged, to act for a time as a center of decision-making and assemblage in the civilization. Such cities, of course, were "open," as Lewis Mumford (1961) called the cities of ancient Egypt. They waxed and waned with the power of the king; they were "green" in that they had their own palace and crownland fields; they were manned only by the king's officials of the royal clan, farms, and household. They filled up only in the great annual or regnal celebrations. They were places of visitation, not residence. Their "king-doms" were their hinterlands, the zones of their attractions and their command.

Thus the royal city, the capital, of Dahomey, at least, was simply one village among many in its form. It was one village, that of a king and his royal sib and household, grown great. Thus it combined the palace, the residences and family lands of the royal lineage and its ancestral shrine, itself grown to be a temple seat within the palace of the royal cult celebrated by all the kingdom. The palace also had its own market, like any village, but it was the royal market. It housed a household, like any village compound, but it was a household hugely expanded into a "patrimonial bureaucracy" of Max Weber's kind. There, each wife of the king was also a particular royal officer, called "mother of the office," to whom the corresponding officer of a particular local village, sib, or cult must report on the palace visits which all local officers and householders must make, including for all officers down even to village headman their compulsory annual attendance with tribute at the King's Custom, the great climax of the harvest and the ceremonial year. Other king's wives, the "Amazons," and the royal city's own <u>dogpwe</u> militia-men -- the standing army -- were sent round the borders in expansion wars and slave raids each year. The king's village huntsman was the royal hunt-master of the kingdom and the king's village guildsmen were the palace artificers. In every particular the city was a combination of the usual dis-persed institutions of the countryside and like them in essential form. But in function it was a gathering in of them into a single center, a node of ruling power. The reach of that rule was the extent of the kingdom.

The royal city, then, is an attested form of the city, as we see, but different indeed from the industrial and the "preindustrial" city. Like all other forms of the city it is also very much related in form to the other constituent communities of its culture and its society. It is also, of course, hugely modified by its new state functions. In the Dahomeyan case it seems to fit the Weberian patrimonial kingdom -- an early, royal but not imperial or

12

"hydraulic" state -- about as neatly as the "preindustrial city" fits the Weberian and the Wittfogelian "prebendary bureaucracy" and the scribal or mandarin
empire. This may well be the general case: as we come to identify new forms
of the city, perhaps, we shall also identify new forms of the state.

All in all, then, we must seek such comparative and variable definitions as these examples reveal. The city is a permanently massed, large
concentration of people in a community having a nodal function, or functions,
somehow providing for the lacing together (not necessarily the subordination)
of some hinterland of the other, perhaps lesser communities of a society.
The nodal functions can be performed in many ways, and the particular institutions of a culture which are found to perform the nodal integration appear in
different identities and combinations. Our inherited assumption of an urban
society that assembles all such functions must be discarded.

All this is even more true when we come to the changes of modernity.
Today many of the functions that were traditionally urban in our civilization
are no longer so. Their urban character was not intrinsic. It was derived
from the preindustrial concentration of the elite in provincial and imperial
capitals, uniting magistracies, tax-collections, garrisons, markets, and
artisan crafts in the same centers. This may well be a concentration not
duplicated outside the Middle East, China, and the post-medieval European
worlds. The commercial and industrial revolutions modified this city form by
dispersing manufactures to sites of raw material and mill power, and later by
eventually establishing "factories in the fields" and by separating manufacturing, commercial, and administrative capitals. The modern age has further
diminished such concentration, removing political and corporate decision-
making from most cities, leaving only mass-communications functions to the
central city (TV, advertising, some banks, and the stock-market). The removal was perfectly plain this year (1968) in New York, when it took the
Governor in Albany, not the Mayor, to get the New York City garbage collectors back to work.

My long-term colleague Solon Kimball and I have been writing, along
with other pens, of these changes that have been overtaking the American
community form. The factories have left the cities for the fringes and the
turnpikes; the shopping centers have moved to the suburbs and the belt park-
way nodes; the middle classes have fled the inner cities, however "renewed";
the small towns are dead or dying; suburbia, exurbia, and metropolitan culture
have erased the rural world. The urban sociology of today must catch up
with these sweeping cultural transformations. Urban anthropology, as yet
merely fragmentary, is in fact largely concerned with the concentration of
formerly rural elements of culture and population in the cities, new and old.

These once-powerful, urban melting pots indeed may or may not still
exert their former urbanizing power. Cityward migration, by no means a new
phenomenon, nevertheless seems new in the magnitude with which it now
continues to sweep the world. But as Joel Halpern has well said (1965), we
have been too long talking about the urbanization of the peasantry of the
world when we should rather today be speaking of the peasantization of the
cities. Certainly, in North and South America, in Africa and India, in slums,

13

favelas, native "locations," and other "marginal" settlements, whether inner city ghettos or scattered squatter "barrios," the work anthropologists have been doing has been largely devoted to exploring the remains, indeed the continuities through urbanization, of the traditional cultures and social structures of the tribals and the villagers once of the countryside: their cults, their healing sects, their families and social networks of kindreds or client-ships, etc.

It is fitting that this should be the case, as these are the data anthropologists are most qualified to search out and to explain. Yet for all the ethnicities to be reported of this kind, the anthropologist cannot neglect the larger evolutionary picture, the world-wide transformation involved in the birth of the post-urban age. He certainly must treat the culture contact, conflict, and synthesis attendant on this evolution, all processes about which anthropology has much to say, from his world-wide experience of them. His work is now more than ever significant in mediating the dialogue between the transforming citizen populations and their technical, professional, and administrative specialists, the middle and upper classes of our new civilization, the once-urban but now suburban and exurban based officials of metropolis. It is no accident, then, that what used to be called "applied anthropology" -- for want of a better term to describe the study of culture contact between "the moderns" and "the natives" (read "the rurals") -- has now somehow been itself transformed into, even sometimes simply rechristened, "urban anthropology."

REFERENCES

Arensberg, Conrad and Solon T. Kimball
    1965   Culture and Community (New York: Harcourt, Brace, and World).
Banfield, Edward C.
    1958   The Moral Basis of a Backward Society (New York: Free Press of Glencoe).
Barzini, Luigi
    1965   The Italians (New York: Atheneum).
Frankenberg, Ronald
    1966   Communities in Britain (London: Penguin Books).
Halpern, Joel M.
    1965   The Rural Revolution. Transactions of the New York Academy of Sciences, Series II, Vol. 28, pp. 73-80.
Harris, Marvin
    1956   Town and Country in Brazil (New York: Columbia University Press).
Hobsbawm, E. J.
    1959   Primitive Rebels (New York: Frederick A. Praeger).
Miner, Horace
    1953   The Primitive City of Timbuctoo (Princeton: Princeton University Press).

14

Mumford, Lewis
    1961   The City in History (New York: Harcourt, Brace, and World).

Piggott, Stuart
    1945   Some Ancient Cities of India (London: Oxford University Press).

Pocock, D. F.
    1960   Sociologies: Urban and Rural. Contributions to Indian Sociology 4:81. Quoted also in Owen M. Lynch, Rural Cities in India: Continuities and Discontinuities. In India and Ceylon: Unity and Diversity, Philip Mason, ed. (London: Oxford University Press, 1967).

Polanyi, Karl
    1966   Dahomey and the Slave Trade, American Ethnological Society Monograph, No. 42 (Seattle and London: Washington University Press).

Sjoberg, Gideon
    1960   The Preindustrial City, Past and Present (Glencoe, Illinois: The Free Press).

Wagley, Charles and Marvin Harris
    1955   A Typology of Latin American Subcultures. American Anthropologist 57: 428-451.

15

THE ARCHEOLOGICAL CONTRIBUTION TO URBAN STUDIES

Charles H. Fairbanks
The University of Florida

Nothing is more current than a concern with urban affairs and related problems. On the face of it, nothing is more remote from urban problems than dirt archeology. The seeming contradiction in these two statements, however, is a delusion. Because it is customary, even among archeologists, to picture the excavator as dressed in shorts, a pith helmet, and bush-jacket in some far and remote spot, the fact that archeology is deeply and traditionally involved in urban studies is apt to be overlooked. What is difficult to determine is where this _involvement_ may make some scientific _contribution_ to the field of urban anthropology.

Before turning to this problem, it is necessary first to dispose of an area of archeological involvement which makes a considerable contribution to urban life, although it seems to add little to a scientific concern with urban studies, namely the area generally called "salvage archeology." Salvage archeology, by its very nature, can rarely be problem-oriented. We must attempt to gather what data we can before destruction or flooding occurs. As our commitment increases to recover data threatened by construction, we are increasingly able to plan excavations that will solve specific problems. In too many cases, however, we can only manage to save a small sample of the sites threatened by obliteration.

The two most destructive agencies of modern times are clearly the Federal Bureau of Public Roads and the Department of Housing and Urban Development. The destruction of archeologic and historic sites brought about by the Interstate Highway Program seems about to be eclipsed in magnitude by the Model Cities Program. From Alexandria urban renewal and Philadelphia expressways to San Francisco subways, by way of the Olympic Games water system being laid in Mexico City, the archeologists can barely list, much less observe, the rapidly proliferating destruction of America's historic urban heritage. Much of this destruction involves information that is badly needed by the student of urbanism and the historian of the city.

Little is being done with this salvage archeology except to enrich the historic museums of the cities involved. As the educational level increases at the same time as our leisure time expands, Americans are finally becoming aware of their past. The 89th Congress, in 1966, passed Public Law 89-665 establishing a National Register of Historic Sites. Hopefully this register will be completed, funds will become available, and some of the sites will be salvaged as historic spots before the grandiose schemes of HUD or BPR have destroyed them all. It would seem that an informative trip to a reconstructed early industrial section, such as the first porcelain factory in

16

Philadelphia's Southwark, might make some contribution to resolving the frustrations and tensions of the teeming denizens of some future model city. Whenever an archeological report of this kind is completed, man is made aware of some facet of his early urban development that had not been studied by the documentary historian primarily concerned with political events. Thus the archeologist is involved with urban studies as a curator of our historic heritage.

The systematic contributions of archeology to urban studies are three-fold. First, it is generally recognized that the basic theory about how cities first appeared, as presented by V. Gordon Childe (1950; 1952), is very largely based on his attempt to organize and synthesize archeological data. Secondly, archeology can, and already is beginning to, contribute information on the rise of modern, "industrial" cities, which are quite different from the "pristine" cities of which Childe wrote. Thirdly, archeology can, by studying the data preserved in the ground, begin to provide important data which is not otherwise available about the destruction by urban man of his environment. This is, of course, the modern specter of pollution of air, water, and soil. It is likely too that archeology may be able to shed some light on the destruction of the final environmental factor of man, his emotional milieu. Each of these contributions will now be discussed in some detail.

In the latter part of the 19th century, Tylor and Morgan, officiating at the birth of anthropology, created a speculative sequence of stages for cultural evolution proceeding from savagery through barbarism to civilization. Morgan in Ancient Society discussed the appearance of civilization in terms of the cumulative growth of technology and the development of "a few primary germs of thought" (1963:4). He also placed considerable emphasis on the value of "survivals" among those less technologically complex cultures known to the Victorian anthropologists. In the last hundred years anthropologists have greatly refined and expanded the ethnographic data available to the discipline.

While some archeological information was available to Morgan and Tylor, it was in general quite imprecise and could be used for little more than to indicate that cultural change had indeed occurred. The imprecise nature of Morgan's evolutionary sequence clearly needed extensive modification. The major evidence for this revision was derived when long, empirically-based archeological chronologies could be systematically compared. Childe attempted to define the complex of cultural features that characterized the sudden appearance of the first urban centers at about 4000 B.C. in Mesopotamia. His diagnostic features of the Near Eastern Urban Revolution were derived almost entirely from archeological data, as the cuneiform texts were not then widely available. Revolution in Childe's sense applied to a complete turnover in the Neolithic way of life rather than to the political activism so often associated with the term today.

Childe defined the Urban Revolution as the sudden appearance of the following: (1) the rise of large urban communities, (2) the imposition of tribute and taxation producing centrally controlled capital, (3) public works (agricultural and civic), (4) writing, (5) the beginning of exact sciences, (6) long-

17

distance trade, (7) full-time craft specialists, (8) emergence of a hierarchy of social classes, (9) formal territorial states replacing kin based groups, and (10) representational, narrative art.

The items in this list can be archeologically documented to varying degrees. Monumental public works such as temples or palaces are much studied by the excavator. The presence of craft specialists or of exact sciences is much more difficult to demonstrate. Of course, from the cuneiform tablets of the Mesopotamian area many of these more subtle criteria can be described. Such contributions, however, lie in the realm of the historian, even though they may have been uncovered by an archeologist. A more serious defect of Childe's criteria is that some of them may be fundamental factors in the emergence of cities while others are rather the results of urban life. While Childe wrote within the framework of materialism, he did not really succeed in discussing cultural events in terms of the uniform results of cultural causes. It is true that he did see the Urban Revolution as largely characterized by the growth of social classes which in turn rested on the proliferation of craft specialization. His proposal remained, however, in the nature of a brilliant hunch, rather than a demonstrated mechanism.

It remained for another generation of workers to demonstrate the validity of the concept. Wittfogel (1957) argued that the complex civilizations dependent on irrigation for their agriculture had special requirements in the form of authoritarian leadership that made them a special case of civilization. Aside from his discussion of Oriental Despotism, what is of interest is that he offered a model which included cultural response to ecological factors in explaining the emergence of a new stage. At about the same time, a number of anthropologists had begun to seize on the long, adequately demonstrated, American archeological sequences as data allowing them to compare the rise of civilization in the Old and New Worlds. Julian Steward (1955) in a series of papers asserted that the two areas had the same fundamental character of evolutionary growth. He pointed out that these civilizations had passed through approximately the same series of stages. Especially in the case of Steward, these constructions were based on archeological data and on generalizations of archeologists. They have become more refined with each successive revision until the recent examples by Adams (1966) and Braidwood and Willey (1962).

These studies in the genesis of urbanism have taken the form of more or less detailed comparisons of the two major sequences: Mesopotamia and Mexico. Most authors have considered that these two chronologies represent the development of the pristine civilizations from the first village settlements up to full urbanism (Fried 1960). For Mesopotamia there is a long, regionally diverse, adequately documented chronology supplemented by extensive contemporary documents. If too many palaces and too few artisans' hovels have been excavated, it is possible at least to reconstruct the behavior of the elite. For Mexico, the picture is somewhat simpler as there are more abundant and better controlled archeological materials, supplemented by an important body of ethnohistorical documents. This coordination of Mexican archeological information with Spanish ethnohistorical data has been especially

18

rewarding. The work of Sanders in reconstructing the settlement pattern of ancient Teotihuacan has amply demonstrated how these two sorts of information supplement each other (1956; n.d.). It has been possible to compare the Mesopotamian and Mexican sequences in some detail and to demonstrate how cultural traditions and environments brought about specific differences in the two regions.

The discussion of the rise of urban complexes has thus been based at first on the Mesopotamian archeological sequence. Later comparisons between Mesopotamia and Mexico broadened the scale. Most writers have felt that the Egyptian, Indus, and Chinese sequences were either derived from Mesopotamia, or so heavily influenced by that center, that they did not really constitute independent sequences. So little is known of developments in Southeast Asia that we cannot really tell whether this is another pristine sequence. This lack of usable information on Southeast Asian urbanism is especially critical in the realm of archeology. In the case of the New World oikoumene, the Mexican chronologies are the best documented archeologically. Peru may be another pristine sequence, but the lack of long archeologically valid chronologies and extensive exposures in the highland area present some problems. Adequate sequences and settlement studies are available for the coastal areas, but these seem to present special adaptions to a highly specific set of environmental situations. Comparisons between other sequences are also possible. While Mumford (1938) and others have pointed out that there are many different "kinds" of cities, one particular comparison seems especially rewarding. This is the contrast between the pristine cities in Mesopotamia or Mexico and the industrial city characteristic of countries around the North Atlantic Basin from the eighteenth century to the twentieth.

The pristine cities of antiquity differed in a number of respects from the recent industrial city. They were characterized by a compact area and a dense settlement pattern, a seemingly unified culture in spite of class stratification, various cultural mechanisms to assure adherence to the patron diety, or at least to the city as a unit, a strong local tradition which changed very slowly, and designation as the political capital. In addition they were centers for metropolitanism as expressed in learning and the arts. The Mexican city differed from its Mesopotamian counterpart in that it possessed a larger hinterland and consequently a more intensive development of market integration. The industrial city, in its turn, differs in a number of ways from both of these early types. It is characterized by an industrial core rather than by a sacred or political center. Where compact plans are found, they are not primarily defensive but are functionally related to the presence of prime movers such as waterpower or steam engines. Industrial cities may be trade centers, but this is primarily because they are productive centers rather than ports or caravan termini. Because they are parts of a national state, they do not have the need for the integrative loyalty mechanisms that characterized the ancient cities. While there is certainly an individual tradition adhering to each city, these separate traditions do not seem to have the permanence or rigor found in Ur, Eridu, or Sumer. The industrial city is linked to the factory and does not rest on slave labor or the guild system. Thus it contains within itself

19

ethnic enclaves, ghettos, and suburbs which create a heterogeneity foreign to any ancient city. The most typical examples are not even local capitals and tend to be divorced from political control of their own hinterland. In fact, they often must submit to political rule by rural dominated legislatures. The artists would argue that the industrial cities are not artistic centers. In attempting to trace the development of these new cities, archeology combines with history to synthesize a variety of data into an attempt at meaningful generalization.

It may be that the homogeneity of the pristine Near Eastern cities of antiquity was more apparent than real. Certainly modern Near Eastern cities are characterized by barrios, quarters, and ghettos, which seem to extend back to a considerable antiquity. The truly ancient cities, however, seem to have had an organic unity not found in later urban centers. Although stratified into social classes, each city, or city-state, looked to its patron diety, its god-king, and to common religious festivals for a sense of morality and esprit de corps. It is of course clear that these centripetal agencies were cultural devices by which the necessary integration and interaction of social classes was achieved. The very fact that each city-state maintained its identity over long periods and in the face of cyclical conquests, testifies to the efficiency of the integrative mechanisms. With the appearance of conquest states and empires shortly after 1000 B.C., the unity of the ancient cities seems to decrease. The same patron diety mechanism was transferred to the kingdom, but it was less effective over the larger area. Conquests introduced numbers of foreigners into the cities and these soon formed quarters or barrios. Increased specialization was accompanied by exploitation and the inevitable formation of ghettos. The pristine cities had lost their homogeneity, perhaps never to regain it.

The modern city grew out of rural situations in a quite different fashion than did the pristine city, but it did grow out of the peasantry. In large part, the medieval city was in the old Mesopotamian tradition. With the political collapse of the Roman Empire, the old slave-based system was no longer possible. The center of civilization shifted to Atlantic Europe where the old slave system was replaced by new sources of energy. Efficient wind and water machines were the major sources of these new productive energies. While the new prime movers increased in size and number throughout the Middle Ages, they remained largely rural in location. The small villages that grew up at waterpower sites and windmills were widely scattered over the countryside. Only in a very few spots did large concentrations of wind or waterpower occur. This Wind and Water Revolution increased production and certainly entailed a number of social and ideological changes. It did not, however, lead to the appearance of many more cities or any new styles of cities. This stage of technological and social evolution seems to have been little studied by historian or anthropologist, and it is doubtful that archeology can contribute much to such studies, if they are ever made.

Following a period in which the gains made during the Wind and Water Revolution were consolidated, the western world soon entered into another period of rapid change. This came about through the exploitation of a

20

significant new source of energy, fossil fuel or coal. Beginning in the early
part of the 16th century in southern England and northern France, it gathered
speed rapidly. At first, coal could be used only for the simpler heating jobs
of production, but with the discovery of the coking process it entered into
all industrial activities including smelting. The Fuel Revolution reached high
gear with the development by Newcommen in 1720 of the first steam engine.
Designed at first to pump water out of coal pits so that more coal could be
mined, the Newcommen engine largely revolutionized industry. Because it
worked best in large units, it rapidly produced the great factory complexes
so characteristic of the western world (Cottrell 1955). Transformed by rapid
transport, electricity, the internal combustion engine, and the managerial
revolution, the modern megapolis is the successor to the industrial city of
the mid-eighteenth century. Just as archeology has been the foundation for
an understanding of the rise of the ancient city, so also can archeology contribute much to an understanding of the emergence of this third type of city.
By detailed comparison of the Mesopotamian, Mexican, and industrial cities
it is possible to arrive at a much broader understanding of urbanism as such.

Archeology means the knowledge of the past. In England today "industrial archeologists" do not interpret this to mean that archeology signifies
"digging up the past." They confine themselves to the recording, largely
through architectural techniques, of the details of rapidly disappearing
early industrial sites. While this sort of archeology must join hands with
industrial history, it can contribute much to a knowledge of the process by
which England was transformed during the Fuel Revolution. A great deal of
bomb-damage archeology in England has been done. While much of it has
been concerned with Roman temples, it has shed a good deal of light on the
frequency, layout, and production processes of postmedieval factories.
Archeology remains consistently the study of artifacts. This is the sort of
data that is largely lacking from historic written documents precisely because
it was so well known that no one ever thought to record it. The details of
industrial city plans, arrangement of factories, disposal of wastes, and many
other vital details have so far only been recorded by archeological methods,
including the resort to shovel and trowel.

Most archeologists will continue to believe that the characteristic
stance of their profession is that of leaning on the shovel. Yet in this country
we are well on the way toward the development of an American variety of
industrial archeology. Excavations at Hopewell, Pennsylvania, by the National Park Service during the 30's laid the foundation for the restoration of
the early forge and iron works at that site. Recently, Vincent Foley has begun an ambitious archeological excavation of the industrial section of colonial
Bethlehem, Pennsylvania. In hundreds of sites throughout the country less
ambitious excavations in our cities are taking place. When an urban renewal
project devastated the ancient section of Alexandria, Virginia, archeological
salvage began late but in time to recover some information. In many cases
this work has revealed little-expected facets of our early industrial life,
and often precisely those aspects which are not available from the written
historical documents.

21

The archeological analysis of both artifactual and written data reveals facets which the non-anthropologically oriented historian is unaccustomed to examine. As a consequence, archeology can contribute much in this area to urban studies. That it may not have contributed much so far is due to the fact that archeologists have only just begun to give their attention to these matters. Nevertheless it seems certain that the contribution of archeology will grow and expand. At present, for example, a catalogue of the New England textile industry is underway using both archeological and architectural techniques. While the architect records building plans, the archeologist collects the available details of artifacts, relation to terrain, use of the econiche, and so on. The contribution to an understanding of industrial cities is expected to be a major one.

To turn finally to the ultimate area of archeological contribution, that of man's destruction of his environment, it is evident that archeology is potentially in a position to make a major contribution. For many years it has been clear that the archeologist could partially answer such questions as the reasons for the abandonment of the Old Maya Empire area, or the collapse of the Hohokam settlements in the Salt and Gila valleys of Arizona. Even more important than these specific studies, however, are a number of broad general problems. In the United States today a major development in archeology has been the viewing of cultural process as the interaction of the cultural system with the natural environmental systems (Coe & Flannery 1967). This is an extremely promising development in archeology and one that can offer great rewards. By studying in archeological detail the way in which our cities have exploited their human and environmental resources, it is possible that archeologists may be able to offer some valid generalizations about the rate and direction of environmental deterioration.

To summarize, anthropology has made significant contributions as a comparative science. Ethnology compares cultures through space. Archeology has been concerned with comparison through time. "What is past is Prelude, Study the Past." Unless man is able to study the past of his cities, he may be faced with the prospect of cannibalizing his own past to erect ever more spectacular examples of previous errors.

REFERENCES

Adams, Robert McC.
    1966   The Evolution of Urban Society. Early Mesopotamia and Prehispanic Mexico (Chicago: Aldine).
Braidwood, Robert J. and Gordon R. Willey, eds.
    1962   Courses Towards Urban Life: Archeological Considerations of Some Cultural Alternates. Viking Fund Publications in Anthropology no. 32.
Childe, V. Gordon
    1950   The Urban Revolution. Town Planning Review 21:2-17.
    1952   New Light on the Most Ancient East (London: Routledge and Kegan Paul).

22

Coe, Michael D., and Kent V. Flannery
    1967   Early Cultures and Human Ecology in South Coastal
                Guatemala. Smithsonian Contributions to Anthropology,
                Vol. 3 (Washington, D.C.: Government Printing Office).

Cottrell, Fred
    1955   Energy and Society (New York: McGraw-Hill).

Fried, Morton H.
    1960   On the Evolution of Social Stratification and the State. In
                Culture in History: Essays in Honor of Paul Radin, Stanley
                Diamond, ed. (New York: Columbia University Press).

Morgan, Lewis H.
    1963   Ancient Society, Eleanor B. Leacock, ed. (Cleveland and
                New York: World Publishing Company, Meridian Books).

Mumford, Lewis
    1938   The Culture of Cities (New York: Harcourt, Brace and
                Company).

Sanders, William T.
    1956   The Central Mexican Symbiotic Region: A Study in Pre-
                historic Settlement Patterns. In Prehistoric Settlement
                Patterns in the New World, Gordon R. Willey, ed. Viking
                Fund Publications in Anthropology, no. 23.
    n.d.   Teotihuacan Valley Project: Preliminary Report, 1960-1963
                Field Seasons, (mimeographed).

Steward, Julian H.
    1962   Theory of Culture Change (Urbana: University of Illinois
                Press).

Wittfogel, Karl A.
    1957   Oriental Despotism: A Comparative Study of Total Power
                (New Haven: Yale University Press).

23

SOCIAL ANTHROPOLOGY AND URBAN STUDIES

H. W. Hutchinson
University of Miami

It has been pointed out that "the United States was born in the country and moved to the city" (Hofstatder 1955:1). Although most U.S. anthropologists were probably born in the city, it is clear that in terms of their research they moved to the country. But now that the country folks are all getting sophisticated and citified, the anthropologist is making noises that indicate that perhaps he ought to also. In spite of the work of a few pioneers who have scouted out the urban situation in advance, the proposed move seems to raise all kinds of doubts in the minds of anthropologists as to their role in the city and their scientific identity when dealing with urban affairs. It is as if anthropologists, in moving to the city, were no longer dealing with man and his culture.

It is probably for historical reasons that the anthropologist has remained in the rural setting. First, he has been about the only one to study the way of life of indigenous peoples and to follow them through extinction or acculturation into some other form. Now that even the folk or peasants are exhibiting urban characteristics, it is time for him to make a change. With hindsight, it is possible to say that he should have done this long ago.

Two major factors, other than his substantive area, seem to have operated in keeping the anthropologist out of the urban sector until now. First, in his long association with non-urban peoples, the anthropologist acquired a rural ethos of his own. Secondly, the anthropologist was able to find a methodological justification for maintaining that ethos.

Moreover, during the 1930's the non-urban stance of the anthropologist was reinforced by the rather strong statements concerning the rural-urban dichotomy by Redfield in 1934 and Wirth in 1938. These statements resulted in two views of the city which have characterized most anthropological research and analysis ever since.

The first of these views formally acknowledged that the city was a prime source of social and cultural innovation and that the effects of this innovation could and should be studied as they affected the rural areas. This view gave anthropology license to continue the study of rural communities, with the idea of capturing traditional patterns and structures before they disappeared under the impact of change from the urban area, and it provided a theoretical nexus for the study of the process of change itself in the rural

24

social and cultural microcosm.

A second view of the city, common in the 30's, was essentially a re-affirmation of the U.S. agrarian myth (Hofstatder 1955) and the concomitant idea that the city is "abnormal" (Lampard 1961:58), the scene of anomie, personal and familial breakdown, loss of values, and almost total disorgan-ization. Even today, the overall opinion of many people about the urban condition is that it is essentially "non-human." For example, a recent state-ment by Mumford (1967) describes it as "a life so empty of vivid first hand experiences that it might as well be lived in a space age capsule, travelling from nowhere to nowhere at supersonic speeds." How one can escape "vivid first hand experiences" in the contemporary urban scene is not explained, un-less it means experience with "mother nature." At the same time, experimental psychologists working with rats offer the information that too much personal experience (presumably analogous to the urban scene) results in the rats' equivalent of insanity! In any event, the result of this attitude has been that the anthropologist has for the most part left the study of urban pathology to the urban historian, the sociologist, the city planner, and the journalist.

It was an easy matter for the anthropologist, who was never able to separate his theoretical stance from his methodology anyway, to take refuge in his methodological approach to the study of man and his culture in order to remain outside the rapidly growing and somehow unreal urban scene. His argument was that the great size of the city would negate the holistic approach of the anthropologist to his material. Since he primarily used the community study method, it was necessary for the anthropologist to choose a community which he felt he could get to know intimately through participation-observation and interviewing, plus a few other bows to sociological methodology. This obviously meant the study of small-size and fairly rural communities. On the whole, the anthropologist prides himself on the production of qualitative data, and he seems to be fearful that urban research will take this away from him. Whiteford (1960:2) sums up this anti-urban point of view as follows: "Such approaches as sampling techniques, the use of census data, and statistical analysis of masses of data would appear to be absolutely necessary for under-standing, but their use also tends to impersonalize the research and deprive the worker of his most satisfying experience, the personal identification with the people being studied."

In our times, impersonal statistical data keep revealing that the world is becoming increasingly urban, and it is increasingly evident that the city is the link between the rural areas and their people and the larger entity, the state. The city is, in fact, rapidly becoming a major demographic and social characteristic of many national cultures. As a result, it has become obvious that even the anthropologist must begin to reckon with the city in an active fashion, through field work and analysis, rather than trying to hold it off as a far distant variable as he has been doing for so long. However, considerations of the urban scene often tend to make anthropologists as well as others un-comfortable, for in dealing with the city one must get into larger questions having to do with bigness, sameness, democracy, social control, and other ideological forces which are antithetical to the traditional rural ethos of the

25

social scientist.

The study of the urban scene by social scientists in a systematic fashion is in itself not very old, dating back to about the time of the folk-urban statements referred to above. They were for the greater part pioneered by sociologists, even though Sjoberg (1965) has recently taken sociologists to task for their persisting anti-urban tendencies. Therefore, presumably the anthropologist would have the advantage of the work done by others in this substantive field to use as a guideline in the never ending study of the human condition. There are many areas in which he can bring his hard-won insights to bear on society and culture in its urban manifestation if he will truly abandon his rural ethos and rural ethnocentrism.

However, when confronted with the necessity to undertake urban studies, whether in our own society or crossculturally, anthropologists tend to become anxious and worried about methodology and identity, and to ask what the relevance of anthropology is to the urban scene. It seems to me that the relevance of anthropology to the urban scene is the same as it has always been -- i.e. to describe systematically, to analyze or translate in Bohannan's terms (1963), and hopefully in some near future be able to predict. Antithetical to anthropology's rural ethos is the applied nature of urban studies, especially those carried out in one's own society, for it implies giving direction or taking a hand in determining the nature of the overall society. This aspect is one which will have to be resolved eventually by each anthropologist.

The trouble, in part, probably also lies in the conceptualization of what lies ahead. A survey of the literature regarding the urban scene reveals no agreement concerning many of the words used in the field: urbanism, urbanization, city, metropolis, etc., a situation which is nothing new to anthropologists who have lived comfortably for a long time with vague terminology. However, when anthropological attention is turned to the urban scene in one's own society, the vagueness must perforce be turned into clear and concrete language. The remainder of this paper will attempt to point out some of the many areas in which the anthropologist can transfer his hard-won insights in the study of society and culture to the urban manifestation of contemporary life.

If the process of urbanization is viewed solely in terms of the definition given it by Tisdale in 1942 (Hauser 1965) as a process of population concentration, which takes place in two ways -- the multiplication of points of concentration and the increase in size of individual concentrations -- its study perhaps more properly belongs to demographers. However, the anthropologist doing regional or national studies crossculturally may want to attempt a taxonomy of urban subcultural types, always a useful gimmick for ordering large amounts of data and not too different from the older natural and culture area approach of the heyday of diffusion. At least there can be no argument but that this process is taking place, for the demographic concentration of population has changed the face of the map. Furthermore, the concomitant technological advances of contemporary urbanization have changed the face of urbanization as a simple phenomenon of demographic concentration. The contemporary United States is perhaps the most outstanding example of the directions of that change. If we exaggerate a little for effect, it is

26

possible to view the U.S. as composed of three differently used types of
land areas: (1) areas of concentrated, scientifically controlled, agricultural
and stock production; (2) areas of recreation and reserve, also scientifically
controlled through the methods of modern conservation, preserving the natural
heritage to as great an extent as urban citizenry will allow; and (3) areas of
more or less contiguous settlement patterns -- the urban scene or megalopolis --
the only part of the picture which is not yet entirely scientifically controlled,
but may be well on the way to becoming so.

Europe may undergo a somewhat similar process before too long, but
as a result of directed population change rather than a "natural" urban flow,
in order to bring about economic equilibrium in Europe. Bell (1964) describes
Colin Clark's calculation of the numbers of people (eight million) who must
be moved out of agriculture into the urban setting and the number of years it
will take in each country.

The devastation of natural resources in much of the rest of the world,
especially in Latin America and the Caribbean, and the growing necessity to
bring land under scientific recuperation and management, thereby treating the
land as a factor of production rather than as a domestic site in Bohannan's
terms (1963:222), in order to feed a rapidly growing population will undoubtedly
result in directed movements of people to urban areas. Obviously, here it
becomes difficult to separate urban studies from the larger context of society
and culture for they are intimately bound up together.

The point is that urbanization as it occurs today is quite probably
a different phenomenon than it was in previous times, such as in preindustrial,
prescientific societies. The study of urbanization in contemporary societies
by the anthropologist must be carried out within the context of the concomitant
social and cultural forces. The interrelationship of urbanization as concentration and scientific rationalism will most probably provide the nexus for
future studies, since this is what population concentration is primarily linked
to. The urbanization process, whether "natural" or directed, will, in terms of
sheer numbers as well as cultural background, be productive of social "problems." This brings us to another area of the urban scene -- the study of
urbanism or of urban problems.

Let us look first at problems in urbanism or the nature of urban society,
the first category of problems to be tackled by social scientists. This kind of
problem stems from the theoretical postulates of Wirth and Redfield, and has
to do with anomie, personal and familial breakdown, loss of values, and so
on. Hauser has pointed out that this particular aspect of the old dichotomy
has either been radically changed or even "junked" since it did not hold up
(Hauser 1965). It is interesting to trace out what has been accomplished from
this starting point, especially by the work of Oscar Lewis, and to speculate
on how much more productive work could be accomplished in this line. Through
the technique of tracing small-town people to the large urban scene, Lewis,
after discarding the idea of breakdown, went on to describe a subcultural
type, which he named the Culture of Poverty (Lewis 1963:xxiv). In so doing,
he provided a new dimension in urban studies -- a subcultural typology to
replace the former, unusable and ungeneralizable "urban proletariat." In

27

crosscultural work it should be possible to delineate other such subcultural types in the urban setting: for instance, the much cited "latifundista" or large-landholder, who may also be involved in the move toward the city and his relationship to industrialization; or white-collar workers from small towns whose roles have become dysfunctional and who in the urban setting become part of management, either in the bureaucracy or in burgeoning industry. Much more research is possible and necessary along these definitely anthropological lines of inquiry.

On the other hand, almost all contemporary urban agglomerations present some highly visible problem areas, such as slums, lack of services, transportation snarls, pollution, crime, and riots. Here the concern is with problems generally stated as issues, meaning conflict situations which are not due to urbanism itself, but rather to factors in the total social and cultural fabric, a very different phenomenon than the above. For example, Davis (1967:26) notes that "The causes of urban congestion are twofold: democracy and reproductive freedom." He goes on to point out that:

> . . . clearly, the notion that one can solve social problems
> by studying society, just as one solves medical problems
> by studying the body is a false analogy. Applied science
> by definition is instrumental. When the human goal is given,
> it seeks a solution by finding what effective means can be
> manipulated in the required way. Its function is to satisfy
> human desires and wants; otherwise nobody would bother.
> But when the science is concerned with human beings -- not
> just as organisms but as goal-seeking individuals and mem-
> bers of groups -- then it cannot be instrumental in this way,
> because the object of observation has a say in what is going
> on and, above all, is not willing to be treated as a pure
> instrumentality.

This is a challenging area of urban research for the anthropologist as well as for other social scientists. Because the anthropologist studies "people" or "culture," at the very least his opinion or advice may be asked regarding the solution of the problems. But as has happened in similar circumstances regarding community development, the provision of services, in the rural areas, and so on, his advice will probably not be taken. Nevertheless, this is an area, which if logically pursued, would cause the anthropologist to leave his ivory tower and to join "the establishment" with hopes of being able to in-fluence it in the direction of social or cultural solutions to social or cultural problems rather than the prevalent tendency which as Davis points out, is to offer engineering or managerial solutions to problems which are basically not amenable to them.

As for the urban scene studied in the holistic, personal, intimate, and qualitatively descriptive manner which the anthropologist has customarily provided in his rural community studies, this is probably also possible in a modified form even in areas of the megalopolis. The city is, after all, a form

28

of human community, and as such provides a proper scene for anthropological inquiry.

Arensberg and Kimball (1965:1, 192-193) have pointed out the inadequacy of viewing any community, whether simple or complex, as an object, with identifying attributes. Rather, they insist, community should be viewed as a process -- that on-going thing which actualizes social structure and cultural behavior for the individual and the family. This approach has the advantage of freeing us from placing arbitrary boundaries in order to define the community, and allows us to arrive at a definition and description of the urban community (as well as any other) derived from within the community itself. An appreciation of this approach may remove one of the major stumbling blocks to anthropological urban research. Abrahams (1964) in his study of Negro folklore in Philadelphia used this approach very tellingly.

Arensberg and Kimball indicate, furthermore, that each culture has its characteristic community form. Sjoberg (1965) has provided a preliminary typology of urban cities using the technology of the culture as the primary indicator or variable. Thus he speaks of the preindustrial city, the transitional city, and finally the industrial city. Recently, Brzezinski (1967) in speaking about contemporary United States, pointed out that it has now gone beyond the industrial variable, and he characterizes it as the first technetronic society. Presumably the technetronic city can eventually be defined, and it may be found at that point that city and society and culture coincide.

In conclusion, it may be noted that many fascinating questions have already been posed in regard to cities: Do they tend to become alike? How many class systems are there? How does one deal with the parallel vertical systems of personal life and public superstructures? To what extent is instrumentalization of people possible, or already achieved? What is the meaning of communication in relation to the social structure? Who are the mediators, and what do they mediate? None of these questions is easily answered, and certainly not by the anthropologist seeking answers in the study of the small rural community. The study of the urban scene will be carried out by members of many different disciplines, forgetting disciplinary boundaries, borrowing methodologies and techniques, and joining forces in general. The anthropologist and his particular insights and methodology has much to offer to this effort.

REFERENCES

Abrahams, Roger D.
    1964   Deep Down in the Jungle (Hatboro, Pennsylvania: Folklore Associates).
Arensberg, Conrad M. and Solon Kimball
    1965   Culture and Community (New York, N.Y.: Harcourt, Brace and World).
Bell, Daniel
    1964   Twelve Modes of Prediction. Daedalus 93:853.
Bohannan, Paul
    1963   Social Anthropology (New York, N.Y.: Holt, Rinehart and Winston).

29

Brzezinski, Zbigniew
  1967   The American Transition. The New Republic, p. 18.
Davis, Kingsley
  1967   The Perilous Promise of Behavioral Science. In Research
                in the Service of Man (Washington, D.C.: U.S. Govern-
                ment Printing Office).
Hauser, Philip M.
  1965   The Folk-Urban Ideal Types. In The Study of Urbanization,
                Philip M. Hauser and Leo F. Schnore, eds. (New York,
                N.Y.: John Wiley & Sons, Inc.), p. 508.
Hofstadter, Richard
  1955   The Age of Reform (New York, N.Y.: Vintage Books).
Lampard, Eric E.
  1961   American Historians and the Study of Urbanization.
                American Historical Review 67:58.
Lewis, Oscar
  1963   The Children of Sanchez (New York, N.Y.: Vintage Books).
Mumford, Lewis
  1967   Statement. Senate Subcommittee on Executive Reorgani-
                zation. Mimeo.
Redfield, Robert
  1934   Culture Changes in Yucatan. American Anthropologist
                36:57-69.
Sjoberg, Gideon
  1965   Cities in Developing and in Industrial Societies. In
                The Study of Urbanization, Philip M. Hauser and Leo F.
                Schnore, eds. (New York: John Wiley & Sons).
Whiteford, Andrew H.
  1960   Two Cities of Latin America (Beloit, Wisconsin: The Logan
                Museum of Anthropology).
Wirth, Louis
  1938   Urbanism as a Way of Life. In Cities and Societies, Paul
                K. Hatt and Albert J. Reiss, Jr., eds. (New York, N.Y.:
                Free Press of Glencoe).

30

THE ANTHROPOLOGY OF CITIES: SOME METHODOLOGICAL ISSUES

Anthony Leeds
University of Texas

This paper is concerned with what an anthropologist is to do in a field situation when carrying out ethnography in any given city, i.e., with what knowledge is to be acquired about a city rather than with the theory of cities. The two are intimately connected since the latter specifies what knowledge is to be sought, but, nevertheless, they involve quite different concepts and thoroughly different methodologies. The paper, then, is concerned with some theoretical considerations regarding the content of cities, rather than the theory of cities.[1]

The considerable amount of anthropological or closely related field work dealing with social and cultural phenomena observed in cities has done mainly one of two things.

On one hand, it has dealt with social phenomena which, like kinship, are not restricted to the city or even to urban society (including its country aspect). In such studies,[2] the question asked has generally been, "How is kinship operating in this city?", not, "What is the effect of cityness on the operation of kinship?", i.e., what systemic and characteristic aspects of kinship -- if any -- are elicited or forced into being in the city, and only in the city, as a function of specifiable features, or variables if you will, characteristic of the city. They have been studies of kinship in the city, not of the city in kinship. Generally, they have been (a) particularistic; (b) in the mold of kinship studies carried out in the country areas and among "primitivos"; and, (c) evasive of dealing with the urban ambience as such, to which the kinship organization is related. Studies of other kinds of social life -- networks, associations, etc. -- have tended to take the same approach. In short, all such studies have, as far as the city aspect is concerned, tended to be non-generalizable, not related to generalizable theory, models, or hypotheses, and hence not generative of broader theory as to cities, urban society, or the social evolution of urbanized societies.

On the other hand, anthropological work has been the kind of community study approach exemplified by Leeds, Lewis, Mangin, Padilla, Patch, and others.[3] Here, some segment of the society, like the Puerto Rican minority, which is not even necessarily a city phenomenon, or some specialized housing settlement type like Lewis's or Patch's _vecindad_ or _callejon_, or Clifton's, Leeds's, Lewis's, or Mangin's squatments (_callampa_, _favela_, _arrabal_, _barriada_, respectively) is chosen for study and treated as if it were a self-contained, more or less autonomous community. It may indeed be such a community in the city, but this cannot be _assumed a priori_ as these studies have tended to do. Rather, the fact that it _is_ a community must be _empirically_

31

shown, and the mechanisms which create and maintain the boundaries of that community as over against the rest of the city empiricaliy analyzed in detail as part of the total social process. Failure to do this has led to a thorough failure to justify the units of study used and failure to show mutual effects between the asserted "units" of study and the city in which they are immersed.

Further, it has led to the creation or perpetuation of prevalent myths concerning the continuity of the entity of study for autonomous cultural reasons (e.g. "culture of poverty," "marginalidad") rather than to the achievement of insights as to the continuity of the entity as a socio-economic and political reflex, dependent variable, or coordinate sub-segment of the larger city and national society of which it is part.[4] Finally, there is the failure to see, or even look at, the city as an entity.[5]

In sum, anthropologists have tended to perpetuate traditional concerns -- kinship, the community, child training, study of associations, etc. -- trans- ferring these, first, forty to fifty years ago, to the quite different societal context of rural communities and then, more recently, to the drastically dif- ferent context of the city in large-scale society. Some of the methodological problems regarding tribal societies were never resolved, and sometimes never even raised, though they closely involved both theoretical models and field work procedures. In this transference of traditional concerns from tribal ex- perience to city studies, these problems were perpetuated and intensified.

Perhaps one of the most important of these was the implicit mental model, accompanied by its explicit field work practice, which treated the tribe or the "rural" community as if it were an autonomous unit. Its role as merely one of a population of tribes in a larger ecology (cf. Leeds 1964b) or as a constituent element of a larger society was treated as more or less an epiphenomenon while its autonomy was conceived of as a necessary result of its essential, unique, internal characteristics. That this "essence" itself might be a result or function of its place in a population or as a constituent element is an hypothesis which has scarcely been formulated, let alone inves- tigated theoretically, methodologically, or empirically in the field.

The failure even to raise this question in tribal and "community" studies has been transferred to the city studies, where it has become a yet greater failure because the justification for treating the units under description as autonomous is still less self-evident, while the blindness to the complexity of interrelation within the encompassing social entity or entities (e.g. city, nation) which includes the unit as one of its variables is even vaster. In the case of the city, the blindness leads to its atomized treatment, as if these variables (kinship, associations, housing, etc.) were separable, discrete, and unrelated elements -- as it were, accidents of the city rather than caused and linked manifestations of the city (and national) process.

Essentially what is involved are the methodological and theoretical issues inherent in such questions as "Why the city at all?", and, at a lower level of generalization, "Why this city?" The answer to the first question would have the form of a general law whose content, I believe, would refer to hypothesized universal functions of cities in the context of a consideration of the range of major socio-cultural and ecological variables of human popu-

32

lations and their societal units.

The answer to the second question involves this general law and some corollary or corollaries of limiting reference which should predict the characteristics of this city, or, possibly, at least a class of such "This Cities," for example, a class of administrative cities (non-industrial capitals like Brasília or Canberra) or a class of heavy-industry towns in "developing" countries (like São Paulo). Additional questions such as "Why this city here?" introduce additional variables, relating to the entire city system, which have relevance to the study of any given variable in that city system.

These questions have not been asked in anthropology and its urban field studies, except in the most obvious and everyday sort of way, as, for instance, in the writings about the "urban revolution."[6] Even this broad and rather shallow kind of generalization is not used, or the questions themselves are simply not asked, in the empirical city studies so that it is impossible to assess whether the data observed are caused by, related to, affected by, or independent of, other variables at work in the city system.

For example, in the city of Lattakia, Syria,[7] it seems clear that the shape-up procedure for employing dock workers through kinship and home-town ties was obviously related to the town's location at the seaside and causally related to residence patterns and location of workers, many of whom were rural immigrants. In the system of exchange which ties the Syrian polity to many other polities, Lattakia operates as a point of both physical and juridical transfer. Policies with respect to both types of transfer, set both by the national and municipal governments and conditioned by the geographical-ecological considerations, as well as foreign interests, have direct and indirect effects on the patterning of kinship behavior. To describe kinship behavior without reference to those potent variables of the national and local institutional and geographical conditions is to fail to see the dynamics of the social process and of change.

Another example is afforded by favelas (hereinafter treated as an unitalicized English word) in Rio de Janeiro. Almost without exception, all literature on favelas treats them as enclaves having their own unique internal characteristics in all respects: they are self-maintaining, culturally autonomous outsiders; strangers to the city; in fact, they are rural migrants who have squatted in the physical confines of the city, remaining isolated in it, but not of it.[8]

Virtually none of the studies of favelas (or barrios, barriadas, ranchos, corticos, callejones, vecindades, etc.) deal systematically with the relationships of the favela or cortico to a series of variables which describe the city system, and, quite as important, to the state or condition of those variables. This failure is due to the absence of adequate sociological models, theoretical and descriptive of the city as such, when analytically or empirically examining the favelas or other delimitable entities in the field or in the library. Such variables include the interests of the social and political elites of the city and the mechanisms for their fulfillment, the intensity of action of such mechanisms and the threats, if any, to them; the conditions of the labor market with special reference to pressures varying the rates of unemployment

33

and underemployment and to barriers to attainment of specialized training; the structure and operation of the rent and labor laws, especially the salary structure, including differential pay rates; the structure, accessibility, and costs of the metropolitan transportation system, and so on.

Boundary conditions which delimit a favela population and give it some coherence as an aggregate or as a sub-community are created and maintained by variables such as these. They also define the kinds of action which take place over boundaries: which are impossible, which are possible, and which are probable and likely to be frequent. In general, these variables delimit, either directly or indirectly, the parameters of action and relationship inside the favela or other unit of study.

Variations over time of certain basic variables, such as national salary structures and national salary policy (e.g. prohibiting or delaying salary increases in an inflationary situation; cf. O'Neil, 1966), as these are manifested in the city labor market, govern, on the one hand, the relations of favela residents to the economy generally and specifically. Thus, for example, national salary policy sets minimum wages and the entire wage scale based on it, as well as schedules for different types of professions and occupations. Obviously such scales correspond to jobs in the labor market absorbing workers from the favelas as well as from the rest of the city. Depressed wage structures, especially under inflationary pressure, are chiefly and specifically related to residence in favelas. In turn, there is some evidence that residence in favelas tends to make more difficult the tasks of job-hunting and job-holding, because of the discriminatory and abusive practices of employers against favela residents who are "illegal," "marginals," "squatters," "irresponsibles," "untrustworthy," etc. There are specific institutions or customs to circumvent such discriminations. Again, there is also some evidence that the existence of favelas per se helps reduce the general wage level of the city by making possible the more successful maintenance of a pool of cheap labor for a labor-intensive production system.

On the other hand, these basic variables also govern discrete and predictable relationships inside the favelas, describable with game theory models, such as a series of dyadic, triadic, or similar reduced types of groupings. These include the paternalistic creditor-debtor relationship, the matri-centered mother-child household, a series of types of marital relationships, reciprocal friendships, dyadic or small pluradic neighbor groups, patron-client/client-sub-client, and other chained dyadic relations (cf. Leeds 1964a), etc.

In sum, the states of the variables relevant to the city as a whole (viz., the labor market and its intra-city variations; the transportation system and its differential costs and accessibilities inside the city; the distribution, costs, and accessibilities of urban facilities such as light, water, sewerage; the intra-city topography; special legislation, decrees, and ordinances referring to the city as a whole, and so on) have direct and indirect institutional effects -- indeed molding effects -- on the internal characteristics of the unit of study which cannot be understood at all without reference to these variables.

34

All the foregoing considerations have major implications for the anthropologist carrying out field work in cities. Given the general precepts of
anthropology and its methods regarding all field work (e.g., participant-
observation, thorough ethnography), the anthropologist working in the city is
logistically constrained to working at most in two or three sites given any
standard amount of time that he is likely to have. This constraint is the more
severe, the larger the city and the fewer the co-workers he has, and especially
if he is alone.

I can, perhaps, exemplify these points with my own case. I found
myself -- a single field worker with thirteen months of field time ahead of
me for the study of favelas in Rio de Janeiro (1965-1966) -- confronted with
300 highly differentiated possible units of study. My previously developed
hypotheses indicated I should pick four, each with certain characteristics.
Given (a) the vast number from which to choose these four; (b) the virtually
total lack of any useful information for Rio's favelas regarding the characteristics which interested me; (c) the cost in time entailed by Rio's transportation,
which would have had to be used while trying to identify the appropriate favelas,
the universe of which is spread over the length and breadth of a topographically very difficult city; and (d) a number of other considerations involving
time, my own manpower, available information, and so on, I decided to focus
ethnographically on three or four favelas and attempt to control the variation in
the entire population of favelas by other means, primarily through thorough
documentation (such as it might be).[9] It should be noted here that one's resources tend to set the limits for one's field strategies, but also that changes
in resources, even during the field session, may permit one to shift strategies
advantageously.

It might be asked of me "Why did you insist on studying favelas in a
city as large as Rio de Janeiro whose metropolitan area contains about
7,000,000 people? Why did you not choose a city of perhaps 100,000 like
Ilheus or Itabuna, which, in any case, you have known for fifteen years
since doing your initial Brasilian field work?" The answer is that, except
for particular hypotheses that might revolve about specified city sizes, a
somewhat unlikely possibility at present, I was constrained by the theoretical
conceptions underlying my research, especially regarding power distributions
(cf. Leeds 1964c). These indicated the desirability of a field work site which
presented various politico-economic and administrative levels of organization
at one and the same time. Rio de Janeiro is ideal: it is still, partially, the
de facto national capital; it is the capital of the city-state of Guanabara; it
has subdivisions called regional administrations, equivalents of the standard
Brasilian municipalities; and finally, it has semi-conventionalized, non-
official subdivisions, the bairros, the favelas, and the like, more or less
equivalent to natural localized "community" entities. I was able, therefore,
to get a cross-section of the entire hierarchy of power-distribution, based on
different resources of power and reflecting a larger variety of power relations
growing out of the differentiated kinds of power.

As I remarked above, unless he has indefinitely long time, almost
unlimited resources, and a large personnel, the anthropologist in the city

must limit himself, ethnographically, to one locus or a very few loci of intensive field work. But, as can be deduced from the comments in the first pages and was quite clear from my actual field experience (indeed from all my field experience in quite different kinds of situations), no one locus can be understood without reference to (a) the other examples of the same type of locus, i.e., in my study, other favelas; (b) other loci of related types, e.g. the other types of intra-city settlements or other proletarian housing aggregates; (c) other examples of the same class of locus contexts, in my case other Brasilian, Latin American, and similar "underdeveloped" cities.

It is only with reference to each of these cross-cutting sets of comparisons that one can confirm theoretically indicated variables or discover empirically the most significant variables affecting the locus of ethnography. It is only by reference to the other examples from the same and related classes and the city context of the field work site and comparisons with other cities that one can determine the range of variation of the variable, discover the pressures which bring about or the factors which cause the variations, and establish the essential relationships among the variables.

Put another way, the study of a single example or a very few examples of the class of entities chosen is methodologically erroneous. It either prohibits or limits examining similarities and differences to be found in the full range of examples, an examination of which allows one to isolate the relevant fundamental features of the system of which they are manifestations. Thus, even the study of an entire class of entities, such as the entire universe of favelas of Rio, is inadequate, because it is, in fact, a single example of several larger universes; that of differentiated and interdependent settlement types, that of differentiated and interdependent power aggregates and groups, that of differentiated and interdependent economic aggregates, etc., in the city.

Because of the differentiation and interdependence, no one example from any of these universes can be fully understood alone. They are all variables of the system which is the city under study for which the field worker, before and during his study, must develop a special model. This model will indicate the fundamental features, referred to above, which relate all the kinds of entities, their characteristics, and their mutual effects.

Even this cannot be adequately done unless the ethnographer has some comparative or contrastive foundation for designating the fundamental features. He must keep in mind such usually unasked questions -- Whiteford (1960) being a rare exception -- as "How and why are such-and-such two cities different from each other as a whole or with respect to some specified feature?" -- a question to be asked in the context of the generic question, "How is one to account for the difference of any two cities from each other?"

For example, the ethnographic fact, which the field ethnographer studying a favela in one city, Rio, must know both by reading and some minimal ethnographic observation, is that in São Paulo, a city somewhat larger than Rio (ca. 8,000,000 in the metropolitan area), there are about 1/6 the number of favelas in Rio, and these are on the average about 1/4 to 1/3 the size of those of Rio. This fact raises some extremely interesting questions

36

as to the relationship between those variables which generate favelas -- the labor market, migration, housing conditions, etc., -- and other variables comprising the city, e.g., the prior history of the city growth, the degree of industrialization, the skill level and educational facilities for the working population, and the overall role of the city in the inclusive body politic.

Again, apropos of my general theme and the foregoing example, the field ethnographer must ask himself specific questions about his city of study as a whole: "Why does this city have such and such characteristics?" Such a question is, in fact, a comparative or contrastive question in the same way that those mentioned above are, and the answer helps determine significant features of his locus of study.

By way of what may seem a rather esoteric example, he may ask a question such as "Why the intense level of sexuality of Rio de Janeiro society (as contrasted with, say, São Paulo or Belo Horizonte)?" The answer to this specific question, I believe, lies in the role that the city of Rio de Janeiro -- and, by contrast, the role that the city of São Paulo -- plays in the body politic as a whole. Rio, I believe, constitutes an institutional nexus for a privileged, patrimonial, governing elite occupying public positions whose symbols of office must constantly receive overt validation as part of the mechanism of maintaining, power, authority, influence, and prestige. The sexuality and sensuality seem to me part of a complicated system of mate selection through public offering mediated by a subtle cue system which indicates both availability and social status exclusiveness. The resort-town atmosphere and economy (beaches, Carnaval, vistas, and outlooks) are both physical arenas for the specialized social drama of Rio and part of the actual economy of the courtly-patrimonial elitism which permeates all sectors and activities of Rio's population.

São Paulo's role, in contrast, is that of an institutional nexus of private governing elites occupying private positions in big business and big industries, most of whose basic operations, interests, knowledge, and so on, are enhanced by privacy. The operations of home life, courtship, sexuality, are correspondingly private.

These differentiated roles relate to the historical origins and continuities of each city including the institutional conditions of its founding. It is interesting, in this connection, that, in 1890, Rio and São Paulo had about 523,000 and 64,000 people respectively, while today São Paulo is larger than Rio, as the figures cited above indicate. In other words, Rio, as capital during 100 years of the colonial status and throughout the empire, was already a very substantial city at the end of the 19th Century, while São Paulo, founded at about the same time as Rio, was still a provincial capital beginning its surge of growth about the explosive expansion of coffee and early industrialization. Though Rio, too, has since then industrialized heavily, it has also maintained much of its original administrative role and ethos in contemporary Brasil.

The various social classes and other possible entities of study (e.g. favelas) orient themselves with respect to the differentiated roles in the national society about which the two major cities are focally structured. Such

37

differential orientation is reflected in a variety of ways. One example is the absolute and relative size of the body of public functionaries in Rio: till 1960, when the official capital was removed to Brasília (although Rio for many purposes continues the de facto capital), about 40 percent of the labor force in the city! Anybody working for any public body, especially if he has one tenure (estabilidade), considers himself a funcionário público, a prestigeful status even for the tenured janitors of a ministry or the pick-up drivers of a repartição pública (a public agency), especially if compared with their non-tenured equivalents in private employ. Though there is a large public bureaucracy in São Paulo, it is relatively much, much smaller, and the ethos of being a funcionário público much less important. The ethos and its action manifestations permeate all associational life in favelas and other delimitable aggregates.

Another example is the difference in intensity and elaborateness of the Carnaval in the two cities, and the extreme imitation, among the lower "classes" in Rio, of elite public privilege and prestige in the popular carnaval,. especially the blocos and escolas de samba with their themes (enrêdos) dealing with public, literary, or artistic personages, the Academy of Letters, the 400th Anniversary of the founding of Rio; with their bewigged, bejeweled Louis XIV-XVIth baroque parade figures; with their imitations of wealth, splendor, courtliness, and elitism. São Paulo has its Carnaval, but it is no parallel to Rio's in its much more plebian and unstructured kermesse (cf. Morocco 1966).

The point is that the highly differentiated roles in the nation of these two cities (here used simply as particular examples of the generic problem in question) seen as total systems significantly affect what happens to the specific variables or entities under study. The field ethnographer is obligated to ask himself, therefore, "What are the generic and particular variables affecting, and the generic and particular relationships among, any of the entities of study (mentioned in the opening paragraphs) for all cities, for designated classes of cities, and especially for the city I am now studying?" He must have some ethnographic control over all these variables and the different kinds of entities involved because he cannot understand the ethnographic data of his particular entity of study without such control.

Thus, one cannot properly understand, that is, give an account of, the favelas without understanding the dynamics of migration; residence in other types of proletarian housing such as rooming houses, housing projects, backyard favelas, tenements, and so on; rent patterns; land tenure; inheritance; litigation; and so on. That this methodological point is not self-evident is amply demonstrated by the great majority of the documents on favelas which do not touch on these subjects at all. Since the favela populations mostly hail from, and frequently return to, such other forms of housing-settlement types, respond to rent laws and conditions, and are involved directly with land tenure and litigation problems, the omission of these considerations contributes drastically to the mythology already extant about favelas, as in the works of Bonilla, Pearse (to some extent), Goldrich, and any number of Brazilian writers.[10] These remarks apply, with very few exceptions, to the literature on housing-settlement types in urban centers for México, Perú, and

38

Puerto Rico, including such well-known works as those by Oscar Lewis, except his article of 1952 from whose stance he subsequently departed.

The questions raised above, in their generalized form, require the generation of a general theory of the relationship between the structure of society in all its aspects and its nucleated settlements, on one hand, and, on the other, from such theory, the generation of differentiated models describing different categories of cities. From among such differentiated models (e.g., as unsystematized and incipient examples: the industrial city, the preindustrial city, the parade city, the administrative city, etc.)[11] the ethnographer must choose the appropriate one from which to generate a specific model relevant to the description of his city of study.

The appropriate category model and the specific model together will guide him in his ethnographic field work, indicating to him the significant variables to be examined, desirable quantifications, types of evidence for relationships among the variables, and so on. The models will set forth the hypothesized relationships and effects, mutual or otherwise, in a total system, among the entire range of entities and variables that have been mentioned above. They will indicate, too, the pressures, the constraints, the demands, which, it seems to me, have largely been disregarded in the studies of cities so far carried out by anthropologists and for which quantitative measures are desperately needed.[12]

In conclusion, I think the future of anthropological studies of cities lies in dealing with the multiple variables of the city system in a single synthetic framework. In any case, the ethnographer dealing with some specific aspect of the city must keep this framework in mind and, to some extent, attain some ethnographic control over all the significant entities to which it refers. In the generation of such a synthetic framework and, more sophisticatedly, the theory behind it, the anthropologists' evolutional, ecological, and holistic perspectives should contribute significantly.

NOTES

1. I have dealt with some theoretical aspects in Leeds (1968).

2. See Bott; Clifton; DESAL (1966); Epstein (1961); Firth; Goldrich; Leeds (1964a); Lewis (1966a, 1966b); Mangin (1965); Meillassoux; Patch (1967); Pearse (1957); Warner and Lunt; Whiteford; Willmott and Young; Young and Willmott; the studies on the educational system in New York carried out by Eleanor Leacock and associates, and innumerable others.

3. Banton; Bonilla (1961); Cardona G. (1968a, 1968b); Clifton, Leeds (in press); Leeds and Leeds (1967); Lewis (1959a, 1959b, 1961); Lynd and Lynd (1929, 1937); Mangin (1967a, 1967b, 1967c); Matos (1960, 1961, 1967, 1968); Mayer; O'Neil; Padilla; Patch (1961); Pearse (1958, 1961); Seminário; Southall; Turner (1965, 1966, 1967); Warner and Lunt.

4. Abrams (1966); Bonilla (1961, 1964); Cardona (1968c); Cardona and Simonds;

39

DESAL (1965, 1966); Goldrich; Goldrich, Pratt, and Schuller; Lewis (1959a, 1959b, 1961, 1966a, 1966b); Patch (1961); Pearse (1957, 1958, 1961); Seminário; etc., etc.

5. In my experience, the persons with the clearest view of the city as an entity, a system, are some of the urban planners (cf. Modesto 1968).

6. See V. G. Childe (1936, 1942).

7. These comments are based on Baggett (1965) who got her ethnographic information from Ghassan Arnaoot, a former resident of Lattakia, and on my own subsequent interviews with and his draft of a study of that city.

8. On theoretical grounds, had these been developed or even had very un-developed theory been brought to bear on the favela phenomena, these views should have been considered, at the very least, doubtful. I would say that with any reasonable development of city theory, they should have been thrown out altogether. But they were not, and data collection, including, to some degree, the first stages of my own, went on in the framework of the myth out-lined above. In other words, the myth perpetuated the questions asked, which perpetuated the reception of only certain kinds and interpretations of data, which perpetuated the myth.

9. That, in fact, this latter policy was only partially adhered to is irrelevant to the present argument and has to do with accidents of the local situation, especially with the presence of the Peace Corps Volunteers, selected Brasilian social workers, and sociologists working in the favelas, and the emergence of a working field seminar among all of these. Ethnographically, I did, in-deed focus intensively on only five favelas -- a study carried further in the summers of 1967 and 1968 and by my wife in February of the latter year. My wife and I also carried out the documentation (ca. 40,000 microfilm frames of all sorts of published and unpublished materials, statistical and qualitative, plus acquisition of books, magazines, journals, and newspapers). At the same time, these accidents of the local situation permitted me sufficient free-dom to move away from the five favelas in order to make visits of varying duration to a total of fifty other favelas as well as to other types of housing-settlements. This gave me an additional direct experiential control over the range of variability within the class of entities on five of whose exemplars I was concentrating.

10. Bonilla (1961); Goldrich (1965); Pearse (1957, 1958). Seminário provides a typical if extreme version of the myth. This astonishing publication was produced by the magnificent rectors of six of the major universities in and around Rio de Janeiro with the assistance of a number of professionals such as geologists and others. The following quotation from this "authoritative" statement about favelas will illustrate the remarkable persistence of the myth, in one of its most virulent forms, as late as 1967; "The favelas leap out at

40

the eyes of all not only as a social cancer -- incubators of rebels and gang-
sters -- but also as urbanistic monstrosities destroying one of the most beautiful landscapes of the planet. Rio de Janeiro, with its bay, its beaches, its
belt of steep, verdant slopes, is universally considered the most beautiful
city of the world, a patrimony for humanity which we have in custody without
the right to mutilate it. "Cidade Maravilhosa" was its nickname before the
invasion of the barbarians.... ⁄The favelas⁄ appeared evilly, expanded, and
proliferated like the true cancers that they are" (1967: 76-77, translation mine).

11. See Sjoberg, Mumford, and many others.

12. It is too early yet to present such models. However, a sketchy sort of
thing of what I have in mind may be useful for discussion. In "developing
societies," at least those whose central organizing principle is capitalistic,
the following appear to be the fundamental characteristics of the total society:
(a) the society as a whole is undergoing a basic reorganization of the institutions of the economy, e.g. by introduction of price-making markets, of
planning, of new forms of finance, of new transaction procedures, etc.;
(b) concomitantly, sharp changes in the system of property and its inheritance
are taking place, eliciting extensive confusion and concurrent litigation with
respect, for example, to land claims, usufructs, tenure systems, rent forms,
etc., themselves linked with new transaction procedures; (c) extensive elaboration, revision, recasting, and experimentation with law and the legal system occur, producing very considerable confusion and contradiction which
provide a basis for quite characteristic abuses and manipulations; (d) centralization of the power system accompanied by breakdown of ecological localism
(cf. Leeds 1964a:1321-2), a process usually referred to as "integration," unfortunately, because it implies that prior states were not integrated; (e) institution of national (total-societal) systems of taxation (e.g., imposts, income
tax), social welfare, administration, etc.; (f) shift in basic technology,
towards increasing mechanization, capital-intensiveness, large-scale operations,
"efficiency," and "rationalization"; (g) increasing specialization and linkage
among specializations, necessitating rapid and short-distance transportation
and communications, i.e. localization as in cities which are also the locales
for providing the welfare services, the transactional services, the information
circulation for the ever-more complicated economy and for the power system,
etc. (cf. Leeds 1960).

   These conditions generate surplus labor throughout the society, tending
to draw it towards the sites of welfare distribution, authority (which may solve
problems), economic elaboration (which may provide jobs), and population
growth (which may provide better possibilities for marginal types of work such
as peddling), i.e. towards the cities. The surplus labor itself reduces wage
levels and depresses and restricts the markets, setting limits on production
and productivity levels -- hence on the job markets in the cities. A partial
response to this is the hypertrophy of welfare systems. The hypertrophy of
the unskilled labor force, of low-paid domestic services, of marginal peddling,
odd-jobbing, and the like, in confrontation with the changes, confusions, and

41

manipulative opportunisms of the property systems, especially in landed property, land payments, real estate, and so on, and of the employment system, particularly under a legislative and juridical system controlled by the propertied elites, generates such phenomena as squatter settlements and a considerable number of their internal characteristics, e.g. factionalism, patron-clientism, and others.

Specific historical and ecological conditions should permit us to specify the distinctive states of the variables more closely. Thus, the recency of São Paulo's growth -- after it had already begun to develop an extensive industrial base and after sizable European immigration, but without a history of extensive use of slaves in the production system -- contrasts with the much earlier, imperial and patrimonial growth of Rio with its sizable slave population, freed as late as 1888, a reduced immigrant population, its courtly life, and its fundamentally administrative rather than productive economy. These conditions appear to have profound influences on the demography and subsequent settlement characteristics, especially the favela pattern mentioned above in the text. It should be predictable from these specific models that the cultural characteristics of the favelas of Rio and those of São Paulo should be different in important respects, proletarianized versions of elitism and the patrimonial attitudes prevailing in the former; plebian and industrial types of proletarianization prevailing in the latter. At this time, preliminary inspection seems generally to confirm these predictions.

REFERENCES

Abrams, Charles
    1964   Man's Struggle for Shelter in an Urbanizing World (Cambridge: M.I.T.-Harvard).
    1966   Squatter Settlements: the Problem and the Opportunity. (Washington: Department of Housing and Urban Development, Division of International Affairs).

Baggett, Susan
    1965   The City as Transactional System: A Case Study of Lattakia, Syria. University of Texas, Department of Anthropology, typescript.

Banton, Michael
    1957   West African City (London: Oxford University Press).

Bonilla, Frank
    1961   Rio's Favelas: the Rural Slum Within the City. Reports Service, East Coast of South America Series, 3(3), Brasil (New York: Amer. Universities Field Staff).
    1964   The Urban Worker. In Continuity and Change in Latin America, J. J. Johnson, ed. (Palo Alto: Stanford University Press), pp. 186-205.

Bott, Elizabeth
    1957   Family and Social Network: Roles, Norms, and External Relationships in Ordering Urban Families (London: Tavistock).

42

Cardona Gutierrez, Ramiro
    1968a   Barrio de Invasión Juan XXIII (Monografia). Bogotá:
                  Asociación Columbiana de Facultades de Medicina,
                  División de Estudios de Población, Bol. 19 (mimeo).
    1968b   Barrio de Invasión Policarpo Salivarrieta. Bogotá:
                  Asociación Columbiana de Facultades de Medicina,
                  División de Estudios de Población, Bol. 20 (mimeo).
    1968c   (ed.) Migración, Urbanización, y Marginalidad. Bogotá:
                  Asociación Colombiana de Facultades de Medicina, Di-
                  visión de Estudios de Población.
Cardona Gutierrez, Ramiro and Alan Simonds
    1968   Investigación Nacional Sobre Urbanización y Marginalidad.
                  Bogotá: Asociación Colombiana de Facultades de Medicina,
                  División de Estudios de Población (mimeo).
Childe, V. Gordon
    1936   Man Makes Himself (London: Watts).
    1942   What Happened in History (Harmondsworth: Penguin).
Clifton, James A.
    1966   "A Petition for a Grant-in-Aid of Research" to Wenner-
                  Gren Foundation for Anthropological Research (mimeo).
                  Title of Project: "A Study of Processes of Urbanization
                  and Adaptation in a Chilean Callampa Community" (cited
                  with permission). Lawrence, Kansas: University of
                  Kansas.
Delhi Pradesh, Bharat Sevak Samaj
    1958   Slums of Old Delhi: A Report of the Socio-Economic Survey
                  of the Slum Dwellers of Old Delhi City (Delhi: A. Ram).
DESAL
    1965   Poblaciones Marginales y Desarrollo Urbano, el Caso
                  Chileno (Santiago: Centro Para el Desarrollo Económico
                  y Social de América Latina).
    1966   Antecedentes para el Estudio de la Marginalidad en Chile
                  (Santiago: Centro para el Desarrollo Económico y Social
                  de América Latina).
Epstein, A. L.
    1958   Politics in an Urban Community (Manchester: Manchester
                  University Press).
    1961   The Network and Urban Social Organization. Rhodes-
                  Livingstone Journal 29: 29-62.
Firth, Raymond, ed.
    1956   Two Studies of Kinship in London. London School of
                  Economics Monographs on Social Anthropology, No. 15
                  (London: Athlone).
Goldrich, Daniel
    1965   Toward the Comparative Study of Politicization in Latin
                  America. In Contemporary Cultures and Societies of Latin
                  America, D.B. Heath and R.N. Adams, eds. (New York:
                  Random House), pp. 361-378.

43

Goldrich, Daniel, Raymond B. Pratt, and C. R. Schuller
    1967-68   The Political Integration of Lower Class Urban Settlements
            in Chile and Peru. Studies in Comparative International
            Development, 3 (1) (St. Louis: Washington University,
            Social Science Institute).

Leeds, Anthony
    1964a   Brazilian Careers and Social Structure: An Evolutionary
            Model and Case History. American Anthropologist 66:
            1321-1347. Reprinted in Heath and Adams, cited in Gold-
            rich (1965), supra, pp. 379-404.
    1964b   Some Problems of Yaruro Ethnography. In Actas y Memorias
            del 35º Congresso Internacional de Americanistas, Mexico,
            1962, pp. 157-175.
    1964c   Locality Power in Relation to Supra-Local Power Institutions.
            In Urban Anthropology, E. Bruner and A. Southall, eds.,
            in press.
    1965   "As Variaveis Mais Importantes na Ecologia das Favelas."
            Paper presented at 1º Seminário Nacional de Estudo do
            Problema Favela. São Paulo: Movimento Universitário
            de Desfavelamento.
    1968   "Specialization, Transaction, Location, and Power -- Some
            Theoretical Considerations Regarding Towns and Cities."
            Paper read at Rutgers Seminar on Urban Studies, March.
    In Press   (ed.) Rio's Favelas (Austin: University of Texas, Institute
            of Latin American Studies).

Leeds, Anthony and Elizabeth R. Leeds
    1967   "Brazil and the Myth of Urban Rurality: Urban Experience,
            Work, and Values in 'Squatments' of Rio de Janeiro and
            Lima." Paper for Conference on Urbanization and Work in
            Modernizing Societies, Nov. 2-4, St. Thomas, Virgin
            Islands.
    1968   "System Continuity in Brazil." Paper read at Conference
            on Political Parties and the Search for Institutional Stability
            in 20th Century Latin America. Buffalo: New York State
            University, Department of Political Science.

Lewis, Oscar
    1952   Urbanization without Breakdown. Scientific American 75:
            3-41.
    1959a   La Cultura de Vecindad en la Ciudad de México. Ciencias
            Políticas y Sociales 5: 349-364.
    1959b   Five Families: Mexican Case Studies in the Culture of
            Poverty (New York: Basic Books).
    1961   The Children of Sanchez (New York: Random House).
    1966a   The Culture of Poverty. Scientific American 215: 19-25.
    1966b   La Vida, A Puerto Rican Family in the Culture of Poverty
            (New York: Random House).

44

Lynd, Robert S. and Helen M. Lynd
    1929   Middletown, A Study in American Culture (New York: Harcourt, Brace).
    1937   Middletown in Transition: A Study in Cultural Conflict (New York: Harcourt, Brace).
Mangin, William
    1965   The Role of Regional Associations in the Adaptation of Rural Migrants to Cities in Peru. In Heath and Adams, cited in Goldrich (1965), supra, pp. 311-323.
    1967a   "Political Implications of the Barriadas in Perú." Paper read at Latin American Colloquium, Brandeis University, May.
    1967b   Squatter Settlements. Scientific American 217: 21-29.
    1967c   Latin American Squatter Settlements: A Problem and a Solution. Latin American Research Review 2: 65-98.
Mangin, William and John C. Turner
    1968   The Barriada Movement. Progressive Architecture, May, pp. 154-162.
Matos Mar, José
    1960   La Urbanización "Simon Rodriguez" (Caracas: Banco Obrero de Venezuela).
    1961   Migration and Urbanization. The Barriadas of Lima - an Example of Integration into Urban Life. In Urbanization in Latin America, Philip P. Hauser, ed. (New York: UNESCO), pp. 170-189.
    1967   Estudio de las Barriadas Limeñas (Lima: Instituto de Estudios Peruanos).
    1968   Urbanización y Barriadas en América del Sur (Lima: Instituto de Estudios Peruanos).
Mayer, Philip
    1961   Townsmen or Tribesmen (Cape Town: Oxford University Press).
Meillassoux, Claude
    1968   Urbanization of an African Community; Voluntary Associations in Bamako. AES Monograph 45 (Seattle and London: University of Washington Press).
Mitchell, J. Clyde
    1956   Urbanization, Detribalization, and Stabilization in South Africa: a Problem of Definition and Measurement. In Social Implications of Industrialization and Urbanization in Africa South of the Sahara, D. Forde, ed. (Paris: UNESCO).
    1964   Distance and Urban Involvement in Northern Rhodesia. In Bruner and Southall, eds., cited in Leeds (1964c), supra.
Modesto, Hélio
    1968   Favelas; Reflections Regarding the Problem. In Leeds, ed. (in press).

45

Morocco, David
1966   Carnaval Groups - Maintainers and Intensifiers of the Favela
Phenomenon in Rio de Janeiro. In Leeds, ed. (in press).

Mumford, Lewis
1938   The Culture of Cities (New York: Harcourt, Brace).
1961   The City in History: Its Origins, Its Transformations, and
Its Prospects (New York: Harcourt, Brace and World).

O'Neil, Charles
1966   Problems of Urbanization in Rio Favelas. In Leeds, ed.
(in press).

Padilla, Elena
1958   Up From Puerto Rico (New York: Columbia University Press).

Patch, Richard
1961   Life in a Callejón: A Study of Urban Disorganization.
Reports Service, West Coast of S. Amer. Series 8 (6) (New
York: Amer. Universities Field Staff).

1967   "La Parada, Lima's Market - A Study of Class and Assimilation."
      Part I: "A Villager Who Met Disaster"
      Part II: "Serrano and Criollo, the Confusion of Race
        with Class"
      Part III: "Serrano to Criollo, A Study of Assimilation."
Reports Service, West Coast South America Series 14
(1,2,3). (New York: American Universities Field Staff).

Pearse, Andrew
1957   Integração Social das Famílias de Favelados. Educação
e Ciências Sociais, Ano 2, 2(6): 245-277.
1958   Notas sobre a Organização Social de Uma Favela do Rio
de Janeiro. Educação e Ciências Sociais, Ano 3 3(7):
9-32.
1961   Some Characteristics of Urbanization in the City of Rio
de Janeiro. In Urbanization in Latin America, Philip
Hauser, ed. (New York: UNESCO).

Seminário Interuniversitário
1967   Seminário Interuniversitário para o Exame das Consequên-
cias das Chuvas e Enchentes de Janeiro de 1966 na Região
da Guanabara e Áreas Vizinhas (Rio: Universidade Federal
do Rio de Janeiro).

Sjoberg, Gideon
1960   The Preindustrial City: Past and Present (Glencoe: Free
Press).

Southall, Aidan
1956   Determinants of the Social Structure of African Urban Populations with Special Reference to Kampala. In Social
Implications of Industrialization and Urbanization in Africa
South of the Sahara, D. Forde, ed. (Paris: UNESCO).

46

Southall, Aidan and P. C. W. Gutkind
   1957   Townsmen in the Making. East African Studies No. 9
                 (Kampala: East African Institute).
Turner, John F. C.
   1965   Lima's Barriadas and Corralones, Suburbs vs. Slums.
                 Ekistics, Vol. 19, March.
   1966   "Uncontrolled Urban Settlements, Problems and Policies."
                 Paper for the U. N. Interregional Seminar on Development
                 Policies and Planning in Relation to Urbanization. Pitts-
                 burgh.
   1967   "Autonomous Urban Settlements, Problems or Solutions."
                 Paper read at Latin American Colloquium. Waltham:
                 Brandeis University.
Warner, W. Lloyd and Paul S. Lunt
   1941   The Social Life of a Modern Community (New Haven: Yale
                 University Press).
Whiteford, Andrew H.
   1960   Two Cities of Latin America: a Comparative Description
                 of Social Class (Beloit, Wisconsin: Logan Museum).
Willmott, Peter and Michael Young
   1960   Family and Class in a London Suburb (London: Routledge
                 and Kegan Paul).
Young, Michael and Peter Willmott
   1957   Family and Kinship in East London (London: Routledge and
                 Kegan Paul).

47

THE REORGANIZATION OF COUNTIES IN THE BOLIVIAN HIGHLANDS:
AN ANALYSIS OF RURAL-URBAN NETWORKS AND HIERARCHIES

Hans C. Buechler
Syracuse University

Two major approaches to urban anthropology are represented in contemporary research. The first attempts to isolate the "urban phenomenon" and to analyze its common characteristics; the second maintains that universally valid criteria for defining urbanism cannot be established. The second approach implies that urbanism must be viewed in its wider cultural context which includes both large agglomerations and rural settlements. It attempts to analyze both continuities and differentiation within sub-systems such as political hierarchies and markets in cities and rural settlements in a given area, as well as the linkages between such sub-systems.

In this paper we will follow the latter approach to discern the ways in which certain social forms link Bolivian cities with the rural areas. We shall analyze these rural-urban connections within a specific organizational process: the formation and transformation of cantones, i.e. political units encompassing a small number of peasant communities, in the Bolivian highlands. This particular problem was chosen first because county organization provides a focal point for a variety of social forms represented both in the city and in the country, and second because we believe that it is in such changing situations that structural characteristics are most readily observed.

In order to present structural analyses of complex changing societies, a framework must be discovered which takes change into account directly rather than regarding it as an intrusive phenomenon which transmutes social structure, as it were, from without. Such a framework should allow for differences between groups and for inconsistencies between sub-systems. We propose an approach similar to Martinet's (1955:60) model of phonological change. According to Martinet, language structure never reaches a permanent equilibrium. The physical structure of the speech organs (e.g., their assymetry), the very complexity of language with its different semi-dependent levels, and the continuous contact between languages and dialects, etc. preclude completely equilibrated systems.[1] Despite the foregoing, he still finds it possible to plot and even to predict the processes of change in a linguistic sub-structure such as the vowel system because the direction of change depends on previous relationships between the elements of a system. Similarly in the study of complex societies, instead of perpetuating the myth that social systems ever attain a permanent equilibrium, one may see them as a multitude of sub-systems, i.e. as complexes of interpersonal relationships, which never attain full stability either within themselves or vis-à-vis other sub-systems. From this vantage point, one may speak of the structuring of complexes of relationships rather

48

than of systems in equilibrium.

Ideally one would begin a dynamic analysis of a social system with a description of prior transformations. However, if ethnohistorical material is insufficient or lacking, one must begin not with a hypothetical system in equilibrium but with the actual state of a system (or sub-system) at a given point in time. Such a dynamic structural approach permits the analysis of the creation of new political units like the post reform counties in the Bolivian highlands as the result of transformations of a number of loosely interrelated sub-systems.

The Bolivian social revolution and agrarian reform of 1952-53 altered the relationships between the national government and political organization on the community level. During these years all unremunerated labor was abolished and a large proportion of the land was distributed among the former serfs and landed estates, or haciendas. At the same time, attempts were made to bring the peasant into a more direct relationship with the La Paz government. One of the consequences of this revolution was a profound change in political relationships between communities and county seats which were the deepest extension of the national government into the peasant community.[2]

The official hierarchy prior to the reform is shown in the following diagram:

Official Political Hierarchy prior to the

Agrarian Reform

National Government

Departmento (State)

Provincia (Province)

Cantón (County)

haciendas   communidades
(landed estates)   (free communities)

However, the system was both more complex and varied in reality than in its official form. In actual fact, cantón authorities possessed little authority over haciendas which functioned as more or less autonomous political units. Although cantón authorities did on occasion judge individual hacienda serfs, only free communities sent representatives to executive sessions in the cantón capital, and only they were obliged to provide free labor for public works in the county seat and services for the parish priest and cantón judge. Furthermore, communities in a cantón held different positions within the county. For example, communities near the county seat furnished more important aides to

49

the county judge than did the more distant ones. Thus, the components of the system were in a disjunctive, rather than in a harmonious or mutual relationship.

The agrarian reform abolished the hacienda system and with it the political power of the hacienda owners and mestizo administrators. The traditional cantones, however, did not inherit their power. On the contrary, the former cantón capitals lost much of their influence. The traditional mestizo authorities could not represent the interests of the emancipated peasants adequately, for they now lacked governmental support to control any sizeable area. After the reform, the government established a number of competing hierarchies which made it possible for individual peasants or communities to bypass traditional authorities and seek justice elsewhere. It instituted not only peasant syndicates on the ex-hacienda, the regional, and the national levels (sindicatos, sub-centrales, centrales, and federaciones campesinas) but also a number of offices which depended directly on the Ministry of Peasant Affairs and the National Council for Agrarian Reform (Buechler 1963; Léons 1966:166-171). In addition, a peasant could bring his case directly to a variety of institutions in the capital.[3] None of these alternative systems was completely congruous with the units of the former political hierarchy. Thus the sub-central campesina, a unit comparable in size to the cantón, usually did not coincide with it.

Despite the above developments, cantonship continues to be of extraordinary importance in the Bolivian highlands. Everywhere both free communities and ex-haciendas are vying for the position of cantón capital. As a matter of fact, a common belief is that if one "recreates" a traditional cantón capital in miniature, complete with a central plaza surrounded by two-storey houses, a church, a town hall, a weekly market, a few stores, a telegraph connection, and perhaps a major school, one has the indisputable right to the honor of being named a capital. This is considered to be the most coveted position with respect to neighboring communities.

The foregoing belief is also fostered by La Paz migrant organizations. Their charters stress the development of the home community which includes support in the attainment of higher political status. Many communities which achieved these objectives did actually become cantón capitals. However, a "cantón ideology" cannot explain their success. Rather, the explanation lies in the fact that these new villages are the focal points for recently established institutions, e.g. schools; focal points in the widening of pre-existing networks of relationships, e.g. markets; and focal points in the struggle for political position. These we will discuss in more detail in the subsequent paragraphs.

Education is one of the most important issues for the modern Aymara. Schools are being built in practically all communities. The teachers are usually of peasant extraction schooled in rural teacher's colleges. They often teach in their communities of origin, but many also come from widely scattered communities on the altiplano. Except for the teachers who have returned to their home communities to teach, there is a rapid turnover. The schools are supervised by directors who live and teach at the largest ones, called núcleos escolares. They are usually mestizos trained in La Paz. Directors with their

50

La Paz backgrounds are in a good position to obtain aid for school construction and other types of educational aid from La Paz authorities. Thus the peasants go to considerable lengths to satisfy their demands for food, etc. Although their power is curbed by the fact that their positions, like those of the teachers, are impermanent, they sometimes gain almost dictatorial powers. Since the núcleo escolar controls the schools in all its member communities, it becomes a focal point for a wider area.

In addition to the expansion of educational institutions, Aymara peasants are also involved in a distribution network of increasing complexity and scope (H. Buechler 1963, 1966; J-M. Buechler 1967; Léons 1966). With access to more land, peasants sell more produce, either directly in the cities or in local markets. At the same time the local markets serve as outlets for a variety of manufactured goods and produce from other areas. These markets attract not only peasants and middlemen, but also storekeepers from La Paz who rent buildings around the market places. These factors have created a proliferation of weekly markets.

Finally a community may become a capital of a regional peasant syndicate. These syndicates group together a number of local peasant syndicates which were created to govern ex-haciendas. The latter are patterned after industrial unions, but in their actual functioning they more closely resemble the traditional governments of free communities. The leaders of regional syndicates often act as the representatives of their local syndicates when dealing with outside authorities as well as on the behalf of the entire grouping of syndicates. The secretary-general of a regional syndicate may gain considerable importance in his jurisdiction.

If a newly established village acts as a nodal point for two or more systems: education, marketing, and/or peasant syndicates, it may gain sufficient power to assert itself as cantón capital. Each of these systems includes persons from both city and country and from different rural areas. A cantón therefore does not function as a closed unit. This is reflected in the personnel involved in the formation of cantones. On the one hand, store owners are frequently returned migrants from La Paz who combine commercial activities in the capital with similar activities in their home cantón (J-M. Buechler 1967). Cantón judges have often lived in La Paz where they acquired the necessary education for their office and established important political connections. School directors are frequently Pazeños too. On the other hand, lower level political authorities in La Paz often are themselves second or third generation descendants of migrants. These persons create a closely meshed network which includes both the city and cantones.

Three concrete cases will serve to illustrate the process of cantón reorganization. In the first case, the peasants of Jank'o Amaya,[4] an ex-hacienda on the shores of Lake Titicaca, established a village in 1955 on former hacienda property. The richer peasants from the six sections of Jank'o Amaya built houses around the plaza. In 1960 a weekly market was brought into existence by forcing the women from the community to sit with their wares in the central plaza every Thursday morning. This practice soon attracted peasants from the neighboring area who previously had to walk to a market four

51

or five hours away. Altiplano staples as well as tropical fruit, bread, manufactured goods from La Paz and Peru, etc. were offered to both consumers and
middlemen in ever increasing quantities. Thus between 1965 and 1967 the
number of persons selling factory-woven cloth and ready-made clothing more
than doubled. Three stores, owned by migrants who returned from La Paz,
were installed in the houses around the plaza. These houses were also used
as storehouses by vendors from La Paz who arrive on Wednesday in order to
sell early on Thursday morning. Many of these vendors were Jank'o Amaya
migrants.

In 1960 this community was accorded the status of _cantón_ capital by
the incumbent president during an election campaigning tour. Later a church
was built and a telegraph service installed. For all but one year of its existence, former migrants from the community who have returned from La Paz held
the position of _intendente_, or judge, the highest political office in Jank'o
Amaya. (During that year a Pazeño nominated by La Paz officials held the
office.) In a number of cases, higher syndicate leaders influenced the choice.

However, Jank'o Amaya has not been able to hold its privileged position
as capital without opposition. The other communities which had pledged their
allegiance to the county felt that most advantages of cantonship accrued to the
capital alone. First Jank'o Amaya had promised house-sites around the central
plaza to all member communities of the _cantón_. In actual fact, however, only
peasants from the capital were permitted to build there. Then, persons from
member communities of the county other than Jank'o Amaya were allowed to act
as judge for only two years. Furthermore, a person from another community
could gain prestige and money as a judge, but any material improvements, such
as telegraph service, were felt to be to the sole benefit of the _cantón_ capital.
As a result, two member communities, Compi and Chua, tried to usurp the
power of the county seat. Neighboring Compi even assigned an area for the
construction of a village and attempted to establish a market. Perhaps economic considerations have thwarted the Compeños' bid for cantonship. Their main
cash crop is onions which each family sells in La Paz. Jank'o Amaya produces
potatoes which are almost invariably sold through middlemen at the local fair.
Thus Jank'o Amaya has a more solid basis for a market than Compi.

Political considerations aided Chua in its bid for power. Chua had been
the seat of a _sub-central_ _campesina_ since the agrarian reform. The secretary-
general of this regional syndicate has wielded considerable power during the
first years of the _sub-central_'s existence. At present a number of persons,
especially from his own community, bring their cases to him rather than to the
county judge. In 1966 all _sub-centrales_ were accorded the status of "acces-
sory _cantón_" by the government. This has produced a split in the _cantón_. One
section of Compi has decided to join the newly formed sub-county while the
others continue their allegiance to Jank'o Amaya. At the same time, however,
Compi is attempting to establish a _núcleo_ _escolar_ as a new bid for power. Thus
it is difficult for any community to maintain its supremacy for any protracted
period of time because of the continuous splitting of _cantones_ and reshuffling
of allegiances.

The power of a Jank'o Amaya judge is seriously curtailed by rival

52

"judges," heading splinter groups and by the fact that he can always be bypassed. A person may use his connections with migrants to La Paz to have his case judged directly in the capital.

Turning to the second case, Cruz Loma, a community in the sub-tropical Yungas valleys studies by Mangudo, has a very different history from that of Jank'o Amaya.[5] The village of Cruz Loma was built around a núcleo escolar instituted immediately after the agrarian reform by members of two adjacent ex-haciendas.[6] Practically no one stays in Cruz Loma during the day. At night only a few persons in each family sleep there; the remainder return to their dispersed homesteads.

Cruz Loma is also the seat of the regional federation of peasant syndicates which adds to its prestige. On several occasions the town has attempted to gain the position of a cantón capital. A town council was formed to initiate the legal proceedings, but the plan did not materialize. Recently there has been a new impetus to acquire cantón status. Cruz Loma has set aside a plot of land for an administration building and has inaugurated a weekly market. Moreover, a migrant from the altiplano has established a store. However, Cruz Loma has experienced setbacks in its bid for cantonship. The three ex-haciendas who sent their children to school in the núcleo became involved in a serious quarrel; one of them accused the others of stealing the rafters which it had provided for the school. This dispute resulted in an armed struggle. A potent political figure of the ruling party supported one side, and a leftist peasant syndicate leader the other. Then the parents in the wronged ex-hacienda took their children out of the Cruz Loma school and sent them to Coroico, a nearby mestizo village. Thereby they threatened the very existence of the núcleo escolar. Since none of the peasants from that ex-hacienda owns a house in Cruz Loma anyway, they are even less inclined to repair the rift. Cruz Loma peasants continue to dream about becoming a cantón partly because the village would then obtain a share of taxes levied on coca. But the proximity of Coroico may permanently inhibit the realization of their dream.

As a third example we may consider Arapata, studied by Léons (1966), a cantón which is situated a few miles from Cruz Loma. Unlike Jank'o Amaya and Cruz Loma, Arapata was a cantón capital prior to the agrarian reform. However, the cantón authorities did not have much power since there were only haciendas in the area, which as we have indicated earlier, settled most disputes through their mayordomos, or administrators. Even when the cantón judge was called upon to act, he followed the recommendations of the mayordomos. Moreover the cantón judge was himself recruited among the mayordomos, and thus he was an equal of the hacienda administrators. A village was constructed only after the agrarian reform, but it gained importance rapidly due to its weekly market where many altiplano peasants sold their produce. Its importance was further enhanced by a number of stores which purchase coca from the peasants and provide them with goods from La Paz. Half of these stores were established by altiplano peasants who migrated from communities which engaged in commercial activities with the Yungas for many generations.

Today the leader of the cantón is usually a peasant rather than a mestizo. Apart from the cantón officials and the sindicatos, the former mayor of a nearby

53

village wields considerable power. He occupies the position of "provincial coordinator of peasant affairs" and is responsible only to higher officials in the capital and thus bypasses the cumbersome bureaucracy. Thanks to this privileged position, he can bring about more rapid action on the part of La Paz authorities; thus he has gained widespread influence, and he has held an important political position in Arapata for years.

Like Jank'o Amaya, Arapata is splitting further. Three ex-haciendas which officially form part of the cantón pledge their allegiance to Trinidad Pampa, a new peasant town which has gained influence by establishing a núcleo escolar and its own central campesina. (Arapata is a central as well.) Trinidad Pampa wants to become a cantón too.

Even the village of Arapata itself does not constitute a harmonious entity; its inhabitants, which belong to two ex-haciendas, form two major factions. Few decisions regarding the progress of the village can be reached because of factional differences. This probably contributes to the fact that Arapata's political influence is very limited beyond the village proper, in spite of its paramount commercial position.[7]

The complex structure of the cantones described in the preceding pages does not lend itself to a traditional structural-functional approach. If we had examined our data in this manner, we would no doubt have attempted to establish an equilibrium model of a pre-reform and a contemporary cantón first. Then, however, the transformation from one model to the other would have appeared as the disintegration of the old cantón system and the subsequent integration toward a new equilibrium, and thus the nature of the processes involved would not have become apparent. Instead, we adopted an entirely different procedure. We began our analysis with a description of the actual state of the cantón system with all its inconsistencies. The relationships between cantón and hacienda provided at best for a compromise solution and not a fully integrated structure. Once the hacienda system was abolished, cantónes were transformed in a number of ways depending on their relationships to other sub-systems. The former cantón capital, usually a mestizo village, could continue to exert some influence on the surrounding area. Cruz Loma, for instance, has not yet been able to become a cantón, in part because of the proximity of Coroico whose weekly market continues to be important and whose schools provide an alternative for dissident communities. Jank'o Amaya, on the other hand, has been very successful in establishing a local market due to the fact that there are no nearby markets and due to its production pattern. The booming market will probably attract a clientele for the local judge irrespective of competing judgeships in neighboring communities. Finally, Arapata was a cantón capital previous to the reform, but because there were no free communities in the area it could gain influence only after the reform. However, it did not fully accomplish its political potential, in spite of its paramount economic position, partly because of schisms within the village itself. In all three cases, the power of centers of political influence is limited on the one hand by the establishment of rival markets, centrales, etc. in other communities -- for all communities strive to gain political importance -- and on the other hand by the fact that local rungs in the political ladder may be

54

bypassed and relationships with the highest rungs established more directly by means of migrants residing in La Paz.

Cantón reorganization must then be understood processually as the constant manipulation by groups of individuals (whose positions are themselves defined by social forms) of a variety of political hierarchies. A community's success in political maneuvering will depend on the relation it has established with respect to other nodes in the networks, hierarchies, and institutions. Some of these sub-systems are loosely interconnected; others are in direct competition with each other. Some, such as the market, are expansions and elaborations of traditional systems of distribution; others, like the syndicate organizations, are recent developments. Still others, the judgeships which provide the most coveted positions, are continuations of old institutions adapted to recruit personnel from the peasantry. The cantón then is not simply a closed system which has been subjected to disorganization and subsequent reorganization, but a major intersection of a variety of sub-systems. These extend over a much vaster area than the county. They include both the cities and the rural areas which do not constitute two specialized poles.[8] Rather the city simply occupies a privileged position in an otherwise undifferentiated system.

The study of major sub-system intersections in complex societies leads us away from a typological approach where urban and rural areas are defined as discrete entities to a dynamic structural one which analyzes topological transformations of sub-systems. As we have seen, these sub-systems need not be described by equilibrium models but as a plurality of both coordinated and competing social forms which are in constant flux.

NOTES

1. See, for instance Martinet (1960 chapter 6, especially paragraphs 6-1, 6-23, 6-24, and 6-31). The comparison with Martinet is made on a purely structural level. There is no simple analogue to Martinet's functional characteristics of language in social systems.

2. We have attempted to give a processual definition of the "community" elsewhere (Buechler 1966; 1967).

3. Fieldwork in the cantón Jank'o Amaya was carried out by the author from November 1964 to February 1966 and in summer, 1967. It was supported by a Columbia Travelling Fellowship, by the Research Institute for the Study of Man, by Peace Corps Grant No. PC (W) - 397 and by The Canada Council.

4. Bailey (1963:128-133) describes the emergence of caste associations which although they seem to be genetically connected to traditional caste assemblies have entirely different purposes and functions. A similar process is transforming indigenous political units (Bailey 1963:Chapter 4). Thus, just as in Bolivia, a variety of indigenous forms and their transformations play simultaneous roles in modern politics.

55

5. From field notes, Research Institute for the Study of Man, and Peace Corps. Mr. Felix Mangudo gathered material on Cruz Loma under the direction of Dwight B. Heath.

6. Cruz Loma had a private school even previous to the agrarian reform. In 1953 this school was transformed into a state school.

7. For other examples of cantón reorganization, cf. H. Buechler (1966:79-80; 1963:61-62). Dandler-Handhart (1967) gives an account of the manipulation of political hierarchies in pre-reform times from the vantage point of a Cochabamba hacienda. Here the political foci were a school on the one hand and the haciendas on the other.

8. Cf. Judith-Maria Buechler (1967) who considers the markets in La Paz and in the country as a communications network integrating market women in a single economic and social system.

REFERENCES

Bailey, F. G.
    1963   Politics and Social Change, Orissa in 1959 (Berkeley:
                    University of California Press).
Buechler, Hans C.
    1963   The Altiplano and Adjacent Temperate and Sub-tropical
                    Valleys. In Land Reform and Social Revolution in Bolivia,
                    Dwight B. Heath, Charles Erasmus, and Hans C. Buechler,
                    eds. (m.s., in print).
    1966   Agrarian Reform and Migration on the Bolivian Altiplano.
                    (Columbia University, Ph.D. dissertation).
    1967   Dynamic Models in the Analysis of Peasant Societies:
                    Aymara and Quechua Communities in Bolivia and Ecuador.
                    Paper presented at the conference of the Northeastern
                    Anthropological Association, Montreal, Canada, April, 1967.
Buechler, Judith-Maria
    1967   "To Market, to Market...": An Evaluation of Changing
                    Market Relations of Aymara Women in La Paz. Paper pre-
                    sented at the 66th Annual Meeting of the American Anthropo-
                    logical Association, Washington, D.C., Nov. 30-Dec. 3,
                    1967.
Dandler-Hanhart, Jorge
    1967   Local Group, Community, and Nation: A Study of Changing
                    Structure in Ucureña, Bolivia (1935-1952) (University of
                    Wisconsin, M.A. thesis, mimeograph).
Léons, Madeline B.
    1966   Changing Patterns of Social Stratification in an Emergent
                    Bolivian Community (University of California at Los
                    Angeles, Ph.D. dissertation).

56

Martinet, André
    1955   Economie des changements phonétiques: traité de phonol-
                ogie diachronique (Berne: A. Francke).
    1960   Eleménts de linguistique générale (Paris: Armand Colin).

57

CULTURAL CONTINUITY AND AFRICAN URBANIZATION

Brian M. du Toit
The University of Florida

More than half of the world's population lives in towns and villages or dispersed in scattered homesteads. Least urbanized of the world's continents is Africa, where a mere thirteen percent of the nearly three hundred million population live in population concentrations of thirty thousand or more (Hance 1965:52). Yet the definition of the city in Africa needs some clarification. Population concentrations of considerable size have been present in north and west Africa for a long time (Sjoberg 1955). The industrial urban center, however, with its wage labor potential and modern industry coupled with associated socio-economic conditions is a recent innovation.

For a long time after the industrial revolution had changed living conditions in western European countries, African territories which were administered and used as colonial areas supplied the raw material for the industries of Britain and Europe. The demand for labor was present but concentrated in nonindustrial undertakings and especially at ports where raw materials were shipped out and imported products received. It is not strange therefore to find that the first and largest cities grew, for economic and historical reasons, at coastal ports. Linked to this same set of historical conditions, African cities were also located at the sources of mineral wealth and at river and lakesides where internal shipping could be handled. Only recently have independent industrial and commercial centers developed.

In addition to the above general typology of urban centers in Africa, the major urban concentrations can be organized into four agglomerates. Three of these, the Nile-Delta (with about seven million people), the Atlas region (five million), and the Transvaal complex (three million) are really non-African in terms of Negro-Africa, even though the latter agglomerate affects most of southern Africa. The fourth agglomerate extends along the coastal area of West Africa and finds its highest concentration in Nigeria where more than two and a half million people live in urban conditions. When discussing the African in the city, we must primarily deal with the region south of the Sahara -- the region which includes the Transvaal and West African agglomerates.

It has been pointed out that these urban concentrations were new to south and east Africa and that industrial growth was new to all of Africa. This implies that those who lived in large population centers had to adjust to the novel conditions created by industrialization, while in those cases where new industrial centers grew the population had to be attracted from elsewhere. The Kano which was visited by Hugh Clapperton in 1824 was inhabited by thirty to forty thousand residents (Clapperton 1961:90). It was the mercantile hub of the region and visited regularly by traders from Lake Chad, Timbuktu,

58

and the region to the south. But this trade center produced conditions which differ basically from a city like Ndola today. While their population sizes do not differ that much, the industrial and mining life in the latter creates expectations, routines, and institutional needs of a different nature than the preindustrial city, the nonindustrial city, or the nonindustrial village. The preindustrial and industrial types of population concentrations differ in kind rather than in degree, and while earlier population centers may be industrialized, thus changing their nature, new industrial cities have to be populated from elsewhere. This population mobility may of course be either permanent or temporary, but in both cases a degree of adjustment is required of the people and their life ways.

The purpose of this paper is to show the kinds of mobility which are called for and which mark the African scene. The kinds of changes or adaptations which occur when the "proto-peasant" -- as Fallers (1961) refers to the African tribesman -- leaves the village to become an urban laborer or urban resident, or possibly even committed to urban living, will also be discussed.

Types of Human Mobility

The distinction made between urban laborer and urban resident is not intended to suggest that there are major differences between these two categories of persons. Rather, the distinction is made for the sake of clarity. In the case of the urban laborer, a man comes to the city to work and may even bring his wife and family with him -- though this happens very rarely -- but his sojourn is temporary. He is in the city for a one or two year contract and will then return to his rural origins. In contrast, the urban resident is one who may have been born in the city or who has lived there for a great number of years. Despite his more permanent residence in the city, however, he is in many cases still rurally oriented, still shares village or tribal loyalties, and still participates in the obligations of kinsmen and village members. He returns in many cases to his village even after an absence of half a lifetime.

It should be kept in mind that human mobility has been an important characteristic of Africa. Large population movements as well as the migration of families and individuals have long marked the continent, especially in recent years in the area south of the Sahara (Prothero 1961; Prothero 1964; Soper 1959). This migration aspect of human mobility has become more pronounced as modern industrial and mining centers have arisen, or as old population concentrations have been modernized. Although the urban populations increase very rapidly, the number of jobs increases at no more than five percent annually (Mercier 1963:55), allowing, among other things, for some of the conditions which give rise to a new social stratification. But the jobs and the stratification are tied causally and effectually to the presence of an urban population composed of permanent or temporary urban residents. Hence it is necessary to distinguish aspects of mobility other than migration.

Meyer Fortes (1967) suggests that the aspect of mobility and the aspect of migration be seen as elements of the same thing. He states that migration

59

is the "movement of people -- individually or in groups -- across boundaries,"
while mobility is the "movement within boundaries." The boundary may be
geographical, structural, ethnic, or cultural, as long as it is recognized as
a boundary by the actor. In urban anthropology there is a need to focus on
this mobility, first of all the aspect of migration, and secondly the horizontal
and vertical mobility of the man in the city. Since urban concentrations are
relatively novel to Africa and their membership is still being drawn from a
rural and village reservoir, the kinds of migration which bring Africans to the
cities should be analyzed.

Many people see the city as a place where needed cash can be earned
but a place which can offer only temporary residence. They work there but do
not live there; the city offers a house, not a home. Theirs is a temporary
migration as they return to peri-urban or rural conditions weekly, seasonally,
or at least periodically. In this category of temporary migrants there are three
distinct groups.

The first group is comprised of those people who work in the city --
even in industries -- but live on the borders of the city proper. They travel
to and from their work during the week, spending their weekends in the non-
urban conditions while planting a field or tending a flock which is otherwise
cared for by a wife or relatives.[1] The migrant in this category is exposed to
the urban influences but not permanently. He may even be in regular contact
with kinsmen or fellow tribal members who are urbanized. He is one of the
links in an important chain of communication to be elaborated on in a later
section of this discussion. While it is not the same kind of influence, the
distinction between Gulliver's "low-wage, rural employment" and "higher
wage, industrial employment" (1960:159), is important in understanding this
type of migrant. Both rural and industrial employment remove the men from
their homes for periods of time; both are major factors in cultural change
even though the former does not take the men to a city -- or at least not right
away.

A second important group of migrants are those adult males who go to
the city for five or six months when rural agricultural undertakings do not require their presence. This seasonal migration (Prothero 1957; 1962; 1965)
does not disrupt the rural or village economy and allows the man to earn additional income. This kind of migration differs only slightly from the first
in that temporary urban residents may now be spoken of. Persons in this
second group of migrants may return to the city every year, establishing a
regular channel of communication between kinsmen or tribal group members
who reside in the city and those in rural areas. These regular seasonal migrants who are very common in West Africa are even recognized terminolog-
ically in certain cases. Berg notes, for example, that "throughout northern
Nigeria seasonal migrants are apparently referred to in the local language as
"men who while (eat?) away the dry season," and R. C. Abraham's Dictionary
of the Hausa Language gives a definition of 'migrant' as follows: 'In order
to eke his corn out, he has gone to spend the hot season elsewhere in exercise
of his trade'" (1965:166).

The third group of temporary migrants into the urban areas includes all

60

those persons who come from the rural setting to work for periods up to two years. This type of temporary migrant is found in most of Africa, but especially in south and central Africa where the city has come to be identified with a preponderance of adult males, mining compounds, and typically urban situations of time clocks and machines. The males who make these migrations become temporary urban residents, but their orientation is rural; they live and work in the city, but they are not committed to it; they may become urbanites in due course, but for the time being they are migrants and contemplate their return to the village. Watson (1967) speaks of this as oscillatory migration. In some cases such a man may return home even after twelve years of absence (Fortes 1965:76). While tribal loyalties are maintained, migrants frequently retire to the village after a lifetime in the city (van Velsen 1961).

The three types of migrants noted above are only general types which apply generally to Africa. Different parts of the continent -- and even different countries -- exhibit these types in varying intensities. The urban migration in West Africa differs from that in South Africa, and while the cities in both cases are industrial centers, the stimuli which prompt migration in the first place cause exposure in varying degrees of intensity and duration to urban conditions.

In addition to the temporary kinds of migration already outlined, there is a type of migration which brings people to the city on a more or less permanent basis. This may be termed urbanization, or at least the establishment of the necessary condition for this process to take place. Prothero (1965:2) speaks of definitive movements in which "people sever completely their links with rural areas and settle permanently in towns." While one may agree in principle with people relocating themselves more or less permanently, links with rural areas are seldom severed, and even when they lapse due to minimal communication they are still present and may be reactivated by persons in both directions. Although temporary migrants constitute an important group in urban centers, it is important to realize that for urbanization to occur, there must be permanent migrants to the city. The more or less permanent migration of people to the cities is primarily responsible for the growth of African cities, and while natural increase soon takes over as a contributing factor to a permanent urban population, it is this population movement which is of great interest.

In summary, urbanization has two basic criteria: the presence of a large population living in a relatively high density, and the commitment of these people to urban conditions in terms of industry, time schedules, class hierarchy, social structure, and similar criteria which are distinctly urban. Hence, urbanization contains an element of process and an element of condition; it requires the process of arriving in or growing up in urban conditions, and it requires a process by which people come to accept, identify with, and gradually become committed to these conditions and ways of life. It implies, too, a condition of relative population density and the commitment of persons to the amenities and conditions which are industrial and urban.

61

The fact that urbanization in Africa does not entail a complete rupture between the urban population and the town folk and a complete severance of links between city and country, urban and rural, or urban culture and tribal or village culture has been noted by several scholars. Every study dealing with urbanization in Africa speaks of "loyalty to the home country and culture" (Fortes 1967:25), of a continuous "feedback process" (Epstein 1967:282) to the rural areas, or at least of some variation of "family parasitism" (Mercier 1963:52) by which migrants to towns join relatives already living there. This produces in many cases what Gutkind calls "the formation of tribal settlements -- little pockets of intense overcrowding where members of the same tribe live and find comfort in one another's presence in an otherwise alien environment" (1960:130). Even long after the process of urbanization has been completed and people are committed to urban ways and conditions, one still finds residential areas, societies (Marris 1962:39) and associations (Little 1965:85), "urban tribalism" (Epstein 1958), "super-tribalism" (CSA 1961:20) or "ethnicity" (Wallerstein 1960) which follow traditional lines of loyalty and contrast sub-groups of the urban population.

A number of researchers have given their attention to this aspect of cultural continuity. Just how much contact is maintained, and what forms of communication mark these bonds? In dealing with African industrial workers in South Africa, four criteria were employed by Glass (1960:21). She measured the degree of urbanization of subjects in terms of: place of birth, the place of residence of dependents, whether land rights were being retained in the rural area, and the period of continuous urban residence. She accepted ten years as "qualifying a man for such a socio-psychological transition" needed for assimilating into the new ways. [2]

This latter aspect, namely the socio-psychological transition, is that element which permits the urban resident to become committed to the urban life. "Industrial commitment has been conceived as involvement in an industrial work environment through the performance of new industrial work skills and conformity to new work norms, relations and expectations," (Glass 1962:16; see also Feldman and Moore 1960).

Looking at this question from a different point of view, Reader has established six indices of tribalism. In addition to those criteria which were outlined above, he notes sociometric visiting relations, the transfer of cash or clothes, and the practice of sending children to the rural areas for various reasons. [3] Measuring these indices allows one to make general statements about the rural or tribal orientation of the subject and to decide whether a person is a migrant in the city or an immigrant to the city (1966:18). The question being asked is whether or not the subject is committed to urban life, roles, and values. But in all of this -- as was the case with Hellman (1948: 116) -- one gets the idea of detribalization being somehow synonomous with urbanization. At least there is an underlying assumption that the move to the city produces an urbanite who is no longer socially or psychologically identifiable with the tribe and the tribal culture.

62

This is, of course, an unnecessary deduction. While people who settle in urban centers enter into urban socio-cultural situations, it does not logically follow that they are detribalized. If the argument were to be turned around, we would expect that all persons who were not urban dwellers would then have to be tribalized. One finds persons in rural as well as in urban areas who express loyalty to and participate in "tribal" culture. But logically the person who is removed geographically from the political community identified as a tribe also tends to decrease his participation in tribal affairs. The point is that migration is not equivalent to detribalization. The first is measured purely by geographical distance, the latter by social, cultural, and other distances and loyalties. These two concepts must be approached on different levels of analysis.

The first level which states only the factor of geographical distance satisfies migration, but for detribalization to be measured it is necessary to move up a level to measure other kinds of distances. The first is migration, the latter is an aspect of mobility. The first has been present in all parts of the continent since the country was first populated; the latter is something which is essentially recent. Mitchell explains it in the following way:

> Tribalism as a significant factor in human relationships, in fact, only arose in situations where people from widely different backgrounds were thrown together in social interaction. In other words, tribalism is a phenomenon arising out of culture contact: it comes into being when people of different origin are thrown together in industrial areas and other labour centers, in schools, in farms, or similar situations. It is then that differences in language, beliefs, values -- in short, in culture   become immediately apparent. The anthropologist could only be expected to develop an interest in tribalism, therefore, when he set about studying people in modern industrial centres (1962:2).

But it would once again make a difference whether one is concerned with a culturally relatively homogeneous urban center, or with a city where a number of linguistic and cultural groups interact.

The first is the mono-tribal arrangement of which Mayer speaks in his Townsmen or Tribesmen (1961), while most other cities are marked by different groups of people, each group having its own language, traditions, and loyalties. A city with such a composition is marked by multi tribalism as each of these groups is contrasted with other such groups. This means furthermore that in terms of an ideal model of urbanisation each of these city-based groups would be linked to a rural reservoir where the same tribalism is present. Additional criteria, however, would be needed to measure this aspect.[4] This kind of natural move to the city produces a geographical proximity on which new arrivals can draw by traveling to persons they know and settling near them, but it also allows for a continuous flow back to the rural center. This kind of model is inherent in the development of the Zambian mining centers (Mitchell 1953),

63

of Stanleyville in the Congo (Pons 1965), and in the early growth of Dar-es-Salaam (Leslie 1963) where there is even a geographical proximity between the tribal area and the part of the city where members settle. The model, however, not only suggests geographical proximity but also a continued interaction. This is the factor recognized in the indices of tribalism mentioned by Reader above. Thus Rotberg (1962:589) discusses the market system which is developing in Zambia and the new "entrepreneurial role" which has been created. In this instance the urban African plays a new role but continues to buy the produce from his relatives in rural villages or to write for supplies "to his relatives at home." Further, the rural village serves as a retreat for the young (to live with their grandparents), for the old (who retire among kinsmen), or for those in crises. Fortes states the situation as follows:

> . . . . the preservation by migrants and mobiles of their distinctive tribal and family ties and values can serve as a social and psychological sheet anchor, or perhaps better still mooring rope, so to speak, for them. . . . Having a home to go back to in crisis or personal disaster, a community and a culture that serves as an independent focus of their cohesion and a sanction for their mutual support, can provide a secure basis for their sense of identity and unity as a group, face to face with the long vested interests and organized unity of the host society as well as, often, with the solidarities of other immigrant elements (1967:29).

It is not suggested that all urban Africans are rurally oriented, have loyalties in rural communities, or even maintain kinship and friendship ties in a particular rural or tribal community. As a temporary resident, the migrant has many of his social network relations with persons in the rural region from whence he comes; these latter have been replaced by urban ties for the urban African. There is a need to postulate a hypothetical continuum among the urban African population: at one pole those oriented and tied to the tribal area and at the opposite pole those completely committed to urban life. Second and third generation Africans in many cases have no specific links with a traditional homeland or rural community. Consequently the urban population includes at least three categories of persons: people who are rurally oriented and maintain strong bonds with that community; people who represent what Mayer calls "the cultural turncoat" (1962a:588) who adopt urban values and loyalties; and a last group of persons who are basically urbanites. This latter group of persons have little or no interest in the rural area from which their parents or grandparents came.

The above three categories constitute an urban community. They are the categories which together constitute one end of a "tribe" -- a tribe which has a rural footing and an urban footing.[5] A number of these tribes comprise the urban complex which is multitribal in the sense of social network relations and loyalties, rather than in terms of traditional, primitive, or non-western elements (vide Mayer 1962b:v). This ethnic, linguistic, and cultural continuum -- a continuum which is composed of circulating personnel -- raises an important

64

analytical question. How is this subject matter to be conceptualized and approached? Related to this question is the important one as to whether urban Africans are primarily urban or primarily African -- meaning by the latter a particular tribe and culture. It is to these questions that the remainder of this paper now turns.

Cultural Continuity

The issue which arises is whether "tribalism," as it exists in African cities, produces any distinctively African institutions and modes of life. Is the man in the city to be understood solely in terms of a tribal cultural background, solely in terms of an urban system, or in terms of a combination of these which recognizes various situations and roles which he can occupy?

Gluckman, who has been one of the important contributors to a knowledge of central and south African conditions of urbanization, states that "the starting point of our analysis of tribalism in the towns is not that it is manifested by tribesmen, but that it is manifested by townsmen. The African newly arrived from his rural home to work in a mine, is first of all a miner. . . . An African townsman is a townsman, an African miner is a miner" (1960:58; 1961: 68-9). This means that the urban resident must be seen primarily in terms of urban systems and only secondarily in terms of the tribal associations in which he interacts. Gluckman further explains that "the moment an African crosses his tribal boundary to go to the town, he is 'detribalized,' out of the political control of the tribe" (1961:69). Gluckman contrasts this model of alternating roles with the older approach to a gradual cultural change especially inherent in the writings of Malinowski and many of his students. Thus, the fact that a tribesman is involved in a labor union predisposes him for the actions and values of a union member and discounts the tribal values and background which he may have. The social field in which a man is involved while in the urban center is distinct from the social field in which he will be involved should he return to the village.

Somewhat in contrast to the position of Gluckman, Mitchell and Epstein postulate an involvement by the actor in a variety of sets of relations, each of which occurs in a different situation. This situational approach allows for Gluckman's position only in that when a tribal man is participating in a union meeting he acts in accordance with the roles prescribed by the situation. When he leaves the meeting and joins kinsmen or linguistic group members for a beer, he enters a different situation and must perform a different role. During a day a man switches back and forth between participating in contrasting and often contradictory roles due to the situations he finds himself in. Obviously, the village institutions cannot be transplanted exactly to the new situation of urban living and scheduled working hours. Mitchell in fact even states that "It is fallacious, therefore, to think of rural institutions as changing into urban types of the same institution. The fact is rather that urban dwellers develop institutions to meet their needs in towns and these, because of their different contexts, differ from rural institutions meeting the same needs in the tribal system" (1966:47-48, italics mine).

65

This point of view sees each institution in an urban setting as a completely novel development which is specifically developed to meet the needs of the people in this new situation. It assumes that a person or a group of persons enters a new situation without any traditional background and with no prototypes which predispose them for a certain type of association and a certain type of institution. But we find in all cases that people enter the new situation from a tribal culture from which they have migrated. They retain not only indirect but frequently even direct contact with kinsmen and fellow villagers who participate in institutions and hold values which are incompatible with the new situation of urban living. While it is not possible to transplant a rural institution to the urban situation, it is this very rural institution in which people had participated which serves as prototype for the formation of new associations and institutions. Elsewhere (du Toit 1968) I have attempted to show how this process takes place. Mutual aid societies in urban communities are not transplanted from the rural areas, but new kinds of these societies are fashioned in the city. In all cases they are based on the rural and traditional prototype. Speaking of voluntary associations in West Africa, Little shows that "adaptation proceeds through modification of the traditional institutions and their combination with Western cultural values, technology, and economic practices into a new social structure" (1965:85, italics mine). In both these latter cases, it is recognized that something new is formed, that the situation of urban living calls for a new kind of institution. To suggest that all that is urban is uniquely urban due to the situation seems fallacious.

Epstein prefers to speak of different sets of social relations in the urban setting which all constitute a social field. Since each of these sets is unique, it is possible for some of them to be exclusively urban in context and nature while others may be tribally oriented. By this he is speaking of tribalism in the urban context. When he discusses the unions which developed among the miners on the Copperbelt he shows that unions themselves are novel associations of urban origin. Since they were strictly urban in type, they could not be based on traditional associations but "at a later date, the cleavages developing within the Union appeared to follow tribal lines. . . . Thus we have the strange paradox of 'tribalism' reappearing in situations in which a man's tribal affiliations would appear to be completely irrelevant" (1958:235). It would seem furthermore that tribalism and tribal cultural patterns are of greater significance on the personal and interpersonal level than on the institutional and political level. Mitchell, for instance, reports that the African in Salisbury "takes his ancestor spirits to town with him" and continues to interpret his experiences and misfortunes in the urban setting in personal terms and based on assumptions and categories which are rooted in tribal and rural culture (1965).

It seems then that it is necessary to distinguish between the personal level and the interpersonal level to measure the significance of tribalism and to distinguish between the sets of interpersonal relations and patterns which emerge, and the structure of institutions which are situationally adapted. The more novel an urban institution, the further removed it will be from anything found in the tribal culture. This does not suggest that marriage, or religion,

66

or beer drinks are going to be the same as they were in tribal village conditions. It has already been emphasized that each will differ in style, in structure, and even in function due to the situational changes, but they will be closer, in terms of building on a prototype, to the rural tribal institution or association than will a banking system, a labor union, a university faculty, or even a church community.[6]

Conclusion

African urban anthropology must approach its subject matter, at least for the present, in terms of a model which recognizes fields of social interaction. This is the most fruitful approach to the conceptualization of the existing socio-cultural situation and also the most rewarding for reasons of research.

In the accompanying figure an attempt is made to represent this model. The urban complex is represented as consisting of a number of micro-fields, each of which is basically introverted as fellow linguistic group and tribal members interact, intermarry, and assist each other. Each of these micro-fields has a minimum of contact with persons belonging to other such tribal micro-fields as people work together, meet in the business section of town for meetings, belong to labor unions, and similar associations. But even this aspect of urban living will differ from group to group as the tribal culture from which these people come may predispose toward lesser or greater contact with non-group members. Parkin (1966) has given a very good case for Kampala. Urban sub-fields consist in one case of members of centralized tribes with many specialized roles and much value placed on individualism, in contrast to uncentralized tribes who paradoxically are more conservative. In the urban situation then it is the members of centralized tribes who show a higher rate of intertribal marriage than the uncentralized tribes with their high value on bride wealth and little value on initiative and individualism. But each of these tribal micro-fields in the urban setting is in continuous and even intense contact with the tribal base in a village or rural environment.

The communication between an urban micro-field and a rural micro-field has already been discussed. In nearly every case which has been studied, urban communities have continuous contact and communication with rural village communities. Members visit back and forth; old linguistic group loyalties remain; people in the urban centers are able and expected to keep a steady stream of gifts and money flowing to the rural kinsmen. Van Velsen (1961:235) tells of Tonga women who return from the city for childbirth. In some cases children are sent to the village because "it is not good for young children to be in a city," or they may be sent to school in the city because better facilities are offered there. In many cases marriage ties link males in the city with women and families in the village, or a man might even have a wife in the city and one in the village. Both Marris (1962) and Little and Price (1967) remark on the changes which are taking place as new values influence the choice of a wife, and we find this kind of polygyny, or at least concubinage, being accepted in West African cities.

67

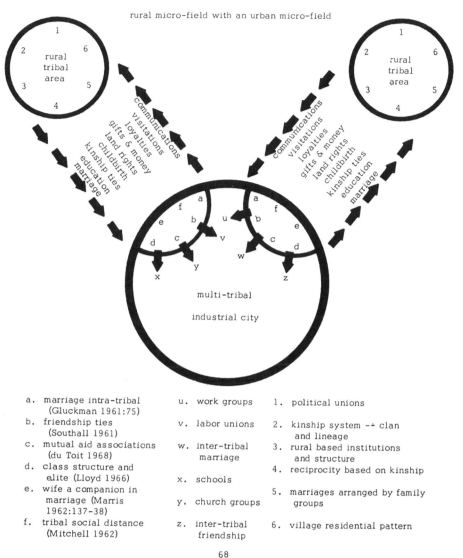

FIGURE I

The tribal social field linking a

rural micro-field with an urban micro-field

a. marriage intra-tribal
    (Gluckman 1961:75)
b. friendship ties
    (Southall 1961)
c. mutual aid associations
    (du Toit 1968)
d. class structure and
    elite (Lloyd 1966)
e. wife a companion in
    marriage (Marris
    1962:137-38)
f. tribal social distance
    (Mitchell 1962)

u. work groups

v. labor unions

w. inter-tribal
    marriage

x. schools

y. church groups

z. inter-tribal
    friendship

1. political unions

2. kinship system –→ clan
    and lineage

3. rural based institutions
    and structure

4. reciprocity based on kinship

5. marriages arranged by family
    groups

6. village residential pattern

68

Urban anthropology in Africa must perforce recognize the existence of a variety of situations, each of which is going to influence and even decide the behavior of an actor. This aspect of situational variation has much in common with reference group theory as it is employed by sociologists. It differs, however, in that the situational approach is much wider and takes into consideration not only the reference individuals and reference groups, but the very situation in which a man from the village finds himself when he stands in new situations of time and space. Although his actions and behavior are not basically affected while he is in the home, his behavior is influenced when he stands in a factory next to a machine. This behavioral aspect ties in also with role theory, for the actor is going to perform different roles depending on the situation in which he finds himself. He may be expressing values and loyalties in accordance with his traditional social organization while he is at home with his family -- even though this may be in the city -- and then when he leaves his home to spend a day next to the machine his role changes. This kind of role playing is also basically involved in the social relations and fields of interaction which each person develops.

It should be emphasized that the kind of interpersonal relations and the institutions which are formed in rural villages differ fundamentally from the developments in the urban micro-field. While they differ, they do serve as the prototype from which new institutions and new kinds of associations develop in new situations. Since there is this degree of cultural continuity it is possible to distinguish between micro-fields in the multi-tribal city. Logically then, the study of the African city will present us with varieties of relationships, types of institutions, and kinds of associations which are distinctively African. The African city must be seen as one end of a cultural continuum which produces a kind of urban culture which differs from other urban cultures, such as Latin American, only in that they draw on different reservoirs and grow from different rural bases. Situationally they are the same. Depending on the situation and on whether one looks at the actor as performing tribal or urban roles, the urban African may be seen in terms of Gluckman's "townsman and miner" or in terms of my "tribesman in the city."

NOTES

1. Vide Mayer (1962a) regarding the Xhosa in East London.

2. For the Tonga, van Velsen (1961:232) states that "the number of years spent in the towns by a person is not a reliable index of that person's 'urbanization.'"

3. Some of these same criteria were employed by Wilson (1942.40) to distinguish between "labour migration" and "temporary urbanization."

4. See also Lloyd's discussion of "the elite in traditional and modern association" (1966:27-40), and the fact that strong ethnic allegiances are retained by individual members of the elite. The author tells us that hotel registers in

69

Nigeria frequently list "Yoruba," "Ibo," etc. in the column asking for "Nationality."

5. A similar point is made very explicitly by Bruner (1961) for urbanization in Sumatra when he speaks of "the village-city network."

6. This latter category, however, may not be a very good example, for separatist and independent churches are frequently tribally oriented. See, among many studies on this subject, Sundkler (1961:350-353; 1965) and Pauw (1965).

REFERENCES

Africa Institute
    1962   *Africa*, Maps and Statistics, No. 1, (Pretoria: The Africa Institute).

Berg, Elliot J.
    1965   The Economics of the Migrant Labor System. In *Urbanization and Migration in West Africa*, Hilda Kuper, ed. (Berkeley: University of California Press), pp. 160-181.

Bruner, Edward M.
    1961   Urbanization and Ethnic Identity in North Sumatra. *American Anthropologist* 63:508-521.

Clapperton, Hugh as quoted in Margery Perham and J. Simmons
    1961   *African Discovery* (London: Faber & Faber).

C. S. A.
                      See Scientific Council for Africa.

du Toit, Brian M.
    In Press   Co-operative institutions and culture change in South Africa. *Journal of Asian and African Studies*, special issue.

Epstein, A.L.
    1958   *Politics in an Urban African Community* (Manchester: Manchester University Press).
    1967   Urbanization and Social Change in Africa. *Current Anthropology* 8:275-295.

Fallers, L.A.
    1961   Are African Cultivators to be called 'Peasants.' *Current Anthropology* 2:108-110.

Feldman, A.S. and W.E. Moore
    1960   Commitment of the Industrial Labour Force. In *Labour Commitment and Social Change in Developing Areas*, W.E. Moore and A.S. Feldman, eds. (New York: Social Research Council).

Fortes, Meyer
    1965   Culture Contact as a Dynamic Process. In *Methods of Study of Culture Contact in Africa*, L.P. Mair, ed. Memorandum XV (International African Institute), pp. 60-91. First published, 1938.

70

Fortes, Meyer
1967   Aspects of Time, Space and Human Mobility. Paper presented at the Latin American African Studies Conference. University of Florida, November.

Glass, Y.
1960   The Black Industrial Worker: A Social Psychological Study. Preliminary Report. National Institute for Personnel Research, Johannesburg.

1962   Industrialization and Urbanization in South Africa. Paper contributed to Social Science Research Conference, Durban.

Gluckman, M.
1960   Tribalism in Modern British Central Africa. Cahiers d'Etudes Africaines 1:55-70.

1961   Anthropological problems arising from the African Industrial Revolution. In Social Change in Modern Africa, Aidan Southall, ed. Studies presented and discussed at the First International African Seminar, Makerere College (Oxford: Oxford University Press), pp. 67-82.

Gulliver, Philip H.
1960   Incentives in Labor Migration. Human Organization 19: 159-163.

Gutkind, Peter C.W.
1960   Congestion and Overcrowding: An African Urban Problem. Human Organization 19:129-134.

Hance, William A.
1965   The Geography of Modern Africa (New York: Columbia University Press).

Hellman, E.
1948   Rooiyard: A Sociological Survey of an Urban Native Slum Yard. Rhodes Livingstone Papers, No. 13 (Capetown: Oxford University Press).

Leslie, J.A.K.
1963   A Social Survey of Dar-es-Salaam (London: Oxford University Press).

Little, Kenneth
1965   West African Urbanization (Cambridge: Cambridge University Press).

Little, Kenneth and Anne Price
1967   Some Trends in Modern Marriage among West Africans. Africa 37:407-424.

Lloyd, P.C.
1966   Introduction. The New Elites of Tropical Africa, P.C. Lloyd, ed. Studies presented and discussed at the sixth International African Seminar at the University of Ibadan, (Oxford: Oxford University Press), pp. 1-62.

Marris, Peter
1962   Family and Social Change in an African City (Northwestern University Press).

71

Mayer, Philip
    1961   Townsmen or Tribesmen (Capetown: Oxford University Press).

    1962a   Migrancy and the Study of Africans in Towns. American Anthropologist 64:573-592.

    1962b   Introduction. The Multitribal Society, A.A. Dubb, ed. Proceedings of the Sixteenth Conference of the Rhodes-Livingstone Institute (Lusaka: Rhodes-Livingstone Institute), pp. v-x.

Mercier, Paul
    1963   Urban Explosion in Developing Nations. UNESCO COURIER 7-8:50-55.

Mitchell, J.C.
    1953   A Note on the Urbanization of Africans on the Copperbelt. Rhodes-Livingstone Journal 12.

    1962   Some Aspects of Tribal Social Distance. In The Multitribal Society, A.A. Dubb, ed. Proceedings of the Sixteenth Conference of the Rhodes-Livingstone Institute (Lusaka: Rhodes-Livingstone Institute), pp. 1-17.

    1965   The Meaning in Misfortune for Urban Africans. In African Systems of Thought, M. Fortes and G. Dieterlen, eds. Studies presented at the Third International African Seminar in Salisbury (London: Oxford University Press), pp. 192-203.

Parkin, David J.
    1966   Types of Urban African Marriage in Kampala. Africa 36:269-284.

Pauw, B.A.
    1965   Patterns of Christianization among the Tswana and the Xhosa-speaking peoples. In African Systems of Thought, M. Fortes and G. Dieterlen, eds. Studies presented at the Third International African Seminar in Salisbury (London: Oxford University Press), pp. 240-257.

Plotnicov, Leonard
    1967   Strangers to the City (Pittsburgh: University of Pittsburgh Press).

Pons, V.G.
    1956   The Growth of Stanleyville and the Composition of Its African Population. In Social Implications of Industrialization and Urbanization in Africa South of the Sahara, D. Forde, ed. (UNESCO), pp. 229-249.

Prothero, R.M.
    1957   Migratory Labour from North-Western Nigeria. Africa 27:251-261.

    1961   Population Movements and Problems of Malaria Eradication in Africa. Bulletin of the World Health Organization, No. 24. pp. 399-403.

72

Prothero, R.M.
    1962   Migrant Labour in West Africa. Journal of Local Adminis-
                  tration Overseas 1:149-155.
    1964   Continuity and Change in African Population Mobility. In
                  Geographers and the Tropics, Steel and Prothero, eds.
                  (London).
    1965   Socio-Economic Aspects of Rural/Urban Migration in
                  Africa South of the Sahara. Scientia.

Reader, D.H.
    1966   Tribalism in South Africa. In Scientific South Africa,
                  3:No. 4. .

Rotberg, Robert I.
    1962   Rural Rhodesian Markets. In Markets in Africa, P. Bohan-
                  nan and G. Dalton, eds. (Northwestern University Press).

Sjoberg, Gideon
    1955   The Preindustrial City. The American Journal of Sociology
                  60:438-445.

Scientific Council for Africa
    1961   C.S.A. Meeting of specialists on Urbanization and its
                  Social Aspects. Publication No. 75.

Soper, T.
    1959   Labour migration in Africa. Journal of African Administration
                  11:93-99.

Sundkler, B.
    1961   Bantu Prophets in South Africa, 2nd. ed. (Oxford Univer-
                  sity Press).
    1965   Chief and Prophet in Zululand and Swaziland. In African
                  Systems of Thought, M. Fortes and G. Dieterlen, eds.
                  Studies presented at the Third International African Seminar,
                  in Salisbury (London: Oxford University Press), pp. 276-
                  287.

van Velsen, J.
    1961   Labour Migration as a Positive Factor in the Continuity of
                  Tonga Tribal Society. In Social Change in Modern Africa,
                  Aidan Southall, ed. Studies presented and discussed at
                  the First International African Seminar, Makerere College
                  (Oxford University Press), pp. 230-241.

Wallerstein, L.
    1960   Ethnicity and National Integration in West Africa. Cahiers
                  d'Etudes Africaines 3:129-139.

Watson, W.
    1967   Migrant Labor in Africa: A consideration of Its Various
                  Forms and Their Relation to Traditional and Bureaucratic
                  Socio-Economic System. Paper read at the Tenth Annual
                  meetings of the African Studies Association, New York.

73

Wilson, G.
 1942   An Essay on the Economics of Detribalization in Northern
         Rhodesia, Rhodes-Livingstone Papers No. 6 (Cape Town:
         Oxford University Press).

74

URBAN CLASSES AND ACCULTURATION IN LATIN AMERICA

Emilio Willems
Vanderbilt University

Among the various alternatives open to anthropologists who wish to concentrate on Latin American cities, the study of social class seems to be one of the most obvious possibilities. Although there is nothing new about the conceptualization of social class as subculture, very few studies of class actually live up to what anthropologists consider a descriptive or analytical investigation of subcultures. The sociological approach to class has been almost exclusively concerned with a few selected aspects of culture, such as occupation, income, education, ethnicity, race, and perhaps a few others. Consideration of these variables, singly or in association, may provide a few glimpses rather than a full understanding of the lifeways of the aggregate under scrutiny.

There are at least two specific reasons why the urban classes of Latin America constitute a particularly tempting topic to the anthropologist. First, class cleavages in Latin America are so striking that Maurice Halbwachs' characterization seems fully applicable. Class, he writes "determines the conduct of its members and imposes definite motivations on them; it stamps each category with such a peculiar and distinctive mark, so forcibly, that men of different classes, even though they live amid the same surroundings and are contemporaries, sometime strike us as belonging to different species of humanity" (Halbwachs 1958:4). Secondly, the class structure of many, perhaps most, Latin American cities is complicated by the presence of a variety of subcultures alien to urban life, or to the general culture a particular city stands for, or to both. The bearers of these subcultures are migrants who have settled in the city without surrendering their own cultural identity.

This paper is concerned with the relationships between these cultural groups and the urban class structure. Based on facts known at least in a general way, it presents hypotheses designed to call attention to the rich research potential inherent in the topic which is submitted here for preliminary inspection. The underlying hypothesis is that the acculturation of these groups, regardless of their cultural origin, may be considered synonymous with their adsorption into the existing class system which in turn does not remain unchanged in the process.

It is suggested here that the location of the migrant within a given urban area constitutes the first step in a series of adjustments to a particular class culture. Location does not proceed at random, nor is it a matter of free choice, except perhaps in the narrowest possible sense of preferring one shantytown to another. Location is inevitably the outcome of ecological competition for a scarce commodity: housing, or at least an unoccupied piece of land on which to build a hovel from whatever scraps may be available. Unless

75

the migrant succeeds in moving out and "up," he and his family are bound to be absorbed by the lower class culture of their habitat to the extent that they are acculturated at all. Acculturation may be impeded or accelerated by a number of factors. Of these, this paper will especially consider the urban settlement patterns of migrants, the rapidly changing urban environment in which migration occurs, the relationship between the city and its surrounding countryside, and the role of the mass media in the acculturation process.

The fact that migrants of differing cultural provenience tend to cluster and to occupy distinct zones within given city areas is well known. Clustering makes it possible for the group to perpetuate its cultural identity and thereby to perform the function of cushioning the initial shock which exposure to a strange culture involves. If the group feels discriminated against, or if leading members develop a vested interest in its continuance, the culture of the group may acquire a defensive character and prepare itself for indefinite resistance. In Latin American cities, however, available evidence suggests that the ethnic ghetto is a transitional rather than a permanent phenomenon.

Urban settlement patterns and acculturation processes both occur within the context of an often rapidly changing urban environment. In Latin America, industrialization has been accompanied by major changes in cities, and the nature and rhythm of these changes makes the industrializing city considerably different from the pre-industrial cities described by Sjoberg. One of the characteristics of the pre-industrial city is a "perpetual state of depression" manifest in chronic unemployment and underemployment (Sjoberg 1960:17). Both terms suggest anomaly and therefore fail to satisfy the anthropologist who perceives these phenomena, within the context of the pre-industrial city, as definite components of lower class culture rather than as a deviation from normality. A brief discussion of the biscateiro in Brazil will provide an example of the potential effects of industrialization on the type of chronic unemployment and underemployment characteristic of the pre-industrial city.

In Brazil the term biscateiro is widely applied to men who hire themselves out to perform a variety of unskilled jobs, none of them implying any degree of permanency or particular skill. In the city of Fortaleza, Ceará, a recent survey of Pirambú, a lower class suburb, counted 1,026 biscateiros out of a total of 7,992 heads of households (Ribeiro: 13). Biscateiros are predominantly bearers of folk cultures, and their marginal role in the economy of the city may be considered as a barrier to acculturation. It would seem that the preservation of certain aspects of their original peasant culture has distinct survival value. They may raise poultry, pigs or goats, tend a few banana trees, or a tiny manioc garden. Witches and curandeiros are much sought after, and beliefs in the sacy, the werewolf, and the evil eye are very much alive.

A comparison of figures on underemployment in a number of Brazilian cities indicates that industrialization of a city tends to absorb an increasing proportion of the marginal labor force and consequently reduces the incentives to preserve cultural values alien to urban lifeways. Juarez R. Brandão Lopes recently discovered that underemployment decreases with the degree of industrialization. In São Paulo City, for example, 16.1 percent of the 1950 labor

76

force were classified as underemployed; in Belo Horizonte, with its then incipient industrialization, the figure was 27.4 percent; and in Salvador it reached
32.1 percent (Lopes 1966:32). Thus if there is such a thing as a biscateiro
culture, it would seem to be disappearing gradually as industrialization increases.

In addition to urban settlement patterns and the rapidity of changes in
the urban environment, an examination of the acculturation process must also
consider the way in which the city proper is related to the surrounding countryside. In some cases, as in Panama City for example, there is no transitional
zone at all, while in other cities, such as San José (Costa Rica), the urban
area proper gradually merges into the countryside. The transitional sector is
inhabited by a population predominantly engaged in farming and perpetuating
a peasant-like subculture (Sandner 1967). Here ecological conditions seem
to delay the absorption of a folk culture into the lower class of San José.
Somewhat similar conditions prevail in peripheral areas of São Paulo City
with the difference however, that the interstitial population is primarily composed of Japanese and Portuguese peasants.

The main difference between marginal and interstitial populations seems
to lie in the fact that the former is predominantly composed of newcomers who
have not found a definite niche in the urban structure, while the latter have
moved into a pre-existing semi-rural setting, the viability of which is related
to the (largely unknown) morphological development of certain cities. In
either case, acculturation is slow.

Little attention has been paid to the changing ecology of the fast
growing Latin American cities. The residential distribution of social classes
in the traditional Latin American city "where the elite were clustered near the
central plaza and the lower classes were found at the edge of the city"
(Schnore 1965:47-48) is rapidly becoming a thing of the past. In a recent
study of the Central American capitals, Gerhard Sandner calls attention to
"growing disintegration" of these cities. "Within the last three to four decades
the large cities of Central America have lost that compactness which was inherited from colonial times and which manifested itself in far-reaching integration and in an obvious orientation toward an urban center characterized by
a concentration of functions. In the meanwhile the expanding urban area, the
rapidly following cellular fragmentation of the urban organism in the peripheral
zones, and the differentiation of the urban population have generated structures
which sometimes resemble the 'suburbanism' of the modern city in highly industrialized countries" (Sandner 1967.13).

It would seem that the disintegration of the traditional urban structure
has gone even farther in South America than in Central America. In cities
like Bogotá, Cali, Lima, Santiago, Buenos Aires, Pôrto Alegre, Curitiba,
São Paulo, Rio do Janeiro, and many others, centrifugal developments affect
all social classes and actually dominate the scene of urban expansion. Two
characteristics of these suburban developments seem to be relevant: They
are becoming increasingly independent from the old center and, as Claude
Bataillon indicated for Mexico City (Bataillon 1965:172-73), they are inhabited by different social classes. In fact, they are probably more effective

77

in segregating the social classes than the traditional city with its single multi-functional gravitation center.

There are various ways in which these ecological changes may be related to the problem under scrutiny. Whether a suburban development -- "suburban" in the sense of being located well outside the perimeter of the traditional city -- may hinder or further the transition from an ethnic or folk culture to a class culture seems to depend on several variables. It is hypothesized here that if a suburb develops as a primary settlement of an ethnic group it would seem to act as a barrier to acculturation. However, if it emerges as a secondary settlement, designed to attract people already located in other zones of a given urban area, it will probably stimulate transition to a class culture.

Some years ago in Santiago, Chile, government agencies began to carry out the relocation of a shantytown population in a carefully selected area designed to become the new suburb of San Gregorio. House sites were allocated without giving consideration to the regional origin of the individual householder. Although the transfer proceeded smoothly enough, many people complained about the destruction of their neighborhood groups which had been homogeneously comprised of people of the same regional background. This is but one instance of the frequent observation that the lower class housing provided by governments, industrial companies, or other agencies often makes it difficult or impossible to reconstitute subcultural groups which may have flourished in previous locations. Loss of residential propinquity gradually tends to dilute cultural traits alien to the new environment in which the migrant now lives. Suburban development in São Paulo, Curitiba, and Porto Alegre, suggests that the eventual outcome is a rather homogeneous class culture which may have absorbed fragments of architectural styles, consumption habits, food items, speech patterns, gestures, and so on which were formerly associated with distinct ethnic groups. Another development, typically observed in fast growing metropolitan areas, is the transformation of formerly isolated folk communities into residential or industrial suburbs. The banlieue of São Paulo City presents several instances of these sorts of rather complicated structural changes which tend to convert folk cultures into class cultures.

In addition to the factors described thus far, the role which modern mass media play in the urbanization of folk cultures has not yet been fully understood. Instead of changing them, they are sometimes used to perpetuate values alien to a supposedly secularized urban society. With reference to São Paulo City, Roger Bastide observed that "modern means of information, such as newspapers, radio and television, far from creating a new mentality, are put at the service of messianic and thaumaturgic rural movements in order to disseminate them in the city, even in the middle classes. Thus in Brazil a thaumaturgic priest of a small rural town performed the blessing of miraculous water on television, and in São Paulo people put a glass of water in front of the little screen to have tap water transformed into a miraculous medicine" (Bastide 1965:80-81).

Sometimes elements of folk cultures present in the city do change

78

indeed, but such changes, far from destroying the identity of these elements, are merely adaptions to a changing lower class culture. A major instance of this process may be seen in the gradual transformation of Brazilian Camdomblé, Macumba, or Xangô into Umbanda. The traditional African cult centers attracted a limited number of colored Brazilians whose acculturation had been arrested, primarily because the pre-industrial city offered little opportunity for social ascent. With the emergence of an industrial civilization and the concomitant rise of the working class, macumba began to rid itself of what was considered crude and to adopt certain traits of the more sophisticated Spiritualist movement. Formerly based on oral traditions, it began to develop its own scriptures. According to one estimate, there were about 400 books available in 1961, written by followers of Umbanda (Camargo 1961:41). Umbanda literature and cult paraphernalia may now be purchased in specialized stores in any major Brazilian city. Numerous formerly autonomous terreiros or cult centers joined larger associations offering medical and social assistance to their members. One of these associations, the Spiritualist Federation of Umbanda, claims control of over 260 centers in São Paulo City alone (Camargo 1961:53).

The following facts suggest that Umbanda has become one of several religions of the lower urban classes without relinquishing some basic African and Indian traits of the macumba:

(1) In the cities of Southern Brazil Umbanda attracts the masses regardless of ethnic origin and color. It has ceased to be a "Negro" religion (Camargo 1961:34-35).

(2) In São Paulo City, the diffusion of Umbanda seems unrelated to the previous existence of macumba centers (Camargo 1961:34).

(3) In contrast to Camdomblé practices "each cavalo or medium, in the Umbanda of São Paulo, bears the wisdom of the spirits which he receives. The division of labor extant within the 'phalanges' (of spirits) makes it possible for all to have access to spirit contact; thousands of mediums assist their distressed clients every week. This is democracy in religion. This is a far cry from the superior gods that only condescended to dance haughtily in the midst of the men" (Camargo 1961:37).

(4) The spirits possessing the Umbanda medium are invariably those of humble negros velhos (old negroes) or caboclos (Indians) as they are called in Umbanda terminology. They rank highest in the spirit hierarchy of the Umbanda, while those of their former masters, the slave-holding landowners, are demoted to the lowest rank. From the standpoint of orthodox Spiritualism, this is subversive ranking which may be considered a symbolic expression of discontent with the existing class system. By preserving African and Indian traits -- particularly the extremely popular cult of Iemanja -- the followers of Umbanda attempt to validate the cultural heritage of the lower classes (Bastide 1960:468).

Although this paper has primarily discussed the acculturation of lower class migrants into cities, the anthropologist's concern with urban phenomena need not be limited to the lower classes. The previously stated hypothesis postulating a relationship between ecological change and the acculturation of ethnic groups already suggests possible applications to the middle and upper

79

classes. It is my contention that European and Asian immigrants and their descendants develop a high degree of awareness of their emerging class position, especially if it differs from their previous status or from their own expectations, which may or may not be exceeded by actual opportunities. While still clinging to their ethnic identity, some of these groups institutionalize their defenses in various ways, one of these being the ethnic club.

In all metropolitan areas of Latin America there are associations of Italians, Portuguese, Germans, Syrians, Lebanese, Japanese, and so forth, whose stated objectives range from those of a country club to those of a charitable or literary society. It seems that these clubs can be divided into two broad membership categories. First, there are those immigrants of middle class extraction who feel superior to the native middle class and gather together in order to protect their allegedly superior ethnic values from "assimilation." Primarily this means the prevention of intermarriage between their native-born children and nationals of the country. Individuals of the same ethnic group of lower middle or upper lower class extraction, who do not wish to belong to the corresponding native strata, frequently seek to join the ethnic club, an accomplishment which is valued as an upward step in the process of social mobility. In cities with a highly successful and prosperous native middle class (São Paulo, for example), the ethnic club often fails to satisfy the aspirations of its highest-ranking members, and identification with the native upper middle or upper class through intermarriage or business association (or both) may become desirable.

The second category of ethnic clubs is comprised of those clubs whose members wish to protect their actual desired middle class status against alleged or actual discrimination. These clubs are frequently formed by individuals of Syrian, Lebanese, or Armenian extraction who, all over Latin America, are summarily and somewhat contemptuously referred to as turcos and excluded from the first type of club described above. Clubs constituted by oriental minorities thus may be interpreted as a response to prejudice, while all other ethnic clubs tend to be rather expressions of prejudice against "the natives."

The numerous unexplored opportunities to study the more advanced phases of the dynamic interrelationships between acculturation and social stratification are especially apparent in the industrial cities of Southern Brazil. The almost continuous flow of European immigrants over a period of at least one hundred years, and the gradual absorption of these groups into the social structure cannot be interpreted as a social ascent of ethnic groups in corpore. As a matter of fact, all the ethnic groups have been widely distributed over the class system, and their gradual integration into the different classes has not only changed the composition of each class, but has altered the system as a whole.

Without going into the complexities of this phenomenon, I wish to suggest the hypothesis that somewhere along the tortuous lines of this process class comes to be more important than ethnicity. One expression of this crucial change may be seen in the breakdown of ethnic endogamy. Studying intermarriage of German-Brazilians in São José, an industrial and mostly lower class district of Porto Alegre, between 1930 and 1950 (the study was carried out in 1951), I discovered that in 1930 the number of in-group marriages was higher than that of inter-ethnic marriages. In 1940, however, there were only 47 in-group marriages as contrasted with 76 inter-ethnic unions, and in 1950 the number of inter-ethnic marriages was three times higher than that of in-group marriages (Willems 1953:96).

I have no data on inter-ethnic marriages in the middle and upper classes of Southern Brazil beyond the general impression that they are commonplace, particularly among ethnic groups characterized by a high degree of cultural affinity with Brazilians of Portuguese stock. In a recent study of the upper class of Chile, I found that 80 (26.5 percent) out of a total of 319 family names were English, German, Italian, French, Slavic, or Jewish. The bearers of these non-Spanish names were, with very few exceptions, descendants of immigrants who married women of traditional upper class families (Willems 1967:44) In the course of the study, it became quite obvious that for immigrants who were socially acceptable, membership in the upper class country club (acting as a boundary-maintaining device) was preferable to membership in an ethnic club.

In summary, I should like to submit that the incorporation of the numerous and widely differing subcultural groups of Indian or Mestizo peasants, and of European and Asian immigrants into Latin American cities, proceeds along the lines of social class. The rhythm of acculturation is presumably dependent on the capacity of the city to absorb the flow of migrants. In contrast to the lower class districts of industrial cities, those of preindustrial cities offer little incentive for peasant and Indian migrants completely to surrender their cultural identity.

Another variable, not necessarily related to industrialization, is to be seen in the changing ecology of the Latin American city. Large scale suburban developments which are becoming increasingly independent of the traditional center, seem to be highly effective in segregating the social classes, but their role as vehicles of acculturation appears to depend on whether they are primary or secondary settlements. The way in which the mass media may affect the transition of an ethnic subculture into a class culture may be observed in the transformation of traditional Afro-Brazilian cult centers into the Umbanda movement.

To the extent that ethnic groups claim middle class status, the ethnic club seems to play the role of a way station in the acculturative process. It is suggested that eventually social class tends to become more important than ethnicity, a trend which is confirmed by the increase of inter-ethnic marriages.

The few facts presented in this paper provide no more than glimpses into the complexities of urban stratification in Latin America, but inadequate as they may be, they at least suggest the viability of the proposed hypotheses, as well as the diversity of research possibilities which the study of urban class systems in Latin America offers to the anthropologist.

81

REFERENCES

Bastide, Roger
  1960   Les religions africaines au Brésil (Paris: Presses Univer-
              sitaires de France).
  1965   Ethnologie des capitales latino-américaines. In Le
              problème des capitales en Amérique Latine, Colloques
              Internationaux du Centre National de la Recherche Scien-
              tifique (Paris: Editions du Centre National de la Recherche
              Scientifique).
Bataillon, Claude
  1965   Mexico capitale métis. In Le Problème des capitales en
              Amérique Latine, Colloques Internationaux du Centre
              National de la Recherche Scientifique (Paris: Editions du
              Centre National de la Recherche Scientifique).
Camargo, Candido
  1961   Kardecismo e Umbanda (São Paulo: Livraria Pioneira
              Editôra).
Halbwachs, Maurice
  1958   The Psychology of Social Classes (Glencoe: The Free
              Press).
Lopes, Juarez R. Brandão
  1966   Desenvolvimento e Mudança Social: Formação da Socie-
              dada Urbano-Industrial no Brasil. Primeira parte. (São
              Paulo)
Ribeiro, Favila
  s/d   O latifúndio na conjunctura urbana. MS
Sandner, G.
  1967   Gestaltwandel and Funktion der zentral-amerikanischen
              Grosstädte aus sozial-geographischer Sicht. Paper pre-
              sented at the Segundo Colóquio Científico de Ultramar.
              University of Münster, Germany.
Schnore, Leo F.
  1965   The Study of Urbanization: Report of a Council Committee.
              Items. Social Science Research Council, Vol. 19, No. 4.
Sjoberg, Gideon
  1960   The Preindustrial City (Glencoe: The Free Press).
Willems, Emilio
  1953   A miscigenação entre brasileiros de ascendência germânica.
              Sociologia XV, No 2, São Paulo.
  1967   A alta classe chilena. América Latina, Ano 10, No. 2
              Abril-Junho, Rio de Janeiro.

82

LEVELS OF URBAN RELATIONSHIPS IN A COMPLEX SOCIETY:
A COSTA RICAN CASE[1]

Michael D. Olien
The University of Georgia

The city is not an isolated community. Instead, the urban community
lies in a nexus of interrelationships. Not only are there relations between the
subcultures of the community, but there are also relations between the city
and the rural areas, between the city and the nation, and even international
relations. In part, it is this very network of relationships which makes an
understanding of the city possible. Describing the context in which an urban
area exists may allow anthropologists to approach the same level of totality
in their studies of cities as has been reached in the studies of isolated primitive groups.

In this paper the context in which one Latin American city exists will
be explored. The paper will examine the relationships between Puerto Limón,
Costa Rica, and larger more inclusive units at various levels of analysis. It
is necessary first, however, to briefly review the development of urbanization
in Costa Rica as a whole in order to understand the somewhat unique line of
development found in Puerto Limón.

Urbanization in Costa Rica

During the pre-contact period, Costa Rica was marginal to both the
Meso-American and South American tropical forest areas; pre-industrial cities
such as Teotihuacan never developed in Costa Rica. The first area of Costa
Rica to be discovered by the Spanish was Cariay, in 1502, by Columbus, the
site of what is today Puerto Limón. However, the Caribbean coastal area was
not settled by the Spanish.

Following the period of early Spanish exploration, Costa Rica developed
as an extremely poor agricultural colony with no true urban center. The Spanish
speaking white settlers lived in small villages and were basically engaged in
subsistence agriculture. Only one community was slightly larger than other
communities of the early colonial period, Cartago, situated in the central highlands. Cartago was founded in 1563 and was named the capital of the province
of Costa Rica, under the Captaincy General of Guatemala. Although a capital,
Cartago had a limited population; 83 in 1569, 330 in 1611, and 600 in 1675
(Nunley 1960:17). Throughout the colonial period the Spanish speaking white
population remained settled in the cool, comfortable highlands and made little
attempt to settle the hot humid lowlands, except for small cacao plantations
in the area of the Matina Valley, situated in the eastern lowlands and owned
by absentee-landlords who lived in Cartago (Olien 1967:57-80). In 1736 the

83

parish of Villa Nueva de la Boca del Monte was established. It consisted of a church and twenty-six houses in 1751. By 1783 it had grown to a community of more than 4,000 persons, and in 1813 it was given the title "city" and renamed San José.

After independence, in 1823, a short-lived civil war broke out over the question of whether or not to join the newly formed Mexican empire. The republicans won the dispute and proceeded to move the seat of national government from monarchist Cartago to San José, the republican stronghold (Nunley 1960:17, 20). San José has remained the capital ever since.

Until the end of World War II there was a gradual, rather slow increase in the population of Costa Rica. San José served as an administrative center for the agriculturally based country. Since the end of World War II population growth has been extremely rapid, especially in San José. San José has grown to a primate city of over 172,000 persons, with a surrounding metropolitan area of over 327,000 (Ministerio de Economía y Hacienda 1964:18). All of the cities of Costa Rica, except the two major ports, are located in the highlands within 10 miles of San José, connected by well-paved highways. In many ways these larger highland communities are extensions of San José.

It was not until after Costa Rica gained its independence that the white settlers began to move out of the highlands. Puntarenas was established as a port on the west coast in 1814 (Bode and Richardson 1968:2). Between 1844 and 1864, it developed into the principal Pacific port. Puntarenas prospered as a port for shipping coffee, the main export crop of the highlands.

The last of Costa Rica's urban centers to develop was Puerto Limón, Costa Rica's east coast port, built in the 1870's. It became important to Costa Rica's economy as a banana exporting port at the turn of the century. Because of its post-colonial founding and because of the influence of the United Fruit Company in its formation and growth, Puerto Limón has developed a network of relations which are different from those found in any other Costa Rican city. These relations can be discussed at a number of different levels. In this paper, relations at four levels will be examined: intra-community relations, urban-rural relations, urban-national relations, and urban-international relations.

Puerto Limón: a Costa Rican Port City

Puerto Limón is the principal port on Costa Rica's Caribbean coast, with a population of about 20,000 inhabitants. The city was built by Minor C. Keith, the founder of the United Fruit Company, under a contract from the Costa Rican government. By 1914 Puerto Limón had developed into the world's leading banana exporting port. The Puerto Limón of the early twentieth century was a company town controlled by the North American managers of the United Fruit Company.

Under the domination of the United Fruit Company, the lowlands of Costa Rica developed in a somewhat autonomous manner from the highlands. The highland whites were concerned with growing coffee in the valleys surrounding San José. As long as economic opportunities existed in the highlands, the

84

Spanish-speaking whites were reluctant to migrate into the lowlands.

The United Fruit Company imported Negro workers from the West Indies to work on its banana plantations, as there was no ready supply of labor in the lowlands. These West Indian Negroes were restricted by Costa Rican law from migrating into the highlands. During this plantation period, as many as 60 percent of the inhabitants of the lowlands were Negro. There were 2.2 foreigners in the lowlands for every Costa Rican (Ministerio de Economía y Hacienda 1960:63).

With the collapse of the plantation system by 1942 due to banana diseases throughout the eastern lowlands, the Negroes were isolated in the lowlands without a major employer. Although the United Fruit Company attempted to relocate some of the Negro laborers as it moved its operations to the Pacific coast, the Costa Rican government would not allow it.

During the last two decades, due to increasing population pressure in the highlands, there has been an influx of white settlers into the Caribbean lowlands. However, the lowland area is still considered a Negro area in the belief system of many highland white Costa Ricans, although the Negroes no longer constitute a majority of the population.[2]

Today, although less important as a banana exporting port, Puerto Limón is Costa Rica's major port and plays an important role in the importation of consumer products from other countries.

The network of relationships which developed as a result of Puerto Limón's particular ethnic composition, history, and function, will be described in the next section of this paper, beginning with the relationships which have developed between the various ethnic groups living in the city today as they relate to the wealth, authority, and prestige substructures. Then, several levels of supra community relations will be examined.

1. Intra-Community Relations. The interaction of three ethnic groups form the basis of Puerto Limon intra-community relations -- the Spanish speaking whites, the Negroes, and the Chinese. The whites, for the most part, represent the cultural brokers of the highland Costa Rican culture. Many have filled positions at the top of the local wealth, authority, and prestige substructures vacated by the North Americans of the United Fruit Company. Other whites have filled middle positions in the substructures. Most numerous, perhaps, are the peons who no longer find employment on the highland coffee farms and have migrated to the lowlands to fill positions at the bottom of at least the wealth substructure.

The upper class whites make up the membership of the Miramar Club, an exclusive club organized originally to exclude Negroes from a previously public club. The Miramar Club is patterned after the North American country club. It is a place in which members can play cards, swim, play table tennis, drink, eat, hold dances, and entertain friends. The membership, while it excludes Negroes, does include some of the prominent Chinese businessmen. The upper class whites also belong to the local Rotary Club, the (white) Masons, and the Garden Club.

The upper class whites interact socially almost exclusively with persons of the same social standing. They maintain ties with influential families

85

in San José, and often travel to San José to shop and to visit relatives. Some of the Puerto Limón upper class whites live in a section of the city, the <u>Zona Bananera</u> or Company Point, made up of houses originally built by the United Fruit Company for its managers. This section of the city is conspicuously separated from the rest of the community by a fence.

The majority of the upper class whites, however, live scattered throughout the various <u>barrios</u> (neighborhoods) of the city. Outside of the <u>Zona Bananera</u>, there are no <u>barrios</u> in Puerto Limón which are made up exclusively of upper class families. Many of these Spanish speaking whites of the upper class speak English and maintain ties with the few North American and other foreign managers still living in Puerto Limón. Some of these upper class whites also maintain households in San José, as well as in Puerto Limón. The people in this class hold the following types of positions: lawyers, doctors, school officials, government officials, store owners, and other types of managerial positions. Some also own land in the rural areas, but are absentee owners.

The middle class whites form the clerical and lower echelon managerial staff of the city. Many are owners of small shops and school teachers. The unskilled, urban proletariat form the lower class sector of the Spanish speaking whites. Many of these people take any job which is available, including employment on Negro-owned or Chinese-owned farms.

Negroes can be found at all levels of the wealth, authority, and prestige substructures, but the number of Negroes near the top of the hierarchy is considerably restricted. Only ten professionals, who were Negro, were discovered in the course of a year's investigation: four lawyers, five professors, and one civil engineer. For the most part, these persons are excluded from the white upper class, and may best be categorized as upper middle class. Most Negro professionals leave Puerto Limón because they are accorded less prestige than whites with the same occupations. Negroes are forced to leave Puerto Limón and move to San José in order to complete their professional training because the only university in Costa Rica is in San José. Once they leave Puerto Limón, they do not return. As a result, there are no professional people to assume roles of leadership within the Negro population.

Leadership, as it does exist, comes from the middle class Negro group. The president and vice-president of the Universal Negro Improvement Association, which is the most active and influential Negro organization in the city, are, respectively, a barber and an undertaker. The middle sector of the Puerto Limón Negro population includes shopkeepers, school teachers, nurses, railway foremen, clerks, and secretaries.

For the most part, the Negro population forms part of the lower class of Puerto Limón. The lower class Negroes are unskilled laborers, and there is little demand for unskilled labor, especially unskilled Negro labor, since the United Fruit Company left the area. Many of these Negroes are hired by the day to work on the docks. Most are partially or totally unemployed.

The Negro no longer has an economic advantage in Puerto Limón as he once had under the United Fruit Company because of his ability to speak English. His employers are no longer English speaking North Americans. Instead, they are Spanish speaking Costa Rican whites. At the same time, many Spanish

86

speaking whites have learned English in secondary school and can fill positions in which Negroes used to be employed on the basis of their knowledge of English.

The most important formal group among the Negroes of Puerto Limón is the Universal Negro Improvement Association (U.N.I.A.). The U.N.I.A. sponsors cultural programs, dances for young people, and an annual May Pole dance and lawn party. The U.N.I.A. is also one of the two organizations in Puerto Limón which has a burial plan for Negroes.

The young Negroes of Puerto Limón are not active joiners of formal organizations. A few belong to church youth groups sponsored by the Methodist and the Anglican church. The adults, on the other hand, normally belong to a number of organizations. The Negro males belong to more than one lodge. The Negro women belong to the Women's Auxiliary of the U.N.I.A., as well as to auxiliaries of many of the lodges to which their husbands belong. The Negro females are also active in Protestant church organizations.

The third ethnic group in Puerto Limón, the Chinese, are engaged in commerce. Almost all are owners of grocery stores, bars, or restaurants. Two of the three movie theaters in Puerto Limón are owned by Chinese. There are several Chinese cacao exporters who are marginal members of the same upper class as the whites. They have considerable economic power and are members of the Miramar Club, although lacking the same prestige as the whites. They tend to interact less frequently with the members of the club than do the whites.

The Chinese are less likely to conspicuously display any wealth they may have accrued, and they are extremely reluctant to answer questions concerning income. As a result, it is difficult to relate the Chinese to the wealth, authority and prestige substructures. There are overt differences in wealth among the Chinese, but these differences seem to correlate more closely with age than with any type of class differences. The young Chinese merchant is less likely to be wealthy.

The Chinese in Puerto Limón tend to interact among themselves. Many are members of the Chinese Association (Asociación China). This association sponsors fiestas in Puerto Limón for visiting Chinese Nationalist dignitaries, teaches Chinese culture to Chinese school children, sends money to needy families in Puerto Limón, and sends money to Taiwan to support the invasion of the mainland. The Chinese maintain a separate section of the Puerto Limón cemetery for their dead which is fenced off from the rest of the cemetery.

In general, the Spanish speaking whites control the positions of power within the community which were vacated by the North American managers of the United Fruit Company. The Negroes on the other hand, face greater economic competition from whites than ever before. There are no longer many occupations which are filled only by Negroes. During the United Fruit Company's domination of the city, Negroes were used exclusively for many positions. An important factor as to why the Negro is losing the economic advantage he once had is the lack of Negro influence in the authority substructure. The Chinese seem to have made a more successful adaptation in the economic sphere by establishing almost a monopoly over theaters, bars, cantinas, pulperías, and restaurants. An understanding of intra-community relations reveals only a partial picture of the city. Another aspect of the urban network involves supra-

87

community relations. The first of these to be described are the urban-rural relations.

2. <u>Urban-Rural</u> <u>Relations</u>. Like Puerto Limón itself, most of the Atlantic lowlands were developed by the United Fruit Company. Until the beginning of World War II, the hinterland derived its livelihood from the production of bananas. After the United Fruit Company left the area, the Negroes, who formed the bulk of the lowland labor force, changed from a plantation subculture type to a rural proletariat. There is, however, really little distinction between rural and urban labor in the lowlands today.

Many workers easily move back and forth between the rural hinterland and Puerto Limón, the urban center, searching for any available work. Sometimes the difference between rural labor and urban labor is a seasonal one. Laborers work on rural plantations during the cacao harvest, near the city during the lobster season, and in the city whenever ships are in port. Other individuals work full time in Puerto Limón, but own farms in the hinterland which they visit on weekends.

The railroad, built by the United Fruit Company in the 1870's, is the main means of travel in the hinterland. It is usually easier for most individuals of the hinterland to travel to Puerto Limón in order to fulfill various needs than it is to travel to the highlands. Many of the rural children attend school in Puerto Limón, traveling to the city each day on the train. The only high school in the lowlands is located in Puerto Limón.

Although only a few relations can be described in this brief paper, the hinterland, Limón Province, and the urban center, Puerto Limón, are intimately linked together. Urban-national relations, however, present quite a different situation.

3. <u>Urban-National</u> <u>Relations</u>. The focus of Costa Rican culture from the period of initial white settlement to the present has always been the Central Plateau (<u>Meseta</u> <u>Central</u>) on which is located San José, the nation's capital, and Costa Rica's other major cities, Cartago, Heredia, and Alajuela. The Spanish speaking whites of the highlands have engendered an economic system based on small-scale, family-owned farms. In general, they have never been eager to settle the lowlands. During the colonial period much of the lowland area was controlled by English buccaneers. Following independence, the lowlands were developed by the North Americans of the United Fruit Company and their Negro laborers.

The collapse of the plantation system and the abandonment of the lowlands by the foreign plantation managers of the United Fruit Company marked the initial step in the integration of the West Indian Negroes with Costa Rican institutions and culture patterns. It marked the end of the United Fruit Company's <u>de facto</u> control of the lowlands and finally marked the beginning of control over the region by the Costa Rican government. Costa Rican whites replaced the North American managers in the top positions of the region. By this time the Chinese also had risen to considerable economic power throughout the country, especially in the lowlands where they supplied many of the services which had been provided by the United Fruit Company. The Negro, however, no longer filled a vacuum in the lowlands, in terms of a labor force.

88

The Revolution of 1948 brought about sweeping social reforms, including the removal of the law which prohibited colored persons from settling in highland communities. This action marked the beginning of equal legal status for the Costa Rican Negro.

Since 1948 the Negroes of the lowlands have come under increasing influence from Costa Rican society and culture. The Negroes have begun to absorb more of the values of the highland whites and have obtained a position in the Costa Rican society as a whole, and not just within the context of a single region. The people of Puerto Limón and the lowlands have become Costa Rican citizens. Today there are approximately three Costa Ricans for each foreigner in the lowlands (Ministerio de Economía y Hacienda 1953:105).

In the lowlands during the United Fruit Company's control of the region, private English schools reinforced the cultural differences between the West Indians and the Costa Ricans. Today public education has become a strong integrating force. All classes are taught in Spanish, and attendance is compulsory through six years of primary education.

Nevertheless, the lowlands and highlands are still separated topographically and socially. A range of volcanoes and lowland swamps separate Puerto Limón from the Central Plateau. The only major connecting link is by railway.[3] There is no road connecting the lowlands with the highlands. Because of the limited size of the lowland population, it receives little representation in national decision-making. There is a strong "we-they" feeling separating the inhabitants of the lowlands from those of the highlands. A lowland esprit de corps has developed in opposition to the highland population, the so-called "people of the other side." The focus of this opposition is the refusal of the National Assembly, controlled by the highland population, to build a road linking the lowlands with the highlands. Although widespread acculturation has taken place in the lowlands, the process of assimilation has proceeded at a much slower pace. Another important aspect of Puerto Limón urban relationships are the relations on an international level.

4. Urban-International Relations. Since its inception, Puerto Limón has had important international ties. Today foreign vessels arrive in Puerto Limón each week. On the streets, in the bars, and in the restaurants, one finds sailors of many nations. German, Dutch, Colombian, Greek, and Norwegian sailors are the most frequent visitors to the port. The people of the port have developed stereotypes of persons of each nationality. The foreigner is not a stranger in Puerto Limón.

Although the number of North Americans and British in Puerto Limón has been greatly reduced since the United Fruit Company left the area, the Anglo-American influence is still strong. English is still widely spoken throughout the lowlands, especially among the older Negroes. In fact, more than half of the inhabitants of the lowlands over 55 years of age consider English as their mother tongue. Although the public schools have had a great acculturating effect on the Negroes and Chinese, private schools are still maintained in Puerto Limón, supported by the Protestant churches, especially the Anglican and Methodist churches. Many Negroes, and some Chinese, attend these schools every day after they have finished public school. Jamaican Independence

89

Day is observed by the Negroes. The older Negro women still wear West Indian dress. The influence of the United Fruit Company and of North America can be seen in the movies shown, the baseball stadium, the number of short-wave radio sets used to receive the Voice of America and the U.S. Armed Forces Radio Station, and in the number of persons who have direct contact with the United States through relatives from Puerto Limón who have moved to the United States. A contract agency located in Puerto Limón has recruited a number of people from Puerto Limón to work for a period of one year in the United States as domestics. Many of the people living in the United States send money to Puerto Limón relatives each month. Migration to the United States has provided a temporary stop-gap to the conditions of unemployment within the community. The United States Information Agency sponsors a Cultural Center to promote the learning of English and to spread American ideals. The ties between Puerto Limón and the United States most directly affect the Negroes, but most of the inhabitants of the community have been influenced by North American culture in one way or another. The Chinese maintain a Nationalist Party (Kuo Ming Tang) headquarters in Puerto Limón, as well as several family associations. Urban life in Puerto Limón, then, cannot be understood without regard for ties that extend beyond the borders of Costa Rica.

Summary and Conclusions

This paper has briefly outlined some of the important levels of relations between an urban community and the complex context in which it exists. Four levels were discussed: intra-community relations, urban-rural relations, urban-national relations, and urban-international relations. Within the scope of this paper it has been possible to describe only a few of the relations.[4] An adequate study would involve an interpretation of various social, economic, and political relations. To understand the nature of an urban community, it is necessary not only to describe the interrelation of the subcultures of the community, but also the relationship of the city to a series of hierarchical supra-community relations. Analysis of these networks of relations will allow anthropologists to approximate something of the totality, or holistic approach, found in the study of isolated primitive groups.

With urban anthropology in its infancy, there has been a tendency to concern ourselves with problems of "the city," treating urban areas as if all were basically the same. Certainly differences between cities have been recognized. Whiteford's (1960) study of Popayán, Colombia, and Querétaro, Mexico, for example, is a contrastive study of social class. But in general, possibly as a result of Redfield's folk-urban continuum, the differences between types of cities have not played as important a role in anthropological theory as has the difference between the urban and the rural.

There are many differences between cities in terms of ethnic composition, history, and function. Puerto Limón, for example, cannot be understood in terms of generalizations about urbanization in the highland cities of Costa Rica. Instead, the development of Puerto Limón and the particular context in which it is found today are unique in Costa Rica. Instead of concen-

90

trating on urban-rural differences, further refinement in method and theory will come from an awareness of the differences between cities. Attention to the types of intra-community and supra-community relations described in this paper may provide the most effective means of comparing cities.

NOTES

1. The field work upon which this paper is based was carried out during July and August of 1963 and from June, 1964 through June, 1965. The research undertaken in 1963 was made possible through a Carnegie Overseas Summer Fellowship, awarded by the Latin American Studies Program of the University of Oregon. Field work during the 1964-1965 year was undertaken while the author served as a Rotating Staff Member of the Central American Field Program of the Associated Colleges of the Midwest. The program was sponsored, in part, by a National Science Foundation Grant, GE-5205.

2. In the last Costa Rican census to distinguish racial categories, the population composition of Limón Province, the Caribbean lowland area, was 63 percent white, 33 percent Negro, 1 percent Chinese, and 3 percent Amerind. However, 90 percent of all Negroes living in Costa Rica live in Limón Province (Ministero de Economía y Hacienda 1953:34-35).

3. There are two airplane flights between San José and Puerto Limón daily, but this type of transportation is much too expensive for anyone but the very wealthy.

4. The leader is referred to Olien (n.d.), where the network of relationships in Puerto Limón are given more detailed treatment.

REFERENCES

Bode, Barbara and Miles Richardson
    1968   Health and Disease in Puntarenas, Costa Rica; A People's View (Manuscript).
Ministerio de Economía y Hacienda
    1953   Censo de Población de Costa Rica (22 Mayo de 1950) (San José, Costa Rica: Dirección de Estadística y Censos).
    1960   Censo de Población de Costa Rica, 11 Mayo de 1927 (San José, Costa Rica: Dirección de Estadística y Censos).
    1964   Anuario Estadístico de Costa Rica, 1963 (San José, Costa Rica: Dirección General de Estadística y Censos).
Nunley, Robert E.
    1960   The Distribution of Population in Costa Rica (Washington, D.C.: National Academy of Sciences-National Research Council).

91

Olien, Michael D.
    1967   The Negro in Costa Rica: The Ethnohistory of an Ethnic
                Minority in a Complex Society (Ph.D. Dissertation,
                Department of Anthropology, University of Oregon, Eugene).
    n.d.   Puerto Limón: Urban Relations in Lowland Costa Rica
                (Manuscript in Preparation).
Whiteford, Andrew H.
    1960   Two Cities of Latin America: A Comparative Description
                of Social Classes (Beloit, Wisconsin: The Logan Museum
                of Anthropology).

92

THE OUTLOOK, RESEARCH STRATEGIES, AND RELEVANCE
OF URBAN ANTHROPOLOGY: A COMMENTARY

John Gulick
University of North Carolina at Chapel Hill

    This paper bears only incidental resemblance to the comments which I made at the session in Gainesville when the papers by Arensberg, Fairbanks, and Hutchinson were originally presented. While those comments were part of the program, they were largely extemporaneous, owing to the fact that I had read in advance only the full text of one of the papers and the abstract of one of the others. Now, having read the final versions of these papers along with the five others, I find it necessary to broaden and alter my horizons.

    In my original comments, I devoted considerable attention to the anti-urban, polarized mental set which has dominated so much urban research and by which urban anthropology must not be entrapped. I was expanding on a point made by Hutchinson. I shall not repeat myself on the subject here. Happily, there are no signs that any of the authors in this volume is so entrapped. Whether or not the issue itself is really dead is another matter, but I have been criticized for belaboring it, and so shall hold my peace and wait and see.

    The present condition of urban anthropology is well represented by several topics which are dealt with by these papers: (a) the general outlook of urban anthropology; (b) research strategies; and (c) the "relevance" problem. These are not themes of this volume, for they were not developed intentionally by any of the authors alone or in concert. Nor are they common denominators of all the papers. They are simply the most important issues concerning urban anthropology which precipitate out of this collection as far as I am concerned.

General Outlook: The Varieties of Urban Experience

    There is a great variety of cities, of urban subcultures. It follows that any research or argumentation is fallacious which is based on the assumption that there is a single, fixed, standardized phenomenon called "urban society." Arensberg, Leeds, and Ullen all seem to be making this point, each in his own way.

    It is consistent with the anthropological tradition of identifying and comprehending cultural variations while at the same time not being blind to essential similarities. It is contrary, however, to a recurrent attitude among urban sociologists, urban political scientists, and others, which is that all cities are basically the same (i.e., any differences are unimportant), or that they soon will be when Western industrialization hits them (implication: Western industrial cities themselves are all the same). This viewpoint is certainly ethnocentric, and one wonders whether it may not also be due to a

93

powerful impulse statistically to control complexity by, ironically, reducing it to manipulable (i.e., deceptively simple) variables.

Anthropologists themselves, though, have their own characteristic weaknesses which they must try to counteract. One of them is the tendency to resort to typologies with evolutionary implications. None of the efforts to typologize cities has so far been very successful, and probably none which is really satisfactory will soon be developed. However, I do not think that we should give up trying as long as our arguments about proposed types add to our knowledge.

For example, Fairbanks contrasts the early, homogeneous Pristine city with the modern, heterogeneous industrial city, but he acknowledges (in response to one of my original comments in Gainesville) that there also are non-industrial cities which are heterogeneous. The latter, "preindustrial" city has been carefully delineated by Sjoberg, but Arensberg correctly observes that Sjoberg dealt only with cities associated with the so-called "hydraulic" cultures, neglecting many others including the native sub-Saharan African cities of which du Toit writes. So we have two types at least (very likely more) of preindustrial city. Leeds, comparing two huge industrial metropolises, identifies significant differences in ethos between them even though they belong to the same national culture. If such differences occur between São Paulo and Rio de Janeiro in Brazil, many more must occur among industrial cities elsewhere, and with sufficient knowledge many types of industrial city could probably be suggested.

Anthropologists should be clear about the purposes of urban typologies. Is the need to "order the data" sufficient by itself to warrant all the effort? I think not, particularly considering the probably inevitable imprecision of our typologies at any time in the foreseeable future. In working with typologies, we should also keep in the forefront of our thinking those urban conditions which seem to be especially important as limiting or facilitating elements in the lives of the inhabitants. Leeds gives some examples, but the array of possible factors is very large. For instance, much more research needs to be done on the effects of such obvious phenomena as the sheer mass of the city, the various population densities within it, housing styles, etc. Some city planners are interested in these things, but very little is known about them as elements in the environment which may affect other aspects of culture.

Typologies based on function (e.g., college town, mill town, shrine city, etc.), mentioned by Arensberg, seem to be of limited value. Single-function typologies are increasingly meaningless the larger and more complex the cities in question are, and multi-function ones easily become unwieldy, losing their heuristic value. Nevertheless, the ascertaining of what those functions, or predominant institutions, are is an indispensable part of the study of cities.

An underlying difficulty is that urban scholars have tended to embark on their subject with the unstated "common sense" notions of their own culture as to what a city is. In American cultural terms, a city is a big settlement which is different from "the country." How big? Different in what respects? These questions can be avoided fairly easily if one limits oneself to studying only the largest cities. Yet in so doing, an unbalanced view of urban conditions

94

in the culture as a whole can be, and often has been, generated and perpetuated. Hence such characterizations of urbanism in general as sophisticated, dangerous and/or exciting, and accommodating to various sensual gratifications (all in contrast to the country) when in fact such features are found only among certain people or in certain locations in the largest cities.

It is more difficult to evade the questions of "how big" and "why different from the country" the more one shifts one's attention to cities of less than maximum size. Timbuctoo, Mali, has a population of only 6,000-7,000, yet Miner calls it a city because its culture is heterogeneous and its ecology is nonagricultural (Miner 1965:xviii). Yet there are settlements three times as big in the Nile delta which are considered to be villages, not cities, because they are culturally homogeneous farming communities. Cultural heterogeneity (begging the question of how heterogeneous!) seems to emerge as a salient criterion of urbanness when the issue of minimum size is forced as far as possible. Yet would not this very criterion disqualify Fairbanks' Pristine "cities" as such?

Dilemmas of this sort (due primarily to imprecision of terms, insufficiency of operational concepts, and lack of good information) have led some scholars to despair of typologizing altogether. What would they do instead? I shall have more to say about this, but I do not retract what I have already said about the usefulness, within limits, of typologizing.

Urban anthropologists should make a point of eliciting the native definitions of the city in the cultures they study. Eventually, an analysis of such definitions might be of assistance in establishing the boundaries of cross-cultural urban research. That such inquiry will present its own puzzles and challenges is illustrated by this item from the Middle East. Farmers in a part of southern Iraq live and work in small hamlets which have no other occupational specialists than themselves (in contrast to many other Middle Eastern villages where there are specialists like blacksmiths, carpenters, and shopkeepers). For such services, the farmers go to a settlement of about 3,000 people which is itself a farming community but, besides having the specialists, is also a minor administrative center with a police station. Some natives refer to it as garya, "village," giving priority to its small size and agricultural character. Other natives, however, refer to it as madina, "city," giving priority to its administrative functions and the presence of certain locally elite persons (Fernea 1967:29).

Such examples can probably be multiplied many times over, and regular meditation on them should prevent anthropologists from ever again becoming rigid adherents of dogmas of the "folk-urban" sort. But will it?

Research Strategies

Three research strategies emerge from these papers. All of them, it seems to me, are indispensable for the progress of urban anthropology, and all should be encouraged. Some will undoubtedly be more appropriate for certain situations than others, and individual anthropologists will undoubtedly differ in their preferences for them. Urban anthropology should benefit from this

95

diversification.

The first is simply the use of "traditional" anthropological methods in the city, investigating familiar topics such as kinship and culture and personality. Hutchinson emphasizes that the holistic, personal, and intensive approach is feasible in city research. None of the papers, however, deals with the question of participant observation (necessarily involving a small sample) versus survey methods. However, I know of no anthropologist who has done urban research who does not feel that the two methods must be used together, supplementing each other.

Leeds sounds a very important warning: that the tendency of anthropologists to assume (or seek) maximally autonomous cultural conditions must be resisted and counteracted in urban research. Indeed, to be faithful to the holistic tradition, urban anthropologists must take into account their subjects' relationships to the total city environment. The papers by Willems, du Toit, and Olien seem to meet these standards well.

This is an appropriate point at which to raise an issue which may become troublesome if it is not clarified. Anthropologists not heeding Leeds' warning, deliberately or otherwise, can quite easily do research in cities which is not, I would argue, urban anthropology. For example, formal analysis of kinship terms used by city dwellers could quite conceivably be done in such a way that it would contribute little or nothing "to a better understanding of the complexities of the urban environment" (Gulick 1963:445). Only urban field work which makes such a contribution is "urban anthropology." Others may disagree, and if there is enough divergence of opinion, the matter should probably be argued out.

The second research strategy might be called an institutional inventory of the city, including mapping (literal and figurative), relevant historical materials, relationships of the city and its institutions to the larger society, and elements of ethos which seem outstanding. Without this information, the contextual requirement emphasized by Leeds cannot be met.

Also, macrocosmic information of this sort is essential raw material for comparative analysis in urban anthropology, including the refinement of typologies. Urban anthropologists need to beware, however, of social scientists who see little value in such "descriptive" material and disparage publications which feature it. My book on Tripoli, Lebanon (Gulick 1967) has already been subjected to unappreciative comments on this account.

The third research strategy is mentioned by Arensberg who recommends studies of the "deployment" of institutions over a given area. As I understand it, this kind of study would, initially, disregard rural or urban boundaries and concentrate instead on institutional networks. Such phenomena as population concentrations and community identities would become clear inductively. This approach would have the advantage of obviating entanglement in definitional problems such as community boundaries, what is urban and what is rural, etc. Buechler's paper is, I think, an approximation of this kind of research.

96

The "Relevance" Problem

Anthropologists have been accused of being professionally "aloof and preoccupied" as far as major social problems of their own contemporary culture are concerned. Archaeology, one might suppose, would be even more aloof and preoccupied than social anthropology. Be that as it may, it is interesting, and rather delightful to me, that it is the one archaeological paper in this collection which shows professional concern for serious problems in present-day American cities. Fairbanks discusses the possibilities of archaeology's being used to cast some light on the growth patterns of American industrial cities and on the problem of environmental pollution.

Urban anthropologists show every sign of wanting to devote major attention to the contemporary problems of other cultures than their own, as Leeds' concern with shanty-town dwellers and Willems' with the adaptation of migrants to the city well illustrate. This, however, is not "relevant" in the sense used currently by many American critics of their own culture. They ask, is American anthropology going to address itself to American problems, as sociology, political science, and social psychology have been doing for some time? This is what "relevance" means to them. The issue has already generated controversy in the profession -- stimulated especially by reactions to the war in Vietnam -- and there is probably more to come.

I raise this matter because I do not think that urban anthropologists can legitimately avoid confronting it. Already, it seems, there are those to whom the phrase urban anthropology means, not cross-cultural studies, but studies of modern American culture in cities. And there are bona fide anthropological studies, like Liebow's in Washington, D.C. (Liebow 1967), which would seem to reinforce this point, as does Oscar Lewis's work in New York City. American urban anthropologists should at least answer for themselves the question of whether they should work professionally on contemporary American urban phenomena and problems. Does anthropology have something to offer in this regard or doesn't it?

Lastly, I would like to raise the question of what contributions urban anthropologists could or should make to the increasing activities in the profession concerning anthropology and American secondary and primary education.

The value of anthropological concepts in educating for more acceptance and understanding of human differences, for example, is widely acknowledged. And anthropology could certainly contribute more than it does to such subjects as what it really means to be male or female and how to channel aggressive impulses, subjects in which there is intense interest and on which there is much sensational misinformation. One of the weaknesses, it seems to me, of school programs in anthropology is the illustrative materials. American children may be entertained (or bored) by descriptions of Eskimos, Australian aborigines, and Plains Indians, but these cultures are too different from their own to have very much educational impact, for there is no transferability. I would like to suggest that the development of new materials from urban anthropology might help greatly to provide greater empathy for the increasingly urban schoolchildren of America. To cite just one example: the sectarianism of Middle Eastern cities

97

could be used to impart a number of lessons for youngsters struggling with their own social identities. And before anthropology surrenders completely to Ardrey, Lorenz, Morris, and Co., perhaps urban anthropological materials could help save the day by showing what a wide variety of workable options human beings really have in the matter of sex roles and the constructive utilization of basic energy.

REFERENCES

Fernea, Robert A.
1967   Shaykh and Effendi: Changing Patterns of Authority among the El-Shabana, a Settled Tribe of Southern Iraq. Typescript. To be published by Harvard University Press.

Gulick, John
1963   "Urban Anthropology: Its Present and Future." Transactions of the New York Academy of Sciences, Ser. II, Vol. 25, No. 4, pp. 445-458. Reprinted in Readings in Anthropology, Morton H. Fried, ed., revised edition, Vol. II (New York: Thomas Y. Crowell Co., 1968), pp. 552-564.
1967   Tripoli: A Modern Arab City (Cambridge: Harvard University Press).

Liebow, Elliot
1967   Tally's Corner: A Study of Negro Streetcorner Men (Boston: Little, Brown and Co.).

Miner, Horace
1965   The Primitive City of Timbuctoo, Revised Edition (Garden City: Anchor Books).

98

THE CONTRIBUTORS

Conrad M. Arensberg is professor of anthropology in the Department of Anthropology at Columbia University. Author of many books and articles, Professor Arensberg was a pioneer in the study of complex societies and urban anthropology, and he was one of the founders of the Society for Applied Anthropology. He is currently writing on India and on comparative and operational models of social structure.

Hans C. Buechler is assistant professor in the Department of Anthropology at Syracuse University. His theoretical and areal interests are structural anthropology, culture change, ritual, and the Andean area.

Brian M. du Toit is assistant professor in the Department of Anthropology at the University of Florida. He is associated also with the Africa Studies Program at the same institution. His main interests are urbanization, urbanism, and community studies in Africa and Melanesia.

Elizabeth M. Eddy is Director of the Urban Studies Bureau at the University of Florida. She also holds an appointment as associate professor in the Department of Sociology. Her research interests are in urban education, community health programs, and the study of complex organizations.

Charles II. Fairbanks is Chairman of the Department of Anthropology at the University of Florida. His primary interests are Southeastern archeology, including colonial archeology, cultural evolution, and revitalization movements in the Southeastern United States.

John Gulick is Chairman of the Department of Anthropology at the University of North Carolina. He is a specialist in the social structure and community organization of the Middle East and in urban anthropology.

H. W. Hutchinson is professor of anthropology in the Center for Advanced International Studies at the University of Miami. His major research areas are Brazil and the Caribbean, and his main research interests are in family organization and the community.

Anthony Leeds is professor of anthropology in the Department of Anthropology at the University of Texas. He is best known for his publications on field work in Brasil and Venezuela and for his theoretical contributions on the topics of cultural evolution, cultural ecology, complex social structure, and ideological systems.

99

Michael D. Olien is assistant professor of anthropology in the Department of Sociology and Anthropology at the University of Georgia. His primary interests are in ethnohistory, the study of complex societies, the New World Negro, and Latin America.

Emilio Willems is professor of anthropology in the Department of Sociology and Anthropology at Vanderbilt University. His interest is in Latin America, primarily in Brazil.

100

Proceedings No. 3.
Concepts and Assumptions in Contemporary Anthropology

Edited by Stephen A. Tyler

SOUTHERN ANTHROPOLOGICAL SOCIETY

Founded 1966

<u>Officers 1969-70</u>

John L. Fischer, President

John J. Honigmann, President Elect

Michael D. Olien, Secretary-Treasurer

John Gulick, Councilor 1969-70

Arden R. King, Councilor 1969-70

Harriet J. Kupferer, 1969-72

Charles Hudson, Editor

David J. Hally, Program Chairman

CONCEPTS AND ASSUMPTIONS
IN CONTEMPORARY ANTHROPOLOGY

Table of Contents

Preface

Page

Cover: shell mask from the Little Egypt site at Carters, Georgia; courtesy David Hally. Photo by Joyce Rockwood Hudson.

214

PREFACE

Anthropologists must not only keep a critical eye on the concepts they use in analyzing their universe of discourse, they must also examine the basic assumptions which lie behind everything they do. While concepts are explicit, accessible, and continuously examined, assumptions are implicit, difficult of access, and infrequently examined. These assumptions lie at both ends of anthropology, as it were, implicit in our most abstract theories at one end and in our most highly specified handling operations at the other end.

We examine our assumptions infrequently because it entails what Edmund Leach has aptly called "rethinking," a process that is always intellectually bruising and sometimes excruciatingly painful. The anthropologist is a scholar, and this means that he must to some extent be insulated from society, but he is also a fieldworker, and field work is supremely social. Perhaps this is the reason why we are shocked when we find that we have been operating all along with both the intellectual and moral assumptions of our society. It is obvious that if our society changes, and if the position our society occupies with respect to other societies in the world changes, then anthropology must also change. Rethinking is not easy, but we cannot evade doing it.

Eight of the papers in this volume were presented at the key symposium on "Anthropologists and their Assumptions" at the fourth annual meeting of the Southern Anthropological Society. Stephen Tyler's "Introduction" and "A Formal Science" were written especially for this volume. This meeting was held jointly with the American Ethnological Society in New Orleans, March 13-15, 1969. We of the Southern Anthropological Society owe our greatest debt to Miles Richardson, who served as program chairman, helped organize the key symposium, and took care of many details at the meeting itself. We owe a similar debt to Arden King for serving as local arrangements chairman and for acting as liason between the Southern Anthropological Society and the American Ethnological Society. The Department of Anthropology at Tulane and the Department of Geography and Anthropology at Louisiana State University are to be commended for supplying equipment, personnel, and a part of the financial support for the meeting.

Many others, whose names do not appear here, gave generously of their time in helping to make the meeting a success. The Department of Sociology and Anthropology at the University of Georgia has once again provided material and financial support toward the preparation of these papers.

v

Annelle Nelms typed the final photo-ready manuscript expertly and cheerfully. I am grateful to my wife, Joyce Rockwood Hudson, who helped in several ways.

Charles Hudson
SAS Editor

vi

INTRODUCTION

Stephen A. Tyler
Tulane University

Is anthropology merely an "interstitial science" characterized by a habit of ferreting out problems that somehow get lost in the interstices between other disciplines; is it simply a technology whose function is to "test" the findings of other disciplines in exotic "laboratories"; or does it have a uniquely defined subject matter of its own? Perhaps it represents only a point of view -- a peculiar mental attitude whose source is the anthropologist's experience of other people, other places, and other times.

To say that anthropology is this or that to the exclusion of something else violates its richness and variety. What to an outsider may seem an anarchic disregard for the legislative role of disciplinary boundaries is to an anthropologist the bread and wine of intellectual life. Possibly anthropologists pay a heavy toll for their freedom, but the price of a narrow and categorical specialization is even higher. For once we have decreed that only certain things are relevant, that the universe is segmented in just one way, then we have sacrificed the impulse to think about the non-relevant things, or to conceive of the universe in some other way. We become unwitting prisoners of our own categories, languishing for some creative spirit to change the structure of the jail.

The papers in this volume testify that this state of affairs has not yet come to pass. There is still an anthropology for every anthropologist. Where Banks identifies the concept of culture as the single most important unifying construct in anthropology, Edmonson rejects it in favor of a science of man that would be more biologically sophisticated and would deal with man in all his aspects. In a complementary fashion, Johnston documents the utility of a biological concept of man that draws its information from a wide range of behavioral and ecological sources. In contrast, Wolf abandons the idea of a science of man and argues that anthropological thought is a reflection of prevailing power relationships. Opposing this position, Brukman makes a convincing case for the attempt to discover internally consistent and publicly attainable procedures which will produce replicable statements held to be true by native speakers. Fischer maintains that anthropologists have neglected the Negro as a subject of research because the study of Negro society does not fulfill professional goals and because Negro society does not conform to generalized anthropological assumptions about primitive culture. Haag feels that archaeologists in assuming evolution, the comparative method, the concept of culture, and cultural determinism are committed to the search for scientific generalizations about human behavior. King perceptively argues that the chief result of anthropology has been the continuous expansion of the consciousness of man.

1

Because these papers represent a wide variety of different and sometimes conflicting opinions, they challenge our natural predisposition to look for unity within diversity. But perhaps we should question our predisposition. That anthropologists should not agree is not surprising. Agreement may be a sign of scientific maturity, but it can also be a mark of conceptual senility. We should rejoice in the fact that anthropology is youthful and vigorous.

2

AMERICAN ANTHROPOLOGISTS AND AMERICAN SOCIETY

Eric R. Wolf
University of Michigan

I shall argue that in the period of the last hundred years there have been three major phases of American anthropology, and that these three phases in the development of our discipline correspond largely to three phases in the development of American society. Such a triadic scheme represents, of course, an oversimplification, but the oversimplification will serve its purpose if it leads us to think about problem-setting in our discipline not merely in terms of the truth and falsity of answers to questions asked, but about our whole intellectual entorprise as a form of social action, operating within and against a certain societal and cultural context. I must also caution you that in this attempt I cannot help but be idiosyncratic, though our common acquaintance with our professional literature renders my idiosyncrasy intersubjective, that is, amenable to discussion by others who, in turn, hold their own idiosyncratic positions. My purpose in this presentation is not to defend a new interpretation of American anthropology, but to generate an interest in the sociology of anthropological knowledge.

The oversimplified periods into which I want to break down the development of American society during the last century are, first, the period of Capitalism Triumphant, lasting roughly from the end of the Civil War into the last decade of the 19th century; second, the period of intermittent Liberal Reform, beginning in the last decade of the 19th century, and ending with the onset of World War II; and, third, the America of the present, characterized by what President Eisenhower first called "the military-industrial complex" in his farewell address of January 17th, 1961. Each of these periods has been characterized by a central problem and a central set of responses to that problem. There were of course numerous subsidiary and peripheral problems and subsidiary and peripheral responses to them; and there were more often than not divergent and contradictory responses. But I want to argue that even the divergent and contradictory responses possessed a common denominator in that they addressed themselves to the same central issue of the day, and that they were marked by a common intellectual mood, even when directly opposed to each other in suggesting possible solutions.

The phase of Capitalism Triumphant witnessed the construction of American industry by our untrammelled entrepreneurs; its dominant mode of intellectual response was Social Darwinism. The period of reform was marked by the drive to democratize America; the dominant mode of intellectual response was to explain and justify the entry of "new" and previously unrepresented groups into the American scene, and to adumbrate the outlines of a pluralistic and liberal America. The period of the present is marked by the extension into

3

all spheres of public life of a set of civil and military bureaucracies, connected through contracts to private concerns. I shall argue that the dominant intellectual issue of the present is the nature of public power and its exercise, wise or unwise, responsible or irresponsible.

To each of these three phases American anthropology has responded in its own way: it responded to the intellectual mood of Social Darwinism with the elaboration of evolutionist theory; it responded to Liberal Reform with theories which stressed human flexibility and plasticity; and it responds to the present phase with uncertainties and equivocations about power. Intellectual responses fed theory, and theory, in turn, fed practice; concern with the central issues of each period did not mean that anthropologists abandoned their technical tasks. Under the impetus of an evolutionist philosophy, Lewis Henry Morgan studied the Iroquois and collected the data which underwrote Systems of Consanguinity and Affinity, just as John W. Powell embarked on a vast effort to study Indian languages, institutions, arts, and philosophies. The emphasis on human plasticity and flexibility similarly prompted numerous technical investigations, especially in the field of culture and personality, a mode of inquiry which made American ethnology distinctive among the ethnological efforts of other nations. Nor does the character of the present inhibit technical skill and cumulation; indeed I shall argue that it is the very character of the present which causes us to emphasize technique, and to deemphasize ideas or ideology. Yet in no case could American anthropology escape the dominant issue of the time, and its intellectual responses could not and cannot help direct themselves to answering it, or to escaping from it. To that extent, at least, the problems of the day enter into how we construct the picture of reality around which we organize our common understandings. As that reality shifts and changes, so our responses to it must shift and change.

Of Social Darwinism, the intellectual response of the first phase, its historian, Richard Hofstadter, has written that

> Darwinism had from the first this dual potentiality; intrinsically, it was a neutral instrument, capable of supporting opposite ideologies. How, then, can one account for the ascendancy, until the 1890's, of the rugged individualist interpretation of Darwinism? The answer is that American society saw its own image in the tooth-and-claw version of natural selection, and that its dominant groups were therefore able to dramatize this vision of competition as a thing good in itself. Ruthless business rivalry and unprincipled politics seemed to be justified by the survival philosophy. As long as the dream of personal conquest and individual assertion motivated the middle class, this philosophy seemed tenable, and its critics remained a minority (1959:201).

To the extent that American anthropologists were primarily concerned with the Indian, this general view also informed their own. It was anthropology, above

4

all, which had contributed the realization that "savagery is not inchoate civili-zation; it is a distinct status of society with its own institutions, customs, philosophy, and religion," but "all these must necessarily be overthrown before new institutions, customs, philosophy, and religion can be introduced" (John W. Powell, quoted in Darrah, 1951:256).

Such an overthrow of one status of society by another involves numerous processes -- the process of power among them -- but it is a hallmark of Social Darwinism that it focused the scientific spotlight not on the actual processes -- the fur trade, the slave trade, the colonization of the Plains -- but on the out-come of the struggle. This allowed Americans -- and American anthropologists among them -- to avert their eyes from the actual processes of conflict both morally and scientifically. Hence the problem of power -- of its forms and their exercise -- remained unattended. Unattended also remained the problem of the power relationship which would link victor and defeated even after savagery had yielded to civilization. This basic paradigm did not change even when it was extended from Indians to Negroes, immigrants, Mexicans, or Filipinos by equating the spread of civilization with the spread of the Anglo-Saxons. When Theodore Roosevelt exclaimed (quoted in Hofstadter, 1959:171-172) that

> The Mexican race now see in the fate of the aborigines of the north, their own inevitable destiny. They must amalgamate or be lost in the superior vigor of the Anglo-Saxon race, or they must utterly perish,

he was merely elaborating an already familiar argument. The civilized are more virtuous than the uncivilized; the Anglo-Saxons are the most capable agents of civilization; ergo, the non-Anglo-Saxons must yield to their superior vigor. Here moral judgement masked, as it so often does, the realities of power, and Americans -- including American anthropologists -- emerged into the next phase of their intellectual endeavors with appreciably less concern and understanding of power than their British confreres. The victim could be censured or he could be pitied (Pearce, 1953:53), but as an object of censure or pity he was merely an object lesson of history, not an object himself.

We have said that the next stage in American history was the movement towards reform. It began around the turn of the century and found its most substantial expression in the New Deal. On the one hand it asserted the claims of society as a whole against the rights of the untrammelled and individualistic entrepreneur. On the other hand, it sponsored the social and political mobility of groups not hitherto represented in the social and political arena. On the wider intellectual scene, the assortion of a collectivity of common men against the anarchistic captains of industry was represented by Beard, Turner, Veblen, Commons, Dewey, Brandeis, and Holmes; in American anthropology, the reaction against Social Darwinism found its main spokesman in Franz Boas. His work in physical anthropology furnished some of the initial arguments against a racism linked to Social Darwinist arguments. In his historical particularism he validated a shift of interest away from the grand evolutionary schemes to concern with the

5

panoply of particular cultures in their historically conditioned setting. If we relate these anthropological interests to the tenor of the times, we can say that the renewed interest in cultural plurality and relativity had two major functions. It called into question the moral and political monopoly of an elite which had justified its rule with the claim that their superior virtue was the outcome of the evolutionary process -- it was their might which made their right. If other races were shown to be equipotential with the Caucasians in general and the Anglo-Saxons in particular, if other cultures could be viewed as objects in themselves and not merely as object lessons in history, then other races and other cultures could claim an equal right to participate in the construction of an America more pluralist and more cooperative in its diversity. For the intellectual prophets of the times the pre-eminent instruments for the achievement of this cooperative participation among new and diverse elements were to be scientific education and liberal reform achieved through social engineering. The major protagonist of this faith in education as a means of liberating men from the outworn canons of the past was John Dewey who saw in the union of education and science the basis for a true association of equals, sustained through the freely given cooperation of the participants. In anthropology, this concern found its expression in the variety of approaches to culture and personality. These celebrated the malleability of man, thus celebrating also his vast potential for change; and they pointed to the socialization or enculturation process as the way in which societies produced viable adults. Each culture was seen, in fact, as one large schoolhouse instead of a little red one; the plurality of cultures constituted a plurality of educational institutions. The tool for the discovery of the manifold educational processes -- and hence also for a more adequate approach to the engineering of pluralistic education -- was science, that is, anthropology. The faith in social engineering and in the possibility of a new educational pluralism also underwrote the action programs among American Indians, who by means of the new techniques were to become autonomous participants in a more pluralistic and tolerant America.

But like the anthropology of Social Darwinism before it, the anthropology of Liberal Reform did not address itself, in any substantive way, to the problem of power. Humankind was seen as infinitely malleable, and the socialization processes of personalities in different cultures as enormously diverse in their means as well as in their ends. But only rarely -- if at all -- did anthropologists shift their scientific focus to the constraints impeding both human malleability and malleability in socialization from the outside. At the risk of overstating my case I would say that the anthropology of the period of Liberal Reform placed the burden for change on the freely volunteered participation of the participants, drawn from both the culture under consideration and from among their neighbors. It might no longer deal with a given culture as an object lesson in history, but as an object in itself. Yet just as the Social Darwinists had made a moral paradigm of the evolutionary process, so the culture-and-personality schools of the 30's and 40's made a moral paradigm of each individual culture. They spoke of patterns, themes, world view, ethos,,

6

and values, but not of power. In seeing culture as more or less of an organic whole, they asserted some of the claims of earlier intellectual predecessors who had seen in "political economy" an organic model for the explanation of a vast range of cultural phenomena. But where "political economy" explicitly emphasized the processes by which an organization of power is equipped with economic resources as central to the organic constellation to be explained, the anthropologist's culture of the 30's and 40's was "political economy" turned inside out, all ideology and morality, and neither power nor economy. Neither in the 19th century nor in the first half of the 20th century, therefore, did American anthropology as such come to grips with the phenomenon of power. It is with this legacy of unconcern that we enter the period of the present, a period in which the phenomenon of power is uppermost in men's minds.

This period, it seems to me, is characterized by two opposing and yet interconnected trends. The first of these is the growth of a war-machine which is becoming the governing mechanism of our lives. Whether we are radicals or liberals or conservatives, we have a prevailing sense that knowledge is not sufficient to put things right; we have come up against institutional restraints which may have to be removed before changes can occur. Gone is the halcyon feeling that knowledge alone, including anthropological knowledge, will set men free. On the other hand, the pacific or pacified objects of our investigation, primitive and peasants alike, are ever more prone to define our field situation gun in hand. A new vocabulary is abroad in the world. It speaks of "imperialism," "colonialism," "neo-colonialism," and "internal colonialism," rather than just of primitives and civilized, or even of developed and under-developed. Yet anthropology has in the past always operated among pacified or pacific natives; when the native "hits back" we are in a very different situation from that in which we found ourselves only yesterday. Thus the problem of power has suddenly come to the fore for us; and it exists in two ways, as power exerted within our own system and as power exerted from the outside, often against us, by populations we so recently thought incapable of renewed assertion and resistance.

Yet neither the intellectual endeavors of Social Darwinism nor the period of Liberal Reform have equipped us to deal with the phenomenon of power. In these matters we are babes in the woods, indeed, "babes in the darkling woods," as H. G. Wells entitled one of his last novels. We confront the problem of understanding power at a time when the very signposts of understanding are themselves growing confused and irrelevant.

This is not only our own situation. Stillmann and Pfaff, political scientists, write of this as an age in which

> the world practices politics, originated in the Western
> historical experience, whose essentially optimistic and
> rationalistic assumptions fail utterly to account for the
> brutality and terror which are the principal public ex-
> periences of the twentieth century... neither tragedy nor

7

irrationality are to be understood in terms of the political philosophies by which the West and now the world, conducts its public life (1964:238).

Daniel Bell, in a similar vein of ambiguity, entitles a book of essays The End of Ideology, and subtitles it On the Exhaustion of Political Ideas in the Fifties; and John Higham summarizes the mood of present-day American historians by saying that

> Most of the major postwar scholars seem to be asking in one way or another, what (if anything) is so deeply rooted in our past that we can rely on its survival. This has become, perhaps, the great historical question in a time of considerable moral confusion, when the future looks precarious and severely limited in its possibilities (1965:226).

Yet where some are lost in doubt, others assert a brutal return to Machiavellianism, to a naked power politics, abstracted from the social realities which underlie it. "The modern politician," write Stephen Rousseas and James Farganis,

> is the man who understands how to manipulate and how to operate in a Machiavellian world which divorces ethics from politics. Modern democracy becomes, in this view, transformed into a system of techniques sans telos. And democratic politics is reduced to a constellation of self-seeking pressure groups peaceably engaged in a power struggle to determine the allocation of privilege and particular advantage (1965:270-271).

On the international plane, this has meant recourse to a "new realism," most evident in the application of game theory to what the Germans so charmingly call the international "chickenspiel." This new realism emphasized technique over purpose, the how of political relations over their whys and wherefores. Where opponents of this approach argue that such a new emphasis sacrifices the hope of understanding the causes of such politics, its defenders argue, as true American pragmatists, that what matters is the world as given, and what counts is the most rational deployment of our resources to respond to present-day dilemmas. What counts in Viet Nam is not how "we" got there, but that "we" are there. Two kinds of rationality thus oppose each other, a substantive rationality which aims at a critical understanding of the world, and perhaps even at critical action, and a formal or technical rationality which understands the world in terms of technical solutions.

In this argument social scientists find themselves heavily involved. Some feel, with Ithiel de Sola Pool (1967:268-269), that

8

The only hope for humane government in the future is through the extensive use of the social sciences by government.... The McNamara revolution is essentially the bringing of social science analysis into the operation of the Department of Defense. It has remade American defense policy in accordance with a series of ideas that germinated in the late 1950's in the RAND Corporation among people like Schelling, Wohlstetter, Kahn, and Kaufmann. These were academic people playing their role as social scientists (whatever their early training may have been). They were trying to decide with care and seriousness what would lead to deterrence and what would undermine it. While one might argue with their conclusions at any given point, it seems to me that it is the process that has been important. The result has been the humanization of the Department of Defense. That is a terribly important contribution to the quality of American life.

Others will echo C. Wright Mills when he described the selfsame set of social scientists as:

...crackpot realists, who, in the name of realism have constructed a paranoid reality all their own and in the name of practicality have projected a utopian image of capitalism. They have replaced the responsible interpretation of events by the disguise of meaning in a maze of public relations, respect for public debate by unshrewd notions of psychological warfare, intellectual ability by the agility of the sound and mediocre judgement, and the capacity to elaborate alternatives and to gauge their consequences by the executive stance (1962:610-611).

Anthropologists, like other social scientists, cannot evade the dilemmas posed by the return to Machiavellian politics. Yet our major response has been one of retreat. This retreat is all the more notable when we realize that wholly anthropological ideas have suddenly been taken over and overtaken by other disciplines. Political scientists have appropriated the anthropological concept of "tradition" and used it to build a largely fictitious polarity between traditional and modern societies; Marshall McLuhan has made use of largely anthropological insights to project the outlines of the communication revolution of the present and future. In contrast to the 'thirties and 'forties when anthropology furnished the cutting edge of innovation in social science, we face at the moment a descent into triviality and irrelevance. This descent into triviality seems to me, above all, marked by an increasing concern for pure technique; important as our technical heritage is for all of us, it cannot in and of itself quicken the body of our discipline without the accession of new ideas. Technique without ideas grows sterile; the application of improved

9

techniques to inherited ideas is the mark of the epigone. This is true regardless of whether anthropologists put themselves at the service of the new realists, or whether they seek refuge in an uncertain ivory tower.

Someone who diagnoses an illness should also prescribe remedies. If I am correct in saying that anthropology has reached its present impasse because it has so systematically disregarded the problems of power, then we must find ways of educating ourselves in the realities of power. One way I can think of accomplishing this is to engage ourselves in the systematic writing of a history of the modern world in which we spell out the processes of power which created the present-day cultural systems and the linkages between them. I do not mean history in the sense of "one damned thing after another"; I mean a critical and comprehensive history of the modern world. It is not irrelevant to the present state of American anthropology that the main efforts at analyzing the interplay of societies and cultures on a world scale in anthropological terms have come from Peter Worsley (1964), an Englishman, and from Darcy Ribeiro (1968), a Brazilian. Where, in our present-day anthropological literature, are the comprehensive studies of the slave trade, the fur trade, of colonial expansion, of forced and voluntary acculturation, of rebellion and accomodation in the modern world, which would provide us with the intellectual grid needed to order the massive data we now possess on individual societies and cultures engulfed by these phenomena? We stand in need of such a project, I believe, not only as a learning experience for ourselves, but also as a responsible intellectual contribution to the world in which we live, so we may act to change it.

REFERENCES

Bell, Daniel
   1960   The End of Ideology (Glencoe: Free Press).
Darrah, William C.
   1951   Powell of the Colorado (Princeton: Princeton University Press).
Higham, John
   1965   History (Englewood Cliffs: Prentice-Hall).
Hofstadter, Richard
   1959   Social Darwinism in American Thought (New York: Braziller).
Mills, C. Wright
   1963   Power, Politics and People (New York: Ballantine Books).
Pearce, Roy H.
   1953   The Savages of America (Baltimore: The Johns Hopkins Press).
Pool, Ithiel de Sola
   1967   The Necessity for Social Scientists Doing Research for Government. In The Rise and Fall of Project Camelot, Irving L. Horowitz, ed. (Cambridge: The M.I.T. Press), pp. 267-280.

10

Ribeiro, Darcy
    1968   The Civilizational Process (Washington: Smithsonian
                Institution Press).
Rousseas, Stephen and James Farganis
    1965   American Politics and the End of Ideology. In The New
                Sociology, Irving I. Horowitz, ed. (New York: Oxford
                University Press), pp. 268-289.
Stillmann, Edmund and William Pfaff
    1964   The Politics of Hysteria (New York: Harper Colophon Books).
Worsley, Peter
    1964   The Third World (London: Weidenfeld and Nicholson).

11

THE PERSONALITY AND SUBCULTURE OF ANTHROPOLOGISTS
AND THEIR STUDY OF U. S. NEGROES[1]

Ann Fischer
Tulane University

The outstanding fact about anthropological studies of U. S. Negroes is the paucity of community studies based on participant observation. Herskovits complained of this in The Myth of the Negro Past nearly 30 years ago, and Charles Valentine (1968) and Margaret Mead (1968) are still complaining about it today. Anthropologists have skillfully avoided the social life of the U. S. Negro as a subject for study, while Trinidad, Jamaican, and Colombian Negroes do not lack for eager participant observers. Even in these more distant places, however, the student of Negro life often seeks out the folklore, music, religion, and history for study -- all subjects which might be called Culture with a big "C".

Avoidance of field work among U. S. Negroes can be explained in terms of the anthropologist, his personality and his professional culture. If the psycho-social professional needs of the anthropologist are listed on one side of the balance, and what studies of Negroes have to offer in satisfying those needs on the other, it is clear that studies of Negroes could generally not be very rewarding to anthropologists. This paper is concerned with the problem of why we have avoided ethnographical studies of Negroes in the U. S. It will also consider the studies which have been done in relationship to the general avoidance pattern.

Except for very recent times, most interest in Negroes on the part of anthropologists was shown in the 1930's when Hortense Powdermaker and Melville Herskovits did studies of major interest. At that early date, due to the Great Depression, money was even scarcer than anthropologists. The Negro presented an inexpensive field experience, but a field experience that could never really be complete. In doing field work in Negro communities, Powdermaker, Dollard, and Davis all had to conform to the mores of the day and had to live in the appropriate caste section of the towns they studied rather than in the most propitious locations for good observation. Inevitably, this led to shaping the field problems to the possible rather than to problems of interest to the anthropologist. The procedure always seemed to arrive at the same end -- the same matter for study -- that is, the problem of race relations or racial comparisons, for it was always this that furnished the field worker the greatest discomfort and, as a result, kept his attention.

Hortense Powdermaker, for example, went to Indianola intending to study the Negro community. Living and interacting with the whites, by the end of the first month she writes, "I soon realized that an understanding of [the whites] , their behavior and their attitudes was essential. I knew, too, that they had to trust me as a person if I was to work freely with Negroes and if no harm was to come to the Negroes " (Powdermaker 1966:149).

12

Herskovits, who had done field work elsewhere among Negroes, did not have very much actual contact with southern U. S. Negroes. The Myth of the Negro Past was written largely out of information obtained in libraries -- an even more appropriate technique than field work when funds were scarce.

The above remarks are not intended to reflect on the research done among Negroes by Powdermaker and other anthropologists of that day. Such research was dangerous and those who tried it deserve great admiration. The field work problem is one reason Negro studies have failed to attract many anthropologists. The heart and soul of the profession is the field experience. It comes very close to being a sacred experience. It is certainly an initiation rite, and it is almost a "vision" quest. Field work is thought to accomplish a great deal in terms of the world view of the anthropologist and is even considered capable of bringing about basic personality changes in him. Clyde Kluckholm used to say in lectures that field work in a number of cultures was equivalent to a full-fledged psychoanalysis.

Although field work is a general requirement in anthropology, the evaluation of any particular field work experience varies according to the location and situation. Field work among U. S. Negroes does not fare well if it is evaluated on a number of dimensions used to evaluate a field experience with regard to its contribution to professional status. These include: (1) distance from the U. S. (both geographical and cultural), (2) the degree of cultural shock value of the culture studied from the point of view of Westerners, (3) the primitiveness of the culture studied, (4) the value of the culture in terms of theoretical problems of interest to anthropologists, (5) the number of anthropologists who have done field work in the culture or in adjacent regions (the fewer the fieldworkers the higher the status of the experience), (6) the physical difficulties involved in doing field work in the culture, (7) the time spent in the field, and (8) the comparative excellence of the field work, which may be disguised to an extent by excellence and speed in reporting if no other experts are available to dispute the report.

One of the most problematical factors in doing field work among Negroes is that professional status is not enhanced by field work in a culture not considered foreign to the anthropologist. That research must be focused on foreign people or subjects is the professional anthropologist's equivalent of the surgeon's custom of not operating on members of his own family. All professions eschew any emotional involvement that is likely to influence objectivity. If the anthropologist studies Negroes, or for that matter, Americans, he is put on the defensive. I myself have done three studies which immediately put an anthropological audience on alert for attack on any possible weakness. These were: (1) a study of a New England village and the child training practices there, (2) a study of New Orleans Negroes, and (3) a study of women in anthropology. This latter was perhaps the most sensitive subject matter of the three studies; the role of women is a very dangerous topic for a professional woman to investigate. The audience was small and might be said to have been frightened to be there. On the other hand, audiences for papers on the American Negro used to be small, but over the last several years they have drawn increasing numbers at annual meetings of anthropologists. Over the last five years the

13

size of rooms for groups of papers on Negroes has grown increasingly large. The audiences, by the way, tend to be exceptionally argumentative and often hostile. The subject matter which draws most hostility is that of sex roles. This fact in itself, in my opinion, settles the question of whether or not the Negro has "a culture" which is foreign to American culture as a whole. Only a close similarity in culture could arouse such heated debate.

The anthropologist's dictum about studying cultures which are foreign to one's own is aimed at professional objectivity -- a defense against the interference of emotions in scientific judgement. Following the rules of objectivity in the large gray area in which the Negro falls culturally is one factor leading to avoidance of the subject altogether. An interesting analogy with music was suggested to me by Norma McLeod, who maintains that music involving values which cannot be clearly categorized as either representative of Western musical values or definitely different from Western musical values makes her physically ill, and she says that other ethnomusicologists have reported this same experience. The problem of Negro culture is equally irritating.

According to the dictums of professional anthropology, then, the Negro must have "a separate culture" and "a foreign culture" to be a suitable subject matter for professional study. Many studies of the U. S. Negro show this professional concern with defining Negro culture and a certain defensiveness in establishing the Negro as an appropriate subject for study. I myself have spent some time on the question of whether the Negro has a culture which is separate from general American culture. Herskovits' effort is also an example. He tried to place the origins of at least some of Negro life in Africa and searched diligently for evidences of Africanisms. As Miles Richardson (1968) pointed out to me, Herskovits did this at a time when Negroes themselves were completely unconcerned with their African origins. Their efforts at that time, Richardson said, and I agree, were simply to make Negroes more like whites. In retrospect, Herskovits furnishes comfort to Negroes trying to re-establish their African ties today. Richardson sees some guilty colonialism in this approach which seems to say that the histories of Negroes were not completely destroyed with the move to American plantations. At present, when Negroes wish to be more African, the general trend is to show them to be American. As Richardson points out, anthropologists seem to be "contrarions." To me, Herskovits' position in professional anthropology seems a more plausible explanation for his choice of subject matter. He seems to have felt that if the Negro were to be a suitable subject for him as an anthropologist, it first had to be shown that the Negro had his own foreign culture or at the very least, and as a less desirable alternative, his own sub-culture.

This problem of whether the Negro has a culture has been a major concern -- anthropological as well as sociological -- of those who have studied the Negro. The solution proposed has a number of versions. Walter Miller finds adolescent Negro gang culture a "variant" lower class culture. The special variation he mentions is the originality and inventiveness in the areas of language and clothing. Others say that Negro culture is the same as lower class culture. It is a good guess that those who contend that Negro and lower class culture are equivalent have never been involved in studies of a Negro

14

group, for this point of view disavows the Negro as a subject in need of primary anthropological attention.

In recent years I detect a new point of view regarding the existence of Negro culture. The new view tends to imply that Negroes throughout the Americas have a common culture which is caused by adaptation to the socio-environment of slavery. The resulting culture in this view represents the limited number of solutions to this adaptational problem. Regardless of the model of causality or the definition of Negro culture the student arrives at, the problem of a culture for Negroes is still a paramount concern in anthropological studies of American Negroes.

Aside from the need of the anthropologist to have the group he studies represent some kind of definite cultural entity, other factors in doing field work among Negroes are not favorable to attaining status in the anthropological profession. One factor is that the shock value of Negro life for the profession has been fairly well exploited and understood by Kardiner (1951), Rainwater (1966), and others in studies of sex relations and family life. Another factor is that any particular anthropologist is not the sole expert on the subject of Negro life. Anyone who thinks otherwise will be quickly disillusioned on this score by delivering a paper at a meeting, where almost any statement is readily challenged by an audience of experts.

Another factor in avoidance of Negro communities as matters for study is the problem of rapport. The loss of rapport in field work is a major anthropological sin. Your informants must love you. The modern Negro community offers a tremendous risk in this regard. The love of Negro informants for white anthropologists is tempered by the times and by the needs of the Negro community itself. Rapport in the Negro community cannot be gained with gifts of glass beads or pieces of cloth or cigarettes. It can occasionally be gained by working for the socio-economic advancement of the community, but even here the field is crowded with local talent.

Above all, avoidance of Negro studies may be due to the fact that the doctrine of cultural relativity is challenged by their case. Margaret Mead came to the heart of the problem in a recent lecture at Tulane. Her partial answer was that "the ethos of anthropology requires us to respect and value the cultures of those we study. Anthropologists would never be able to convince ghetto residents that we respect or admire their way of life. Ghetto residents would feel that anyone coming to live in the ghetto voluntarily was out of his mind" (1968).

The question then arises: Are we unwilling to study the U. S. Negro because his place in our society challenges the very foundations upon which anthropology has become such a popular science? Certainly Negro social life still fits the doctrine of cultural relativity in the broad sense that it represents a fairly good, perhaps the very best possible, social adaptation to conditions as they are in our society for the Negro. But does Negro social life fit the picture of culture as a cohesive, coherent way of life with beautiful, if puzzling, patterns wending their way through the institutions of the group? There is evidently a flaw somewhere in our theory of cultural relativity. Can it be that

15

the responsiveness of culture to the environment is one thing, while the benevolence of that responsiveness for the development of man and for his pleasure or even for his survival is another? Is the view that makes culture an "object of art" not reminiscent of the use of anthropological data or principles in preserving colonialism?

In their theoretical approach anthropologists have not allowed for flaws in culture. Recognition of flaws leads too readily into activist roles in relation to society -- roles which anthropologists as scholars have long avoided and thought distasteful. An architect or an artist does not expect to build the perfect building or paint the perfect picture and may even assume that perfection is not desirable in any case. Anthropologists have been more idealistic in this regard and have not allowed for imperfections in culture in their theories.

Culture considered as an admirable and beautiful object seems reasonable enough when dealing with a primitive group far from civilization, particularly where the anthropologist cannot hope to effect changes in those conditions to which the group must adapt. Yet when one environmental reality is clearly more beneficial to its constituents than another, the doctrine of cultural relativity becomes repugnant to an environmentally deprived group. It is perfectly obvious in the case of the Negro that social rather than physical conditions are causal to his harsh environment. Under these circumstances, the anthropologist, as a representative of the oppressive cultural majority, cannot very well play the role of defender of his people so often played under colonial conditions.

On the positive side, studies of Negro communities offer the opportunity for anthropologists to get at the core of some important theoretical problems. The Negro community is a perfect setting for studies in the developing field of urban anthropology. Existing theories in anthropology face some exciting challenges when applied to urban life.

In summary, anthropologists have avoided the study of the U. S. Negro generally. Where the Negro has been studied, procedures or theoretical problems have focused on shaping the Negro up as an appropriate subject for anthropological study: giving him a culture, studying those aspects of his culture which are clearly good in our terms, studying the more shocking aspects of Negro life, and studying Negroes with reference to adaptations to an unfortunate environment. While building their intellectually beautiful but often unreal patterns of culture, anthropologists leave aside the whole irritating problem of why man makes himself miserable and presents obstacles to the adaptation of the total human species.

NOTES

1. The term Negroes is used here instead of the presently preferred term, Blacks. The reason is that the title of Herskovits' book, about which this paper is largely concerned, used the term Negro.

16

REFERENCES

Davis, Allison and John Dollard
    1940   Children of Bondage (Washington, D.C.: American Council
                   on Education).
Davis, Allison, Burleigh B. Gardner, and Mary R. Gardner
    1941   Deep South (Chicago: University of Chicago Press).
Herskovits, Melville J.
    1958   The Myth of the Negro Past (Boston: Beacon Press).
Kardiner, Abraham, and L. Ovesey
    1951   The Mark of Oppression: A Psychosocial Study of the
                   American (New York: Norton).
Mead, Margaret
    1968   Lecture at Tulane University.
Miller, Walter B.
    1959   Implications of Urban-Lower-Class Culture for Social Work.
                   Social Service Review 33:219-236.
Powdermaker, Hortense
    1966   Stranger and Friend (New York: W. W. Norton and Company,
                   Inc.).
Rainwater, Lee
    1966   The Crucible of Identity: The Negro Lower Class Family.
                   Daedalus 95:172-216.
Richardson, Miles
    1968   Personal Communication.
Valentine, Charles A.
    1968   Culture and Poverty: Critique and Counter-Proposals
                   (Chicago: University of Chicago Press).

17

THE CONCEPT OF A CULTURE

E. Pendleton Banks
Wake Forest University

It is perhaps too soon after the American Ethnological Society symposium on the concept of tribe (Helm 1968) to re-open the question of the validity of the concept of a culture, since many of the considerations relating to the concept were discussed ably by the participants in that symposium. But it may be of value to restate the problem, review some of the solutions that have been suggested, and explore the implications of some previous contributions in the context of a critical examination of other assumptions that underlie anthropological research.

It is fashionable these days to bemoan the methodological naiveté of anthropologists (Moerman 1968:166). Whether this represents a case of diffusion from other disciplines, such as sociology, where methodological breast beating has been fashionable for decades, or whether it is a case of innovation traceable to a single source, such as Kluckhohn's (1940) critique of Middle American studies, I will not attempt to decide. It is no doubt a healthy activity, even though the recency of the fashion obscures the fact that individual anthropologists have been concerned with methodological problems far longer and more constantly than the literature would suggest. No research experience that I know of is so conducive to prolonged and profound self-examination as anthropological field work, and the marginal position of anthropology (Is it a natural science, a social science, or a humanity?) guarantees sensitivity to methodological and conceptual points that is perhaps rare among ordinary practitioners of the natural sciences.

When it comes to the concept of a culture -- what Taylor (1948) called the partitive, in contrast to the holistic, meaning of the word -- there is no doubt that we have been naive. While good ethnographers have acknowledged the problem of identifying the cultural units they are describing and have often furnished careful and detailed accounts of the cultural, linguistic, social, and geographic boundaries of their units of study (cf. Moerman 1967, 1968), most of us, I suspect, use terms like "Navaho culture" and "Japanese culture" (or worse, pairs like "Pueblo culture" and "Zuni culture") without clarifying for ourselves or our hearers what we mean. In defense of the practice I might point out that it occurs most often in informal discourse, in lectures, and in non-technical writing, that is, in contexts in which precise and therefore cumbersome syntax is inappropriate.[1] It is entirely too convenient a practice to give up.

But to remain uncritical about the term in the context of professional discourse is indefensible. The time has passed when any proposition containing references to "a culture," "culture x," or "cultures" can be taken seriously unless the terms are carefully and explicitly defined. Now, there is no doubt that the terms can be defined on an ad hoc basis as needed: we have no real

18

difficulty in explaining the differences between the meaning of "culture" in the phrase "Navaho culture" and the phrase "Japanese culture," nor in discussing the differences in the basis of our knowledge about these entities.

The real problem that has not yet been resolved is whether it is possible to give a general definition of the term "culture" in the partitive sense -- or if you prefer, a general set of instructions for delimiting a culture. I propose to discuss some of the proposed solutions to the problem. These usually fall under three headings: (1) social definitions, that is, those derived from definitions of societies or other social units; (2) linguistic definitions, those derived from linguistically defined groups or those based on linguistic analogies; and (3) cultural definitions, those based on a theory about culture.

Social Definitions

> A culture is a historically derived system of explicit and implicit designs for living, which tends to be shared by all or specially designated members of a group (Kluckhohn and Kelly 1945:98).

This is a typical social definition, and it is interesting that the parts of the definition that have been considered controversial -- "explicit...implicit," "designs for living," "shared" -- do not include the word "group." It has been taken for granted that the group exists or can be defined with precision; yet if that assumption is shown to be faulty the entire definition falls.

In fact, no one has demonstrated that mankind comes in neat packages, whether called groups or societies. Those social scientists who deal with such topics have found it necessary to resort to all kinds of conceptual and methodological subtleties merely to identify and delimit such social units as "social systems," "societies," or "communities." Meanwhile some argue that culture and society are not separate entities and that to define one in terms of the other is tautological (Levy 1952). Even if we do not accept this position Sapir has exposed another weakness:

> The so-called culture of a group of human beings, as it is ordinarily treated by the cultural anthropologist, is essentially a systematic list of all the socially inherited patterns of behavior which may be illustrated in the actual behavior of all or most of the individuals of the group. The true locus, however, of these processes which, when abstracted into a totality, constitute culture is not in a theoretical community of human beings known as society, for the term "society" is itself a cultural construct which is employed by individuals who stand in significant relations to each other in order to help them in the interpretation of certain aspects of their behavior (Sapir 1932:515-516, quoted in Kroeber and Kluckhohn 1963:247).

19

And Kroeber and Kluckhohn (1963:367) point out that a culture may outlive its original society (e.g., Roman culture) or may overlap social boundaries of whatever degree (Mohammedan culture).

We may adopt one of the following positions: (1) wait for someone to produce a defensible formula for identifying a society, or (2) accept the fact that a group can be delimited arbitrarily and agree to consider its shared patterns as a culture. The first solution seems unsatisfactory because it evades responsibility, and the second confronts us with the existence of cultures within cultures <u>ad infinitum</u>. If there are as many cultures as there are human groups we might as well abandon the use of culture in the partitive sense. Perhaps there is another way out.

<u>Linguistic Definitions</u>

Cultural anthropologists have often looked to linguists for help in solving their own problems. Practically they have made use of linguistic behavior in the field to identify social and cultural boundaries. This approach assumes that those who speak different languages carry different cultures and may lead to the assumption that for every language there is a culture. This requires a basic assumption that languages exist as separate and identifiable entities.

Hymes (1968) has given a thorough critique of this approach, and I will not attempt to repeat all of the criticisms. Briefly, this approach ignores such problems as the mutual intelligibility of adjacent languages; the problem of whether a language is a language or a dialect (it is instructive to hear Sinologists debate the issue of whether Chinese is one language or many); and the fact that even when linguistic boundaries can be determined they do not necessarily coincide with cultural boundaries. As Hymes (1968:36) puts it: "...to rely on facts of language to determine boundaries of cultural communication amounts to a form of strong linguistic determinism." And he summarizes the basic reason for questioning this approach: "...<u>any language-involving term in any definition of ethnic or cultural unit -- is to be regarded, not as a constant, but as a variable</u>" (Hymes 1968:30).[2]

Thus when a cultural anthropologist goes beyond the pragmatic level to make linguistic features a part of a general definition of a cultural unit he is building upon sand. Take Naroll's definition, the fruit of one of the more ambitious recent attempts to settle the problem:

> Cultunit -- People who are domestic speakers of a common distinct language and who belong either to the same state or the same contact group (Naroll 1964:286; see also Naroll 1967).

Following Hymes we must question "common," "distinct," and "language," not to mention the problems raised by the final clause.

It is ironic that those areas where cultural anthropologists may look to linguists for valid conceptual and methodological assistance -- in the search for cultural regularities or units comparable to the phoneme and morpheme --

20

are precisely the areas of least value for defining cultures.

Cultural Definitions

It is not necessary to postulate the complete autonomy of cultural phenomena in order to produce relatively independent conceptual models of culture. Cultural anthropologists have not hesitated to compose definitions of culture in the holistic sense that omit references to society or even to man. For example, "Culture is an organization of phenomena -- material objects, bodily acts, ideas, and sentiments -- which consists of or is dependent upon the use of symbols" (White 1943:335, quoted in Kroeber and Kluckhohn 1963:137). They have even assigned a derivative status to society (see Sapir's comment quoted above) and sometimes to man himself.

There is no shortage of propositions that impute some kind of inner organization to individual cultures. The structuralist or configurationist theorists from Benedict to Lévi-Strauss have generated numerous propositions of this type. If culture has structure, and if the structure is not universal -- if we can distinguish between an "Apollonian" and a "Dionysian" culture -- then structural properties should provide a basis for delimiting cultures. Unfortunately the structuralists have not as far as I know addressed themselves to the task of making the delimiting procedure systematic. Thus Kroeber and Kluckhohn (1963:367):

> ...the lines of demarcation of any cultural unit chosen for
> description and analysis are in large part a matter of level
> of abstraction and of convenience for the problem at hand.
> Occidental culture, Graeco-Roman culture, nineteenth-century
> European culture, German culture, Swabian culture, the peas-
> ant culture of the Black Forest in 1900 -- these are all
> equally legitimate abstractions if carefully defined.[3]

In short, when it comes to designating a specific culture one proceeds without necessary reference to the conceptual apparatus of structuralism. Surely this is a remarkable statement following, as it does, a paragraph and a footnote arguing that "patterning is what gives to each culture its selective and distinctive life-way" and that "only particular cultures have structure" (Kroeber and Kluckhohn 1963:366-367).

Actually the impetus to look for a rigorous technique for delimiting cultures has come from an entirely different source: the field of quantitative cross-cultural research. From the beginning this field has been plagued by "Galton's problem": the necessity of demonstrating the independence of cases and the validity of sampling if statistical measures of correlation or association are to be used. Recently a number of publications have dealt with Galton's problem and possible solutions (Köbben 1952; McNett and Kirk 1968; Murdock 1966, 1967; Naroll 1964, 1967; Naroll and D'Andrade 1963). Since most of these solutions employ rather large geographic distances between cultures as guarantees of independence, they are of limited use. While reference may be

21

made to purely cultural considerations, as in Murdock's (1967:3) concept of "clusters, whose cultures are genetically closely related and hence merit at most but a single representative in any world sample," at least one anthropologist interested in the problem of delimiting cultures denies that cross-cultural techniques have anything to contribute (Moerman 1967).

Some interesting possibilities have been suggested by two recent studies. In one, Hackenberg (1967) has used aerial photography, computerized data processing, and the genealogical method to define a total tribe. While his purpose does not coincide exactly with ours, he may have solved the methodological problem of finding the boundaries of a social entity and thus contributed indirectly to the solution of our problem. And if similar techniques could be adapted to the study of the distribution of culture traits rather than of people, we might find an operational if not a theoretical solution. The other study, by Hoffmann (1968), offers a program for doing just that in the context of set theory. While his vocabulary of "phase spaces," "transforms," and "trajectories" confronts the anthropologist with the problem of learning yet another foreign language, his approach offers at last an empirical technique of establishing clusters of traits or invariants that might serve to define discrete cultures.[4]

Consistent with the demand of the "new ethnography" that cultures be described in terms used by the bearers of the culture, Moerman (1965, 1968) argues that native ethnic categories should be utilized by ethnographers. His attention was drawn to the problem while doing research in Southeast Asia, an area that others have found especially confusing in this regard. He points out:

> It is often difficult to discern discontinuities of language, culture, polity, society, or economy with sufficient clarity to draw boundaries. It is this which makes me suggest that the delimitation of ethnic identities is especially problematic in all parts of the world which are continuously inhabited but not divided into either sharp ecological zones or strong and durable states (Moerman 1965:1215).

He goes on to indicate that the problem is probably more widespread than has been recognized. The essence of his recommendation is that the existence and nature of ethnic, social, linguistic, and other groupings be made a proper topic for field study, and that the formulations thus established will have a validity superior to the formulations imposed by the ethnographer on a priori grounds: "In order to identify and account for the survival of ethnic entities, I would suggest that we discover the criteria used for ethnic labelling at different taxonomic levels, compare the criteria used by entities that interact, determine whether such criteria are consciously manipulated, and analyze the mechanisms which maintain and inculcate the practice of the criteria through which members identify themselves or are recognized by others" (Moerman 1965:1225).

22

Conclusion

In my opinion the problem of the validity of the partitive concept of culture has not been solved. The concept has been shown to rest on shaky assumptions, whether leaning on concepts borrowed from other fields, such as sociology and linguistics, or on the theoretical foundations of cultural anthropology itself. Yet I do not propose that we abandon it. We will continue to speak of this culture and that culture, and it is hard to imagine how we could communicate otherwise.

I offer the following suggestions: (1) that whenever a culture is referred to in professional discourse, its referent should be carefully defined, whether by social, ethnic, linguistic, spatial, or temporal co-ordinates; (2) that we remind ourselves periodically of the heuristic, ad hoc nature of the usage; and (3) that we continue to search for both theoretical and practical solutions with emphasis on leads suggested by the theory of culture. This is an enterprise that structuralists, functionalists, specialists, generalists, old ethnographers, and new ethnographers can take part in. We may find in the end that culture is a continuous variable and that the postulating and delimiting of culture areas, clusters, whole cultures, part cultures, and subcultures must be an arbitrary operation. But if we do we will at least be able to perform the operation with confidence and honesty.[5]

NOTES

1. Imagine using Naroll's complete definition of a "cultunit" (1968:286-287) every time we wish to say "a culture."

2. Hymes' discussion of the problems involved in looking at linguistic phenomena associated with the communication of cultural material is valuable (Hymes 1968:36-37).

3. Italics mine.

4. Trait distribution studies have been used in the past to delimit culture areas, but Hoffmann's technique would require a considerable refinement of the traditional method as well as a new mathematical framework.

5. On the subject of the arbitrary identification of culture patterns that vary through space and time, see Ford (1954) and Steward (1954).

REFERENCES

Ford, James A.
 1954   On the Concept of Types: The Type Concept Revisited.
     American Anthropologist 56:42-54.

23

Fried, Morton H.
1968   On the Concepts of "Tribe" and "Tribal Society". In _Essays on the Problem of Tribe_, June Helm, ed. Proceedings of 1967 Spring Meeting of the American Ethnological Society (Seattle: University of Washington Press), pp. 3-20.

Hackenberg, Robert A.
1967   The Parameters of an Ethnic Group: A Method for Studying the Total Tribe. _American Anthropologist_ 69:478-492.

Helm, June, ed.
1968   _Essays on the Problem of Tribe_. Proceedings of the 1967 Spring Meeting of the American Ethnological Society (Seattle: University of Washington Press).

Hoffmann, Hans
1968   Mathematical Structures in Ethnological Systems. In _Essays on the Problem of Tribe_, June Helm, ed. Proceedings of the 1967 Spring Meeting of the American Ethnological Society (Seattle: University of Washington Press), pp. 49-57.

Hymes, Dell
1968   Linguistic Problems in Defining the Concept of "Tribe." In _Essays on the Problem of Tribe_, June Helm, ed. Proceedings of the 1967 Spring Meeting of the American Ethnological Society (Seattle: University of Washington Press), pp. 23-48.

Kluckhohn, Clyde
1941   Patterning as Exemplified in Navaho Culture. In _Language, Culture and Personality_, Leslie Spier, et.al., eds. (Menasha, Wisconsin: Banta), pp. 213-227.

Kluckhohn, Clyde and William H. Kelly
1945   The Concept of Culture. In _The Science of Man in the World Crisis_, Ralph Linton, ed. (New York: Columbia University Press).

Köbben, A. J.
1952   New Ways of Presenting an Old Idea: The Statistical Method in Social Anthropology. _Journal of the Royal Anthropological Institute_ 82:129-146.

Kroeber, A. L. and Clyde Kluckhohn
1963   _Culture: A Critical Review of Concepts and Definitions_ (New York: Vintage Books).

Levy, Marion J.
1952   _The Structure of Society_ (Princeton: Princeton University Press).

McKern, W. C.
1939   The Midwestern Taxonomic Method as an Aid to Archaeological Culture Study. _American Antiquity_ 4:301-313.

McNett, Charles W., Jr., and Roger E. Kirk
1968   Drawing Random Samples in Cross-Cultural Studies: A Suggested Method. _American Anthropologist_ 70:50-55.

24

Moerman, Michael
    1965   Who Are the Lue? American Anthropologist 67:1215-1230.
    1967   Reply to Naroll. American Anthropologist 69:512-513.
    1968   Being Lue: Uses and Abuses of Ethnic Identification.
                  In Essays on the Problem of Tribe, June Helm, ed., Pro-
                  ceedings of the 1967 Spring Meeting of the American
                  Ethnological Society (Seattle: University of Washington
                  Press), pp. 153-169.
Murdock, George Peter
    1966   Cross-Cultural Sampling. Ethnology 5:97-114.
    1967   Ethnographic Atlas (Pittsburgh: University of Pittsburgh
                  Press).
Naroll, Raoul
    1964   On Ethnic Unit Classification. Current Anthropology
                  5:283-291.
    1967   Native Concepts and Cross-Cultural Surveys. American
                  Anthropologist 69:511-512.
Naroll, Raoul and Roy G. D'Andrade
    1963   Two Further Solutions to Galton's Problem. American
                  Anthropologist 65:1053-1067.
Steward, Julian H.
    1954   On the Concept of Types: Types of Types. American
                  Anthropologist 56:54-57.
Taylor, Walter W.
    1948   A Study of Archaeology. Memoirs of the American Anthro-
                  pological Association, No. 69.

25

A SCIENCE OF MAN AND OTHER POSSIBILITIES

Munro S. Edmonson
Tulane University

Even the purveyors of textbooks who visit my office each spring have now become aware that anthropology has passed from a period of rapid growth into one of downright confusion. To those of us in the profession, who must cope personally and directly with the modern trends and development of the science, a measure of real disorientation attends the contemplation of our colleagues riding off in all directions while our own earnest efforts and particular interests seem only to increase our distance from one another at an ever-accelerating rate. A measure of such centrifugal movement is obviously necessary to a maturing science, but in recent years the question of what anthropology is and where it is going has been raised more often and with more anxious insistency than ever before. It is not too early to inquire whether the field is doomed to be dismembered into separate specialties, the autonomy of some of which is already considerable. It is not too late to suggest that perhaps we have a joint future as anthropologists despite the immense magnitude of our problems and the enormous scope of our interests and the necessarily forbidding specializations into which these have led us.

In some part our very commitment to anthropology leads us to the past for possible answers to these questions. For surely what anthropology has been is one of the most important factors in determining what it can become. Yet for an historical science, anthropology is not particularly rich in histories of itself. Those we have tend to be partial or dated, or both, and there is as yet no comprehensive source in which the history of the discipline can be extensively examined. We are, indeed, rapidly approaching the point where such a history will be beyond the capacity of any scholar.

Meanwhile I should like to offer some modest data which, I believe, give some perspective to our present situation and our prospects. This paper is a survey of the general interests of anthropology as indicated by the titles and subtitles of anthropological books and monographs as they have changed through time. I can, of course, claim neither completeness of coverage nor lack of bias, but I believe even these sketchy data may be of some interest in relation to our current reappraisal and reexamination of our subject.

From a general bibliography of anthropological works containing some 7,500 titles, I have selected for examination all those books and monographs whose titles do not restrict them geographically. I have, thus, a list of some 2,200 works of a "general," "topical," or "theoretical" character which I believe to be representative of the technical literature of anthropology, broadly conceived, though not exhaustively sampled. The longer list includes all works cited in the standard histories of the field, as well as the complete bibliographies of a number of other standard works. Suspecting the inevitable

26

ethnocentric bias of my own cultural and geographic location, I have made little systematic effort to fill in American sources, but on the other hand I have worked hard on the non-English sources in more or less direct proportion to their inaccessibility to me. Although this bibliography was compiled for general purposes, I suspect that Spanish sources are overrepresented because books in that language come readily to my attention. I suspect that the minor European languages and others are seriously underrepresented. At no point, however, has the compilation been influenced by selection directly relevant to the facts here reported. Doubtless, the list is weaker in archaeology, prehistory, and physical anthropology than it should be, but I do not believe that even this bias is material to my conclusions.

Personally, I find it reassuring to discover that incomparably the commonest word in the titles of general anthropological works is "man" (homo, hombre, homme, Mensch, uomo, chelovek) (217). "Anthropology" (114) itself shares second place with "culture" (115). "Race" (94) and "history" (95) tie for third, followed by "origin" (75), "primitive" (65), "evolution" (57), "prehistory" (40), "archaeology" (40), "social" (38), and "society" (36) in that order. Other frequent terms are "civilization," "ethnology," "language," "myth," "psychology," "religion," "nature," "science," "people," and "ethnography." I believe these words describe the perennial interests of anthropology reasonably well.

"Man" has not always stood at the center of anthropology. Indeed, he does not now. In fact, from the completion of Magnus Hundt's Anthropologium de hominis dignitate in 1501 until 1900, the concept of "history" had that honor. From 1900 to 1910 "race" was the most frequent title word. But from 1910 to 1950 ours had indeed been the science of "man." Since 1950 "man" has been displaced by "culture." I do not believe any serious student of anthropology would consider this gross finding to be indicative only of fortuitous fads of title selection.

So much for words. The most frequent title words of general anthropology may be grouped at a slightly more abstract level around four root concepts -- anthropos, ethnos, cultura, and societas -- each of which has been, and remains today, the center of a particular conception of anthropological science. I omit the concepts of "science" and "history," which occupy, I think it will be agreed, a somewhat special position. I believe it is substantially accurate to say that anthropology has tried at various times to be a science (or history) of man, peoples, culture, and society, and that these are still the most general choices which confront us.

The gradual apposition of the concept of science with the concept of man has been one of the great intellectual adventures of modern times. In the crowded history of the last two centuries so much has been done with these ideas that it is easy to forget the considerable development they had already been reached by the end of the eighteenth century. Yet the proto-anthropology of that early period had already explored the comparative anatomy of man and other primates and of various races, the potentialities of natural, universal, and philosophic history, the character of the human body, the "keys" to human

27

languages, and the customs of primitive men. A distinguished place in this early anthropology must be reserved for the educated chroniclers, historians, and relacionistas of the Spanish Empire whose trickle of often excellent descriptive and interpretative ethnography, united with scattered accounts of travelers in many lands, has swollen into the flood of modern data which is one of the glories of anthropology.

There can be little doubt, nonetheless, that the center of gravity of anthropological curiosity in 1800 lay in a natural history of man, nor that the nineteenth century brought sweeping changes to this conception. Problems of history, origins, and beginnings remained dominant in anthropological literature, but they were supplemented by new sciences and new concepts. Ethnography, archaeology, ethnology, sociology, anthropometry, folklore, prehistory, human geography, mythology, comparative religion, and comparative law were born, stimulated by comparable growth in other fields of inquiry. Culture, civilization, heredity, society, the primitive, and evolution became current, well-known, and influential ideas. Through all of these developments the counterpoint of history and science, Kulturgeschichte and Kulturwissenschaft Naturgeschichte and Naturwissenchaft, flickers through the intellectual history of the nineteenth century until it emerges ambiguously in most fields of anthropological work in the evolutionary synthesis at the end of the century.

The twentieth century reaction to this synthesis is too well-known to require comment. The distinctive character of twentieth century anthropology is reflected, however, in our increasing preoccupation with psychology, organization, and structure. Peoples displace races; genetics displaces heredity; linguistics displaces the study of language; and continuation of well-established nineteenth and even eighteenth century concepts rounds out the complex body of anthropological thought that is our heritage.

Throughout the corpus of our literature these various concepts overlap and fuse in intricate patterns of mutual influence in the works of various scholars. Nonetheless, it is my thesis that it is a different thing to study man and to study culture or primitives or society or evolution or structures, and I should like therefore to state the case for an anthropology which is the science of man. Let us consider some of the alternatives.

A Science of Ethnos

Even very early attempts to define our species reflect a concern for the differences among groups of men. Type (Menschenart), variety, subspecies, and race were necessary constructs for even the earliest essays at a description of man. These concepts have undergone considerable change, development, and refinement, but they are still with us. By 1822, Maupied could write a Prodrome d'ethnographie in which, as for a considerable period thereafter, the central meaning of ethnos was approximately what we should now call race. After Darwin, the biological content of the concept became ever more clearly divorced from the cultural content, until ethnology became nearly synonymous with culture history or the comparative study of ethnic cultures. Eventually a new term, raciology, would have to be coined for what ethnography

28

had once been.

In the later nineteenth century, race, folk, people, nationality, culture group, ethnic group, and kindred idioms in various European languages reflected the rapidly diversifying conceptions of ethnos. In a context dominated by the ancient, early, exotic, and primitive, "ethnic" came to connote strongly the natural cultural groupings of primitive peoples and folk communities, to which the national affiliations of Europeans were loosely analogized. Many scholars came to regard the special province of anthropology as the study of primitive peoples, and these words found their way onto the covers of increasing numbers of books of the period.

Evolutionary theorists of an earlier day had a special reason for considering primitive peoples or barbarians or savages apart from civilized man. Primitive people were a window to the past. Twentieth century anthropology has rejected this conception, but found new grounds for the distinction in relation to conceptions of complexity and simplicity, primary and secondary groups, Gesellschaft and Gemeinschaft, folk and sophisticate. Thus we became specialists on ancient or isolated groups of men, leaving civilization substantially to the historians and industrial societies to the sociologists. Profound and persuasive members of our profession continue to urge this convenient division of labor upon us in a new and more sophisticated evolutionism. In this connection "ethnic" continues to connote, somewhat ambiguously, the primitive, the folk, the popular, and the traditional.

An anthropology of ethnicity is urged upon us in a more universalist form by modern cultural psychology. An early Soviet review which accused Kardiner of racism badly misses the point in one dimension but is quite suggestive in others. For surely our studies of character and personality are predicated on the premise that some dimensions of ethnic culture can be remarkably stable, almost as stable as biological features, perhaps, even though they depend upon the stability of family life and unconscious but patterned learning. In considerable part it is this premise which has enabled the anthropologist to move comfortably from primitive to complex cultures, carrying with him expectations of similar, perduring, ethnically structured cultural situations. He is not always disappointed.

The concept of folklore has also been a nucleus of effort of some importance to the tasks of anthropology and a center of interest for scholars who find in folk communities and peasant populations a satisfactory base of intellectual operations. The distinctive character of folk literature, as of folk institutions, has become a matter of considerable controversy, and it seems apparent that anthropological folklorists are pulled in contrary directions to the interests of their belletristic colleagues in a degree which is tantamount to schism. Whether the operations of oral traditions are sufficiently distinctive from those of literate traditions to constitute a separate field of inquiry remains at this date at least an open question.

Whether we consider it evolutionally, psychologically, or folkloristically, ethnicity does not appear to be in any sense a permanent resting place for our science. For while the reflections of ethnos in both the biological and cultural spheres are distinctive and recognizable, its laws are not unique nor

29

its characteristics distinctive except in some matters of degree from those of other factors structuring the bio-social inheritance of mankind. Indeed, the study of ethnicity demands expansion. We cannot assert the peculiarity of the folk without studying the sophisticate; we cannot differentiate the primitive without appreciating what is not primitive; we cannot study cultural psychology as though men were influenced by only one social institution. An interest in the varieties of human groups is necessarily coupled with an interest in the qualities common to the species. An anthropology of differences complements but cannot replace an anthropology of similarities.

The study of ethnos is a long and illustrious anthropological tradition which has proved a vital and stimulating part of our science. Unlike Lévi-Strauss, I can foresee no end to its utility. I conclude, however, that to confuse this fruitful specialty with the whole of anthropology, whether in its biological or cultural dimensions, would be a serious retreat from our most central concerns and problems and an abandonment of some of our most promising hypotheses.

A Science of Culture

The mid-nineteenth century saw the almost simultaneous rise of two concepts which have aided and plagued us ever since: culture and society. Following Klemm's Culturwissenschaft in 1852, the concept of culture came gradually to occupy a central position in German and English anthropological work, and by 1950 it had swept the field in a large part of the world. Cultural development, primitive culture, culture history, cultural studies, cultural conflict, culture area, cultural cycles, material culture, cultural patterns, cultural diffusion, folk culture, cultural psychology, culture change, acculturation, enculturation, and transculturation are but a few of the concepts which reflect the flexibility of the idea of culture and the vicissitudes of its history. Indeed, for some time now the proposition has been before us that cultural anthropology, Culturwissenschaft, or culturology secede from the anthropological union and set up shop as an independent science unburdened by connections with extra-, non-, or precultural phenomena.

The idea of culture has enormously expanded the horizons of anthropology. By systematic and comparative study it has yielded us a rich harvest of increasingly coherent theory in which time and space, social and psychological process, have been combined into a comprehensive method for classifying the endless variety of the human scene and in some measure understanding and predicting it. It is usually agreed that our greatest successes in cultural theory are findings and theories relating to that most human of phenomena, language. And much of the present promise of a cultural science still lies in that research direction.

In another perspective, culture theory seems somewhat disappointing. We have found some plausible analogies in culture for processes of growth and change which appear in organisms -- evolution, function, organization, cycles. We have uncovered level upon level of meaning in the mediation of culture in

30

other processes and phenomena -- social, psychological, political, economic, geographic, literary, philosophical, even geological. With the possible exception of linguistics, we have found no laws and few if any concepts useful to other sciences. Very much of our knowledge of culture remains a lore rather than a systematized body of principles and relations. And we still argue about the epistemology of culture itself.

We have some rough working agreement that culture is coterminous with man. Bur our agreement on the stigmata of culture which would give body to such a statement is vastly less. Our disagreement on what is essential to a definition of culture is, in fact, simply chaotic in comparison with the unanimity possible on basic concepts in a mature science. The emphasis upon system and structure in recent years seems to promise much towards a resolution of these difficulties, but we have as yet little solid achievement. The concepts of pattern and drift, though not yet applicable in any precise way to all of culture and by no means exclusive to it, yet hold a similar promise.

The most serious difficulties posed by the prospect of a science of culture, however, are perhaps the practical ones. How can an anthropologist, whose interests almost inevitably span several different culture areas, hope to compete with the historian or other scholar who chooses to dedicate himself to the deeper, fuller knowledge of one? A first-rate anthropologist is doomed to being not more than a second-rate Sinologist or Americanist, and vice versa, by simple economic choice. How can the anthropologist's general cultural knowledge compete in depth or competency with that of experts on specific phases of cultural activity -- politics, economy, art, or botany? It obviously cannot. A cultural science is conceivable which could overcome these difficulties, but it is not yet an achieved reality. And meanwhile many anthropologists are threatened with assimilation by Egyptology, Classics, Islamic studies, sociology, political science, philosophy, medicine, or other fields of study. Whether this infiltration exemplifies anthropological imperialism or disintegration will depend finally upon the ability of the field to hold together at the center while these activities transpire on the various frontiers. Though central to it, culture has never been a monopoly of anthropology and is not now. And while our knowledge of culture is extensive, it is not so specialized that it cannot be readily borrowed as appropriate by other disciplines, many of which, indeed, have already pilfered heavily from anthropology.

The case for a science of culture has not infrequently been additionally weakened by plans for a cultural anthropology of ethnic, folk, or primitive cultures, leaving the complex cases to more specialized scholars. To begin with a science of ethnic culture is to end with a science of not much culture and very little ethnicity. A bolder proposal -- that we undertake the systematic study of all of culture and of all cultures -- would seem to be the minimal requirement for a sound specialization. Most of us draw back at this prospect, boldly stated, yet we are pushed toward it by our problems and traditions. I believe we have good grounds for hesitation at taking on a task of such enormous scope with so little promise of immediate synthesis.

Despite its weaknesses, the concept of culture is surely one of the strongest, yet most delicate, of the weapons of anthropology. I do not for a

31

moment suggest that we abandon it. But culture is an aspect of the life of man -- not the whole of it, and I believe it to be as useful to the study of man as metabolism is to the study of organisms without being any better suited to serving as the cornerstone of a separate science. In fact, the significance of that small but precious store of cultural universals which have survived our exposure to the full range of cultural variation represented in world history may be said to rest precisely on the light they shed, not upon the nature of culture, but upon the nature of man and his cultural capacities.

A Science of Society

The concept of society (Gesellschaft, obschestvo) has undergone a development only roughly parallel to that of culture, despite the contemporaneity of the two terms. Society is less intimately coupled with history (cf. Sozial-wissenschaft, Kulturgeschichte); it is more closely identified with social (sic) issues, problems, disorganization, and conflict; it has been subject to more abstract and analytic definition and is less tied to human contexts, even though it is mainly studied in human situations; it has unequivocally become the focus of an autonomous science, at least in most parts of the world. Whether anthro-pology should be a science of society, as is proposed in effect by some schools of social anthropology, is essentially a question of abdicating or seceding in favor of sociology. In view of the subtlety of interplay between the concepts of society and culture theoretically and historically, this is a most complex pro-posal. The complexity is only compounded by use of terms like "socio-culture," and by the division of labor, now traditional, through which sociologists commonly undertake the study of complex cultures while anthropologists take on primitive societies.

Obviously disciplinary labels and traditional differences are not the essential problem in this connection. Sociology does not appear to be entirely clear about its own center of gravity, as is evidenced by its diversification and exploratory activity, which are scarcely less marked than those of anthropology. But if there is some confusion in the field etymologically designated to be the science of society, how much greater is the uncertainty in social (or socio-cultural) anthropology, in which both etymology and strong traditions pull in other directions. It may be doubted that either field can ever successfully become the science of some societies.

Under the circumstances it seems somewhat remarkable that sociology and social anthropology have grown so separately and so differently even in the face of strong mutual influence and constant contact. With varying degrees of clarity, the family is a sociological province, while kinship is an anthropological one; race is an anthropological problem, but race relations is sociological; language is a sociological interest, but languages an anthropological one; social movements are sociological, while nativistic ones are anthropological; primitive societies are anthropology's territory, but industrial societies are sociology's; folk communities belong to the scholar who gets there first. It is difficult to imagine that interests so capriciously distinguished could ultimately do anything

32

but coalesce.

In the meantime there can be no question about the importance of social dimensions to all aspects of anthropology and the consequent necessity for involvement of anthropology in social theory and social problems, whatever the disciplinary locus of such involvement. The concept of culture supplements but cannot supplant that of society in these connections. The comprehensive understanding of the social life of our species in its constancy as in its variation is a task conceivably peripheral to a science of society but central to a science of man.

It is difficult to pinpoint the specifically anthropological contributions to our understanding of society, but it is perhaps in the field of kinship that anthropological studies of social form become most specialized, most distinctive, and most inaccessible to the general sociologist. Such studies have made a considerable contribution, which, coupled with comparably broad but less specialized studies on other aspects of social organization, illustrate some of the strengths of studying society in the traditional anthropological setting. It is doubtless no accident that British social anthropology, which has recently entered the strongest claims for autonomy, centers its case emphatically on kinship structure.

Social psychological considerations lead us to much the same point, since they too tend to emphasize, with or without a Freudian bias, the primacy of the family as a learning context and the relative specificity of patterns and roles acquired through kinship. The social psychology of class, of mental illness, of marital and professional choice also tends to underscore this relationship.

More recently geneticists and physical anthropologists have come to have a lively interest in problems of social groupings, centering of course on those relevant to mating and descent, and this, too, has strengthened the anthropological emphasis on kinship in social organization. While the anthropologist's view of society is in no sense unique, therefore, his commitment to ethnicity, his interest in folk and primitive cultures, and his biological interests conspire to direct his attention towards a social organization theory built around kinship. Such considerations might help to explain to our sociological colleagues their own mystification over Murdock's selection of the title Social Structure and other analogous phenomena.

Anthropological studies in the sociology of religion have, albeit more diffusely, a similarly distinctive character. The study of magic, totemism, witchcraft, divination, and many kindred phenomena is more or less peculiarly anthropological. More strategically, the anthropological conceptualizations of cult movements, nativism, messianism, and millenarianism are in themselves strong arguments for an anthropological sociology.

In short there are good reasons for the most intimate intellectual contact between sociology and anthropology. There are even good reasons why anthropologists should do sociology, and vice versa. But this partial synonymy of problems and specific congruences of interest should not lead us to identify or to confound the two fields. A science of society is not a science of man.

33

A Science of Man

Something of the scope of a possible science of man is indicated by the context in which the word "man" (homo, anthropos, etc.) has been used in the past in titles of anthropological works. "Early man," "primitive man," and "fossil man" figure prominently. "Human nature" and "human races," "human habitat" and "human fertility," "human genetics," "human physique," "human behavior," "human relations," "temperament," "development," and "growth" also recur and clearly demand some place in any general scheme. On the whole, studies of man as such emphasize the biological dimensions of anthropology.

I have used the term anthropology throughout in the most general American (or Mexican) sense, as equivalent to "the science of man." The term has of course a specifically biological reference in many European languages and even in much of Spanish and some English usage. Such terms as social or cultural anthropology, physical, general, theoretical, chemical, psychological, criminal, synthetic, medical, applied, or pedagogical anthropology direct our attention to the possibility of a science of man which is both biological and non-biological, and such usages are now becoming common in many parts of the world.

It seems clear that books about man have long been influenced directly by books about culture, society, ethnicity, and other dimensions of human experience, as well as reflecting similar indirect influences of general cultural background. Studies of human origins and history have given way to studies of human development and evolution, and these have yielded in some measure to studies of human genetics and human ecology. Descriptive and metrical work on comparative morphology has led inexorably to functional and structural theory. Since 1950, the fundamental theoretical concepts of biological and cultural anthropology have been similar and parallel rather than opposed and disparate ab definitio. I believe that the logical conclusion to this long and complex development lies in the creation of a body of theory whose central consideration is the nature of man -- not early, fossil, or primitive man, but the whole, complex, bewildering animal.

It may be objected that human nature is traditionally a philosophical or theological problem. So were matter, heavenly bodies, and disease in former times. What we need to study is a researchable problem on which we have already made considerable progress. Admittedly the term "human nature" is tainted with non-empirical vagueness and extra-scientific subjectivism. It seems to me to be the duty of anthropology to reclaim it. If we are not entirely prepared for this task, we are at least better prepared than any other group of men, for we have data and a tradition of objectivity in its interpretation. We represent the only science of man there is.

It may be objected that the study of human nature overemphasizes the constancies of the human phenomenon at the expense of the variations. I do not believe that it must do so. On the contrary, only the rigid application of a categoric causality which we no longer employ in any aspect of our science would force us into descriptions of mode without matching descriptions of distribution.

34

It is hard to imagine any competent use of contemporary genetic conceptions, for example, which would not have to give full weight to the polytypicality of the species.

It may be objected that the study of human nature would force us into a reductionist biologism. Again I do not believe so. If there is one fundamental tenet of the anthropological work of recent decades, it is that man's nature is largely cultural. I do not see how this fact can be subverted merely by being considered in relation to human biology or evolution or genetics. On the other hand, the understanding of human biology as of human culture may be considerably enhanced by correlative consideration of both.

It may be objected that we can make man the central object of our concern without the complex assumption that he has a "nature." I find no other convenient concept, however, for describing the perduring structure of biochemical, genetic, behavioral, and moral events on which alone a science of man may rest. At some point in the future we might be able to agree on a study of human structure or human dynamics, the human process or the human pattern, but I see no immediate prospects of such agreement. Conversely, I think we are within striking distance of a science whose central problem is the nature of man.

In a brief sketch of this type I can do no more than to suggest what such a science would look like and what directions it might take. I need hardly say that I do so with humility in the face of the enormous complexity our science has already attained and my own consequent ignorance of the larger part of it.

The boundaries of the human phenomenon have proved somewhat elusive in many dimensions although clear in others. The difficulties and obscurities of interpreting the scanty fossil remains of early man and the archaeological record of his cultures leave us even now with more questions than answers about the origins of the genus, the species, and the races. On the other hand, the promise of biochemistry that we shall soon have a complete map of the chemical transformations peculiar to human physiology, coupled with the breathtaking advances of contemporary human genetics, create a new field for the study of human growth, adjustment, maturation, and evolution. We need to find means of ready access to assimilation of this order of information from genetics, nutrition, physiology, endocrinology, neurology, epidemiology, and other medical and quasi-medical specialties. The tiny band of able physical anthropologists working in medical contexts appears to me to be in need of extensive reinforcement if the present promise of synthesis in human biology is to be realized. For this communicative and synthetic purpose a medical anthropology is at least as vital to the science as a whole as an anthropological psychology or sociology. Despite the considerable difficulties of the clinical research context and the sometimes profound traditional and institutional barriers to interdisciplinary communication in these areas, a science of man needs much more of the information already known about the structure and functioning of the human body than it has so far been able or willing to assimilate.

A deeper grasp of comparative morphology in its genetic, nutritional, and behavioral aspects over a broad phyletic range is equally essential. The day has long since passed when every anthropologist can be a competent general biologist. We need more of those rare individuals who have some ability to

35

communicate with both culturology and herpetology. We need to maintain the broad perspective on the place of man among living organisms, which is one of our great traditions, but in the face of the expansion and specialization of the biological sciences this can only be done with specifically directed effort. The ecological and ethological character of our species should come to be well understood by all of us, regardless of our particular specialties and research interests. Clearly we are progressing in this direction.

Such a background reveals clearly the awkwardness and the doctrinaire narrowness of driving any deep wedge between the biological and socio-cultural sides of human nature. We can do full justice to the complexity of human society and the uniqueness of human culture without denying ourselves the broader comparative view of humanity that is deeply woven into our scientific past. We need have no confusion between the communication of genes and germs and the communication of symbols, but in other contexts we find it possible to discriminate concepts without insisting that they be enshrined in separate disciplines. It will be apparent that a science of man can no more avoid being a social and cultural science than it can avoid being a biological one. But it must be all of these at once if it is to be a science of man at all.

Possibly our closest scientific allies in this problem area are psychologists. Comparative, differential, social and cultural psychology, physiological, historical and depth psychology, and studies of human learning and behavior are so directly germane to various anthropological problems that close contact is ultimately inevitable and mutual influence unavoidable. Indeed, some psychologists have occasionally addressed themselves to the study of human nature. The possibility of a synthesis within that field of a specific human psychology seems now to have gone glimmering. However closely it has on occasion approached it, psychology is not a science of man. Nonetheless, the bio-socio-cultural range of psychology gives it a structure parallel to that of our own science and confronts it today, perhaps even more acutely, with the dilemma of synthesis or segmentation.

In the psychological field as in those of social and cultural phenomena, I can see no possibility of integrating anthropology through retrenchment. On the contrary, it is my belief that the ultimate achievement of a systematic science of man can only follow further and yet more ambitious expansion of our interests as anthropologists and of the scope of our activities. We cannot be a science of only some men nor of men under only some conditions. We must learn from pathology and psychopathology; we must know human behavior under artificial laboratory conditions as well as under the natural artificiality of general conventions; we must swallow modern history as we have already downed the Pleistocene; we must understand the city as well as the tribe; and we must examine existentialism as well as totemism or double descent. But in this range of infinite complexity we must always return to man.

This review of the potentialities of a science of man may appear incautiously sanguine, visionary, or even naive, in view of the limitations I have myself noted in the current state of anthropological theory. Science, however, is by nature optimistic and grows by the occasional success of such extra-

36

polations. To resort to a tired analogy, if physics can take on the infinity of time, space, energy, and matter, I see no intrinsic reason for us to balk at man. Timidity and diffidence are not the highest of scientific virtues.

Furthermore, I do not believe we are in any sense starting from scratch. While even a superficial survey of our past preoccupations reveals the highly distinctive and occasionally distorted interests which have shaped the anthropological tradition, we have strengths and solid achievements behind us even though we are not in general agreement in identifying them. We have made errors which we need not repeat. And we are now expanding into a scholarly community capable of meeting expanding tasks and challenges.

Though we can know much more, we now know a great deal about the history of the human body and the forces that have shaped it. We have even reduced some of these forces to precise and predictive laws. We can calculate mathematically the likelihood of various kinds of short and middle range changes in human biology under specified conditions. We have learned a vast amount about the limits of evolution and function, those slippery biological analogies, as they bear on human affairs, and we can make precise, if often qualitative, predictions about social forms, psychological attributes, styles, and values as regressions on one another and on other variables. We have discovered and partly codified an enormous amount of human variability, individual and collective, historical and environmental, biological and cultural. We can predict mathematically (though we haven't agreed how precisely) some aspects of linguistic change, characterology, and social structure. While, therefore, we have achieved only a limited success in the theoretical integration of our far-flung science, its problems are not yet so disjunctive nor so complex as to make such an achievement impossible. In fact, the simultaneous elaboration of comprehensive theory and expansion of substantive scope of anthropology is almost a better description of its history than a forecast of its future.

Conclusions

We commit ourselves daily to a science of man, but when we actually <u>do</u> anthropology, our history shows that we have been constantly involved in other matters -- race, language, culture, society, history, primitive people, institutions, systems, religion, and so on and on. Obviously these are closely related matters, but they will not in themselves add up to a science of man in any automatic way. Quite the contrary, there are some signs that these special interests, coupled with geographical subdivision, are in imminent danger of tearing anthropology apart. Continued lip service to our common label will not prevent this. Possibly it should not be prevented. While we have a number of subfields capable of carrying on piecemeal many of the tasks of anthropology, I believe a strong case can be made for a science of man, broadly, comparatively, systematically, and integrally conceived.

Such a synthetic study cannot replace, of course, the desirable division of labor which alone can make possible competent scientific treatment of the complexities of the human animal. I do not believe we need to abandon our

37

traditional concern with <u>ethnos</u>, culture or society, or any other of our now thriving specialties. Consequently it may legitimately be asked whether a commitment to a science of man involves any real consequences. I believe that it does.

I believe that a successful anthropology will have to be far more sophisticated biologically and more committed to extensive research in all areas of human biology than is our present science. I believe that we must be more daring in expanding our interests in many areas, explicitly abandoning any commitment which restricts us to the primitive, the ancient, the exotic, the rural, the simple, or the traditional. I believe we must use our sub-disciplines -- cultural, social, physical, and historical anthropology, linguistics, folklore, ethnography, and ethnology as means to the comprehension of man rather than as ends in themselves. I believe we need more specialization along fresh lines to illuminate with ever increasing competency the manifold intricacies of human nature. And I believe we must shape our science in this direction before either our necessary expansion or an efficient specialization can take place. I believe, in sum, that we must bend our efforts to the creation of an explicit and comprehensive science of man, or we shall shortly have no science at all.

38

HUMAN BEHAVIOR, HUMAN CULTURE, AND HUMAN BIOLOGY

Francis E. Johnston
University of Texas at Austin

Physical anthropology may be dying; in fact, it may already have died. If so, it has perished not because of any cataclysmic development within scientific technology nor even through some noble effort at upholding scientific truth against the distortions of some sick society. Rather, its death will come about quietly and unnoticed, and its epitaph will be: "How wistful it was that no one really cared about what it was doing."

The truth is that physical anthropology, as viewed by others and as practiced by most, has traditionally been concerned with the reconstruction of historical events and the description of static phenomena in loosely drawn samples, and it has been in isolation from much of the progress of biological and behavioral sciences. The treatment of data has been so far removed from their reality that the conclusions have been of interest to fewer and fewer scientists.

The loss of interest in topics and approaches such as this has been evident in the papers reported in our two major English language journals, the American Journal of Physical Anthropology and Human Biology, although the latter has always had a much broader orientation conceptually and a much wider audience. For example, fewer and fewer papers are written on the subject of fossil man, and fewer and fewer anthropologists are conducting research in this area. Interpretation of the data is left to a very small band of specialists who can make authoritative pronouncements which can be read quickly and incorporated into the smaller numbers of lectures devoted to the topic in our classes. The other articles which appear on the subject are almost exclusively "position papers" generated by seminars and presenting little in the way of new information. The same is true for much of the other temporally sanctified ground of physical anthropology.

Let us not, however, regret the passing of the old, even if it means the death of what we have come to regard as fixed and unchanging and of what we have looked to as our academic "security blanket." What is presently replacing physical anthropology may be one of the most exciting developments in the bio-behavioral realms of science in many years. I am speaking here of the appearance of "human biology" as an identifiable discipline, one which represents the merging of efforts of a number of varied sciences which are concerned with man as a physical being.

The focal point of human biology is human variation. No longer do we accept the pre-Darwinian idea that the average is the reality. We know now that it is but an abstraction of very limited use. Human groups are no longer seen as the arithmetic means of a set of observations, with the variation of such groups viewed as an unreality to be ignored. What is real and what is

39

important is the diversity itself and its meaning, which one can observe in any biological system.

How different an approach it is to inquire, albeit at times descriptively, into the distribution and components of variance rather than to combine averages into a "type" composed of "little men who aren't there." The sin of typology, which is the "original sin" of physical anthropology, has left a scar upon our discipline which is very difficult to remove, although human biology repudiates all it stands for and, more important, all that it is supposed to stand for but doesn't.

How different a conceptual approach it implies to understand that the differences among human groups which we see are really patterned by the mechanisms of evolutionary change. The traits once eagerly sought for as non-adaptive characters of ultimate taxonomic significance are, in fact, dynamic indicators of adaptive responses to past and present ecological pressures. If they are seemingly unchangeable, it is because they are kept in equilibrium by the balance of opposing pressures. How much more meaningful it is to inquire into the forces which generate, pattern, and maintain human diversity.

Finally, how meaningful it is to realize that man really is unique. To understand him as a biological being requires, to be sure, the utilization of the techniques of other bio-physical sciences, but it also requires the utilization of the techniques of the cultural anthropologist. Culture is a powerful adaptive mechanism, one which interacted with the more purely biological aspects during the course of organic evolution and one which evolved along with man. Culture is also an effective agent in promoting variability and in channeling it, thereby becoming a force significant in the operation of ongoing evolutionary changes.

Human biological variability can only be understood by a human biologist. Such a person must be trained in both the biological and the behavioral sciences, which he must weld into an effective approach to the study of the variation which seeks, through a comparative and experimentally-oriented methodology, to reach a deeper understanding of the human condition in space and time. As most human biologists, he may have his training primarily in physical anthropology, but this is not necessary and often not even desirable.

Although the appearance of human biology as a separate discipline is recent, its roots are old, extending in time back to the pre-Darwinian nineteenth century, when writers such as Samuel Stanhope Smith (1810) inquired into the cause of biological differences among groups of men. Unfortunately, these most pertinent questions were lost in succeeding generations of physical anthropologists, who became mired in the biometric morass of the nineteenth and early twentieth centuries.

More immediate developments can be seen in publications which appeared almost twenty years ago. Genetics and the Races of Man, by William Boyd (1950) turned the attention of some anthropologists to the necessity of separating genotypic and phenotypic components of population variance. Coon, Garn, and Birdsell's Races: A Study of the Problem of Race Formation in Man (1950) demonstrated that the static taxonomic categories called races, whose delineation obsessed the time of so many, were, in fact, major adaptive

40

constellations of geographically-ordered groups characterized by traits which were neither fixed in time nor sacred in concept. Finally, Washburn's rather brief paper, "The New Physical Anthropology" (1951), showed that the questions raised by these developments could be answered by a sound, hypothesis-oriented, comparative-experimental approach.

The most recent developments are occurring right now. We find that more and more scientists are becoming involved with human biology despite their diverse backgrounds. For example, evolutionary biologists such as Dobzhansky and Mayr have dealt tellingly with many of its questions; human geneticists have but recently gone through their "Age of Discovery" by learning of the existence of primitive man, and the same is increasingly true of environmental physiologists as well.

We also find a proliferation of courses of this nature in our colleges and universities and a flood of students taking them, demonstrating the coming of age of human biology as a recognized academic subject. Many of these courses entitled "Human Origins" or "Introduction to Physical Anthropology" were previously composed of four unrelated areas: monkeys, bones, fossils, and races. If any efforts were made to provide a laboratory, it consisted of bone identification and Martin anthropometry. Now we find newly organized courses oriented around a broader and more inclusive approach to man and which, though often still called physical anthropology in the catalogues, are nonetheless dealing with human biology as conceived and as practiced. New textbooks appear, such as those by Laughlin and Osborne (1967) and by Bleibtreu (1969), which are composed of readings from a variety of disciplines all relevant to the subject. Laboratory sessions do not involve students in the arduous and unrewarding task of differentiating between the right and left capitate bones nor of the subjective appraisal of the slope of the forehead. Rather, they now learn, for example, that skin color is a measure of light reflectance which within an individual varies with exposure and which varies among peoples and groups independently of exposure to the sun. They learn that body fat can suitably be estimated in living men and that its phenotypic expression varies with the interaction of population genotypes and several environmental agents.

It is of the greatest significance, perhaps, that the development of human biology has resulted in more effective collaboration between students of biology and those of behavior than has existed at any time in the past. Human culture is not another parameter which may or may not be related to a particular observation; it is a basic element in man's ecology and probably the most significant aspect of any human eco system. The fish-out-of-water is no more ridiculous than the man-apart-from-culture.

There are several ways in which man's cultural component is important to human biologists. The evolution of culture proceeded hand in hand with the evolution of man's physical being. To be correct, we must back up even more and say that this relationship existed before the appearance of man. Studies of infra-human primates are clear in pointing to the evolutionary feedback between pre-cultural behavior and somatic changes. The manipulative ability of creatures whose thumbs were becoming increasingly more opposable was enhanced by

41

behavior patterns which stressed hand use. Primates explore with their hands, not their noses. They remove parasites by mutual grooming, a practice which not only is related to manual dexterity but which also increases social interaction. The level of culture of the pre-human Australopithecines was more than fortuitously related to the evolution of bipedal locomotion. By the time that man is first taxonomically recognized, palaeolithic archeologists recognize two different cultural traditions. Even before our own species has appeared, we find ourselves able to make some inferences concerning non-material culture.

We must conclude that the hominid ecology was a cultural one even before the appearance in time of the genus Homo. The irreversible bond between our evolutionary predecessors and the patterning of their behavior is indeed a very ancient one.

From paleolithic to modern man, culture serves as an adaptive mechanism of paramount importance. All life evolves through the selection of forms more highly adapted to specific environments, acting upon a genetic pool creating variable genotypes through mutation and recombination. Vertebrate evolution is characterized by increasing plasticity, also called phenotypic adaptation, which permits environmental independence to a degree through individual modification of environmental response. Acquired through genetic evolution, the ability to maintain homeostatic conditions in the face of drastically changing environments finds its highest expression in mammalian life. Primates display a continuation of this trend, with emphasis upon the evolution of behavioral responses to environmental changes. Human culture has permitted man to live in a truly remarkable range of temperatures, altitudes, disease conditions, and population densities without being forced to adapt genetically. Genetic adaptation would undoubtedly result in speciation and create barriers to gene flow. By allowing maximal cultural diffusion across a broad geographical expanse, the absence of biological barriers is, in itself, a positive feedback.

Culture has also permitted man to exist successfully in areas whose environmental stresses are too great for biological adaptation. It is difficult to conceive of the Eskimo in his present Arctic habitat without the assistance of a technology which affords sufficient protection against the cold. Although Eskimos display physiological responses not found in Caucasian controls, they are not so efficient as to allow them to withstand their environment without considerable cultural help.

On the other hand, we must not automatically jump to the conclusion that man's sole adaptation to temperature stress is a cultural one. The Alacaluf of Tierra del Fuego and the aborigines of central Australia are classic examples of marked biological adaptation to cold stress among peoples with rather minimal technologies. In other words, as the human biologist views human adaptation, he sees it as a complex interaction of, first, genetic responses through time (that is, evolution in the neo-Darwinian sense); second, phenotypic responses of individuals to changes in their own environments; and finally, the mediating effects of culture in permitting a broad range of responses to environments, the responses themselves being altered through the conscious (or perhaps the subconscious) efforts of the individuals.

42

Consequently, the human biologist studies human diversity from the standpoint of the total ecology of a specific population, in which there is a complex interplay of factors of both cause and effect. Even when it is impossible to view the ecology in anything approaching a totality, he still sees the problem as a multi-variate one involving several components which, in themselves, may display a good deal of co-variation.

Culture also serves to create genetic variability by injecting a non-random element into genetic processes. For example, the social structure of any group interferes with random mating. Rules of marriage, rules of residence, systems of kinship, all restrict the random process and may create genotypic distributions which deviate greatly from those to be expected. The same is true of inbreeding, which will increase homozygosity in a population. Alteration of genotypic frequencies in this way can alter the effects of natural selection and create micro-evolutionary changes. Genetic variance is also affected by assortative mating, the measurable tendency for greater similarity between a husband and his wife than between random pairs. Significant assortative mating exists in certain populations for variables such as age, education, religion, and so forth. It also exists for others such as stature and weight.

Selective mating, the greater opportunity for marriage of certain genotypes, can have genetic effects. Where polygyny is significantly practiced, certain males have more wives and greater numbers of offspring than do other males, and all males have more children, on the average, than do the females.

Differential migration is another culturally determined process which can create major genetic differences among groups. When a population splits into two units, they are never random samples of the original one. Instead, migrations of major groups, or even of small segments, tend to be composed of kin groups such as extended families. Such groups will be composed of constellations of more similar genotypes and hence may not be representative of the population from which they departed nor of any other migration from it. Many attempts by geneticists to demonstrate genetic drift in a human population have simply demonstrated the effects of differential migration.

In short, among men, culture interrupts the operation of random process and creates different genetic patterns in human groups. This increases the differentiation of our species, which can serve as a course of future adaptation through the operation of more conventional evolutionary mechanisms.

As I mentioned earlier, physical anthropology may very well be beyond help. The identification of its practitioners with the problems of the past may prove to be too great a handicap to overcome. The entry of scientists trained in other disciplines into its once exclusive preserves may have destroyed the identity of the developing science of human biology with any single discipline. But above all, let us not be sad. If we must cease being physical anthropologists, as many already have even in name, then we may still apply many principles which we have been taught, as well as the newer ones still being formulated, to those problems which have intrigued man since the days of Samuel Stanhope Smith. Regardless of developments, our understanding of man will be the better for them.

43

REFERENCES

Bleibtreu, H. K.
    1969   Evolutionary Anthropology: A Reader in Human Biology
                (Boston: Allyn and Bacon).
Boyd, W. C.
    1950   Genetics and the Races of Man (Boston: Little, Brown,
                and Company).
Coon, C. S., S. M. Garn, and J. B. Birdsell
    1950   Races: A Study of the Problems of Race Formation in Man
                (Springfield: C. C. Thomas).
Laughlin, W. S., and R. H. Osborne, eds.
    1967   Human Variation and Origins: An Introduction to Human
                Biology and Evolution (San Francisco: W. H. Freeman).
Smith, Samuel Stanhope
    1810   An Essay on the Causes of the Variety of Complexion and
                Figure in the Human Species (New Brunswick: J. Simpson).
Washburn, S. L.
    1951   The New Physical Anthropology. Transactions of the New
                York Academy of Science 13:298-304.

44

THE ARCHAEOLOGISTS' PRESUPPOSITIONS

William G. Haag
Louisiana State University

A few years ago Eric Wolf wrote a small volume about anthropology (1964). In its several dozen pages are to be found a wealth of critical interpretation of our science. One of the most obvious aspects developed in this monograph is the notion that a distinguishing feature of anthropology is its ever-widening scope of interest. A half century ago, perhaps, it was tacitly assumed that anthropologists were interested in the primitive, the exotic, or the ancient. Today anthropology has moved far from that designation, perhaps so far as to have more interest in the study of modern complex societies by anthropological techniques than it does in the remnants of primitive people still to be found. Even archaeology has undergone great change, not the least example of which is the expanding interest in historical archaeology. These new movements in the field are indicative of the directions in which anthropologists cast their eyes today. A readily apparent aspect of this is the fact that the endeavors of many are becoming more and more humanistic with every decade. Among many happy phrases in Wolf's book is one he uses to characterize anthropology -- "the most scientific of the humanities, the most humanistic of the sciences."

One of the arresting features of anthropology is this scope. It was distinguished from its inception by the broadness of its interests. It has ever been a generalizing science as compared to some of the more specific endeavors. However, anthropology is constantly moving in new directions, and this very fact is one that threatens the distinctiveness of the discipline. The appearance of a series of new journals that are exclusively devoted to subdivisions of anthropology is indicative of the trend toward fragmentation. Archaeology is no exception to this development. Sometimes archaeologists feel alienated from their fellow anthropologists and even become the objects of some disdain. Our esteemed past-president, Dr. Frank Essene, while a graduate student at Berkeley, was conducting a visiting European ethnologist through the museum. When he pointed out the innumerable drawers of potsherds in storage and remarked that archaeologists were interested in such because they were virtually indestructible, the visitor murmured, "What a pity." Of course, many mature archaeologists are in complete sympathy with this feeling.

As suggested before, archaeology is by no means free of these new trends toward fragmentation. Historical archaeology is so developed now that a new international organization devoted to this subfield has been founded in the last three years. In recognition of this splinter, the literature suddenly blossoms with references to "anthropological archaeology," meaning that branch in which the archaeologist is a trained anthropologist rather than a subverted historian or even post-graduate pot hunter. No matter what our individual specialization, all kinds of archaeologists share certain basic assumptions, and it is these assumptions with which we are here concerned.

45

Most anthropologists are agreed that the discipline of anthropology is moving increasingly in the direction of scientification of our methodology. It is also agreed that there is a conflicting nonscientific humanistic aspect to anthropology. This humanism makes itself manifest on such occasions as the frequent deploring of our activities in molding the policies of given primitive societies. Some practitioners are vaguely disturbed by this apparent nonobjective attitude. However, if there is one major premise that we may say all anthropologists embrace, it is that the discipline is the science of man. We may use a variety of suitable synonyms, but they all add up to a science of human behavior (Phillips 1955).

For archaeology to have a goal beyond just antiquarianism demands that we embrace the concept that we are ultimately looking for evidence of human behavior out of which we may make generalizations that are applicable today. As Rouse states it, "...people are the proper subject of prehistoric research" (Rouse 1965:13). In this sense, the archaeologist operates as any two-dollar horse player who looks at past performance of the object of his affection, compares it with present situations such as soundness of limb, et cetera, and predicts what will happen in the seventh race. If he does this often enough with a variety of horses, he will eventually be enabled to make some laws of horse behavior -- rather gloomy laws, to say the least, but still they are regularities that he has noted.

What the foregoing implies is that archaeologists are unanimously committed to the idea that theirs is a scientific endeavor, that archaeological data are amenable to scientific analysis, and that our pursuit of predictability is tantamount to rendering us a science. Despite this fact, some non-archaeological members of the anthropological profession have concluded that archaeology is the antithesis of the scientific approach (Lowther 1962). These persons often argue that a science is a discipline capable of laboratory procedures that will test hypotheses. These critics aver that archaeology is almost "a mystical wresting of meaning from fragments" (Adams 1968:1187). It is certainly a basic assumption of archaeologists that all sciences operate in identical fashions. Despite the pious protestations of scientists in general that they operate in a wholly inductive atmosphere, it is obvious that most move in an entirely opposite manner, namely, they have a conception and demonstrate its validity by empirical data derived for the purpose of bolstering that conception.

One of the oddities of archaeological research is the fact that most practitioners share with their fellow anthropologists an abhorrence of the biological model for explanations of culture change through time. Despite this, nearly all Americanists are unconsciously committed to evolutionism in culture history. Both Stanley South (1955) and I (1959) have noted in separate articles that evolutionary theory largely permeates American archaeological writings. In other words, it is a basic assumption that American culture history has unfolded, stage by stage, in serial relations. Commitment to evolutionism has been rather unpopular in recent decades, and this has led to a seemingly anomalous position for many archaeologists. It may be judged that the crux of

46

the matter is not so much that evolution has taken place but, rather, what have been the causal agents. Many, but not all, archaeologists have been reluctant to accept the view that pots breed pots, but again this is an almost inescapable conclusion that would be reached from an examination of American archaeological writings.

We are almost entirely committed to the notion that the comparative method is a guiding light in archaeology. Modern students of archaeology have somewhat lost sight of what is implied by "the comparative method." They assume that this means one compares his archaeological manifestations with others and calculates a degree of similarity or dissimilarity. As originally stated, the comparative method stipulated that one would find explanation for his prehistoric material by comparison with living ethnic groups. Thus, more Paleolithic manifestations in the Old World could be illuminated by an examination in the light of the living Australian aborigines. In historical perspective, it is readily apparent that the impetus for embracing the "direct historical method" in American archaeology was the realization that prehistoric materials could be rendered more intelligible by comparing these with living Indian materials (Stewart 1942). We may not be able to realize fully the import of this now, but at that time archaeologists were bowing to the strong wind of Boasian philosophy that demanded an explanation and understanding of the psychological behavior of non-Western man.

Some recent writings concerned with the possibility of trans-Pacific contacts in the introduction of various items in the New World have caused archaeologists to examine again some fundamental assumptions. The idea, considered patently absurd by some (Rowe 1966), that pottery in the New World was introduced onto the coast of Ecuador by a chance visit of shipwrecked Japanese fishermen has, nonetheless, caused a reexamination of certain ideas that we hold rather dear in American archaeology. Heretofore, it has been concluded that pottery was independently invented in the New World, perhaps even several times. Now comes a view, and evidence to support it, that pottery was introduced once into South America and that from that initial impregnation came a veritable potpourri. One of the interesting and exciting aspects of this relatively new idea is that it has forced archaeologists to take a long, hard look at the effectiveness of diffusion. If one were to reject the idea of diffusion as the most cogent factor in the development of pottery traditions in the New World, then he is almost inevitably thrown back on another basic presupposition of the archaeologists: namely, the "psychic unity of mankind." This theme is about the only thing that can be evoked to explain a series of closely similar independent inventions. Of course, every archaeologist subscribes to the theory that diffusion takes place now and did so in the past. It is conclusions concerning the extent to which it is effective that find archaeologists divided.

The single most basic assumption of archaeologists throughout the world is the acceptance of the concept of culture. In verbal commitment archaeologists are not unified, but in actual application of a concept of culture they are essentially of one mind. That concept is one that accepts the definition of Tylor in which culture embraces all of the manifestations of human

47

behavior, including the so-called products of culture. Some may vow adherence to the concept that culture is a stream of ideas, but their utilization of artifacts suggests a much more prosaic and a much broader definition. Artifacts are reflections of the ideas that dominate a given cultural configuration. Artifacts are the keys that enable us to develop the whole or near-whole of a given culture. We view culture "as if" it had an existence of its own, and material objects must remain the "handmaidens" of archaeologists.

With such a concept of culture it more or less logically follows that we are again committed to the idea that cultures are composite in character yet patterned and integrated. We do divorce cultural items from the cultural whole for the purpose of study, but at the same time we recognize the fact that each item is a part of a greater configuration.

Any student of archaeological research within even a confined area must become aware that there is a constant refinement of its reconstructed history. This applies to the Lower Mississippi Valley, to the Nile Valley, or to any other culture area. If archaeologists do make a somewhat vague commitment to the idea that they know everything about the prehistory of any given area, it is never really very vigorously voiced. If anything, we are increasingly aware that relatively important segments of the prehistoric picture may be overlooked. An impressive example is the Poverty Point culture. Several times I walked over the enormous earth works that are so dramatic a part of the type site of the culture without realizing that these structures were man-made. Once we became aware of the features that were integrated into a single culture unit, we began to find similar evidences widespread through the southern United States from Florida to Texas and from Louisiana to Missouri. Now, in the light of these new awarenesses, we are conceiving of Poverty Point culture as basic to several later regional developments. Seriations or cultural grades can be opened at many levels and new manifestations inserted. Certainly we no longer blandly assume that we have completely documented the extent and direction of aboriginal prehistory in the several areas. No longer do archaeologists assume that they know more than they do.

Fifty years ago a rational assumption of all prehistorians was that the geographic setting in which a given culture operated was about as important a factor in molding the configuration of that culture as might be conceived. Twenty-five years later disillusionment had set in, and this assumption was largely wiped from the practices of archaeologists. Now we are faced with a revival of a new brand of geographic determinism, or at least a realization that we must grapple with the environment in the understanding of any cultural configuration. We no longer think of the environment as a determining factor, but we certainly conceive of it as a limiting factor. Again, many archaeologists feel that it is incompatible with their theoretical position to openly accept the notion that the physical environment is a controlling factor. Whereas archaeologists formerly only described the setting in which a given culture operated, now they are avidly making soil analyses, collecting every shread of evidence of floral and faunal surroundings, and utilizing all geological and geomorphological evidence that may be had. In essence, archaeologists

48

completely reject geographic determinism, yet at the same show their awareness that it is a real, systematically integrated world in which each culture unfolds (Flannery 1968).

A commitment to evolutionary theory leads almost inexorably to an evocation of cultural determinism. It seems so simple to utilize what seems obvious: namely, that the cultural configuration at any given time is the product of the preceding cultural configuration. Associated with the idea of cultural determinism is the relatively new idea that there are systems so basic in nature that they can be seen operating in virtually every field. In the words of a distinguished American archaeologist, "Culture is about as powerless to divert these systems as is the individual to change his culture" (Flannery 1967). It is this kind of cultural determinism that seems obvious and useful to the archaeologist.

Archaeologists, then, are among other things noteworthy for several assumptions about their science which they share with other anthropologists. They are scientific in attitude and are motivated by the belief that they will cast some light on the general topic of human behavior. They take it as given that cultural evolution has transpired in much the same way that biological evolution has. They assume that knowledge of the lifeways of numerous ethnic groups will enable a more fruitful interpretation of their own lifeless data. Few archaeologists believe that their interpretation of a given artifact or other trait is the ultimate truth. All take for granted that the future will produce better evidence and modify present interpretations. Above all, archaeologists are committed to the concept of culture and regularly produce works that demonstrate their adherence to the concept that culture is a thing sui generis.

REFERENCES

Adams, Robert McC.
 1968   Archeological Research Strategies: Past and Present.
             Science 160:1187-1192.
Flannery, Kent V.
 1967   Review of "An Introduction to American Archaeology," by
             Gordon R. Willey. Scientific American 217:119-122.
 1968   Archeological Systems Theory and Early Mesoamerica. In
             Anthropological Archeology in the Americas, B. J. Meggers,
             ed. (Washington: Anthropological Society of Washington),
             pp. 67-87.
Haag, William G.
 1959   The Status of Evolutionary Theory in American Archeology.
             In Evolution and Anthropology: A Centennial Appraisal,
             B. J. Meggers, ed. (Washington: Anthropological Society
             of Washington), pp. 90-106.
Lowther, Gordon R.
 1962   Epistemology and Archaeological Theory. Current Anthro-
             pology 3:495-509.
Phillips, Philip
 1955   American Archaeology and General Anthropological Theory.
             Southwestern Journal of Anthropology 11:246-250.

49

Rouse, Irving
1965 The Place of "Peoples" in Prehistoric Research. Journal of the Royal Anthropological Institute 95:1-15.

Rowe, John H.
1966 Diffusionism and Archaeology. American Antiquity 31:334-337.

South, Stanley
1955 Evolutionary Theory in Archaeology. Southern Indian Studies 7:2-24.

Steward, Julian
1942 The Direct Historical Approach to Archaeology. American Antiquity 7:337-343.

Wolf, Eric
1964 Anthropology (Englewood Cliffs, N. J.: Prentice Hall).

50

THE OLD ETHNOGRAPHY: THE CONSCIOUSNESS OF MAN

Arden R. King
Newcomb College, Tulane University

I have no intention of engaging in a repetition of recent criticism of the "new" ethnography, nor do I feel the necessity to evaluate the conceptual and theoretical systems of the "old" ethnography. The latter have already been discussed continuously for the past eighty years. The former is really a case of beating a dead horse, for it is apparent that the seeds of the "new" ethnography, if indeed not considerable detail of method and conceptualization, were present in the "old" ethnography. I am more concerned with changing orientations in cultural anthropology and in the expanded conceptualization of man resulting therefrom. I am concerned with the ways the constantly developing new ethnography has exemplified the processes of the historical approach to culture by deriving conceptual systems from the past, sometimes refurbishing them, sometimes refining them, and occasionally rearranging their parts to devise new approaches to the study of man, as Paul Mercier (1966) has so insightfully noted. But more than that, I am interested in the development of the consciousness of the nature of man. Hence the reason for the sub-title of this paper. I shall attempt to clarify the rise of new concepts of man reached through the methods, goals, mistakes, cultural and individual prejudices, and passions of the old ethnography. For me the old ethnography gave rise to the anthropologist as intensified man.

It is extremely difficult to define just exactly what the "old" ethnography was. It is also difficult then to decide if one can attach a date to the rise of the new ethnography. Voget (1960) does attempt this, although with some diffidence, by noting a post-World War II reorganization of concept and theory. Consequently, I shall not attempt a definition of either old or new ethnography at this point.

When Western men self-consciously began to term themselves anthropologists, a number of primary interests evinced themselves. A great deal of energy and concern was spent in the search for theories of total explanation in order to understand newly encountered cultures as well as the total phenomenon of culture. The increase in knowledge of and experience with other cultures, however, should not be expected to have evoked theories emphasizing process and function, although these points of view were not lacking. Being men of western European culture, these early ethnographers acted as all men that is, they utilized their own culture's means of characterizing the totality of experience and knowledge. The way any man deals with such new knowledge and experience is to look for such theories of total explanation. Thus, there was an emphasis on general theory rather than theories of particular cultures or parts of cultures. They were concerned with the totality of culture and of man and were rapidly disenchanted with the involution of the classical

51

functionalists.

In striving for theories of total explanation the "old" ethnographers laid great emphasis on causes of behavior rather than relationships. This, in a simplistic sense, fostered the development of historical reconstructions and the search for single causal events as the instigators of long chains of sequential cultural events. As it were, a demand for determinism of cultural behavior, rather than the enchantment and fascination of a well-functioning Chinese puzzle,dominated the scene.

In the pursuance of such goals it was soon apparent that the aid of several fields of investigation had to be sought as tools of anthropological understanding. Thus, ethnography and historical linguistics, and ethnography and history and archaeology were soon cooperatively involved not only in the investigation of particular phenomena but, more importantly, in the development of the idea of the compleat anthropologist. As the range of knowledge of man expanded, and as this was more and more identified with his concern, the anthropologist achieved a professional identity, albeit only by assuming an imperialistic stance.

The early interest in total explanations for cultural behavior and the implementive concern with causes led to the identification of causes with origins. Thus, the concern with cultural content led to a search for historical origins, the rise of diffusion and distribution studies, as well as the conceptualization of cultures consisting of discretely comparable parts. This coordinately allowed for the application of evolutionary concepts to the data of the ethnographer. Once sequential histories of parts of cultures became possible, or at least more demonstrable, similarities between cultures could more easily be explained. This did not, however, lessen the importance of the search for total explanations, for at the same time as ethnographic information became more available, as the idea of discrete cultural parts became current, so too did schemes of total explanation rise through concepts of cultural evolution.

Counterposed to these historical and evolutionary emphases, the results of ethnographic fieldwork intensified ideas of cultural integrity and uniqueness. At the same time, when historical and evolutionary orientations led to and sought structural similarities of human behavior, the necessity for more detailed information concerning the variability of cultural behavior brought a recognition of the distinctiveness and unity of each new culture reported. In the search for universals and total explanations the exigencies of the collection of new data forced the consideration of process and function. The seeds of destruction of the older goals of ethnography were present in the procedure for their elucidation. The bases of new ethnography were thus laid.

From the foregoing cursory statements certain basic ideas concerning the nature of man are apparent. An underlying assumption that man possesses only limited potential for new behavior is clear, especially in the search for causes of present behavior in single origins. The emphasis on the historical approach not only directed interpretation this way, it also made much of the retention of culture as opposed to the differential interpretation of each culture by each new generation. Evolutionary concern, it goes without saying,

52

implicitly assumed a similar stance. The emphasis on the description of individual cultures leading to functional analyses and structural concepts were also similarly limited, and to an important extent the "new" ethnography is a continuation of this point of view. But, of course, this is not the entire story.

Certainly the temporal circumstances of the development of ethnography were peculiar to the history of man. For the first time the entire gamut of the variety of human behavior was within the reach of experience. It has perhaps been rightly argued that the systematization of the anthropologist that is part of every man could not have come into being at any other point in human history. But then so too were those men and women who began and developed the first systematization of the discipline peculiar to the experience of man. They arrived at a point in the history of Western cultures wherein they could ignore the demands of their own culture by pointing to the exigencies of the accumulation of knowledge.

We hear much today concerning the motivations leading to the development of field work by anthropologists of western European cultures. It is now fashionable to indulge in a great deal of ex post facto breast beating about the evil purposes to which such work was employed -- colonial expansion and exploitation. However, although anthropological knowledge emerged from colonial administration in the 19th century and in pre-World War I times, anthropologists were not conceived to be of any particular use as professional men until the 1920's. But certainly the utilization of ethnography and its development was affected by the country of origin of the anthropological field worker. Wilhelm Mühlmann (1968) has perspicaciously indicated an important difference between the American and Russian anthropologists on the one hand and those of European countries with colonial territories on the other. For the former it was a case of the primitive at home, albeit the circumstances of the utilization of this fact were often very different. Foreign cultures within the anthropologist's own national boundaries meant that one's own culture was always within easy reach; the manifest safety of home accompanied manifest destiny. Compared with the study of the primitive in a foreign clime and/or in a colonial context, this has a certain psychological ease. The preservation of knowledge of cultures which were disappearing before the ethnographer's eyes in North America was conducive to a different ordering of urgency than was found in a region where there was little evidence that such extinction was either likely or deplorable.

Then there is the matter of cultures and cultures: those of the ethnographers and those being learned by them. It should not be news to anyone that the cultural terminologies of the ethnographer have very often been imposed upon those studied. Even with the recognition of this fact by the "old" ethnographers, the problem was not solved. Our discipline has been characterized by the rise of national schools of ethnography. Under such circumstances the description and analysis of other cultures reflect the ethnographer's own view of man. It is possible to use our stereotypes of other western European national cultures to arrive at an approximation of the influence of these national schools. For example, the expressed French concern with logical organization and intellectually justified efficiency of

53

centralization, with all parts operating in a highly integrated fashion, sounds like a caricature of Durkheim. Despite all this, with the increased knowledge of other cultures, the overriding concern with historical reconstruction -- along with the unexpressed value of limited human potential for new behavior relative to the search for single origins, with the definition of the stages of cultural evolution, and with total explanations -- disappeared before the rise of field work studies of single groups and settlements. With these came a clearer realization of the cultural complexity existent among human societies. The functional approaches of Radcliffe-Brown and Malinowski were pioneer reactions to the consciousness of this complexity. But even so, there was a persistence of the assumption of limited human potential in the necessity of devising structural approaches to accommodate the plethora of new data.

If there was an effect of the ethnographer's culture upon that culture which he was investigating, then most certainly that culture affected him -- even if it was to the point of alienation. We have paid little attention to the effect of the cultures studied upon the body of anthropological theory. One important recognition was brought about by the rise of field work: the realization that all cultures have their own theory of culture and that all men are anthropologists. The fascination of anthropologists with Australian kinship systems, the influence of Central Polynesian theories of status and social control on hypotheses about the function of religion, and the effect of Meso-American Indian theories concerning the relationship between man and the universe on the definiton of the nature of civilization are some cases in point. The anthropological possessive is a field work addition to the anthropologist's personal grammar. As such, the influence of these is rarely assessed. I hasten to add, however, that I would not necessarily expect a Crow to feel apotheosized if he encountered a Crow system in an introductory anthropology textbook -- let alone recognize it.

All the foregoing factors played important roles in the development of ethnography, but none of these have any meaning unless one attempts to place these in the context of the personal and social nature of the ethnographers themselves. And this in turn enables us to have some understanding of the rise of new ethnography in our times. We are all more or less aware that the history of ethnography derives from the upper and middle class background of the Europeans and North Americans who first explored the non-European cultural world and then systematized its description and analysis. In the beginning it was simply a matter of well-educated men seeking a profession. In one sense, the history of ethnography has been a process of professionalization as knowledge of other cultures accumulated and attempts at its ordering were made. Of course, this is not too different from the history of other professional disciplines. It has been my contention that the development of such knowledge brought about a condition in which the ethnographer, and inter alia the anthropologist, could be described as an intensified man. Certainly the acquaintance with and then the deep knowledge of other cultures developed a radically different view of man than heretofore had existed in any culture. The necessity of adopting a cross-cultural view of man and the drive towards a

54

systematization of this knowledge in the universal search for regularities of human behavior evoke new images of man. Once having put this process into train, the question has always been why the ethnographer continues his quest for experience with cultures other than his own. Why could not the principles developed in these comparative analyses of human behavior be as comfortably used with regard to their own culture? We all know the various reasons given for continued research and investigation of other cultures. I would boil these down to two important motivations: curiosity and the joy of the unique and, second, the alienation of the ethnographer from his own culture.

I would not judge either to be more important. Besides the desire to gain knowledge of other cultures while it was still possible, despite the conceptual frameworks used to organize this knowledge, the "old" ethnographers were well-educated persons who increased their education through the knowledge of other cultures. In some sense the rise of the old ethnography was a reflection of the social class from which most came. It was far easier to gain insights into the nature of human behavior from newly encountered cultures than to investigate the cultural differences expressed by their own social classes. The sense of stability imparted by Euro-American culture in its optimism concerning the future of man, which was current in the late 19th century and lasted until the time of the second World War, was just as important, if not more so, in the motivation of fieldworking ethnographers. This is not to say that many did not concern themselves with their own culture and that some were not alienated from it. Nevertheless, the curiosity about and enjoyment of other cultures, given one's own cultural security, imparted a degree of impartiality toward and appreciation of both cultures. However, in a contradictory fashion, this contributed to a broader view of man in the abstract and an unconcern with man in the particular. One could ignore his own culture with intellectual impunity. It was only after field work became attached to the study of whole cultures and after sufficient knowledge of other cultures had accumulated that the impulsion of alienation could assert itself.

With this I am saying that ethnography, and especially ethnographic field work, as a means of self-therapy cannot be dismissed as misplaced and meaningless Freudian nonsense. This would hold whether the ethnographer was a fieldworker or not. The concern with the cross-cultural view and with intense knowledge of other cultures, all with the purpose of arriving at valid generalizations about man as a whole, would certainly tend to alienate one from one's own culture. Cultural relativity and the horrors of ethnocentrism could well bring about this alienation, and I suspect that this state of affairs did not assume importance until these phenomena became conscious values of the ethnographer. But I would argue that, equally, the ethnographer became alienated from all cultures -- in a far wider context of knowledge he was seeking universal man. Perhaps an analogy is appropriate. Andreas Lommel (1967), in an otherwise undistinguished book, puts forth the hypothesis that the shaman represents a man alienated from his fellows, psychotically or otherwise, and that through self-therapy he achieves a creative act applicable to the totality of things. This allows him not only personality integration, but

55

having encountered experience foreign to others of his society, he also serves to mediate the unknown but apprehended world for others. If it is true that the anthropologist has become a stranger to his own culture, if not to all distinct cultures, then might it not be possible that through his adventures on the wilder shores of human behavior he is seeking the same ends as the shaman?

All the ethnography before our time is the old ethnography. A historical treatment of its development may reveal temporal emphases of particular conceptual and theoretical viewpoints. The ethnocentrisms of western sub-cultures may have had their way from time to time. But taken overall, the old ethnography is a pheonomenon characterized by the continuous expansion of the consciousness of man. That it has been a terrifying experience is only verified by our repeated efforts to reduce it to as simple a set of principles as possible.

REFERENCES

Lommel, Andreas
    1967   Shamanism: The Beginnings of Art (New York, Toronto: McGraw Hill Book Company).

Mercier, Paul
    1966   Histoire de L'Anthropologie. Collection "Le Sociologue" No. 5 (Paris: Presses Universitaires de France).

Mühlmann, Wilhelm E.
    1968   Geschichte der Anthropologie, Second edition (Frankfurt am Main, Bonn: Athenäum Verlag).

Voget, Fred W.
    1960   Man and Culture: An Essay in Changing Anthropological Interpretation. American Anthropologist 62:943-965.

56

ON THE NEW ETHNOGRAPHY[1]

Jan Brukman
University of Illinois

I would like to preface my remarks with an apology to all ethnographers, both old and new, who may come to feel that I have misstated their case in some way. I make this apology at the outset because it seems to me that we are not in a position at this time to fully catalogue either the assumptions we bring to our work or the implications of that work for future ethnographic undertakings. I simply ask your indulgence as I try to outline what I believe some current assumptions are and what I think they ought to be as well. If a note of finality is apparent in what I say, it is the fault of my style and not of my intent.

Let me begin then with what I believe is a generally adequate substantive definition of the new ethnography, and a kind of summary statement of what new ethnographers are up to as well:

> The new ethnography is an attempt to discover and utilize procedures which are both internally consistent and publicly attainable, and which produce valid and replicable statements held demonstrably to be true about the world by native speakers of some language L.

Worded this way, the definition in a loose sense incorporates what one might call an evaluation procedure for descriptive adequacy. Within the definition there is a specification of what a description shall be ("valid and replicable statements held demonstrably to be true about the world") as well as an indication of how we might evaluate the accomplishment of the description (it must be "internally consistent and publicly attainable"). That is to say, a description will be highly valued just to the degree that the procedures utilized are made explicit. In any reasonable view this is a necessary condition for an adequate description, but certainly not a sufficient one. Note that no reference is made to the way such a description shall be elaborated. For example, nothing is said about the manner in which statements made in an exotic language will be transformed by the ethnographer into statements interpretable by one's colleagues. These statements will be, in one form or another, in an analytic language, or in other words a meta-language, a subject to which I shall return below.

With this definition and its entailments in mind, I believe it is important here to make a distinction between two enterprises which are certainly related but which represent very different ways of conceiving of primary data. I mean particularly that we must keep separate what we might call the formal analysis of ethnographic materials from the generating of those materials themselves. In the former case, the analyst is concerned with accounting for

57

data already present in what we might designate the anthropological discipline's ethnologic record. Some of the work of Buchler, Hammel, Kay, Levi-Strauss, Lounsbury, and Romney, for example, is of relevance here. The latter case, the generating of ethnographic materials, and practically speaking, the simultaneous analysis of these materials, is the concern of men who pursue a particular kind of research strategy that generally fits the definition I have proposed for the new ethnography. And here the work of Berlin, Conklin, Frake, Geoghegan, Goodenough, and Metzger seems to apply.

Now what these two approaches (and their varying mixtures) have in common is their overwhelming focus on language as the source of primary data as well as the very data itself of ethnography. Whether in fact this interest in certain aspects of natural language is predated on the part of some scholars by an interest in linguistics as such or vice versa is immaterial; it seems clear to me that practically every theoretical and methodological assumption underpinning this position in anthropology stems from a prior understanding of the nature of linguistics as a discipline.

I think it not unfair, then, to examine as the central issue of this paper the ongoing relationship between linguistics and anthropology as disciplines -- as well as the assumptions of the two -- from a kind of microhistorical viewpoint. I will be bold and say here that I will use the term anthropology on occasion to mean whatever it is that the new ethnography, ethnoscience, ethnographic semantics, componential analysis, and so on have in common. I could of course use some current locution such as linguistic anthropology. In any case, I do not have space to characterize the different kinds of work that might appropriately be labelled by one of these terms; I assume that the assumptions of new ethnographers are shared by those who do these other labelled things.

It is difficult to briefly characterize precisely what this prior understanding of linguistics seems to be and what the particular intellectual sources of this viewpoint are. I will only try to point out here without going into too much detail a few examples of what this anthropological conception and use of linguistics appears to be.

There are four readily apparent concepts, procedures, ideas -- call them what you will -- which have been dominant in the thinking of formal analysts and new ethnographers alike and which have been borrowed by analogy from a particular kind of linguistics. (I will return to this issue "kind of linguistics" shortly). These four principles are: (1) the availability of a mechanical discovery procedure; (2) the distinction between the etics and emics of language; (3) the idea of distinctive features and/or semantic markers or components; (4) and the concept of complimentary distribution.

Of these four principles the first is probably the only one that is exclusively associated with the new ethnography. Metzger's eliciting heuristic, illustrated and developed in a series of recent papers (c.f. Metzger and Williams 1963a, 1963b; Black and Metzger 1965), and Frake's (1964) interlinked queries and responses are two of a variety of explicit techniques designed to attain a high level of descriptive adequacy in the sense indicated above. Insofar as they generate "new" data with the use of a sentence frame

58

technique, these eliciting procedures are parallel to the way a linguist might discover, for example, new tokens of some form class ("noun," "verb," "adjective," etc.).

The remaining principles, when they are utilized in anthropology, are invoked quite consciously as being applicable to cultural domains by analogy with descriptive linguistics. In the analysis of kinship semantics emic distinctions are made on the basis of culture-specific semantic markers or components. This sort of analysis parallels a componential description of pronominal systems where the markers may be, for example, singular, dual, plural, first person, or second person. In the case of kinship semantics, the markers may be sex, generation, degree of collaterality, and so on. In both kinds of analysis a pronoun or a kin term is in theory uniquely defined by the intersection of the markers. We know, however, that the application of pronouns is highly determined (that is, obligatory in the grammar of a particular language), whereas the application of kin terms is much less so and presents many problems for analysis that are as yet unresolved.

Coming relatively late but clearly in association with the development of formal analysis itself has been a serious and rather more concerted effort to evolve a logically rigorous metalanguage with which to display all the data of anthropology, and not just that which relates to kinship terminological systems. Such a concern probably stems from an overall interest in scientific rigor, although it is an interest greatly affected by the assumed rigor of linguistics. In this context I need hardly mention the reason for bringing these concepts to the collection and analysis of ethnographic data in the first place; it is simply that the search for a paradigm of sufficient scientific power and precision that could account for certain natural language data such as kinship terminologies and folk taxonomies led necessarily to the scholarly source of our knowledge about language -- linguistics. This is the position taken by Goodenough who first began to explore the analogy between the structure of language and the structure of culture as a language-like system. On the other hand, Lounsbury, a linguist, was concerned with the semantics of particular kinship terminologies, and fortunately the fit between a particular kinship terminological system and behavior manifested relative to it had always been a major topical area of interest for anthropologists.

Now, if one even casually examines the bibliographies appended to work produced by the scholars I have mentioned here, certain names crop up again and again. Among the more frequently occuring are those of Bloomfield, Pike, Morris, Harris, Zipf, and Jacobson. With the exception of Jacobson, all of these men, as linguists or semanticists, are part of the mainstream of what is often called the American structuralist school of linguistics. That is, they represent, after Bloomfield, the culmination of a kind of linguistics whose historical roots we may trace to Boas. Considering, then, the very real and frequently acknowledged debt the kind of anthropology I am concerned with here owes to linguistics for its methodological and theoretical insights, I am particularly struck by the fact that names such as Chomsky, Katz, Postal, Lees, and Fodor are rarely if ever cited, even in publications as recent as 1965.

59

Let us take up for a moment the character of this structuralist or taxonomic school of linguistics. What were some of its assumptions, both implicit
and explicit?

It seems clear that insofar as these linguists thought of themselves as
scientists, the paradigm of science that they brought to their work was radical
empiricism; and insofar as they thought of themselves as behavioral scientists,
they adopted the paradigm of the behaviorists. We are all familiar with
behaviorism; it is in fact the scientific paradigm with which most of us have
grown up. We have been taught the basic tenet of S-R theory "that human
knowledge is derived purely from experience" (Sklar 1968:217); that it is essentially "an adventitious construct (hence the lack of concern for psychological
reality on the part of some componential analysts?) which has developed
through association and habit and so on from an essentially unstructured organism which has as its structure only the ability to perceive certain impressions --
and ability to carry out induction -- which Hume quite honestly said must be
just animal instinct; there is no explanation for it" (Chomsky, quoted in Sklar
1968:217). This is, I think, a not inaccurate statement of the structuralist-
empiricist position. It was made by Noam Chomsky, in the Fall of 1968. In
another context, Chomsky, then a student of Zellig Harris at the University of
Pennsylvania, has this to say about the status of linguistics in the mid-1950's:

> I remember quite clearly my own feeling of uneasiness as a
> student and the fact that, so it seemed, the basic problems
> of the field were solved, and that what remained was to
> sharpen and improve techniques of linguistic analysis that
> were reasonably well understood and to apply them to a
> wider range of linguistic materials. In the post-war years
> this was a dominant attitude in most active centers of re-
> search. I recall being told by a distinguished anthropologi-
> cal linguist, in 1953, that he had no intention of working
> through a vast collection of materials that he had assembled
> because within a few years it would surely be possible to
> program a computer to construct a grammar from a large
> corpus of data by the use of techniques that were already
> fairly well formalized. At the time, this did not seem an
> unreasonable attitude, though the prospect was saddening
> for anyone who thought, or at least hoped, that the re-
> sources of human intelligence were somewhat deeper than
> these procedures and techniques might reveal. Corre-
> spondingly, there was a striking decline in the study of
> linguistic method in the early 1950's as the most active
> theoretical minds turned to the problem of how an
> essentially closed body of technique could be applied to
> some new domain -- say to analysis of connected dis-
> course, or to other cultural phenomena beyond language
> (Chomsky 1968:2).

60

I do not need to document here the revolution in linguistics that has occurred since the appearance of Chomsky's Syntactic Structures in 1957, nor to illustrate the impact that the brilliant and complex beauty of the transformational generative approach to grammar has had on philosophy and psychology, as well as linguistics. Its assumptions, however, are of a totally different kind. Let me again quote Chomsky:

> It has, I believe, become quite clear that if we are ever to understand how language is used and acquired, then we must abstract for separate and independent study a cognitive system, a system of knowledge and belief, that develops in early childhood and interacts with many other factors to determine the kind of behavior we observe; to introduce a technical term, we must isolate and study the system of linguistic competence that underlies behavior but that is not realized in any direct or simple way in behavior. And this system of linguistic competence is qualitatively different from anything that can be described in terms of the taxonomic methods of structural linguistics, the concepts of S-R psychology, or the notions developed within the mathematical theory of communication or the theory of simple automata. The theories and models that were developed to describe simple and immediately given phenomena cannot incorporate the real system of linguistic competence; "extrapolation" from simple descriptions cannot approach the reality of linguistic competence; mental structures are not simply "more of the same" but are qualitatively different from the complex networks and structures that can be developed by elaboration of the concepts that seemed so promising just a few years ago (Chomsky 1968:4).

If we accept the truth of what Chomsky is saying here, we cannot fail to note the irony that what anthropologists call the "new ethnography" has its roots squarely in what has been an old linguistics for at least 10 years. Specifically, we have not isolated and studied the systems of linguistic competence. We have indeed been able to describe certain domains of linguistic behavior in ways very much like the taxonomic methods of structural linguistics; every such description contributes to the store of knowledge that we have about behavior we observe. Yet what is the characterization of the system that underlies behavior?

Reference is made occasionally to the "cognitive maps" of culture-bearers. Such a map is supposed to be the collective representation of the knowledge and beliefs members possess about the world. In the context of the argument presented here, I find the metaphor to be particularly apt, since a map is by definition the representation of the surface of something, a little picture of parts of the "full-sized" world, scaled down so that spatial relationships between and among entities in the real world can be seen all at

61

once. If this view is correct, then a cognitive map is clearly nothing more than a convenient way of picturing already apprehended phenomena and tells us nothing about the system which underlies the map.

So it seems we must ask several questions: whether developments in linguistics somehow invalidate what has gone before in the new ethnography, or whether in fact these new developments are at all related to the descriptive task ethnographers have set for themselves? And we must ask the most crucial question of all: what can generative transformational grammar contribute to the task of the ethnographer as it stands?

Now, these questions are interrelated in an important way, because they reflect upon what our conception of Science is. If we believe, for example, that an elegant, parsimonious, non-redundant, internally consistent descriptive statement, designed to impart to our colleagues how both they and the producer of the described phenomena would apprehend the "truth" of the phenomena is a scientific statement, then none of these questions apply. However, if we wanted to characterize how the phenomena described got to be that way -- and no other -- (that is, to explain it), we would have another kind of scientific statement, and we might then think about these questions seriously.

Stephen Tyler (1969) has recently put forth an important distinction between natural and formal sciences in discussing the emergence of what he calls cognitive anthropology (which could well be another term for the subject matter of this paper). Inherent in this distinction, he quite rightly says, is the difference between data that have their representation as discrete material phenomena and whose explanation lies at some other level in the sense that, for example, the data of zoological taxonomics is explained biochemically, and data that have their representation as mental phenomena, such as language, whose explanation is not at some other level but in fact is in some more abstract set of logical operations whose domain remains that of the phenomena explained. That is to say, we must explain mental phenomena (whose manifestation is language) in language, but in some language other than natural language, that is, in a metalanguage. In this regard, we should not confuse achieving some kind of descriptive adequacy in a metalanguage and using the metalanguage as a tool for revealing (not "discovering") relationships that are not obvious in the descriptions themselves, a point to which I shall make reference below.

But even granting this, it seems to me that the issue which the new ethnography must face squarely is this: Some day soon, perhaps even now, we must stop the inordinate worrying about descriptive adequacy as an end in itself, because if the generative approach to grammar is correct in its essentials, then descriptive adequacy in the present frame of reference is not only practically but theoretically an impossibility, since no list, no matter how extensive, can incorporate the potentially infinite variety of appropriate behaviors in some domain or another. When we talk of getting inside people's heads or of the organizing principles underlying behavior, we must be prepared to eventually explain how a certain kind of ordering of data comes about.

There are inherent differences between, on the one hand, organizing, and on the other, displaying knowledge and beliefs. Do we believe that

62

the thing displayed is ultimately what is of interest? I think not. The thing displayed in the generative view is, after all, only a manifestation of some deeper, underlying structure. In taking a position similar to this, Lévi-Strauss is essentially correct, but the assumption underlying his analyses is too conservative. More than just binary structures exist, as the formal analysis of various hierarchic and componential semantic sets has shown. We know that even at the very lowest levels of description it is at least the combinatorial possibilities of binary oppositions and hierarchic and componential sets that are organized for display and which must ultimately be accounted for. Even so, the structure of a kinship system or a folk taxonomy (or something more complicated than either of these, which we cannot yet describe) is of very little interest as a formal object. What can be said of significance about a set of terms cross-classified by a set of features (Chomsky 1968:65)?

However, when we suppose that a genealogical grid is in some way analogous to the phonological grid, in the sense that a fairly small number of features are specifiable in absolute, language-independent terms, and that these features form the basis for the organization of all kinship systems, certain interesting consequences follow within the metalanguage we use to express the relationships among the features of particular kinship systems. These consequences are investigated in the most recent work in the formal analysis of kinship, that of the transformationalists. In general, this sort of analysis has been treated as another kind of descriptive technique, with many ad hoc rules needed to describe a given system, but also with many rules which are potentially universal. If the latter were true, such a discovery would not be trivial. Although I think the jury is out on the matter, a great deal of significant and highly suggestive work in this area is being produced. But we must note, however, what does happen when an explanation is attempted for the universality of certain rules. We are returned to the so-called "extensionist" hypothesis of Malinowski. What is this hypothesis? It is a restatement of the pernicious behaviorism of stimulus-response psychology in which something is generalized and comes to stand for something else. There is no indication that the mind has ever worked like this, except in trivial and unrevealing ways. And certainly the complex domain of kinship, considering the degenerate nature of the input (that is, time and access to data, as generative grammarians put it), cannot work this way. If so, our ability to use genealogy as a source for our descriptive techniques may be an epiphenomenon of some other deeper reality, an order of a kind that genealogy hints at but does not reveal. We know, after all, that phonology as such tells us virtually nothing about language. We must ask: what does kinship analysis tell us about culture? (cf. Lounsbury 1965; Coult 1967). I propose, then, that we begin to think now about what a universal ethnography (that is, a theory of Culture) might look like, just as linguists seriously look forward to a universal grammar. It is clear that we must also continue to refine our formal descriptive techniques and to apply them to symbolic systems of all kinds. And it seems to me quite necessary that we do so because of the unquestionable importance of that premise underlying the definition of the new ethnography which I offered at the beginning of

63

this paper. In Frake's words: "To produce ethnographic statements that can be demonstrated to be <u>wrong</u>, (emphasis his) and not simply judged to be unpersuasively written, is...some advance over the production of most current statements" (Frake 1964:142-143). Explicitly derived descriptive statements which can be proved wrong, and explanatory hypotheses rich enough to account for newly encountered data ought to go hand in hand in anthropology, just as they have come to do in linguistics. They ought to because, in truth, a theory of culture, like a theory of grammar, is within every man as a species-specific, innate capacity.

NOTES

1. I want to acknowledge the debt I owe Paul Kay who first articulated for me many of the ideas presented in this paper. A view parallel to the approach taken here is most clearly manifested in Kay (1966).

REFERENCES

Black, Mary and Duane Metzger
    1965   Ethnographic Description and the Study of Law. <u>American Anthropologist</u> 67:141-165.

Chomsky, Noam
    1968   <u>Language</u> and <u>Mind</u> (New York: Harcourt, Brace).

Coult, Allan D.
    1967   Lineage Solidarity, Transformational Analysis and the Meaning of Kinship Terms. <u>Man</u> 3:26-47.

Frake, Charles
    1964   Notes on Queries in Ethnography. <u>American Anthropologist</u> 66:132-145.

Kay, Paul
    1966   Ethnography and Theory of Culture. <u>Bucknell</u> <u>Review</u> 19:106-113.

Lounsbury, F. G.
    1965   Another View of Trobriand Kinship Terms. <u>American Anthropologist</u> 67:142-185.

Metzger, Duane and G. E. Williams
    1963a   A Formal Ethnographic Analysis of Tenejapa Ladino Weddings. <u>American</u> <u>Anthropologist</u> 65:1076-1101.
    1963b   Tenejapa Medicine I: the Curer. <u>Southwestern</u> <u>Journal</u> <u>of</u> <u>Anthropology</u> 19:216-234.

Sklar, Robert
    1968   Chomsky's Revolution in Linguistics. <u>The</u> <u>Nation</u>, September 9, 1968.

Tyler, Stephen A.
    1969   Introduction. In <u>Cognitive</u> <u>Anthropology</u>, Stephen A. Tyler, ed. (New York: Henry Holt and Co.), pp. 1-23.

64

A FORMAL SCIENCE

Stephen A. Tyler

We have found a strange footprint on the shores of the
unknown. We have devised profound theories, one after the
other, to account for its origin. At last, we have succeeded
in reconstructing the creature that made the footprint. And
Lo! it is our own.

Eddington (1966:201)

Anthropologists persist in believing they are scientists. They persist
in this belief despite the intractability of their data, the chaos of their methods,
and the paucity of their results.[1] It is this assumption more than any other
that articulates the diverse approaches to the study of man.

Determinism, Materialism, and Mechanism

Like the 19th century biologist, the anthropologist is committed to a
science that is deterministic and materialistic. The anthropologist has a
Laplacian view of the world. He believes that a complete description of some
instantaneous state of nature together with all the laws of nature would enable
him to calculate any event of the past or future. This kind of assumption is
most obvious in the doctrine of evolution -- biological, cultural, or otherwise.
An essential ingredient is the belief in causation, and more particularly, in
the uniformitarian view that like causes produce like effects.
It is not necessary to here document the vicissitudes of the concept of
causality since Hume's rejection of the component of necessity. It is important
to observe only that the "purified" notion of causality as predictability is
dependent on a very unlikely set of circumstances. If a causal relation is to
be found between two events, then the preceding event must be the whole previous situation. Given the whole previous situation and all the relevant laws
it is possible to assert a causal relation between two events (Carnap 1966:191-
5). It is conceded that such predictability is only potentially possible since
no one could know either the whole situation or all the relevant laws. It is
obvious that such a truncated version of causality is hardly compatible with
the anthropologist's more simpleminded version of the relations between stages
in an evolutionary sequence.
The materialist biases of anthropologists are most apparent in the frequently expressed opinion that anthropology is a "behavioral science." A
chief tenet of behaviorism is that behavior is explicable in mechanistic terms.
From this point of view behavior is simply a series of reflexes exemplifying

65

the law of cause and effect. The movements of bodies are always determined by preceding movements and these by still preceding movements in a continuous chain of bodily movements culminating in the original movement which was itself simply a response to some external stimulus. A further tenet of behaviorism is that even though humans may have minds, it is impossible to observe a mind. All that can be observed is the movements of human bodies -- behavior. And even if there are minds attached to these bodies, they do not affect what bodies do. Consequently, such things as minds -- even if they exist -- do not alter the operation of causal laws. In its insistence that the object of study must always be some observable phenomenon independent of the observer, and that the law of cause and effect governs the relations among these phenomena, behaviorism represents a materialist point of view.

We have already seen that the concept of causality involves something more than the behaviorist's purely mechanistic version, but what of the proposition that the object of study is some observable phenomenon? Inasmuch as this penchant for observable phenomena represents a belief that the only things we can have knowledge about are physical objects perceived by our senses, it is an oversimplified account of knowledge, perception, and the external world. We have knowledge of physical objects only as the result of an inference. When we have the sensation of "seeing" something, we are led to infer that there is some physical object which is in some way responsible for the sensation. In effect, we make a double inference. We "perceive" a sensation, the sensation leads us to infer an object, and this leads us to infer a causal relation between the object and the sensation. Consequently, we do not have direct knowledge of physical objects. The inescapable conclusion is that the event which is the immediate cause of our sensations is one that occurs in our own heads (cf. Russell 1929:25-103). From this point of view, the behaviorist's adamantine observable phenomena disintegrate into certain "fancies" projected into the external world by the mind.[2]

Behaviorism asserts an identity between movements and behavior, that is, movements of bodies are behavior. If it is true that movements and behavior are identical, then the study of behavior should have a sound physical basis. It should, in fact, be mechanistic, for studying the movements of bodies (human or otherwise) is precisely equivalent to classical mechanics. In essence, the behaviorist's stimulus-response theory is nothing more than a qualitative rephrasing of Newton's third law of motion: To every action there is always opposed an equal reaction: or, the mutual actions of two bodies upon each other are always equal, and directed to contrary parts (1725:14).

The behaviorist reformulation of this principle necessarily deletes the second phrase and the condition of equality in the first phrase.[3] In the behaviorist's version: "to every stimulus there is always an (opposed) response." If behaviorists actually study movements, then behaviorism is at least conceptually on a par with other physical sciences, differing from them only in manner of quantification. It must be emphasized that this whole scheme hinges on the identity between movements and behavior. Is it the case that movements and behavior are identical? Is it the case that behaviorists really

66

study movements of bodies? The answer to both questions is decidedly "no." It is readily apparent that the datum of behavior is something more complex than a mere movement. When I say, for example, "He is running up the street," I am reporting a "piece of behavior" (running up the street) which involves a complex of many specific movements. Assuming, for the sake of argument, that there is some analytic or observable phenomenon (like running up the street) corresponding to the phrase "piece of behavior," then this phenomenon must consist of some subset of the set of all observable movements in some unspecified time dimension. A "piece of behavior" is consequently not identical to a simple movement; it is rather some set or collection of simple movements. Since this is the case, behavior and movements are not identical.

Even if behavior and movements are not identical, it still seems possible that behavior is at least reducible in some sense to movement. This is simply another form of the identity argument. Since all reductionistic arguments involve identity, the identity between behavior and movement can be saved if it can be demonstrated that behavior is reducible to movement. That the reductionist argument fails can be demonstrated by posing the question of whether any given "piece of behavior" is always reducible to the same set of movements. That is, does the same set of movements always occur when I report "running up the street"? This is not only a logical impossibility, it is empirically the case that we identify two pieces of behavior as identical even when the hypothetically corresponding movements are not identical. In other words, there are no certain criteria which enable us to say what particular series of movements constitute a given "piece of behavior." What seems to be involved then is not an identity between behavior and movement, but possibly a weak form of an equivalence relation. The implication, however, is clear: If behavior and movement are not identical, we cannot account for behavior in terms of the purely clock-like mechanical models that are appropriate only to movement.[4] The seemingly sound physical basis of behavior is a mere chimera.

Since behaviorists do not study movements, what do they study? After more than 50 years of behaviorism it may seem ridiculous that such a question should be asked, but it is even more ridiculous that there is no obvious or ready answer. Tolman (1961:6-7), for example, maintains that "behavior acts" constitute the fundamental "bits" of behavior. "Behavior acts" are such things as "....to 'sniff,' to 'sit,' to 'scratch,' to 'walk,' to 'gallop,' to 'talk.'" In moving from the "molecular" level of direct physiological events characteristic of Watson's behaviorism, Tolman (1932:6-10) suggests that these behavior acts are "molar" wholes "....in one-to-one correspondence with the underlying molecular facts of physics and physiology...," but with "....emergent properties of their own." We can agree that behavior or behavior acts are not reducible to physiology, but what are these "emergent properties," and what do they have to do with such verbs as "sniffing, sitting, scratching"? When Tolman speaks of "emergent properties," he is at least in part talking about the classification of movements. To be more precise, behavior acts are simply linguistic conventions whose relation to observable phenomena entails, as a minimum, a referential theory of meaning. The behaviorist is presented

67

with an unsegmented flow of observable movement. He precedes to break up or
segment this flow by imposing on it arbitrary linguistic categories like "sniffing"
and "sitting," but he never asks the more fundamental question of what it is
that constitutes "sniffing" and "sitting." Consequently, behavior acts turn
out to be not acts at all, but mere "verbal reports" about acts. This may seem
to some to be of little consequence when we are talking about such things as
"sniffing" and "sitting" since we are tempted to believe that everyone knows
what we are talking about when we use such "low level" descriptions, but what
are the implications when the verbal reports are of the form: "x dominates y,"
or "the x worship their ancestors," or "x has power over y." We are led to ask:
"What constitutes 'dominating,' 'worshiping,' 'ancestors,' or 'power'?" After
all, it is demonstrably not "dominating," "worshiping," "ancestors," or
"power" that we observe, but something else for which we infer these linguistic
categories as appropriate designations. Consequently, we should direct our
attention not to the categories, but to the process by which we derive them, a
process intimately connected with the semantics of natural languages. In
other words, a behaviorist account is dependent on a semantic theory; without
a theory of semantics, a behaviorist account is impossible. And it follows
logically that the theory of semantics cannot be derived from behaviorism. All
attempts to build a semantic theory from behaviorist presuppositions are doomed
simply because these behaviorist presuppositions are not prior to semantic
theory, but are anterior to it.

I have answered the question with which I began: behaviorists study
their own linguistic classifications of events. However, if they do their job
properly, they are inexorably driven to repudiate the most fundamental tenets
of behaviorism. Paradoxically, one cannot be a behaviorist and study behavior.

The Empiricist Dogma and Loquacious Facts

Field work is an integral part of the anthropologist's experience, and
the movement from armchair to field is universally hailed as a turning point in
the history of the discipline. It is not my intention here either to belittle or
discount the necessity for field work. Yet, it must be pointed out that the
anthropologist's commitment to field work is part and parcel of an empiricist
dogma. If you want to know what the universe is like, the only way to find
out is to go and look. Useful as this conception has been for the collection
of certain kinds of natural history data, it has had pernicious effects in other
realms. Because of it, anthropologists are still in the thralls of a tyrannical
inductive method. "Let the facts speak for themselves" might well have been
emblazoned on the banner under which anthropologists fought their battles
against unilineal evolution, racism, armchair sociology, and prejudices against
primitives. From acute observation of numerous instances theoretical generalizations should emerge unaided by prior conceptions or anything more active
than a sort of placid midwifery on the part of the anthropologist. In part,
anthropologists have adhered to this doctrine of loquacious facts because they
believe that external phenomena exhibit a natural order, and this natural order

68

is <u>discoverable</u> if one applies objective techniques. The aim of anthropology, then, has been to devise a set of objective discovery procedures which would more or less automatically reveal the natural ordering of external phenomena. The absurdity of this position should be apparent to anyone who has contemplated a pile of facts. It is a shattering experience from which one emerges impressed with just how mute data can be unless they are plied with questions. Paradoxically, however, answers turn out to be functions of questions. That is, the kind of question you ask determines the response. This strongly implies that any order <u>discovered</u> by such a technique resides in the structure of the question and is not necessarily inherent in the data. Such natural order as there is, then, is in the concepts expressed by questions (Collingwood 1939: 29-43). Whether one also wishes to believe that the data are ordered in the same manner as one's questions is largely a matter of taste.

<u>Universals</u> and <u>the</u> A <u>Priori</u>

Since anthropologists have endorsed the empiricist dogma that observation or sense experience is the basis of all knowledge, they have naturally avoided the "contamination" of rationalist arguments for the existence of a priori knowledge. To admit a priori knowledge is to affirm that humans have incontestable knowledge independently of sense experience. Even though anthropologists might admit that logic and mathematics qualify as a priori knowledge, they would still deny that any significant part of the universe was of fundamentally the same nature as mathematics. Curiously, however, the denial of a priori knowledge of a sort other than mathematical condemns man to a partial and fragmented kind of knowledge. In fact, it can hardly be said to account for knowledge at all. If all knowledge is derived solely from sense experience, then it is difficult to understand how we are able to extrapolate beyond the confines of experience. How do we account for the fact that we can and do know more than we have directly experienced? The doctrine of sense experience does not take into account our ability to grasp the general truth of a proposition on the basis of a limited number of actual instances. Since a general proposition embraces instances of things that have not been directly experienced, it cannot be based entirely on experience. In short, our minds make a jump from actual instances derived from direct experience to general propositions. In the terminology of modern linguistics, we are able to generate propositions that we have not directly experienced. Such a Kantian view neither necessarily invalidates the importance of sense experience, nor neglects the importance of a priori knowledge. We can still assert that a priori knowledge is in some way elicited by experience. In some sense, it seems necessary for us to have sense experience before we can have a priori knowledge. This is not to affirm a developmental priority for sense experience, but is only an assertion that a priori knowledge must have something to operate on. In fact, what we call sense experience presupposes a priori principles which organize the fragmentary data we are given in sensation. When we perceive an object in the external world, we never experience the whole object. We

69

regularly infer the other sides of tables, chairs, people, dollar bills, and other objects. Our sensory experience of these things presupposes the principle of induction and consequently our knowledge of the validity of the principle. Yet, we cannot demonstrate that the principle of induction is in any way derivable from or validated by experience. Similar arguments can be adduced for the principle of inference. Such "laws of thought" are a priori processes by which we categorize and generalize the partial and incomplete knowledge given in sensory experience.

Anthropologists have been chary of a priori knowledge because they see it as a threat to the concept of human plasticity and thereby to political liberalism. It is felt that a priori knowledge is in some way inimical to the doctrine of human malleability. Since the human is molded by his environment, he is capable of change and betterment. Since his knowledge, and by inference, his habits and customs, are derivable from sense experience, it is only necessary to change the character of his experience in order to change his character. It is unquestionable that a priori knowledge places a constraint on this anarchic conception of human knowledge, but that it in any way controverts the plasticity and variability of humans is ludicrous.

More important in accounting for this flight from the a priori is the anthropologist's commitment to the doctrine of cultural relativity. Anthropologists are justifiably infamous for their penchant for the disconfirming case, the one instance that will invalidate some proposed universal. Inasmuch as this attack has been directed toward the demolition of "substantive universals," it is a legitimate scientific procedure. "Substantive universals," however, are not universals in the proper sense; they are merely empirical generalizations.[5] Like all empirical generalizations, they are disconfirmable by non-conforming facts. But, if universals are something other than empirical generalizations, that is, if they are abstract ideas, then they are not subject to disconfirmation by empirical facts. Since it is a characteristic of a universal that it is not an object experienced by means of our sense organs, to concede knowledge of universals is to admit a priori knowledge. It seems to me that anthropologists ought to follow the lead of linguists in the search for universals of this sort. As a partial list of these universals, I suggest the following pan-human modes of thought: categorization (classification), induction, causality, inference, analogy, and metaphor.[6] It is even possible that all of these could be reduced to classification and relationship (classes and relations), or as Lenneberg (1967:331-336) has suggested, to categorization, differentiation, and transformation.[7] When we study a particular culture, we are interested in the way these formal modes of thought are used by natives to generate a set of propositions about the world.

Contingency and Necessity

Anthropological thought is pervaded with a persistent duality that has taken many forms of expression.[8] As the ancient Vedic seers said of God, even though we know him by many names, he is one, so too this duality has

70

many names for a single underlying concept. We have known it variously as: competence vs. performance (Chomsky 1965); la langue vs. la parole (de Saussure 1959); mechanical vs. statistical (Lévi-Strauss 1967); ideological vs. phenomenal (Goodenough 1964); formal vs. functional (Lounsbury 1964); eidos-ethos vs. sociology (Bateson 1936); jural vs. domestic (Fortes 1949); culture vs. patterns of observed behavior (Schneider 1968); sacred vs. profane (Durkheim 1915); deterministic vs. stochastic (Buchler and Selby 1968). In Kantian terms, all of these are more or less equivalent to the distinction between phenomenal and noumenal orders. The phenomenal order is the world as we know it; the world our minds have transformed in the process of knowing. The noumenal order is the world as it is independent of our knowledge. These distinctions also roughly correspond to the broader philosophical divisions of rationalism vs. empiricism. The fundamental distinction, however, is between necessity and contingency; that is, between those things that, as Leibniz observed, are "true in all possible worlds," and those that are merely true given the current state of affairs. Closely allied to this conception is another distinction that has to do with the nature of our knowledge of the world. I refer here to Kant's (1787:16-19) distinction between analytic and synthetic knowledge. Analytic judgements are those in which the predicate B belongs to the subject A as something covertly contained in the concept A. In synthetic judgements the predicate B lies outside the subject A. Analytic judgements, Kant declared, add nothing through the predicate to the concept of the subject. An often cited example of an analytic proposition is: "all unmarried men are bachelors." "Bachelors" conveys no information not already present in the subject "unmarried men." As Ayer (1952:77-80) and others have demonstrated, even though Kant's explicit use of analytic and synthetic was often inconsistent, the distinction is still valid. In Ayer's terminology, an analytic proposition is one whose validity depends solely on the definitions of the symbols it contains, whereas the validity of a synthetic proposition is determined by the facts of experience (1952:78-80). Or, in Carnap's formulation, there is L truth, that is, logical or necessary truth established on the basis of the semantical rules of the system without reference to extra-linguistic facts, and F truth (factual or synthetic or contingent truth) established on the basis of the observation of the relevant facts (Carnap 1947:8-13) [9]

Deriving from this distinction between analytic and synthetic propositions is a classification of the sciences as formal (e.g., logic, mathematics) and factual (e.g., physics and chemistry). As Carnap (1953:123-128) notes, it is precisely the fundamental difference between analytic and synthetic propositions that accounts for the difference between formal and factual sciences. The propositions of mathematics and logic do not owe their validity to empirical verification, but the generalizations of the factual sciences do. We have known since Hume that no general proposition whose validity is subject to a test of experience can ever be logically certain. Even if an empirical generalization holds up in n-1 cases, there is still the possibility that it will be disproved in the nth case. It is always contingent. On the other hand, if the truths of logic and mathematics had factual content, they could not be

71

necessary and certain. Thus, in attempting to reduce all knowledge to sense data, Mill held that the truths of mathematics and logic were simply inductive generalizations based on a large number of instances. They were a kind of habit of thought. This, of course, is the empiricist bind. Either the truths of logic and mathematics are not necessary truths, or they do not have factual content. If they do not have factual content, then the empiricist must admit at least a portion of the rationalist's case for purely a priori mentalistic knowledge.

The point of all this, then, is that some kinds of anthropology are formal sciences and others are factual. Table I shows the formal/factual classification of anthropological sub-disciplines.

Table I. Distribution of Formal and Factual
Sciences in Anthropology

	Formal (Necessary)	Factual (Contingent)
Cultural Anthropology	+	−
Ethnoscience	+	−
Linguistics	+	−
Ethnomusicology	+	−
Folklore	+	−
Social Anthropology (Sociology)	−	+
Archaeology	−	+
Physical Anthropology	−	+
Psychological Anthropology	−	+
Psycholinguistics	−	+
Sociolinguistics	(+)	+

I have included cultural anthropology, ethnoscience, linguistics, ethnomusicology, and folklore in the formal category because their subject matter is the mental codes of other people. This subject matter does not consist of

72

entities with observable physical properties. Consequently, we attempt to understand these codes by means of logical and semantic interpretations of their symbolic expressions. Sociolinguistics is in a special category because it can provide a means of articulation between some of the formal and factual sciences. This articulation is discussed in the following section.

A strict empiricist will immediately object to this formulation. If cultures are mental constructs, then how can I have knowledge of them, since I can only have knowledge of sense data. In response to this question, we either insist with Lévi-Strauss that all a priori mental constructs are pan-human and therefore knowable simply as a function of our common "humanness," or that they are knowable only by analogy. To put the matter more succinctly, "How do we know that other minds exist?" I have argued elsewhere that native cognition (other minds) is an abstract entity (Tyler 1969a). What I meant by this designation was that it was something for which we could not formulate synthetic propositions at all, and for which we can formulate analytic propositions only by analogy. I am willing to concede only metaphysical status to such abstract entities as culture, language, native cognition, other minds, and the like. Since abstract entities cannot as such be observed, verification cannot be effected by reference to empirical data; it can only be effected by the disconfirmation of alternative analytic models.

For cultural anthropology, the implications of this position are far-reaching. It implies that cultural anthropology is not concerned with empirical data in the usual sense. It also implies that cultural anthropology is not con-cerned with natural laws or empirical generalizations. Finally, it implies that cultural anthropology is not a social or behavioral science. The implications for general anthropology are that it is not a unified discipline, even in the rather broad and vague sense of adherence to a common scientific method. Anthropology contains within itself a seemingly irreconcilable duality.[10]

Beyond Duality

One other aspect of this hypostasized duality is relevant to this dis-cussion. Is it not possible that there is some systematic relationship between necessary and contingent facts? To posit such a relation immediately opens the door to a consideration of dialectical and therefore "dynamic" properties of systems and of analysis. Where anthropologists have held to a distinction between necessary and contingent facts, they have either attempted to relate the two in some deterministic fashion, or they have discarded one in favor of the other. Thus, for Marxists (and cultural materialists) contingent facts determine necessary facts. In Durkheim's system, the reverse is true.[11] Most anthropologists have been content to let the causal arrow point in both directions. Despite the continuing popularity of such formulations, they are valueless, or worse, because they obscure the real problem. If we grant that it is possible to formulate a set of empirical propositions referring to contingent facts as well as a set of theoretical propositions referring to nece-ssary facts, then the question is not whether one determines the other, but

73

more simply, "how can one set of propositions be related to the other set?" (cf. Carnap 1966:232-250). What we want is a set of correspondence rules which connects a term in one terminology with a term in another terminology. The correspondence rules have the function of connecting the terms of a necessary model with the terms of a contingent model.

To give a concrete example: when an informant asserts that some person is such and such a kinsman designated by a kin term, we translate the kin term into genealogical notation, attempting to determine the class of genealogical positions denoted by the term. When we attempt to write a formal rule for this process we are not interested in such contingent facts as the social situation or the speaker's intention. We are concerned only with the process of genealogical extension. The end result is a purely formal, non-contingent account of this process. That is, we have constructed a formal (necessary) model. Yet, our informants persist in taking into account things that we have neglected to build into this model. We discover that their use of terms (performance) is sometimes governed by contingent facts. We then derive a model to cover these contingencies. The next question is "how do we relate the formal model to the contingent model?" My suggestion here is that we relate the two models by developing a third model -- a conformance model. This model consists simply of a set of correspondence rules which transform the variables and relations of the formal model into those of the contingent model, or vice versa.[12] The model of the system, then, is neither the formal model nor the contingent model. It is instead the conformance model.

It is of interest to note that such a model also seems to parallel the kind of processes individual speakers take into account in communication. That is, it corresponds to the fact that no two speakers of a language share identical semantic structures (Wallace 1961:29-41). What must happen in communication is that hearers have access to some kind of conformance model which enables them to establish formal equivalencies between their own semantic decoding and the speaker's semantic encoding. A conformance model from the communications point of view mediates between both the speaker's competence and the hearer's competence, but it does so in terms of estimations of competence inferred partially from a performance model. A conformance model in this sense is what Chomsky and Miller (1964) called a comprehension operator.[13]

In this formulation, at least, a conformance model represents an attempt to create a rapprochement between contextual and referential theories of meaning. In brief, a contextual theory encourages us to look for "rules of use" and identifies meaning with the response an utterance elicits from the perceiver. As a consequence, meaning varies with context. A referential theory asserts that an utterance "refers" to or is about something. The English word "tree," for example, denotes or refers to those features characteristic of all trees. Whether the "tree" referred to is an object or a mental construct (an idea) is a matter of some dispute, but in the sense of my use there is no real distinction between objects and ideas about objects. Consequently, what an utterance refers to is an idea.

74

Since the semantic codes (ideas) of any two individuals can never be identical, solipsism is true, and "private languages" are possible. The later Wittgenstein (1958) maintained that such private languages were impossible. In its most succinct form, Wittgenstein's view is that I cannot know if I have used a term correctly in my private language, that is, I cannot know if my use is consistent with my own definition. Thus, the rules of my private language are only impressions of rules. Since Wittgenstein equates language with rules, it follows that my private language cannot be a language. All I can say is that I have an impression of language or that I think I understand it. I agree that this is the case, but only where "public language" is concerned. In the first place, it is not necessary to assume that language (or at least its semantic aspect) consists merely in agreed upon rules of use. Secondly, if I am to endorse this view, I must be willing to agree that I am incapable of thinking about my private language. But since I maintain that I am perfectly capable of inventing a second private language which interprets or explains the first private language, then it is obvious that I can invent or discover what-ever set of rules I may find necessary for my private language.[14] Private languages are possible, then, even under the stricture of rules of use. It is paradoxical that Wittgenstein's strictures on private languages actually pertain only to "public language." It is self-evident that public languages do have this quality of indeterminateness in their semantic aspect. In a public language it is only necessary that I have or give the impression of understanding language; whether I really understand it in Wittgenstein's sense is irrelevant. What this implies is that people do not actually communicate; they only give the appearance of communicating. This appearance, however, may be adjudged more or less adequate as a performance depending upon how well it conforms to the rules of my private language.

Despite its behavioral predisposition explicit in the idea that meaning is equivalent to the response it elicits in the perceiver, the contextual theory of meaning also curiously contains an Hegelian proposition. The slogan that meaning varies with context is a form of holistic argument. Like Hegelian holism it is workable only if it can be demonstrated that contexts are finite. Note also that if rules of use are to incorporate contextual features, it is not even possible to formulate rules unless contexts are finite. It does not need demonstration to prove that the total physical surroundings or context of any utterance are never exactly the same on two different occasions. Thus, con-texts cannot be finite. This is the paradox of the contextual theory. Since the notion of context violates the idea of rule, we cannot properly speak of meaning as a rule of use. Yet, since humans do seem to take contextual features into account, they must have some means of establishing equivalencies among non-identical contexts. Just as the more general problem of behaviorism can only be resolved by a phenomenological approach, so too with context.

Holism and Eclecticism

Most anthropologists at least pay lip service to the belief that the anthropological discipline has an underlying unity expressed in a shared

75

preoccupation with the phenomenon of man. Lacking common axioms, methods, and results, anthropologists are bound together only by their object of study. The primary corollary to this belief in unity is that the understanding of man will be the result of combined evidence from psychology, biology, history, economics, sociology, religion, philosophy, and art. It follows from this that the anthropologist is free to draw on any or all of these disciplines in formulating his own views of man. In endorsing this holistic approach to the study of man the anthropologist is a committed, but irresponsible, eclectic. To many this looseness of the disciplinary strait jacket is a positive asset, and to the extent that commitment to holism is founded on the presupposition that the whole is greater than the sum of its parts, no one would disagree with the implied need for a view of man that transcends and integrates the partial, incompete, and fragmented views of man represented by other academic disciplines. The problem is whether the implications of holism are consistent with science. Both Hegel and Whitehead (among others) have argued not only for a holistic view, but have also demonstrated the inherent incompatability between holism and science.[15] That this problem has not perturbed anthropologists is testimony to the fact that the anthropologist's attempts at holistic interpretation have either been entirely mechanical (and therefore not genuinely holistic) or artistic (and therefore not genuinely scientific). The dilemma of contemporary anthropology derives from its pursuit of science. If we want a science of man, then we must be content with a relativistic account in which the nature of man is determined by the academic and disciplinary viewpoint of the observer. We will have not only economic man, but psychological man, biological man, artistic man, and anthropological man. On the other hand, if we wish to preserve the uniquely anthropological commitment to a holistic view of man, we cannot allow ourselves to be fettered by the preconceptions of a materialistic and empirical science.

NOTES

1. I wish to thank Marshall Durbin, Charles Hudson, and David Schneider for their helpful comments on an earlier version of this paper.

2. For a penetrating discussion of the behaviorist position in linguistics, see: Chomsky (1959).

3. As Haring (1956:107-8) notes, the "dynamic equivalence" between stimulus and response does not obtain.

4. This discussion derives from Hamlyn (1962).

5. This seems to be the source of some of the confusion about the role of universals in transformational grammar. Chomsky sometimes talks as if universals were empirical generalizations (1965:35-36) but at other times (27-30, 117-118) clearly specifies the distinction between universals and empirical

76

generalizations. On the other hand, Greenberg's (1963) so-called universals are really empirical generalizations.

6. If it is argued that inclusion of causality commits me to a Kantian synthetic a priori (that is, an a priori concept derived from experience), I would not deny it. What I would deny is that the dissolution of the synthetic a priori in modern physics and philosophy (cf. Reichenbach 1953:202, 208-211) implies its dissolution as a cognitive universal -- even for modern physicists and philosophers. This is an important point because it provides the key to a primary distinction between philosophy and anthropology. I think it is fair to say that the whole history of philosophy can be regarded as an attack on commonsense notions of the world. One of the chief functions of philosophy is to scrutinize commonsense views of the world and evaluate their truth or falsity. Anthropologists, however, are interested in describing commonsense views of the world, but are not primarily interested in assessing their truth of falsity.

7. It is interesting to note that James (1891:867-78) derived all of these functions from the mind's ability to compare. According to James, it is this ability to establish resemblance and difference relations between ideal objects that enables us to classify. Since the operation of comparing can be repeated on its own results, the mind becomes aware of series and eventually of the principle of "skipped intermediaries." That is, skipping intermediate terms in a series leaves the relations the same. Similarly, substituting classes for terms enables us to apply the principle of skipped intermediaries to propositions. This in turn enables us to relate things so naturally remote that we would never have thought them comparable.

8. This section and parts of the one following were originally given as a talk before the Tulane University Anthropology Colloquium in February, 1969. It has benefitted from the suggestions of my Tulane colleagues.

9. Carnap (1966:259-60) later modified this view by introducing a category of "A" (analytic) truth to cover those propositions which were not L true, but were true because of the meanings assigned to their descriptive terms as well as the meanings assigned to their logical terms. I mention this change here because "A" truth seems especially pertinent to the problems that interest anthropologists and linguists.

10. The distinction between formal and factual sciences is difficult to maintain if the arguments against causality, mechanism, and materialism are accepted, for, in a sense, the force of these arguments is to reduce all factual sciences to formal sciences. This is the case both developmentally and in terms of what so-called empirical (factual) scientists do. The history of all factual sciences is merely a record of increasing approximation to the certitudes of mathematics. In essence, the goal of any respectable factual scientist is to turn his science into a formal one. Factual sciences are ranked as more or less developed

77

depending on how much of their content can be stated in purely formal, mathematical terms. Since I have already demonstrated that an empiricist view of the relation between the perceiver and the external world cannot be supported, it follows that the factual scientist actually manipulates concepts and symbols whose ontological status is at least dubious. All of the supposedly sensible experiences of the factual scientist are necessarily translated into other terms which exemplify the ideal relations of kind, number, and form no different from those of the formal scientist. Despite these facts, I still maintain that there is a difference between formal and factual sciences. The difference is that the knowledgeable factual scientist operates *as if* a materialist view of the world is correct (the ignorant factual scientists *believes* that the materialist view of the world is correct), while the formal scientist need not, and in fact cannot make this assumption.

11. Durkheim was not always consistent on this point.

12. A more detailed example of the use of a conformance model in anthropology can be found in Tyler (1969b).

13. Because they assume an isomorphism between encoding and decoding, information-processing approaches to cognition incorrectly assumed that both speakers and hearers have identical semantic structures (Cf. Reitman 1966:230-40). Some anthropologists commit this same error when they assume that their decoding of a kinship terminology is isomorphic with the native speaker's encoding processes.

14. Note that I make no claim for the completeness or consistency of the ideal language whose function is to explain my private language. Thus the question of whether a language can both be consistent and say something about itself is irrelevant.

15. In James' (1891:862) terms, "The reality *exists* as a *plenum*. All its parts are contemporaneous, each is as real as any other, and each as essential for making the whole just what it is and nothing else. But we can neither experience nor think this *plenum*."

REFERENCES

Ayer, A. J.
    1952   Language, Truth and Logic (New York: Dover).
Bateson, Gregory
    1936   Naven (Cambridge: Cambridge University Press).
Buchler, Ira R., and Henry Selby
    1968   Kinship and Social Organization (New York: Macmillan).
Carnap, Rudolf
    1947   Meaning and Necessity (Chicago: University of Chicago Press).

78

1953   Formal and Factual Science. In Readings in the Philosophy of Science, Herbert Feigl and May Brodbeck, eds. (New York: Appleton-Century-Crofts).

1966   Philosophical Foundations of Physics (New York: Basic Books).

Chomsky, Noam
1959   Review of B.F. Skinner, "Verbal Behavior." Language 35: 26-58.

1965   Aspects of the Theory of Syntax (Cambridge, Mass: M.I.T. Press).

Collingwood, R.G.
1939   An Autobiography (New York: Oxford University Press).

Durkheim, Emile
1915   The Elementary Forms of the Religious Life, J.W. Swain, trans. (London: Allen).

Eddington, Sir Arthur
1966   Space, Time and Gravitation (Cambridge: Cambridge University Press).

Fortes, Meyer
1949   Time and social structure. In Social Structure, Meyer Fortes, ed. (Oxford: Clarendon Press).

Goodenough, Ward H.
1964   Introduction. In Explorations in Cultural Anthropology, Ward H. Goodenough, ed. (New York: McGraw-Hill).

Greenberg, Joseph
1963   Some Universals of Grammar with Particular Reference to the Order of Meaningful Elements. In Universals of Language, J. H. Greenberg, ed. (Cambridge: M.I.T. Press).

Hamlyn, D.W.
1962   Behavior. In The Philosophy of Mind, V.C. Chappell, ed. (Englewood Cliffs, New Jersey: Prentice-Hall).

Haring, Douglas G.
1956   Science and Social Phenomena. In Personal Character and Cultural Milieu, 3rd revised edition, D. G. Haring, ed. (Syracuse: Syracuse University Press).

James, William
1891   The Principles of Psychology (Chicago: Encyclopedia Britannica), 1952.

Kant, Immanuel
1787   The Critique of Pure Reason, 2nd. ed. (Chicago: Encyclopedia Britannica), 1952.

Lenneberg, Eric H.
1967   Biological Foundations of Language (New York: Wiley).

Lévi-Strauss, Claude
1967   Structural Anthropology, Claire Jacobsen and Brooke G. Schoepf, trans. (New York: Doubleday).

Lounsbury, Floyd
1964   The Formal Analysis of Crow- and Omaha-Type Kinship

79

Terminologies. In Explorations in Cultural Anthropology, W. H. Goodenough, ed. (New York: McGraw-Hill).

Miller, G. A. and Noam Chomsky
1964   Introduction to the Formal Analysis of Natural Languages. In Handbook of Mathematical Psychology, Vol. II, P. Luce, R. Bush, and E. Galanter, eds. (New York: McGraw-Hill).

Newton, Sir Isaac
1725   Mathematical Principles of Natural Philosophy, 3rd ed. (Chicago: Encyclopedia Britannica), 1952.

Reichenbach, Hans
1953   The Philosophical Significance of the Theory of Relativity. In Readings in the Philosophy of Science, Herbert Feigl and May Brodbeck, eds. (New York: Appleton-Century-Crofts).

Reitman, Walter R.
1966   Cognition and Thought (New York: Wiley).

Russell, Bertrand
1929   Our Knowledge of the External World (New York: Norton).

Schneider, David M.
1968   American Kinship (Englewood Cliffs, New Jersey: Prentice-Hall).

Saussure, Ferdinand de
1959   Course in General Linguistics. Wade Baskin, trans. (New York: Philosophical Library).

Tolman, Edward C.
1932   Purposive Behavior in Animals and Men (New York: The Century Co.).

Tyler, Stephen A.
1969a   The Myth of P: Epistemology and Formal Analysis. To be published in the American Anthropologist.
1969b   Comments on Alan R. Beals, "Dravidian Kinship." To be published by the University of Texas Press.

Wallace, A. F. C.
1961   Culture and Personality (New York: Random House).

Wittgenstein, Ludwig
1958   Philosophical Investigations, 2nd edition, G.E.M. Anscombe, trans. (New York: Macmillan).

80

THE CONTRIBUTORS

E. Pendleton Banks is chairman of the Department of Sociology and Anthropology at Wake Forest University. He has done field work in the Lesser Antilles, Burma, and Yugoslavia, and currently is doing research on sociocultural change in Yugoslavia. His theoretical interests include values, structural theory, and cultural ecology.

Jan Brukman is instructor of anthropology in the Department of Anthropology of the University of Illinois. His topical interests include formal semantic analysis, descriptive and analytic techniques in ethnography, social structure, and sociolinguistics. His area interest is South Asia.

Munro S. Edmonson is chairman of the Department of Anthropology at Tulane University and past president of the American Ethnological Society. He has done field work among New Mexico Spanish Americans, New Orleans Negroes, and Guatemala Mayans. He has published on topics including status terminology, kinship, folklore, race, nativistic movements, linguistics, pottery, and most recently a translation of the Popol Vuh and a general book on lore. He is currently working on a dictionary of Yucatecan Maya.

Ann Fischer is a professor in the Department of Anthropology at Newcomb College, Tulane University. She also holds an appointment in the School of Public Health and Tropical Medicine. She has done field work and published on her experiences in Truk and Ponape in Micronesia, Japan, New England, and among the Houma Indians. Most recently she has been completing a study of family structure through two generations in New Orleans. Her main interests are in culture and personality, socialization, family studies, and medical anthropology.

William G. Haag is professor of anthropology in the Department of Geography and Anthropology at Louisiana State University. His main interest is the archaeology of the Southeastern United States, and he has done extensive field work there as well as in St. Lucia and Martinique.

Francis E. Johnston is associate professor of anthropology at the University of Texas at Austin. His interests are primarily in two areas: the interaction of bio-cultural factors in the creation, patterning, and maintenance of genetic variance; and the adaptive nature of human development. He has conducted field work in Peru, Guatemala, and the United States.

Arden R. King is professor and head of the Department of Anthropology, Newcomb College, and research associate of the Middle American Research

81

Institute in Tulane University. His primary interests are in Nuclear America, especially Meso-America, and anthropological theory.

Stephen A. Tyler is associate professor of anthropology at Tulane University. His theoretical interests are cognitive anthropology, kinship, language and culture, and comparative Dravidian linguistics. His area interest is India.

Eric R. Wolf is professor of anthropology in the Department of Anthropology at the University of Michigan. He has done field work in Puerto Rico, Mexico, and the Italian Alps; his main interest lies in the comparative study of peasant populations. Together with Dr. Sylvia Thrupp, he is co-editor of Comparative Studies in Society and History.

82

Proceedings No. 4.
The Not So Solid South
Anthropological Studies in a Regional Subculture

Edited by J. Kenneth Morland

SOUTHERN ANTHROPOLOGICAL SOCIETY

Founded 1966

Officers 1970-71

John J. Honigmann, President

Arden R. King, President Elect

Miles Richardson, Secretary-Treasurer

John L. Fischer, Councilor 1970-71

Harriet J. Kupferer, Councilor 1970-72

Francis Johnston, Councilor 1970-73

Charles Hudson, Editor

Joseph B. Aceves, Program Chairman

Copyright © 1971 by
Southern Anthropological Society
LC 70-1429122
ISBN 8203-0304-6
Printed in the United States

Contents

v

Preface

WITH the publication of this volume the Southern Anthropologica
Society inaugurates two changes in its program of publication. One
change is to a more compact and more attractive format, and the
other change is in the number of Proceedings published. The Society
will continue its established policy of publishing a Proceedings each
year consisting of papers presented at the "key symposium" of each
annual spring meeting. The Innovation is that when funds permit the
Society will publish additional Proceedings numbered consecutively
with the others. Like the present volume, these additional Proceedings will usually consist of collections of papers dealing with a particular subject or problem. The papers in this collection were selected
from those presented at recent American Anthropological Association and Southern Anthropological Society meetings and
from a conference sponsored by the Center for Southern Studies
at Duke University. However, this need not be the case in the future:
the policy will remain flexible, and other kinds of manuscripts will
be considered. This collection, *The Not So Solid South*, is an appropriate beginning for this new program of publication. In an era
in which college students are questioning the relevance of anthropology
to contemporary society, the papers in this collection show in a
rather direct fashion how anthropology can be not only relevant but
readable.

This volume owes much to the editorial criticism of my wife, Joyce
Rockwood Hudson.

Charles Hudson
SAS Editor

vii

Introduction

J. KENNETH MORLAND

AT the 68th Annual Meeting of the American Anthropological Association in New Orleans in November, 1969, one of the resolutions presented to the membership called for support of anthropological studies of American society. Overwhelmingly approved, the resolution stated:

> Whereas anthropological studies of contemporary American society are essential to the advancement of anthropology as a science and to the well being of the society,
>
> And whereas increasing numbers of students entering anthropology wish to undertake research on contemporary American society,
>
> And whereas such studies, and the training of students to undertake them, have been relatively neglected,
>
> Therefore,
>
> Be it resolved that the American Anthropological Association recognizes the legitimacy and importance of such research and training, and urges the active development of both.

Actually, the papers included in this volume anticipated the resolution, for they are anthropological studies of American society that were well under way prior to November, 1969. Most of the papers were selected from those presented in a symposium on the American South at the annual meeting of the Southern Anthropological Society in March, 1969, and from another symposium on the same topic at the 68th Annual Meeting of the American Anthropological Association. In addition, two were first presented at a conference sponsored by the Center for Southern Studies at Duke University in January, 1969.

The papers in this volume are significant for several reasons. First, they demonstrate a considerable range of possibilities for

1

anthropological research in present-day American society, particularly in the South. They deal with such varied groups as a healing sect, gypsies, coal miners, peasants, urban mill workers, moonshiners, a hippie ghetto, and a remnant Indian tribe; and with such cultural phenomena as pottery traditions, funeral practices, religious disease, and techniques for eluding the sheriff. They are therefore suggestive of the kinds of projects close at hand that may be utilized in the training of graduate students and as the objects of field work by seasoned anthropologists. These research undertakings show that it is not always necessary for anthropologists to go to remote places or to find exotic peoples in order to do research.

Second, these research papers illustrate the complexity of the Southern regional subculture. They show that the South is far from being as homogeneous or "solid" as it has sometimes been called. It is to be noted that these studies are termed research *in* rather than *of* the region, for there is no pretense that they represent the study of the South as a whole. Indeed, some might say that the groups dealt with in these papers are not in the mainstream of the regional sub-culture, and that their very differences and relative isolation make them amenable to anthropological research. All we can say at this point is that these groups do exist in the South and are presumably part of the regional subculture. The papers are offered as beginnings of what might be extensive anthropological research to establish just what is held in common by Southerners. It is true that at least three of the studies point to regional subcultural characteristics: Crocker's "The Southern Way of Death," Peacock's "The Southern Protestant Ethic Disease," and Sayers' "The Southern Pottery Tradition"; and most of the other studies imply characteristics that appear to permeate the region. However, these regional generalizations are stated as hypotheses that require testing through further research.

Third, these research undertakings demonstrate that participant-observation, the hallmark of anthropological method, can be employed in the culture of which the researcher is a part. It is evident that the groups described in these papers have been observed and analyzed with objectivity and that the cultural background of the researchers has not hindered their perception. At the same time, they have realized one great advantage from studying within their own culture, namely the understanding of the language, making it unnecessary to resort to interpreters. Admittedly, these studies cannot hope to succeed fully in being "holistic," that is, in being related to the entire society and culture of which the group or phenomenon studied is a part. When anthropologists do research on relatively small, isolated, homogeneous societies, the problem of showing the inter-relatedness of culture patterns is not so great. With a large, heterogeneous society, however, trying to deal with the cultural context of the behavior being described and analyzed is difficult indeed. Nevertheless, it is something with which the anthropologist must deal if his study of American society and culture is to be successful. More will be said about this in the concluding chapter. In addition to the use of anthropological method, it is to be noted that the authors of these studies apply to American society concepts developed in traditional anthropological study of smaller, more homogeneous folk societies. Thus, one of the papers employs "rites of passage" and "revitalization process," two deal with "peasantry," and another relies on "symbolic behavior" as an organizing concept. The assumption is that American society is as amenable to the use of such terms as any other society.

Fourth, it is significant that most of the contributors to this volume are relatively young. Some have only recently acquired their graduate degrees, and some are still in the process of doing so. In accord with the resolution of the American Anthropological Association calling for more studies of American society, these authors represent a considerable number of anthropologists who at the very beginning of their careers share a strong interest in increasing the understanding of their own culture through anthropological research. Anthropologists have much to learn about American society and culture, and with many younger anthropologists showing strong interest the future of the research necessary to such learning is bright.

The papers are arranged so that studies of specific groups precede studies that look at aspects of behavior which are assumed to characterize the South as a whole. Once more, it is to be emphasized that the authors of these research reports present highly tentative generalizations about what they have studied. The papers are offered as starting points of what the authors hope will lead to more extensive research by themselves and by others.

All of the contributors, including the editor, are especially indebted to Charles Hudson, Proceedings editor, for his encouragement, helpful suggestions, and skillful guidance of this volume into print.

Higher on the Hog

HELEN PHILLIPS KEBER

THE following pages are an attempt to substantiate the position that black divine healing in a southeastern United States town does not pose a barrier to sociocultural change but rather encourages such change among its members. I have conducted research on a group of black divine healers in Oakboro from May 1968 continuously to the present.[1] Oakboro, located in the Piedmont of the Appalachians, is composed of three major social segments—low-income whites, the blacks, and university personnel and students. The group I have been studying is numerically small. Those in regular attendance at the weekly healing meeting include about eleven women, ten men, and their children. A few others come less regularly. It is entirely a volunteer group and forms only a small portion of the black community of which it is a part. The leader is a black woman, Sister Thompson, from another town, who leaves her family every weekend to come to Oakboro. Every Friday night she holds a healing meeting in the home of one of the "Saints," the term by which I shall refer to Sister Thompson and her followers. During the rest of the weekend she spends the nights in the Saints' homes, has the members come visit with her to discuss their problems, goes shopping with them, and, in general participates in their activities. She is essential to the group; without her it would disband.

There is little agreement upon the best label for, and by implication the best way to conceive of, the sociocultural situation of the Saints.[2] Whether to term it lower-class culture (Frazier 1966), a culture of poverty after Oscar Lewis (1966), an American subculture or subsociety, or black culture *per se* (Keil 1966) is currently debated because it is an issue that is both central to research and to methodological and theoretical orientations. Terming the Saints low-income blacks is appropriate in one sense; yet it suggests similarities with blacks throughout the United States that I have not found to

4

be valid (Young 1970). My solution is to utilize an approach appropriate for delimiting sociocultural variables in developing nations. The Saints are definitely responding to sociocultural change which is best characterized as a shift from a more "traditional" life—farm-reared, white-dominated—into a more "modern" one—dependence on cash, the securing of material goods, and the development of a self-image as equal to whites. The following paragraphs outline some aspects of this change.

Sister Thompson and the Saints are confronted with the surrounding society's many specialized organizations and institutions. They must adapt to some of these; others they ignore or avoid. Hence, the degree to which they participate in this surrounding society must be investigated.

Compared to United States society as a whole, the Saints are poorly educated. The adults themselves have in no case completed high school, all having grown up on farms and moved to town as adults. However, their children are being sent through the school system.

The Saints possess skills which are unspecialized in comparison with those of many people in the United States. All utilize the same skill—menial or manual labor in a variety of jobs. The men work as janitors at the university, at a grocery store, or at the Town Hall. The women work as maids in private homes, in schools, or in businesses. With this same unspecialized skill they can and have worked in a variety of jobs. Their employment periodically shifts, especially in the case of the women. Basically, obtainment of jobs follows the modernized pattern of universalism; i.e., obtainment of jobs is based on ability rather than on ascribed status. Referral is by word-of-mouth or by formal application and is not handed from kin to kin or gained through "pull." Nevertheless, in one important aspect obtainment of jobs is particularistic. They obtain these jobs by being who they are—by being black.

Politics, whether local, state, or national, is a topic I have rarely heard mentioned, despite admiration for both Martin Luther King, Jr. and the Kennedys. The racial riots are viewed as an effective political instrument, but the Christian outlook of the Saints leads them to disagree with violence as a means to an end. In their opinion one should act with love towards all one's fellow men, yet they believe the riots brought about changes which King and other peaceful civil rights workers were unable to accomplish. Occasionally they talk of formulating a petition to have their dirt roads paved. Such talk is closer to overt political action than anything I have encountered. Even in the November 1968 local, state, and national elections not one of the members voted, despite a suspicion that if Nixon were elected it would be detrimental to blacks.

The Saints participate in formalized churches with the encouragement of Sister Thompson but with the warning that not all ministers are honest and sincere. Their churches appear to be a potent factor in their adjustment to modern life. For one thing, the minister of the largest black church in town, and the one to which the majority of the Saints belong, is a civic leader in addition to being a religious leader. In both capacities he is involved in many committees and other community activities. As their leader he provides his congregation with a model after which they expect to pattern their lives. The bureaucratic nature of his activities provides for his congregation a role model that is not a part of their "traditional" life.

In addition to the minister's role, the structure of the formalized church offers its congregation an experience in modern living. Based on state and national church institutions, many committees and organizations in which the members participate compose the structure of the church. Rather than conducting solely business meetings, their meetings take the broad form of a church service interrupted for the business sessions which substitute for the sermon and are conducted by parliamentary procedure. My contention is that familiarity with the existence of these church organizations and with their manner of operation provides the members with a means of comprehending and handling the many specialized organizations, including bureaucratic systems, which they encounter in their surrounding society, a means which again is not in evidence in other aspects of the life of the Saints.

Kinship among blacks is a difficult subject with which to deal. Keil's characterization of black kinship as a battle of the sexes is manifest in the kinship of the Saints. Their marriages are more permanent than those that Keil (1966) and Liebow (1967) describe for the ghetto. The men stay with their families, perhaps because they are able to obtain regular employment and are thereby encouraged to "sink roots into the world in which they live" (Liebow 1967:70). Nevertheless, relationships between the sexes appear to be governed by what Keil terms "variations of the finance-romance equation" (Keil 1966:9) rather than by a concern for the primacy of the nuclear family. The men do not fit the white middle-class husband's role of provider; rather they aspire to the role of their culture hero—the hustler, the good preacher, or the entertainer who is financially well-off without having to undergo regular work for an employer. With no loss of respect to the husband, the wife contributes as much to the cash income as he does, if not more, regardless of whether they have children to support.

With this brief entrance into the lives of the Saints, I will now turn attention to their Friday night healing meeting. I will attempt to convey to the reader the experience of the Friday night meeting through a description in print. The medium of print is, however, ironically unsuited to this purpose. Most of white America reveres the printed word, the literary tradition, and its attendant values. On the other hand, among the Saints the spoken word and the oral tradition carry more power. Their modes of perception and expression and their channels of communication are primarily auditory and tactile rather than visual and literate (Keil 1966:16-7). It is essential in the description which follows to pay attention to the auditory and tactile activities of the healing meeting rather than to view the description as a transcription of a hypothetical meeting.

There are three parts to the healing meetings: the devotional, the testimonial, and the healing. The healing meeting is unlike many middle-class, white liturgical church services for which a printed program maps beforehand in minute detail the order, the content, and the form of the many parts. In the healing meeting the boundaries between the three parts are only sometimes enunciated and clear cut. At other times one part flows into the other or the testimonials and the healing may become intertwined. Not only are the boundaries indefinite but the procedure and the outcome are not planned beforehand. The boundaries remain fluid as the members respond to Sister Thompson, to one another, and to the Holy Spirit within themselves.

The setting is a house of one of the members. Some houses are large enough to comfortably accommodate everyone; others are small, so that everyone is crowded together with the children on each other's or an adult's lap. Even in the heat of summer the doors and windows are closed and the drapes drawn, although strangers are welcomed. Not only does this prevent the devils who are upon the earth from using what goes on during the service to their own evil ends, but it also prevents distractions from outside the circle in which everyone is seated.

The members arrive and enter the living room around eight o'clock at night. Rather than assuming a reverent attitude, they talk with one another, discussing the cars outside, what went on last week, the dog next door, the milkman, or joke with each other, or watch television. Sister Thompson goes into the back bedroom where the people may follow to talk with her. Perhaps someone starts a song.

Perhaps Sister Thompson reappears, asking someone to read the scripture and lead the prayer, the events which constitute the devotional. Usually it is a group prayer, signaled by the phrase, "Let every heart in the building pray," so that everyone gets down on his knees and addresses the Lord directly. In this short and informal manner the stage is set for the rest of the evening.

Usually somewhere near the beginning Sister Thompson will stand up and take over leadership by announcing that the service is open to testimony. She says: "Let every heart sing, pray, dance, do whatever the Spirit leads you to do. If the Spirit says 'Shout,' you shout. If it says, 'Sing,' you sing. Let's not clap our hands lightly and half-heartedly, but loudly and from our hearts. And stomp your feet. If you do, it won't be long until you are out there shouting for the Lord."

She encourages, cajoles, coaxes, and reprimands the members into participating not only with their spoken testimonies but with their entire bodies.

The testimonial is directed towards praising the Lord. It is not a confession of sins. The several attempts at turning it into confession that I witnessed were unsuccessful and unapproved. Everyone is patient with a confession, since one direction of the meeting is that everyone always—within the limits of what is considered moral—gets to do and is encouraged to do what he wants. Yet, after a confession, Sister Thompson will say, "Let's not confess our sins. Let's praise the Lord. Let's tell what the Lord has done for us. The Lord has done so many things. Let's praise his name." Thus, the testimonial is a praising of the Lord, a listing of blessings received. It is an activity in which everyone present must participate.

The general pattern is to begin one's testimony with a song. One person will begin the song and lead it, although leadership may be taken over by someone else at any time during the song. When the song is well underway (and it can go on as long as is wanted) the individual who started it stands up. He testifies, usually relating the first part of his testimony to the theme of the song. The rest of the testimony may continue on an entirely different tangent. A person can give a short, formalized testimony or a long, personal testimony. Sometimes the long testimonies actually become narrative story-telling, as when one individual recounted all the events of his long trip to and from California. Or a person can simply list all the things which the Lord has done for him. The individual may also lead a prayer in his testimony.

The testimonies are earthy and mundane, bringing to mind daily, non-ritual life with its struggles and conflicts, its good and bad sides, its miracles and simple happenings, its successes and hopes. Sometimes they are monotonous and ticked off mechanically; but then again they are told with enthusiasm and fervor so that everyone responds with "Amen, Yes Sir, Tell it like it is," with a clapping of hands to the rhythmical rhetoric or with shouting. If the individual becomes so enwrapped in his testimony that it is obvious the Lord is going to bless him at that moment instead of during the healing, Sister Thompson will take the lead, starting a song which everyone takes up while the individual dances and shouts, rejoicing in his contact with the Lord.

Usually near the beginning—although she may do this more than once—Sister Thompson gives a testimony which approaches being a sermon. It is impromptu, for written speeches are not considered to be the Lord's words. Sister Thompson tells the Saints how to live by giving examples of how the Lord has told her to live. Yet the members may revere her words not so much from the logic of what she says as from the manner in which she tells it. Keil writes regarding blue-singers that "It is the intensity and conviction with which the story is spelled out, the fragments of experience pieced together, rather than the story itself" (1966:17) by which performances are measured. The same may be true of Sister Thompson's testimony. It is usually long, with no central theme but with many subjects, the fragment of one leading to a related other. Her approach to validation is a frenzied one. She will lull through an extended interval with side-stories and occasional jokes. But when she reaches her point, her voice becomes louder, her emphases stronger, she repeats phrases, and slides into a rhythmical rhetoric which borders on being a song. She leads, clapping at the end of each phrase and tapping her foot throughout; the members form the chorus, affirming her every phrase through their hands, feet, and voices. As a leader her sense of timing is superb. She knows how to phrase, when to pause, where to accent, how to hold and bend a word, a note, or her body.

The climax of the meeting does not come until the healing. The point of it is to receive a blessing from the Lord. That is what the members say they come for and why participation is encouraged. The blessing comes when Sister Thompson lays her hands on the individual, thereby transferring the power of the Lord which resides in her to the individual and taking on any demons that may be in his body. It is a tactile experience, for the individual feels the power, the spirit of the Lord, move through his body. The Saints say it is similar to an electric shock.

Sister Thompson might pray over each individual as all stand in a circle. She might make them form a long line or form several lines, each having a special purpose. Sometimes she simply says one prayer that applies to everyone. Sometimes she has each person approach her. As everyone touches a part of her body, she bends and sways. Sometimes blessings are obtained by touching her hands as the olive oil with which she has been anointed runs down her arms. Sometimes she has everyone place their purses and wallets or their shoes in a pile and she says a blessing over them.

During the healing there is much support and participation from those who are not being prayed over at the moment. Everyone will be singing, shouting, and clapping. Someone will have started a song, in which everyone joins. Usually the song is fast-moving with only one or two lines that are repeated again and again and again. With repetition the bodily movements, the clapping, and the foot-tapping require less and less effort as they flow with the music. Usually the same song continues throughout the healing; occasionally it is changed. Sometimes there is a leader, sometimes there is not. People clap, tap their feet, shout, suddenly dance and get into frenzies, which are outside the song and the beat; and people pass out in a trance on the floor. A beat permeates the atmosphere, the floor sends it through one's feet, the chairs reverberate, the clapping encourages it, the song can not break from it, the rise and fall singsong of those praying is formed by it. The praying is a request for a blessing made by Sister Thompson for the individual she is praying over. Each request has the same rhythmical refrain; they are matched. The request begins on a high note from which she glides down about three or four notes to a level on which her vibrato sustains and draws out the prayer. Lorrine and Jack, her assistants, carry on their own singsong which they synchronize to fit that of Sister Thompson. Theirs, each of which is different, are not identical to hers but fit the same rhythm, so that the prayer becomes a trio. The shouts of "Glory, hallelujah," "Amen," "Yes, Jesus," are caught in the beat of the song and the trio. As Sister Thompson reaches the pinnacle of her request, she grippingly lays on her hands; the individual jolts as the "electric shock" of his blessing from the Lord shoots through him, while the beat and the song endure.

The rest of the meeting is anticlimactical. An informal atmosphere with small talk among various members pervades the offering and its blessing. There is a request for any additional remarks (in which members who were late or did not get to testify can do so), for announcements, for telling about a particularly good blessing received during the healing, followed by the benediction and the farewell handshaking.

The healing meeting encourages the members to new behavior in their daily lives rather than encouraging them to continue in a subordinate relation to whites or strengthening their attachment to "traditional" life. To understand the meeting as such it is necessary to view the ritual as action and form rather than as the mapping out of an ideology. The final paragraphs suggest the processes by which participation in the healing meeting offers an effective means of coping with modern life.

When I meet one of the Saints the day after, or several days after the Friday night meeting, or when I overhear several of them discussing the meeting, talk always centers on how "good" the meeting was. If a person was not there, his first question will be, "Was it a good meeting?" If he was there, he will begin the discussion by declaring "Wasn't it a good meeting!" "Good" meetings are desired and some meetings are "better" than others. The Saints say they are "out to have a good time in the Lord" at the meeting; they are there "to enjoy" themselves. Yet, "good" meetings do not just happen. They occur when the spirit is high. A high spirit is created in the following manner.

As I noted above, Sister Thompson usually gives a testimony early in the meeting, shortly after the devotional. In it she encourages everyone to participate vigorously, explaining to them all the ways that one can "make a joyful noise to the Lord" and reminding them that if they participate "from the heart," they will soon be filled with the Lord—i.e., obtain a blessing. She also testifies to the many blessings she has received, thereby pointing out the wide range in their testimonies, drawing from all sorts of daily experiences, to make their testimonies intimate, creative, and insightful rather than rattling off a string of formalities. If encouragement is not enough, when the individual finishes his testimony Sister Thompson will often require him to stand up again and tell such-and-such a tale to the glory of God. She is very concerned that the spirit of the meeting not be broken. The only instances in which I have seen her interrupt the service is to give this instruction. Her efforts to elicit meaningful testimonies are efforts to raise the spirit, to create a "good" meeting. A meaningful testimony includes references to gaining that which is desired—health, money, clothes, houses, cars, tires, food, employment, a saved spouse, the outwitting of a policeman, a safe journey, an equitable outcome in a struggle with an employer. As opposed to confessing one's sins, bemoaning how miserable the world is, monotonously rattling off formalities, bringing up these successes evokes excitement in the others because they seek gratification in similar successes. They can identify with the conflict and vicariously enjoy the outcome. Their excitement is manifest in the animation during meaningful testimonies—in the responses from the others and, if the teller's enthusiasm is great enough, in the occasional outburst into song, dancing, clapping, tapping, and shouting during the testimony instead of during the healing. A meaningful testimony elicits more animation just as enthusiastic singing with accompanying loud clapping and hard and rapid foot tapping does between testimonies. Also, greater activity in singing leads to more sincere testimonies and vice versa. The more animation, the greater is the spirit, and, hence, the better is the meeting.

Participation seems to breed more participation. Yet the structure of the testimony is extremely fluid. A testimony inciting the members to action may be followed by a stirring song, but the next four or five testimonies may be formalities and the songs limp. Sister Thompson may stand up and give another talk or begin and lead a propelling song. It is in essence the last chance to create a high spirit verbally before the healing. As does the testimony in general, her talk consists of a series of highs and lows in spirit but tends before the end to develop into rhythmical rhetoric with much participation from the group. Thus, a rise and fall in the amount of participation and involvement by the members, a rise and fall in the degree of spirit, punctuates the testimony. In order to sustain a generally high level of spirit throughout, individual effort must be put into the testimonies and the songs.

The testimony contributes much to the healing. Throughout the healing the spirit is on a much higher level than it was during the testimony. If the meeting is a "good" one, the contrast between the testimony and the healing in intensity of spirit is much greater than when the meeting is "poor." A "poor" meeting is characterized by having approximately the same—generally, low—level throughout. Thus, the more the testimony creates a high spirit, the greater is the ikelihood of a high spirit during the healing.

Besides the influence of the testimonial, another factor heightening he spirit during the healing is the degree to which individuals act ıpon the spirit as it enters their bodies. If one individual goes into a frenzy, others are likely to follow suit. If another starts beating the ambourine rapidly, the others will clap harder. If someone begins dancing and continues unable to get the satisfaction of his blessing, the others will stomp their feet until the floor sways with the beat. In a "good" meeting, participation does indeed breed participation, for the more one person acts out his blessing, the more others will act out theirs, and the more still others will contribute to the singing, clapping, and stamping. These, in turn, move someone to be more active in receiving his blessing. In a "good" meeting, the members participate to a greater extent and more intensely during the healing.

The healing is the climax of the meeting, for it is both the point of greatest participation—everyone acting in unison to the beat for a prolonged period of time—and the time for consummating the participants' goal in coming to the meeting—i.e., receiving a blessing. When a "good" meeting is created with a high spirit throughout the healing, the chances are better for many individuals to consummate their goal, to receive a blessing.

To be rational is to have a goal in mind for which one is willing to change his behavior in order to attain it. I would argue that the healing service encourages the members to act rationally to attain their goal, the blessing. In order to attain it they must change their means of attaining a blessing; means which include participation in the testimonies, the songs, and the healing. They must strive to delve into their daily lives and interpret situations through the framework of God's rules during the testimony and they must strive to put more effort into the singing, dancing, shouting, clapping, and tapping. Too, the individual must learn to adjust himself to a delayed gratification before attaining his goal. He requests the blessing during his testimony and must wait for his chance to receive a blessing through the lulls of the meeting, through others' testimonies, through the songs, through Sister Thompson's sermon, and while others before him are being prayed over. Finally, when his chance comes, he must struggle to dispel the devil that is within him and that causes him to resist, allowing the spirit to enter his body. The healing meeting thus provides the individual with a goal and with a means of attaining it, but with a means that involves changing his attitudes and behavior towards more constructive participation.

Rationality, it can be argued, is necessary for successful adjustment to modernized society. By necessity and by choice the Saints have become and are becoming more dependent on their surrounding society. They no longer grow most of their food as they did on the farm, either to consume or to sell for cash. Instead they rely on their menial services in jobs controlled by their employers. Cars, telephones, clothes, refrigerators, stoves, and houses are necessary for existence in modern society. Yet the Saints' means of attaining them are limited. By choice they desire a comfortable house, reliable car, an education for their children, a television set, employment which would not be so utterly dependent on their employer's whims, a free choice of food, and self-respect. Recent civil rights legislation has served to reinforce their desire for the fruits of modern society and has encouraged them to feel it is their right to attain them. Yet it has been the position of the black in the United States to "stay in his place," to accept his lot without trying to change it, to feel he is a second-class citizen with no other alternative, and to feel lucky to have a shack, a run-down car, hand-me-down clothes, or "kind" employers. In other words, there is a discrepancy now between what the Saints found to be true of life in the past and hints of what life could be in the future. Sister Thompson encourages her followers to believe in the hints, to act in a free and equal manner, and to participate in modern life— to buy a car, a house, obtain a better job, and so forth. Nevertheless, legislation only paves the road. A means of traveling over it is also necessary. It is not enough to feel that one has a right to modern life and to want to participate in it. One must also be willing to find a means and to change his life by utilizing the means. One must plan for the future and be able to cope with delayed gratification, struggles, and striving in order to attain one's goal.

I have argued that Sister Thompson's healing meeting encourages utilization of one's means and this kind of coping. However, it not only encourages such coping, but also paints the process of coping as a desired and joyful process with its bright sides and rewards. Moreover, the outcome of the process of coping—the blessing—is not limited to a religious ceremony or to religious action. Rather, it is the promise of a success in daily life.

It is during the meeting when the Spirit is high and God is within their bodies that the attitude of equality as brothers under God is made emphatic, that problems in changing their lives are made clear, that resolutions are proposed, and that they are taught the means to participate actively in solving their problems. Thus, the prospect of a different future is opened and planning for it encouraged. It is then that they say:

> If you go into a grocery store and you see a steak and you want that steak, then you buy it. God didn't put steak on the earth just for the rich people. He put it there for His people. It's time we quit eating chitterlings and hog's feet and moved higher on the hog.[3]

NOTES

1. My entrée as a white into the black group came by a 'Godsend.' Before I knew anything of Sister Thompson or the Saints, I had become interested in a Church of God campgrounds close to Oakboro. A friend introduced me to his black maid whom he knew to be religiously inclined, in order that I might learn about the campgrounds. When I told her I wished to study divine healing, long discussions ensued. The maid, a Baptist, had little to do with the campgrounds, but was eager to discuss the merits of various divine healers and the effectiveness of divine healing. She found that my interest was sincere and noted that as a college graduate I could read and write well. While not a healer herself, to serve the Lord she held small evening gatherings during which she read and fathomed the meaning of the Bible. Because she reads and writes slowly and has never learned many Biblical words, she had been praying to the Lord for someone to assist her, so that she might better accomplish His work. Obviously to her, I had been sent by the Lord as His answer. Her account of this story when introducing me to Sister Thompson, the Saints, and others in the community explained the anomaly of my being with her, as well as establishing my interest in divine healing. Sister Thompson, the Saints, and the town have been given fictitious names.

2. See Valentine (1969) for a synopsis of implications of various labels.

3. In my experience, the Saints eat as little of chitterlings and hog's feet as they do of steak (virtually none). They choose other foods over steak, given comparable amounts of money. Sister Thompson's use of these terms in the concluding statement may thus be interpreted as expressing symbolically the desirability of adopting modern ways and putting aside traditional ways.

REFERENCES

Frazier, E. Franklin, 1966. *The Negro Family in the United States* (Chicago: University of Chicago Press). First published in 1932.

Keil, Charles, 1966. *Urban Blues* (Chicago: University of Chicago Press).

Lewis, Oscar, 1966. *La Vida* (New York: Random House).

Liebow, Elliott, 1967. *Tally's Corner: a Study of Negro Street-cornermen* (Boston: Little, Brown, and Company).

Valentine, Charles A., 1969. Culture and Poverty: Critique and Counter-Proposals. *Current Anthropology* 10:181-201.

Young, Virginia Heyer, 1970. Family and Childhood in a Southern Negro Community. *American Anthropologist* 72:269-288.

"Gypsy" Research in the South

Jared Harper

One group of people largely neglected by anthropologists interested in Southern studies, or for that matter, by anthropologists in general, are the gypsies. Many articles on gypsies have appeared in the popular press, but to my knowledge there have been only two articles on gypsies appearing in anthropological journals, and neither of them is about gypsies in the South. One appeared in the *American Anthropologist* (Bonos 1942), while the second, a sequel to the first, appeared in the *Southwestern Journal of Anthropology* (Çoker 1966). Publications on gypsies in the South are limited to a few articles in popular magazines, religious periodicals, newspapers, and in a little known, non-anthropological, specialist journal. Of these, only three are worthy of note, consisting of one article each in *Reader's Digest* (Muller 1941), the *Journal of the Gypsy Lore Society* (Boles and Boles 1959), and in *Ave Maria* (Ryan 1967). We should not, however, overlook the recent papers by Harper (1968; 1969a; 1969b) and Harper and Hudson (1971; n.d.). The dearth of professional literature on gypsies and gypsies in the South in particular seems incredible since there are, I would estimate, from fifteen to twenty thousand people in the South alone labeled "gypsy" by the layman and perhaps from three to four times that number in the United States as a whole. These belong to four fairly distinct groups: the classical or Continental European Gypsies, the English Gypsies, the Scottish Gypsies, and the Irish Travelers, these being only general categories, each with several subgroups. Yet, despite the lack of professional literature on these groups, there are indications that any of them would provide a veritable storehouse of anthropological data relevant to the linguist, the ethnographer, the ethnomusicologist, or any other anthropological specialists.

16

THE IRISH TRAVELERS

My own Southern gypsy research has placed me in contact with one of these four groups—the Irish Travelers. Field work, so far, has been limited to only one Irish Traveler community numbering approximately twelve hundred people.[1] Entrée into the community was gained through a Catholic Father who served for nearly twenty years as their pastor and priest. It cannot be overemphasized that without his initial endorsement and support I could never have broken through the barrier of suspicion the Irish Travelers have built between themselves and outsiders. With his help I assumed the role of historian, there to write a history of the Irish Travelers. Similar barriers, no doubt, would be encountered by anyone attempting research with any of the so-called Southern "gypsy" groups, although such barriers are by no means insurmountable, as I have shown.

Because of a lack of available quarters in the community I was studying, it was necessary for me to rent quarters about ten miles away and to commute from there to the community. This hampered my research somewhat but did not prove to be a major barrier. My field technique consisted primarily of participant observation and interviewing. I found that many informants were unwilling to record on tape, fearing that I would, perhaps, use the recordings to inflict harm upon them, although the same informants were perfectly willing for me to write down verbatim everything they said. Most informants even showed concern if it did not seem to them that I was writing fast enough to record all their statements.

Of the four gypsy groups mentioned earlier, the Irish Travelers seem to have played the largest part in the economic and social history of the rural South. Like the Yankee Peddler who supplied rural Southerners with the industrial products of the North, the Irish Travelers, too, served as middlemen, furnishing the Southern farmer with the mules so essential to his agricultural economy. Farmers who could not make the trek to one of the large Southern stock centers such as Memphis, Nashville, or Atlanta to purchase draft animals for their farms depended instead upon the itinerant Irish Traveler mule traders to come year after year "sellin' 'em and tradin' 'em," supplying the farmers with stock to carry them through planting and the harvest.

The Travelers, as they are commonly known, and it is the collective name which they themselves prefer, are not Romany Gypsies as are the members of the other three groups mentioned earlier, but are of Irish Stock. In fact, among the Irish Travelers "gypsy" is a fighting word, indeed many a fight has started between a Traveler and non-Traveler or "Country Person," as non-Travelers are called, when the latter inadvertently used "gypsy" as a term of reference. According to Traveler tradition, they emigrated from Ireland about 1847, during the Irish Potato Famine, driven to a better life in America by hunger and disease. Upon their arrival in America, so the Travelers say, the immigrants settled first in upstate New York, near Buffalo; near Pittsburgh and Germantown, Pennsylvania; and near Washington, D. C.

In Ireland, the Travelers were commonly known as "tinkers," although according to Patrick Greene this was somewhat of a misnomer since they performed any number of other itinerant occupations such as chimney sweeping, selling knick-knacks, clothespins, and baskets (usually handmade), swapping livestock, and as the occasion demanded they relied on petty swindling, thievery, and begging (Greene 1933-34:262). They traveled about the countryside with cart and horse living in tents and in the open air (Greene 1933-34:259-63). It might be said, however, that despite their Irish beginnings, the Travelers today seem to retain little that might be identified as Irish.

About the time of the American Civil War, my informants state, they abandoned all other occupations, moved to the South, and specialized in the mule and horse trade until about 1955 when that business virtually ceased. In those days boys learned the trade from their fathers by accompanying them on their trading forays into the countryside, a form of occupational training used by the Travelers today. They camped by the roadside in a friendly farmer's field, living in wagons and tents, and in later years in house trailers. Marriage was only within the group—arranged by the parents—a custom that continues to be practiced today and which shows no signs of changing. The Travelers of today practice uxorilocal residence after marriage, and this too is probably an old pattern.

At present, the Travelers live in several permanent and semipermanent communities in Georgia, South Carolina, Mississippi, Louisiana, Texas, and Tennessee, numbering about five thousand—a rough estimate. Their way of life has changed somewhat since the mule trading days, which many Travelers look back upon with nostalgia as the "good old days." As a rule only the men travel today, while the women and children remain at home in modern house trailers. This has been necessitated in part by their living in large mobile homes which are difficult and expensive to move. Also the cost of living on the road and compulsory school attendance laws are major factors in their traveling less.

Since the demise of the mule trade the Travelers have developed two new itinerant occupational specialties: peddling linoleum rugs from door to door and spray-painting barns and houses. The latter originally consisted only of spraying the metal parts of buildings with aluminum paint, although today Travelers are beginning to paint the wooden parts of buildings as well. Both of these specialties are not really new, however, but grew out of a need for summer employment in the mule trading days. Mule trading was a seasonal occupation lasting from the middle of September to the end of April. When the season was over, Travelers took their families to one of the Southern stock centers to camp for the summer. About the time of the appearance of automobiles and trucks, the men began to go out into the countryside near to where they were camped to peddle and paint. As the mule trade breathed its last, many traders found it necessary to adopt as fulltime employment what was once only a summer diversion from the normal routine of the mule trading way of life.

Today painting and peddling have no season as such, although Travelers tell me there is less to do in winter generally because of inclement weather. As in the mule trading days, the men in their new occupations often form partnerships and share their profits, though this is much more common for painters than for peddlers. During the part of the year the children are in school, the men go into the countryside with pickup trucks and ply their trades. Sometimes the men will be gone as long as a month or more at a time, although some return to their homes and families every weekend. During the summer months the men often take their families with them, and painters go as far north and west as Michigan and Minnesota. Painters say business is better "up country" where the farm buildings are bigger, and they can get a better price for painting them. Rug peddlers, on the other hand, tend to restrict their travels primarily to the southern states of Georgia, North Carolina, South Carolina, Mississippi, Alabama, and Kentucky, where they can still find unpainted shacks along unpaved country roads. "Up country," peddlers say, "people don't use linoleum rugs no more."

Today the Travelers are a rapidly changing people. They are losing the old ways and are taking up new. Perhaps the two greatest forces for change are education and an increasingly intimate contact with middle class American values through such sources as the mass media. Also, occupations such as mule trading, painting, and linoleum peddling are dying out so that most Travelers feel that these occupations will soon be gone. Some Travelers are finding other things to do. In their own community, for example, there are two stores owned and operated by Travelers. Another Traveler works for a fuel oil company, while others have driven cookie and milk trucks, and every day more Travelers make similar outside contacts.

Education is one of the most potent forces in changing Irish Traveler society. There are probably more Irish Travelers in school today than at any other time in Traveler history. Furthermore, a few high school age boys even aspire to attend college.

The greatest barrier now remaining between the Travelers and the outside world is their "Travelerness," for lack of a better term. Although all Travelers consider themselves good Americans, none wants to be cut off from the security and sense of community that his village or group has to offer. Parents who want their boys to attend college want them to go no farther than the local community college, for to go farther would separate them from the warmth and security of their people. Parents are very much afraid that their children will fall under the bad influences of hippies, marijuana, and wild women. Summing it up, one Traveler woman said, "At home they have the best of everything. They want the opportunities of . . . the Village. They don't want to take a chance."

IRISH TRAVELER CANT

So far my research on the Irish Travelers has been primarily linguistic (Harper and Hudson 1971). While conducting field work among the Travelers, I discovered that this group still retains an argot, a mode of disguised linguistic communication which they call "the Cant." I first learned of the existence of Cant when some Traveler children plied me with the question: "Hey Mister! Do you know the Cant?" and then proceeded to spout a list of strange words, an episode that would be repeated, perhaps, a dozen times while I was in the field.

Cant uses the phonology and morphology of the host dialect of English and is not a language in the conventional sense, but a jargon akin to pig-Latin. In fact, the Travelers themselves regard it in this light. As one Traveler stated:

> Cant . . . it's more of a damned dog-Latin than anything else. It originated right out of the original Irish language. Of course, there's none of us that can really talk that—the Irish Brogue. Of course, we might have sometimes a touch of it, more or less, but that's as far as we can go. But we can't talk the real brogue, so we just pick up what they call Cant.

Traveler children confuse Cant with pig-Latin and are often hard pressed to differentiate the two, indicating again that in the Traveler way of thinking they are not radically different. As a nine-year-old Traveler boy stated, "Cant and pig-Latin are sort of the same."

The difference between the two, basically, is that pig-Latin is a systematic modification of English for the purpose of disguising meaning from those who do not understand the modifications. Cant on the other hand, although it began as a systematic modification of Irish Gaelic, has now become frozen into a set of variant words. Thus the Cant speaker can simply plug these words into an English sentence, as is necessary, to disguise meaning from non-Travelers.

Cant, therefore, is a secret mode of communication, and this secrecy is of primary importance to understanding its function (Harper and Hudson n.d.). Traditionally, Cant was passed from generation to generation serving to isolate the Travelers from non-Travelers economically and socially. One Traveler said, "The word 'Cant,' to us, means you can't understand us." This emphasis upon secrecy was further expressed in statements made by other Traveler informants when asked to give examples of Cant.

Originally, according to informants, Cant was used by the Travelers to communicate with each other in their business dealings. In fact, when the Travelers were asked how they use it they replied, "Oh, it was a talk we used in tradin' but we don't use it much any more." However, a semantic analysis of sentences and phrases of Traveler origin indicates a much wider and more important usage for Cant than the purely economic one suggested in the Traveler statement. Out of the approximately two-hundred fifty sentences and phrases I collected, no more than twenty deal specifically with the mule and horse trade or any other common Traveler occupations, while over one-hundred and twenty, or nearly half, are in the nature of warnings and commands. This suggests that Cant also has the function of aiding the Travelers in situations of danger, stress, or adversity coming from outside their community. This distinction between the two functions of Cant, however, may be one the Travelers themselves do not make. It is probable, in fact, that in the Traveler way of thinking, the two functions are inseparably intertwined in that the second function developed as a result of the first.

To understand what I mean, you have to understand the manner in which the Travelers conduct their business affairs. Traveler business practices are reminiscent of the kind of barter economics practiced by our American forebears and are similar to those of practically any traveling salesman or used car salesman today. Their objective is to make the best deal possible. In other words, in an economic system

with a sliding price scale, to stay in business it is sometimes necessary
to take a loss which is made up on subsequent sales. However, as
in all such shrewd business dealings, the customer sometimes feels,
after it is all over, that he has been cheated, whether it is necessarily
true or not. In his anger, he may seek some sort of recourse by finding
and confronting the person who sold him the merchandise. Yet, the
salesman, having realized a profit, will not want to lose it. Thus, it is
in connection with such confrontations that Cant is most effectively
used by the Travelers. In other words, Cant is not used to cheat
people but is simply used to maintain the economic advantage in
business dealings.

To illustrate one of these situations, imagine an angry farmer
approaching within earshot of an Irish Traveler encampment. He
feels cheated in a mule trade and wants his mule and money back.
Upon noticing the farmer's approach and wanting to retain possession
of the mule and whatever he got to boot (that is, money or barter
beyond an even swap), the trader tells his partner, "Put the *mayler*
(mule) in the *kul* (swamp), the *gyuk* (man) is *thawriyin araysh*
(coming back)."[2] When the farmer reaches the camp, the trader
tells him that the mule has been traded off. He then makes every effort
to placate the farmer and to convince him that the trade has not been
such a bad one after all and that the farmer should go home and
forget the whole thing.

Rarely, the situation would arise where the farmer was not to be
satisfied with anything short of the trader's arrest. In such a case,
Cant served as a warning device. When a Traveler saw the farmer
approaching with the sheriff in tow, he would say to the trader,
"*misliy* (go) the *sheyjog* (sheriff) is comin'" or "I saw the *sheyjog*
(sheriff) up there an' he is *thawriyin* out (swearing out a warrant)
an' he's gona *sawlk* your *jiyl* (take you away)." Thus, if the farmer or
sheriff or anyone else were within hearing distance, they would not
understand what the Travelers were saying, and the trader could get
away unscathed.

Finally, Cant has one more important function, that of identifying
its speakers as members of a particular group. Thus when the boys
asked, "Hey Mister! Do you know the Cant?" they in effect were
inquiring "Are you one of us—are you a Traveler?" In fact, the
Travelers themselves have described to me situations where Cant
was used to identify fellow Travelers.

In summary, Cant is a secret argot brought to America by Irish
itinerants during the Irish Potato Famine. In the Old Country it was
known as Shelta and was used by Irish itinerants in their business

dealings and as a warning device in much the same manner Cant is used by the Irish Travelers today. There are indications, however, that Cant is being used much less now than in the past. While Travelers thirty-five years of age or older may know from one hundred to one hundred and fifty words, the younger generation retains fewer than seventy-five words. And there are indications that the number of Cant words retained will grow fewer as the years go by. The Travelers state that non-Travelers are suspicious of people who talk differently and that keeping secrets really is not the proper thing to do. Also, the priest discourages the use of Cant as one of those old customs the Travelers ought to forget.

CONCLUSION

As evidenced by my data on the Irish Travelers, Southern gypsy research is a fertile field of investigation, and is one that has barely been researched. Yet, at the same time I indicated that the Irish Travelers are undergoing rapid changes. Future changes will probably occur in the form of out-marriage, the loss of their uxorilocal residence pattern and the loss of their Cant, all of which will have very definite negative effects in terms of Traveler group cohesiveness and identity. This is especially true when combined with the other factors previously mentioned—education and increasing contact with middle class American society. Referring to the Traveler way of life and to past and future changes one Traveler said, "It's coming when they will have to get off the road. The road is expensive with all the motel bills and gas and other things. They don't make buildings with metal roofs anymore. The rug business is going out too, going to tile and hardwood floors. In ten years it will be gone unless they find something else to do."

My limited information tells me that the other Gypsy groups in the South are undergoing similar rapid changes. No doubt much of their traditional way of life will be lost in the next decade. The burden of recording these life ways before they are gone will rest upon the shoulders of the anthropologist, whose field techniques are uniquely suited to the research demands of gypsy studies.

In conclusion, I would like to raise several basic questions, each of which would be a good beginning point for further research: (1) Are there more than four gypsy groups in the South, and how are they related to one another? (2) Do the Romany Gypsy groups still retain and use the Romany Language; and how do they use it? (3) Exactly what part did the Romany Gypsy groups play in the history of the rural South? (4) How do traveling peoples such as the gypsies appraise the personalities of prospective customers in order to gain the advantage over them? (5) Exactly how many "gypsies" are there in the South? Undoubtedly there are many other questions that might be raised concerning the Southern gypsy groups, but it is by now obvious that here lies a fertile area of anthropological research in the South.

NOTES

1. My field work began in January of 1968, continuing with several interruptions until June of that year. Subsequently I returned for short visits and a ten-day period of field work in August, 1969. I plan to do additional field work and research on the Irish Travelers in the future.

2. Unfortunately it has not been possible to indicate the correct phonetic values for Cant words. The interested reader should refer to Harper and Hudson (1971).

REFERENCES

Boles, Don and Jacqueline Boles, 1959. The Gypsies' Doctor in Georgia. *Journal of the Gypsy Lore Society* 38:55-62.

Bonos, Arlene Helen, 1942. Roumany Rye of Philadelphia. *American Anthropologist* 44:257-75.

Çoker, Gülbün, 1966. Romany Rye in Philadelphia: A Sequel. *Southwestern Journal of Anthropology* 22:85-100.

Greene, Patrick, 1933-34. Some Notes on Tinkers and Their "Cant." *Béaloïdeas, the Journal of the Folklore of Ireland Society* 4:259-63.

Harper, Jared, 1968. Tinker Cant in the South. Current Research Report presented at the 67th annual meeting of the American Anthropological Association, Seattle, Washington.

————————, 1969a. Irish Itinerants in the South. A paper presented at the 68th annual meeting of the American Anthropological Association, New Orleans, La.

————————, 1969b. Irish Traveler Cant: An Historical, Structural, and Sociolinguistic Study of an Argot. A master's thesis, University of Georgia, Athens, Georgia.

Harper, Jared and Charles Hudson, 1971. Irish Traveler Cant. *Journal of English Linguistics*, in press.

————————, n.d. Irish Traveler Cant in its Social Setting. Manuscript.

Muller, Edwin, 1941. Roving the South with the Irish Horse Traders. *Reader's Digest* (July, 1941), 59-63.

Ryan, George, 1967. The Irish Travelers. *Ave Maria* (March 18, 1967), 16-18.

The Impact of Coal Mining on the Traditional Mountain Subculture

Edward E. Knipe and Helen M. Lewis

This paper developed from a recent study of the effects of mechanization on coal miners and their families in the Southwest triangle of Virginia[1] (Lewis and Knipe 1969). In order to determine the impact of mechanization upon underground work organization and the social life of miners and their wives, nine mines, representing the major coal-getting technologies were sampled. The data for the study came from underground observations in each mine, taped interviews with each miner, and semi-structured interviews with each wife.

We had assumed that coal miners and their families, because of the nature of coal mining itself, would exhibit patterns of behavior and thoughts which differed from the older mountain patterns. We found, however, many parallels between our sample responses and what has been written about traditional Appalachian culture. We became interested in distinguishing traditional mountain ways and the effects of coal mining. Since our sample lived in the same region as the traditional highlander, it would be an easy matter to dismiss these similarities between miners' responses and traditional mountain values as nothing more than the "perpetuation of the mores" or simple diffusion.

Rather, we will try to show how and what structural changes occurred in this particular area of Appalachia as a result of coal mining and what resulted from these changes. It is our contention that coal mining reinforced and helped preserve certain traditional mountain ways while at the same time it changed other relationships. It is a fundamental point of this paper that coal mining created a system of "peasant-like" structures over the traditional Appalachian culture. We will also attempt to show how changes in coal mining with the introduction of modern technological processes have been

25

responsible for the transformation of these peasant-like characteristics into what might be called urban patterns, thus resulting in peasantry being lost.

TRADITIONAL APPALACHIAN CULTURE

Southern Appalachia cannot be thought of as a unified region having a homogeneous culture (Campbell 1921; Vance 1960). However most studies of isolated communities or counties in the Southern Appalachians find very similar orientations and characteristics of the inhabitants. Ford's "Passing of Provincialism" (1962), Pearsall's *Little Smoky Ridge* (1959), Brown's *Beech Creek Studies* (1950; 1952), Weller's *Yesterday's People* (1965), and Stephenson's *Shiloh* (1968) find quite similar orientations of persons living in the area. Among these orientations are: traditionalism, individualism, fatalism, and a present-orientation. Howard K. Beers (1946) felt that the general isolation of mountain people and their strong kinship affiliations and orientations placed them into a "folk-like" category. Cressy (1949) spoke of the area as an "arrested frontier culture" having many characteristics of a folk culture but lacking the stability and class stratification of a peasant culture.

That part of the Appalachians with which we are concerned is the portion of the Alleghany-Cumberland mountains in which bituminous coal mining developed. Portions of southwest Virginia, eastern Kentucky and southern West Virginia form this area. It is an area which was the most isolated portion of the Southern Appalachians and which developed and maintained for a longer period of time those patterns referred to as "traditional mountain culture."

The area had a relatively long period of virtual isolation in the nineteenth century. Up until the Revolution it was an area to pass through or skirt around, since it was covered by extensive forests, the soil was poor, and there was little level land. Those seeking good farmland went farther into the Blue Grass, the Tennessee Valley, or farther north (Lewis 1968).

Since the bottom lands near the rivers and streams provided the only acreage suitable for agricultural use, original settlements followed "line" patterns. With population increase the settlers moved farther up the hillsides and hollows, usually along kin lines so that one finds even today valleys and hollows named after and resided in by extended kin. Moving away from the arable river bottoms meant moving onto lands less suitable for traditional agricultural practices. Without knowledge of terracing and crop rotation the land soon became barren and subject to erosion and flooding. The indiscriminate cutting of lumber and general exploitation led to devastation of the natural environment. It is not difficult to explain the fatalistic orientation attributed to the Southern Highlander. The inability to predict the future because of complete dependence upon the environment presents one with little alternative but to be present-oriented. Within a subsistence economy there is little need for a complex system of social organization. With limited contact with the outside world there are few from whom one can "borrow" practices or beliefs; therefore tradition can be the only source for present practices. Because of this traditional and kin orientation, the placing of outsiders into meaningful social categories is useless. Given the level of technology of the original settlers and the nature of the environment, these orientations "fit" the situation.

THE COAL MINING CULTURE: A CASE OF PEASANTRY GAINED

Ford (1965) draws a parallel between the values of rural Appalachia and those of a Mexican peasant society, attributing similarities to the conditions of poverty which exist in the Mexican village of Azteca and in communities of eastern Kentucky. Although isolated rural mountain people and Mexican peasants may share certain values, we suggest that something more than poverty link the two together and this something did not appear in Appalachia until after the introduction of coal mining. According to Eric Wolf (1955) the criteria by which a society is defined as peasant are *both* economic and socio-political. The peasant society is defined through its relationship to the larger urban society, and only when there is subjugation to the larger society is one able to state that a condition of peasantry exists (Foster 1967). Some of the same values existed in the isolated mountain area where living was meager, but the structure which produces peasantry was not present until coal mining.

Looking specifically at southwest Virginia, we find that the first load of coal was shipped from Wise County in 1892. With the introduction of mining, mining camps were built near the mines, up the hollows, some being more isolated than the original farming settlements. Instead of following the stream beds like the residence patterns of the original settlers, the camps were built along the railroad tracks leading to the mine tipple.

The fertile bottom land where the best farms had been located were often the only land suitable for the erection of mine offices and houses. The former independent landowners either sold at a profit and retired or parted with their land and became day laborers. The wage system replaced barter and exchange. The commissary or company

store substituted imported food and store goods for household manufactures of the past. Roads were poor or non-existant. Some mountain
men were attracted to the coal mines. Hillside farming produced a
meager, difficult existence, and the wages, the goods, the houses,
and the pleasures of the mining camps were attractive. Others were
forced into mining by fraudulent land sales and soil depletion.

The coming of the coal industry did not open the mountains to the
mainstream of modern society. The markets, ownership, and control
of the coal operations were in Pittsburgh, New York, and the industrial centers of the East and Midwest. While the coal moved out to
supply the industrial centers of the country, the miners became more
isolated and less able to move because of the elaborate system of paying
in scrip and forced patronage of the company stores which kept the
miner in "debt peonage."

In addition to the physical isolation and the dependency of the
miner upon the coal companies, there developed a stratification system
which made the miner socially isolated. Mining brought in social
class distinctions unknown to the mountain culture. Trading centers
and residential towns were developed for the managers, chemists, engineers, geologists, and other personnel brought in to provide professional services to the mining companies. These towns and villages
were not large, most of them around 2,000 population, but they were
connected with the outside world. Surrounded by mountain settlements and mining camps, they were middle class islands, bringing
"civilization" from the outside world to the crude and harsh life of
mountain farming and coal mining. Like colonists in a foreign land,
the owner-operators and their wives developed country clubs, ladies
literary clubs, and Episcopal and other "establishment" churches
which contrasted with the informal sectarian religion or the unclassified "company church" of the coal camp.

Although some may object to our use of the term peasantry or
peasant-like to describe the situation of the early coal miner in the
region, we feel that Firth's extension of peasantry to non-agricul-
turists has merit, especially when one defines as peasantry those
situations characterized by certain structural relationships to a larger
society (1952). For example, the central theme of Foster's approach is
that those in peasantry have very little control over the conditions
which govern their lives (1967). Looking at the traditional Appalachian,
we note that very few if any of his ties were to social units outside
the immediate geographical area in which he resided. Although the
traditional highlander was subject to the rigors of his environments—
poor land, primitive technology—he was nevertheless somewhat in-

dependent. Once he moved into the coal camps, however, the only decision he made was to stay or to leave. While in the camp he had no choice over the house in which he would live, the place in which he would work, where he would buy his groceries and other commodities, or how much he would be paid. In other words there were no alternatives. Decisions about his life were made by others. If he went to church, that church was provided by the company. If he or his children were sick, he went to the company doctor or to no doctor at all. The doctor's pay, the pay of the man who checked the cars of coal he loaded during the day, the cost of dynamite, and the cost of carbide used in his lamp were all deducted from his wages. In early coal camps there were no unions, and companies were often very lax in maintaining safety conditions. If the miner felt that conditions were unsafe underground, he had no recourse other than to quit. If the company docked his pay because he loaded too much slate, he had no appeal. The money he received for his wages were subject to markets at the national level and to the caprice of the local managers. While the traditional highlander could decide not to work one day, the coal miner could not. If he did not show up for work, he might find himself and his family moved out of the company house.

Those mountain men who remained on their subsistence farms and worked sporadically in the mines were more independent. They were not, however, considered desirable workers by owners and operators (Verhoeff 1911).

Foster points out that the peasant is poor. Although the traditional mountain family had a meager subsistence, they were not economically dependent. There were few economic differences among members of the population. Poverty, as we perceive it, is relative rather than absolute. Persons brought in with the coal industry—owners, managers, professional people—enjoyed a level of living higher than the Appalachian who left his farm to work in the mines and live in the coal camps. Without some type of standard the highlander did not know he was poor.

Foster presents the idea that peasant leadership is weak or nonexistent because "the more powerful extra-village leaders who hold vested interests in peasant communities cannot afford to let local leaders rise, since they would constitute a threat to their control" 1967:8). It has been suggested that the low standards of education provided by coal companies, the resistance by the coal companies to pay any local school taxes, and the system of debt peonage maintained by the use of scrip and the later "unlimited credit" were effective means of preventing the emergence of local leaders. What strong leadership did emerge was through the unions, which developed later and on the national level.

Foster says that the powerlessness inherent in peasantry leads to a search for structures which will permit a maximizing of limited opportunities. Two such patterns are suggested—the patron-client relationship and fictive kinship. In the patron-client relationship the peasant seeks out those who are links to the outside, those associated with or attached to the "Great Tradition" (1967:9). Accounts of the early coal camps picture owners and operators as either highly exploitative of their labor or very paternalistic (Ross 1933; Lantz 1958; Caudill 1962). The paternalistic owner-operator was one who looked after his people and who was concerned with the welfare of each miner and his family and who, in turn, received the undivided loyalty of his workers. In some of the small mines in our study we found owners who assumed a very paternalistic attitude toward their miners. They paid them whenever they needed money, extended loans, co-signed notes, and took a great deal of interest in the welfare of the miner's family.

Some of the intense hostilities and bitter conflicts which developed in the unionization process in the area can be seen from this "personalistic" attachment the miner had to the operators and the later feeling that his personal loyalties had been betrayed. Personal behavior can be violent as well as friendly. Mining resulted in the development of strong peer-groups of miners with strong identification and loyalties, which may be considered as substitute kin groups and support structures in the face of this powerlessness.

The introduction of mining also affected non-miners in the region. Those who attempted to maintain traditional rural patterns of agriculture were in many cases forced off the land, and the poorly educated sons of rural people were lured into mining.

Some of the characteristics of traditional mountain culture were encouraged and maintained by coal mining, fitting in well with peasant-like dependency or maintained by the social and physical isolation of mining. Suspicion of outsiders was reinforced after the traditional highlander had been exploited by large coal interests. The individualism of the mountaineer, which has been described not in terms of independence but as avoidance of social responsibilities, was also encouraged by the paternalism of the coal camps (Weller 1965). There was some breakdown of the extended family due to the mobility of families within the coal fields, but loyalties shifted to the worker peer-groups and did not extend relationships to heterogeneous outside groups.

Handloading, the simplest and earliest technology of coal mining, helped maintain some of the mountain man's individualism. In the handloading mine each man works his own "place." He is isolated from his fellow workers and generally sees the foreman or other miners only once or twice a day. Goodrich (1925) calls this isolation the "miner's freedom" and maintains that the miner was a free agent underground. Our data from handloading miners showed they preferred to work alone rather than with a "buddy." Owners of some of the handloading mines complained that many miners would set a quota for the day and when this quota was completed they left. Some operators of these small handloading operations tried to win the loyalty of their men through "old fashioned" paternalism or by such economic controls as money lending or the operation of small credit groceries.

CHANGES IN MINING: PEASANTRY LOST

Changes in mining technology increased the productivity of the miner and resulted in widespread unemployment in the coal fields. With the introduction of conventional mining techniques in the 1920s and continuous mining after World War II, the productivity rose from 4.47 tons per man day to 17 tons per man day in 1964. The number of miners decreased from 704,793 in 1923 to 131,752 in 1966 (National Coal 1964; 1968).

The changes in mining technology also resulted in changes in worker organization. Unlike handloading methods of mining, in both conventional and continuous sections men work together as teams. The exact relationships between miners in these two technologies would differ, but the fact that a machine is operated by two or more men and has to be supported continually through contact with other miners brings the miner into very close relationship with others (Knipe 1967). In conventional and continuous mines there is no self-determination of work pace. This is either established by the work group or by the design of the machine. Another result of this working together is the increased bond of solidarity for safety reasons. Coal mining is the most dangerous occupation in the United States. It has the highest fatality and accident rate as compared with any other occupation or industry. With an increasing division of labor as a result of changing technology, men became increasingly dependent on others. The men who bolt the roof or set safety timbers have to be trusted to do their job. The man operating a machine has to be felt competent enough to control that machine so as not to hurt others working nearby. This interdependency is reflected in the question concerning working alone or with others. Only 14 per cent of the conventional miners said they would rather work alone, while 9 per cent of the continuous miners felt this way (Lewis and Knipe 1969).

Probably the most significant consequence of changes in technology was the trend toward increasing stability in employment. The market was leveled somewhat with the loss of the home consumer of coal and the increasing demands for coal as a fuel in generating electrical power. Because of this, mines and mining companies could predict future needs, thereby guaranteeing to the miner future employment. The mechanization of mining increased predictability underground as well. The mining of coal became a more rational process in which the machine created regularity in mining procedures.

Along with these changes in technology, other changes in community patterns occurred (Lewis 1967). After 1940 the companies began selling the company-owned houses to the individual miners and the stores to outside businessmen. There were several reasons for selling the houses: the companies found the houses expensive to keep up, and making the miner a property owner and taxpayer relieved the operator of the obligations for repairing, installing, and maintaining roads, water supplies, sewage and garbage disposal facilities, and other public facilities. The building of roads and the ownership of automobiles by the workers reduced the necessity for housing close to the mines.

These changes were not without their problems. Residents reported the great "panic" of the housewife when announcements were made that the company store would be closed (Evanoff 1960). Some of the coal camps were completely demolished by the companies, others became smaller home-owning communities made up of working and retired miners, and some changed into dilapidated rural slums.

Accompanying the changes in mining and mining communities was the development of several types of occupational family types in the area (Lewis 1970). One is the unionized, skilled mechanized miner who works in the larger mining operation. This miner and his family with the independence of stable employment at relatively high wages and union contract have approached the more urban patterns of living.

Another type is the "independent" handloader who works in the small, marginal truck mines and shifts from job to job. His work is intermittent due to his own work patterns and the shifting nature of small marginal truck mines in which capital investment is low and movement is frequent. Although he gives the appearance of operating like the old independent mountain man, the independent handloader no longer has his subsistence farm to return to; thus he is more tied to the job for survival. His work patterns may be interpreted not as a sign of independence, but as a form of sabotage to express his frustrations, or it may be an expression of his lack of commitment to "getting ahead" so that he works only enough to maintain his meager but acceptable standard of living. We found the handloaders less likely to own their homes and maintain family gardens than the stable, mechanized miner (Lewis and Knipe 1969).

Intermediate between these two types is the non-unionized miner who works in small mechanized truck mines. These mines work less productive seams of coal leased from larger companies. The whole operation is dependent upon the larger mines and moves frequently due to leasing arrangements or physical conditions. The miner's lack of education and his ties to his kin still hold him to the area and to coal mining because it is the only job available. Although Cressey (1953) suggested that coal mining resulted in the loss of ties to extended kin, we found that the coal mining families of the area belong to large kin groups, and they live and interact in a world of kin (Lewis 1970). It seems likely that differential migration from the coal fields has occurred so that those with less education and larger kin groups have remained in the area. Those who had moved into the area from outside to enter mining, thus breaking their ties with extended kin, were probably more mobile and left the area when mechanization resulted in large scale unemployment. This is obvious in the case of Negro and foreign born miners who migrated out. In some ways the kin ties may hold the miner to the area and to the job, but in other ways it also frees him from complete dependence upon the job, for he has the resources of his extended kin groups to give him assistance in times of unemployment.

EMERGENCE OF URBAN PATTERNS

One indication of the change to more urban values and patterns of interaction by those employed in the stable mechanized mines are the differential attitudes which indicate fatalism on the part of the miner and his family. We mentioned earlier that one of the values of the rural mountain subculture and of peasantry was fatalism: man has no control over his environment; he is subjugated to environmental forces or supernatural will, unable to control his destiny; death, illness, and accidents occur when it is "your time," and there is nothing you can do about it.

In opposition to this, the value orientation of urban middle class America defines a person's position as one of directing life; nature is something to be controlled, God works through man, and man is

charged with the responsibility of changing his condition and controlling the world about him.

In reply to questions concerning control over life, satisfaction
with life as it is, and ability to plan for oneself or one's children,
those mining families who had had a longer period of steady employment at relatively higher wages and had enjoyed a higher standard of
living for a longer period of time were less fatalistic. While 93 per
cent of the handloaders' wives felt that man should be satisfied with
his condition, only 43 per cent of those stably employed in mechanized
mines expressed these views. Intermediate types of truck miners whose
employment had been less stable were in between. Age did not
affect this; both young and old in unstable situations were fatalistic
(Lewis and Knipe 1969).

In terms of ambitions and plans for children, handloaders' wives
were much less optimistic about being able to encourage their children
to remain in school. While 75 per cent of the mechanized miners'
wives felt that they would have some success in encouraging their
children to finish school, only 45 per cent of the handloaders' wives
felt they could plan or help their children in this way.

The mechanized miners were no longer dependent on company
stores and small credit groceries, and they were able to budget, save,
and pay cash for groceries. The truck miners' wives continued to
be dependent on the credit grocer, who was an important resource
in times of unemployment. They could not afford the luxury of
giving up these informal networks of obligations and responsibilities
which the ties to the small market represented.

The increase in community participation—ties to the greater society
—also reflected these differences. The economically secure were the
highest participators in church activities, politics, and community organizations. Fifty per cent of the wives of mechanized miners participated in clubs or organizations as compared to 18 per cent of the
truck miners' wives. Seventy-nine per cent of the mechanized miners
voted as compared to 36 per cent of the handloaders.

CONCLUSIONS

We have illustrated some of the changes associated with the
introduction of coal mining in one part of the Southern Appalachians.
We have suggested that these changes account for or explain the
various social types found in this area. In doing so, the concept of
"peasantry" has been used to identify some of the main structural
dimensions associated with these types. We have suggested that the
stably employed mechanized miners have moved toward urbanized
values and social organization, while the truck miners, both hand-

loaders and mechanized miners, represent various degrees of peasantry.

Although some may feel that we have extended the concept of peasantry far beyond its usual reference to agricultural peoples, we feel that such usage is justifiable if one is to become sensitized to those underlying structural dimensions which have explanatory value. To label a social configuration as peasant does not explain it; to restrict the usage of the term gives it little analytical value. If, as Foster suggests, peasantry is characterized by dependency, powerlessness, and lack of autonomy then we can apply it to a wide variety of social phenomena. This study illustrates such an application.

NOTES

1. A somewhat longer version of this paper was read at the 1969 meeting of the Southern Anthropological Society, New Orleans, Louisiana, March 14, 1969.

This study was made possible through two grants from the U. S. Bureau of Mines: Grant EA-7, "A Pilot Study of Methods to Determine the Impact of Changes in Mining Technology on the Attitudes, Behavior, and Productivity of Bituminous Coal Miners" and Grant EA-12, "A Pilot Study of Techniques to Analyze Data on the Impact of Changes in Mining Technology on the Attitudes, Behavior and Productivity of Bituminous Coal Miners." The research was carried out between June 1, 1967 and August 31, 1968.

REFERENCES

Beers, Howard W., 1964. Highland Society in Transition. *Mountain Life and Work*, (Spring), pp. 1-27.

Brown, James S., 1952. The Family Group in a Kentucky Mountain Farm Community and The Farm Family in a Kentucky Mountain Neighborhood. Kentucky Agricultural Experimental Station Bulletins, 587-588.

———————— 1962. *Eastern Kentucky Resources Development Project* (Lexington: University of Kentucky Press).

Caudill, Harry, 1962. *Night Comes to the Cumberlands* (Boston: Little, Brown and Co.).

Campbell, John C., 1921. *The Southern Highlander and His Homeland* (New York: Russell Sage Foundation).

Cressey, Paul F., 1953. Social Disorganization and Reorganization in Harlan County, Kentucky. In *Sociology: A Book of Readings*, Samuel Koenig, et al., eds. (New York: Prentice Hall), pp. 576-582.

Evanoff, Vonda Sue, 1960. Dunham, Kentucky. Community Studies. Library, Clinch Valley College, Wise, Virginia.

Ford, Thomas R., 1962. The Passing of Provincialism. In *The Southern*

Appalachian Region, Thomas R. Ford, ed. (Lexington: University of Kentucky Press), pp. 9-34.

————————, 1965. The Effects of Prevailing Values and Beliefs on the Perception of Poverty in Rural Areas. In *Problems of Chronically Depressed Rural Areas* (North Carolina State University: Agricultural Policy Institute), pp. 33-43.

Foster, George M., 1967. What is a Peasant? in *Peasant Society: A Reader,* Jack M. Potter, May N. Diaz and George M. Foster, eds. (Boston: Little, Brown and Co.), pp. 2-14.

Firth, Raymond, 1963. *Elements of Social Organizations* (Boston: Beacon Press).

Goodrich, Carter, 1925. *The Miner's Freedom: A Study of the Working Life in Changing Industry* (Boston: Marshall Jones Company).

Knipe, Edward E., 1967. Changes in Mining and Worker Interaction. Paper presented at the International Seminar on Social Change in the Mining Community, Part I, Jackson Mill, West Virginia.

Knipe, Edward E. and Helen M. Lewis, 1969. Toward a Methodology of Studying Coal Miner's Attitudes. PB 184665, U. S. Dept. of Commerce, Springfield, Virginia.

Lantz, Herman R., 1958. *People of Coal Town* (New York: Columbia University Press).

Lewis, Helen M., 1967. The Changing Communities in the Southern Appalachian Coal Fields. Paper presented at the International Seminar on Social Change in Mining Community, Part I, Jackson Mill, West Virginia.

————————, 1968. Subcultures of the Southern Appalachians. *The Virginia Geographer* 3:2-8.

————————, 1970. Occupational Roles and Family Roles: A Study of Coal Mining Families in the Southern Appalachians. Ph.D. dissertation, University of Kentucky.

Lewis, Helen M. and Edward E. Knipe, 1969. The Sociological Impact of Mechanization on Coal Miners and Their Families. *Proceedings of the Council of Economics,* American Institute of Mining, Metallurgical, and Petroleum Engineers, 268-307. And PB 183849, U. S. Dept. of Commerce, Springfield, Virginia.

National Coal Association, 1964. *Bituminous Coal Data* (Washington, D. C.: National Coal Association).

————————, 1968. *Bituminous Coal Facts* (Washington, D. C.: National Coal Association).

Pearsall, Marion, 1959. *Little Smoky Ridge* (University, Alabama: University of Alabama Press).

————————, 1966. Communicating with the Educationally Deprived. *Mountain Life and Work,* (Spring), pp. 3-11.

Ross, Malcolm, 1933. *Machine Age in the Hills* (New York: Macmillan).

Stephenson, John B., 1968. *Shiloh: A Mountain Community* (Lexington, Kentucky: University of Kentucky Press).

Vance, Rupert B., 1960. The Sociological Implication of Southern Regionalism. *The Journal of Southern History* 26:51-52.

Verhoeff, Mary, 1911. *The Kentucky Mountains, Transportation and Commerce, 1750-1911* (Louisville: Filson Club Publication 26).

Weller, Jack, 1965. *Yesterday's People* (Lexington: University of Kentucky Press).

Wolf, Eric R., 1955. Types of Latin American Peasantry: A Preliminary Discussion. *American Anthropologist* 57:452-471.

The Darlings Creek Peasant Settlements of St. Helena Parish, Louisiana

Milton B. Newton, Jr.

In 1821 the *American Farmer*, a journal devoted to rural life, published "The Peasant and His Wife," which in part ran as follows (Anonymous 1821):

> He: The long, long day again has pass'd
> In sorrow and distress:
> I strive my best—but strive in vain,
> I labor hard—but still remain
> Poor and in wretchedness.

At least since that time, the term "peasant" has not been considered applicable to citizens of the United States. People feel that the term "peasant" is derogatory; avoidance of the term extends, as well, into the ranks of the literati. Reference to standard surveys of peasantry, such as Eric R. Wolf's *Peasants* (1966), shows that the United States is lily-white on distribution maps—in other words, there are no peasants in the United States, or so it would seem. For example, George Foster states categorically, "American farmers, even prior to the introduction of elaborate machinery, were not peasants . . ." (1967:7).

The cultural geographer, E. Estyn Evans, might have had tongue in cheek when he explained: "We may find peasant values persisting among farmers who would resent the term 'peasantry'. . . . The word has always carried an implication of rustic inferiority, and we tend to apply it to countries other than our own" (1956:220). It seems that peasants are what *others* have. Failure to admit that a peasantry exists or existed in the United States makes the many, varied, and excellent studies of peasantry in other places unavailable as theoretical and practical aids in dealing with the complex society of the South.

This is not to say that the peasants of the South have not been

38

studied; indeed, they have been examined many times over. Actually, a number of scholars have touched upon the Southern peasant, but under a variety of names. The historian Owsley, after examining several possible names, settled upon "Plain Folks" (1949), while the agricultural historian Gray subdivided them into poor whites and yeoman farmers (1933). Other historians, such as John Hebron Moore (1958) and Herbert Weaver (1945), have dealt with the people we should call peasants. A few, such as Raper (1936) and Raper and Reid (1941), have spoken specifically of Southern peasants.

A variety of terms have been used to denote the Southern peasant and to connote varying degrees of approval. Most of these are folk terms and can be used only with the greatest care because they are emotionally loaded. The terms include: Hill-Billy (Tennessee), Red-Neck (northern Louisiana), Piney-Woods Folk (wide spread), Sand-Hiller and Clay-Eater (Carolina), Cracker (Georgia and Florida), Cedar-Chopper (central Texas), Congaree (Blue Ridge), Southern Highlander (Appalachia), and many others. With this array, it is not surprising that Owsley chose "Plain Folks" as an over-all term, especially in view of the pejorative quality of many of the other terms.

But the real question at hand is whether any of the people of the South can be classed as peasants. We can, for the moment, accept several leading definitions as valid for their specific purposes and simply use a tabulation of criteria as a check list to judge whether and to what extent some Southerners can be classed as peasants. By this means we may be able to avoid some of the disagreement concerning the traits of peasantry. If the people in question exhibit all or most of the significant traits suggested by each authority, and if these function in the manner implied by the over-all view of peasantry, then we are indeed dealing with a peasantry.

The following table presents the specifically stated positive criteria abstracted from definitions of peasantry by eight authorities. The group includes anthropologists, geographers, and an economist, covering all inhabited continents and spanning publication dates from 1939 through 1967.

Ignoring for the moment pre-peasants (Fallers 1961), post-peasants (Foster 1967:7), sub-peasants (Raper 1936:4), fisher-farmers, hunter-farmers, cuckoo-clock makers, and other folk groups, perhaps we might agree that, based upon this tabulation, a consensus would re-assemble these traits into a functioning whole as follows. A peasant is a member of a rural community of rustic agriculturists, horticulturists, or stockman, who individually or collectively have sufficient

Tabulation of specifically-stated, positive criteria of peasantry as stated by eight authors.	Redfield (1960:19)	Evans (1956:220-1, 237)	Pfiefer (1956:242ff)	Wolf (1966:2, 8-9, et passim)	Warriner (1939: passim)	Kroeber (1948:248)	Foster (1967:2-13)	Diaz (1967:50-56)
Agricultural occupation	X	X	X	X	X		X	X
Part-society, part-culture	X	X		X	X	X	X	X
Subsistence w/some market	X	X	X	X	X		X	X
Self-employed/control of land	X	X	X	X	X			X
Customary technology/"conservative"	X	X	X		X			X
External controls		X	X	X			X	X
Rustic/rural		X			X	X	X	
Man-land bonds	X	X	X					X
Way of life, not business	X		X	X				
Hostility to commercial culture	X		X				X	
Market transcends local dealings						X	X	X
Stockmen may be included		X	X					X
Family labor as capital		X	X					
"Estate"/Bauernstand			X					
Relate to pre-industrial cities							X	

control of the land to carry on largely traditional methods of producing mainly customary crops. Such a community supports its labor-supplying households importantly from the land as well as produces certain specific staples demanded by the dominant sections of a larger society and culture in which they participate only partially. The latter partialness stems, on the one hand, from a historic status occupied by the peasant with regard to a historic nobility if the noble shared title to the peasant's land. On the other hand, partialness stems from equally historic relations with the elite of the market town (pre-industrial city) where there originate external economic, political, and religious demands upon the peasant, his community, and his produce. Peasant farming is part of a way of life ("*estate*" or *Bauernstand*) involving a series of historically derived man-land relations which have value in themselves, not merely in their potential for profit. In the partial conflict between these rustic lifeways and the demands and values of the elite of the market town lies the source of hostility toward commercial culture and cities. From the geographical point of view, the peasant community is interesting not only because of its occupying an area of the earth's surface and a segment of the economic network, but also because of its continuing customary manner of altering the landscape and because its simple technology and long tenure point up variation in earth qualities.

THE DARLINGS CREEK SETTLEMENTS

Turning to a specific group of peasants, the Negroes living along Darlings Creek in northwestern St. Helena Parish, Louisiana, will serve as a convenient example. Though these people are black in a white-dominated society and though they seem to hold certain traits peculiar to themselves, they can serve as samples of a larger, mainly white, Upland South Culture.

Upland South Culture—the Scotch-Irish-and-German frontier— spread in the century from 1750 to 1850 to settle the area from Pennsylvania to central Texas and from southern Illinois to northern Florida (Kniffen and Glassie 1966; Evans 1965 and 1969). It occupied Darlings Creek between 1800 and 1805. The black segment, or caste, in Upland South Culture continues more of traditional practices than does the white group in this region, though there is no clear dichotomy between the cultural forms of blacks and whites, especially in the material and landscape aspects (Newton, 1967). Indeed, black peasants in their relationship with the white elite are quite similar to white peasants in the same relationship. Both also share a single complex of man-land relations which spread and developed from its eighteenth century origin in southern Pennsylvania. Evidence consisting of letters (Anderson Papers n.d.), an unusual farm diary (Lewis n.d.), succession and probate records (St. Helena Parish n.d.), and field investigations reveal not only temporal continuity in the culture of the Upland peasant of St. Helena and continuity between white and black peasants, but also a cultural lag of about one generation between whites and blacks. Historical studies of small farmers support the notion of continuity through time and space for the St. Helena Parish aspect of Upland South (Wailes 1854; Gray 1933:437-82; Moore 1958; Weaver 1945).

At two places along Darlings Creek in the vicinity of Chipola are churches which serve as focal points for two hamlets of black farmers: to the north lies St. Helena Baptist Church; to the south, Pipkin Chapel. Near these two churches are scattered the farmsteads of the families making up the hamlets which are not mutually exclusive nor completely included within these two church-memberships. In each area the leaders in social, economic, and political matters are often important in the church, though male leaders may not attend regularly. Leadership tends to cluster around one or two families and the elders of these families are frequently consulted on personal and community matters such as new church projects, support of political candidates, techniques of crop raising, and marketing arrangements. The eminence of these families is based upon at least three interrelated considerations: (1) the capacity of the family leader to deal with the white elite of the parish (county) and the market; (2) the size and success of the leader's farming enterprise and of the farms of his close relatives; and (3) the historic status of that leader as descendant of the founder of a "settlement."

The ability to mediate the demands of parish (county) officials and to obtain information and favors for one's own is an important skill, but a demanding role. The status of the leader assures him of considerate and fairly respectful treatment by both his clients and his patrons so long as he is successful and so long as the general, regional sociopolitical situation is stable. The hamlet leader supports the Police Juror (County Commissioner) of his ward if the parish official obtains favors and concessions for the hamlet leader and his clients. These channels are built up through a variety of personal contacts and include the following: (1) There are legal kinship bonds recognized between white farmers and the white elite, and illegal kin bonds between blacks and whites. The latter are "recognized" in many ways, for example, by false deeds of sale in which a white person conveys land to a black. Blacks speak frankly of their white kinsmen; whites speak frankly of others' black kinsmen. (2) Faithful service and participation in an almost proprietary bond is a relation sometimes overtly expressed as "so-and-so's man." The debt of the patron is recognized through favors and even deeds of property. (3) The farmer-leader often permits or arranges rustic favors such as hunting, fishing, and camping activities for his patron. (4) Preferred-purchaser-preferred-seller relations often reinforce bonds as in the case of a parish official of long standing, who owns a produce market. In addition to being a profitable business, his market represents a conscious effort at getting all of each of his clients' produce sold. The skill shown by a hamlet leader in obtaining and maintaining these and other contacts is one of the determinants of his status.

The success of the leader's farm is at least as important as the size. In one instance, the hamlet leader farms only about 35 acres, but quite successfully; he has bought a small tractor, built a new house, and holds the regional record for cotton production per acre. No less important is the need for the leader's close relatives to be successful. To be a big man, one's advice must not only be sought; it also must work.

The historic status of principal descendant of the founder of a settlement is important. The "settlement," in local terminology, is the intermediate level of social integration in a hierarchy including the "homeplace" (family farm), the "settlement" (hamlet), and the "community" (dispersed village).

The settlement is a loose clustering of several peasant family farms, most or all of which belong to kinsmen. It amounts to a dispersed, extended family because it is presided over quite unobtrusively by the eldest male; most of the inhabitants are his sons, brothers, or cousins and their wives and children. Women are nearly the equals of men and, at times, may serve as family heads. Since land is freely salable, non-family members may purchase plots adjacent to or in the midst of the settlement. Settlements are usually named for the principal or founding family, though some are named for the church which includes most of the people in its membership.

While the settlement does not usually have a church at its center, the church is probably the most important single building that is built and maintained by the inhabitants of the settlement. The state of repair of the church is the best single criterion for judging the vigor of the settlement as a social unit. The settlement seems to be the largest entirely peasant unit; it includes no professionals; and it tends to become endogamous. After the third generation, goods and services are exchanged within the settlement with a minimum of money, and such exchanges reinforce social relations.

Several settlements tend to be oriented around a more prosperous settlement, and collectively these are called a community. In or near the community center are located a number of functions missing or infrequent in the settlement. These may include several churches, several cemeteries, a Masonic temple, a post office, scout troops, public schools, retail stores, and service stations.

A community is less populous and more scattered than a town, of which there are two types, both being non-peasant forms belonging to each of the two elites making demands on the peasants. The oldest town in time and function is the courthouse-market town—in this case, Greensburg. Around its courthouse square the main routes of the parish converge, and there too clusters the old elite and its landscape forms: courthouse, newspaper, lawyers' row, county agent's

office, clinic, larger stores, and so forth. Peasants—white or black—
do not live in the courthouse town, and Negroes—peasants or not—
do not live there. Clustering at the edges of the town along the
principal routes are "quarters" of Negroes, some of whom work
in the town and some of whom are even professionals. The courthouse town is a current-day descendant of the pre-industrial city
(Sjoberg 1955).

The second kind of elite center is often the successor to the
courthouse-market town and in many cases has taken on the market
functions and often the court functions of the older type of town.
These more advanced elite centers are the railroad towns, riven apart
by the rails that gave them life. The railroad town with its ware-
houses, double main streets, tracks in the middle of side streets, and
huddles of small factories and poor houses next to the tracks is the
legitimate envoy of "commercial culture" sent into the rural, peasant-
and-courthouse landscape. In the case of St. Helena, there are no
railroads remaining today and, hence, no railroad towns.

The Use of the Land

Each family enterprise is a farm ranging from a minimum for
independence of about 25 acres to about 200 acres. However, these
figures can mislead because the areas under cultivation usually vary
between 25 and 35 acres, regardless of total holdings. Furthermore,
the family with only the minimum total acreage must have access
to many additional acres of unimproved land, a continuation of the
ancient commons available for use by all villagers. The uncultivated
woodlands serve as pasture for livestock; as foraging grounds for
gathering firewood, berries, nuts, and herbs; and as hunting and
fishing grounds. For the titular owner, woodlands provide all of
the above as well as new land for use while "resting" other plots
and income from sales of posts, pulpwood, and select hardwoods for
lumber. He may also give part of the woodland to his sons or
sons-in-law, or he may sell it. But so long as it is not under cultivation,
the people of the settlement, especially kinsmen, regard the woods as
open to their uses. (Interestingly at this point, the ward through which
Darlings Creek flows is one of the last to effectively resist closed-
range laws.) As is usually the case with peasants, possession of land
is a primary goal for the individual, but use of that land is participated in by the local group.

The land-use pattern is similar to that followed by some European
peasantry, especially the infield-outfield system of Atlantic Europe.
While there is some shifting of crops in the fields, the more important

aspect is land rotation, a kind of slash-and-burn land management. Any given plot, except those close to the farmstead, may be used for up to 20 years; as it "gets tired," it is abandoned, first to cleared pasture, but gradually returning to forest. As each plot loses productivity and is about to be left idle, similar amounts are cut from the woodland. The clearing is accomplished by deadening trees and burning the slash. Much of the surrounding forest is also burned clear of undergrowth that hinders its use as pasture. Each fall and winter the landscape is dotted with smoke plumes from burning woods.

Fields near the house, as well as the gardens, are seldom taken out of cultivation so long as the farm continues. This is true as well for all of the fields of the smallest farms, for they have no land to rotate. The fertility of these infields is maintained by commercial fertilizer, stockpenning, limited mulching, and burning of grass and stubble before planting.

The Darlings Creek peasant follows a system of crude mixed farming which Wolf might classify as "mesotechnic," or between neotechnic and paleotechnic. Such a classification seems necessary following Wolf's criteria (1966:18-59) and based upon the following traits.

The Darlings Creek farmer spends most of his farming effort on a historic food-and-feed (or subsistence) complex including corn, peas and beans, squash, sweet potatoes, greens, and the raising of pigs. Nearly all of the production of these crops is consumed on the farm as food for man or feed for animals. Cotton, green beans, cucumbers and a few calves are raised for sale.

A customary annual round is followed in which for four months fields lie idle, in the sense that no crops are being grown. However, cattle and mules are penned on the idle fields to forage on the stubble. Pasture grasses are planted only on the most progressive farms or on those specializing as dairies or stock farms, and these would be classed as neotechnic.

The Darlings Creek farmer is aware of basic notions of breeding both plants and animals. He selects seeds following modified folk practices, such as choosing long-kerneled, straight-rowed, large-eared corn for seed. He frequently renews crops with bought seed, choosing varieties that experience or neighbors approve. In the case of commercial crops such as beans, the desires of the commercial buyer are also given weight, largely as a result of instruction by the market owner in Greensburg. The value of improved or hybrid forms is understood, but so is the frequently unprofitable nature of such improvements: yield increases may not be great enough to make acceptance worthwhile. The market must be able to reward the innovation by purchasing the produce, but necessary arrangements do not always exist.

New commercial crops and animals have been accepted in the past and continue to be adopted as profitability becomes apparent. Recall for example, that in their turns corn, sweet potatoes, beans, squash, cotton, bell-peppers, peanuts, and many others were each new crops. New agricultural practices and new machines have also been accepted, including contour plowing, a variety of fertilizers, small tractors, and a host of plow forms. Innovations have been accepted when they have proven useful in terms of local desires, fertility, and access to market. Tradition is important in this as in any other peasant system of tillage; however, it is a realistic traditionalism, willing to accept locally viable innovations.

CONCLUSION

In summary, important data for classifying the Darlings Creek people as "mesotechnic" peasants, following Wolf (1966), are these: 1. They practice permanent cultivation of favored plots (in field-out field). 2. They have a mixed farming ecotype (neotechnic-paleotechnic, or mesotechnic) in which they (a) eat part of their produce; (b) practice seasonal farming and planting ("idle" fields); (c) give some attention to breeding and limited acceptance of hybrids; (d) accept new crops when clearly profitable; and (e) adopt new machinery when clearly profitable and when capital is available. 3. They recognize mercantile domain with both patrimonial and prebendal tendencies. 4. They are organized into extended family clusters of conjugal families changing to nuclear-family units. 5. They practice partible inheritance with some tendency to sell small inheritances to one of a few close relatives. 6. They have many-stranded, dyadic, vertical associations in which both families and family-clusters develop bonds with social, political, and economic superiors, supplemented by many-stranded, polyadic, horizontal associations among co-residents of open country neighborhoods.

As anthropologists would certainly suspect, the significant point is that new tools, crops, and animals have been adapted to the pre-existing system. And since the economic development of the region has been slow, abundant time has been available to integrate these innovations without destroying the peasant character of the culture. Indeed, historical descriptions of the crop complex, garden practices, the system of tillage, the settlement pattern, house and out-building types, and many other traits of the cultural ancestors of Darlings Creek farmers are little changed in their descendants.

Further study of the South as complex society or as a cultural landscape must be aimed, in part, at the question of the role and extensiveness of this peasantry.

REFERENCES

Anderson [Mollie E.] Papers, n.d. File B-16-1, Archives Room, Louisiana State University Library, Baton Rouge.

Anonymous, 1821. The Peasant and His Wife. *American Farmer* 1:60.

Diaz, May N., 1967. Economic Relations in Peasant Society. In *Peasant Society: A Reader*, Jack M. Potter, May N. Diaz, and George M. Foster, eds. (Boston: Little, Brown, and Co.), pp. 50-56.

Evans, E. Estyn, 1956. The Ecology of Peasant Life in Western Europe. In *Man's Role in Changing the Face of the Earth*, William L. Thomas, Jr., ed. (Chicago: University of Chicago Press), pp. 217-39.

———————, 1965. Cultural Relics of the Ulster-Scots in the Old West of North America. *Ulster Folklife* 11:33-38.

———————, 1969. The Scotch-Irish: Their Cultural Adaptation and Heritage in the American Old West. In *Essays in Scotch-Irish History*, R. R. Green, ed. (London: Routledge & Kegan-Paul), pp. 69-86.

Fallers, L. A., 1961. Are African Cultivators to be Called "Peasants"? *Current Anthropology* 2:108-110.

Foster, George M., 1967. What is a Peasant? In *Peasant Society: A Reader*, Jack M. Potter, May N. Diaz, and George M Foster, eds. (Boston: Little, Brown, and Co.), pp. 2-14.

Gray, Lewis Cecil, 1933. *History of Agriculture in the Southern United States to 1860* (Washington, D.C.: The Carnegie Institute of Washington).

Kniffen, Fred and Henry Glassie, 1966. Building in Wood in the Eastern United States: A Time-Place Perspective. *The Geographical Review* 56:40-66.

Kroeber, A. L., 1948. *Anthropology* (New York: Harcourt, Brace, and Co.).

Lewis [Jones] Diaries, n.d. Manuscript Farm Diaries, 1910-1962. Microfilm Room, Louisiana State University Library, Baton Rouge.

Moore, John Hebron, 1958. *Agriculture in Ante-bellum Mississippi.* (New York: Bookman Associates).

Newton, Milton B., Jr., 1967. The Peasant Farm of St. Helena Parish, Louisiana: A Cultural Geography. Ph.D. dissertation, Louisiana State University, Baton Rouge.

Owsley, Frank L., 1949. *Plain Folk of the Old South* (Baton Rouge: Louisiana State University Press).

Pfiefer, Gottfried, 1956. The Quality of Peasant Living in Central Europe. In *Man's Role in Changing the Face of the Earth,* William L. Thomas, Jr., ed. (Chicago: University of Chicago Press), pp. 240-77.

Raper, Arthur F., 1936. *Preface to Peasantry: A Tale of Two Black Belt, Counties* (Chapel Hill: University of North Carolina Press).

Raper, Arthur F., and Ira DeA. Reid, 1941. *Share Croppers All* (Chapel Hill: University of North Carolina Press).

Redfield, Robert, 1960. *Peasant Society and Culture* (Chicago: University of Chicago Press).

St. Helena Parish, n.d. Records of the Parish Clerk of Court, Succession and Probate Records, Greensburg, Louisiana.

Sjoberg, Gideon, 1955. The Preindustrial City. *American Journal of Sociology* 60:438-45.

Wailes, Benjamin L. C., 1854. *Report on the Agriculture and Geology of Mississippi* (Jackson: E. Barksdale).

Warriner, Doreen, 1938. *Economics of Peasant Farming* (New York: Oxford University Press).

Weaver, Herbert, 1945. *Mississippi Farmers, 1850-1860* (Nashville: Vanderbilt University Press).

Wolf, Eric R., 1966. *Peasants* (Englewood Cliffs, New Jersey: Prentice Hall, Inc.).

Living in Urban Milltown

Ronald J. Duncan

Mill man makes money. And from this vital essence men were created. Men who could work with their hands and their backs. Men whose minds dimmed with age. Mindless chores. Repeated. Repeated. The loom thumps.

Their minds churned. In the same repetitive acts. The same stories are told when the same group of men gather. The same chores are done every day. The same stories are told every night. It is satisfying to do the same things over and over and over.

Their minds churned. In the same repetitive acts. To come home at night to rock and rock and rock. On the porch, in the living room, in the bedroom. To be more than mindless would be intolerable tomorrow.

Their minds churned. In the same repetitive acts. To come home with no feeling left. A mill is not a place to live. A woman and kids are repetitive acts. A mill town is not a place of love.

Their minds churned. In the same repetitive acts. But, man's mind does not die. On Sunday he is told that he is right. And he needed that. Sometimes man lives by rectitude alone. Calvin is our Savior. To live in grey is not totally colorless.

Their minds churned. In drunkenness. The good Lord gives him a little drink every night. And in the morning he is gone. To the mill? The good Lord? The mill man's world is alone. The little drink. A machine. A bird, maybe a bird.

And the TV roared. And the gas heater mightily conquered the seeping cold. And the seasons passed. And grandmother died. We are not sure where she came from, but we know where she went. And the seasons passed.

JAKE'S BOTTOMS

Jake's Bottoms is ordered rows of former mill company houses,

49

crazy quiltwork patterns of shotgun shacks, and white cottages with neatly trimmed lawns built on and around a low rolling hill and tied together by being cut off from everything else in the city. Railroad tracks are on one side. A cemetery, a major thoroughfare, the ever looming mill complex, and black neighborhoods complete the isolation. From one crest of the little hill, looking past the corner of the mill one can see the skyline of the city less than a mile away. The gold capitol dome gleams on the sunny days. On the foggy days the 30 story buildings can still be seen in the haze.

But, that is a world that is so far away that no one from Jake's Bottoms ever goes there. Downtown, people get disoriented and lost. It is a foreign and uncomfortable feeling. Nothing good comes from down there, so no one bothers to go. Everything that one could want is within walking distance in Jake's Bottoms. Few people have cars.

Mack's store on the corner has good streak-o-lean bacon and Cokes and just about anything else that one could want. There is a liquor store just down the way. Four generations of family live in the neighborhood, frequently next door to each other, or in the same house. And, no one has to walk more than a block to find a church.

One literally does not have to leave this community of 2,500 souls for anything. Indeed, entering and leaving is rather difficult. Two sides of the community are blocked off, forming a dead-end corner. The streets are narrow and irregular and one-way. One can come to believe that it is impossible to extricate oneself from the maze.

Billy Joe

When I was 18, a wife came. At $63.80 a week from the mill I couldn't lose. She came from across the street. She lived with her grandmother. She was sixteen and was unhappy at home. We rented the house next door. Her old man came drunk one night and busted the door. She had a kid the first year we were married. The kid died.

Her brother is pretty good at pool. He and I used to go down in the afternoon, and we'd play till they closed at midnight. He'd hear that some guys had come into town from Moffit, and no matter what he was doin' he'd get up and go down and shoot with them. Sometimes he'd win fifty, maybe hundred dollars a night. He liked tattoos. He had his wife tattooed in the nude on his left arm. Later he had "hell" tattooed there. On his right arm he had tattooed "born to lose."

I've worked off and on at the mill since, I guess, I was 16. My first job was when I was 14. I've worked quite a bit over at Henry's Grocery. He has always been good about taking me back on when I need a job. The only thing about Henry's is that you have to work on Saturday, and you have to work longer every day. At the mill you go at 7:30 and get off at 3:30 if you are on the day shift. But, at the mill you don't ever get to let up. You can't stop what you are doing for a single minute. You don't even get off for lunch. I really don't like working an 8 hour shift without gettin' off at all.

I worked at the mill all summer. Not long ago I quit. I had left the loom, and I stopped just a minute to talk to a guy that I know there. About that time a boss came by. He wasn't even my boss. He asked me what I was doing; I told him. He said that I had been leaving my job too much. He told me to get back to work. Well, I didn't like the way he was talkin'. And, he wasn't even my boss. I told him that he could take his damned job and ram it up where it belonged. And, I left right there on the spot. I didn't even go back to get my check, I just let 'em mail it to me.

I could've gone to one of the big bosses, and they would've straightened things out. But, I didn't like the way the guy was doing. I wasn't goin' to take that, so I just quit.

That Woods family is no account. It's families like that that is makin' our neighborhood go down. This used to be a pretty place to live. The Woods have got a house full of kids, two houses full, and they'd all just as soon kill you as look at you. Kids is runnin' wild. People seem to have lost control.

There are some boys down here that are my age that cause trouble sometimes. They get to drinkin' and get mean. They'll fight a little. My in-laws are like that. It's kinda bad livin' in the same house with them sometimes. They'll start fightin' each other and cussin'. It'll sound like they are tearing the place apart; Lucille will want to do something because its her brothers. I've told her to stay out of it. I don't want to get into that. If she gets her head busted, she'll just have to take whatever happens to her.

I've seen my brother-in-law cuss his own mother to her face. And he lives with her! I'll bet he would hit his own mother. He does a little bootleggin' on the side on the week-ends. He always has beer and wine around. And when they get started drinking, they get mean.

I don't mind drinkin' a beer or two. I used to get drunk. I told the Lord when our first baby died that I'd never touch another drop. And, I didn't for a long time. But, I really got to missin' it. I talked to Mother about it, and she said that the Lord would understand. Sometimes His children make promises that they just cannot live up to.

I really don't think that it is so bad to drink. It is not what goes into a man, but what comes out of him. Take my ol' Dad for instance. He gets drunk every night of the world. But, every morning he gets up and goes to work. And, he is as good as he can be.

He has been that way as long as I have known him. He never does no harm to nobody. He wouldn't hurt a flower. But some people, when they get drunk, they get mean.

My older brother, James, has always had a lot of trouble with his legs. When he was little, he had polio. One of his legs now is no bigger than my arm. But, you hardly ever notice it. He doesn't let people know. When he was in the seventh grade, he had a lot of trouble with his legs. He missed a lot of school that year. And so, he quit. When he got better, he got a job as a roofer. Later on he got me a job with him. Then, I quit school too.

I never was too much on school no way. Why, my Dad never went to school but one day in his life. He didn't like it and ran away. They never did make him go back. He can count and add and figure things as good as anybody. He learned it himself. He educated himself.

I didn't get along too well down at school. I never did like to read too much. Now, I'll read something like the sports in the paper, but nothing like school books. Those teachers always gave me a lot of trouble. They never did like me down there no way. And, I guess you'd say it was mutual. I'd rather a been out playing ball anyhow.

My old man never had much to do with us kids. He was always awfully strict on us. Mother used to try to get him to let us do things, but he never would. He wouldn't let us go out and play with the other kids because he was afraid that we might get hurt. I wanted a bicycle, but he wouldn't buy one because he was afraid something might happen. When I got old enough, I used to go over and spend all my time at my Aunt Chloe's. I'd lived over there if they had let me. But Mother always wanted me to spend time at home. She said it didn't look right. So I'd come home.

When I got old enough, I started spendin' all of my time over at the ball park. When I got off work, I'd go over and play until it got dark. On Saturdays I'd spend the whole day playin' ball. I wouldn't even come home to eat. I've always had to watch how I played because I have heart trouble. I guess that is one reason why Dad never would let me play with the other kids.

I've never had nothin', never did expect nothin', and the good Lord has taken care of me. Riches are a burden to the spirit, and I guess the Lord knows what he was doing by never giving us much.

I've lived in this same ol' house for twelve years. The man who owns it comes by and collects the rent every month. He owns lots of houses around here. He's a crazy old man, a millionaire. He never spends a penny. That's how he got rich. He rides a bicycle and wears the same old clothes all the time. That's a rich old man.

We've always had plenty of beans in the pot and cornbread in the oven and clothes on our backs. We've never really been wantin' for anything. The Lord has been good to us.

Johnny, the one that's four, has been sick an awful lot. When my wife was pregnant with him her teeth got brittle and whitish, and it wasn't long before they started coming out. She is almost as toothless as her old Mother now. Then, after Johnny was born we had trouble after trouble with him. I guess he is going to be the unlucky child of this family. We've had him in the hospital four or five different times. This last time he was in for a month and a half, off and on. He has a hole between the two sides of his heart, and it don't pump right. The doctors thought they might have to operate. But, they didn't. They sent him home. He's got a machine and a tent that he has to stay in sometimes. And, my wife has to beat him in the chest part of every day.

The Lord always carries us through every sickness. I've spent an awful lot of time sittin' up in hospitals, prayin', and the Lord hasn't let us down yet.

THE ANTHROPOLOGIST

The emotionally significant symbols around which people in Jake's Bottoms organize their behavior are the Lord (not the church), the family, the community (not as a structured place but as a familiar place), the mill, and fate. These symbols become the foci for the organization of a way of life that is paced by biological events. The resulting behaviors look away from the larger society in which they are meshed. Social change in terms of the larger society is not cultivated. Indeed, the world may be seen to drop off at the edge of Jake's Bottoms.

The organization of behavior is community specific, even family specific. The primary contact with the outside comes through the mass media, the mill, and schools. But, these are bothersome influences that are either encysted or ignored and seldom responded to positively. Usually the outside is associated with authority; authority that is illegitimate to community members.

This paper is an attempt to portray the major areas of symbolic behavior that are characteristic of the men and women inhabiting one urban mill village. My attempt has been to project the actual thoughts and ideas of specific individuals living there, rather than to abstract these into a terminology that sacrifices realism.

As anthropologists have turned to urban, complex societies for field research, a number of new approaches to ethnography have been tried. The work of Elliott Liebow (1967) and Oscar Lewis

(1959; 1961; 1965) demonstrate some of these approaches. Working from a community point of view has been feasible with small populations and relatively isolated groups of people. This approach seems to become more untenable as social scientists analyze the behavior of groups that are closer to their own (Valentine 1968:174). The complexities of behavior become more apparent, and perhaps more real because of the mass society. So, the search is for a unit of behavior that is feasible for observation, analysis, and realism.

In this paper I have tried to blend three goals of description: empirical, realistic, and sentient. Focusing on the actual behaviors that are generated by specific individuals seems to be the best way to achieve this blend. The individual is the unit of behaving. This is an attempt to conceptualize culture as an "existential attribute of actual men in society" (Bidney 1967:xv).

Are these behaviors typical of all the individuals who live in Jake's Bottoms? Is Jake's Bottoms typical of all lower white communities? The concept "typical" does not adequately describe the behavior here. Many life problems and assumptions about behaving are similar for lower class white people. But, the behavioral responses may vary.

Thus, the question becomes whether the behavior is generic to the group, i.e. does the behavior described come out of the cultural assumptions and premises generally used and understood in the group? Individuals generate behavior from certain cultural assumptions and premises which exist in their group (Wallace 1962:351). More than one action may be generated from one cultural assumption.

These behaviors are generic to Jake's Bottoms. Everyone in the community shares or understands both the behaviors described here and the emotionally significant symbols from which they are generated. Because of role differences a person may not be in a position to generate some behaviors. But, he will understand these behaviors sufficiently to mesh his own with them. Billy Joe may not behave like his in-laws, nor approve of their behavior, but he knows that some people are like that.

As a respectable member of his community, there are certain behaviors (excessive drunkenness, fighting, tattoos) that he may shun. But, he knows some people will do those things. The emotionally significant symbols and the behavior Billy Joe derived from them are shared by most of the respectable people. As a person becomes peripheral (either disreputable or upwardly mobile) he will increasingly generate other behaviors and acquire additional emotionally significant symbols.

Each incident, idea, and action portrayed here I have collected in the course of eighteen months of participant observation and interviewing in Jake's Bottoms. The substantive material is empirical; some of the wording and organization are mine.

NOTES

1. I wish to thank J. Kenneth Morland and Charles Hudson for their comments on an earlier version of this paper.

2. Parts of this paper were delivered at the 68th annual meeting of the American Anthropological Association in New Orleans, Louisiana, in November 1969, under the title 'Symbolic Behavior in Urban Milltown."

REFERENCES

Bidney, David, 1967. *Theoretical Anthropology*, Second, augmented edition (New York: Schocken Books).

Lewis, Oscar, 1959. *Five Families* (New York: Basic Books).

———————— 1961. *The Children of Sanchez* (New York: Random House).

Liebow, Elliot, 1967. *Tally's Corner* (New York: Little, Brown, and Co.)

Valentine, Charles, 1968. *Culture and Poverty* (Chicago: The University of Chicago Press).

Wallace, Anthony F. C., 1962. Culture and Cognition. *Science* 135: 351-357.

Slingings and High Shots:
Moonshining in the Georgia Mountains

John Gordon

Moonshining, or the making of illicit liquor, is an activity that comes to mind when one mentions mountain people; and indeed it should, for the development of illegal distilling in this country got its start in the isolated mountain areas of Appalachia.[1] The production of moonshine has now become such a large scale business in many Southern states that the federal government has, in addition to employing hundreds of Alcohol and Tobacco Tax agents, actually launched a concerted campaign (involving modern advertising techniques) aimed at drying up the production of illicit liquor in these states. Although moonshining is by no means confined to the mountain areas, it is still very much alive in the mountains and much can be learned about moonshining from the mountain people. A well developed folklore of moonshining exists in the highlands, and one can hardly spend any time there without contact with moonshining in some form.

In spite of the uniqueness of moonshining, its traditions, and its effect upon mountain subculture, little has been written on the sociological and technological aspects of the activity. Winston and Butler published an article in 1943 on Negro moonshiners in eastern North Carolina, and Loyal Durand, Jr. has written on the mountain moonshining of east Tennessee in the *Geographical Review*. The classic work by Horace Kephart, *Our Southern Highlanders*, contains two humorous chapters on the history of mountain moonshining and the state of the art in the early decades of this century. The most thorough account to date of the technology of moonshining was published in 1968 in an article by the staff writers for *Foxfire*, a quarterly magazine published by high school students in the Rabun Gap School in north Georgia.

56

My purpose in this paper is to briefly describe the technology of moonshining and then to examine some of its sociological and economic implications. Specifically, I shall attempt to explain the popularity of moonshining as opposed to other types of work which are safer and less demanding.

Mountain people know how to build many different types of stills; the type selected for use is determined by the speed at which the operator wants to produce and the quality desired in the final product. One of my main informants was a fifty-one year old ex-moonshiner who had begun making liquor when he was eight years old. Doc was a specialist at making the type of still known as the "blockade" or "rerun" still. Although this type of still has been one of the more popular varieties, several other kinds are often used; and the desire for quick profit with these other stills has, in many cases, resulted in a product that is not far removed from pure poison. If the blockade still is properly constructed and run with care, however, the operator can produce a liquor of very good quality.

The basic parts of the blockade still are the still itself,[2] the furnace (which is built around the still), the cap and cap stem, the thump post and thump barrel, the headache piece, the pre-heater box and trough, the slide connections, the flake stand, and the condenser. (See diagram.) After the still is constructed, the first step in the distilling process is the making of the mash, or beer, which will be run through the still. Several different "recipes" for making the beer are used by various operators. Generally, to make the mash, the operator fills the still full of water and adds the proper amount of corn meal. The furnace is fired and this mixture of meal and water is cooked. It is unnecessary to connect any of the still's parts during this procedure. The boiling mixture is then drawn out of the still into barrels or into the box dug in under the slop arm. Corn malt and rye meal are then added to the cooked meal. This starts the mixture to "working." The malt contains the enzyme diastase which saccharifies the starch of the raw corn meal. To obtain the corn malt used in this process, the moonshiner often had to sprout and grind his own corn. This complicated the distilling operation because it is a federal offense (just like moonshining itself) to grind sprouted corn. A miller who was a trusted friend was a necessity.

After the mixture has set for a day or so, it is stirred up again and sugar is added. Sugar increases the yield, but it is not used by all moonshiners because with its use the product is not considered "pure corn whiskey" (*Foxfire* 1968:102). While the mixture is fermenting, a crust or cap forms on the surface. When the mixture

works off—that is, when the cap has disappeared—the beer is ready
to run; the alcohol in the mixture has eaten off the crust.

When I asked Doc to give me his "recipe" for the mash, this is
what he said:

> O.K. John, you want me to give you a recipe how to make
> moonshine, so I can't write so I guess I'll just tell you how you do
> this and you can put it on your tape here. So the way you do that
> now, you get your meal, you get your still, and you put it in the fur-
> nace and you build a fire under it. So you fill it about ⅔ full of
> water, a fifty gallon still we'll say, a 'pacity fifty gallons. So you put
> a bushel a meal in it and you stir it up good with your scrape paddle.
> And you keep your fire under it and when it goes to boilin—then,
> you cap it, with the cap, and the steam comes out the stem thar.
> You let it boil fifteen minutes. O. K., and then you draw it over
> in your boxes, now that's the box that's dug in under your slop
> arm where you make your beer. So you push your swab stick up
> and you draw your beer over into the box, ah, your meal or water
> you've cooked, and so you have your corn malt thar and on this 38
> square box you put ½ bushel of dry corn malt and a gallon of rye
> meal. You stir it up good, and that's in the evening, or the morn-
> ing, and you let it set about twelve to twenty hours and then you
> go back and stir it up good and you put about one hundred pounds
> of sugar on this box. Then you stir it up good and go back in about
> twelve hours and stir it up again. And then when it works off,
> you, ah—when it clears off like water on top—then you put
> it in your still and you go to running it just like usual.

With the beer ready and the still parts connected, the operator
can begin the run. A fire is built in the furnace and as the beer begins
to heat, the operator must periodically stir the mixture to keep it
from sticking to the bottom and sides of the still. A duck nest furnace
of the type Doc builds, by recirculating its heat, is said to "burn its
own smoke." This lessens the danger of discovery of the operation.
After the beer has come to a boil, steam will begin to flow through
the connections. From the still, steam goes through the thump barrel
and headache piece into the pre-heater box. The thump barrel also
contains beer, and the steam bubbling through the beer makes a deep
thumping noise. The pre-heater box contains a copper ring similar
to the condenser. At the beginning of the run, beer is put in the box
to cover the ring. Steam going through the copper heats the beer,
and when all of the beer in the still has boiled away a trough is then
placed between the heater box and the uncapped still. The gate
on the box is opened and the pre-heated beer flows into the still.

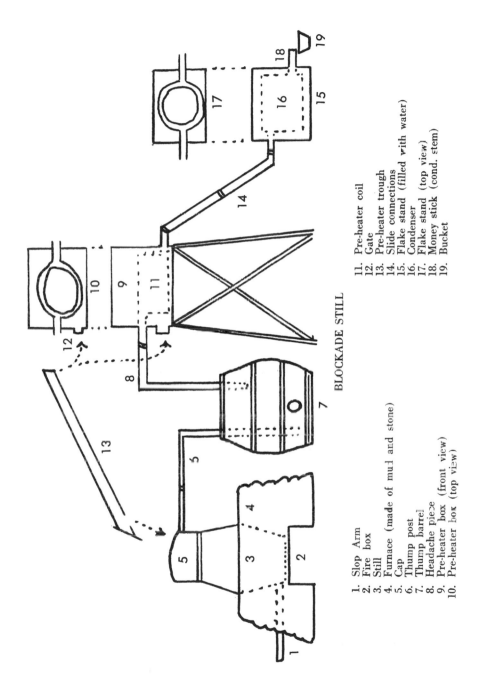

BLOCKADE STILL

1. Slop Arm
2. Fire box
3. Still
4. Furnace (made of mud and stone)
5. Cap
6. Thump post
7. Thump barrel
8. Headache piece
9. Pre-heater box (front view)
10. Pre-heater box (top view)

11. Pre-heater coil
12. Gate
13. Pre-heater trough
14. Slide connections
15. Flake stand (filled with water)
16. Condenser
17. Flake stand (top view)
18. Money stick (cond. stem)
19. Bucket

Because the beer is already hot, little time is lost waiting for the beer to boil. This makes the operation, therefore, almost continuous.

From the pre-heater box the steam goes into the flake stand. The flake stand, a wooden box similar to the pre-heater, contains the condenser. During distillation, water (usually from a nearby stream) runs through the box and condenses the steam into alcohol. The product trickles out the condenser stem and is caught in a bucket or barrel. A funnel inserted in the bucket or barrel contains a filter of charcoal wrapped in cloth which strains the fusel oils out of the alcohol.

The first run usually does not produce any whiskey strong enough to "hold a bead."[3] The product from the first run of a fifty gallon still should be about ten gallons of weak liquor. To start the next run, the still is drained and re-filled with fresh beer. The thump barrel is also emptied and the ten gallons from the first run, known as slingings or backings, are put in the thump barrel. On the second run the product will be much stronger because the steam is going through the alcohol in the thump barrel and being "doubled." The second run should produce about two gallons of good alcohol and around eight weak gallons. The weak gallons, as before, form the backings for the next run. This process is continued until all the beer is used. After about seven runs, the result will be seven to ten gallons of pure corn whiskey. This whiskey is close to 200 proof and is called "high shots."

Doc describes how he makes liquor:

> So the way you do, John, you make the mash, that's in boxes as we do back in the mountains. So you cook your meal and mash it up and you put your corn malt or any kind of malt you want to on it. Well, when your beer works off, it usually takes seventy-two hours on up to three or four days according to how many hogs fall in it, and possums, so forth and so on. So anyway, John, now the way you do this, son, you fill up the still here with the beer and take the beer here and put it in this heater, it's a pre-heater, what it is, a double condenser, it's a quick way of makin' it. So why we invented this heater it's much faster and much easier, and while you rest you take off a keg of liquor and bring back a load of wood.
>
> So, haint nothing to it, and then you fill up the heater with beers. You got a trough over here in the flake stand, you run the water right down through it, and so now what happens when it goes to boilin', you can use wood or coal or anything you want to, but we usually back in the mountains use wood, such as sourwood, fence rails, so forth and so on. So the way you do this now, when it goes to boilin', you cap it and you pour a couple a gallon of

beer in your thump barrel to start off with. So then, when it goes to runnin whiskey you take up a little proof vial, we call it out there, under the condenser stem. And then you check it, you shake it down to a bead and it gets down to about 100 proof then you stop an put the bucket, a bucket's usually what we use, or a tub, or a keg, or a barrel, and you change and you catch the backings. Well the backings is a low grade of whiskey, it's alcohol, and you catch 'em as long as it burns. The way you tell, when they get weak you throw 'em under the furnace and when they blaze, they still good. So you catch what backings you get there and then you go to changin' and you switch it from one to another. And then you pour, refill it back up, and you start the same operation over and over, again and again.

So, I have the names here on this little still, very 'cular names, they true. The names on these stills, here are the slop arm, that's where the slop comes out, we call it slop, after it's boiled down into whiskey then it goes back to make re-mash again. The slop arm is where you put the swab stick, a swab stick is a mallet or a forked stick with a tow sack wrapped on it, ever body that's ever made any whiskey knows what I mean. And then we come on up to the still, and the duck nest furnace is a new model furnace that burns its own smoke. So we used to make 'em old groundhog furnaces, two or three different ways you make furnaces. But we invented this duck nest furnace, it burns its own smoke, and the man won't see you—you know how it is—you gotta be careful when you're makin it; ah, I tried to be—seven times I learnt better.

So, the way you do it, go on down the cap stem on down into the headache piece, thump post go down in the barrel and thumps the backings into processed whiskey. And why they call it a headache piece, that's the one that goes up here, John, out of the thump barrel up here into the pre-heater, and it's the headache piece now, son, and the reason I know this *is* the headache piece, if you've drunk as much of this pop-skull as I have, you'll find out exactly what I mean. Well, it goes on down and the water it runs into the slide connections, and the condenser is what condenses steam into alcohol. I'll tell you now about this condenser business, ah, we used to make 'em with old worms, coil worms, foil worms, and all that. So my grandfather invented this condenser; it's a quick, easier way to make it. So the way the whole set up goes, the pressure, John, pushes the steam through this rotation, on through the thump barrel over into the pre-heater, right on down in the condenser. And the pressure, or the temperature, is about 480 degrees, so I've been told. And the pressure from this fire pushes it right on down and the steam goes right on through all these connections, right on down through the slide connections into the condenser, and the water condenses this into liquor—alcohol—and it comes out here at the money stick.

The most frequent explanation for the popularity of moonshining in the mountains is couched in economic terms. The marginal mountain farmer, so the argument goes, can clear practically no profit from selling his poor quality corn on the open market. But when the corn is concentrated into liquor, its value jumps many times and the mountaineer can thus realize a good return. No doubt the economic factor is a very important (perhaps the most important) motivation to engage in illicit liquor production. It has certainly been stressed by those who have written on this subject, as we shall see below. It is my contention, however, that other factors must also be considered in any explanation of the appeal of moonshining. My experience suggests that were the economic factor the sole justification for moonshining, the practice would virtually die out.

Historically speaking, moonshining was greatly stimulated by economic pressures. All sources seem to agree on this. Campbell (1921:106) states that, "Moonshining is due primarily to economic reasons." Winston and Butler (1943:692) contend that the Negro moonshiners of eastern North Carolina have "drifted into the business because the amount of poor land they cultivate is not sufficient to keep them and their families employed steadily and profitably." The writers of *Foxfire* (1968:38) agree with Horace Kephart, "He [Kephart] argues most effectively that the primary reason for all this [moonshining] was economic, and we agree completely." Kephart (1913:122-123) relates his findings through the words of one of his mountain friends:

> . . . the main reason for this 'moonshining,' as you-uns calls it, is bad roads . . . . From hyar to the railroad is seventeen miles, with two mountains to cross; and you've seed that road! I recollect you-uns said every one o' them miles was a thousand rods long. . . . Seven hundred pounds is all the load a good team can haul over that road, when the weather's good. Hit takes three days to make the round trip, less'n you break an axle, and then hit takes four. When you do git to the railroad, th'r ain't no town of a thousand people within fifty mile. Now us folks ain't even got wagons. Thar's only one sarviceable wagon in this whole settlement, and you can't hire it without team and driver, which is two dollars and a half a day. . . . The only farm produce we-uns can sell is corn. You see for yourself that corn can't be shipped outen hyar. We can trade hit for store credit—that's all. Corn *juice* is about all we can tote around over the country and git cash money for. Why, man, that's the only way some folks has o' payin' their taxes!

Within the last twenty-five or thirty years a fairly extensive system of highways has penetrated Appalachia. Many areas still remain isolated, but in north Georgia the highway system is quite extensive. Now if the economic argument based on "bad roads" was valid, then moonshining should have disappeared in these areas when good roads were built. It obviously has not. One may counter, however, that the better road network simply made distribution of the product easier and therefore moonshining became more profitable. This no doubt is true. As Durand (1956:178) states, "Good roads, nearly all of them gravelled and many of them paved, have been provided by the respective states. The moonshiner is able to dispose of his product several hundred miles from its region of manufacture. . . ." The fact remains, however, that making illegal liquor is an extremely exacting, as well as a dangerous, business. Raine (1924:132) comments, "The making of moonshine is sleepless, nerve-racking work, and produces comparatively little return for the long days and nights of strain." Furthermore, in the counties where I worked, better employment (in terms of pay and less strenuous work) was available. It stands to reason, then, that the economic aspect of moonshining cannot be its sole appeal. If it were, then the moonshiners should have long ago switched over to work in the various light industries (textiles, shoes, etc.) of the area.

Why, then, do some mountain people prefer the relatively insecure life of the moonshiner to the relatively secure life of the factory worker? Winston and Butler (1943:693) have come close to what I believe may be the answer in saying that, "A small proportion of bootleggers enjoy their trade and actually get a 'thrill' out of the suspense and uncertainty and danger connected with it." They contend that this group is in the minority. But I believe this thrill factor is, on the contrary, of great importance. Winston and Butler further state that, "The manufacture and sale of bootleg whiskey is not sufficiently exciting or remunerative to induce the Negro youth to engage in such activities unless there are no alternative economic opportunities in the same community or section of the State." This observation does not hold true for the area in which I worked. As mentioned previously, better employment was available in the area to the extent that moonshining should have ceased to be a significant activity.

Herbert Gans has developed a conceptual framework which attempts to explain the type of thrill seeking behavior mentioned above in the statement by Winston and Butler. In his study of Italian-Americans in a Boston slum (1962), Gans describes the slum dwellers in terms of several differing behavior styles, the two most important categories being "action-seekers" and "routine-seekers." The routine-seeker feels comfortable when he has established a fairly definite and repetitive living pattern, such as working each day from nine to five, attending church every Sunday at 11:00, and watching the same television programs every Tuesday night. The action-seeker, at the opposite end of the spectrum, enjoys more thrilling and spontaneous activities. He tends to live episodically.

Jack Weller in *Yesterday's People* (1965:40-43) has applied Gans' concepts to the mountain people of West Virginia. Weller describes the action-seeker as one whose "jobs are often the unstable ones, or those offering excitement or change." He contends that coal mining, as a dangerous activity, appeals to those with action-seeking personalities. "Many a coal miner will leave a steady, routine factory job in the city any time to take back a job in the mines." Weller believes that mountain people as a group are predominantly more action-seeking than routine-seeking. My observations tend to support this belief, and I contend that the action-seeking personality is a characteristic of the average mountain moonshiner. Moonshining, like coal mining, is a dangerous, thrilling activity.

By this I do not mean that all moonshiners, or even all mountain moonshiners, should be considered action-seekers. I do not deny that some moonshiners are purely economically motivated. My observations indicate, however, that in most cases, something in addition to the profit motive is at work; and I suggest that it is the action-seeking aspect of the mountain personality that drives men to risk their fortunes and even their lives in the making of illegal liquor.

NOTES

1. The original version of this paper was presented at the 1969 annual meeting of the Southern Anthropological Society in New Orleans, Louisiana. The paper itself is a modified portion of an undergraduate honors thesis written at the University of Georgia. This thesis is presently being published in four installments in *The Georgia Review;* all installments have been published to date (Gordon 1970). Permission from *The Georgia Review* to reproduce part of this material here is appreciated.

The research for the paper was conducted in the Appalachian region of Georgia during the summer of 1968. My major informant was a garrulous ex-moonshiner who was always eager to tell of his past accomplishments in the "moonshine life." He was happy to record his methods and techniques on my tape recorder, and most of my information was, therefore, collected this way. My general research method was participant-observation. I am grateful to Charles Hudson for his helpful comments.

2. The term "still" can refer to the entire unit, as in "moonshine still," or merely to the metal container in which the beer is boiled.

3. To check the strength or proof of the liquor, the operator fills a small bottle (called the proof vial) with the product and thumps the bottle in the palm of his hand. If the bubbles that rise remain steady in the center of the bottle, then the liquor is of proper strength and it is said "to hold a bead."

REFERENCES

Campbell, John C., 1921. *The Southern Highlander and his Homeland* (New York: Russell Sage Foundation).

Durand, Loyal, 1956. Mountain Moonshining in East Tennessee. *Geographical Review* 46:168-81.

Foxfire, 1968. The End of Moonshining as a Fine Art. *Foxfire* 2, nos. 3 and 4.

Gans, Herbert, 1962. *The Urban Villagers* (New York: Free Press of Glencoe).

Gordon, John L., Jr., 1970. Up Top Amongst None: Life in The Georgia Appalachians. *The Georgia Review*, 24, No. 1, pp. 5-28; No. 2, pp. 183-199; No. 3, pp. 337-348; No. 4, pp. 483-494.

Kephart, Horace, 1913. *Our Southern Highlanders* (New York: Outing Publishing Co.).

Raine, James, 1924. *The Land of Saddle Bags* (Richmond, Va.: Presbyterian Committee of Publication).

Sheppard, M. E., 1935. *Cabins in the Laurels* (Chapel Hill: University of North Carolina Press).

Sherman, Mandel and Thomas R. Henry, 1933. *Hollow Folk* (New York: Thomas Y. Crowell Co.).

Weller, Jack E., 1965. *Yesterday's People: Life in Contemporary Appalachia* (Lexington: University of Kentucky Press).

Winston, Sanford and Mosette Butler, 1943. Negro Bootleggers in Eastern North Carolina. *American Sociological Review* 8:692-7.

How to Lose the Hounds: Technology of the Gullah Coast Renegade

H. Eugene Hodges

The Gullah Coast is a distinctive cultural area noted in the literature for its richness in folklore and folk music. It encompasses the geographical area from Charleston, South Carolina to Kingsland, Georgia and includes the offshore islands, the pine forests, and swamps of the coastal plains. While interviewing in a rural section in this area, I discovered a social type designated by members of the community as "renegades". The first time I heard the term "renegade" was during an interview session with an informant whose primary source of income was the manufacture of illegal whiskey. When the interview session was concluded and I was about to leave, I asked my informant for directions to Mr. X's house. My informant became visibly upset and responded, "You ought not to go to those people's house. They're a bunch of renegades." I did not attach any significance to the term, but I was curious about the reason for his hostility towards Mr. X. When I asked him what he meant by renegade, he gave me a rather confusing description of a person who lives outside the law. Since he himself was a moonshiner, his explanation made little sense to me.

During an interview with another informant I again brought Mr. X into the conversation. The response was "If you are going to visit that family you better not go by yourself. Those people are renegades." It was at this point that I began to see that perhaps I had uncovered a social type. I postponed my visit to Mr. X's house until I could discover what a renegade was. The definition which emerged was that the renegade is, first of all, a person who has broken the law and has been found out. But this in itself was certainly not unusual in the population I was studying. Most of my informants were making their living by either illegal fishing or by moonshining. The thing

66

that made the renegade distinctive was that when he became a fugitive from the law, he ran to the swamps, the pine forest, or the offshore islands where he remained isolated from the necessities of civilization and feared by members of the community. In contrast, when other members of the community became fugitives, they would leave the county to reside in one of the fishing communities in Savannah, Charleston, or Jacksonville.

Two families were designated as a "bunch of renegades" by my informants. The label seemed to apply not only to specific members of the family but to the entire family. And of these two families there was no living member who had actually been a renegade. The renegade label meant only that the family had produced renegades in the past but the last renegade anyone could name lived in the area about 1915. This renegade was related to Mr. X and was described as a real renegade, who, when the hounds were after him, would drink cow's blood by cutting the vein on a cow's neck, drinking his fill, and then sealing the vein back up by pressing on it. "He would just keep on running."

The content of this paper is from separate interviews with the male heads of the two renegade families. In no instance did either of the two informants mention specific members of their families who were renegades in the past, and after several "polite" attempts to probe this met with failure, I let it drop. The interviews were characterized by an easy, flowing conversation in which I played the part of an interested listener, asking questions to direct the informant to particular subjects. The two families knew each other by name and sight, but had never interacted. But both informants knew how to lose the hounds and "how to live out there." The combination of these two bodies of knowledge is what I refer to as "the technology of the renegade"; it includes techniques of food gathering, food preservation, and cooking as well as the procedure for losing the hounds. The focus of this paper is on the procedure for losing the hounds which the sheriff placed on the fugitive's trail.

LOSING THE HOUNDS

The renegade's strategy for losing the hounds is based on a number of "tricks" or ploys which are designed for particular purposes. There are tricks designed solely to lose the hounds, but are not expected to confuse the sheriff. There are tricks designed to exhaust the hounds, and tricks designed to confuse, exhaust, and lose the hounds as well as the sheriff.

Once the hounds are placed on the renegade's scent, the renegade perceives that he is locked in combat with not one, but two rather formidable opponents. First of all there are the hounds themselves, which have the ability to follow an invisible scent, which can run at least three times faster than a man, and which have tremendous stamina. In addition they have a voice, a bark which relays to the sheriff information such as the direction of the fugitive's flight or contact with the fugitive. But, the hounds by themselves are the least of the renegade's problems. It is the sheriff, referred to by the renegade as "the Man," the human intelligence behind the hounds, who is the major opponent. In the renegade's words, "Any damn fool can outsmart a hound, but you have to lose the Man behind the hounds to be home free." It is with this definition of the situation that the renegade joins combat.

When the hounds pick up the fugitive's scent, the sheriff and his posse will not follow behind the hounds, but will attempt to follow the hounds' barking in their automobiles as long as the roads permit. When the hounds are on the scent, their barking takes on a muffled quality as a result of their noses being almost on the ground. The hounds will also be in a tight pack, barking in unison and moving swiftly. If the hounds lose the scent, the pack will disperse, attempting to pick up the scent, the barking will be irregular, and the muffled quality will be absent. The hounds will mill around, roughly in the same spot, until they are put back on the scent. If the hounds catch the fugitive on the ground, they will attack and hold the fugitive at bay. In such a case the noise produced will be unmistakably clear. But generally the fugitive will climb a tree to avoid being caught on the ground and injured. In this case the hounds bark the "treed" bark which is characterized by a long, hollow howl. The hollow quality is due to the hounds' heads being skyward as they are looking up into the tree.

The significance of the hounds' voice is that the sheriff does not have to follow on foot behind the hounds, but can remain on the ridge roads, and by interpreting the hounds' bark he can follow in an automobile. He can also anticipate the direction of flight and head the fugitive off. The renegade is aware of this and will change directions at irregular intervals to avoid being headed off. He also knows that as long as the Man is on the ridge road "sitting high, dry, and rested," he will have to keep running forever. One part of the renegade's strategy is to exhaust the sheriff: "He'll call off the hounds when he's had enough." One informant explained how to do this: "You have to keep the Man off the hill, in the swamp, wet and working." Any simple trick which can lose the hounds will require the sheriff to leave the hill and walk the distance to where the hounds are in order to place them back on the scent. For example, the renegade may find two trees which are in contact so that he is able to climb up one tree, cross over, and climb down the other. The hounds will follow the scent to the tree and voice the "treed" bark. When the sheriff arrives, he will instantly see what has happened and place the hounds back on the scent. But in the meantime the renegade has accomplished two things: he has gained the extra time it takes for the sheriff to walk from the hill to the trick, and the sheriff is no longer sitting high and dry on the ridge road, but is now "wet and working."

The renegade repeats this trick every time the situation presents itself and the sheriff and posse fall in behind the hounds to add the now necessary commodity of human intelligence to the chase. The renegade had gained time to rest and the added time to pull off a more elaborate trick, one designed to fool both the hounds and the sheriff.

It seems to be the popular opinion that all one has to do to lose the hounds is to run into a stream, but this disregards the fact that there is human intelligence behind the hounds. In a situation where a fugitive destroys his scent by wading in a stream the posse searches both sides of the stream and finds where the fugitive exits and then places the hounds back on the scent. The renegade's tricks take this into consideration, and he therefore attempts to confuse the Man as well as to lose the hounds.

It should be noted at this point that the renegade seems to be working on the basis of something on the order of a folk psychology. His perception of the view of himself in the eyes of the other becomes an instrument which he uses to aid in his escape. A clear example of this came to light when the discussion touched upon the stream trick. Both informants agreed that upon entering the stream the fugitive should at first go with the current, not against the current, because "the Man always thinks that you are lazy and that you'll take the easiest way."

When the hounds lose the scent at the stream, the Man will at first go with the current expecting to find the exit path in that direction. The renegade goes with the current several hundred feet and exits on the opposite side of the stream. After running through the woods for a way, the renegade will re-enter the stream and wade further down stream and exit on the opposite side from the one he has just entered. The object of these maneuvers is that once the first exit is found the sheriff will have to carry or drag the hounds across the stream in order to place them on the scent, and this has to be repeated each time a new exit is found. This, of course, is consistent with the strategy of keeping the Man wet and working.

The number of exits and false trails which the renegade leaves is dependent upon the amount of time and energy he possesses. He knows something of the amount of time he has, for he too can hear the hounds.

Upon making the final entrance into the stream, the renegade double tracks against the current and passes his original entrance. Now he goes as far up stream as he has time and exits without leaving visible signs. To do this, he looks for an overhanging limb by which he can pull himself into a tree without setting foot on the bank. When he jumps from the tree he attempts to land as far away from the water's edge as possible, for it is at the water's edge that the sheriff and the hounds are patrolling. If he can put distance between the water's edge and his exit from the tree, he may be home free. However, if the Man is persistent he may still pick up the trail, but it will take considerable time for the Man to handle this trick, and the renegade has time to rest and prepare for the next round.

In passing, my informant noted that the final exit from the stream had to be a great distance from the first false exit, because if the posse happened to be very large, it could be split into four groups, and both sides of the stream could be covered in both directions. But when the first false exit is found, the smaller groups will be called together, and the chase will be carried in that direction.

Another trick designed to exhaust the hounds and lose the Man can be performed if the renegade happens upon a field fence. The procedure in this trick is to cross the fence, but double back and cross to the other side again. He lays down a false trail parallel to the fence and again cuts back to the fence. He climbs and walks the fence back to the middle of his previous parallel trail. He then exits from the fence and makes a new trail out from the fence to his parallel trail and then retracks his other entrance back to the fence. This lays down so many overlapping trails that both the hounds and the Man are confused. If the renegade has time he may just walk the fence, jumping off each time on the side opposite to his last exit, laying down false trails, but always doubling back to the fence. This last trick was given as one which will wear out the hounds. While a man may not expend much energy climbing a fence, the hounds have a great deal of difficulty. The object of the trick is to make the hounds cross the fence as many times as possible. This trick was considered to be especially effective in exhausting leashed bloodhounds and exhausting the hound's master, who has to constantly lift the animal across the fence.

The final exit from the fence should be made in the same manner as the exit from the stream, by means of an overhanging limb or by simply jumping as far as possible from the fence. Again it will be at the edge of the fence that the Man will be looking for the exit.

In the event that the renegade happens upon an area of hard ground in which he will not leave footprints, he is prepared with a special trick. This trick involves laying down a false trail for several hundred feet and retracing his steps. He then repeats this at least twice, taking care to stay on his original trail as best he can. Once he has laid down a strong scent by means of this double tracking, the renegade starts down the trail again but begins to veer from the original trail so that he ends up a hundred or so feet away from the end of his false trail. He then takes off running. This trick is designed to lose both the hounds and the Man. The hounds will take the strongest scent, and when they reach the end of the false trail they will retrack, but will again take the stronger of the two scents. And since this trick occurred on hard ground which does not leave footprints, the Man may be unable to perceive what has happened.

From the minute that the renegade knows that the hounds are on his trail, he begins to look for something which will "wear out the hounds' nose." This involves rubbing on the bottom of his shoes something which would destroy the hounds' ability to smell. Wild onions or turnips repeatedly rubbed on the shoe soles were said to wear out the hounds' nose. One informant mentioned that if you happened to run across a skunk, "just go up and kick him in the butt and there ain't no hound in Georgia that'll follow you."

It is significant that a large array of household goods were mentioned, such as red or black pepper, pine-oil and turpentine; kerosene and gasoline were also considered effective in destroying a hound's sense of smell. At the very time a person becomes a fugitive, the commodities of civilization take on new and instrumental significance. This is the point at which a bottle of pine-oil is perceived as being the difference between life or death, freedom or imprisonment, and the difference between a picturesque character and a desperate man becomes clear.

Perhaps this in some way explains the antipathy found in the community towards this type of deviant. When the renegade becomes isolated from the commodities of civilization but chooses to continue living in the geographical area, perhaps he can realistically be perceived as a serious threat. One informant in the community referred to a renegade as a person who would "kill you for the nails in your shoes" and then added, "or for your boat." The renegade is perceived not so much as a killer but as a desperate person.

CONCLUSION

The purpose of this paper has been to call attention to the existence of a social type who is so much on the fringe that he possesses a specialized technology for avoidance of capture by the law. The possession of such a technology implies a degree of alienation which one would not expect to find among indigenous, white, Southern people. However, it is not only present, it is several generations deep. The cause of this alienation, then, cannot be credited to the recent encroachment of industry and the means of mass production upon a simple and unassuming folk way of life. This alienation also existed in the agrarian society of the late 1800s.

There is another interesting aspect of the alienation of the two renegade families which should be pointed out. The renegade informants considered themselves alienated from society and this was manifested in their possession of a technology for avoiding capture. This is alienation in a strict sociological sense, in that sociology treats the alienated person as being aware of his alienation. But the renegade's alienation does not take a revolutionary form. It is more like the "amoral familism" Edward Banfield (1958) found in South Italy, a moral system characterized by the belief that any act which is committed by a family member or any act which promotes the family's interest is justifiable. If the renegade's stance towards the larger society is seen as being basically anti-social, then it must be seen as being completely so, and the renegade can best be described as a person who will take a shot at any passing army, be it Federal or Revolutionary.

A question which remains to be answered is how this detailed information entailed in the procedure for losing the hounds could have been maintained in a family even though the procedure has not been used in over 50 years. A partial answer can be found in the fact that this information was passed down by means of the oral tradition, which stresses the spoken word above and beyond the written word. The oral tradition is one in which the form of communication, as opposed to the content, becomes almost an end in itself. The stories which are part of the oral tradition become structured through innumerable repetitions, and the story eventually assumes a form in which one theme leads into the next in such a smooth and easy manner that any attempt to diminish its content interrupts the pattern and distracts from the story. Therefore, even though the content is subordinate to the form, the content can be quite detailed in nature and yet remain unmodified in the innumerable retellings of the story.

The two renegade informants presented the information in the true style of the oral tradition, but unfortunately I did not use a tape recorder and I am consequently unable to reproduce the "telling" of the procedure in the manner in which the informants relayed the information to me. Only occasionally do I include the neat and precise statements which are characteristic of the oral tradition. For example, "you have to keep the Man off the hill, in the swamp, wet and working" is such a statement.

As mentioned earlier, the procedure for losing the hounds is only one aspect of the technology of the avoidance of capture which the renegades possess. Even though the many procedures of the technology are not a monopoly of the renegade families, I suspect that the manner in which they have organized all of the components necessary to avoid capture is unique. I would also hypothesize that the procedure for losing the hounds was developed originally by the field slaves on the large rice plantations in the area and that the renegade families are just the carriers of the body of knowledge. The suggestion that the renegades themselves did not originate the technology does not diminish the significance of the fact that in the second half of the twentieth century my informants still considered the technology relevant to their situation.

REFERENCES

Banfield, Edward C., 1958. *The Moral Basis of a Backward Society* (Glencoe, Ill.: The Free Press).

The Hippie Ghetto

William L. Partridge

THE hippie ghetto in which I was a participant and observer is located in the low-rent fringe area between the white and Negro sections of a small southern town.[1] The main industry of the town is the large state university; signs at the city limits say "Welcome to University City." The residents of the ghetto are all either students or former students. They are adolescent to young adult in age, of middle class background, of both sexes, and white. The population numbered on the average about forty to fifty in 1967 and 1968, although it should be noted that it was expanding rapidly and that there were other areas of the town in which hippies lived.[2] The majority of the residents are transient, staying in the area for perhaps a year or more and then moving.

In the spring of 1967 I became interested in the phenomenon labeled as the "hippie movement" by the media and moved into the neighborhood called the "ghetto" by the students who lived there. As a participant and observer I was concerned with recording the movement of ghetto residents through time and space, the fluctuating levels of interaction intensity, and the events which defined and gave meaning to their lives.[3] Some of the conclusions which can be drawn from this study and their anthropological implications are the subject of this paper.

First, the social process of hippie ghetto life will be described as a rite of passage in which the nature of the ghetto and the relationship of the ghetto to the larger American society are defined. In this way the hippie ghetto is understood within the context of an ongoing cultural process and not simply in terms of flat, often pejorative, statements about characteristics. The ghetto will then be viewed from the perspective of the revitalization process. Certain similarities and differences between the data examined here and Wallace's (1956) processual structure will be noted. Attention will be given the role of the prophet in revitalization movements.

74

The hippie movement is a peculiarly American phenomenon, although it does have political counterparts in France, Japan, and other modern industrial nations (Califano 1970:60-61). It is common to refer to students on university campuses throughout the world as "alienated" and involved in youth movements. The extent to which hippies can be called alienated is of importance. The group studied here is disconnected from American society in a physical, psychological, and social sense. The name used by residents to identify their neighborhood, the "ghetto," expresses the depth of this separation. Psychologists (Keniston 1960:56) have noted the inclusive or total nature of the alienated mental state, embracing not only the self, others, and society, but the very structure of the universe and the nature of knowledge, i.e. the total cultural *Gestalt*. At the level of observable behavior it can be seen that interaction in the straight world is largely irrelevant to residents of the ghetto. Newspapers, magazines, television sets, and so on are scarce. Interaction takes place almost entirely within a tightly defined social network. The most credible sources of information are the subjective views of the novelist and the experiences of fellow residents. These are credible because it is the reader or listener who judges credibility. And credibility is important if one is to see the world "as it really is."

The continuing estrangement of hippies from American society is partly a function of the continuing rejection and condemnation which they experience. *Reader's Digest* (January 1968:59) put it this way: "Murder, Rape, Disease, Suicide. . . , The dark side of the Hippie moon has become increasingly visible." But such campaigns only partly account for the mental state of alienation. To paraphrase Goffman (1961:148), hippie behavior must be understood not only in terms of interaction with straight society but as a product of the social arrangements which evolve among hippies in response to straight society. And these social arrangements are best understood from the perspective of the natural history method (Arensberg and Kimball 1965:4-5).

By observing the social life of ghetto residents through time and space it becomes evident that the social process of ghetto life is born of the educational institution in American society. This is not to say that the phenomenon is a product of American educational institutions, but rather to say that it is a product of the role education plays in the larger American society. That role is defined here as a rite of passage, a ceremony which eases transition from one status to another (Chapple and Coon 1942:285; Turner 1969:69). The rite has three stages: separation, liminality, and incorporation. First, the initiate leaves his previous status, ceasing previous patterns of interaction and structured behaviors appropriate to that status. He moves from the confines of the nuclear family and the high school peer group into a university where he initiates new and often foreign patterns of interaction. Second, upon separation he begins a period of liminality or limbo in which his status is no longer "son of ...." or "daughter of ...." but simply student or neophyte. Along with other neophytes of differing ages, talents, and backgrounds he learns new behaviors and the traditional knowledge of "elders." He is held in this state of limbo for a specified period of time during which he experiences various tests and examinations which he must pass before he is allowed to exit. Third, the rite is completed when individuals leave the educational institution and take on a new status, different from both previous ones, which incorporates them into the larger society (Kimball and McClellen 1962).

The hippie ghetto population, then, consists of liminal individuals or students who consciously involve themselves in seeking alternatives to the larger society, or more accurately, in seeking alternatives to the status for which the educational rite has prepared them. They evolve for themselves systems of interaction which make the discovery of alternatives possible. Hippie life can be understood as a secondary rite of passage out of the large institutionalized American rite known as education.

This secondary rite, as is true of the primary one, is marked by the three stages of separation, liminality, and incorporation. First, the initiate moves out of the university and the larger society, cutting his ties with parents and friends. Second, no longer bound by the responsibilities, structured behaviors, and values associated with his previous status, he enters the stage of liminality. During this stage he begins interaction in a new social network, entering a variety of tentative associational groups made up of fellow neophytes and "elders" of the ghetto. Problems of subsistence, sex, housing, and so forth are now solved in the context of the elder-neophyte relationship as those with more experience in the subculture are able to offer assistance and support to the neophyte. The solutions to these problems often spark the formation of new associational groups based upon the male-female relationship. And third, the rite of passage is complete when the individual is incorporated into one of the several groups who have discovered some feasible adjustment to the larger society.

Turner's (1968; 1969) extended treatment of the second stage of the rite of passage is useful here, for it is the liminal period and its distinctive symbols which have caught the attention of the media. The state of liminality is characterized by "structural impoverishment and symbolic enrichment" (Turner 1968:567). Symbols of a previous status are cast off and insignia which are wholly unintelligible to former associates are taken on. More significant, perhaps, than shoulder length hair on males and hemlines which fall at the pubic area of females is the absence of structured, differentiated, hierarchical behavior and the presence of "undifferentiated *comitatus* (Turner 1969:96). I prefer using a different Latin word *comitas*, meaning politeness, civility, and kindness. Spontaneity is the vehicle for self-discovery, for being fully alive and fully human. All manner of behavior is "beautiful" if it is understood to represent a spontaneous eruption of the self. Even hostile and aggressive acts are received in the spirit of *comitas*, for they teach an individual about himself and others; not only are they welcomed but they are encouraged since they are interpreted as evidence of trust in one's fellows and commitment to what two sociologists have seen as a "quest for self-knowledge" (Simon and Trout 1967:52).

Liminality is "essentially a period of returning to first principles and taking of the cultural inventory" (Turner 1968:577). Spontaneity and experimentation deliver a host of stimuli heretofore sublimated by the demands of a previous status and structure. For to be outside of a particular social position, to be in a state of limbo, is to cease to have a specific perspective.

> [It is] in a sense to become (at least potentially) aware of all positions and arrangements and to have a total perspective. What converts potential understanding into real gnosis is instruction (Turner 1968:577).

The kaleidoscope of new stimuli is transmuted into knowledge and imbued with meaning through ceremonial communication with elders. Urges, fantasies, and fears press for recognition; these may spark insights and as such are encouraged and even directly produced by ceremonial sacraments and ceremonial behaviors. A "good head" is someone who uses drugs for the purpose of self-discovery, according to Davis and Munoz (1968:160).

The period of liminality is a time of freedom, a time when the normal moral codes have little validity and are transgressed (Turner 1969:577). Sexual relationships are not binding; friendships do not imply responsibility, and interactions fluctuate with need and temperament rather than custom. For example, the individual who is ejected from the associational group is the one who seeks to formalize and organize relationships by virtue of moral codes and sanctions. Those who transcend the moral codes of straight society remain secure in liminal freedom. Likewise, the essence of a bad trip with LSD is the inability to give in freely to the effects of the drug and the reliance upon traditional mechanisms of control in an effort to avoid unfamiliar stimuli.

It is in the nightly rites of intensification (Chappel and Coon 1942:507) of the associational group that one finds natural expressions of liminal symbols. Feelings of *comitas* are induced by ritual acts, such as sharing the sacramental drug and voicing expressions of satisfaction and contentment, and by ritual beliefs, such as the expectation that the sacrament will produce a shared psychic state in which all the participants are drawn together. Ordinary communication is held in abeyance while ceremonial communication symbolizes "honesty," a truer expression of the self, or in Turner's (1969:103) more lyrical words, "whole men in relation to other whole men." And it is in the nightly rituals that the mythology of the associational group is aired. Stories involving "ancestors" who have since moved on are related, linking those present to the almost legendary individuals whose adventures and exploits return to the ghetto through the grapevine of travelers. At a later time these may have practical value to the neophyte in that many alternatives to the larger society are revealed, but much of their significance in the rite of passage lies in their ontological value. For liminal wisdom "refashions the very being of the neophyte" and infuses him with the power to make a transition or change (Turner 1968:577). Cloaked in nonresponsibility, innocent of guilt or shame, invulnerable to the threats that stem from moral sanctions, the individual is prepared to leave the ghetto.

This second stage of the rite of passage is particularly complex and lengthy. It may last for only a few months or for several years. There are two reasons for this. First, the belief in the ideal of self-fulfillment, as evidenced by the quest for self-knowledge, demands experimentation. Solutions to problems, then, are often tentative. Secondly, the neophyte is made aware of a great number of alternatives to straight society in terms of sex, subsistence, residence patterns, and so forth. These are primary areas for self-fulfillment; a certain degree of adjustment and readjustment must take place since the population is largely transient. Movement into the third stage, incorporation, is not possible until one knows the nature of the self and how to go about fulfilling his own demands and urges.

The third stage of the rite of passage appears to be fragmented, for there are various alternatives open to the ghetto resident. Upon leaving the ghetto he may enter a variety of subcultural associational networks which may lead him to Boston, Atlanta, New York, Taos, Denver, Miami, and many other cities and towns. Some residents move to communal farms, others move to university education once again. Still others may innovate businesses, marketing the trappings of the subculture. Others may join the networks of drug dealers and learn one of the most lucrative of the alternate means of survival. And some seek out addictive drugs which work to separate them even further from straight society. It is apparent, however, that the rite does not smoothly deliver up all neophytes to a single subculture, nor does it prohibit part-time commitment to several.

Building upon this description of the social processes of hippie ghetto life, it is now possible to go on to a consideration of theoretical interpretations. It is apparent even upon cursory examination that those who seek to discover alternatives to straight society, to obtain knowledge of the self, and to live a more satisfying life are making an effort at revitalization. As defined by Wallace (1956:265), a revitalization movement is a "deliberate, organized, conscious effort by members of a society to construct a more satisfying culture."

Wallace (1956:269) indicates that revitalization efforts grow out of conditions of chronically high individual stress in which major stress-reducing techniques appear worthless. "Admission that a major [stress-reducing] technique is worthless is extremely threatening because it implies that the whole mazeway system may be inadequate" (Wallace 1956:269). The mazeway is the "total *Gestalt*" of one individual, "his image of self, society, and culture, of nature and body, and of ways of action" (Wallace 1956:267). One will note the similarity between the psychological characteristics of alienation (Keniston 1960:56) and Wallace's conception of mazeway reformulation. Likewise, Turner (1969:121) has called attention to the "peculiar linkages between personality, universal values, and 'spirit' or 'soul' that appear to be the stigmata of communitas." The period of increased individual stress is followed by a period of cultural distortion in which,

> Rigid persons apparently prefer to tolerate high levels of chronic stress rather than make systematic adaptive changes in the mazeway. More flexible persons try out various limited mazeway changes in their personal lives, attempting to reduce stress by addition or substitution of mazeway elements with more or less concern for the *Gestalt* of the system (Wallace 1956:269).

Revitalization actually begins after this period of mazeway reformulation. Wallace (1956:270) notes that in all cases with which anthropologists are familiar mazeway reformulation occurs "as a moment of insight" to a prophet or "in one or several hallucinatory visions by a single individual" in which the supernatural explains current troubles as resulting from the violation of certain rules. The prophet then reveals his insights to potential converts as doctrine and organizes his followers; the doctrine is adapted to the resistance such efforts inevitably meet, transforms the culture, and finally is routinized (Wallace 1956:273-74).

Of particular interest in the present context is the role of the prophet, for one finds little evidence of prophets in the hippie ghetto. Ritual behaviors and beliefs engage the neophyte in the "quest for self-knowledge" or personal vision seeking, but no single vision points the way to doctrine and no single person is treated with special respect in this regard. There are only "elders" in the ghetto who by virtue of longevity command a great knowledge of the mythology of the associational group and who are known to have confronted previously many of the problems which may appear new and frightening to the neophyte. Elders may act as guides or models, but their "teaching" does not involve well defined practices and programs through which the good life may be achieved. Moreover, the paths out of the ghetto are numerous and most are forked; so in this sense each individual must choose his own alternatives according to the promptings of the self and the knowledge of the experiences of others gained from the "elders."

The hippie ghetto, therefore, probably represents the period of cultural distortion in the revitalization process structure. The rite of passage may function for those who return to the larger society as "milieu therapy," much the same as Werner (1963:259-67) has observed in the case of student religious centers. This is implied, in any case, since some adjustment of the cultural *Gestalt* must take place if those who were formerly alienated now find the straight world palatable. Still, incorporation into the larger society is not desired for a significant number. And those who seek and find viable alternatives to the larger society will probably rise in number in proportion to the level of stress and distortion which they experience. The rite of passage will then deliver up the majority of those who pass through the ghetto into a revitalization movement, and the "elders" of an earlier time will become prophets.

NOTES

1. My role as researcher was ambiguous for several reasons, foremost of which was the fact that I was a student and knew many of the residents previous

to the period of study. I identified myself as an anthropology student doing research for my MA thesis. This created no obstacles until I encountered a network of drug dealers who handled and used heroin. Access to these groups was of course denied. By moving into the ghetto area and fully participating in the subculture I became a participant.

2. This situation changed dramatically during the time I lived in the area; so dramatically that by the time I was ready to leave I would estimate that the population had doubled several times over. My sample is bounded in time, 1967-1968, and is geographically limited to the area known as the ghetto during that time.

3. While the method used was that of community studies, after Arensberg and Kimball (1965), the area and population studied can not be defined as a community in terms of the criterion that three generations be present.

REFERENCES

Arensberg, Conrad M. and Solon T. Kimball, 1965. *Culture and Community* (New York: Harcourt, Brace, and World, Inc.).

Califano, Joseph A. Jr., 1970. *The Student Revolution: A Global Confrontation* (New York: W. W. Norton and Company).

Chapple, Elliott D. and Carleton S. Coon, 1942. *Principles of Anthropology* (New York: Holt, Rhinehart, and Winston).

Davis, Fred and Laura Munoz, 1968. Patterns and Meanings of Drug Use Among Hippies. *Journal of Health and Social Behavior* 9:156-64.

Goffman, Erving, 1961. Asylums (New York: Doubleday and Company, Inc.).

Keniston, Kenneth, 1960. *The Uncommitted: Alienated Youth in American Society* (New York: Harcourt, Brace, and World, Inc.).

Kimball, Solon T. and James E. McClellen Jr., 1962. *Education and and the New America* (New York: Randon House).

Simon, Geoffery and Grafton Trout, 1967. Hippies in College—From Teeny-boppers to Drug Freaks. *Transaction* 5.27-32.

Turner, Victor W., 1968. Myth and Symbol. *International Encyclopedia of the Social Sciences* (Macmillan Company and the Free Press).

—————————, 1969. *The Ritual Process: Structure and Anti-structure* (Chicago: Aldine).

Wallace, Anthony F. C., 1956. Revitalization Movements. *American Anthropologist* 52:264-81.

Werner, Fred, 1963. Acculturation and Milieu Therapy in Student Transition. In *Education and Culture*, George D. Spindler, ed. (New York: Holt, Rhinehart, and Winston).

A Remnant Indian Community:
The Houma of Southern Louisiana

Max E. Stanton

THE federal census of 1960 reported over 2,000 Indians living in the coastal marsh and swamp areas of southern Louisiana, most of whom were living along the bayous which fan out toward the Gulf of Mexico from the city of Houma.[1] Terrebonne Parish had a total of 1,980 Indians, and another 241 Indians were reported in Lafourche Parish, most of them near Bayou Lafourche, which is the boundary between the two parishes.

There is no collective name used by these people to identify themselves other than "Indian." The word "Sabine" is sometimes used, but in a derogatory sense. They prefer to be called Indians and resent, even among themselves, those who use the term Sabine. In the historical and descriptive literature, they are often referred to as Houma Indians, but this researcher was not able to find any Indians who used this designation, although some have heard it used by non-Indians. For the sake of brevity and clarity, "Houma" and "Indian" will be used interchangeably throughout this report to refer to these people.

HISTORICAL SETTING

There is a historical connection between the present Indians of southern Louisiana and the traditional Houma Tribe. Until the eighteenth century, the Houma lived along the Mississippi River in what is now the border area of the states of Louisiana and Mississippi (Swanton 1911:285). In the first decade of the eighteenth century they were reduced in population by warfare with other Indian groups and by disease. As a result, they fled down the Mississippi to seek a more secure place in which to live. They spent the next one hundred years in the swamps of Ascension Parish, west and south of the Mississippi

82

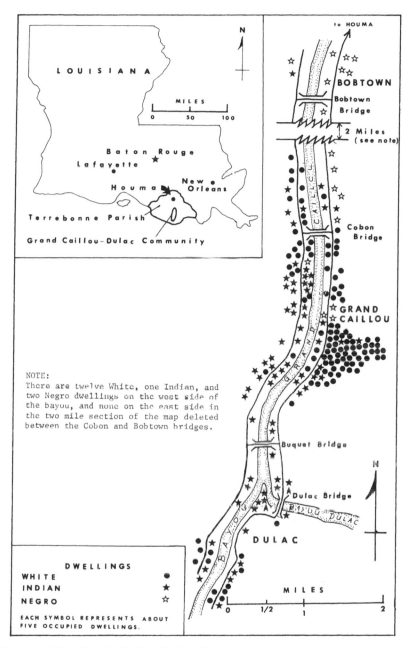

Figure 1. The Grand Caillou-Dulac Community: the approximate location of dwellings showing the ethnic identity of the occupants. The scale of the map does not allow for the actual spatial placement of each individual dwelling. Isolated symbols represent, in a few isolated cases, one or two more or one or two less than five dwellings.

River. During this time, they were joined by remnants of other tribes. Most of the new arrivals spoke Muskogean languages closely related to the Houma dialect (Swanton 1911:292). Escaped Negro slaves and Europeans (mostly French trappers and some fugitives from the law and from the military) were also accepted into the group.

In the latter part of the 1700s, French refugees from Acadia (the present-day Maritime Provinces of Canada) began to settle in southern Louisiana.[2] Some of them took Indian wives. A record dated 1795 states that land in the southern portion of Terrebonne Parish was granted to French settlers who had married local Indians (Parenton and Pellegrin 1950:149).

In the early part of the nineteenth century, large tracts of land in southern Louisiana were cleared and drained for planting sugar. Negro slaves were brought in to work on these plantations. The influx of French refugees from Acadia and the creation of large plantations brought an end to the isolation of the Houma. The main body of the tribe moved back up to the Mississippi River and have become lost to the historical record. Three bands are known to have moved into the present area of Terrebonne Parish (Swanton 1911:292). The present city of Houma was established in 1834, taking its name from a group of Houma Indians living in the vicinity. The present Indians of the area are presumed to be descendants of this Houma group.

As pressures for land and living space became more demanding, the Indians were forced to move into the brackish marsh and swamp country adjacent to the Gulf of Mexico. It was fortunate that this land was thought to be (at the time) useless by the non-Indian population, for these people were not seafarers and they had reached land's end. The sojourn in Ascension Parish had conditioned the Houma to a life of hunting, fishing, and trapping in swampy land, and they survived where others could not.

The isolation of these remaining Houma Indians was brought to an abrupt end in the late 1920s when oil and natural gas were discovered under their land. Being largely illiterate, disfranchised, and impoverished, the Houma quickly lost their rights to the now valuable land (Fischer 1968). They also were never formally associated with the federal or state government, so they were denied even what little help such formal recognition might have given them.[3]

As a result of an upset in the balance in the ecosystem by the oil companies, the fauna of the marshes and swamps began to decline. The Indians could no longer make a living in their scattered homesteads. They began to congregate in settlements at the termini of the roads along the bayous. Here they found occasional work in the oil fields, in the newly established fish and shrimp canneries, and on the commercial fishing boats. They could also supplement their income as part-time hunters and trappers and as guides for sportsmen.

By congregating into their six present locations, the Indians have become part of a larger socio-cultural unit.[4] None of these communities were unsettled before the Indians moved in, for there were Whites (mostly Cajun French) and Negroes living there as well. Of the six communities, only one, the small and semi-isolated Champs Charles (Isle St. Jean Charles), has a majority of Indian residents. Over half of all the Indians in the area live in or near Dulac on Bayou Grand Caillou, about twenty miles south of the city of Houma. There are sections in these communities, especially Dulac, which have Indian majorities, but there is no strict residential segregation. Indians, Whites, and Negroes can be found living as neighbors.

No such organization as a Houma Indian Tribal Council or any similar body representing all of the Houma exists, and there is no strong feeling of tribal or intra-group unity. The Houma live in the six communities mentioned above and have only limited contact with each other. There is, however, some small degree of inter-community contact as a result of the recent consolidation of the Terrebonne Parish high school system and the construction of new all-weather roads which offer fast and direct routes between the settlements.

PRESENT SITUATION

Today the Indian stands as middleman in a three-tiered hierarchy, with the White (mostly Cajun French) occupying the level above and the Negro the level below. These groups live in close geographical proximity but have only limited inter-group contacts. The situation is not (as yet) tense or marked by hate and strife, but it is not one of accord either. Jealousy, discontent, scorn, and rejection are not far below the surface.

The Indians have mixed with the other two racial elements in the community, but there is strong evidence to refute claims of substantial Negro ancestry among the Houma (Roy 1959:120). Speck (1943: 215) states that they have some Spanish-French, English, and other White progenitors with no reference made to Negro admixture. He is quoted by Fischer as having said:

> In my judgment, as based upon comparisons with Indians of the southeastern tribes over a number of years, I should rate the Houma as a people possessing Indian blood and cultural characters to a degree about equal to that of the Creek, Choctaw, Catawbe [*sic*], and Seminoles (Fischer 1968:135).

It is not to be denied that these people do have some degree of Negro ancestry, but this element is not as strong as has been inferred in some earier works (such as Parenton and Pellegrin 1950: 148). As a result of racial mixing, many Indians are phenotypically indistinguishable from many Whites or Negroes in the area, but because of their social connections in the community they are "Indians" (Speck 1943:137). Family, tradition, society, genealogy, and history are far more cogent factors in determining one's status as Indian than is biology. Surnames are often indicators of an Indian background. Some of the more common names which are either exclusively Indian or tend to be Indian are: Billiot, Deon (Dion), Gregoire, Naquin, Parfait, and Verdin. An Indian can move away from his home area and "pass" as a White, or be mistaken for a Negro, but when he returns, he is an Indian (Roy 1959:89). Some intermarriage does occur but it is, as a rule, into the Negro group. This is usually by Indians who have suspected Negro ancestry and who are therefore not fully comfortable in the Indian community. The children of such a union are accepted into the Negro community and are not socially "Indians." If an Indian marries a White, the couple will generally leave the community and settle elsewhere.

The hospitals in the area no longer use the "Indian" category for their birth records. A child born of an Indian mother is now automatically classed as "White" on its birth certificate. Until recently, the option of racial designation was left to the judgment of the person who recorded the birth. As a result, individuals within a single family who are all recognized in the community as being Indians have birth certificates designating them as either White, Negro, or Indian—depending on when they were born and the judgment of the person who recorded the birth (Roy 1959).

Culturally, the Indians are quite close to the local Cajun French, for they have lost their traditional Indian culture and have adopted the rural Cajun French ways. Their religion, folklore, language, dwellings, surnames, and occupations are mostly Cajun. Even when Swanton visited these people in 1907, he could find little of cultural significance that connected them with their Indian past.

The most significant social group among the Houma is the extended family. An Indian identifies with his kindred and finds security and support in this association. Siblings, cousins, uncles, and aunts, all are central elements in an Indian's social life, and loyalty to the kin group is his primary social responsibility. Some find this situation to be a restriction on their private affairs and try to break out of it, but they usually return to it when they need help,

especially in finances. There are few Indians who have become independent of their kin group. Those few who have succeeded have
either turned their back on the Indian element in the community
or left the area entirely.

It is difficult to be well-to-do and still maintain strong ties with
kinsmen. Still, no man is expected to subsidize everyone in his extended family. A handful of men have been sufficiently generous to
satisfy their kinship obligations and still be moderately successful
in their personal financial affairs. These men are admired because
they must be hard-working and thrifty in order to maintain such a
balance. They are the unofficial spokesmen for the Indian community
because non-Indians can appreciate their achievements and other
Indians trust their judgment.

The general poverty level of the Indians has put them in a
precarious position with the local non-Indian merchants and storekeepers. The seasonal and sporadic nature of employment of so many
of these people forces them to buy on credit, and most families
are deeply in debt to the local store. Any money that a person earns
must be used to pay part of the debt owed to the merchant, for not
to do so would risk the cancellation of credit privileges in the future.
This is the familiar merchant-creditor relationship. Since so many
Indians have hopelessly overdrawn accounts, the merchant has considerable influence in their affairs. He can exert strong pressures
on those who are in debt to him. He also uses his influence to protect their economic welfare when it is to his long-term advantage,
not because of a feeling of compassion, but for his own interests.

In the last decade much has changed in the Houma situation.
All of the children now have access to schools, although the quality
of education in some of the schools is questionable. Still, attempts are
being made to improve education. The schools in the area are now
fully integrated along geographic lines, thus putting Indian and Negro
children in classrooms with White children. Various private and
religious groups are working to provide recreation, skills improvement, and adequate health treatment for all underprivileged persons
in the community, regardless of race or social background. Employment opportunities are more plentiful now than ever before. To be
sure, many of the jobs offer low wages and require long hours of
hard work, but work is available to those who want a job. Private
ownership of small businesses and shrimping boats is now a reality
to a few Indians; a generation ago it was only a distant hope.

CULTURAL CHANGE

The Houma Indian situation offers an interesting case in the study of the movement from isolation into more and more integration with the larger society. This movement can be traced through three different stages, although the changes have been gradual, and, therefore, the chronological cut-off points are somewhat arbitrary.

The first stage can be termed social and geographical isolation, an extension of the earlier pattern of settlement developed by the Houma during their sojourn in Ascension Parish. The people lived as semi-nomadic hunters, trappers, and fishers, and drifted rather freely through the marsh and swamp country of southern Louisiana (Speck 1943:141). They were a self-contained community existing in relative isolation. The main reason for contact with the non-Indian community was for trade in order to get cloth, metal artifacts, and some foods which could not be produced locally. Otherwise, these people were self-sufficient and independent of the outside culture. This type of a community began to break up when professional trappers entered the area in the early part of the twentieth century. Further disturbance came with the establishment of fish and shrimp canneries which began to attract Indian laborers. The final blow came in the latter part of the 1920s, when the rich oil and natural gas fields were discovered in the area.

The second phase, social isolation, began as the Indians left their semi-nomadic hunting camps and settled in clusters at the termini of the roads which had been built into the swamp and marsh country. This clustering was the result of the establishment of the oil and gas fields in the area forcing the Indians to leave their isolated camps in the swamps and marshes. It was a gradual movement which began in the 1920s and continued until the late 1950s, and it was greatest just prior to and during the Second World War. In 1940, it was estimated that there were 700 Indians within walking distance of Dulac (Speck 1943:215), and by 1960, the movement into more accessible, permanent communities was complete.

In this second phase, the Indians came into casual contact with non-Indians, but these were of no great significance in their lives. Their home life and most intimate personal contacts were with other Indians. As general and unskilled laborers, the Indians worked in subordinate positions, having only limited contacts with their non-Indian employers and co-workers. Some religious groups did establish churches and schools in the Houma settlements, but these were attended exclusively by Indians (Fischer 1968:139). The parish made only feeble attempts to help Indian children obtain an education.

School attendance was difficult, and there was very little effort made by the parish school officials to enforce truancy laws against the absentee children. The Indian schools were substandard and under-financed, and during this period very few Indians received an adequate education (Fischer 1968: 140-41).

The pressures of the Second World War and the great industrial, technical, and economic "boom" which followed finally brought the Indians into the third and present stage of a closer association with the rest of the nation. Increasing petrochemical operations, both on land and in the Gulf of Mexico, have resulted in the establishment of supply depots and satellite companies to support their needs. The commercial fishing fleet has greatly expanded; the existing fish canneries have enlarged and new ones have been established. There has been a significant influx of Whites and some Negroes into the area to work and operate these new facilities and to open busi-nesses to serve the growing population. However, good land for settlement and commercial use is still severely limited because of the swampy nature of the area, and all six of the communities concerned in this study stretch out in line settlement fashion along the bayous. The Dulac-Grand Caillou community is over eight miles long but extends only a few hundred yards wide on either side of the bayou, and newcomers have built their homes where space could be found. This has resulted in a generally desegregated situation, although there have been more than a few cases in which Indians lost title and deed or rights to use their land and have been forced to settle elsewhere.

With the expansion and growth in these communities Indian life has changed considerably, and the Indians are now a minority in all but one community. Even in Dulac, their largest settlement, there are twice as many Whites as Indians. Many of the new arrivals are from outside Louisiana and even from outside the South. The French language and customs are no longer a general part of the total cultural milieu, and the institutions of the Houma Indians have become integrated into a larger whole. Schooling is available to those who want it. There has been a change in the legal system in which Indians are beginning to have faith in the protection of their rights. An intensive voter registration drive has finally given them some small measure of political influence. Improved literacy, health, and transportation have opened new job opportunities. Some Indians now own small businesses and commercial fishing craft, and Indian youth can now pass the minimum physical and mental qualifications of the armed forces, which enables them to turn to the military for vocational training.

THE FUTURE OF THE HOUMA

The Houma Indians are now a part of the greater cultural community of southern Louisiana and of the nation. Circumstances and events have made a return to their former free-roving, semi-nomadic life impossible. The current trend seems to indicate an even greater association with the non-Indian community and a steady decline of the traditional Indian norms and values.

A vital question generated by the rapidly changing situation concerns the effect of such change on group cohesiveness. Kinship ties and the French language still bind the Houma together as a group distinct from their non-Indian neighbors (Fischer 1968:147; Parenton and Pellegrin 1950:152). Nowadays, however, the individual finds increasing pressures from outside the Indian community which make him less dependent on his kindred and more attracted to non-Indian lifeways. Schools, the military, outmigration, the automobile, television, Protestant missionaries, community centers, better jobs, integrated neighborhoods, fluency in English, and other related factors have all had their role in breaking down the traditional Houma society. The individuals who have readily accepted the changing conditions often find themselves at variance with others who would wish to maintain a more traditional orientation. The close social bond of the Indian community is not so significant to one who can successfully function in the context of the greater, non-Indian community. The material improvements of the mid-twentieth century have, therefore, made the individual less dependent upon the group. Some who can leave the area because of acquired skills do, and as such are no longer primary members of the local community. Many emigrés contribute to the support of their kinsmen who remain in the Indian community, enabling even more individuals to gain the skills and ability to leave, especially if they are young. Most of those who leave go to urban areas.

By the late nineteen-sixties, this rural to urban migration was well under way with a predictable increase in intensity as more and more people found that they could function in a non-Indian world. This type of process will tend to leave the older and more conservative individuals behind as a majority within the Houma community.

Most Houma would prefer to remain among their friends and relatives, but there are not enough jobs to support them. The future does not offer an easy solution to the problems raised by rapid cultural change. What it does offer is a chance to feel a sense of individual worth and dignity, and to be free from poverty, ignorance, and debt.

The question may now be asked as to what the over-all and lasting consequences of such a change to the Houma Indian community will be. Will the group continue to be socially identifiable with its close kinship ties and basic Cajun French culture? Or, will it gradually fade into the larger "mega-culture" of America? These questions must wait to be fully answered by the passage of time.

NOTES

1. The background data for this study were gathered by the researcher at Louisiana State University. The actual field research was conducted during a six-week period in the summer of 1969. The project was funded through a National Science Foundation Summer Traineeship. The researcher lived in the Dulac Community Center, which is supported by the United Methodist Church, and he gathered the data in the capacity of a community worker. No attempt was made to conceal the fact that the researcher was an anthropologist involved in a community study, but the local residents thought of him and accepted him as a community worker. The Center and its workers are accepted and respected by the local people, and this enabled the researcher to make meaningful contacts.

2. The term "Cajun" is a corruption of the French pronunciation of the word "Acadien." It is freely used by both the French-speaking and English-speaking people in the area and does not have a negative or derogatory connotation.

3. John Swanton visited these people in 1907 (Fischer 1968:6) in an official capacity for the federal government and reported that they were not "pure" enough to qualify for federal help. His visit was brief and his conclusions are debatable. Still, as a result of his recommendations, the Houma were not given any recognition by the government.

4. These settlements, from west to east are: DuLarge, along Bayou DuLarge; Dulac, along Bayou Grand Caillou and Bayou Dulac; Pointe au Barree (Lower Montegut), along Bayou Terrebonne; Lower Pointe au Chien, along Bayou Pointe au Chien; Champs Charles (Isle St. Jean Charles), along Bayou St. Jean Charles; and, Lower Bayou Lafourche, along Bayou Lafourche (in both Terrebonne and Lafourche parishes).

REFERENCES

Fischer, Ann, 1968. History and Current Status of the Houma Indians. In *The American Indian Today*, Stuart Levine and Nancy O. Lurie, eds. (Deland, Florida: Everett/Edwards).

Parenton, Vernon J. and Roland J. Pellegrin, 1950. The Sabines. *Social Forces* 29:148-154.

Roy, Edison Peter, 1959. *The Indians of Dulac*, unpublished master's thesis (Baton Rouge: Louisiana State University).

Speck, Frank G., 1943. A Social Reconnaissance of the Creole Houma Indian Trappers of the Louisiana Bayous. *American Indigena* 3:134-146, 212-220.

Swanton, John R., 1911. Indian Tribes of the Lower Mississippi River and the Adjacent Coast of the Gulf of Mexico. *Bulletin of the Bureau of American Ethnology*, no. 43.

——————————, 1946. The Indians of the Southeastern United States. *Bulletin of the Bureau of American Ethnology*, no. 137.

United States Department of Commerce, Bureau of the Census, 1963. United States Census of Population: 1960. *Characteristics of the Population*, vol. 1, part 20, Louisiana.

Potters in a Changing South

Robert Sayers

The general character of the South today might best be conveyed in a single theme: "A region in transition."[1] One need only look to the large store of current literature concerned with developments in the economic and technological spheres, urbanization, and the Civil Rights movement to draw truth from this statement. And yet, for all of this emphasis on broad regional modification, we still find a considerable number of instances on the local level where change is only grudgingly acknowledged. Indeed, certain institutions or traditions which appear to have passed from the scene without fanfare elsewhere have managed in many quarters of the South to hold their own, even in the face of growing obsolescence. This "conservative bent" became particularly evident to me when in 1968 I visited and interviewed at length numbers of Southern hand-craftsmen who were caught between the times but were trying to shore up rather than abandon their faltering trade. Because I see in this response much to suggest a regional phenomenon inextricably tied in with the area's history and sociocultural organization, I should like to say more about these artisans and their craft.

Pottery manufacture has long been an important domestic hand-craft industry in the Southern states, even after the trade faltered elsewhere. In 1940, Helen Stiles accounted for some 200 working potters in North Carolina alone (1941:166); and similar numbers probably were to be found elsewhere in the region at that time. Today "old-time" potters are still plentiful, though perhaps not quite so numerous. What is interesting to note, however, is that the widespread proliferation of glass and tin containers into all but the most isolated of Southern communities shortly after the turn of the present century should have spelled the end of the rural ceramist's art. But, as I have just implied, it did not.

Before I attempt to explain why potters still abound in the

93

region, I would first like to present brief sketches of two families
of present-day Southern potters, the Meaders and the Browns.
Hopefully, from these sketches some of the important elements of
the craft tradition will become obvious. The following features are
noteworthy: each family's efforts to maintain the institution; accom-
modations to changing markets, technologies, and the physical environment; and finally, similarities and differences between the two
families.

THE MEADERS POTTERY

The town of Cleveland sits in a piedmont area just south of the
Smoky Mountains in northern Georgia. A rural hamlet until early
in the century, Cleveland is situated at the top of the cotton belt and
was once a center for north Georgian pottery manufacture. Cleveland now appears headed on a downhill drift. Young forests cover the
surrounding countryside revealing here and there a reminder of the
cotton era. Kudzu (*Pueraria thunbergiana*), a vine introduced in
the 1940s to check erosion, has largely taken over whole sections
of the land adding to the forbidding "feel" of the outlying region
where few people still live, I was told, "because of a lowered water
table."

Cleveland itself with its courthouse, town square, historical society,
and various small businesses, is much like any other settlement in
that part of the state. Religious activity, where it is apparent, is of
the fundamentalist sort, characterized by large evening revivals. Unemployment is widespread, and I saw few young people. Attempts on
the part of the city chamber of commerce to attract a tourist trade
seem to be less successful than similar attempts made by nearby
Dahlonega.

Today the only working potteries in Cleveland are the Cheever
Meaders Pottery and the Robert Owens Pottery, the latter developed
and run by a young college instructor and consequently of little
concern here. The former establishment, on the other hand, has been
standing in its present location south of town since 1887. Rich in
pottery lore, the shop is one of many with the Meaders name that
have dotted north Georgia since 1830 or before, the first member
of the clan having migrated to nearby Banks County from Virginia
about that time (Ramsay 1939:237).

The Meaders, however, were not the only potter family in the
region. Through the late 1920s, many other working potteries were
to be found scattered throughout White, Hall, and Banks Counties.
Early in the present century there were at least eight individual

shops in Cleveland alone, two belonging to Meaders boys and the others belonging to Dorseys and Pitchfords. Of all of these north Georgia potteries perhaps three remain.

It was in this section of the country that potters took to the open road as "wagoners," often peddling their produce as far distant as North Carolina before returning home. Most of these men farmed or tended livestock in their spare hours away from the pottery. Families ranged on the large side, as is common in nearly all rural communities.

Common tools of the Georgian trade included mule-drawn pug-mills, hand-cranked glaze-mills (these look like a millstone set into a flat-horizontal slab), treadle kick wheels, outdoor tunnel kilns, and row upon row of large stoneware churns, crocks, pitchers, and jugs. These vessels were glazed with flint, feldspar, iron-sand, and sand-and-ash glazes as well as with the conventional Albany Slip, the latter probably introduced into the region at some point after 1890. It is unlikely that any of the ware was ever stamped.

By the time of the Great Depression, a decline in the region and the degeneration of the cotton trade had forced most of the potters out of business. Only the Meaders Pottery along with a handful of others survived. Interestingly enough, Cheever Meader's son, Lanier, sees the Depression as a time of productivity rather than decline for his "daddy":

> People at that time was all out of work and didn't have anything to eat and nowhere to go. And this business here—my dad was making churns. That's all he ever liked to make anyhow. For some reason I can't understand it he really had a heyday with it: five to ten cents per gallon (and now it's seventy-five cents). People used more of our ware then and somehow they managed to find a nickel or a dime or a quarter to buy a four-or-five gallon churn. If anybody didn't have a job, they'd have a garden. And if they didn't grow it, they didn't eat. If they didn't *preserve* it after they growed it, they didn't have it to eat then. And that's the reason, I reckon, the churns sold so well. And we didn't go hungry either!

Up until this point all of the Meaders males had made a career of pottery-turning. However, following the hard times, only Cheever and Lanier continued the family operation. Two of Lanier's brothers found work in a lumber yard and a poultry farm respectively, a third learning the electrician's trade. Even Lanier himself occasionally took time off from the pottery to seek work in a local metalshop and in surrounding textile mills. Asked whether his father intended that he become a potter, Lanier replied: "Well, I wouldn't say that for not knowing. It's more circumstance than anything else." This answer is probably a considerable understatement in light of what we shall see later.

In 1952 Lanier Meaders built a new shop for his father to replace the older building, which was in a state of disrepair. He also continued working at a local metalworks and tended the farm. Upon Cheever Meader's death in 1967, Lanier returned full-time to the family industry. Today, at age 53 and still single, he turns ware at the pottery alongside his mother. Sometimes he has only to work but two or three hours a day. Because there is virtually no competition for his kind of ware and because he is a skilled artisan, Cheever's son is able to do amazingly well for himself.

Minor changes in the shop in the past two years have included a new oil kiln and a small mechanical clay grinder which Lanier devised and built himself from scraps he brought home from the metalshop. The mule is gone but the old pugmill remains. The glaze-mill also stands as usual but is seldom used. Lanier is hesitant to dispose of it, although at least one state museum is interested.

Clay is difficult to obtain these days even though a rich deposit sits within a few hundred yards of the pottery shed. The proprietor of the land it rests on would probably be willing to let the Meaders mine the pit in return for rent except that another man has a lien on the land and will not let the "owner" use any of its resources. Such a situation is not uncommon around Cleveland.

Another feature of the Meaders Pottery that has not changed appreciably over the years is the product. Lanier still turns large, heavy churns as did his father and his father before that. In addition, he makes an occasional "face" jug, part of a long tradition in Southern pottery-making. His mother has been turning ornamental pieces such as bird-houses and decorative vases since around 1950, but Lanier does not consider these things "old-time" or traditional— much the same reaction he displays toward Bob Owen's ware.

Customers who patronize the Meaders Pottery are mostly local residents who buy churns in which to pickle beans and sauerkraut and to store meat, both common activities in rural areas of the South. Glass bottles and tin cans are readily available these days, but Lanier's stoneware "churns" do the trick more efficiently, as they always have. Mr. Meaders also attracts a great many tourists and a small group of folk art collectors, but he appears bothered by these, especially the former.

Asked to characterize his life as a potter, Lanier Meaders has these words:

> Well, it's just a trade. It's a gift that a person comes by. I could no more stop this than I could fly an airplane. All my movements, all of my work that I've done all my life has led one way or another straight to this place right here and every time I come about it, I'm just a little bit deeper into it. If a man's really farming, he's got a job every day, rain or shine. But if he don't farm no more than I do—no more than he has to—then this pottery makes everything balance out. This is quick money. I used to think that it was hard, but it's not. It's easy work.

THE BROWN POTTERY

Arden, North Carolina, unlike Cleveland, lies in close proximity to a small urban center. Stretched out along State Highway 25 traveling in a southbound direction from Asheville, the town is predominantly an area of light industry (paper mills) with some small businesses and a remnant of a former farming economy. Several trucking concerns, machine shops, and dragstrips are nearby, and most of the men in Arden are skilled auto mechanics. The Asheville Airport, a half-mile distant, also affords some employment opportunities. By and large, Arden seems to be a modest, low-middle income community in transition from a traditional rural economy to a semi-industrial one, even though the nearness of Asheville has probably always lent the town some familiarity with urban ways.

Those persons whom I met in Arden were generally conservative, religious (though not fundamentalist), and showed an interest in other regions beyond their own, many of the men having served overseas duty during the World War or having vacationed up North. Teenagers around Arden are fond of cars, often joining together in informal auto clubs. Few Blacks were encountered, although a great many live in Asheville. The Cherokee Indian Reservation is just to the west, and occasionally Indians come down to the pottery for trade but have little other interest in the town.

Three Brown potteries stand in and around the local area today. Of these, the oldest (and the one I shall speak the most about) is the Davis Brown Pottery just off to one side of Highway 25. Originally founded in 1923 by Davis and his brother, Javan Brown, it was maintained by the former until his death in 1967. Now Davis' son, Louis Brown, operates the pottery with his family. Javan Brown, on the other hand, is still alive at age 72 and has his own shop in

Valdes. His son, Evan Javan Brown, Jr., runs the third shop, Evan's Pottery, in nearby Skyland.

One more pottery, and perhaps the original establishment in the region, belonged to a Mr. Stevens who died some years ago at an advanced age. Steven's Pottery now belongs to a pair of young men who have renamed it the "Pisgah Forest Pottery." Like Bob Owens, these men did not grow up in the potter families (which I shall henceforth refer to as "dynasties").

Like the Meaders, the Browns were settled in various parts of the South by 1830. The first Brown potter in the United States seems to have been an English immigrant tradesman named John Henry Brown. Whether this man settled immediately in the South or not is unknown. However, by the time he fathered a son, he was living in South Carolina. The present Brown potters in Arden, Louis Brown and his sons, represent the sixth and seventh generations of ceramists in direct line from this man.

At the time the Arden pottery was built, conditions remained much the same as those described for the Meaders pottery. As in Cleveland, part of the year the men would take to the road as wagoners, peddling their stoneware to merchants in not-too-distant communities. On occasion such trips were not necessary, for a trader would come by the shop and buy all the ware the potters had stock-piled, but this did not happen too often. When Davis and Javan Brown's brothers would travel up to the shop from Georgia (some worked at potteries around Atlanta; others worked in and around Cleveland), the men divided their time between the pottery and a baseball team that would play all comers from the local textile mills.

As the Great Depression swept through the South, the brothers scattered, leaving again only Davis and Javan, the original founders. (Unlike the Meaders, none of the Brown boys gave up the craft at this point; they simply moved elsewhere, often hiring out as pottery-turners in other men's shops). When Javan Brown, too, left for a time to build kilns for artisans elsewhere, the remaining Brown potter was left much to his own devices. Here the Browns diverge from the Meaders, for Davis Brown sought to restructure his formerly traditional industry.

Before the nation found itself involved in another world war, Davis had remodeled his machinery and introduced to his pottery the new manufacturing techniques of jiggering and slip-casting. He even renovated the large wood-burning kiln so that it would fire coal, since good pine wood was becoming scarce. In 1939 the original Brown Pottery was torn down and a larger, more efficient building constructed to house both the machines and the kilns.

The most important contribution that Davis Brown made in "modernizing" the pottery, however, was in terms of the product. He began production of a new line of ware to be sold directly to department stores in the large cities—coffee cups, mugs, flower pots, vases, ash trays, pie plates, tea pots, cups and saucers, and any custom item which might be in demand. Each piece bore the stamp: BROWN POTTERY. ARDEN, N. C. In addition, Davis systematized his ware into categories, listing some 120 different shapes and sizes.

Early during World War II, Mr. Brown also began experimenting with a French style of cooking ware dubbed "Valorware." Created after painstaking trials with local clays, the new casseroles readily found a market through a New York distributor who could no longer import similar ceramics from overseas. By 1942 Davis had as many as twenty-six persons working for him making Valorware at the shop in Arden. But the boom did not last.

After Japan surrendered, laborers in the pottery, who had found plenty of work during tough times, began drifting away. Innovations came more slowly, even with the shift from coal to oil and, ultimately, to gasoline fuel in the big kiln. Davis's own two sons, Louis and Edward, like the rest (and like Cheever Meader's boys following the Depression) began to take an interest in other endeavors. Louis had served in the Armed Forces during the War and was now working on diesel engines, formally learning the trade in Chicago. Returning to Arden sometime in the late 1940s, he put this knowledge of mechanics to practical use by accepting a job with a local trucking firm where he remains employed to this day.

However, with his father's death in 1967, Louis Brown fell heir to the family pottery. Because his seven-day-a-week job at the trucking plant cuts into so much of his time, his nearly-grown boys, Charles and Robert, have been left with most of the daytime chores around the shop. They turn out orders as they come in and prepare demonstrations for the daily busloads of tourists who pass through to see the well-known Brown Pottery, home of the "original" Little Brown Jug. As such, the family manages to attract a modest tourist and mail order market for their heavy patent-glazed ware. Little about the shop has changed since World War II. Even the building is something of an anachronism, surrounded as it is by numerous filling stations, motels, taverns, and small businesses.

Nevertheless, Louis Brown has plans for the shop "when it'll be possible to give more time to it." He reads ceramic trade journals and makes minor alterations here and there such as replacing the old glaze buckets with marshmallow topping containers for the benefit of their teflon linings. Looking toward the future, Mr. Brown has the following to say:

> In my opinion the shop can be improved and updated. I like to see modern things and I like to see old-time things, and in the pottery business you can see both. If a machine nowadays will do the job better, I believe in using that machine. We still have the old kickwheel here [actually a treadle-type wheel]. I think the kick-wheel is fine, but I'd hate to know that I had to make 500 gallons of churns a day on the kickwheel like those old-timers used to have to do. We don't really have that type of work to do and it would be unnecessary if you did it nowadays that way, because they've got power wheels and better machinery. We should use those new inventions as time goes on to keep intact [sic] with time and keep production up with the demand.
>
> I don't think the craft and the potter's wheel and the potter is going to go completely out, although in our lives and the generations behind us there's not been near as many potters as other skilled trades, because it takes so long to learn. That's why I think it helps in a long period of time to get potters encouraged to keep changing.

THE SOUTHERN POTTERY TRADITION

From these two thumbnail sketches, we can see that change has taken place to varying degrees and with varying results in both instances over the past 70 years. But where do the two families converge? Is there any basic similarity between the Meaders and the Browns beyond the fact that they share the same trade? Here I believe it would do well to look to the region's past.

Several important factors affected the course of Southern history in a fashion unlike that in other parts of the country. Predominantly a producer of a few plant staples and allied products—cotton and tobacco, textiles and petrochemicals—the South on the whole proved mainly a builder of small, isolated communities rather than large-scale cities (Reissman 1965:80). In addition, these communities were relatively static—almost homogeneous in ethnic and religious background (at least for whites) and uncontaminated by alien influxes from the outside, both in terms of human immigration and in terms of "culture capital" flow, that is, knowledge. Indeed, what movement there was seemed to proceed in the opposite direction, ". . . including [emigrants] who might have questioned or challenged the [standing] traditions" (Reissman 1965:81).

And yet there is a third element in the South's past that has the most bearing on contemporary potters. Colonial historian Carl Bridenbaugh notes the unusual dearth of middle class craftsmen in the lower colonies during the formative stages of "regionalization" ". . . whose skills and solid worth as citizens would have contributed greatly to the common weal" (1950:32). Instead, it appears that skilled handcraft labor was virtually non-existent in the area at a time when, by comparison, craftsmen comprised close to eighteen percent of the general population in the settled colonies of the North, next only in numbers to husbandmen (Bridenbaugh n.d.:1). There are several reasons behind this interesting phenomenon.

In the first place, many successful Northern craft industries were initiated by immigrant tradesmen or others newly apprenticed on these shores. Clustering around moderately large communities, these men enjoyed a prosperous business and a respectable status as suppliers of the everyday items common to nearly all households. Even though the domestic product rarely equalled in quality that made overseas, it found favor with a sizable portion of the populace who deemed it troublesome, expensive, or unpatriotic (during the American Revolution) to import all their ware. Therefore, the crafts provided a livelihood for large numbers of colonists who did not farm.

By contrast, the South attracted few experienced artisans from outside until a late date. The isolated, primitive complexion of Southern settlements, the limited amount of capital resources, and the disinterest of the landed gentry in locally-made ware—all of these factors discouraged the formation of an immigrant middle class (Ramsay 1939:28).

Southern society militated as well against the spontaneous growth of its own indigenous body of skilled craftsmen. Patrons, who occasionally subsidized artisans in the North, were unknown, even in cities like Charleston and Atlanta. Apprenticeships too were seldom to be had except by orphans and other unfortunates who were simply bound over to a trade until maturity for the sake of convenience (Bridenbaugh 1950:30-31).

Moreover, as land holdings in the region began to increase, Black labor was imported in large numbers. Rather than serve as field-hands, many Negroes in the pre-Revolutionary period learned semi-skilled crafts and turned out crude ware for local consumption (Bridenbaugh 1950:15). Therefore, of those white artisans who were attracted to the South at this early date, few remained craftsmen for very long. Cheap land and social standing usually meant more than the prospect of competing with Blacks.

To be sure, white hand-craftsmen, including potters, were established in the South after the middle 1700s (probably because utilitarian ware had to be made and could not always be imported or manufactured by slaves), but these men had neither the skill nor the status of their Northern counterparts. Rather, it is more likely that they were typical of some of the "low-lifes" of the region. Potters throughout north Georgia today remark, though mostly in jest, that their forebears likely were refugees from some British debtor's prison.

By the time of the Civil War, potters who were not conscripted into the Confederate Army did their share for the war effort by turning medicine jars, mugs, bowls, and chamber pots for the Southern hospitals (Spargo 1948:96). After the conflict, the number of small establishments increased markedly throughout the entire region, since outside sources for ceramics were largely closed off. A unique feature of the Southern craft at this time was the emergence of countless "jugtowns" in response to the demand from local distilleries for liquor containers, a demand which continued unabated until Prohibition. From this period down through the earlier part of this century, the same isolation and independence of foreign innovation and idea that had characterized the Southern potteries for nearly 200 years still prevailed.

Taking all of these historical features into consideration then, we might suggest that Southern potteries formed institutionalized identities peculiar to their own region from a very early time— traditions which, when reinforced over several generations, would prove exceedingly difficult to alter or abandon as future conditions and events demanded. And so saying, I wish to return now to the two families of potters as a means for illustrating those structural features which can be said to underlie a "Southern Pottery Tradition." Each category has a basis in historical fact, although some are more important to the maintenance of the industry than are others, and some are no longer applicable (as noted). However, I think all are important to an understanding of the change situation.

1. Male potters. Without exception, men have always been the pottery-turners in the South, although their wives often help around the shop. And though a woman might try her hand on the wheel (like Lanier Meaders's mother), she will never be considered a genuine potter. Interestingly enough, this situation frees the females in potter families from the "dynasty" while the men remain bound, as we shall see presently.

2. A low social position. In neither Arden nor Cleveland could I determine that members of potter families were ever ascribed a status lower than that of their non-ceramist neighbors. Therefore, I would assume that this trait—if, indeed, it ever existed as Bridenbaugh suggests—had disappeared before the time of those craftsmen and family members with whom I talked. Perhaps it was the demise of the plantation system after the Civil War and the subsequent dimming of distinctions between planter, merchant, sharecropper, artisan, slave, and so on that brought about this change.

3. A lack of formal training. Genuine apprenticeships have been the exception to the rule in the South, since most technical learning occurred in the home. Many potters like Javan Brown spent time working for other concerns besides the family shop, but they usually learned the basic skills of the trade from their fathers beginning at a very early age. Also this training was more the "learn as you go along" variety than it was the "do as I do" sort, if my observations are correct. I asked both Louis Brown and his sons at separate times about firing the big gas kiln. Their answers differed markedly as to what happens—even down to the procedure for bricking up the door —and this in spite of the fact that the older boy, Charles, has been working in the pottery for almost fifteen years.

4. Isolated shops with local markets. Through the early part of this century, all potters turned ware for the local community (excepting those instances already mentioned). On the other point, however, one might question whether or not the shops were truly isolated from one another in view of the many potteries in and around Cleveland, Georgia. And yet it seems that the craftsmen—even brothers—rarely interacted, preferring to remain fairly close to their own shops most of the time. This peculiar behavior might relate to competition for customers as Louis Brown supposes: "I don't think that any potters ever stuck together. If they had, they would have cut one another's throats with prices." Rivalry and trade secrecy might enter the picture as well.

Another possible reason for this anti-social posture would be simply that the potter was too busy to socialize. It is significant that George Foster, speaking about Mexican peasant artisans, should offer: "In my experience, it is the rare potter who, without unusual stimulus, is much interested in how other potters work or what they make (1965:55)." Even today the point may be well taken as regards Southern potters. Louis Brown, when driving me to the Pisgah Forest Pottery some few miles distant from Arden for an interview, mentioned that he had not been out that way for years.

Even more improbable, while Louis and his uncle, Javan, have always known of the Meaders Pottery a hundred miles to the southwest (Javan having even worked there), no one has been down to Cleveland for at least three decades. Nor have the Meaders placed any calls with the Browns in all that time.

5. A utilitarian product. All ware turned prior to this century (with the exception of that made for the Confederacy during the War Between the States) was made for local use and consisted of those same kinds of articles that Lanier Meaders still favors: churns, crocks, pitchers, jugs (including "face" jugs), and so forth. Later we see the development of trade with local distilleries and, still later, a tourist orientation.

6. Dynastic regeneration. This is certainly the most important feature of the Southern craft, and for nearly 200 years has contributed to the continued maintenance of artisans in a region basically hostile or indifferent to their presence. And it is this aspect of the Southern pottery tradition that is presently making it exceedingly difficult for young members of potter families to break with the craft altogether, even in the face of its increasing obsolescence.

What the process means, ultimately, is that *all* sons of potters were trained from a very early age to continue the family craft when their father died—in other words, "like father, like son." Until quite a late time, this was the rule. However, the young man's fate was usually accepted, since in the rural South of some forty or fifty years ago, he had few other alternatives besides farming. Besides that, potters still speak of an intangible: "Pottery gets to you!" And anyone to whom pottery had "got" at the age of five or six was probably pretty well stuck until more glamorous occupations coupled with a decline in the craft's utility came along. And even then it might prove difficult to turn one's back upon six generations of forebears.

CHANGE IN THE TRADITION

Just as the process of dynastic regeneration served to accommodate the region's need for artisans whom it could not attract from elsewhere, it did one other thing: it chained these same craftsmen to a trade that was gradually losing its usefulness. Held captive to a limited and poorly-championed technology, a slow inflow of new ideas, a local market which demanded a specific utilitarian ware for home use, and a unique social and cultural tradition that placed severe limits on male members of the family, the craft was slowly strangling in the wake of industrialization. However, it was only

when clay products began to give way to glass bottles and tin
cans and when this trend was taken in combination with the
development of new employment opportunities in the local community that we see potters quitting (as in Cleveland). Probably even
this was not enough—it took a catastrophic event like the Great Depression or World War II to convince many younger potters that
their place was no longer in the work shed.

A second response to a changing economic milieu, and perhaps
more common than that just described, was an attempt to alter either
one's product or one's market orientation—or both. Most of the
older, established potters did this, some faring better than others.
Davis Brown, combining genuine innovative abilities with foresight
and a fortuitous location for his pottery, was the most spectacularly
successful of these. The rest, like Cheever Meaders (and now Lanier)
made little concession to change but sold their ware to tourist and
neighbor alike for as long as they were able.

But what of the future? That some persons seem determined to
further the tradition is fairly clear. One son of each of the older
potters (Cheever Meaders's son, Lanier; Davis Brown's son, Louis;
and Javan Brown's son, Evan) is doing what he can to preserve the
craft. This suggests that the dynasty is breaking up in its original
form, but that it is continuing to insure each family pottery's survival for a while. That both Louis Brown and his cousin Evan hold
second jobs, however, is going to make a difference. Nevertheless
both men are training their children as potters—Louis has his two
sons who work alongside him in the shop; and Evan, having no sons,
has sent his daughter to college to learn ceramics. It seems likely
that these individuals will have a greater right to self-determination
than did their fathers and grandfathers when it comes to choosing
an occupation.

Assuming that a seventh generation of Brown potters does find
its place at the wheel (and I believe this will occur), we can look
for still further divergence from the traditional norm to compensate for ever-increasing social and economic change in the region. As I
see it, aside from the large, industrialized manufacturer of ceramic
tableware (who does not concern us here), tomorrow's potter in
the South will have to depend even less upon the once-stable market
for general household goods (cooking and storage vessels, decorative
vases, lamp bases, etc.) than at present and more upon specialized
ware (unglazed garden pottery) and novelty items (tourist knick-
knacks). The former of these two alternatives is still fairly secure;
the latter much less so though perhaps catering to a more visible

and attractive market initially. Nevertheless, there are just so many tourists, and the better potter is the only one who will be able to earn a living day in and day out. Therefore, family tradition will no longer be enough to hold the craftsman to the task and Southern institutions will no longer demand that the region produce potters. Skill, creativity, and competitive spirit will better characterize the survivor, much the situation that remains for the small businessman or artisan elsewhere in the United States.

CONCLUSIONS

It is implicit in my introduction that the South, until recent times, has undergone a unique historical experience quite apart from the mainstream of industrial American life and that the consequences of this distinct regional "imprint" have often been a slowness to innovate and an overall tendency toward conservatism. Even by 1940, "the South [when compared with the national average] consistently showed a lower level of economic productivity, and a lower proportion of people living in the cities" (Reissman 1965:81). I have here attempted to demonstrate how the structuring of a particular institution when combined with a long period of social and cultural stability (those centuries of Southern experience prior to the advent of industrialization) might hinder any such forces of change once they are introduced into a region.

This point assumes particular importance when we begin to compare other formerly stable, agrarian societies only now beginning to experience urbanization and industrialization with the situation just described for the South. It is my hope that someone might find useful a modified folk society model (after Foster's [1953] "folk culture" configuration) to describe and predict what happens when industrialization displaces a rural system with the pre-industrial city as a focal point. Because this is occurring among peasant and other pastoral peoples throughout the world, the problem should have more than academic interest.

NOTES

1. Field work was undertaken in 1968 while I was a summer intern at the Smithsonian Institution and was directed by Mr. Ralph Rinzler, Division of Performing Arts, and Dr. Sam Stanley, Division of Anthropology. Financial assistance was provided by the National Science Foundation.

REFERENCES

Bridenbaugh, Carl, 1950. *The Colonial Craftsmen* (New York: New York University Press, Washington Square).

———————— n.d. *Myths and Realities, Societies of the Colonial South* (New York: Atheneum).

Foster, George M., 1953. What is Folk Culture? *American Anthropologist* 55:159-173.

————————, 1965. The Sociology of Pottery: Questions and Hypotheses Arising from Contemporary Mexican Work. In *Ceramics and Man,* F. R. Matson, ed. (Viking Fund Publications in Anthropology no. 41).

Ramsay, John, 1939. *American Potters and Pottery* (Hale, Cushman, and Flint).

Reissman, Leonard, 1965. Urbanization in the South. In *The South in Continuity and Change,* John C. McKinney and Edgar T. Thompson, eds. (Durham, North Carolina: Duke University Press).

Spargo, John, 1948. *Early American Pottery and China* (Garden City, New York: Garden City Publishing Co., Inc.).

Stiles, Helen E., 1941. *Pottery in the United States* (New York: E. P. Dutton and Co., Inc.).

The Southern Protestant Ethic Disease

JAMES L. PEACOCK

I WOULD like to report some ideas about Southern religion and Southern mental illness that underlie an exploration I have begun at the state mental hospital at Butner, North Carolina.[1] The mental and cultural complex that I am investigating may be called the Southern Protestant Ethic Disease. The Southern Protestant Ethic Disease differs profoundly from the Classical Protestant Ethic Disease, which is probably better understood by psychiatrists.

Some of the differences between the two diseases should emerge from the following brief sketch, which is preliminary to the more disciplined research planned for Butner. What I have to say is based partly on exploratory interviews and mainly on deductions from premises underlying the Classical Protestant Ethic as defined by Max Weber (1968) and the Southern Protestant Ethic as defined by Samuel Hill (1966). The aim is to deduce the kinds of mental trouble and torment that are likely to come from the Southern as opposed to the Classical Protestant Ethic.

According to Weber, the Protestant Ethic derived from the Calvinistic belief in a terrifying distance between God and man. So distant was God that His will was unknowable to man in any determinate fashion. God had willed that some men be among the saved, others among the damned, but no man could learn definitely into which group he fell. None of the techniques or media of the medieval Church, such as rites or sacraments, could signal or assure a man's salvation. Seeking desperately to discover some sign or assurance, the Calvinist finally concluded that incessantly, methodically, and piously behaving *as if* he were called by God was the surest sign and assurance that he was in fact called by God to serve Him as one of the saved, the Elect.

The search for salvation thus drove the Calvinist Protestant to systematize his entire life into an incessant, methodical, pious, straight

108

and narrow movement serving God's glory and kingdom. Waste of time was the deadliest of sins, since it distracted from this service. Regular and planned work was most desirable. Irregular or casual work was at best a necessary evil. Theater, idle talk, sex, adornment, or elaborate ceremony and ritual were sensuous and sinful distractions from the ascetic and disciplined life of service that thrust toward salvation.

The Southern Protestant faced the same problem: how to assure himself of salvation. The horrors of damnation loomed as vividly to him as to the Calvinist. His solution was, however, different. Instead of idealizing a total life of relentless, systematized, and cumulative service, the Southerner pinned his hopes almost entirely on a single instant of emotional, climactic, conversion experience. This instant need bear no integral relationship to the convert's total life plan, as is illustrated by an anecdote reported by Hill (1966:105). A Sunday school teacher, upon being asked by his pupil if Adolf Hitler was in heaven, replied that it was quite possible that at some point in his childhood Hitler had undergone the necessary conversion experience. The example is extreme, but it serves to illustrate that the Southern Protestant Ethic emphasizes the instantaneous conversion experience rather than the Classical Protestant Ethic of a life-long harnessing of self to God's plan.

Both the Southern and the Classical Protestant Ethic are ascetic. Both call for harsh discipline of body and senses. But the Classical Protestant Ethic defines such asceticism as a rational means toward more efficient service to God's ends. Lacking this orientation, the Southern Protestant Ethic views ascetic prohibitions less as efficient means toward ends than as absolute and unquestioned laws unto themselves. Taboos against drink, sex, and gambling acquire the character of primitive taboos.

The Classical Protestant has felt compelled to ruthlessly systematize more and more of life as service toward God's glory or some secular equivalent thereof: the great Anglo-American system of what Weber called "ascetic and bureaucratic capitalism" and, more recently, the Anglo-American welfare state are products of this compulsion (Peacock and Kirsch 1970: Chap. 6). The parallel compulsion of the Southerner has been to harshly discipline his impulses. Drink, sex, and the other joys have been the Southern Protestant's concern more than sloth, inefficiency, and human messiness that prompt the reforms of Classical Protestantism.

In addition to personal ethics, the Southerner has emphasized an interpersonal ethic whereby the personally righteous and admirable man stands as a model for others to emulate if they like (note the role of men like Robert E. Lee). This personable and voluntaristic ethic contrasts with the more distant and coercive one of Classical Protestantism. Classical Protestants move toward abstract schemes and plans that attack and reform unwilling and distant targets.

Given that a mental patient is strongly oriented in the Southern Protestant Ethic, how might his tensions, anxieties, frustrations, and symptoms differ from those of the Classical Protestant patient? The difference perhaps lies not so much in orthodox psychiatric symptomology and dynamics—which note that some patients suffer from headaches, others from insomnia; that some project, others compensate; that some are paranoid, others schizophrenic. Rather, the difference lies in the life patterns that evoke suffering. Southern Protestant Ethic patients will be bothered by patterns and problems of one type, Classical Protestants by patterns and problems of another type.

Deducing from the Classical Protestant pattern, one might suspect that its adherents will tend to feel guilty about poor planning and poor implementation of plans pertaining to long segments of life— projects and careers. They will see their failurees as composing a methodical and relentlessly cumulative build-up toward collapse. If they worry about drink, sex, gambling and other personal vices, they worry about them specifically as distractions from the straight and narrow path toward achievement and service for God or some secular surrogate of God. Installment plans, savings accounts, career plans, and growth rates are worries to the Classical Protestant Ethic patient.

Deducing from the Southern Protestant pattern, one suspects that its adherents balance hope for instant salvation with fear of instant damnation or secular equivalents thereof. Their guilt or shame derives less from systematic and continuous movement toward collapse than from one or more discrete and traumatic lapses or goofs. A rape of or by oneself, a sexual affair of self or spouse, a drunken episode, a social faux pas, a failure of nerve in a particular confrontation, as in battle, brawl, or football, will torment the Southern Protestant Ethic patient. Such failures occur in relation to specific persons, often hometown neighbors or relatives perceived as either opponents or disapproving spectators. The Classical Protestant patient's failure and guilt are more closely related to an abstract life plan or reference group, such as his profession.

Symptoms of the Classical Protestant patient might tend toward the delusional. He may tend to elaborate goal-oriented schemes, as did one Northern-born patient I interviewed. This fellow literally perceived life as a giant baseball field and was anxious about his inability to reach second base. Obsessive-compulsive scheduling should neatly express the Classical Protestant emphasis on specialized purity. By compulsively meticulous separation of the specialized thrust of work from the diffuse and disorderly miasma of personal relations, the thrust is purified. In Puritan imagery, this thrust is God's tool, so that polishing, purifying, and streamlining it by compulsive scheduling are essential

Symptoms of the Southern patient apparently tend toward conversion hysteria, as in imagined paralysis and pain. The Classical Protestant patient will perhaps tend less toward bodily hysteria. For him, body is merely an instrument of service to God. Bodily adornment is not so much evil as inefficient, and if it should prove efficient it would presumably be allowed. More absolute is the Southerner's attitude toward adornment of body and person. He is either totally for it, as in the Southern Cavalier or Southern beauty queen complexes, or he is totally against it, as in the harsh taboos of fundamentalists. Not surprisingly, the fundamentalists, who taboo makeup, manifest symptoms such as those displayed by one woman I interviewed. Her cheeks ached unbearably where she had worn rouge. Southern patients may generally focus their symptoms more around the adornment and contour of the body than do Classical Protestant patients.

The Classical Protestant patient's anxieties should, according to the logic of the Classical Ethic, flow more from friends, neighbors, and co-workers, whereas the Southerner's anxieties should derive more from blood kin. Social science suggests that the middle-class Classical Protestant son's fears and anxieties will focus around a mother who withholds love except when the son achieves (McClelland 1967:340-362). Research suggests that the Southern patient's fears will derive more from an authoritarian father—the type who administers whippings to a wayward son (Morland 1958:90-92).

The personalistic warp of the Southern Protestant Ethic can be expected to encourage what Tom Wolfe calls a "good ol' boy" ethic (1966). Patients will worry about not being good ol' boys, being mean and ugly instead of nice to people. Classical Protestants are encouraged by their belief to act mean and ugly in the name of reform for the sake of God, or His plan, or some other transcendent purpose; hence they might worry less about being nasty but worry more about not contributing to some abstract godly and social aim. Especially the Classical patient may worry and feel anxious about choosing a socially useless job.

Given the violence of Southern Protestant Ethic patterns of salvation, the Southern patient's disease, conceived as damnation, should tend toward violence. He should display more violent symptoms than the Classical patient, who should tend more toward systematic and compulsive intellectualization and scheduling. A careful analysis of the timing of symptoms might reveal that Classical Protestant patients degenerate more methodically and systematically, whereas Southerners fall apart by violent and erratic outbursts.

A word should be said now about the methods that will be employed to diagnose these two diseases within a population of patients. A questionnaire, partly derived from the foregoing deductions, is being administered to patients entering a certain section of Butner hospital during the next few months. Some of the items on the questionnaire will induce patients to classify themselves as more of the Classical Protestant or of the Southern Protestant religious persuasion. Other items portray life problems that seem logically to derive from one of the other of the two traditions. Possibly patients who classify themselves as Classical Protestant in religious orientation will consistently choose a configuration of life problems that contrasts with the configuration chosen by the Southern Protestant patients. Conceivably these contrasting configurations will resemble the sketch of diseases just presented—but perhaps not.

Turning from method to implication, a theoretical implication of the proposed study can first be noted. If patients embodying the Southern Protestant Ethic do turn out to differ clearly and consistently in mental disease from patients holding to the Classical Protestant Ethic, the utility of Weberian (and Hillian) typologies will be demonstrated in a new sphere—the abnormal. Indeed, it may be that the implications of religious belief in the realm of the irrational, in the spheres of neurosis and psychosis, are stronger than in comparatively rational business, which was Weber's concern.

A second implication of the study is more practical. Some psychiatrists sense that something is different about mental patients who are endowed with the Southern Protestant Ethic. None, so far as I know, have mapped with precision or depth the psychological contours of the Southern Protestant Ethic disease. Failing to understand the sickness, psychiatrists may not fully comprehend the treatment. Psychoanalysis, with its methodical, systematic, and rational progression matches the Classical Protestant pattern of salvation, but not the more episodic, dramatic, and emotional pattern of the Southern Protestant who, according to Hill (1966:85), is accustomed to feel himself "stricken, then released, remorseful then joyful, doomed then pronounced free of condemnation." If patterns of disease match Southern patterns of the Fall, then patterns of treatment should reson- ate with accustomed Southern patterns of salvation.

NOTES

1. This paper was originally presented as part of the conference on *The Bible Belt in Continuity and Change*, chaired by Professors Samuel S. Hill and Edgar Thompson, January, 1969, at Chapel Hill and Durham, North Carolina.

REFERENCES

Hill, Samuel S., Jr., 1966. *Southern Churches in Crisis* (New York: Holt, Rinehart).

McClelland, David C., 1967. *The Achieving Society* (New York: Free Press).

Morland, John Kenneth, 1958. *Millways of Kent* (Chapel Hill: University of North Carolina Press).

Peacock, James L. and A. Thomas Kirsch, 1970. *The Human Direction* (New York: Appleton-Century-Crofts).

Weber, Max, 1958. *The Protestant Ethic and the Spirit of Capitalism* (New York: Scribner's).

Wolfe, Tom, 1966. *Kandy-Kolored, Tangerine Flake, Streamline Baby* (New York: Pocket Books).

The Southern Way of Death

CHRISTOPHER CROCKER

FUNERALS and weddings are the two great rituals in American life which have most relevance to the individual's understanding of himself in relation to his society.[1] The symbols utilized in each of these rituals serve to define the categories and normative relationships of social life in particularly self-contained, systematic fashion. They also reflect certain beliefs about "final causes," God, the meaning of life, and, generally, the epistomological conditions of human existence. As such they are relevant to any examination of what the South understands itself to be. But one immediate problem is the identification of a uniquely "Southern" way of death. Many of the customs discussed here are preeminently American practices in the most general sense. However any judgment as to the extent of specific identity between Southern funerals and those in other sections of the country is hindered by a lack of precise ethnographic information on the subject. While monographs on the "exploitative" aspects of American funerals have had success (Mitford 1963; Harner 1963), and while there are superb sociological studies of "passing on" in the hospital considered as an American institution (Sudnow 1967), there have been no extended analyses of the social matrix of ceremonies involved with death and the collective representation of death in a modern American community.[2]

This paper is a preliminary effort at filling the gap. It is a report on research in progress, which I hope will stimulate further investigation. I shall not be concerned with the controversy over the high cost, the aesthetic taste, or general social validity of modern funerals, except as the general lack of public concern with such topics in the South is an important aspect of the regional deathways. The absence, for example, of memorial societies in the area as a whole reflects the almost total dominion of the churches over funerals. Rather, the paper's emphasis is on the ways in which death is socially handled

114

as reflected in funeral practices in two Southern communities. My particular concern shall be the nature and relationships between social and moral categories as these emerge in the organized, prescribed procedures of deathways. The last section of the paper will attempt to relate some ideologically problematic aspects of death as presented in Southern funerals to a fundamentalistic and presumably Southern Christian belief system. In short, I shall proceed on the classical anthropological dictum that death is a social process as well as a biological event (Hertz, 1960).

The data presented here have come from interviews among middle and upper-lower class whites and from participant observation in two communities in North Carolina, one a relatively small, homogeneous, and tradition oriented town and the other an expanding, industrialized urban center. While there are differences in practices between the two localities and between sub-groups in each of them, such contrasts are surprisingly minor even though they have considerable significance to actors as definitions of critical group boundaries This is true, for example, for variations between the practices of historical churches and the chiliastic sects. However, critical differences, in terms of the actors' perspectives, are found between black and white funeral customs. Indeed, white informants corroborated accounts in the existing literature that a "proper funeral" is defined partly in opposition to the supposed characteristics of black funerals. While a comparison of the two types would be illuminating, black deathways have been excluded from consideration here through lack of space and data.

With this exception, the near identity of the practices of all classes and sects, even Catholics and Jews, has considerable analytical importance. Since there are shared expectations as to the appropriate sequence of events and the "proper" behavior during the funeral, persons from distinct segments of the community may participate in the ritual. But the common definition of a "proper funeral" —that is, one which follows a single prescribed normative pattern— derives from a number of factors and certainly cannot be accounted for on the basis of any supposed functional consequence of fostering community solidarity. Furthermore, the similarity of the deathways in the communities studied should not be taken to imply any such identity throughout the South. Even though references will be made to "Southern" rather than "Carolinian," generalizations from the towns studied to the region as a whole should be made with some caution.

I

The following account shall deal first with the customs surrounding the process of dying and death itself; next, with the separate phases of the funeral as defined by the actors; and last, with the nature of mourning, the status and contemporary relevance of the dead in the community, and the symbolic values reflected in the cemetery. It must first be noted that today nearly all Southerners either die in a hospital or during the process of dying are passed through the organization of the modern hospital. Indeed, "going to the hospital" has apparently come to signify dying for many middle and lower class Southerners. This has considerable significance since the hospital involves a set of structural and ideological elements which serve to interpret and to define the exact nature of dying for society. Sudnow's recent work in a hospital in a large West Coast city is quite relevant here, for the hospital's characteristics do not appear to vary a great deal from region to region. He points out that dying is not a medically appropriate disease category or even symptom in the way that cancer or fibrillation is. The hospital's application of the category of "dying" to a given patient must be carefully judged by the doctors and administrators. If used early in the case it may imply to relatives and others that medical efforts have been curtailed too soon, particularly if the patient continues to live for some time. But it is also crucial that the term be applied in advance of actual death, because it conveys the meaning that all that could be done has been done, and that a natural process is underway that no human agency can control. Therefore the doctor must convey the impression that death is always possible although everything is being done to prevent it (Sudnow 1967:90-99). The doctor's problem of maintaining a credible ambiguity, endemic in his role, seems less acute in the communities studied than elsewhere, perhaps because of the common local belief that illness, recovery, or death are all reflections of God's plan. While the sufficient cause of death is admitted to be an auto accident or cancer or cessation of heart beat, the necessary cause is always divine will.[3] Furthermore, my observations indicate that the common American ambivalence toward doctors is less strong in the South, at least in terms of overt attitudes among lower and lower middle class whites. This in turn may be related to the same belief, in that doctors are regarded as themselves agents of the Holy Will, or to regional notions of the respect due any professional, or combinations of these with other factors.

The actual application of the "dying" category to a patient initiates the rite of passage that is the Southern funeral: it sets in motion a chain of patterned sequential actions and attitudes beginning with preparation for the announcement that death has occurred. Thus, "dying" is regarded as a private rather than a public matter, and therefore only those considered nearest the afflicted person are informed of the gravity of the situation. Most classes in the two communities, however, also felt it very important that the "immediate relatives" (the definition of this category is considered below) be present at the end. Indeed, in the South the horror of dying alone is matched only by that of being buried alone or in an unmarked grave. The former attitude appears based on the assumption that the dying man can be reassured by the presence of his "loved ones." In part, at least, the practice is a Southern one; in larger metropolitan hospitals it has been noted that visiting tapers off sharply after the "dying" category is applied (Sudnow 1967:72-77), whereas in North Carolina the reverse appears to be the case. This, however, is one of the last times in the funeral sequence that explicit attention is given to maintaining or fostering certain states in the dying or dead person. As anthropologists have known since Mauss, funeral practices in many other societies are explicitly devoted to securing various conditions for the deceased's soul in the transition from this world to the afterlife. But in the South, after this first act, the totality of ritual concern is with the living. Even here, certain categories of relatives— among them, young children and the elderly—are exempt from the obligation to be present during "dying." The doctor's problematic tightrope is again encountered by the relatives in their preparations during the "dying" to "dead" period, for it is thought vital that such "readying" actions should not proceed too rapidly or extensively —"After all, what would it be like if he got better and the undertaker was already there?" Hence preparation is likely to be very covert and slow, and the family typically resolves the problem by delaying to contact a minister and mortician until the doctor announces, "It is only a matter of time now."[4]

The insistence on the combined services of an undertaker and a preacher is at once an aspect of and a major element in the maintenance of the expected sequence of events and meanings in the funeral. It is considered essential by all informants that the deceased have a "church funeral," regardless of past religious affiliation, moral history, or circumstances of death. With rare exceptions an alcoholic, a suicide, and a child all have *formally* similar funerals. The minister is usually one associated with the deceased's or a relative's particular church; this selection causes problems when family members belong to different churches. There seems to be less difficulty with the chiliastic sects, perhaps due to a tendency for "family" to be defined by co-membership in the church. The mortician is usually chosen by a combination of criteria, including co-membership with the family in church, lodge, or other associational group and/or evaluation of his past skill at conducting "proper" funerals. Both prior arrangements contracted by the deceased and the process of "shopping around" for the cheapest funeral on the part of the family are evidently rare in the South, and both appear to be viewed as reprehensible. Perhaps this is true because these activities subvert the notion of the "proper funeral." But regardless of the ways in which preparation has been made, as soon as death occurs the community must be notified. The patterned ways in which the news is conveyed to relatives, friends, associates, and others reflect the normative relationships between these persons and the deceased. These ways establish the differing obligations of roles during the funeral and mourning period. The customary Southern ways of spreading news of a death are very much like those described for other parts of the country (Sudnow 1967:154-168), with some exceptions to be given later.

The first persons notified by those in attendance at the death bed or by the doctor are relatives described as "having the right to know" of the death: spouse, lineal relatives (such as parents, children, and grandparents/grandchildren), and immediate consanguineals such as siblings. There is an emphasis on personal notification, by telephone rather than by public media or by card; thus airlines do not release lists of crash victims until the "relatives," those defined as having the right to know, are informed personally. Those persons having this right and those with the right to grieve and to receive public sympathy are virtually identical; together they compose the rather sharply bounded category designated as "the mourners" or "the immediate family." As Sudnow shows (1967:161-162), this group may also be characterized as those who are entitled to an unqualified use of "my" in describing their relationship to the deceased. Thus someone has only to say, "My father died" to be regarded as a mourner, but a more distant relation must qualify the kinship tie, as with the statement, "My dear sister's boy who was like a son to me," in order to establish his character as one who has suffered direct loss.

The relationship of first order collaterals—uncles, aunts, cousins, nephews, and nieces—to this category seems quite ambiguous. Their "right to know," to be categorized as "immediate family," seems to vary according to the particular kinship system operative in the local society. I have neither the space nor the data to explore this problem in detail. However, it is my impression that in those regions where economic matters (including inheritance and labor exchange) along with political and religious activities are identified as being the responsibility of an extended kindred, such collaterals are included in the "immediate family." Concomitantly, as the socially significant kin group is more or less restricted to lineal relatives with an emphasis on the nuclear family, the collaterals are of course excluded. In a very general way, the two modes of grouping might be characterized as rural (and Southern) and urban (and Northern) if it is realized that both modes can be found in the same community or region.

The death practices discussed above constitute one important way in which a person's membership in different kin groups is defined. For example, those relatives who fail to comply with the normative requirements of their kinship relationships lose the right to be relatives, to be regarded as family members. Thus a cruel, profligate, or "sinful" son may not be informed immediately of his parent's death. The manner and time in which persons outside the immediate family are notified of the death is also highly significant. It has been pointed out that, "It is possible to learn a good deal about a person's position in a variety of social structures by mapping out the circles of those persons entitled to learn about his death" (Sudnow 1967: 154). Thus it is considered improper that individuals learn of the death from others more distantly related to the deceased, so that a first cousin should not be told by an in-law. Therefore the family attempts to have each circle of relations inform each other: friends tell friends, cousins tell cousins and so forth. Complex factors of status in the local community, moral judgments, rights and obligations implicit in different roles, all influence the sequence of events.

The process of notification is complicated by the fact, as Sudnow demonstrates, that those who are regarded as immediately bereaved and entitled to sympathy are hindered from informing persons in the non-bereaved categories, for to do so would create a complex problem in interaction. To inform a friend that one's father has died requires the friend to extend sympathy and may be interpreted as a claim to such sympathy. Further, behavior toward the bereaved and acts expressing regard for the deceased should ideally be similar to gifts, things which must have a free, spontaneous quality however much they are normatively enjoined. So while members of "the immediate family" may inform each other, they cannot tell anyone else; the responsibility for imparting the news to the next circle of kin is usually taken by an affinal relative, such as the husband of the deceased's sister. Often there is an explicit division of labor, with the caller instructing the respondent to tell certain others. In this way judgments as to the deceased's position in a variety of social units as well as the nature of his relationships with persons in those units continue to be made throughout the process of notification.

Two final points need to be made here: first, the act of mourning is always associated with "blood ties," with close biological relationships as these are perceived by the local society. The community's loss of a member is portrayed dominantly as a biological matter, not as one of presumed social value. This is related to the insistence that all persons have the right to a "proper" church funeral. Since this ritual is thought more for the mourners' than the deceased's benefit, it is the only appropriate structure for the expression of grief. Second, the obligation to inform certain persons immediately reflects a concern that their social demeanor be congruent with the "fact" of death. This concern, as expressed in such statements as, "She was dancing and singing as her mother lay dead," is related to the problems of ambiguity found in Southern symbolic representations of the dead that shall be discussed at the conclusion of the paper.

II

The funeral itself is separated into four quite distinct phases, each with its particular social configurations and symbolism. These phases are the wake, which removes the deceased along with the bereaved from society and secular existence; second, the "visiting" in the funeral parlor, a period of ambiguous non-social time which continues nearly unbroken into the third phase, the church service. Finally the fourth stage, burial at the cemetery, incorporates the deceased into the company of the dead and signals the beginning of the mourners' assumption of their normal secular roles. These analytical processes of separation from the society, a marginal period of transition, and finally re-incorporation are derived from van Gennep's historic formulation of the sequence in rites of passage (1960).

The wake is an old custom which seems to be common in the traditional community studied but which is disappearing in the urban center. In holding a wake the "immediate family" does not go to bed on the night following the death, but is at home to callers. The underlying assumption is that the bereaved are too upset to sleep and require extensive social support since they are incapacitated by grief and unable to fulfill normal roles. Therefore the visitors bring great amounts of food. Those kin, neighbors, and friends who are considered to be outside the bereaved category assume domestic chores as well as those funeral arrangements not part of the mortician's duties. The mourners, as defined in the ways indicated above, are expected to demonstrate fairly standardized signs of grief. Women should cry and "take on" generally; even mild hysterics are not socially disapproved. Men should exhibit an outward composure while indicating through various recognized and stereotyped signs their actual emotional states. Under no circumstances should mourners attempt to "carry on as usual," nor is the Southern wake ever characterized by the joking and revelry which supposedly occur during similar rituals in other American regions. The stress on the inappropriateness of usual roles is one more reflection of the separation of the mourners from society.

The food brought by the callers at the wake is limited not in quantity but in variety. It appears that in the South, rites of passage are marked by the consumption of special ceremonial foods. These consist, at least for the areas studied, of smoked or country ham, sliced white chicken or turkey meat, potato salad, and cakes and pies of various types. Other items certainly do appear, and there are no explicit prohibitions or prescriptions such as found in the ceremonial diets of other societies. Rather, there is a vague feeling that the above dishes are somehow appropriate to ritual occasions. The reasons for this association are quite complex and deserve further research. One possible mode of analysis would be to focus on the total field of man-animal relationships in the South, endeavoring to discover if pigs and chickens are considered to have any sort of special relationship to their owners.[5]

Interestingly, the social categories expected to attend the wake are not clearly defined, in the sense that there are no normative expectations as to who should or should not come. Attendance, then, becomes another way in which membership in social units can be expressed and the deceased's social position revealed freely, without the constraint of prescribed behavior. In practice, the persons attending the wake are those who categorize themselves, and expect to be classified, as intensely affected by the death due to closeness of relationship to the deceased or to those directly bereaved. The wake is explicitly private, a family matter, and thus contrasts with the public ceremonies which follow it. Thus it is characterized by an emphasis on particularistic and functionally diffuse relationships. It is significant that business associates, friends, lodge members, fellow churchmen and those in other functionally specific roles make an appearance during the Southern wake, for in so doing they stress the diffuse and unique quality of their relations with the deceased and his family. In contrast, those persons who call on the family during the period between the wake and the burial, when the bereaved are similarly at home to the community, are proclaiming a somewhat more distant relationship. These latter visitors, then, may be regarded as members of the broad category of "sympathizers," those who attend the funeral parlor and/or the church service.

III

During the next two phases the family occupies a marginal status which must be demonstrated by aspects of their conduct, such as clothing. Currently in the South, any public viewing of the body or casket, if done at all, occurs at a funeral home rather than in the deceased's own house, as was formerly the case. This event comes from one to three or four days after death, and lasts for only a morning or afternoon. Its public quality is reflected in the announcements of the event through the mass media. Persons of the "immediate family" should be present to receive condolences, although very often the individuals regarded as most afflicted, such as a wife or mother, are exempt from this obligation. The two elements of the ritual viewing which seem most significant to me are the presentations of flowers and the importance attached to a last view of the body, which is made to look as nondead as possible.

It is somewhat surprising that all informants said there was no particular symbolic importance in the variety of flowers used. Rather, it is form, size, and quantity of the "floral tributes" which are emphasized. The different types of such gifts are loosely associated with particular social categories. "Standing wreaths" are given by members of the immediate family, according to the ways in which this group has been defined during the preceding phrase. Therefore the contribution of such displays by others, whether families, individuals, or groups, becomes a social declaration of the closeness of relationship to the deceased and, consequently, of the importance of the loss suffered. That is, to give a standing wreath is to say, "The deceased was like a member of our family." When an important community figure dies he or she may receive wreaths from a variety of organizations, but it may be stretching a point to say that the deceased is thus declared a town father or mother. Sprays, again a unique arrangement used only at funerals, are contributed by relatives, friends, neighbors, colleagues, and the like, those who have suffered loss but who are not regarded as "bereaved." The bier is contributed only by the "immediate family."

The symbolism involved with the "floral tributes" is at least two-fold. First, the specific forms of the wreaths are often explicit statements—a "bleeding heart" or "unbroken circle." Second, the presentation of flowers in American society is generally associated with the affirmation of affectual solidarity, of feeling so intense that it may be expressed in no other type of gift but flowers. Women are usually taken to be vehicles and objects of such feeling, so that the institution of "flower girls" is an important element in Southern working class funerals. These women convey the floral tributes from cars into the church, and from the church to the graveside. They are usually drawn from an important referent group of the deceased, such as an adult Sunday School class, or a school class in the case of a dead child or adolescent, or some club, such as Eastern Star. For male deceased, the group is often chosen on the basis of the wife's associational membership. In all cases, only women actually handle the flowers. On a more sociological level, the flower girls are expected to remove the tags indicating the donor or donors, and note the type of floral offering and its form on the reverse side. These tags are given to the immediate family so that a formal note of appreciation can later be sent to the givers. The analogy to wedding presents is striking.[6] While the general public does not usually see the tags (although in some areas these are left attached), there is a general correlation drawn between the number, size, and approximate cost of the flowers and the deceased's social position. This sort of evaluation of the funeral occurs throughout the ritual, and there appears to be considerable preoccupation on the part of the bereaved with such judgments of size and cost. One of the critical elements of a "proper funeral" is that it be deemed in these terms congruent with the deceased's and his family's social position.

The concern with the lifelike appearance of the corpse, and the stress on the "last view" which accompanies it, is often claimed to be a bit of astute salesmanship by undertakers. I doubt this is the case. Rather, the morticians have responded to a widely held value, particularly in the South. This is not so much an attempt to deny the reality of death as to present it as a phase of life. It may not be too much of an imaginative leap to say that the collective representation of death as a type of peaceful sleep is an assertion that the dead have a special kind of life. This can only be assured them through the cosmetic manipulations of embalming, the purchase of which is a moral obligation of their descendants. Certain aspects of the American cemetery, such as its characterization as a garden and a place of waiting, support, I think, this interpretation.

The visiting period at the funeral parlor shades into the church service, and, in fact, the two rites are often combined. Here the symbols used in hymns and prayers focus on the moral character of death in general, as well as its particular significance in terms of the deceased's life. I will deal with this at the end of the paper, along with the problem of the selection of appropriate eulogies, hymns, and so forth for morally ambiguous categories such as suicides, infants, and alcoholics. But first, the social categories involved in the church service and burial must be examined. In addition to the flower girls, another critical social unit appears at the service itself, the pallbearers. Members of this group are usually selected from among the deceased's close friends, business associates, and nonbereaved kin, or in the case of a dead woman, from her husband's associates and relatives. Again the exact composition of this group reflects the totality of social roles held by the deceased, and of course it forms the masculine counterpart of the flower girls. Older men or those who are regarded as physically incapacitated from carrying the coffin are designated as honorary pallbearers, and in fact this may present a delicate problem since men may object to such a categorization. Generally, the pattern of southern funerals appears to stress the incorporation into the ritual of a great many otherwise discrete, functionally specialized, and well differentiated social groups. The boundaries between these units are eclipsed by the sense of common loss, so that the funeral becomes a time when mechanical rather than organic solidarity is emphasized.

This stress is further reflected in the very strongly enjoined obligation for the deceased's relatives, friends, colleagues, associates, and neighbors—in short all those who are regarded as having participated significantly in the deceased's life—to attend the funeral in a proper ritual condition. By this last term I mean that the appropriate inner emotional state should be reflected in dress and deportment, in the wearing of best clothes, a diffuse attitude of grave seriousness, and so forth. As one informant put it, "Everyone has to have a clean white shirt to go to funerals in." The obligation to attend the funeral is decreasingly binding the further the formal social distance from the deceased, but it obtains for "immediate family" regardless of the actual facts of the relationship. Two brothers may not have spoken for twenty years, but one is obligated to go to the other's funeral. One of the most damning moral classifications a Southerner can apply is, "He's so mean he didn't (or wouldn't) go to his own mother's funeral." Not to comply with this requirement is to place oneself beyond society in a quite definitive way. It is significant that one of the critical episodes in the career of a folk hero-criminal (as presented in a song or movie) is his presence, incognito, at a relative's funeral.

IV

The burial itself is generally regarded as the most traumatic phase of the entire ritual, and during it various kinds of emotional outbursts are expected and usually condoned. This may be due to the character of the burial as the particular rite which begins the process of incorporation of the bereaved into normal society, and which moves the deceased into the company of the dead. The persons who attend the burial are usually those who participated in the wake, so that we find a blurring of the public-private distinction in the concluding as at the initial portion of this rite of passage. The actual location of the plot involves a statement of the deceased's critical social affiliations. Thus a wife is buried by her husband, but a daughter by her parents. It seems clear that American cemeteries emphasize lineal kinship ties. The only exception to this rule occurs not so much as a consequence of moral judgments—for the black sheep of the family ultimately will lie in the family plot—but as when the circumstances of death are thought to involve even higher values than those represented by the family. Soldiers are buried together, patriotism being the highest good of all,[7] and sometimes other associational groups predominate over particularistic values, as when the three or four adolescent victims of an automobile crash are placed in the same separate plot. Above all, however, the deceased's burial site must have some social referent, so that he is assigned at the end, as throughout the funeral, some universal and perpetual category. A pauper's grave, an unmarked site, is hideous because it is a complete end to all the social categories embodied by the dead man. This, as we have known since Durkheim, is a fundamental threat to the very basis of social cohesion.

There are no definite sets of mourning rules, which is surprising until we consider the flexibility such imprecision allows for the demonstration of "actually felt," as opposed to socially enjoined, feelings and attitudes. Up to this point the actions and even the precise social composition of the bereaved group has been restricted by normative expectations. The freedom to mourn allows two things: the socially defined bereaved have the opportunity to demonstrate that they do indeed feel grief and do not merely act a role. Second, those more distantly related to the deceased may show that in emotional fact the relationship was closer than its formal characteristics indicated, that a business associate was indeed "like a son to me." At the other extreme, and typically Southern, is a normative stress on the consistency of demonstrated grief during the ceremony and of conduct during the following period. For example, a widow who "cuts up awful" during the burial service and then remarries some six months later is subject to considerable adverse sanctions. This appears to be another implicit recognition of the possibility of hypocritical compliance with role expectations. This threatens solidarity, which rests on the paradox that to be an effective base of social cohesion, shared emotional states must be at once free and obligatory.

Perhaps the most striking ideological characteristic of Southern funerals, as represented in the material presented here, is their explicit avoidance of moral or theological judgments. Funerals are for the living, not the dead, and the ways in which these rituals are conducted have only social rather than cosmological significance. As I mentioned earlier, a suicide and even a murderer have the right to "a proper funeral" just like that of an individual revered throughout the community for his saintly conduct. To be sure, the community response may well demonstrate their judgment of the moral worth of such persons, but the point is, first, that each of them receive formally the same kind of treatment, and second, that neither the moral character of the deceased nor the specific incidents of a particular funeral affects the condition of the soul in the afterlife. Each of these elements, from anthropology's perspective, is unusual and intriguing, and in my view they relate first to certain features of Southern religion and next to various aspects of death as a social phenomenon. Charles Hudson has demonstrated that in fundamentalistic Southern Christian belief, illness and dying are held to be the primary instrumentality of supernatural justice.[8] The death of a wild, sinful boy in a car accident and the almost miraculous recovery of an elderly Christian woman are held to be examples of God's judgments and the direct consequence of sin and salvation. At the same time, the proper Christian who is visited by boils, economic calamities, and finally an early death is considered an example of fate, an act of God which cannot, and should not, be comprehended by man. Illness, suffering, and death are represented in the South as human tribulations during which faith may be demonstrated: they are "trials," in a very literal sense.

The important point is that no matter how much sinners as an abstract category may be consigned to everlasting hellfire, in the funeral no *particular* sinner is portrayed as suffering such pangs of the damned. Not only practice, but books of instruction for funerals written by Southern ministers for their regional colleagues insist that the most morally reprehensible of persons should be pictured during the burial service as enjoying the fruits of salvation. This is deemed a proper and fitting response not so much for the immediate family's sake, but in terms of doctrine and faith. The emphasis of hymns and eulogies is on the mysterious ways of God's will, and the necessity of avoiding moral judgments concerning the ontological status of the deceased. In the cemetery the dead are portrayed as morally equal and of similar relevance for the living: they are "all family." This may strike an anthropologist from another culture as an excellent demonstration of the logical inconsistencies in what Levy-Bruhl termed mystical participations, but I do not think this is the case. In Southern society, moral classifications stop at the grave, and this is one particular way of handling a perhaps universal human problem: the ambiguity of death.

From an individual standpoint, social time is serial, non-repetitive, yet from the position of society this must not be the case (Evans-Pritchard 1940:94-95). To admit that what has happened may not happen again, that the passing of an individual creates a vacuum which may never be filled up, is to admit the falseness of social categories and the vulnerability of social processes. This threatens the entire expectational system, which is based on the assumption of cyclic rhythms. Thus funerals must resolve an inherent ambiguity: the sense of uniqueness of an individual's life and the enduring quality of the roles he filled and which may now be filled by others. The emphasis during the funeral on the living and even on their obligation to the deceased to continue the process of social existence is one aspect of the resolution of this ambiguity. In more specific ways, the reiteration of the dead man's character in terms of his specific biological roles, that of father, son, husband, nephew, and grandfather, affirms the universality and inevitability of these positions. At the most, as when a young child dies, the manner and time of death conjoined with the moral *persona* of the deceased may be represented as a trial for the living, a period during which their faith may be tested. But the explicit refusal to judge the dead also carries with it the assertion that life has no definite end either in the glories of heaven or the pangs of hell, but instead continues, indefinitely and ambiguously. Thus we find in the funeral the affirmation of all the statuses and roles through which the deceased played out his social game, along with the assertion that social existence is indeed perpetual, enduring, and cyclic. The Southern way of death is therefore one way of preserving the continuity of Southern life.[9]

NOTES

1. A prior version of this paper was read at a conference entitled "The Bible Belt in Continuity and Change," sponsored by the Center for Southern

Studies of Duke University and held in January, 1969. I wish to express my gratitude to James Peacock, Charles Hudson, and Edgar Thompson for both their general comments on Southern religion and for their suggestions regarding this paper. I am particularly indebted to Mr. Leonard Kovit and to my wife, Eleanor Crocker, for their numerous suggestions and insights concerning Southern funerals. The views expressed here are of course my own responsibility.

2. While various community studies include some notes on the local character of funerals, the topic is not systematically investigated or analyzed. Perhaps the most extended and systematic analysis is to be found in Warner's *The Family of God* (1961:157-260). However, Warner's material is somewhat dated and the treatment neglects the social categories and groupings discussed here.

3. As might be suspected, this faith sometimes encounters difficulties in encompassing suicides, murders, and "freak" accidents. I have heard these tragedies attributed to the Devil's machinations, even though it is generally recognized that this is not accepted by religious authorities. Since the paper was written, a murder has occurred in the traditional community, and public opinion seems to be that the accused (the victim's husband) should *not* have a "proper funeral" whenever and however he dies.

4. It is perhaps obvious that sudden death, particularly when it occurs to the young, is all the more difficult to accept because it has no similar "preparation time." The apparent tendency for the funerals in these cases to be more protracted and elaborate may be an attempt to provide *post facto* a period of adjustment.

5. These comments derive, of course, from recent theories concerning liminal, anomalous animal categories put forward by various anthropologists (Leach 1964; Douglas 1966).

6. There are other analogies between funerals and weddings; perhaps the most striking is the Southern custom of burying women in "peignoirs" especially made for this purpose. This might be interpreted as congruent with the "death as sleep" view discussed below, but several informants made explicit comparisons between this garment and similar ones in a bride's trousseau.

7. Recently some men killed in Vietnam have been buried with their families, with the explicit reason that the war there is "bad" and "wrong."

8. Charles Hudson, "The Structure of a Fundamentalist Belief System," in Samuel Hill (ed.), *Religion and the Solid South,* forthcoming.

9. Comments on earlier drafts of this paper stressed that many of the practices discussed are not unique to the South, and that customs of different social classes are considerably more heterogeneous than I assume. Both assertions may reflect the current situation in Southern urban centers, in which there has been rapid social change for the past two decades.

REFERENCES

Douglas, Mary, 1966. *Purity and Danger* (London: Routledge and Kegan Paul).

Evans-Pritchard, E. E., 1940. *The Nuer* (Oxford: Clarendon Press).

Harner, R., 1963. *The High Cost of Dying* (New York: Crowell, Collier, and Macmillan).

Hertz, Robert, 1960. *Death and the Right Hand* (Glencoe, Ill.: The Free Press).

Leach, Edmund, 1964. Anthropological Aspects of Language: Animal Categories and Verbal Abuse. In *New Directions in the Study of Language*, E. H. Lenneberg, ed. (Cambridge: M. I. T. Press), pp. 23-63.

Mitford, Jessica, 1963. *The American Way of Death* (New York: Simon and Schuster).

Sudnow, David, 1967. *Passing On* (Englewood Cliffs, N. J.: Prentice-Hall).

van Gennep, A., 1960. *The Rites of Passage* (Chicago: Phoenix Books).

Warner, W. Lloyd, 1961. *The Family of God* (New Haven: Yale University Press).

Conclusion: Problems and Prospects

J. KENNETH MORLAND

THE call for more anthropological study of American culture and society has sometimes been put on the basis that it is a necessary move because of the eventual disappearance of the preliterate societies and cultures which have primarily been the province of anthropologists. Thus, both John Gillin (1967) and Leslie White (1965) sounded this note in recent presidential addresses to the American Anthropological Association. Gillin stated that whether they liked it or not cultural anthropologists were being drawn into the study of complex industrial societies. White raised the question of what the ethnographer would do when preliterate societies were gone. He felt that diminishing returns were setting in from continual studies of some tribes and that the remark that a Zuni household consisted of mother, father, children, and a social anthropologist was not entirely a joke. Furthermore, he thought that trivialities were being dealt with in some anthropological journal articles, such as "An Unusual Prayerstick from Acoma Pueblo," and "The Excavation of Hopewell Site Number 793." While disclaiming the intention of saying that anthropologists should not be interested in such details, he wondered if more valuable and significant studies could be made. Both he and Gillin urged cultural anthropologists to study American society, thus enlarging their scope to cover the entire field of culture which is rightfully theirs.

An even more valid justification than moving into its "rightful field" is the special contribution anthropology can make to the understanding of modern, complex societies. These societies have long been the domain of sociology, political science, and economics, and these disciplines have developed concepts and research techniques designed to deal with the complexities of urban societies. We need to make sure that anthropology is not merely duplicating the efforts of sociologists and others, but, rather, that it is making a unique con-

130

tribution. Max Gluckman and Fred Eggan have reminded us of what this contribution can be by pointing out that in addition to their traditional emphasis on tribal societies anthropologists have in common:

> . . . a continuing focusing of interest on customs, as having an interrelated dependence on one another, whether in forming cultural patterns, or in operating within systems of social relations, or in the structuring of various types of personality in different groups. This focus on customs in interdependence has continued to distinguish the disciplines of anthropology from the other subjects with which each branch is increasingly associated (1966:xii).

What Gluckman and Eggan are saying, as I understand it, is that the distinguishing characteristic of anthropological study is the viewing of behavior in its cultural setting. In other words, it is the "holistic" approach. Closely related is the notion of *in vivo* study, as Conrad Arensberg has termed it, that is, study through direct observation and comparison, in contrast to *in vitro* study through isolation and statistical abstraction (1954:110). There are formidable problems in utilizing holistic, *in vivo* research in American society and culture.[1] In the pages which follow we shall look at some of these problems in relation to the papers in this volume, and we shall then consider next steps for anthropological research in the American South.

PROBLEMS OF ANTHROPOLOGICAL STUDY OF AMERICAN CULTURE

The first problem in doing research on American culture is selecting the group or type of behavior to be studied. This is not easily or readily done when one intends to employ anthropological approaches in an industrial, urban society. The reports in this volume offer examples of small, distinct groups that might be studied by lone investigators with a minimum of funds. In addition, there are other occupational enclaves like the urban mill people studied by Duncan and the coal miners studied by Knipe and Lewis, other religious sects like the one observed by Keber, other peasant settlements like those delineated by Newton, and additional "gypsy" or itinerant groups as Harper himself suggested. In the last section of this paper a proposal for more systematic and cooperative research will be given.

Acceptance by those being studied is the next problem in anthropological research. Participant-observation requires that the field worker enter into the lives of those he is studying much more than is the case in *in vitro* study. Of course, this is a problem that faces the anthropological field worker regardless of where his study is being conducted.[2] Whether or not it is a greater problem for the anthropologist studying American society than it is for the anthropologist studying tribal society would itself be a valuable topic for research. Americans have become especially sensitive to being studied, regarding it as an invasion of privacy, and this sensitivity is becoming especially acute among minority and other disadvantaged groups in the United States. Obviously, gaining acceptance is by no means easy for Americans studying their own culture. In this volume Gordon and Hodges had surprisingly little difficulty in gaining acceptance by those involved in illegal activity, while, on the other hand, Harper makes a strong point of the necessity of help from a priest who worked with the Irish Travelers, and Keber tells of the breakthrough when she was vouched for by someone trusted by the healing cult. Stanton reports that his position as a community worker led to his acceptance by the Houma. In my own study of the mill village sections of a Southern town, I encountered a great deal of suspicion at the beginning (1958:3). Towards the end of the twelve months of field work, I learned that there had been rumors at various times that I was a company spy, a labor organizer, a private detective, an F. B. I. agent, and a communist. I also learned that if someone were seen talking to me, he was later taunted by fellow mill villagers with, "I see you've been feeding the spy." Gaining genuine acceptance and trust are things that every anthropological field-worker has to strive for throughout his research, whether it is conducted in his own or in another culture.

Another problem of anthropological study of one's own society is that of familiarity with what is being studied. Many anthropologists have felt that in participant-observation it is not possible for the researcher to have the proper perspective and objectivity when studying a culture of which he is a part. They believe there is a real danger of overlooking significant behavior because of being so close to it. As Margaret Mead has put it, students of anthropology have been sent to live in remote societies "to be exposed to ways of behavior quite different from our own, so different in fact that no effort of mind will work that simply redefines the new ways in terms of the known old ways" (1949:25). However, the reports in this volume give every appearance of objectivity, insight, and perspective. Of course, it might be argued that the ways of healing cult members, gypsies, moonshiners, hippies, renegades, miners, pottery-makers, peasants, and mill workers were unfamiliar to the investigators; yet it must be added that members of these groups share much of their culture. And it might be added further that herein lies a major asset, for one important aspect of the culture shared is language. One might wonder just how much would have been missed by Partridge as he listened to conversations in the hippie ghetto, or by Sayers as he interviewed potters, or by Keber as she participated in healing ceremonies, if they had not known the language and had had to work through interpreters.[3] It might be noted, parenthetically, that in participant-observation studies in remote societies anthropologists frequently rely upon informants and translators who are themselves highly familiar with both the culture and the language. In other words, they must see the culture, in part at least, through the eyes of those who are highly familiar with it. At the same time, anthropologists distinguish between behavior that is observed and verbalizations about behavior. Yet, if one believes that language is a "vehicle of the culture" (Herskovits 1955: 277-301), then the field worker who knows the language, including its shades of meanings, innuendoes, and subtleties, has a distinct advantage in describing and analyzing the culture. Of course, anthropologists studying the kinds of groups reported on in this volume undoubtedly encounter some difficulties in understanding the shades of meaning of the English being used, a problem particularly acute in Keber's study of a Black healing sect; but these investigators no doubt understand far more of the language in these studies of the American South than investigators in foreign societies.

As cited above, Gluckman and Eggan emphasize that a special contribution of anthropology is to show the interrelatedness of customs. If one thinks of interrelatedness in terms of American culture as a whole, or even of the Southern regional subculture as a whole, the task is beyond anthropological *in vivo* study at present. America and the American South are simply too complex, too heterogeneous, too little studied for aspects of behavior to be seen fully in context. Perhaps this is what Margaret Lantis had in mind when she said that some anthropologists think that "when we study complex contemporary civilization, we tend to abandon the tenets of our discipline" (1955:1118). Some anthropologists believe that anthropologists who study American society and culture become, in effect, sociologists, since *in vivo,* holistic studies of such a complex culture are virtually impossible. I do not agree, and I feel that research in this volume gives leads as to how the holistic problem may be approached.

One way is to restrict severely the group or type of behavior being considered, as was done in most of the studies in this volume. Thus the context will be so limited that it is possible to see interrelationships within it. Admittedly, this modifies the usual meaning of "holistic," especially since it is unlikely that the groups that are so distinct are typical of the South. But if enough of these groups and behavior patterns are studied comparatively, knowledge about similarity and difference in relationship can be broadened. A more effective approach to being holistic is to use the community as the context, something that will be considered in the last part of this chapter.

Anthropologists who carry out the kinds of studies found in this volume are sometimes accused of being impressionistic, of generalizing from too few or too imprecise data. The problem of generalizing is a constant one for the cultural anthropologist, as indeed it is for every scientific discipline, although perhaps more for the participant-observer than for those who make extensive use of random sampling and official statistical data. Anthropologists have rightly feared over-simplification in trying to generalize from their limited studies to American society as a whole. However, the accusation of being impressionistic is not justified in the case of careful *in vivo* studies. The papers in this volume are based on extensive, careful observation and not on casual impressions, although some contain more systematic, extensive data-gathering than others—for example, the Knipe-Lewis study of coal miners.

A basic purpose of anthropological research is to delineate the culture patterns in the group. Margaret Mead (1953) has pointed out that sampling for the purpose of establishing patterns is different from sampling to determine the extent of variation within patterns, the kind of sampling with which sociologists are especially concerned. According to Mead, the anthropologist assumes that he is dealing with a system that can be delineated by the analysis of a small number of highly specified cases. As an example, she states that this is what the linguist does in determining the structure of a language. There is some risk in this assumption, as Mandelbaum (1953) points out in his argument that language has far less leeway for variation than other aspects of culture. He goes on to say that the only way to be sure that the pattern is really a pattern is to test to see if it recurs under a range of various kinds of observations.

Admittedly, the generalizations offered in the brief reports in this volume are tentative, and the authors call for further research to test them. It is clear that they recognize the difficulty of generalizing from their observations. Even so, problems arise in their reports, as for example in Duncan's study of urban mill workers. After concentrating his attention on the behavior of one family in the mill village area, he raises the question of whether or not the behavior in that family is "typical" of other mill workers. He then declares such a question to be "incongruous," stating that the behavior of the family derives from "the cultural assumptions and premises generally used and understood in the group." Duncan implies that the behavior is familiar to other families of workers, that is, it is "generic" to their assumptions and premises, but it is not necessarily practiced by them. Yet, in my opinion, he still has the task as an anthropologist of ascertaining what behavior is generally shared and approved of and what behavior is considered to be undesirable or deviant. He must also establish empirically whether or not the cultural assumptions and premises are indeed shared by the mill workers.

The anthropologist who studies his own culture is faced with the special problem of publishing results that will be read by those whom he has studied, as well as by a larger audience. Such publication invariably affects his relationships with the group studied and has consequences for follow-up research. No matter how hard the anthropologist may try, disguising the group and the individuals studied is in fact very difficult to accomplish. Thus, those of us who studied the town of "Kent" gave this community a pseudonym and changed the names of persons reported on in the studies. Nevertheless, a number of those in the town were able to see through the disguises. After my study was published (1958), friends in the mill village section invited me to return for a visit. But they advised me to bring my gun, saying, "it won't be for hunting rabbits either." In another example, publication of the study of a small town in upper New York state (Vidich and Bensman 1958) brought forth this reaction in a newspaper report:

> The people of the Village [Springdale] waited quite a while to get even with Art Vidich who wrote a Peyton Place-type book about their town.
> The featured float of the annual 4th of July parade followed an authentic copy of the jacket of the book, SMALL TOWN IN MASS SOCIETY, done large-scale. . . . Following the book cover came residents of [Springdale], riding masked in cars labeled with the fictitious names given them in the book.
> But the payoff was the final scene, a manure-spreader filled with very rich barnyard fertilizer, over which was bending an effigy with a sign around its neck, 'The Author.'[4]

Such difficulties resulting from publication are not peculiar to *in vivo* studies, for other disciplines also face this problem in publishing research on America. However, *in vivo* studies are especially subject to this problem, since they are more intimate and are limited to relatively small, identifiable groups.

Prospects: A Proposal

Where can anthropological studies in the South go from here? First, there can be a continuation of the two types of research presented in this volume, namely studies of small groups and of specific cultural patterns that appear to characterize the region as a whole.[5] Presumably these kinds of research would be carried out largely as they are now, by interested individuals who can secure financial support. While such studies would be sharply limited in size and confined largely to description and analysis, they would be nonetheless valuable in increasing knowledge about the regional subculture. We are reminded that however large the society being studied, there is always social interaction in small groups reflecting patterns of the society, and that, paradoxically, "only the most intensive studies of very limited areas of social life will make the most extensive comparative work possible" (Frankenberg 1966:149). At the same time, small-scale, individualistic, uncoordinated studies have obvious limitations in the generalizations they can reach and in the research techniques and strategies they can produce.

Another approach is to have teams of anthropologists use entire communities as the object of research. Arensberg contends that communities are the natural settings for *in vivo* study (1961), and Wissler, in his "Foreword" to the Lynds' *Middletown* some forty years ago, said, "Whatever else a social phenomenon is, it is a community affair" (1929:vi). I agree, for it is in the community that the business of life is largely carried on. It is there where parents begin the process of enculturation in their children, where schools continue the process in formal education, where churches and synagogues nourish religious belief and practice, where most occupational, political, and recreational activities are carried out. Such activities extend beyond the bounds of the community, to be sure, but it can be argued that their major focus is in the community, which Arensberg has termed the context "made up of natural and full human cooperative living, of living intergenerational and intersexual relationships, of ongoing cultural and interfamilial communication and transmission" (1954:120). Communities, then, are the units that provide the closest approximations to microcosms of the region and of the larger society. They therefore offer the most suitable settings for holistic study, far more so than the smaller groups within them.

I have previously discussed specific proposals for anthropological

study of communities in the American South (1967), and I will summarize and add to those proposals here. What is needed, I feel, is
to select several communities for systematic, long-range study. Although there have been a number of anthropological studies of
American communities in the past,[6] including some in the South,
there has been only one attempt at a systematic, interrelated study.
This is the one undertaken by John Gillin and the Institute for Research in Social Science at the University of North Carolina in the
late 1940s.[7] The number of communities studied, the particular ones
studied, and the extent of detail in the studies done would, of course,
depend on how much money is available and whether university
departments of anthropology would be interested in organizing such
research. If enough communities could be studied to make generalizations about the region valid, then the characteristics of the regional
subculture could be ascertained. Regardless of how many communities might be selected for study, the content of the studies could
follow this sequence. Initial, or base-line, studies would describe the
major patterns of behavior, belief, and attitudes found in each community. Comparison among the communities could indicate the extent of similarity and variation in what is assumed to be a regional
subculture.

After initial studies have been made, periodic, or time-interval
studies could be utilized to measure socio-cultural change in the communities.[8] If, in the communities studied, family and kinship ties
are still found to be among the special value emphases, as Gillin and
Murphy (1951) reported earlier, time-interval studies could show
what happens to these ties as movement toward the urbanization and
standardization of American culture continues. These and other
studies, done over a period of time and *in community context*, could
contribute a gread deal to our knowledge of how change takes place.
Many of the studies in this volume would lend themselves to time-
interval research; for example, such research could find out what
happens to Newton's peasant settlements as urbanization increases,
how Stanton's Houma Indians adjust their self-identify if they are
absorbed by the larger society, what happens to Harper's Irish
Travelers as their traditional bases of support and separateness change.
However, doing these studies in full community context would not
be possible until the community setting for each of these groups had
been delineated.

Research on Southern communities could also provide for the
testing of generalizations about culture and for the generation of
additional hypotheses. For example, tests for the normative theory

of racial prejudice (Westie 1964) could be undertaken. This theory is sometimes contrasted to psychological theories like the scapegoat theory (that prejudice is a function of frustration and aggression) or the authoritarian personality or psychological syndrome theory (that prejudice is the function of a fascistic or authoritarian personality make-up). The normative theory of prejudice assumes that prejudice is a cultural matter, a part of the normative order in the society in which it occurs. In this sense prejudice is conceived to be normal in that it has been acquired by most of those growing up in society, as have language and other aspects of culture. Prejudice, then, is assumed to be an aspect of the society's system of norms defining what ought to be, particularly in regard to how the individual members of the society ought to evaluate and interact with particular groups within and outside the society. In such a normative system both the person without prejudice and the person with excessive prejudice would be deviants. In testing this theory in the communities under study, the anthropologist would first delineate the patterning of prejudice, seeing to what extent it varied by social characteristics within each community and how it varied among the communities themselves. He could then determine if the norms were related to the patterning of prejudice and to variations in the patterning.

Developing base-line, time-interval, theory-testing studies in Southern communities is admittedly an ambitious program. Kimball (1955) has reminded us of what an enormous, time-consuming undertaking the study even of small communities is. Also, most anthropological community research has been in relatively small towns, and we still have much to learn about what is required for anthropological study of large cities.[9] Yet, I am convinced that such systematic, cooperative, long-term research is necessary if anthropology is to make its full contribution to the understanding of American culture. The enormity of the task could be allayed somewhat by working with social scientists from other fields, something Gillin has often advocated (1967:305). Also, some sort of institute for directing and coordinating such studies of the South, for example the Center for Southern Studies at Duke University, would be most helpful.

In his presidential address before the American Anthropological Association in 1965, Alexander Spoehr spoke about the importance of regional study in anthropology. Although he used as his example Oceania and did not speak about the United States or the South, I think that what he had to say is germane to my proposal for studying the American South:

We cannot get along without regional specialization, so long as empirical observation is the basis of archeology and ethnography. The problem of achieving maximum results is at least partly one of examining what a given region has to offer. Regions differ in their potentialities for fruitful work, and it may well be that in some, the major opportunities already have been exploited. We must spend more time in identifying these varying potentialities (1966:637).

I am convinced that anthropological study of the American South as a regional subculture of the United States offers tremendous potentialities for fruitful work.

NOTES

1. For additional discussions of these problems, see Arensberg (1954; 1961), Colson (1967), Gillin (1949; 1957), Kimball (1955), and Mitchell (1967).

2. For fieldwork experiences of anthropologists, including the problem of acceptance, see Spindler (1970).

3. The complications of translation become particularly acute in cross-cultural research, as I discovered in comparing race-awareness and racial attitudes of Americans and Hong Kong Chinese (Morland 1969; Morland and Williams 1969). The questions that had been used with Americans were translated into Chinese by my 19 Chinese students in a social anthropology class at the Chinese University of Hong Kong. I then asked Chinese colleagues who knew English well to translate the Chinese back into English. Significant differences from the original English appeared, so it was necessary for my students to work out these differences before arriving at a satisfactory translation.

4. Quoted in an editorial, "Freedom and Responsibility in Research: the 'Springdale' Case," *Human Organization*, 17:1-2.

5. Studies of "streetcorner" men by Whyte (1955) and Liebow (1967) are examples of research on small groups in large cities. See van Velsen (1967) and Kimball and Pearsall (1955) for other approaches to delimitation.

6. Most of these are listed in Mandelbaum, *et al.* (1961:265-269).

7. Called "Field Studies in the Modern Culture of the South." Publications include Gillin and Murphy (1951), Rubin (1951), Lewis (1955), Morland (1958).

8. For one such time-interval study, see Morland (1964).

9. Developments in the field of urban anthropology can be helpful with this problem. See, for example, Eddy (1968).

REFERENCES

Arensberg, Conrad M., 1954. The Community-Study Method. *American Journal of Sociology* 60:109-124.

------------------------ 1955. American Communities. *American Anthropologist* 57:1143-1162.

------------------------ 1961. The Community as Object and as Sample. *American Anthropologist* 63:241-264.

Colson, Elizabeth, 1967. The Intensive Study of Small Sample Communities. In *The Craft of Social Anthropology*, A. L. Epstein, ed. (London: Tavistock), pp. 3-15.

Frankenberg, Ronald, 1966. British Community Studies: Problems of Synthesis. In *The Social Anthropology of Complex Societies*, Michael Banton, ed. (New York: Praeger), pp. 123-149.

Eddy, Elizabeth M., ed., 1968. *Urban Anthropology: Research Perspectives and Strategies*, Southern Anthropological Society Proceedings, No. 2 (Athens, Georgia: University of Georgia Press).

Gillin, John, 1949. Methodological Problems in the Anthropological Study of Modern Cultures. *American Anthropologist* 51:392-399.

———————————— 1957. The Application of Anthropological Knowledge to Modern Mass Society: An Anthropologist's View. *Human Organization* 15:24-29.

———————————— 1967. More Complex Cultures for Anthropologists. *American Anthropologist* 69:301-305.

Gillin, John and Emmett J. Murphy, 1951. Notes on Southern Culture Patterns. *Social Forces* 29:422-432.

Gluckman, Max and Fred Eggan, 1966. Introduction. In *The Social Anthropology of Complex Societies*, Michael Banton, ed. (New York: Praeger), pp. xi-xliii.

Herskovits, Melville J., 1955. *Cultural Anthropology* (New York: Knopf).

Kimball, Solon T., 1955. Problems of Studying American Culture. *American Anthropologist* 57:1131-1142.

Kimball, Solon T. and Marion Pearsall, 1955. Event Analysis as an Approach to Community Study. *Social Forces* 34:58-63.

Lantis, Margaret, 1955. Introduction: The U.S.A. as Anthropologists See It. *American Anthropologist* 57:1113-1120.

Lewis, Hylan, 1955. *Blackways of Kent* (Chapel Hill: University of North Carolina Press).

Liebow, Elliott, 1967. *Tally's Corner* (Boston: Little, Brown).

Mandelbaum, David G., 1953. On the Study of National Character. *American Anthropologist* 55:174-187.

Mandelbaum, David G., Gabriel W. Lasker, and Ethel M. Albert, eds., 1963. *Resources for the Teaching of Anthropology*, Memoir 95 of the American Anthropological Association.

Mead, Margaret, 1949. *Male and Female* (New York: Morrow).

———————————— 1953. National Character. In *Anthropology Today: An Encyclopedic Inventory*, prepared under the chairmanship of A. L. Kroeber (Chicago: University of Chicago Press), pp. 642-667.

Mitchell, J. Clyde, 1967. On Quantification in Social Anthropology. In *The Craft of Social Anthropology*, A. L. Epstein, ed. (London: Tavistock), pp. 17-45.

Morland, J. Kenneth, 1958. *Millways of Kent* (Chapel Hill: University of North Carolina Press).

-------------------------- 1964. Kent Revisited: Blue-Collar Aspirations and Achievement. *In Blue-Collar World*, A. B. Shostak and W. Gomberg, eds. (Englewood Cliffs, N. J.: Prentice-Hall), pp. 134-143.

-------------------------- 1967. Anthropology and the Study of Culture, Society, and Community in the South. In *Perspectives on the South*, Edgar T. Thompson, ed. (Durham: Duke University Press), pp. 124-145.

-------------------------- 1969. Race Awareness among American and Hong Kong Chinese Children. *American Journal of Sociology* 75:360-374.

Morland, J. Kenneth and John E. Williams, 1969. Cross-Cultural Measurement of Racial and Ethnic Attitudes by the Semantic Differential. *Social Forces* 48:107-112.

Rubin, Morton, 1951. *Plantation County* (Chapel Hill: University of North Carolina Press).

Spindler, George D., ed. 1970. *Being an Anthropologist: Fieldwork in Eleven Cultures* (New York: Holt, Rinehart, Winston).

Spoehr, Alexander, 1966. The Part and the Whole: Reflections on the Study of a Region. *American Anthropologist* 68:629-640.

van Velsen, J., 1967. The Extended-case Method and Situational Analysis. In *The Craft of Social Anthropology*, A. L. Epstein, ed. (London: Tavistock), pp. 129-149.

Vidich, Arthur J. and Joseph Bensman, 1958. *Small Town in Mass Society* (Princeton, N. J.: Princeton University Press).

Westie, Frank R., 1964. Race and Ethnic Relations. In *Handbook of Modern Sociology*, R. E. L. Faris, ed. (Chicago: Rand McNally), pp. 576-618.

White, Leslie A., 1965. Anthropology 1964: Retrospect and Prospect. *American Anthropologist* 67:629-637.

Whyte, William Foote, 1955. *Street-Corner Society*, Revised Edition (Chicago: University of Chicago Press).

Wissler, Clark, 1929. Foreword. In *Middletown: A Study in Contemporary American Culture*, by Robert S. Lynd and Helen M. Lynd (New York: Harcourt, Brace), pp. v-vii.

The Contributors

Christopher Crocker is associate professor of anthropology at Duke University. He has done field work among the Eastern Bororo Indians of Brazil. His main professional specializations are symbolic behavior, South American ethnography, and kinship systems.

Ronald J. Duncan is assistant professor in the Department of Anthropology and in the School of Urban Life at Georgia State University. He has done field work in Mexico and in black and white communities in the United States. He is currently doing research on cultural influences on social change in urban communities in the United States. His theoretical interests are applied anthropology, culture theory and the individual, the personal experience of culture, and descriptive techniques in ethnography.

John Gordon is a graduate student in social anthropology at Harvard University. He plans to do field work in eastern Indonesia.

Jared Harper is instructor of anthropology in the Department of Sociology and Anthropology at Virginia Commonwealth University. He has done field work among Negroes and Irish Travelers in North Carolina and South Carolina. Currently he is working on a sociolinguistic study of soul lingo.

H. Eugene Hodges is a sociologist in the Georgia Department of Public Health, Division of Mental Health. His areas of interest are in the sociology of deviance and the sociology of mental health. He has done field work in the Southeastern United States on the Southern fundamentalist belief system and popular explanations of the causes of mental deviance.

Edward E. Knipe is assistant professor in the Department of Sociology and Anthropology at Virginia Commonwealth University. His primary interests are theoretical anthropology, urban anthropology, and socio-technical change.

Helen M. Lewis is assistant professor of sociology and anthropology at Clinch Valley College of the University of Virginia. Her main interests are in the Southern Appalachians, especially the coal mining regions. She has carried out research on the family structure of coal mining families and on changes in coal mining communities.

142

J. Kenneth Morland is chairman of the Department of Sociology and Anthropology at Randolph-Macon Woman's College. Most of his field work has been in the American South, but he has also done studies in New England and in Hong Kong. His current interest is in anthropological studies of complex societies, particularly in comparative studies of racial attitudes, connotations of color, and race awareness in young children. Among his publications is *Millways of Kent*, a study of mill village life in a Southern town.

Milton B. Newton, Jr. is assistant professor of geography in the Department of Geography and Anthropology, Louisiana State University. His main interest is in settlement geography approached from the cultural point of view; his main region of interest is the South. Other interests include the history of the frontier and settlement archeology.

William L. Partridge is a graduate student at the University of Florida in Gainesville. His particular field of interest is urban areas and the anthropology of complex societies.

James L. Peacock is associate professor and associate chairman in the Department of Anthropology, University of North Carolina, Chapel Hill. He has done field work in Singapore and Indonesia. His main interest is in the ideological dimension of modernization. Most recently he has been investigating the psycho-social ramifications of Muslim reformation movements in Southeast Asia.

Helen Phillips Keber is a graduate student in the Department of Anthropology at the University of North Carolina, Chapel Hill. Her interests include medical and symbolic anthropology, revitalization movements, and modernization. She is currently doing dissertation research on black divine healing.

Robert Sayers is currently a graduate student in the Department of Anthropology at the University of Arizona. His topical interests are several: folklife studies in rural areas of the United States, craft technologies, cultural change, and North American Indians. He has done field work in various of the Southeastern states. Most recently he has been interested in Southern Athapaskan ethnology.

Max E. Stanton is a Ph.D. candidate at the University of Oregon who is presently a visiting instructor of anthropology in the Department of Anthropology at Southwestern at Memphis. He has done field work among the Crow Indians and the Houma Indians. His topical interests are contemporary culture change among the North American Indians and among the Polynesians and adjacent peoples of Oceania. He is currently investigating sociocultural change among the urban Samoan immigrants in California and New Zealand.

Proceedings No. 5.
Red, White, and Black
Symposium on Indians in the Old South

Edited by Charles M. Hudson

SOUTHERN ANTHROPOLOGICAL SOCIETY

Founded 1966

Officers 1970-71

Contents

vi

Preface

THIS symposium was presented at the 1970 meeting of the Southern Anthropological Society in Athens, Georgia. Its purpose was to explore a subject on which anthropologists have been strangely silent: the Indians of the Old South. Although the Indians of the southeastern United States probably achieved the most complex social and cultural development north of Mexico, and although the Old South was a fascinating and richly documented complex society, our knowledge of both still contains large gaps. Indeed, in organizing this symposium I often encountered extreme difficulty in finding scholars who were willing or able to write papers on some of the subjects that had to be covered. So far as I could determine, disregarding conferences and symposia on Southeastern prehistory, no attempt has ever been made to bring anthropologists and other scholars together on the subject of Indians in the Old South. Therefore, it seemed particularly appropriate that the key symposium of the 1970 meeting of the Southern Anthropological Society be devoted to surveying what we know about the Southern Indians and to charting directions for future research. The symposium was organized with the assumption that the Old South was a complex society and consequently that successful research on it must be thoroughly multidisciplinary, requiring the skills and interests of anthropologists, sociologists, historians, geographers, linguists, and others.

All of the papers in this volume were presented at the symposium itself except the paper by John H. Peterson, Jr., written especially for this volume, and the paper by William S. Willis, Jr., reprinted from *The Journal of Negro History*. One hopes that these essays will make it clear that the Old South is an area where interesting and relevant anthropological research can be conducted. It can even be argued that the South is an area where anthropologists might gain insight into the ethical and moral assumptions that are now troubling

vii

their field. For example, the reluctance of social anthropologists to teach and do research in the South is puzzling in view of their ready willingness to do research in politically repressive societies in all parts of the world.

Many individuals helped in the planning and organization of this symposium. Charles Wynes gave me advice and encouragement from the very outset, and I regret that I was not able to succeed in following through on more of his suggestions. I am grateful to Marion Rice and Wilfrid Bailey and the Anthropology Curriculum Project for financial assistance. The following individuals generously gave me advice on particular matters: Clarence Bacote, Brewton Berry, W. Roger Buffalohead, Rupert Costo, Edward Dozier, Clement Eaton, Edward T. Price, Edgar Thompson, and the late James McBride Dabbs. And for various contributions to the symposium and its outcome I am grateful to Andrew Dreadfulwater, Peter B. Hammond, Scott McLemore, Hubert Ross, Robert Thomas, and Susan Tate. The symposium would have been far less successful had it not been for the hard work of David Hally, program chairman; Walter Ward, local arrangements chairman; and George S. Brooks and the staff of the Georgia Center for Continuing Education. As usual, I am grateful to my wife, Joyce Rockwood Hudson, and her Pollyanna-Episcopal world view.

Charles Hudson
SAS Editor

Introduction

CHARLES HUDSON

THREE Indians were once out hunting. One went after water and found a nice hole of water but was afraid to drink. Another went down to it, dipped his fingers in, and said, "It is good. Let us go into it." So he dived in and came out. When he came out he was white. From him came the white people. The second dived in and came out darker because the water was somewhat [muddy]. From him came the Indians. The third dived in and came out black because the water was now very [muddy]. From him came the Negroes. Just before the first man dived he felt of the rocks and they rattled. He did not tell the others that this was gold. They went on from there and the Indian found something else. The white man was told about this and he picked it up. It was a book. He asked the Indian to read this but he could not. The white man, however, could read it, and it was to tell him about this gold. The book gave him this advantage. "The Nokhlas (whites) were terrible people to take the lead."[1]

In preliterate societies people carry all they know about the past in their heads." This means that they must forget a great deal, committing to tradition only the events that are socially most relevant. Anthropologists who have done research on the historical traditions of preliterate people have found that they do not exclude facts from history randomly, but rather by a process that has been called "structural amnesia" (Barnes 1947; Goody 1968). This means that those events which have little relevance to the structure of their society are relegated to historical oblivion. For example, in preliterate societies in which one's social position depends upon one's genealogy, it is obviously impossible to remember all of one's ancestors. What usually happens is that people in such societies have clear traditions about their most remote ancestors, who lived in mythical time before the present world order began, and they have similarly clear traditions about their ancestors in recent generations, but the genealogy in be-

1

tween is "telescoped." The ancestors in between are shifted around and dropped from memory, the victims of social irrelevance or changed conditions. Traditions about the remote, original ancestors are ideological charters for relationships with various outgroups (strangers, foreigners, enemies), while traditions about the recently dead govern most day-to-day, in-group relationships (kinsmen, neighbors). The ancestors in between, neither distant nor close, bear upon relationships which are ambivalent or changing.

A somewhat different kind of structural amnesia can be seen in the history of the Old South. The whites in the South have had a well-known monopoly on power and wealth, and the history they have written is so white it has become embarrassing. When blacks or Indians show up in the history of the Old South, they show up as objects or as background features, and more often than not they do not show up at all. On the other hand, when one reads the accounts that anthropologists and Indian historians have written about the same period, they are pure red; the whites mostly show up as outsiders, invading and destroying, and the blacks are even less evident here than in the work by white historians. Moreover, the recent florescence of research by black historians, realigning and amplifying history to fit the changing social order in the modern South, is too black, this being an understandable bias, but a bias nonetheless.

What this Southern structural amnesia misses, of course, is that the Old South was a complex social entity composed of three races—red, white, and black, leaving aside for the moment various mixtures—and these racial divisions were cross-cut with cultural and economic divisions. Any approach to Southern history which fails to take account of these complexities in the larger social situation must necessarily fail to adequately account for any major part of the history of the Old South. Although we are like our preliterate brothers in having a biased view of the past, our being literate makes us different from them in enabling us to recover something of the past and examine it anew. And in view of recent social changes in the South and in the rest of the country, this is an opportune time to do some historical re-thinking.

Toward achieving a more comprehensive anthropological and historical understanding of the Old South, the first part of this volume consists of papers surveying research in several specialized approaches to the past, namely two specialized fields of anthropology—physical anthropology and archaeology—and two fields closely related to anthropology—geography and linguistics. Although some historians may question the relevance of these approaches, many other historians are increasingly realizing along with anthropologists that we need to explore every avenue to the past that is available to us. As Louis De Vorsey shows in his paper in this volume, the Old South is a historical period upon which the historical geographer and the anthropologist can fruitfully collaborate, each amplifying the results of the other. Anthropologists have always been concerned with the relationship between man and the natural world, but they have not kept up with historical geographers in exploring all of the different sources which hold this information, and especially they have neglected old maps. De Vorsey calls for collaboration between geography and anthropology like that advocated by Carl O. Sauer and Alfred L. Kroeber at Berkeley several decades ago.

Like De Vorsey, William Pollitzer is concerned with reconstructing a feature of the natural world in the Old South, namely the biological characteristics of the Southern Indians, their morphology, classification, and evolution. Again echoing De Vorsey, he calls for a kind of collaboration between physical anthropologists and scholars in other fields that is all too rare. The complexity of the Old South is evident in Pollitzer's review of research on the physical anthropology of the Southern Indians. Not only were there significant biological differences among the Southern Indians, but the human genetics of the Old South was also complicated by the interbreeding of Indians with whites and blacks.

In Mary Haas's succinct survey of research on Southeastern Indian languages we see that the Old South was also diverse with respect to the languages that were spoken. In fact, she underscores the little known fact that in all of North America the Southeast was second in linguistic diversity only to the west coast of the United States and Canada. The languages spoken by the Southern Indians belonged to no less than four language families, containing languages as different from each other as English is different from Mandarin Chinese, and moreover we have some evidence on about a half dozen additional languages, most of which are remotely related to these four families, but some are perhaps related to even further language families. And the linguistic diversity in the Old South does not end here. Considerable dialectical variation, both social and regional, existed in the English spoken by the colonists (Brooks 1935; Kurath and McDavid 1961; Stephenson 1968), not to speak of French, Spanish, and German, the former remaining an important language in Louisiana to this day (Morgan 1960; McDavid 1967). The black slaves brought here from Africa spoke a variety of African languages (Turner 1949); and an argot derived from Irish Gaelic (Harper and Hudson n.d.) was introduced into the South in the nineteenth century. With all this in mind it would be foolish to conclude that linguistic diversity in the Old South ends here.

That difficult area where prehistoric archaeology touches history is surveyed in this volume by David Hally. Here, even more than elsewhere, collaboration between anthropologists and historians is essential. Good archaeology is both expensive and time-consuming, and Hally makes it clear that both money and time for extensive archaeological excavation of historically identified sites are desperately needed. And this need is made all the more acute as sites are progressively destroyed by pot hunters, construction companies, and the Corps of Engineers. We could almost regard the scandalous destruction of archaeological sites in the South as a second Indian removal. In the first removal we got rid of the Indians, and in the second removal we are wiping out their last *in situ* traces, aborting their last feeble chances of winning a place in history.

Archaeology has had a rather secure place in the Southeast for some time, but an indigenous ethnology or social anthropology (the terms can be used interchangeably) is quite recent. Archaeology took root early for several reasons. For one thing, the large mounds and the "moundbuilder" myths that grew up around them in the Southeast were invitations to treasure-hunters and collectors, thus making a lasting impression on the general public. Along with this the idea of excavating antiquities appealed to elitist intellectuals. Moreover, poverty in the South was an indirect stimulus to archaeology: the first large scale excavations were supported by the TVA and the WPA during the Depression as an ideal way to spend money on "nonproductive" labor. Looking at the other side of the coin, one factor that slowed the development of social anthropology was that it directly challenged the racist ideology that troubled the South in the past and continues to do so in lesser degree in the present (Willis 1970:37). Thus, the social anthropology that has been done on the aboriginal peoples of the South has been rather like that in an under-developed country today, namely the social anthropologists doing the research were all outsiders who carefully avoided asking too many embarrassing questions. The most important social anthropological research on the Southern Indians has been done by three men: Frank Speck, a professor of anthropology at the University of Pennsylvania whose main work was with the Catawbas (e.g., 1913; 1934; 1935; 1939) and the Yuchis (1909); James Mooney, from the Smithsonian, who did excellent ethnographic and historical research on the

Cherokees (e.g., 1891; 1900); and John Swanton, also from the Smithsonian, whose favorite people were the Creeks (e.g., 1922; 1928a; 1928b), but who did research on many other groups in the Southeast (e.g., 1911; 1928c), and who wrote several basic works dealing with the Southeast as a whole (e.g., 1929; 1946).[3]

Our debt to these three social anthropologists can scarcely be exaggerated, but their work suffers from some startling blind spots. One shortcoming is that they examined Indian societies as if they were isolated social entities, existing apart from a complex Southern society. The fact is, the Southern Indians began losing their autonomy as soon as they became entangled in the fur trade, enslaved by planters, or involved as combatants in colonial rivalries. Moreover, as William Willis has pointed out, with few exceptions social anthropologists literally turned their heads the other way to avoid blacks in the South (1970:34).

This is the reason why the second part of this symposium takes the form it does. Our understanding of the Southern Indians and of other social and cultural groups in the Old South will be deficient until we come to understand the complex social situation in which they were all participants. As soon as we begin apprehending it as a complex system, we begin to appreciate some of the striking gaps in Southern history which exist in spite of the great amount that has been written on the subject. One searches Southern history in vain for an adequate account of the mixed-bloods whose descendants live in fairly sizable numbers in the South today;[4] one finds surprisingly little coverage of the Indians themselves, particularly those who remained in the South after removal; and the historians tell us rather less than we would like to know about the non-Plantation whites (Owsley 1949).

The basic structure of society in the Old South resembled the structure of the so-called "plural societies," for the most part products of European colonialism, which economists and anthropologists have decribed in various parts of the world and which may date back to the period of Roman expansion or even earlier (Smith 1965; Morris 1967; Despres 1968). Namely, the Old South consisted of people categorized into several distinct social and cultural sections, each with distinctive social institutions, broadly divisible into red, white, and black, who lived in the same place but who did not mix (at least, not in socially approved ways), and one of these sections, the whites, held a monopoly on power which became more absolute as time went on. One would not wish to draw this parallel between the Old South and various European colonial societies too far, but certainly the comparison gives us categories of social understanding we would not otherwise have (Hudson 1970:52-80). Calling the Old South plural carries with it the recognition that it conformed to this ideal type more closely in the middle period of its history than in the early colonial period or in more recent times, and calling the Old South a society carries with it the recognition that it was beset with deep divisions and bitter conflict.

The apex of society in the Old South was occupied by whites, and the apex of white society was occupied by planters who owned large amounts of land and many black slaves. As F. N. Boney argues in his paper in this volume, when the Southern mystique is stripped away these men were basically capitalists who were out to make a buck. Though small in number, their right to control things, while not absolute, was rarely questioned. The political ascendancy of the planters depended upon their being able to perpetuate the divisions within society while not allowing them to break out in uncontrollable conflict. For example, the planters recognized a possible revolutionary threat in the whites who were less well off than they. This was not so much the case with yeoman farmers operating family farms in the back country, who were occasionally opposed to black slavery but even more opposed to free blacks. But as Joseph Brent points out, the freedmen (poor whites who had worked out their period of indenture) and their descendants were a different matter. Because there was no place for them in the structure of the plantation economy, their alienation was always a threat. Many·of them had come from the slums and prisons of England, and they carried with them attitudes and beliefs learned there. So long as social mobility was possible, they imitated their former masters and tried to become rich and powerful themselves. The poor whites were further appeased by the presence of a large and utterly powerless class of black slaves to which all whites, however poor, felt superior and, hence, in some sense equal to other whites.

The relations between whites and Indians varied as time went on. In general, the whites only tolerated the Indians so long as they had a use for them. They exploited the Indians first of all in the fur trade, and also as slaves, but as slaves they were never as satisfactory as blacks were, partly because when they escaped they could easily live off the land and find refuge with their fellows (Lauber 1913). The more powerful tribes or "nations," as they were called, were useful allies in the rivalry among the English, French, and Spanish colonists. However, John Peterson makes the point that as soon as this rivalry drew to a close, the Indians' days were numbered. It then became expedient to "remove" them to the West, expropriate their land, and turn it over to whites. As Joseph Brent points out, this was yet another way the white elite had of buying off dissatisfaction among the non-plantation whites. Not all of the Indians went west, though the ones who remained behind could live only a precarious existence as squatters on marginal land. Peterson discusses the fact that very little is known about this phase of the history of the Southern Indians, and he is perhaps the first to clearly perceive the dilemma of these Indians who remained behind. It was simply that they could neither be white land-owners nor black slaves, and this left them with essentially nothing.

The relationship between white masters and black slaves has been examined in great detail by historians. What is perhaps not so well known is the fact that even in the early eighteenth century South Carolinians were as afraid of slave revolts as they were of hostile Indians. And the slaves did revolt, the Nat Turner rebellion being only the most well known of several. As a defensive measure, the whites took elaborate precautions to keep the blacks ignorant and divided, even to the point of denying them membership in Christianity.

What the whites feared most was an alliance between blacks and Indians. William Willis in an article reprinted in this volume presents evidence that the whites carried out a policy of divide and conquer by setting the Indians against the blacks, just as they had a more explicit policy of setting Indians against Indians. Nor was this policy of creating antagonisms between blacks and Indians limited to the English: in 1730 Governor Perrier of New France ordered black slaves to attack and kill the handful of surviving Chawasha Indians for the ulterior purpose of creating hostility between the races (Swanton 1911:30-31). Proof that the fear of red-black alliances was well founded came in the bloody Second Seminole War, lasting from 1835 until 1842, in which escaped black slaves and Seminole Indians fought the whites to a standstill in a long, tenacious war somewhat reminiscent of the American military involvement in Viet Nam. When some Southern Indians, notably the Cherokees, themselves adopted the institution of black slavery along with other aspects of Southern culture, the whites must have had mixed feelings. It must have pleased them because the Indians set themselves against the blacks by enslaving them, but it must have angered them because the Indians were by the same token becoming uppity (Abel 1915-1925).

Understanding the Old South as a social system is only part of the problem. The other task is to understand the ideological superstructure of this social system (Jordan 1968). Indeed it can be

argued that the ideology of the Old South was more "peculiar" than
the institution of slavery itself. Joseph Brent comments on the dualism in white thought, the opposition of white to black, and the opposition of both of these to red, a category of humanity that was
literally thought to be a part of nature. In Southern thought these
were "pure" categories, each associated with a distinct stereotype.
It is for this reason, perhaps, that the mixed-bloods—people like the
Lumbee of North Carolina, the Brass Ankles of South Carolina, the
Melungeons of Tennessee, the Cajans of Alabama, the Redbones of
Louisiana, and many others—have always been such puzzling, "mysterious" people (Price 1953; Berry 1963). Because they were anomalous
with respect to fundamental categories, in some sense they threatened
to introduce disorder and chaos into the social universe. They were
not white, but they refused to be treated as blacks, and sometimes,
but not always, they refused to be treated as Indians, while at other
times they asked to be treated as Indians but were refused. Their
solution usually was to stay off to themselves, living poor lives on
marginal land, much as the Indians who escaped removal did. They
are still very much present in the contemporary South, and in many
cases their social isolation continues, as illustrated by the fact that
the names by which they are known generally have local significance
only. It should be obvious that "mixed-blood," as used here, designates
a social category rather than mere genetic intermixture. This becomes
clear when we realize that a number of individuals whose parents
were of different races (usually a white father and an Indian mother)
became prominent among the Southeastern Indians. Some of them became wealthy planters, owning large planations and many slaves.

In general the white stereotype of the Indian was more variable
than that of the black. F. N. Boney mentions the fact that Thomas
Jefferson admired certain features of the Indians' stereotype and suggested that it would be a good thing if poor whites would take Indian
wives. Even elite whites could admit to having a trace of Indian blood,
though it was better if it came from a "noble" strain. Perhaps Jefferson could hold this rather charitable view because Virginia had
long since solved her "Indian problem." Other elite whites who were
closer to the frontier regarded Indians as little better than animals.

Perhaps the most fruitful way of counteracting the Southern
structural amnesia discussed earlier is to scrutinize the official ideology
of the Old South and the elaborate fictions which preserved its integrity, and to use this as a basis for calling existing historical
knowledge and interpretation into question. One ideological assumption in the Old South was that the Indians were a part of nature, and

like beasts they were naturally blood-thirsty, killing for the pleasure of it. Are we to accept this as an explanation of why the Southern Indians were so divided among themselves? What was behind the political divisions among the Southern Indians? Are we to accept A. L. Kroeber's explanation of low aboriginal population in the Southeast as being a result of insane, constantly attritional warfare (Kroeber 1939)?

Another ideological assumption was that the Indians naturally hated the blacks, and the blacks, poor superstitious things, were naturally terrified of Indians. Some evidence suggests that this line of thought explains why South Carolinians tolerated Indians within their borders long after they had the means to drive them out. The rationale was that the Indians could be used as instruments to intimidate the blacks (Hudson 1970:56-58; Willis 1970:45). But was the handful of impoverished Catawbas in early nineteenth century South Carolina as fierce and as loathing of blacks as they were believed to be? And were the blacks truly terrified when an Indian approached? Was the Second Seminole War (sometimes called the Negro and Indian war) as inconsequential as most Southern histories would lead us to believe? Why were the Creeks and Seminoles more tolerant of escaped blacks than the Cherokees were (Willis 1970)?

A further assumption was that the Indians should be kept apart from the poor whites because the Indians, as innocent children of nature, would be corrupted by the uncouth ways of the whites. Historians have, of course, already asked whether elite whites did the Southern Indians a favor by "removing" them to safety on the other side of the Mississippi River, far from the unseemly ways of white trash. We may also ask whether these poor whites did not acquire much valuable knowledge from the Indians, and whether this knowledge did not in fact make a significant contribution to Southern culture. A considerable number of people with a European cultural background, black, white, and mixed-bloods, moved in and lived among the Indians even though doing so was illegal or disapproved. What kinds of social relationships existed between these people and their Indian hosts?

It would be unwise to claim that what has been suggested here is a cure-all for Southern structural amnesia. Perhaps the most important message of the papers included in this volume is that the Old South was full of cultural and social complexities, and that although these complexities are usually concealed or forgotten, many of them can be inquired into and explained in a systematic fashion. And just as one can learn a great deal about the structure of a tent by studying the wrinkles in its fabric, one can learn much about the structure of the Old South by studying these complexities. In particular, further research on the mixed-bloods promises to tell us much about the nature of the Old South. A second message is that if there was ever a fit subject for multidisciplinary research, it is the Old South. Much research remains to be done, and it should be done from as many intellectual vantage points as possible.

NOTES

1. A Creek Indian myth collected by John Swanton (1929:75). It is probably incomplete.

2. I am grateful to Wilfrid Bailey, F. N. Boney, David Hally, and Michael Olien, who read and criticized this introductory essay. However, I alone am responsible for its content.

3. Additional and generally more recent contributions to the ethnography and history of the Southern Indians have come from Leonard Broom, Fred Eggan, Charles Fairbanks, Raymond Fogelson, William Gilbert, John Goggin, John Gulick, Harriet Kupferer, Alexander Spoehr, William Sturtevant, and others. About one-third of them can claim to be "indigenous" social anthropologists, this being some measure of the development of the underdeveloped South.

4. But see the recent study of the Coe Ridge people of Kentucky by William Lynwood Montell (1970) and forthcoming research by Peter B. Hammond.

REFERENCES

Abel, Annie Heloise, 1915-1925. *Slaveholding Indians*, 3 vols. (Cleveland: Arthur C. Clark Company).

Barnes, J. A., 1947. The Collection of Genealogies. *Rhodes-Livingstone Journal: Human Problems in British Central Africa*, V.

Berry, Brewton, 1963. *Almost White* (New York: Macmillan).

Brooks, Cleanth, 1935. *The Relation of the Alabama-Georgia Dialect to the Provincial Dialects of Great Britain* (Baton Rouge: Louisiana State University Press).

Despres, Leo A., 1968. Anthropological Theory, Cultural Pluralism, and the Study of Complex Societies. *Current Anthropology* 9:3-16.

Goody, Jack (ed.), 1968. *Literacy in Traditional Societies* (Cambridge: At the University Press).

Harper, Jared and Charles Hudson, n.d. Irish Traveler Cant. *Journal of English Linguistics*, in press.

Hudson, Charles, 1970. *The Catawba Nation* (Athens, Georgia: University of Georgia Press).

Jordan, Winthrop D., 1968. *White Over Black: American Attitudes Toward the Negro, 1550-1812* (Chapel Hill, N. C.: University of North Carolina Press).

Kroeber, Alfred L., 1939. *Cultural and Natural Areas of Native North America*, University of California Publications in American Archaeology and Ethnology, Vol. 38 (Berkeley: University of California Press).

Kurath, Hans and Raven I. McDavid, 1961. *The Pronunciation of English in the Atlantic States* (Ann Arbor: University of Michigan Press, 1961).

Lauber, Almon Wheeler, 1913. *Indian Slavery in Colonial Times Within the Present Limits of The United States* (New York: Columbia University Press).

McDavid, Raven I., 1967. Needed Research in Southern Dialects. In *Perspectives* on the South: Agenda for Research, Edgar T. Thompson ed. (Durham, N. C.: Duke University Press), pp. 113-124.

Montell, William Lynwood, 1970. *The Saga of Coe Ridge: A Study in Oral History* (Knoxville: University of Tennessee Press).

Morgan, Raleigh, 1960. The Lexicon of St. Martin Creole. *Anthropological Linguistics* 2:7-29.

Mooney, James, 1891. *The Sacred Formulas of the Cherokees*. 7th Annual Report of the Bureau of American Ethnology (Washington: GPO), pp. 301-397.

————— —., 1900. *Myths of the Cherokees*. 19th Annual Report of the Bureau of American Ethnology, Part 1 (Washington: GPO).

Morris, H. S., 1967. Some Aspects of the Concept Plural Society. *Man*. 2:169-184.

Owsley, Frank L., 1949. *Plain Folk of the Old South* (Baton Rouge: Louisiana State University Press, 1949).

Price, Edward T., 1953. A Geographic Analysis of White-Negro-Indian Racial Mixtures in Eastern United States. *Annals of the Association of American Geographers* 43:138-155.

Smith, M. G., 1965. *The Plural Society in the British West Indies* (Berkeley, Los Angeles: University of California Press).

Speck, Frank, 1909. *Ethnology of the Yuchi Indians*. Anthropological Publications of the University Museum, University of Pennsylvania, Vol. 1, No. 1 (Philadelphia).

————— —., 1913. Some Catawba Texts and Folklore. *The Journal of American Folklore* 26:319-330.

————————, 1934. *Catawba Texts*. Columbia University Contributions to Anthropology, Vol. 24 (New York: Columbia University Press).

————— ., 1935. Siouan Tribes of the Carolinas as Known from Catawba, Tutelo, and Documentary Sources. *American Anthropologist* 37:201-225.

—————, 1939. The Catawba Nation and its Neighbors. *North Carolina Historical Review* 16:404-417.

Stephenson, Edward A., 1968, The Beginnings of the Loss of Postvocalic /r/ in North Carolina. *Journal of English Linguistics* 2:57-77.

Swanton, John, 1911. *Indian Tribes of the Lower Mississippi Valley and Adjacent Coast of the Gulf of Mexico*, Bureau of American Ethnology Bulletin No. 43 (Washington: GPO).

—————, 1922. *Early History of the Creek Indians and Their Neighbors*, Bureau of American Ethnology Bulletin No. 73 (Washington: GPO).

—————, 1928a. *Social Organization and Social Usages of the Indians of the Creek Confederacy*, 42nd Annual Report of the Bureau of American Ethnology (Washington GPO), pp. 23-472.

—————, 1928b. *Religious Beliefs and Medical Practices of the Creek Indians*, 42nd Annual Report of the Bureau of American Ethnology (Washington: GPO), pp. 473-672.

—————, 1928c. *Social and Religious Beliefs and Usages of the Chickasaw Indians*, 44th Annual Report of the Bureau of American Ethnology (Washington: GPO), pp. 169-273.

—————, 1929. *Myths and Tales of the Southeastern Indians*, Bureau of American Ethnology Bulletin No. 88 (Washington: GPO).

—————, 1946. *The Indians of the Southeastern United States*, Bureau of American Ethnology No. 137 (Washington: GPO).

Turner, Lorenzo D. *Africanisms in the Gullah Dialect* (Chicago: University of Chicago Press).

Willis, William S., Jr. 1970. Anthropology and Negroes on The Southern Colonial Frontier. In *The Black Experience in America*, James C. Curtis and Lewis L. Gould, eds. (Austin and London: University of Texas Press), pp. 33-50.

Part I

Early Maps As a Source in the Reconstruction of Southern Indian Landscapes

Louis De Vorsey, Jr.

In his recent review article entitled, "Geographic Perspectives In Anthropology," Marvin Mikesell, a geographer, convincingly demonstrated the many close links which have existed between the two man-oriented disciplines—geography and anthropology (1967). He stressed the youthfulness, common ancestry, and the common intellectual roots which have shaped their developments through the past three quarters of a century. Both anthropology and geography were shown to have served as valuable academic bridges in recurring attempts to span the widening gulf between the physical and social sciences.

The concept of culture, which has formed the keystone of anthropology's impressive structure, is increasingly recognized as occupying a like position in modern geography. The academic geographer of the present day has moved far from the overriding preoccupation with the determinative role of the physical environment which characterized his discipline four or five decades ago. Rather, he now tends to shape his research and quest for understanding into the form of questions which ask how a particular group perceives, organizes, and utilizes its physical environment or habitat at any given point in time. Man, operating within the context of a culture group, has emerged as the active agent in the modern geographer's study of areal differentiation. Most modern geographers would agree with Charles Frake in concluding that man is "unique among organisms, [carving] . . . his ecological niches primarily with cultural tools of his own invention rather than with biological specializations" (1962:53). In a large measure this new direction in geographical thought has been due to

12

the lessons which geographers have learned from anthropologists and others. Fortunately, American academic geography, like anthropology, has been characterized by a high degree of eclecticism.

Mikesell concluded his review by expressing concern over the paucity of examples of cooperative studies undertaken by workers in anthropology and geography. He mentioned the fact that over four decades have passed since the eminent geographer Carl O. Sauer called attention to the overlapping interests of geographers and anthropologists. Sauer, in 1925, suggested that a gradual coalescence of the disciplines might "represent the first of a series of fusions into a larger science of man" (Sauer 1963:350n). Mikesell found the absence of this fusion "regrettable but understandable." He observed that "even the most uninhibited scholar is constrained, to some extent, by professional affiliations and the departmental structure of our universities." The boundary separating anthropology and geography departments might be likened to many of those marking the map of modern Africa —more arbitrary than logical. This long-standing academic demarcation has encouraged introspective methodologies and what Mikesell referred to as the "academic counterpart to nationalism."

Academic "nationalism" has given way to "internationalism" in this symposium on Indians in the Old South. Anthropologists are here joined with historians, linguists, and geographers to gain insight into the life and rich culture of the South's first Americans.

HISTORICAL GEOGRAPHY AND HISTORICAL CARTOGRAPHY

Historical geography is a subfield of geography which has traditionally had strong ties with both anthropology and history. Currently the parameters and objectives of research in historical geography are the subject of lively debate by practitioners (Newcomb 1969). Most researchers cultivating this row of the geographic garden would, however, agree that the reconstruction of past landscapes is both a valid and important goal for their research (Broek 1932:7-10). It might be further asserted that the reconstruction of a region's landscape on the eve of its occupation by a new and distinctive culture group would be of considerable value to workers in a variety of disciplines including anthropology and history as well as geography. Such a reconstructed landscape could, in some measure, be viewed as the product of the culture group being dispossessed, in this case the Southern Indians during the eighteenth century. Similarly, such a reconstructed landscape might be employed as a datum base from which to gauge the impact of the dispossessing culture group in its regional setting through time. In our case the dispossessing group would be the Anglo-European cultivators and their African slaves of the same century.

In his attempt to reconstruct a landscape of the past, the historical geographer should employ as many relevant and illuminating sources as possible. The range of these sources is broad and their character is varied. Early maps, showing as they do the spatial arrangement of landscape features, are, however, of particular value as sources in any attempted reconstruction.

Early maps, like maps of the present day, are, in their primary conception, conventionalized pictures of the earth's surface as seen from above, to which lettering, symbols, and color are added for feature identification and clarity. The word "picture" is used here in its broadest sense to include what is believed about any area of earth space as well as what is cognized and objectively determined to exist in the area. Early maps, however, differ from modern maps in many important respects. In the words of R. A. Skelton they are, "the end-product of a complex series of processes—assembly of information from various sources and in different forms, both graphic and textual; assimilation to the mapmaker's geographical ideas, to transmitted cartographic patterns, or to his political interest; and the resultant stages of compilation, control, adjustment, and copying" (1965:4). The collection, study, and analysis of early maps are the essential elements of historical cartography. Historical cartography in turn is frequently an ancillary to the study of historical geography (Koeman 1968).

Researchers interested in past Southern Indian landscapes are fortunate in having an excellent guide to the early maps of the region. This is the volume entitled *The Southeast In Early Maps* (Cumming 1962). Also of considerable value as an introduction to the cartographic history of the South is Volume VI (1966) of the journal, *The Southeastern Geographer*. This was a special topic issue which contained articles by Cumming (1966), De Vorsey (1966a), Friis (1966), and Ristow (1966).

Early maps should be considered as extremely valuable historical documents which require somewhat specialized treatment in their reading and analysis (Harley 1968). As Skelton indicated in the statement quoted above, early maps were seldom if ever constructed out of the rigorously controlled processes of measurement and computation which are taken for granted in our scientifically compiled modern maps. As a result, they frequently show a mixture of fact and fiction, both of which can contribute to a clearer understanding of the geography of the past. Facts, such as coastlines, stream courses, animal licks, vegetation cover, roads, and settlements, are liable to change and alteration through time so a contemporary view of them at selected times in the past is indispensable (Coppock 1968).

Misconceptions such as the locating of deserts, lakes, rivers, and oceans where they did not exist in nature provide equally valuable insights. In this case, however, the insights afford a better appreciation of the motives, beliefs, and biases of those long departed individuals who lent life and significance to the landscapes of the past. Varrazano, in his passion to find an easy route to the Orient, reported the Carolina Outer Banks as a long narrow isthmus which blocked his entry to the "original sea . . . which is the one without doubt which goes about the extremity of India, China, and Cathay." Thus, in his mind the broad waters of Pamlico, Albermarle, and Core Sounds became the eastern margin of a beckoning ocean lapping the Oriental littoral somewhere to the west. This geographical misconception was an exciting idea to the sixteenth century European geographers and cartographers who heard it. It became incorporated in many maps of the period and did much to stimulate an interest in exploratory voyages and enterprises which led ultimately to the establishment of the Roanoke Colony (Cumming 1966:8). The satirist Swift drew attention to such cartographical shortcomings when he penned his now well known quatrain which read:

> So Geographers, in Afric Maps,
> With savage pictures fill their gaps,
> And, o'er inhabitable downs,
> Place elephants for want of towns.

Early maps can be viewed as "Cartographic Portraits" of regions of earth space. Just as a good portrait in its subjective rendering may reveal as much about the artist as about his subject, so an early map can reveal both the qualities of the landscape depicted and its author's background, training, and interests, in nearly equal measure. The understanding of early maps can be enhanced through a thorough knowledge of the historical circumstances surrounding their compilation and execution just as a viewer's appreciation of a portrait is enhanced by a knowledge of the painter and his school. The user of an early map, then, should not rest content with a superficial study of its content of lines and patterns. He should probe into the historical circumstances which surrounded its original creation by asking: Who was the cartographer? Why did he draw this particular map? For whom was this map originally intended? Answers to these and similar questions will enable the researcher to utilize these early "map documents" more effectively.

Early maps represent sources of inestimable value to the researcher interested in both the current and past cultural and physical landscapes of a region. They can show zones of change and dynamism as well as continuity and stability in those landscapes. They can show which features and patterns of the present scene are relics of past periods and conditions. They may suggest the reasons for present day patterns and relationships which are inexplicable in purely contemporary terms. They can help explain human actions and habits which are also not comprehensible in the light of present conditions alone. They can illustrate the process of human modification of the environment in a region. They can illustrate too, the process of natural change in a region. They can remind us of forgotten resources. Finally, they may help us all to come a bit closer to the civilizing realization that the present is but the past flowing into the future.

Employing Early Maps: Two Examples

Early maps exist in a wide variety of formats and scales, depending on the skill and intent of those original cartographers who created them. Some are little more than crude sketches while others are intricately detailed, amazingly accurate, and artistically executed. Some show broad regions or a whole continent while others depict small areas of only a few hundred acres or less. Rather than discuss maps in general terms only, it seems advisable to demonstrate their use and value in two recent attempts to reconstruct aspects of the mid-eighteenth century Southern Indian landscape. The first of these utilized a large number of small and medium scale manuscript and printed maps to reconstruct the boundary line which separated the British colonies from the Indian tribal lands in the pre-Revolutionary Southeast (De Vorsey 1966b). The second utilized many very large scale original surveyor's maps of granted properties, known as plats. With these large scale depictions of a relatively small study area, an attempt was made to reconstruct the aboriginal forest cover on the eve of occupation by eighteenth century European cultivators.

The Southern Indian Boundary Line—A Small Scale Study

At the outset of the American Revolution the Southern Indian Boundary Line separated the British colonies from the territory of the Indian tribes in the Southeast. The climactic twelve year period, which began with the surrender of almost all of the eastern portion of the

executed maps which can be effectively employed to reconstruct the Southern Indian Boundary Line.

Surprisingly, there was no published source, be it historical atlas, reference work, scholarly monograph, or paper, to which the investigator of the Southern Indian landscape could turn to find this significant and extensive element reliably illustrated or described. The task was to translate the corpus of manuscript maps, sketches, and descriptions of the Southern Indian Boundary Line to topographic maps of the present day. Regrettably space does not permit a systematic review of all the original maps employed in this cartographic reconstruction.

Rather than attempt any sort of comprehensive review of the many early maps utilized in reconstructing the Southern Indian Boundary, three are reproduced here with brief comments. It is hoped that anthropologists and others will identify ways in which these and similar maps might be employed in reconstructing other facets of the Southern Indian landscape.

Figure 2 is a photographic reproduction of William Bonar's artistically embellished map of the mid-eighteenth century Creek Indian heartland, along the Coosa, Tallapoosa, and Chattahoochee Rivers. The area shown includes that portion of Alabama which stretches from the Coosa, north of Montgomery, south and eastward to the juncture of the Chattahoochee and Flint Rivers in northernmost Florida. Although distance is badly distorted, the map shows the names and locations of many Creek towns as well as two of the chief routes into the area from Georgia and South Carolina. The "French Fort" shown on the Coosa River near the fork of the Alabama (Moville) River was Fort Toulouse, built by the French in 1716. A plan of the fort was included as one of the six vignettes embellishing the margins of the map. The other vignettes include intimate firsthand views of the Creeks, their structures, and implements of peace as well as war.

Bonar accompanied Samuel Pepper, a representative of the governor of South Carolina, on a diplomatic mission to the Creeks during a period of considerable tension. The resourceful Bonar gained access to the French stronghold, Fort Toulouse, in the guise of a packhorseman. He was discovered by the French and arrested. While enroute under guard to the French headquarters at Mobile he was rescued by a party of pro-English Upper Creeks. His map was intended to give the Carolinians a clearer view of the conditions then existing in the Creek heartland. It was recognized as valuable by his con-

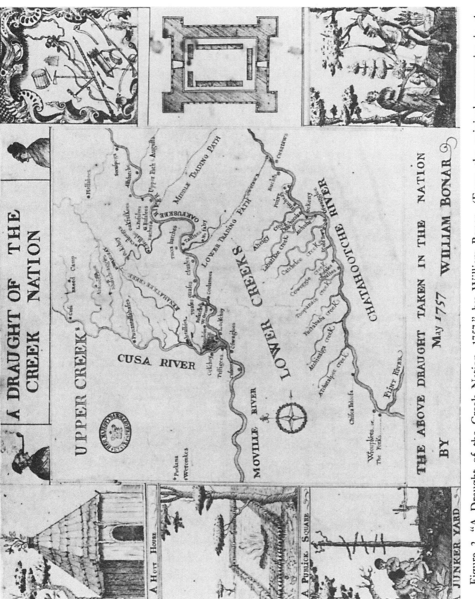

Figure 2. "A Draught of the Creek Nation, 1757," by William Bonar, (From the original manuscript in the British Public Record Office, C.O. 700 Carolina/21. Crown Copyright Material, reproduced with permission.)

temporaries and today represents a rich source for anyone studying the mid-eighteenth century Creek Indian landscape of the Southeast.

Figure 3 is a reproduction of a manuscript draught of the boundary line which was surveyed between the Cherokee lands and the colony of South Carolina in 1766. As can be seen it is an official document, inscribed by the Cherokee representative as well as the Carolina surveyor and commissioner. The line was surveyed from the Savannah River northeastward for approximately fifty-five miles to the Reedy River near the crossing of present day state route 101. The map shows a number of blazed line trees which are identified as to species as well as several named creeks and rivers. Of particular interest is the pair of parallel dotted lines which indicate the route of the "Road to Fort Prince George," the South Carolina outpost in the Lower Cherokee county. The map is of continuing significance since the surveyed line it shows still functions as the boundary between Anderson and Abbeville counties in South Carolina.

The last map in this series relating to the reconstruction of the Southern Indian Boundary Line is Figure 4. For clarity it has been redrawn from Samuel Savery's original manuscript dated January 1769. The area shown lay along the course of the Georgia-Creek Indian Boundary Line in the eastern part of the colony. Included are portions of several present day counties lying along a rough arc about forty miles to the west of Augusta. It is a valuable and interesting map, showing as it does the location of the outermost fringe of the Georgia settlement frontier during the summer of 1768 when Samuel Savery laboriously conducted his survey and boundary demarcation. The surveyor's descriptions of the character and quality of the land near the line are of particular interest. Many of the place names of creeks and other features shown have changed with time so this map would be particularly valuable to anyone attempting to interpret early documentary references or descriptions concerning the area shown. The "Creek Path" indicated is a segment of one of the most important aboriginal routeways in the Southeast. It was known as the Lower Trading Road or Lower Creek Trading Path and crossed the Ogeechee River near the present day Georgia community of Agricola (Goff 1953).

ABORIGINAL FOREST COVER IN GREENE COUNTY GEORGIA—A LARGE SCALE STUDY

In addition to the many hundreds of small and medium scale manuscript maps listed and described by Cumming in his book, *The South-*

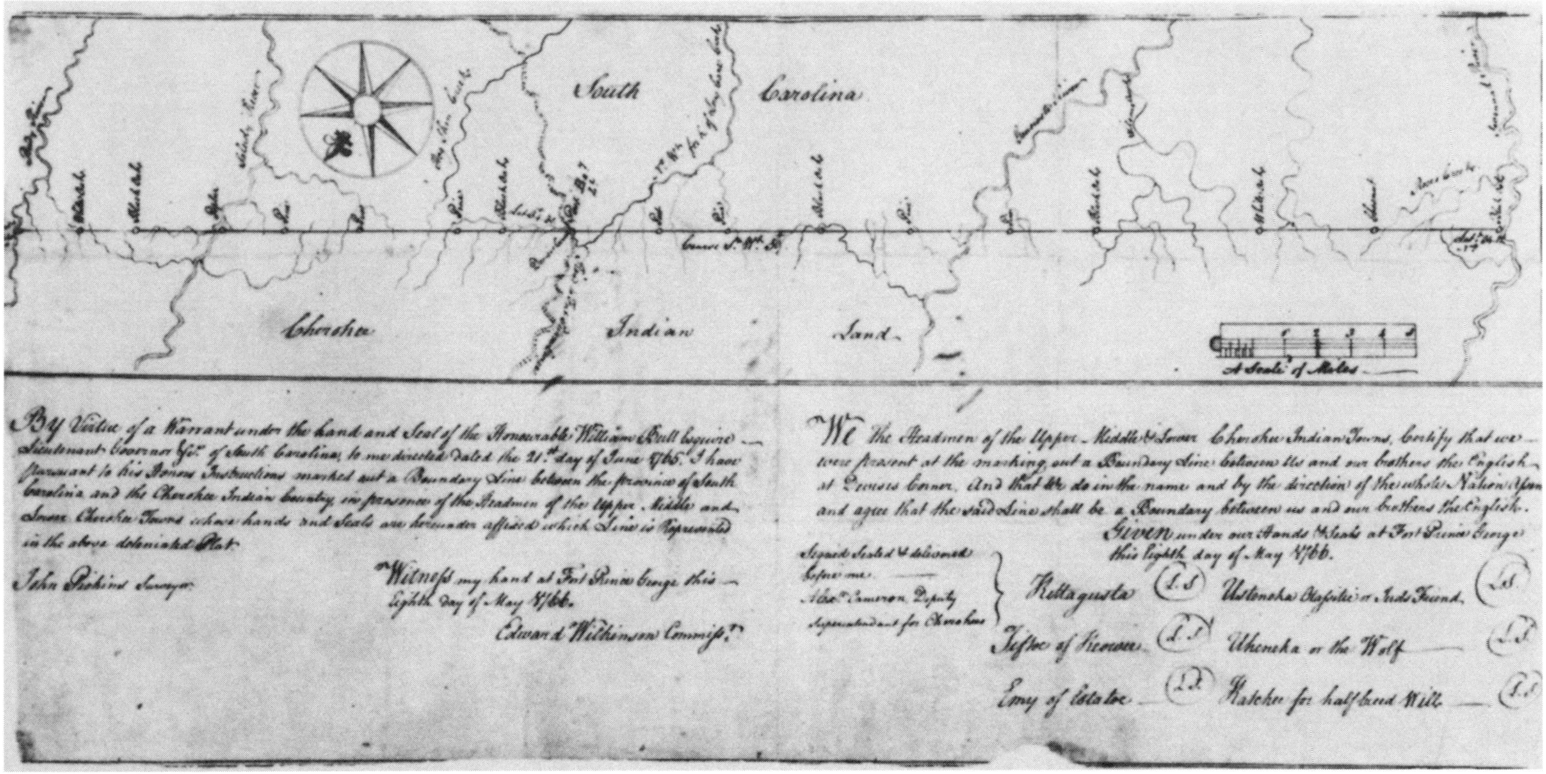

Figure 3. "Boundary Line Between the Province of South Carolina and the Cherokee Indian Country, Marked Out In Presence of the Head Men of the Upper, Middle and Lower Cherokee Towns, Whose Hands and Seals are Affixed. . .," by John Pickens. 1776. (From the original manuscript in the British Public Record Office, C.O. 700 Carolina/26. Crown Copyright Material, reproduced with permission.)

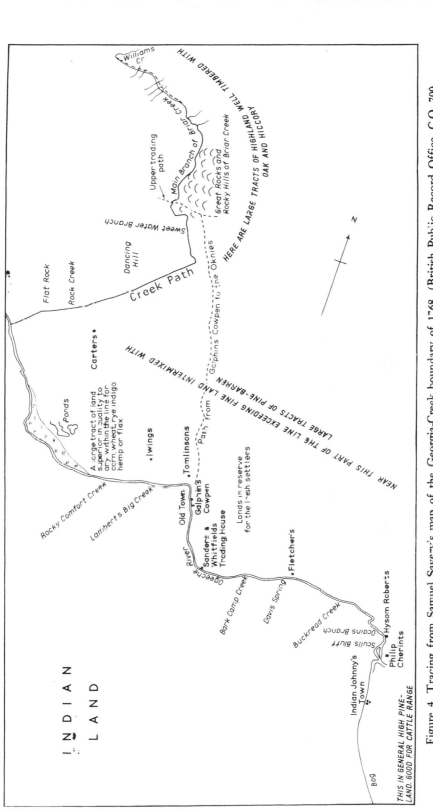

Figure 4. Tracing from Samuel Savery's map of the Georgia-Creek boundary of 1768. (British Public Record Office, C.O. 700 Georgia/14. Crown Copyright Material, reproduced with permission.)

east In Early Maps, there exisits another vast body of primary cartographic evidence which may be valuably employed in efforts to reconstruct past Southern Indian landscapes. This is composed of the several million large scale land maps, called plats, which were prepared as the public domain of the eastern colonies and states was delivered from governmental control into the hands of private citizens and commercial enterprise. This vast corpus of primary evidence is almost untapped at the present time. Its potential value seems enormous.

As might be imagined, the transfer of land, the most fundamental and prized resource of the age, was highly formalized and generally required that an accurate survey and description of the transferred land parcel be prepared and recorded in a central administrative office. The importance of these plats and documents has resulted in their careful preservation to the present day in our state and national archives. The surveyor general of Georgia, for example, maintains approximately one and one-half million survey plats and documents which are available for study and scholarly use.

Figure 5 is a copy made from a particularly interesting survey plat found in the Georgia archives. Thanks to the doodling of one early land surveyor, this plat presents a contemporary view of an eighteenth century land surveying party at work. The surveyor can be seen in frock coat and breeches, sighting on a black oak corner tree through the sight vanes of his circumferentor or surveyor's compass mounted on its "jacobs staff." The chain carriers, following him along his traverse, are shown wearing bits of their Revolutionary War army uniforms. These Revolutionary veterans are measuring distance with a Gunter's chain composed of carefully measured wire links. Edmund Gunter perfected this measuring device in 1620. It was based on the statute rod as a unit of land measurement with 100 links which equalled 66 feet or one rod. Still another member of the party is shown aiming at a deer with a flintlock.

It can be seen that the surveyors noted many landscape features on their plats. These often included such things as tree types, drainage features, soil quality, notable terrain features such as hills, large rocks, swamps, and springs. Many plats showed aboriginal cultural features such as Indian burial and temple mounds, paths, old fields, and villages, as well as fishing and hunting camps. There can be little doubt that these plats may be employed to yield valuable data concerning the landscape of the Southeast on the eve of its occupation by sedentary European cultivators.

Again, rather than describing and discussing the original land

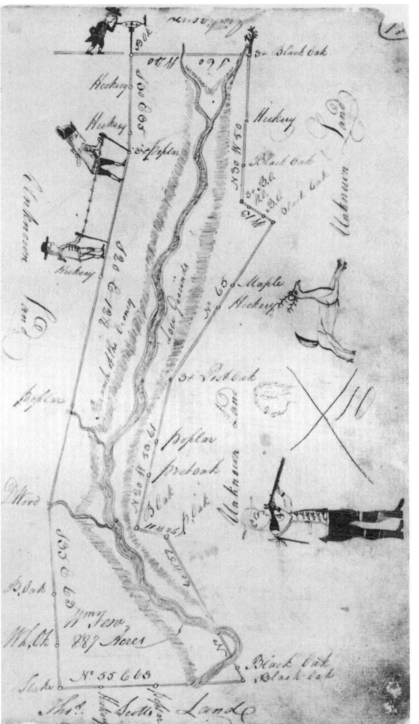

Figure 5. Copy of the survey plat of William Few's grant of 1784. (original scale, 1 inch represents 20 chains). This plat is one of many thousands maintained by the Georgia Surveyor General's Department, reproduced here with permission.

survey plats in general terms only, it seems advisable at this point to demonstrate their value in a more specific way through a large scale study which made use of them. This study is a small portion of a larger effort to gain a clearer and more accurate understanding of the character and composition of the forest cover of eastern America in the late eighteenth century.

Even a superficial examination of the accounts written by early explorers and travelers in the Southeast reveals a view of the forests which is widely at variance with what the present landscape reveals. One of these early travelers through the aboriginal Southeastern forests and glades was the well known Pennsylvania naturalist William Bartram (1958).

Bartram's writings have been extensively utilized by scholars interested in the eighteenth century South. Doubts have arisen from time to time, however, concerning his accuracy as a reporter of the aboriginal southern scene. Who, for example, would not have second thoughts regarding his colorful description of the hardwood dominated forest cover of the area now included in Georgia's Greene and Oglethorpe counties, if they were only familiar with the present day pine dominated scene in the area?

Bartram traveled through this portion of Georgia during the spring of 1773. He was almost rhapsodic in his glowing description of the forest he observed there. He wrote of "the most magnificent forest I had ever seen." He went on to describe

> this sublime forest; the ground perfectly a level green plain, thinly planted by nature with the most stately forest trees, such as the gigantic black oak . . . whose mighty trunks seemingly of an equal height, appeared like superb columns. To keep within the bounds of truth and reality, in describing the magnitude and grandeur of these trees, would, I fear, fail of credibility; yet I think I can assert, that many of the black oaks measured eight, nine, ten, and eleven feet diameter five feet above ground, as we measured several that were above thirty feet girt, and from hence they ascend perfectly strait, with a gradual taper, forty or fifty feet to the limbs (1958:24).

In an effort to check Bartram's description of the aboriginal hardwood dominated forest in Greene and Oglethorpe counties, original survey plats were employed as a source of data for a partial reconstruction.

The original survey plats for the study area, shown in Figure 6, were retrieved from Georgia State Surveyor General's files. The

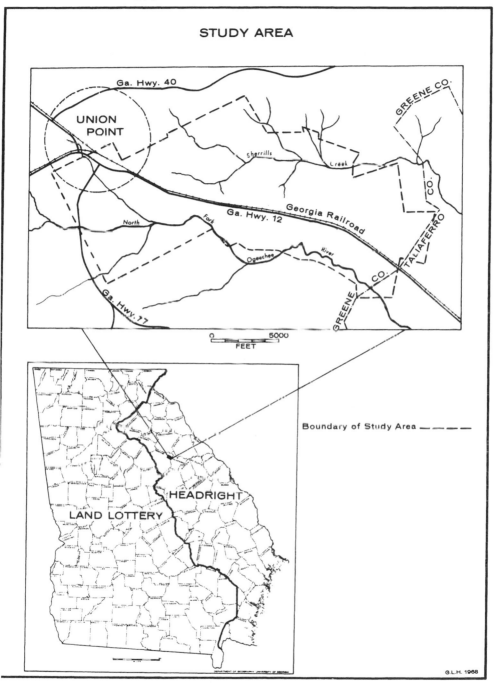

Figure 6. Location Maps Showing the Study Area in Greene County, Georgia. (From an original by Gerald L. Holder.)

several plats covering this area were then mosaicked jigsaw-puzzle fashion. With the aid of a Saltzman projector this mosaic was then keyed to a topographic map of the area. This operation was necessary since the study area is within the Headright region of Georgia and so lacks any regulated cadastral system such as that present in the western two thirds of the state. With the study area correctly located on the map and landscape of the present day, attention was turned to the forest cover (Holder 1968).

It will be recalled that land surveying practices in the eighteenth century entailed the identification, as to species, of several line, corner, and witness trees on each plat registered. In addition to this data, a number of the plats included the surveyor's descriptive commentary on the general character of the forest cover, as he perceived it, on the land surveyed. In all cases where such verbal descriptions appeared they emphasized the hardwoods, oak and hickory, and only occasionally was pine included. When pine did occur it followed oak and hickory. After noting these verbal descriptions, the plats were then scrutinized more closely and the individual tree types were counted. A total of 197 trees were identified on the mosaicked plats of the study area. Of these, 80% were hardwoods with oaks alone accounting for 57% of the total number. Only 18% of the identified trees were pines. A check of recent aerial photography of the study area revealed that hardwoods account for only about 40% of the cover with pines accounting for 60% of the total.

It would seem that the original plats have lent confirmation to William Bartram's account of a hardwood dominant forest in this portion of the eighteenth century Georgia Piedmont. The plats are, however, only one source of data and represent a somewhat biased sample of what the original forest was really like. They are biased because surveyors probably tended to select a hardwood tree on which to strike a blaze rather than a less durable pine, if the choice was available. This fact probably resulted in the inclusion of a higher percentage of hardwoods than a random sample would have produced.

Other data such as maps, documentary accounts, saw mill ledgers, the timbers found in extant old buildings, and pollen grain counts in marshy beds need to be considered before definite conclusions can be framed concerning the forest cover of the study area two centuries ago. It does seem clear, however, that this source of data confirms rather than denies Bartram's accuracy as a reporter of the eighteenth century scene.

CONCLUSION

Anthropologists and geographers share a large common ground in both the material which they examine and the methodology of that examination. In this paper a small part of that common ground has been uncovered through the examination and analysis of early maps of the South. The small and large scale studies discussed here are of limited interest in themselves. What is of major interest, however, is the fact that these early maps represent poorly understood and neglected data sources which may contribute to a deeper understanding of the South's aboriginal heritage. The maps also represent an area of research effort where the expertise of the geographer can valuably contribute to the goals of the anthropologist and vice versa. Perhaps they chart the way toward that fusion of the disciplines to which Sauer alluded so long ago.

REFERENCES

Bartram, William, 1958. *Travels Through North and South Carolina, Georgia, East and West Florida* . . . . Naturalist's Edition, Francis Harper, ed. (New Haven: Yale University Press).

Broek, Jan O. M. 1932. *The Santa Clara Valley, California: A Study in Landscape Changes* (Utrecht: N.V.A. Oosthoek's Uitgevers).

――――――――― 1965. *Geography: Its Scope and Spirit* (Columbus: Charles E. Merrill).

Coppock, J. T. 1968. Maps As Sources For the Study of Land Use in the Past. *Imago Mundi* 22:37-49.

Cumming, William P. 1962. *The Southeast In Early Maps* (Chapel Hill: University of North Carolina Press).

――――――――― 1966. Mapping of the Southeast: The First Two Centuries. *The Southeastern Geographer* 6:3-19.

De Vorsey, Louis, Jr., 1966a. The Colonial Southeast On "An Accurate General Map." *The Southeastern Geographer* 6:20-32.

――――――――― 1966b. *The Indian Boundary In The Southern Colonies, 1763-1775* (Chapel Hill: The University of North Carolina Press).

Frake, Charles O., 1962. Cultural Ecology and Ethnography. *American Anthropologist* 64:53-59.

Friis, Herman R., 1966. Highlights of the Geographical and Cartographical Activities of the Federal Government In the Southeastern United States: 1776-1865. *The Southeastern Geographer* 6:41-57.

Goff, John H., 1953. Some Major Indian Trading Paths Across the Georgia Piedmont. *Georgia Mineral News Letter* 6:122-131.

Harley, J. B., 1968. The Evaluation of Early Maps: Towards a Methodology. *Imago Mundi* 22:62-74.

Holder, Gerald L., 1968. Landholdings Along the North Fork of the Ogeechee River in 1786. Unpublished Seminar Paper, Department of Geography, University of Georgia.

Koeman, C., 1968. Levels of Historical Evidence in Early Maps (With Examples). *Imago Mundi* 22:75-80.

Mikesell, Marvin W., 1967. Geographic Perspectives In Anthropology. *Annals of the Association of American Geographers* 57:617-634.

Newcomb, Robert M., 1969. Twelve Working Approaches to Historical Geography. *Yearbook of the Association of Pacific Coast Georgraphers* 31:27-50.

Ristow, Walter W., 1966. State Maps of the Southeast to 1833. *The Southeastern Geographer* 6:33-40.

Sauer, Carl O., 1963. *Land and Life: A Selection From the Writings of Carl Ortwin Sauer*, John Leighley, ed. (Berkeley and Los Angeles: University of California Press).

Skelton, R. A., 1965. *Looking At An Early Map* (Lawrence: University of Kansas Libraries).

Physical Anthropology of Indians of the Old South

WILLIAM S. POLLITZER

IN a sense the physical anthropology of the Indians of the South begins with the earliest observations of the European adventurers who travelled among them, trading and surveying, and recording the appearance of body and face. Thus, Lawson (1714) not only speaks of the stature of the natives of North Carolina, of their tawny color and their scant facial hair, but also of the deformation of the skull induced by the cradleboard—an early reminder of the influence of culture upon physique and a caution to all subsequent students of skulls. Subsequent to that early contact we have the impressions also of Adair, Bartram, Swan, and many others (Swanton 1946). Swanton's extensive studies of Southern Indians rest largely upon voluminous historical documents, and they understandably contain relatively little detailed account of physical measurements. Boas published on the physical anthropology of the Indians of North America as early as 1895, including measurements on stature and cephalic index among Cherokees, Choctaws, Chickasaws, and Creeks (Boas 1895). In the last decade of the nineteenth century and the first two decades of the twentieth, Clarence B. Moore excavated many sites in the South, sometimes finding and describing skeletal material.

Large scale descriptions of the bones of the dead begin with Hrdlička. In his study of the Lenape or Delawares (Hrdlička 1916), based on 57 skeletons from Mausee near the junction of New York, New Jersey, and Pennsylvania, he characterized these Algonkian people as having good-sized skulls which were oval to elliptical in shape and moderate in length; he found them similar to Iroquois, and different from eastern round-heads. In a subsequent publication (Hrdlička 1927) he reported on similar Algonkian remains from Maryland, Virginia, and Kentucky whose mean cephalic index ranged

31

from 74 to 77, with a high vault and a medium to large face. In his "Indians of the Gulf States" (Hrdlička 1940) he catalogued skulls from many locations in the South, and especially from Florida; on the basis of the almost universal distribution of these broad-heads, he recognized the "Gulf type."

But these early classifications could not take into account the complex relationships between populations and their temporal sequence; it is the work of the modern archeologist which has added the dimension of time to that of space. When Funkhouser (1938) described the osteological material from the Norris Basin in eastern Tennessee, he found the people to be tall, of slight and graceful build, with round heads and broad faces, and considered them as probably of the same stock as those to the north and west in the Mississippi Valley. Skårland (1939) examined the remains from the Chiggerville site in Kentucky and described a population with long, high heads and short faces. When Newman and Snow (1942) investigated the skeletal material from Pickwick Basin near the junction of Alabama, Mississippi, and Tennessee, they differentiated the early, undeformed long heads with high vaults and greater tooth wear of the Shell Mounds from the later, deformed round heads of Koger's Island.

Using Pearson's Coefficient of Racial Likeness, von Bonin and Morant (1938) sought a statistical classification of the Indians based on the series of skulls known at that time. The similarity of the Florida remains to those of California they regarded as in conformity with those peripheral populations that von Eickstedt called "Margids." But they were compelled to separate their Kentucky skulls from Hrdlička's Algonkians on the basis of metrical distinctions. In 1948 Snow gave a thorough report on these abundant Indian Knoll skeletons, dating from the Archaic period. Of 1234 individuals, 521 were measurable, including 475 skulls. These short people had small, ovoid skulls with high vaults and a cranial index averaging 76, and large faces with prominent cheek-bones. One-fourth of them showed signs of flattening at the front of the head and a very few showed flattening at the rear of the head as well. Originally considered dating from the early Christian era they are now generally recognized as being at least 5000 years old. This gold mine of osteology has been reworked since, with studies of long bones being reported as recently as 1968 (Graham and Yarbrough).

Lewis and Kneberg (1961) believe that the people of their Eva Site in Tennessee represent a similar archaic population extending from 6000 to 4000 B.C. Of the 49 measurable skulls, a third are long-headed, only 11% are round-headed, while the majority are intermediate. Further indication of their similarity to the Indian Knoll people is found in their high vault.

When Georg Neumann examined the skeletal remains from Keyauwee in North Carolina (Neumann n. d.), he considered these Catawban people similar to those of Indian Knoll. On the basis of these and other finds he defined the Iswanid variety, the term itself derived from the Catawba word meaning "people of the river." They are characterized by a small, moderately long, ovoid skull with small to medium brow ridges and medium frontal slope. The face is moderate in all proportions and has pronounced lateral zygomatic projection. Neumann believes this variety is represented in the Shell Mound series of Pickwick Basin, in the Chiggerville site, and possibly in sites as widely separated as southern New England and Florida. He sees similarities between the Iswanid and the Basket Makers of the southwestern United States.

In Neumann's scheme the Walcolids are roughly equivalent to Hrdlička's Gulf type or von Eickstedt's Centralids, best represented by the series from the Spoon River focus from Central Illinois. The skull is large, intermediate in length, ovoid, and high, with medium brow ridges and medium to slight frontal slope. The face is largish, rugged, and moderately long. When Snow (1945) described the skeletal remains from the Tchefuncte site on the lower Mississippi, he noted that their skulls were high-vaulted and moderately rounded, that their faces were broad, and that their stature was medium; he saw a closer relationship of them to the early Shell Mound people than to the later Koger's Island people; and he considered them a possible admixture of early longheads and later round-heads. Collins (1941) studied skeletal remains from Copell Place, a Tchefuncte site on Pecan Island, Louisiana, and considered the people a variant of the Indian Knoll group. Neumann thinks that the Tchefuncte population may possibly be Walcolid.

The important Woodland site of Adena in the Ohio River valley was reported by Webb and Snow (1945). They contrast these round-headed people with massive flat faces and broad high foreheads and extensive occipital flattening with the Indian Knollers. Neumann thinks they may have provided a link with the southern Walcolids. Hertzberg has described a series of skeletal material from Ricketts Mound (1940a) and another from the nearby Wright site (1940b) which may also fall into this category. Their large heads are quite broad and with long faces, and the long bones indicate a people of medium stature. More recent excavations in Florida (Jennings, et al. 1957) have revealed further remains from the Woodland stage that fit best into Neumann's Walcolid variety also.

In Neumann's terminology the Algonkians of the East are the Lenapids who entered the archeological scene late and continued into the historic period. Their large, ovoid skulls tend toward long-headedness with brow ridges and signs of muscularity; the face is moderately long and rugged with medium prognathism.

The burials at Hiwassee Island in Tennessee, described by Lewis and Kneberg (1946) include three components which appear to extend from late Mississippian into historic times. The appreciable variability in skulls, especially among the later burials, suggests to the authors admixture of several peoples, although those of the middle or Dallas focus are thought to be primarily Creeks. Deformation, absent in the earliest skulls, is evident in several of the later ones.

Woodland and Mississippian traits were noted in the Peachtree site, whose skeletal remains were reported by Stewart (1941). Located in western North Carolina near historic Cherokee towns, it is possible that that tribe may have been among its occupants. Of 39 individuals, 16 showed cranial deformity, 14 did not, and 9 were too incomplete for information; cranial form was reported as variable.

Hulse (1941) has provided us with a neat analysis of the people who lived at Irene in Chatham County, Georgia, almost into the historic period. Of medium to submedium stature, the people are essentially round-headed but quite variable. Hulse argues that they may show two genetic strains, chiefly on the basis of a peculiar bun-shaped occiput. As is so often the case with later Indians, some cranial deformation shows in one-third of the skulls.

The Stalling's Island Mound, near Augusta, Georgia, has provided information on people who lived into the historic period. Round-headedness, but not usually cranial deformation, is the rule among the poorly preserved skulls from this site (Claflin 1931). Cottier and Dickens (1965) have written of remains of skeletons, also not well preserved, from the Shine Mound Site in Alabama, which apparently extends almost into the historic period.

Near the beginning of the historic period in Virginia are the skeletal remains from the Tolliferro and Clarksville sites in the Kerr Reservoir Basin on the Roanoke River, reported by St. Hoyme and Bass (1962). These two sites were evidently occupied by Occaneechi Indians from about 1500 to 1600 (or earlier) and from 1600 to 1675, respectively. The authors indicate that the Tolliferro crania fit well with such southeastern material as Indian Knoll and Shell Mound. While the Clarksville population are similar, they are more round-headed and somewhat larger. Related material from Mecklenberg, Virginia, measured and described by Sigmon (1963), shows evidence of appreciable admixture. Phelps measured related Tutelo people from Yadkin and Occaneechi from Alamance, both in North Carolina (Pollitzer et al. 1967).

In the Carolinas and Virginia, the Siouan people, of slight frame and small delicate skulls of intermediate shape, were found in the proto-historic period between the tall, long-headed coastal Algonkians and the more rugged, angular, round-headed people near the mountains. The latter, including both the Iroquois-speaking Cherokee and the Muskogean-speaking inhabitants of Town Creek would fall into Neumann's Walcolid variety. The relationship of several of these populations to the living Catawba, survivors of a Siouan-speaking people of the East, will be described presently.

The physical anthropologist is interested in the abnormal as well as the normal variations, and the bones and teeth have provided an opportunity for the study of pathology. Thus, Funkhouser (1938) reported on poor teeth and on bone disease from the Norris Basin; Newman and Snow (1942) noted considerable arthritis at Pickwick Basin; Snow (1948) noted the lumbar arthritis of the Indian Knoll remains and the osteoporosis and osteitis in the Tchefuncte people (1945); Stewart (1941) noted ear exostoses and osteitis at the Peach-tree site; Hulse (1941) reported dental and skeletal anomalies from Irene; Sigmon (1963) wrote of caries and other possible disease; and St. Hoyme and Bass (1962) described the pathology of their Roanoke River sites. Stewart, who called attention to possible pre-Columbian syphilis earlier (1941), has revived interest with his recent report on lesions of the frontal bone (Stewart and Quade 1969), some of which appear to be syphilitic in origin, in Indians of the Archaic in several locations including southern ones.

Mehta (1969) studied the dentition of the Shell Mound Indians of Alabama to test the association of malocculusion and attrition. While the tooth wear was excessive he found crowding in only 29 of 636 teeth studied. In 23 skulls from the site, three had slight and one had moderate overbite. Investigation of Arkansas skulls (Mehta and Evans 1966) revealed similar results which suggest that attrition and malocclusion do not go together.

We must not fall into the habit of thinking that new skulls are produced by the mating of two previous skulls. Our ultimate concern is with the entire organism. Hill (1963) has recently provided us with a detailed dissection of a Cherokee Indian, which he found to be not especially "Mongoloid" in his anatomy.

Few anthropometric studies of living Indians of the South have been done, but Krogman's very thorough monograph on the Seminoles of Oklahoma, derived from the South, is an approximation. From genealogies and measurements he found (Krogman 1935) considerable evidence of admixture of the Seminoles with other Indian groups, especially the neighboring Creeks, and some with non-Indian peoples as well.

How much of the change noted in Indian populations with time is due to displacement of one population by another and how much is evolutionary change? M. Newman (1962) recently addressed himself to this question, examining head form and stature. Citing especially the data from northern Alabama, he believes an increase of 4 or 5 cms. over 5000 years among Indians of the Southeast is an evolutionary change which may be related to climate, perhaps also to nutrition and health, and influenced only slightly by the interbreeding of different populations. He also finds the brachycephalization, the tendency to broader heads, as shown by an increase of six index points over this span of time, further indication of evolutionary change. He would recognize only two major migrations of Indians into America, with subsequent evolution of varieties occurring on this continent. Neumann (1960) apparently accepts the evolution of the Walcolid variety along with the development of the middle Mississippi culture phase.

To understand better the relationships between populations, anthropologists have turned toward those traits with known, precise genetic mechanisms and have attempted to characterize groups by their "gene pools." As races may be viewed as interbreeding populations who share the same genes, an attempt has been made to characterize groups by the frequency of various readily determined traits, such as the blood types, governed by single genes. A large and growing battery of inherited factors of blood are now applicable among the living for a study of their migrations and relationships. One new hemoglobin, $G_{Coushatta}$, was discovered in the Alabama Coushatta Indians on their reservation in east Texas where these Muskogean tribes have lived since about 1800 (Schneider et al. 1964). In this hemoglobin, glutamine replaces alanine in the beta chain (Bowman et al. 1967). Haptoglobins have also been studied among the Alabama Coushatta Indians; their Hp^1 gene frequency of 0.37 is similar to that of most other American Indians (Shim and Bearn 1964).

Cerumen (earwax) can generally be classified into two types that are genetically controlled; the dry variety is dominant over the wet.

Study of 432 Choctaw Indians of Mississippi revealed 21% of the dry type, a lower percentage than that in most western tribes (Martin and Jackson 1969). Investigation among the Seminoles of Florida showed 48% of the dry variety (Hirschhorn 1970).

While the genetics of dermatoglyphics is not fully understood, a well recognized hereditary component in such palm prints permits them to be used in a fashion similar to that of the monogenic traits. Rife (1968) found the pattern of the Seminoles to be similar to those of most other North American Indians, and differences on the three reservations reflect their known genetic relationship.

Our blood type survey of the Cherokee Indians on their reservation in western North Carolina (Pollitzer et al. 1962) provided an opportunity to compare genetically the remnant of this once powerful and flourishing tribe with other Indian populations. In their blood factors, including the high frequency of Group O, of M, and of Rh positive, and their absence of abnormal hemoglobin, they are similar to most other American Indian tribes. The Diego factor found in many other Indian groups was absent, and Rh^1 was more common than in most other Indians studied. The study bore out the conclusion of Glass (1955) that the Indian contributed relatively little to the gene pool of the Negro in America. Gene flow from Negro into Indian, however, is a different question for which our study provides no definitive answers. In our sample the only indication of Negro admixture came from one case each of Hunter and of Henshaw blood types, usually associated with African populations. The absence of Rh_o, Js, S^u, and V blood types and hemoglobin S argue against appreciable Negroid admixture.

Ample opportunities for Negro-Indian admixture in the Old South existed. In earliest colonial days some white owners worked Negro and Indian slaves on the same plantation; runaway Negroes often took refuge among Indian tribes; and Indians themselves sometimes had Negro slaves. Thus, a census report of the Cherokee population in 1835 listed 16,542 Cherokee Indians, 1592 Negro slaves, and 201 whites who had married into the tribe. While matings among all three major groups undoubtedly occurred, our blood type data suggest that the "mixed-bloods" among the Eastern Cherokees are predominantly mixed with whites, probably with the English and Scotch-Irish who prevailed on the frontier. Indeed, the proportion of Indian ancestry estimated by gene frequencies in the "mixed-bloods" on the assumption of admixture with an English stock is almost identical to the 62% actually found. Many of the offspring of Negro-Indian unions evidently went westward in the great forced migration of 1838, while some others remained in small communities bordering the Cherokee reservation.

The Seminole Indians of Florida (Pollitzer et al. 1970) provide a different story, in some ways parallel to the Cherokees and in some ways strikingly different. Like the Cherokees they came into continuing conflict with the need and greed of the white men, and many of their numbers were forcibly removed to Oklahoma on the "Trail of Tears." But whereas the territory and overlordship of the Cherokee was vast at the time of European contact and declined almost to a vanishing point by the mid-nineteenth century, the Seminoles grew by gradual accretion from the early eighteenth century onward as Indians from Georgia, mostly Creek with some Yemassee and Yuchi, moved into Florida and in time successfully challenged the power of the United States in two wars. The Oconee, who had settled at Alachua in north central Florida by 1750, became the Cow Creek Indians and the forerunners of the Seminoles now at Brighton on the north shore of Lake Okeechobee. Related Indians settled around Lake Miccosukee in northwestern Florida, the forerunners of the present-day Big Cypress community bordering the Everglades and the related population at Dania. From the start the lives of these Indians were intertwined with Negroes who joined them, sometimes as slaves and sometimes as free allies.

Our study of the Seminoles in Florida included both physical measurements and blood studies. These Indians are quite variable but most often of copper coloring, moderately tall, round-headed, and intermediate in nose and face dimensions. In blood factors, the very high incidence of Group O, of Rh positive, and of M puts them in line with most other Indian populations. Like the Cherokees they lack Rh_0, but unlike the Cherokees they possess Diego. The presence of hemoglobin S and of G-6-P-D variants is indicative of some Negroid admixture. In general, the distribution of both the physical measurements and the serological factors on the reservations at Brighton on the one hand and at Big Cypress and Dania on the other bears out the historical relationship between the two populations. Moreover, both methods of study agree that the Seminoles are predominantly Indian, with some admixture from both whites and Negroes.

In our research on the Catawba Indians near Rock Hill, South Carolina, we were able to make some estimate of their relationship not only to other present-day populations but also to Indians of the past. During the climactic phase in North Carolina, such Siouan tribes as the Catawba, Saponi, and Tutelo lived along the rivers of the Piedmont. In this proto-historic period the Catawba evidently lost their earlier Uwharrie ceramic traits to a Lamar influence from Georgia, like that of the people at Irene, while a distinctive Muskogean people, bearing the PeeDee culture, had pushed up the river of that name as far as the narrows of the Yadkin (Coe 1952). At the early historic era, some Occaneechi moved on to the Clarksville area from Piedmont Carolina, where their skeletal remains suggest admixture, some of it possibly non-Indian. In time the Catawba moved into South Carolina and absorbed remnants of related Indian tribes. In colonial times they were allied with the English against the Iroquois-speaking tribes. In 1763 they were granted a reservation 15 miles square in York and Lancaster counties, South Carolina. In area, in population, and in the amenities of life, this reserve was steadily reduced in the succeeding years.

In 1962, when the Indians terminated their reservation status, we obtained physical measurements and blood studies (Pollitzer et al. 1967). The serological traits show most clearly that the present-day Catawba are actually about half-Indian and half-white with no significant Negroid admixture. The appearance and the physical measurements, while not as conclusive, are consistent with this estimate, a phenomenon probably due to the influence of the Mormon religion to which they became converted in the late nineteenth century. The Mormons taught that Indians, while not as elevated as whites, could someday become a "white and delightsome people."

In comparing the living Catawba with skeletal populations, appropriate corrections were made for soft parts. In many of their measurements and indices the present-day Catawba still show similarity to remains of the long extinct Indians of the region. The D² or distance measure designed by Mahalanobis takes into account both the difference between the means of traits in two or more populations and the intercorrelations between the traits. By this test, they are most similar to the Tutelo of the Yadkin, and next to the people from Indian Knoll and Clarksville. The Occaneechi at Tolliferro are not far removed, while the mixed population from Mecklenberg is most distant.

Although the attempt at blood typing ancient skeletal remains is a dubious procedure, it is noteworthy that our results on bones of 26 individuals of the Yadkin River sites typed by inhibition techniques show that all except two are in Group O and those two are in Group A—much in line with present Indian populations of the area.

Throughout colonial times population pressures led both to migration of Indian tribes and to their gradual absorption into the expanding white culture. While records are understandably hazy, we have evidence of unions of individual Indians, whites, and Negroes, sometimes "free persons of color." Price (1950) has abundantly documented the formation of such triracial isolates in the Southeast, and Berry (1963) has painted a sympathetic portrait of the "mestizo" who has survived into the present-day. Our own studies of the Lumbee (Pollitzer et al. 1964) and the Haliwa, both in North Carolina (Pollitzer et al. 1966), and of the Melungeons of Tennessee and Virginia (Pollitzer and Brown 1969) bear witness to the survival of Indian strains in these biologic and cultural isolates. The last study also suggests their present-day dissolution.

What are the needs for the future study of the physical anthropology of the Indians of the South? One necessary task is the thorough morphological and metrical analysis of osteological material sequestered in our museums not yet studied and reported. This study must take account of the most recent dating of the material and all relevant data contributed by the archeologist, and previous studies should be adjusted accordingly. But classification alone is not enough. We need more understanding of the nature of morphological change, its rate, and its determinants. We must in time come to understand the people in terms of the selective pressures of the environment, of the demographic variables of fertility and mortality, and the nature of health and disease. We need to compare populations not only within the South but with related ones elsewhere and to contrast them with peoples living under quite different conditions. We must reach out to the historian, ethnographer, linguist, and archeologist on the one hand, and toward the biomedical scientists on the other, to make one unified, yet dynamic, picture of the life of the Indians of the South.

REFERENCES

Berry, Brewton, 1963. *Almost White* (New York: Macmillan Co).

Blackwell, R. Q., I-H. Ro, C-S. Liu, H-J. Yang, C-C. Wang, and J.T-H. Huang, 1969. Hemoglobin Variant Found in Koreans, Chinese, and North American Indians. *American Journal of Physical Anthropology* 30:389-392.

Boas, Franz, 1895. Zur Anthropologie der Nordamerikanischen. *Zeitschrift für Ethnologie* 27:366-411.

Bowman, B. H., D. R. Barnett, and R. Hite, 1967. Hemoglobin G$_{Coushatta}$: a Beta Variant with a Delta-like Substitution. *Biochemistry and Biophysics Research Communication* 26:466-470.

Claflin, W. H., 1931. The Stalling's Island Mound, Columbia County, Georgia. *Papers of the Peabody Museum of American Archeology and Ethnology*, XIV, No. 1 (Cambridge, Mass.: Harvard University Press).

Snow, Charles E., 1945. Tchefuncte Skeletal Remains. In *The Tchefuncte Culture, an Early Occupation of the Lower Mississippi Valley*, J. A. Ford and G. I. Quimby, Jr., eds. *Memoirs of the Society of American Archeology.* Supplement to *American Antiquity* Vol. X, No. 3, Part 2.

——————————————————————————— , 1948. Indian Knoll Skeletons of Site Oh 2, Ohio County, Kentucky. *University of Kentucky Reports in Anthropology*, IV, No. 3, Part II (University of Kentucky Press).

St. Hoyme, L. E., and W. M. Bass, 1962. Human Skeletal Remains from the Tolliferro (Ha6) and Clarksville (Mc14) Sites, John H. Kerr Reservoir Basin, Virginia. In *Archeology of the John H. Kerr Reservoir Basin, Roanoke River, Virginia-North Carolina*, Carl F. Miller, ed. Bureau of American Ethnology Bulletin, 182: 329-400 (Washington, D.C.: GPO).

Stewart, T. D., 1941. Skeletal Remains from Peachtree Site, North Carolina. In *The Peachtree Site*, F. M. Setzler, and J. D. Jennings, eds. Bureau of American Ethnology Bulletin, 131 (Washington, D.C.: GPO).

Stewart, T. D., and L. G. Quade, 1969. Lesions of the Frontal Bone in American Indians. *American Journal of Physical Anthropology* 30:89-110.

Swanton, John R., 1946. *The Indians of the Southeastern United States.* Bureau of American Ethnology Bulletin, 137 (Washington, D.C.: GPO).

Von Bonin, G., and G. M. Morant, 1938. Indian Races of the United States. A Survey of Previously Published Cranial Measurements. *Biometrika* 30:94-129.

Webb, W. S., and C. E. Snow, 1945. *The Adena People.* University of Kentucky Reports in Anthropology and Archeology, Vol. VI (University of Kentucky Press).

Southeastern Indian Linguistics

MARY R. HAAS

IT is a commonplace of anthropological literature that the greatest linguistic diversity of aboriginal North America was that found in the California-Oregon area. But we know this largely because the northern part of the area was little affected by the inroads of European civilization until around the middle of the nineteenth century. By that time some travelers and investigators were accustomed to taking down vocabularies and other notes on the various tribes that they encountered and hence considerable information about diversity was rather quickly acquired.

Another area of great linguistic diversity in North America was certainly the Southeast and the adjacent coast of the Gulf of Mexico. However, it is seldom spoken of in these terms and is certainly not likely to be compared to California. The principal reason for this is the far greater period of contact—nearly five centuries—and the sparseness of information about the most critical period, namely that before the tribes had been seriously dislocated by the pressures of the competing European nations.

Many smaller tribes in the Southeast have almost certainly vanished without a trace. Others are known to us by name only, and in this event (in spite of frequent claims to the contrary) linguistic affiliation is unknown. Our knowledge of Southeastern linguistics, then, is based on information about some of the larger and more powerful tribes of the area, such as the Cherokee, the Creek, and the Choctaw, and only rarely on the much smaller ones, such as the Biloxi, the Ofo, or the Tunica.

Near the turn of the nineteenth century, spurred by the publication of Pallas's *Vocabularia Comparativa*, a great deal of attention among scholars was turned to the problem of classifying North American languages. The determination of "how many principal stocks, or families there are in North America" (Pickering 1831:581)

44

was a pressing problem. In 1787 Jefferson (1964:97) had surmised that their number would be very great. Pickering, unfortunately swayed in part by theological considerations, believed they would be "very few in number." Following Duponceau, he surmised that there were only "three, or at most, four principal stocks" east of the Mississippi (including the Northeast). Most of the Southeast was lumped into one stock, the "Floridian" or "Southern" (Pickering 1833). Although Barton (1797:lxvii-lxviii) had correctly postulated the affiliation between Cherokee and the languages of the "Six Nations" and also that between Muskogee or Creek and Choctaw-Chickasaw as early as 1797, his correct guesses were lost in a maze of incorrect ones and therefore the opportunity to begin a proper evaluation of the Southeastern situation was lost (Haas 1970). Duponceau's Floridian stock ignored Barton's surmises and lumped Cherokee in with Creek and Choctaw and other southern languages.

The first reasonably comprehensive vocabulary of the indigenous languages north of Mexico was that compiled by Gallatin (1836). At that time he believed that he had been able to ascertain the languages of all tribes east of the Mississippi except one. This was the Alabama-Koasati which, though known to be a part of the Creek Confederacy, was not known to have had its language recorded. Gallatin believed that Creek and Choctaw-Chickasaw were related but he kept them separate until 1848, and, still lacking vocabularies of Alabama and Koasati, he left them unclassified.

Gallatin's 1836 classification of the languages of the Southeast was the most accurate that had been achieved to that time. He dispensed with Duponceau's "Floridean" and strictly separated all languages whose affinity was in the slightest doubt. This gave him the following scheme: Atakapa, Chitimacha, Cherokee (possibly related to Iroquois), Choctaw (possibly related to Muskogee), Catawba (and Woccon), Muskogee (Muskogee proper [Creek], Hitchiti, and Seminole; possibly related to Choctaw), Natchez, Tunica, Yuchi, and Timucua. It is interesting that at this time no Siouan tribe was known to live east of the Mississippi, since Biloxi and Tutelo had not yet been identified, and Ofo was not known still to exist. Catawba, though known, was too divergent to be recognized as being related to the known Siouan languages west of the Mississippi. It is also important to remember that Gallatin sagaciously classified only languages for which he had vocabularies, and by 1836 an unknown number of Southeastern languages had already disappeared.

By the time Powell published his comprehensive scheme for

North America north of Mexico (1891), several problems had
been cleared up and his basic results for the Southeast have been
little modified since. Cherokee, thanks to Hale (1883a), was recognized as the southernmost branch of the Iroquoian family; Alabama
and Koasati, thanks to Gatschet (1884), were correctly placed
in the Muskogean family; and Tutelo and Biloxi, thanks to Hale
(1883b) and Dorsey (1893), were correctly identified as Siouan.
Ofo remained unknown except as one of many unclassified Southeastern tribes known by name only.

Within a couple of decades after the publication of Powell's
classification a flurry of reductionism set in. It seems to have started
with Dixon and Kroeber (1913a, b) who, not content to allow
the California languages to be divided up into 22 unrelated families,
sought to establish interrelationships among them. At about the
same time Swanton began trying to find interrelationships among
the language isolates and language families of the Southeast. The
best known language isolates of the Southeast are Tunica, Chitimacha, Atakapa, Natchez, Yuchi, and Timucua. The most widely
accepted suggestions were that Tunica, Chitimacha, and Atakapa
were three branches of a stock named 'Tunican' (Swanton 1919),
that Natchez was a relative of the Muskogean family (Swanton
1924), and that Yuchi was a relative of the Siouan family (Sapir
1921). There was somewhat more uncertainty about Timucua,
though it was suggested that it might be an outlying relative of
Muskogean (Swanton 1929).

The greatest reduction for North America was finally achieved
by Sapir (1929), who divided up all the languages north of Mexico
into six superstocks. The grandest amalgamation of all was the
one called Hokan-Siouan which encompassed not only many California and Texas languages but also all of the various groupings
that had been arrived at for the Southeast. In California, as it
turned out, Sapir's scheme still allowed the appearance of several
different colors on the map (since five of his superstocks were
represented there) but in the Southeast all differentiation was obliterated in the one color assigned to Hokan-Siouan (Voegelin and
Voegelin 1941).

Whatever the final judgment may be about the eventual accuracy
of Sapir's classification, the immediate result was unfortunate for
Southeastern linguistics since it oversimplified the picture. When
this was added to the already complacent attitude toward Southeastern linguistics due to the feeling of familiarity occasioned by
five centuries of white contact, it is scarcely to be wondered that

there was very little interest in studying the languages of this area.

Boas, however, was not inclined to allow himself to be unduly influenced by the classificatory schemes of his famous students, Kroeber and Sapir. It was part of his overall plan that each linguistic family and language isolate should be adequately described, and so it is perhaps to Boas, more than anyone else, we owe the credit for not allowing interest in Southeastern linguistics to die out prematurely. He seems to have been particularly concerned about the language isolates, less about additional languages belonging to already known families. Hence, in the 1920s and 30s he sent out Wagner to do Yuchi, Swadesh to do Chitimacha, and Haas to do Tunica and Natchez. Though much of this material still remains to be published, texts and a grammar of Yuchi have appeared (Wagner 1931; 1933-38), several special studies of Chitimacha are available (Swadesh 1933; 1934; 1946), and a complete grammar, texts, and dictionary of Tunica have been published (Haas 1940a; 1946; 1950b; 1953).

Boas's foresight in regard to these languages was commendable. Atakapa was already gone in the 1930s, though Swadesh and I attempted to find speakers,[1] and today Tunica, Chitimacha, and Natchez are also extinct. Having been exposed to Southeastern linguistics through my work on Tunica and Natchez, I saw that the proposed affiliations of these language isolates could not be validated (or invalidated) without considerably more information about the Muskogean languages, the largest linguistic family existing solely in the Southeast, and so I also worked extensively on Creek (Haas 1938; 1940; 1948), to a lesser extent on Koasati (Haas 1944), and briefly on Hitchiti and Choctaw.

II

World War II was an exceedingly disruptive influence in the study of North American Indian languages. Almost all the linguists who had had field experience with these languages were diverted to the study and teaching of languages of the Far East considered critical for the war effort and some of them were more or less permanently diverted from their earlier interests. Southeastern Indian linguistics was particularly hard hit. After the work of the 1930s little additional field work was undertaken until fairly recently. Frank T. Siebert followed up the work of Frank Speck on Catawba and presented morphological evidence for the Siouan affinity of the language (Siebert 1945). Ernest Bender (1948), Bender and Zellig Harris (1946), and W. D. Reyburn (1953, 1954) have written on the phonology and verb morphology of Cherokee. Hans Wolff collected and published some additional Yuchi materials (1948). David West is working among the Mikasuki and has published on the phonology (1962). Earl Rand has made a brief study of Alabama and published a phonemic treatment (1968). Still more recently T. Dale Nicklas has undertaken fresh field work on Choctaw, a language which has received very little attention since Byington (1915).

In recent years there have also been some changes in our thinking about linguistic classification problems. It was natural that this work should begin with a rechecking of some of the proposals made by Swanton, particularly in regard to Tunican (Tunica-Chitimacha-Atakapa) and to Natchez-Muskogean. Swadesh made a sophisticated study of a part of the first of these in his "Phonologic Formulas for Atakapa-Chitimacha" (1946). Not long after this I proposed putting both of Swanton's groupings into one larger one called "Gulf" (Haas 1951; 1952) and also made note of a few Siouan resemblances. All of this remained ostensibly within the framework of Sapir's Hokan-Siouan superstock. A few years later, however, it became clear that attempts to validate Sapir's far-flung superstock had not been overly successful and that it might be well to look for connections between the Gulf languages and linguistic families outside of Hokan-Siouan. As a result of an effort of this sort it was proposed (Haas 1958) that the Gulf languages might be related to the Algonkian languages (including the Wiyot and Yurok languages of California). Not long after this, following up an earlier suggestion of Louis Allen (1931), Wallace Chafe presented new material supporting the relationship of Siouan and Iroquoian (1964). As a result of these efforts and similar efforts in regard to other parts of North America a considerably modified classification for the continent was set forth in a recent map (Voegelin and Voegelin 1966). The largest of Sapir's six groupings were broken up into smaller groupings, mostly of a more conservative nature. In the Southeast, however, the realignment was partly more conservative and partly more radical, as has just been shown.

Linguistic prehistory is often thought of in terms of language classification, as just discussed, but there are other more painstaking kinds of problems to be attacked by the linguistic prehistorian. The most important of these is the reconstruction of protolanguages. The optimum conditions for the reconstruction of a protolanguage require adequate synchronic descriptions of several languages the

time depth of whose relation is around 2000 years and the reconstructed result is parts of a language that was spoken around two
millennia ago. The only linguistic family lying wholly within the
Southeast is Muskogean and here considerable progress has been
made in reconstruction (Haas 1941, 1946, 1947, 1949, 1950). Much
more remains to be done, however, and for this work fuller descriptive materials on some of the languages are urgently needed,
particularly Choctaw-Chickasaw and Alabama.

Several other linguistic families which have branches extending
into the Southeast have also seen important progress in the reconstruction of their protolanguages. Foremost among these is Algonkian,
for which we have the largest body of reconstructed material of
any protolanguage north of Mexico (Bloomfield 1946, Hockett 1957,
Siebert 1967). Much progress has also been made in the reconstruction of Proto-Siouan, particularly in the work of Wolff (1950-
51) and Matthews (ms. 1958 and 1970). Proto-Iroquoian could
also be reconstructed, though Floyd Lounsbury who has presumably worked out quite a lot of it has published almost nothing
of it (1961).

The work of reconstructing these protolanguages is a new phase
in the progress and development of Southeastern linguistic studies.
Nothing of any significance had been done in the reconstruction
of any American Indian protolanguage prior to 1925 and most of
the work has been done in the past twenty or thirty years. It is
here that the pioneering work of Sapir and Bloomfield assumes great
significance because it is they and their students (and their students'
students) who have made the most important contributions to our
knowledge in this area.

The reconstruction of these protolanguages, and the publication
of the results, is important not only for Southeastern protolinguistics
but for Southeastern protoculture as well, but the development of
this possibility in Southeastern studies has not yet been undertaken
in any serious way. Some idea of the sorts of things that might
be done can be seen in Siebert's careful identification of many
flora and fauna which he used in his attempt to determine "The
Original Home of the Proto-Algonquian People" (1967).

III

The full extent of linguistic diversity in the Southeast may
never be known. Names like Avoyel, Taensas, Koroa, Grigra, Tiou,
Yamasee, and Calusa, and many, many others remain to haunt
us. Even though some of these have been asserted to be the "same

as" or "closely related to" other known languages, we can never be sure in any case where no vocabularies exist. After all, Ofo was thought to be Muskogean because a Tunica Indian recalled one word of the language which began with an /f/ and this was taken to be diagnostic. (Although /f/ is common in Muskogean languages it is rare otherwise.) But when a full vocabulary was finally obtained (Swanton 1909), it was seen to be incontrovertably Siouan. Avoyel and Taensas are said to be related to Natchez on the basis of statements by early missionaries, and Taensas has even been the subject of a grammar generally considered to be a hoax (Brinton 1890:452-67; Swanton 1911:10-13), but whether Avoyel and Taensas were really related to Natchez may never be known. In the same way Koroa, Grigra, and Tiou are said to have been related to Tunica, but again we cannot be sure. But if they were separate languages related to Tunica (and not merely mutually intelligible dialects), their loss is perhaps even greater than if they were totally unrelated, for material on them would have enabled us to reconstruct a Proto-Tunican instead of having to deal with Tunica as a language isolate.

But quite aside from the problem of the unclassified languages of the Southeast, we have good reason to believe that the area was exceeded in diversity only by California-Oregon and the Northwest. If we take a time depth of about two millennia as our base, we find the following families represented in the Southeast, viz:

Algonkian (e. g. Powhatan, Pamlico, and others; Shawnee)
Iroquoian (Tuscarora and Cherokee, and probably some others)
Siouan (e. g. Tutelo, Biloxi, Ofo, and others; more distantly, Catawba)
Muskogean (Choctaw-Chickasaw, Apalachee, Alabama, Koasati, Hitchiti, Mikasuki, Creek, and probably others).

Besides these families we have several language isolates in the area, some of which may be related to one of the above families at a time depth in excess of two millennia, viz:

Yuchi (probably related to Proto-Siouan)
Natchez (related to Proto-Muskogean)
Tunica (part of Gulf, including Chitimacha, Atakapa, Natchez, and Proto-Muskogean)
Chitimacha (part of Gulf, as above)
Atakapa (part of Gulf, as above)
Timucua (of doubtful affiliation, Muskogean? Siouan? Arawakan?)[2]

The answer to the question of what these languages reflect of conditions of four or more millennia ago is suggested by various proposals of wider connections, e. g., Algonkian-Gulf, Siouan-Iroquoian, and even Sapir's Hokan-Siouan. Moreover, even though little has been done in the way of comparisons of North and South American languages, the possibility of finding connections should be good in the Southeast because of its proximity to the Caribbean area. However, greater certainty in regard to any proposals of more distant connections must await a greater accumulation of actual reconstructions in the strategic protolanguages of both continents, a task which may require decades. But this work, as it progresses, will be important for all kinds of prehistorical knowledge of the area, including possible South American connections. Southeastern Indian linguistics is clearly not a thing of the past but an endeavor which is only seriously beginning and which has a very bright future indeed.

NOTES

1. We also attempted to find speakers of other dying languages of the Southeast but succeeded only in the case of Biloxi for which a vocabulary of 54 words was collected (Haas 1968).

2. A possible Muskogean affiliation was suggested by Swanton in 1929. More recently Swadesh (1964) noted a small number of Arawakan resemblances but Siouan resemblances of a similar nature can also be found.

REFERENCES

Allen, Louis, 1931. Siouan and Iroquoian. *International Journal of American Linguistics* 6:185-193.

Barton, Benjamin Smith, 1797. *New Views of the Origin of the Tribes and Nations of North America* (Philadelphia: John Bioren).

Bender, Ernest, 1949. Cherokee II. *International Journal of American Linguistics* 15:223-228.

————— and Zellig S. Harris, 1946. The Phonemes of North Carolina Cherokee. *International Journal of American Linguistics* 12:14-21.

Bloomfield, Leonard, 1946. Algonquian. In *Linguistic Structures of Native America*, Harry Hoijer et al., Viking Fund Publications in Anthropology, no. 6, pp. 85-129.

Brinton, Daniel G., 1890. The Curious Hoax of the Taensa Language. *Essays of an Americanist* (Philadelphia: David McKay), pp. 452-467.

Byington, Cyrus A., 1915. *A Dictionary of the Choctaw Language*. Bureau of American Ethnology Bulletin 46 (Washington, D.C.: GPO).

Chafe, Wallace L., 1964. Another Look at Siouan and Iroquoian. *American Anthropologist* 66:852-862.

Dixon, Roland B. and Alfred L. Kroeber, 1913a. Relationship of the Indian Languages of California. *Science*, n.s., 37:225.

—————, 1913b. New Linguistic Families in California. *American Anthropologist*, n.s., 15:647-655.

Dorsey, James Owen, 1893. *The Biloxi Indians of Louisiana*. American Association for the Advancement of Science Proceedings 43:267-287.

Gallatin, Albert, 1836. *A Synopsis of the Indian Tribes within the United States.* . . . Transactions and Collections of the American Antiquarian Society, 2:1-422.

—————————, 1848. *Hale's Indians of North-West America, and Vocabularies of North America.* . . . Transactions of the American Ethnological Society, 2:xxiii-clxxx, 1-130.

Gatschet, Albert S., 1884. *A Migration Legend of the Creek Indians,* Brinton's Library of Aboriginal American Literature, I, no. 4. (Philadelphia).

Haas, Mary R., 1938. Geminate Consonant Clusters in Muskogee. *Language* 14:61-65.

—————————, 1940*a.* Tunica. Extract from *Handbook of American Indian Languages,* Part 4, Franz Boas, ed. (New York: Augustin).

—————————, 1940*b.* Ablaut and its Function in Muskogee. *Language* 16:141-150.

—————————, 1941. The Classification of the Muskogean Languages. In *Language, Culture, and Personality,* Leslie Spier, A. Irving Hallowell, and Stanley S. Newman, eds. (Menasha, Wisconsin).

—————————, 1944. Men's and Women's Speech in Koasati. *Language* 20:142-149

—————————, 1946*a.* A Grammatical Sketch of Tunica. In *Linguistic Structures of Native America,* Harry Hoijer et al., Viking Fund Publications in Anthropology, no. 6, pp. 337-366.

—————————, 1946*b.* A Proto-Muskogean Paradigm. *Language* 22:326-332.

—————————, 1947. Development of Proto-Muskogean *k^w*. *International Journal of American Linguistics* 13:135-137.

—————————, 1948. Classificatory Verbs in Muskogee. *International Journal of American Linguistics* 14:244-246.

—————————, 1949. The Position of Apalachee in the Muskogean Family. *International Journal of American Linguistics* 15:121-127.

—————————, 1950*a.* The Historical Development of Certain Long Vowels in Creek. *International Journal of American Linguistics* 16:122-125.

—————————, 1950*b. Tunica Texts,* University of California Publications in Linguistics 6:1-174 (Berkeley and Los Angeles).

—————————, 1951. The Proto-Gulf Word for *Water* (with Notes on Siouan-Yuchi). *International Journal of American Linguistics* 17:71-79.

—————————, 1952. The Proto-Gulf Word for *Land* (with a note on Proto-Siouan). *International Journal of American Linguistics* 18:238-240.

—————————, 1953. *Tunica Dictionary,* University of California Publications in Linguistics 6:175-332 (Berkeley and Los Angeles).

—————————, 1956. Natchez and the Muskogean Languages. *Language* 32:61-72.

—————————, 1958. A New Linguistic Relationship in North America: Algonkian and the Gulf Languages. *Southwestern Journal of Anthropology* 14:231-264.

—————————, 1968. The Last Words of Biloxi. *International Journal of American Linguistics* 34:77-84.

—————————, 1969. *The Prehistory of Languages,* Janua Linguarum, series minor, no. 57 (The Hague-Paris: Mouton).

—————————, 1970. Review of Benjamin Smith Barton, New Views of the Origin of the Tribes and Nations of North America. (Ann Arbor, Michigan: University Microfilms, 1968). *International Journal of American Linguistics* 36:68-70.

Hale, Horatio, 1883*a.* Indian Migrations, as Evidenced by Language, Part I: The Huron-Cherokee Stock. *The American Antiquarian* 5:18-28.

—————————————, 1883*b*. The Tutelo Tribe and Language. *Proceedings of the American Philosophical Society* 21:1-45 (Philadelphia).

Hockett, Charles F., 1957. Central Algonquian Vocabulary: Stems in /k-/. *International Journal of American Linguistics* 23:247-268.

Jefferson, Thomas, 1964. *Notes on the State of Virginia.* Harper Torchbooks TB 3052 (New York, Evanston, London: Harper and Row).

Lounsbury, Floyd G., 1961. Iroquois-Cherokee Linguistic Relations. *Symposium on Cherokee-Iroquois Culture.* Bureau of American Ethnology Bulletin 180 (Washington, D.C.: GPO).

Matthews, G. Hubert, [1958]. Handbook of Siouan Languages. University of Pennsylvania dissertation.

—————————————, 1959. Proto-Siouan Kinship Terminology. *American Anthropologist* 61:252-278.

—————————————, 1970. Some Notes on the Proto-Siouan Continuants. *International Journal of American Linguistics* 35:98-109.

[Pickering, John], 1831. Indian Languages of America. *Encyclopaedia Americana* Vol. IV (Appendix), pp. 581-900.

—————————————, 1833. Introductory Memoir. Father Sebastian Rasles, A Dictionary of the Abnaki Language, American Academy of Arts and Sciences Memoir 1:370-574, pp. 371-372.

Powell, John Wesley, 1891. *Linguistic Families of North America North of Mexico.* Seventh Annual Report, Bureau of [American] Ethnology, 1885-1886, pp. 1-142.

Rand, Earl, 1968. The Structural Phonology of Alabaman, a Muskogean Language. *International Journal of American Linguistics* 34:94-103.

Reyburn, William D., 1953. Cherokee Verb Morphology I. *International Journal of American Linguistics* 19:172-180.

Sapir, Edward, 1920. The Hokan and Coahuiltecan Languages. *International Journal of American Linguistics* 1:280-290.

—————————————, 1921. A Bird's-eye View of American Languages North of Mexico. *Science* 54:408.

—————————————, 1929. Central and North American Indian Languages. *The Encyclopaedia Britannica,* 14th ed., 5:138-141 (London, New York, and Toronto: The Encyclopaedia Britannica Co.). Reprinted in *Selected Writings of Edward Sapir,* David G. Mandelbaum, ed. (Berkeley and Los Angeles: The University of California Press, 1949).

Siebert, Frank T., Jr., 1945. Linguistic Classification of Catawba. *International Journal of American Linguistics* 11:100-104, 211-218.

—————————————, 1967. The Original Home of the Proto-Algonquian People. National Museum of Canada Bulletin, 214: Contributions to Anthropology: Linguistics I, pp. 13-47 (Ottawa: The Queen's Printer).

Swadesh, Morris, 1933. Chitimacha Verbs of Derogatory or Abusive Connotation. *Language* 9:192-201.

—————————————, 1934. The Phonetics of Chitimacha. *Language* 10:345-362.

—————————————, 1946*a*. Chitimacha. In *Linguistic Structures of Native America,* Harry Hoijer et al., Viking Fund Publications in Anthropology, no. 6. pp. 312-336.

—————————————, 1946*b*. Phonologic formulas for Atakapa-Chitimacha. *International Journal of American Linguistics* 12:113-132.

—————————————, 1947. Atakapa-Chitimacha *k^w*. *International Journal of American Linguistics* 13:120-121.

—————————————, 1964. Linguistic Overview. In *Prehistoric Man in the New World,* Jesse D. Jennings and Edward Norbeck, eds. (Chicago: The University of Chicago Press), pp. 527-556.

Swanton, John R., 1909. A New Siouan Dialect. *Putnam Anniversary Volume* (New York), pp. 477-486.
--------------------------------, 1911. *Indian Tribes of the Lower Mississippi Valley and Adjacent Coast of the Gulf of Mexico*. Bureau of American Ethnology Bulletin 43 (Washington: GPO).
--------------------------------, 1919. A Structural and Lexical Comparison of the Tunica, Chitimacha, and Atakapa Languages. Bureau of American Ethnology Bulletin 68 (Washington: GPO).
--------------------------------, 1924. The Muskhogean Connection of the Natchez Language. *International Journal of American Linguistics* 3:46-75.
--------------------------------, 1929. The Tawasa Language. *American Anthropologist* 31:435-453.
--------------------------------, 1946. *The Indians of the Southeastern United States*. Bureau of American Ethnology Bulletin 137 (Washington: GPO).
Voegelin, Charles F. and Erminie Wheeler Voegelin, 1941. Map of North American Indian Languages (Menasha, Wisconsin: American Ethnological Society).
Voegelin, Charles F. and Florence M. Voegelin, 1966. Map of North American Indian Languages (Rand, McNally, and Co.: American Ethnological Society).
Wagner, Günter, 1931. *Yuchi Tales*. Publications of the American Ethnological Society, vol. 13.
--------------------------------, 1933-38. Yuchi. In *Handbook of American Indian Languages*, Part 3, Franz Boas, ed. (Glückstadt-Hamburg-New York: Augustin).
West, John David, 1962. The Phonology of Mikasuki. *Studies in Linguistics* 16:77-91.
Wolff, Hans, 1948. Yuchi Phonemes and Morphemes, with Special Reference to Person Markers. *International Journal of American Linguistics* 14:240-243.
--------------------------------, 1950-51. Comparative Siouan I, II, III, IV. *International Journal of American Linguistics* 26:61-66, 113-121, 168-178; 27:197-204.
--------------------------------, 1951. Yuchi Text with Analysis. *International Journal of American Linguistics* 17:48-53.

The Archaeology of European-Indian Contact in the Southeast

THIS paper is intended as a review and critique of historic archaeology in the Southeastern United States. For our purposes here, historic archaeology may be defined, following Fontana (1965:61), as "archaeology carried out in sites which contain material evidence of non-Indian culture or concerning which there is contemporary non-Indian documentary record." In the Southeast, this definition encompasses a period of nearly five centuries, but in the present paper we will be concerned with only the 350 years of European-Indian contact preceding Indian removal in 1838. Our geographical focus will be that area which the historian Verner W. Crane calls the Southern Frontier—"the great area extending southward from Virginia and the Tennessee Valley to the Gulf of Mexico, and westward to the Mississippi River" (Crane 1956:v).

In the Southeast to date, approximately one hundred and forty historic sites have been investigated and described in print.[1] Of these, the great majority, roughly 75%, are aboriginal sites yielding evidence of European contact. The remainder are the direct result of European activity; they include missions, forts, trading posts, habitations, and miscellaneous sites such as fishing camps and ship wrecks of the Spanish Plate fleet.

A number of aboriginal sites can be identified with reasonable certainty in the historical records of the 16th through 19th centuries. A complete inventory of these is not possible here, but some idea of the geographical and cultural range they represent can be given in a selected listing. In the lower Mississippi Valley, several sites can be identified: the Fatherland site, the Grand Village of the Natchez from 1682 to 1729 (Neitzel 1965); the Haynes Bluff and Angola Farm sites, representing historic Tunica from 1698 to approximately 1800 (Ford 1936:101-2, 129-40); and the Bayou Goula

55

Southern Anthropological Society   509

site, with a checkered occupational history spanning the years 1699 to 1758 and including remnants of the Bayogoula, Mugulasha, Acolapissa, Tiou, Taensa, Chitimacha, and Houma (Quimby 1957). Documented Cherokee sites are represented by the lower settlement of Chauga (Kelly and Neitzel 1961), the eighteenth century Overhill towns of Chote and Ocoee (Lewis 1953), and New Echota, the capital of the Cherokee Nation from 1826 to 1830 (DeBaillou 1955). In Georgia, the eighteenth century Lower Creek town of Kasita (Willey and Sears 1952) and Palachacolas, an Apalachicola settlement on the Savannah River dating to 1684-1716 (J. Caldwell 1948), have been identified and reported on briefly. Documented, aboriginal sites in Florida include Safety Harbor, principal town of the Tocobago visited by Governor Menendez in 1567 (Griffin and Bullen 1950) and Mound Key, the Calusa capital visited by Menendez in the following year (Goggin and Sturtevant 1964).

In some cases, sites that are not specifically documented can nevertheless be attributed with reasonable certainty to historically known tribal or ethnic groups. The four sites excavated by Jennings (1941) near Tupelo, Mississippi, and identified as Chickasaw are good examples of this kind of situation.

With these two kinds of identification, it is possible to define the archaeological culture of several tribal groups for at least one point in their historically documented existence. These include Natchez (Neitzel 1965), Taensa (Williams 1967), Tunica (Ford 1936), Coosa (DeJarnette and Hansen 1960), Kasita (Willey and Sears 1952), Apalachicola (Caldwell 1948), Hitchiti (Kelly 1938; Fairbanks 1956), Yuchi (Chase 1960), Tocobaga (Griffin and Bullen 1950), Potano (Goggin et al. 1949), Calusa (Goggin and Sturtevant 1964), and at least one segment of the Chickasaw (Jennings 1941), Choctaw (Collins 1927), Overhill Cherokee (Lewis 1953), Underhill Cherokee (Kelly and Neitzel 1961), Guale (Larson 1958), and Seminole (Goggin 1949; Bullen 1953). These identifications are, theoretically at least, datum points from which further investigations concerned with tribal histories or acculturation processes can be undertaken.

European sites that have been identified and investigated include, among others, the Castillo de San Marcos (Harrington et al. 1955), Fort Frederica (Manucy 1962), the Spanish missions of San Francisco de Oconee and San Luis (Boyd et al. 1951), Charles Towne (Stephenson 1969), and an English trading post, Spaulding's Lower Store, serving the Seminole from 1763 to 1784 (Goggin 1949).

In the past several years, an increasing effort has been devoted to the analysis of European artifacts found on historic sites. Recent typological and documentary studies have provided information on developmental changes that specific kinds of artifacts have undergone and on the manufacturing and trade systems that brought them to the New World. Outstanding studies include those of John M. Goggin on Spanish pottery of the olive jar (1960) and majolica (1968) types, John Witthoft on gun flints (1966), and Stanley J. Olsen on plain clothing buttons of the 18th and 19th centuries (1963). The most immediate reward of this kind of research is an increased precision in historic site chronology. In addition, knowledge of the European origin of trade materials may assist in identifying the nationality of non-aboriginal sites, as well as provide insight into trade patterns within the Southeast. Of potentially great value in this regard is Witthoft's (1966:24-5) recent observation that Spanish gun flints are derived from Albanian quarries and are distinguishable from North European flints used by French and English.

The archaeological literature yields a number of insights into the effect of European contact on aboriginal Southeastern culture. Several researchers have noted the persistence of aboriginal pottery making well into the historic period. At the Upper Creek towns of Nuyake and Tohopeka, both destroyed during the Creek war of 1813-1814, Fairbanks (1962:42, 51) found pottery very similar to that of the related Ocmulgee Fields culture which is dated at approximately 1685-1715. One hundred years of intensive contact with whites seems to have had little effect on the ceramic arts of these people. Fairbanks (1962:51-3) and Mason (1963:73) both attribute this conservatism to the nature of European contact, which affected women's roles little, and to the stabilizing nature of the matrilineal organization of Creek society.

Among the mission Indians of Guale, Apalachee, and Timucua provinces, pottery making continued apparently until the complete destruction of the mission system by English-Indian raids between 1700 and 1725. Unlike the English, the Spanish traditionally used earthenware vessels in food preparation. Majolica and olive jars, the only Spanish pottery occurring with any regularity and frequency in Florida sites, were apparently used for food storage and consumption. Indian pottery seems to have been used for cooking (Goggin 1952:72; Smith 1956:105), and it is likely that the Spanish actually encouraged this aboriginal craft.

Perhaps the contact situation with greatest potential for Indian acculturation prevailed in the Spanish mission system of north Florida. Available archaeological evidence, however, indicates that the missions had relatively little effect on native culture. As noted, aboriginal pottery making continued throughout the mission period. Much of the aboriginal tool inventory seems also to have been retained. Among the artifacts recovered during the excavation of the Apalachee mission of San Francisco de Oconee are stone projectile points, scrapers, and mauls, limestone awl sharpeners, and grinding stones (Boyd et al. 1950:175-7).

The effectiveness of the Spanish policy of Christianizing the native population is difficult to assess archaeologically. A measure of success is perhaps indicated by the cessation of burial mound construction in the Apalachee and Timucua territories by 1600 (Smith 1956:37). To the south, beyond direct Spanish control, this aboriginal mortuary practice persisted well into the 17th century (Smith 1956:64). On the other hand, lack of success can be inferred from the fact that no examples of native made religious articles showing Christian influence have been reported from any site in Spanish Florida.

The extent to which the mission system affected native settlement patterns is uncertain. There were apparently efforts to consolidate the native population in mission settlements, but these seem to have been largely unsuccessful due to the requirements of Indian subsistence practices (Sturtevant 1962:57, 62). Archaeological evidence bearing on this question is inconclusive. At Darien Bluff site (S. Caldwell 1954:15-16), possibly the mission of Santo Domingo de Talaje, we find evidence of a nucleated settlement consisting of fifteen wall trench structures "neatly arranged" in an area to the east of buildings identified as the actual mission complex. The Scott Miller site (the mission of San Francisco de Oconee), on the other hand, did not yield evidence of habitation structures for the Indian neophytes despite extensive testing (Boyd et al. 1950:11-24). Evidence of them may have been obliterated by recent plowing, but it is also possible that this mission was characterized by a dispersed settlement pattern.

Aboriginal culture was not alone in undergoing change as a result of European-Indian contact. There is some archaeological evidence that the Spanish way of life was also being modified. Most striking is evidence from the Spanish frontier outpost, Fort Pupo, on the St. Johns River, which shows the extent to which Spaniards in some situations were utilizing aboriginal material culture (Goggin 1951). So small in quantity and variety were the Spanish artifacts at this fort and so abundant those of an aboriginal nature, that the investigator, John Goggin, is led to observe, "If we had no historical evidence for the nature of the inhabitants at Pupo in Spanish times, the most reasonable assumption would be that the site was one purely of Indian occupation" (1951:186).

From historical records, it is clear that there was considerable movement of tribal populations within the Southeast during the contact period. Some documented movements can be recognized archaeologically. Retreat of the aboriginal population from the Georgia coast province of Guale to the vicinity of St. Augustine in the late 17th century is reflected archaeologically in the appearance of San Marcos series pottery in the latter area (Goggin 1952:60-61; Larson 1958:14). It is also possible to archaeologically demonstrate the later arrival in Florida of peoples that came to be known as Seminole (Goggin 1949, 1958). The movement of remnant Natchez groups subsequent to dispersal by French forces in 1730 is documented in the historical records (Swanton 1911: 253-6) and substantiated archaeologically. In two of the four historic Chickasaw sites he investigated near Tupelo, Mississippi, Jennings (1941: 179-80) found abundant sherds of the Natchez pottery types, Fatherland Incised and Natchez Incised.

From the preceding review, it is clear that much has been accomplished in the field of Southeastern historic archaeology. This pleasing picture must be tempered, however, by a consideration of the shortcomings and inadequacies of the field. These, it should be noted, are by no means unique to the Southeast or to the historic period, but rather are characteristic of American archaeology in general. The research under consideration here may be criticized at three points: inadequacy of investigation, inadequacy of reporting, and inadequacy of interpretation.

The simple fact concerning research conducted to date is that roughly 75% of the sites reported have only been investigated by surface artifact collecting, test pit excavation, or amateur excavation. For an additional 10% of the sites, investigation has been concerned only with burials or mounds. As a result, data available for study from an overwhelming majority of the reported sites is limited in kind and is not representative of total cultures. Much of the value of Goggin's research on Fort Pupo (Goggin 1951), for example, lies in his interpretation of the different degree to which the English and Spanish garrisons were affected by Indian culture. This interpretation, however, is based on only two small test trenches, one of which apparently was located beyond the perimeter of the Spanish fortifications. Adequate sampling of the site might have yielded an entirely different picture of the Spanish occupation than is reported.

In my judgment, only eleven historic sites in the entire Southeast have received an adequate amount and kind of investigation. These are Mle 14 and Mle 90 (Jennings 1941), Bayou Goula (Quimby 1957), Chote (Lewis 1953), Macon Trading Post (Kelly 1938), Scott Miller (Boyd et al. 1950), Darien Bluff (S. Caldwell 1954), Charles Towne (Stephenson 1969), Kasita (Willey and Sears 1952), Fort Frederica (Manucy 1962), and Santa Rosa Pensacola (Smith 1965). Unfortunately, several of these sites have been inadequately reported. At the very least, a site report should contain a detailed description of both the artifacts and architectural features encountered and their assignment to components present at the site. Only a small number of historic sites with any kind of professional field investigation have received such treatment in print.

In the majority of published site reports, interpretation is restricted to identifying the site in historical records and determining the cultural affiliation of its occupants. To some extent these limited goals result from the nature of site investigation. Without extensive excavation of some sort, it is difficult to carry interpretation any further. The relationship between field investigation and interpretation, however, is a reciprocal one. If one is interested only in identifying the cultural affiliation of a site, surface collecting and test pits may be completely adequate.

Site reports containing additional interpretation are worth noting if for no other reason than to give their authors the recognition they deserve. Morrell (1965), Jennings (1941), Goggin (1951), and Fairbanks (1962) have each made observations on the consequences of Indian-European contact based upon field data from a particular site. In a number of reports, historical data is utilized as an aid in interpreting the archaeological record. Outstanding in this regard are the analyses of Neitzel (1965) at Fatherland, Quimby (1957) at Bayou Goula, and Manucy (1962) at Fort Frederica. In the latter, we find archaeology and history working together to provide a detailed description of the fort as it once existed.

Without doubt, the finest comparative synthesis available is that of Hale Smith (1956) dealing with the historic period in Florida. In this study, Smith reviews information available on all known historic sites in the state within a chronological framework of three periods spanning the years 1500 to 1800. Archaeological and historical information is presented to indicate the nature and effect of European-Indian contact during these different periods and a comparison is made between the Spanish-Indian and the English-Indian contact situations.

With this one exception, attempts to synthesize all or part of the historic period in the Southeast are concerned primarily with identifying archaeological cultures with tribal or ethnic groups described in historical accounts.[2] This is certainly an important undertaking, but unfortunately the conclusions offered in such studies are of doubtful validity. For one thing, these syntheses suffer as a result of their reliance on three highly questionable assumptions: that material culture, especially pottery, correlates with ethnic, tribal, political, or linguistic boundaries; that change in the archaeological record is due in the main to movements of people; and that the size, composition, and nature of tribal groups recorded by Europeans were invariant from the late prehistoric period through Indian removal. These syntheses are also defective in that they are concerned almost entirely with political and linguistic groupings such as Creek, Upper and Lower Creek, Muskogean, and Timucuan.

The archaeological literature is full of across-the-board identifications of archaeologically defined cultures and historically documented tribal groups. Frequently, we find the archaeologist paying token homage to the anthropological tenet that there is no necessary relationship between pottery or material culture on the one hand and people on the other, and then proceeding to make just such an identification. In one recently published paper (Bullen 1969:417), the Safety Harbor ceramic complex is equated with Timucua, a language family of uncertain linguistic affiliation, and the Glades pottery complex is equated with Calusa, a political entity. A number of articles (Fairbanks 1958; Sears 1955; Kneberg 1952) have appeared concerning the ceramic complexes characteristic of Creek and Cherokee.

The existence of Creek legends indicating a western origin for Muskogean-speaking tribes and the evident intrusion of Mississippian type culture into the Southeast from that general direction in prehistoric times together encourage the assumption that migration has been a major mechanism bringing about culture change. The archaeological cultures Macon Plateau, Dallas, Fort Walton, Pensacola, and Moundville are frequently cited as evidence for the late prehistoric arrival of Muskogean speakers in the Southeast. In eastern Tennessee, one interpretation (Lewis 1943; Kneberg 1952) equates Creek and Yuchi with Mississippian cultures and Cherokee with cultures related to Caldwell's (1958) Southern Appalachian tradition. Logically, the observed archaeological shift from Mississippian to Southern Appalachian culture type in historic times is attributed to the replacement of Creek and Yuchi by Cherokee (Kneberg 1952:197-98).[3]

The assumption that aboriginal tribal units recognized by Europeans were invariant through time is most thoroughly embraced by researchers working with "Creek" prehistory.[4] Categories such as Creek, Upper Creek, and Lower Creek may have had cultural significance in the 18th century, but there is no guarantee, and in fact it is unlikely, that such was the case one hundred or two hundred years earlier. The Creek Confederacy was a political entity made possible in large part by the degree of cultural homogeneity existing throughout the Southeast in aboriginal times. It represented the last large scale political alignment in the area, but descriptions of de Soto's travels indicate it was not the first. To use these terms and categories uncritically in our research and to assume that they necessarily correlate with archaeological cultures of the prehistoric period can only lead to confusion when we attempt to reconstruct culture history.

I do not think we can make much progress in correlating archaeological and ethnohistorical data in the Southeast as long as we continue to concern ourselves with linguistic categories such as Hitchiti and Muskogee or large scale political alignments such as Creek and Apalachee. Rather, we should focus our attention on the individual tribes or towns that comprise these larger entities.[5] Field research should be concentrated on historically identifiable sites of known ethnic composition with the aim of defining the archaeological culture of such towns. Once they have been identified and defined archaeologically, towns such as Kasita and Ocmulgee or Chote and Chauga can then be compared to determine what, if any, archaeological significance the larger tribal groupings such as Creek and Cherokee have.[6]

At the present time, despite the great amount of work that has been done in Southeastern historic archaeology, the field seems to lack direction. I would suggest that there are at least three tasks which are appropriate and reasonable for it: application of the direct historical approach to specific ethnic groups, investigation of European-Indian acculturation, and investigation of the relationship between archaeological culture units and social or ethnic groups. All three goals complement one another. Furthermore, progress in all would seem to require that we concentrate field research upon the remains of historically documented towns.

Ethnohistorical data indicate the persistence of individual towns as distinct entities throughout much of the contact period, Coosa being a good example. It is logical that they be the subject of the direct historical approach rather than entities such as Creek and Cherokee. If Ocmulgee and Kasita or Tocobaga and Potano are archaeologically distinct on the historic horizon, then culture historical reconstruction should begin with them and work backward in time.

If we are to ever have more than general insights into the nature of European-Indian acculturation in the Southeast, it will be necessary to investigate changes through time in specific ethnic groups. What is necessary is to work with the sequentially related settlements of specific towns. We must, for example, have information on the nature and progress of acculturation among the Kashita not only for 1715, but also for 1680 and 1780.

The relationship of the archaeologist's unit concepts—phase, focus, culture, horizon—to ethnic and social groups has received relatively little attention in American archaeology.[7] Yet if we are ever to do more than construct ceramic histories, we must face this question and attempt to discover what, if any, invariant relationships there are. Obviously, the historic period provides us with the most advantageous conditions for tackling the problem. Only in this period is it possible to compare ethnographically defined ethnic groups with archaeologically defined units.

NOTES

1. For practical reasons, it has been necessary to limit the scope of this paper to published research.

2. Cf. Fairbanks (1952), Lewis (1943), Kneberg (1952), and Sears (1955; 1964).

3. This view of Cherokee history has been recently criticized by Joffre Coe (1961).

4. Cf. Fairbanks (1952:294).

5. I have in mind here the towns or *Talwa* of the Creek confederacy which Swanton (1928:242) describes as consisting of a "body of people who had their own square ground and actually formed a little state." Comparable ethnic units existed among the Cherokee. Gearing (1962:3) refers to them as villages and estimates that they numbered between 30 and 40 in the early 18th century.

6. Bruce G. Trigger (1968:20-23) advocates a similar approach for archaeological reconstruction in general when he recommends that we first identify communities—"the archaeologist's socially defined minimal unit"—and then proceed to investigate the cultural, political, economic, and social relationships existing between them.

7. But see Trigger (1968; Chapter 3).

REFERENCES

Boyd, Mark F., Hale G. Smith, and John W. Griffin, 1951. *Here They Once Stood: The Tragic End of the Apalachee Missions* (Gainesville: University of Florida Press).

Bullen, Ripley P., 1953. Notes on the Seminole Archaeology of West Florida. *Southeastern Archaeological Conference Newsletter*, Vol. 3, No. 1.

————————————————, 1969. The Southern Limit of Timucua Territory. *Florida Historical Quarterly* 47:414-419.

Caldwell, Joseph R., 1948. Palachacolas Town, Hampton County, South Carolina. *Journal of the Washington Academy of Science* 38: 321-4.

————————————————, 1958. *Trend and Tradition in the Prehistory of the Eastern United States*. American Anthropological Association Memoirs, No. 88.

Caldwell, Sheila K., 1954. A Spanish Mission Site Near Darien. *Early Georgia* 1:13-17.

Chase, David W., 1960. *An Historic Indian Town Site in Russell County, Alabama*, Coweta Memorial Association Papers, No. 2 (Columbus, Georgia).

Coe, Joffre L., 1961. Cherokee Archaeology. In *Symposium on Cherokee and Iroquois Culture*, William N. Fenton and John Gulick, eds., Bureau of American Ethnology Bulletin, No. 180 (Washington, D.C.: GPO).

Collins, Henry B., 1927. Potsherds from Choctaw Village Sites in Mississippi. *Journal of the Washington Academy of Science* 17: 259-61.

Crane, Verner W., 1956. *The Southern Frontier: 1670-1732* (Ann Arbor: University of Michigan Press).

DeBaillou, Clemens, 1955. Excavations at New Echota in 1954. *Early Georgia*, Vol. 1, No. 4.

DeJarnette, David L. and Asael T. Hansen, 1960. *The Archaeology of the Childersburg Site, Alabama*, Department of Anthropology, Florida State University, Notes in Anthropology, No. 4 (Tallahassee).

Fairbanks, Charles H., 1952. Creek and Pre-Creek. In *Archaeology of Eastern United States*, James B. Griffin, ed. (Chicago: University of Chicago Press), pp. 285-300.

————————————————, 1956. *Archaeology of the Funeral Mound, Ocmulgee National Monument, Georgia*, National Park Service, Archaeological Research Series, No. 3 (Washington, D.C.: GPO).

————————————————, 1958. Some Problems of the Origin of Creek Pottery. *The Florida Anthropologist* 11 (2)53-63.

————————————————, 1962. Excavations at Horseshoe Bend, Alabama. *Florida Anthropologist* 15 (2)41-56.

Fontana, Bernard L., 1965. On the Meaning of Historic Sites Archaeology. *American Antiquity* 31:61-65.

Ford, James A., 1936. *Analysis of Indian Village Site Collections from Louisiana and Mississippi*, Department of Conservation, Louisiana Geological Survey, Anthropological Study, No. 2 (New Orleans).

Gearing, Fred, 1962. *Priests and Warriors: Social Structures for Cherokee Politics in the 18th Century*. American Anthropological Association Memoirs, No. 93.

Goggin, John M., 1949. A Florida Indian Trading Post, Ca. 1673-1784. *Southern Indian Studies*, 1:35-38.

————————————————, 1951. Fort Pupo—A Spanish Frontier Outpost. *Florida Historical Quarterly* 30:139-92.

————————————————, 1952. *Space and Time Perspective in Northern St. Johns Archaeology, Florida*, Yale University Publications in Anthropology, No. 47 (New Haven: Yale University Press).

————————————————, 1958. Seminole Pottery. In *Prehistoric Pottery of the Eastern United States*, Museum of Anthropology, University of Michigan.

————————————————, 1960. *The Spanish Olive Jar*, Yale University Publications in Anthropology, No. 62 (New Haven: Yale University Press).

————————————————, 1968. *Spanish Majolica in the New World: Types of the Sixteenth to Eighteenth Centuries*, Yale University Publication in Anthropology, No. 72 (New Haven: Yale University Press).

Goggin, John M., Mary E. Goodwin, Earl Hest
 Spangeberg, 1949. An Historic Indian Burial,
 Anthropologist 2:10-25.
Goggin, John M. and William C. Sturtevant, 1
 Nonagricultural Society (With Notes on Sibl
 in Cultural Anthropology, Ward H. Goodenou
 Hill), pp. 179-219.
Griffin, John W. and Ripley P. Bullen, 1950. *Th*
 County, Florida, Florida Anthropological Socie
 ville: University of Florida Press).
Griffin, John W. and Hale G. Smith, 1949. No
 1605 Now in Tomoka State Park. *Florida F*
Harrington, J. C., Albert C. Manucy, and John N
 Excavations in the Courtyard of Castillo d
 Florida. *Florida Historical Quarterly* 34:100-14
Jennings, Jesse D., 1941. Chickasaw and Earlier
 Mississippi. *Journal of Mississippi History* 3:1.
Kelly, A. R., 1938. *A Preliminary Report on*
 Macon, Georgia. Bureau of American Ethnolo;
 ton, D.C.: GPO).
Kelly, A. R. and R. S. Neitzel, 1961. *The Chauga*
 Carolina, University of Georgia, Laboratory
 (Athens, Georgia: Department of Sociology
Kneberg, Madeline, 1952. The Tennessee Are;
 United States, James B. Griffin, ed. (Chicago
 pp. 190-198.
Larson, Lewis H., 1958. Cultural Relationships E
 Area and Georgia Coast. *The Florida Anth*
Lewis, T. M. N., 1943. Late Horizons in the
 American Philosophical Society 86:304-312.
⸻⸻⸻⸻⸻⸻, 1953. Early Historic
 Archaeological Conference Newsletter 3 (3)
Manucy, Albert C., 1962. *The Fort at Frederic*
 pology, Florida State University, Notes in An
Mason, Carole I., 1963. 18th Century Culture Ch
 Florida Anthropologist 16 (3):65-81.
Morrell, L. Ross, 1965. *The Woods Island Sit*
 1625-1800, The Department of Anthropology,
 in Anthropology, No. 11 (Tallahassee).
Neitzel, Robert S., 1965. *Archaeology of the*
 Village of the Natchez, Anthropological Pa
 of Natural History, Vol. 51, Part 1 (New
Olsen, Stanley J., 1963. Dating Early Plain Bu
 Antiquity 28:551-4.
Quimby, George I., 1957. *The Bayou Goula*
 Fieldiana: Anthropology, Vol. 47, No. 2 (Ch
 Museum).
Sears, William H., 1955. Creek and Cherokee
 American Antiquity 21:143-49.
⸻⸻⸻⸻⸻⸻, 1964. The Southeaste
 Man in the New World, Jennings and Nor
 of Chicago Press).

Smith,
 Soci
⸻⸻⸻
 saco
 in A
Stephen
 of ≀
 Note
Sturteva
 Ame≀
Swanton
 Adja
 Bulle
⸻⸻⸻
 India
 Repo.
Trigger,
 York
Willey,
 Indian
Williams
 Confe
 2, Par
Witthoft
 36:12-

Comments

CHARLES H. FAIRBANKS

As a group these four papers are impressive as an inventory of what is known, what is unknown, and what ought to be known about the Indians and early history of the Southeastern United States. I was particularly impressed by the fact that each participant was able to summarize a great deal of information which was probably not familiar even to regional specialists in the specific disciplines. Each generation seems compelled to rediscover much of the work done by previous scholars. A significant function of such a symposium as this is to summarize and list the basic work, thus encouraging pathfinding in new fields. I believe that these four papers will provide this guidance.

Certainly no one is more capable of discussing Southeastern linguistics than Mary Haas. Her paper gives an admirable and thoughtful discussion, largely centered around the theme of linguistic diversity in the area and the history of attempts to classify the many languages there present. It was tantalizing to hear Haas speak of her widespread work in Tunica, Natchez, Creek, Koasati, Hitchiti, and Choctaw.

In talking of reconstructive studies, Haas is really speaking in part about glottochronology. She refers to Siebert's pioneering study (1967) using botanical and zoological terms to suggest the original homeland for the Proto-Algonkian people. Similar studies could be done for Muskogean and perhaps for Cherokee (Iroquoian). For the archeologist, the question is not that Iroquois and Cherokee are related, or that they evidently separated at a particular time, but whether the recovered archeological evidence supports, in detail, such a conclusion. I must confess that I cannot see that it does for Iroquois and Cherokee, which certainly doesn't question either the relationship or the time interval. What does interest me is how Cherokee early historic material, social, and religious cultural elements

67

can relate so closely to their Muskogean counterparts with little or no evidence of linguistic relationship.

Can we but weave a fabric of linguistics, archaeology, ethnohistory, and physical anthropology that will contain these disparate observations, it may well resemble more a straight-jacket than a shopping bag, but the attempt should be made. Even more interesting would be a complex linguistic, ethnographic, and bioanthropological attack on the question of the homeland and migrations of the Muskogean peoples.

Louis De Vorsey's paper was a revelation to most of us of the resources provided by early maps, especially in the hands of such a skilled historical geographer. Most of us have consulted early maps, usually for the purpose of locating Indian villages. It is clear from De Vorsey's work that considerably greater information is available and that cooperation with geographers can be rewarding. The discussion of the Indian Boundary Line, and its delineation from a large series of medium scale local maps, represents a valuable basic document for Southeastern ethnohistorical studies. In addition, it suggests the values that might be derived from similar studies of the later treaty lines in the Southeast. These have been mapped in a general study (Royce 1902), but no detailed analysis of the lines is known to me. Would it be possible to study these treaty lines from the standpoint of conflicting Indian and Colonial concepts of resources and terrain? From the results indicated by De Vorsey, it would seem that such studies are possible and would be rewarding from a cultural standpoint.

The second part of this paper deals with the verification of the original forest cover from the original surveyors' maps. These plats were made when individual land holdings were established and should represent the original condition of the forest. The use of such data was completely new to me, although I had used the original federal survey field notes for the Territory of Florida in site survey and in attempts to locate Seminole communities. De Vorsey here suggests exciting possibilities for combined geographical and archeological studies. As he points out, surveyors generally note the species of trees, especially at corners. The biological scientists should be able, from this data, to reconstruct what resources were available in the specific area. Archaeological studies of food bones and plant remains in the Indian sites would give us an understanding of the local fauna used by the Indians. Up to the present our attempt to define the ecological niche for any aboriginal component has depended almost solely on either archeologic or documentary evidence. Never, as far as I am aware, has there been a coordination of the floral cover such as is suggested by De Vorsey's paper. Should pollen studies and analysis of archeological plant remains become commonly available, we might be able to make significant statements about the Indians' use of selected aspects of their environment.

Impressive as is David Hally's inventory of historic Indian archeology, I was impressed by the fact that unpublished theses and dissertations represent a much broader range of ethnic groups and time periods. It is clear that published materials are only a small part of what we know about the area. All anthropologists in the Southeast must continue to depend heavily on Dockstader's *The American Indian in Graduate Studies* (1957) which is supposed to be updated shortly. A great deal of work has been done which has not been formally published and a number of students are presently at work. Probably the best excavated historic site in the Southeast is Ocmulgee Old Fields on Ocmulgee National Monument. Yet the only significant report so far is in an unpublished dissertation (Mason 1963). There is clearly a need for greater dissemination of the large body of data that has been accumulating over the past forty years.

Hally properly calls attention to the increased precision of dating made possible by recent studies of historic European materials found on Indian sites. It seems clear that continued research, often related to the excavation of European settlements, will yield increased accuracy in these areas. I suspect that new methods of dating, such as thermoluminescence, will also allow us to be much more exact in our dating.

While Hally's discussion of the interaction of Spanish and Indian cultures very adequately summarizes the published literature, recent unpublished work must modify some of his conclusions. It seems to me that documentary and archeologic evidence agree that the mission system did indeed profoundly affect Indian culture. In both the Santa Fe area (modern Gainesville) and the Apalachee area (modern Tallahassee) profound changes are apparent. Most of the Potano and Apalachee sites of the 17th century are single component sites. At least for the Timucua area it is clear that the historic towns represent the end of a long cultural tradition. This Alachua tradition changes through time, yet represents continued evolution along well established trends. Yet the mission sites and Spanish cattle ranches have little stratigraphic depth. We know from documents that the priests tried to establish more permanent villages among their charges. The fact that these communities were built on new sites strongly suggests fundamental changes in the subsistance base. The presence of large quantities of peach pits at Fig Springs seems to be the only direct evidence we have as to the type of acculturation involved. I suspect that similar changes can be demonstrated for Apalachee, and perhaps for Guale.

The Creek and Cherokee areas showed comparable changes, although they seem to have been evoked by the pressures of the Indian trade system. So little seems to be known about the Chickasaw and Choctaw that I feel unsure about the situation in those areas.

Hally calls to our attention the very real needs in Southeastern historic Indian archeology. We certainly need more extensive, rather than intensive, excavations. Equally critical is a planned approach to problem oriented excavation of known towns. The direct historical approach will only work, it seems to me, if it deals with specifically identified sites. This implies a very extensive use of documents and close cooperation between historian, geographer, and archeologist. Hally's plea that the direct historical approach be applied to specific known towns seems to be entirely valid and promises worthwhile results. The implementation of such a program will necessarily involve abandonment of the present pattern of excavation where sites are chosen because of availability or because they are about to be destroyed. Systematic search, in documents and maps, for specific town locations must be followed by extensive excavations that will reveal community plan, burial complex, agricultural plots, and the entire recoverable culture complex. Only then can the archeologist begin to deal with the problems of Indian-European acculturation, community change, and ecological relationships. Without subscribing entirely to Wheeler's (1954) low opinion of stratigraphic test pitting, we have all known that it is primarily useful for establishing chronologies. We now have fairly secure chronologies for most of the major areas of the Southeast. Planned community excavation is long overdue. As far as I know, only Joffre Coe's recent attack on Cherokee origins represents such a systematic approach.

William Pollitzer's paper represents a valuable synthesis of the work so far done in physical anthropology in the Southeast. Like that of Mary Haas, it clearly shows the shift from broad regional, descriptive, classificatory approaches at an early period to specifically oriented functional problems. Once again I am impressed with the amount of material which has been published in recent years. I think that most of us find it difficult to keep up with current literature outside of our own field and area. Papers such as these serve a very useful summarizing purpose.

Pollitzer clearly shows, as did Haas especially, how the style of research and writing has changed in a century or more. Now much of the bio-anthropology is concerned with blood types and characteristics that can be treated as monogenic traits. What has been learned from these studies seems largely to confirm the linguistic, ethnohistoric, and archeologic data which are available. I suspect that it will take some time to satisfactorily project bio-anthropological data back to the older archeological horizons. We do, however, have a solid base on which to build at both ends of the sequences. Pollitzer's recommendations for needed work are entirely sound, and I hope that our current crops of graduate students will not become so enamored with monkey-watching and other glamourous pursuits as to see archeological bones only as examination problems. The body of material is now sufficient so that meaningful studies should be attempted.

These four papers give a comprehensive review of accomplishments in Southeastern Indian studies. They present the first general synthesis in many years, and the first ever to deal with the whole range of studies. A truly satisfactory synthesis will require close coordination between anthropologists and historians. Surely there are historians who have been working in this field, even though they may not be communicating freely with anthropologists. New documents are coming to light, and long familiar ones are receiving fresh scrutiny. The work of Malone with Cherokee sources is highly useful (1956), as are Goaring's excellent papers (1962, 1958). For the Creek area we have an excellent biography of the romantic William Augustus Bowles (Wright 1967) and Cotterill's general summary of the Southern frontier (1954) as well as a broad range of more specific papers. For Florida and the Seminole there has been a continued flow of papers led by the reprinting of many of the earlier works by the University of Florida Press (Giddings, Latour, Cohen, Sprague, Solis de Meras, Forbes, Ribaut).

Space will not permit even a listing of the forty books and papers which have appeared during the past thirty years that have made significant contributions to Seminole ethnography. It would require a lengthy essay to comment in any significant way on them. Here I can only indicate some of the trends that I see developing since John R. Swanton's *Indians of the Southeastern United States* (1946). Two main themes are characteristic of this new body of work. One is the publication of original colonial or territorial documents not previously available. This includes scholarly editions with notes, such as Francis Harper's "Naturalists' Edition" of the *Travels of William Bartram* (1958). These publications include basic source material on the colonial period and for some later periods, especially the Second Seminole War in the 1830s. The major publication is, of course, the five volumes of the *Territorial Papers* edited by Carter (1956-1962). These cover the period 1821 to 1845 in considerable detail. In accord with the established policy for the *Territorial Papers*, they did not publish documents dealing solely with Indian affairs. There is, however, a good deal of Indian material in them and highly adequate footnotes indicate the reference data to a great deal more. These documents represent a major source for a study of Indian-white relations in the early years of the Territory.

A respectable body of newly published documents deal with the Spanish Colonial period. The Jesuit mission field in Florida has been amply documented in three works (Alegre, Zubillaga 1941; Zubillaga 1946). While one of these (Zubillaga 1946) is in Latin, they do present a massive collection of material on the early years of the Florida Colony. A very useful collection of Spanish maps is available which covers not only Florida but the more northern areas as well (Servicios . . . 1953). It is a fitting companion to Cumming's *Southeast in Early Maps*. A somewhat later series represents journals of individuals engaged in the Second Seminole War (Bemrose 1966; Mahon 1960; Sunderman 1953). While the material on Indians in any one of these accounts is rather scanty, they do represent a continued interest in the period. Somewhat later is Sturtevant's report on a trip through the Everglades by R. H. Pratt in 1879 (1956). As a whole these journals and accounts reveal a continued interest by historians and do add valuable data.

In the second realm are reports of recent ethnographic work, along with a few attempts at synthesis. Perhaps the most original contribution is Louis Capron's description of the existence of medicine bundles among the Seminole (1953). More specialized is Densmore's study of Seminole music (1956). Alexander Spoehr made a systematic study of Seminole kinship during the late thirties which gives us an exceptionally solid base to judge changes through time (1941a, 1941b, 1942, 1944). Ethel Cutler Freeman has been working for a number of years among the Seminole and has made a number of valuable observations, among which her studies of cultural change are especially interesting (1960, 1965). Specific studies of particular aspects of Seminole culture have been covered in a large number of papers over the last forty years. To mention only a few, out of

several dozen, will give some indication of the sort of work that
has been done. There has been an excellent study of Seminole patchwork men's clothing that describes in precise detail how this complex
style is made (Anonymous 1959). Additional studies deal with
medicine (Greenlee 1944), Osceola's coats (Sturtevant 1956), and
silverwork (Goggin 1940). More comprehensive treatments are available which approach regional summaries or tribal syntheses. Sturtevant has published a thoughtful analysis of Spanish and Indian relations in the Southeast (1962). Goggin developed the beginning of a
comprehensive classification of style areas in the Southeast (1952).
Goggin and Sturtevant have collected a comprehensive body of
data about the complexity of Calusa social-political organization,
recognizing that it appears to have been of the ramage type (1964).
Unfortunately there is no really modern synthesis of Seminole culture.
McReynolds (1957) is largely a political study of individual events
and largely concerned with the Oklahoma bands. The Indian Claims
Commission studies have resulted in a comprehensive study of Seminole
origins (Fairbanks 1957) which can now be revised and published.
In spite of all this ethnohistorical work, we really need comprehensive summaries of the major tribes of the Southeast, and the material
is available if someone can but find the time to synthesize it.

REFERENCES

Alegre, Francisco Javier, 1960. Historia de la provincia de la Compania de
    Jesus de Nueva Espana, Tomo IV, libros 9-10 (Anos 1676-1766). Nueva
    edicion por Ernest J. Burrus y Felix Zubillaga. *Bibliotheca Instituti Historici,*
    S.J., Vol. 17, Rome.
Anonymous, 1959. Seminole Patchwork. *American Indian Hobbyist* 6:3-18.
Bemrose, John, 1966. *Reminiscences of the Second Seminole War,* John K.
    Mahon, ed. (Gainesville: University of Florida Press).
Capron, Louis, 1953. *The Medicine Bundles of the Florida Seminole and the
    Green Corn Dance.* Smithsonian Institution, Bureau of American Ethnology
    Anthropological Paper No. 35, Bulletin 151 (Washington, D.C.: GPO),
    pp. 159-210.
Carter, Clarence Edwin, ed., 1956-1962. *The Territorial Papers of the United
    States: The Territory of Florida,* Vols. 22-26 (Washington: The National
    Archives).
Cohen, M. M., 1964. *Notices of Florida and the Campaigns.* Reprint of the
    1836 edition, O. Z. Tyler, Jr., ed. (Gainesville: University of Florida Press).
Cotterill, R. S., 1954. *The Southern Indians: The Story of the Civilized Tribes
    before Removal* (Norman: University of Oklahoma Press).
Densmore, Frances, 1956. *Seminole Music.* Smithsonian Institution, Bureau of
    American Ethnology Bulletin 161 (Washington, D.C.: GPO).
Dockstader, Frederick J., 1957. *The American Indian in Graduate Studies:
    A Bibliography of Theses and Dissertations.* Contributions from the Museum
    of the American Indian, Heye Foundation, Vol. XV (New York).
Fairbanks, Charles H., 1957. *Ethnological Report, Florida Seminole.* 300 pp.
    mimeographed manuscript.

Forbes, James Grant, 1964. *Sketches, Historical and Topographical, of the Floridas,* Reprint of the 1821 edition, James W. Covington, ed. (Gainesville: University of Florida Press).

Freeman, Ethel Cutler, 1960. Culture stability and change among the Seminoles of Florida. In *Selected papers of the 5th International Congress of Anthropological and Ethnological Sciences* (Philadelphia), pp. 249-254.

——————————————, 1965. Two Types of Cultural Response to External Pressures Among the Florida Seminole. *Anthropological Quarterly* 38: 55-61.

Gearing, Fred, 1958. The Structural Poses of 18th Century Cherokee Villages. *American Anthropologist* 60:1148-1157.

——————————————, 1962. *Priests and Warriors: Social Structures for Cherokee Politics in the 18th Century.* American Anthropological Association, Memoir 93 (Menasha, Wisconsin).

Giddings, Joshua R., 1964. *The Exiles of Florida,* Reprint of 1858 edition, Emmett B. Peter, Jr., ed. (Gainesville: University of Florida Press).

Goggin, J. M., 1940. Silverwork of the Florida Seminole. *El Palacio* 47(2): 25-32.

——————————————, 1952. Style Areas in Historic Southeastern Art. In *Indian Tribes of Aboriginal America,* Vol. III, Proceedings, 29th Congress of Americanists (Chicago: University of Chicago Press), pp. 172-176.

Goggin, J. M., and W. C. Sturtevant, 1964. The Calusa: A Stratified, Nonagricultural Society (with notes on Sibling marriage). In *Explorations in Cultural Anthropology,* Ward H. Goodenough, ed. (New York: McGraw-Hill), pp. 179-219.

Greenlee, Robert F., 1944. Medicine and Curing Practices of the Modern Florida Seminoles. *American Anthropologist* 46:317-328.

Harper, Francis, ed., 1958. *The Travels of William Bartram,* Naturalist's Edition (New Haven: Yale University Press).

Latour, A. L., 1964. *Historical Memoir of the War in West Florida and Louisiana in 1814-15,* Reprint of the 1816 edition, Jane Lucas de Grammond, ed. (Gainesville: University of Florida Press).

Mahon, John K., 1960. The Journal of A. B. Meek and the Second Seminole War, 1836. *Florida Historical Quarterly* 38:302-18.

Malone, Henry T., 1956. *Cherokees of the Old South: A People in Transition.* (Athens: University of Georgia Press).

Mason, Carol Irwin, 1963. The Archaeology of Ocmulgee Old Fields, Macon, Georgia. Unpublished Ph.D. diss., University of Michigan.

McReynolds, Edwin C., 1957. *The Seminoles.* Civilization of the American Indian Series (Norman, Oklahoma: University of Oklahoma Press).

Ribaut, Jean, 1964. *The Whole and True Discoverye of Terra Florida,* Reprint of the 1563 edition, David L. Dowd, ed. (Gainesville: University of Florida Press).

Royce, Charles C., 1902. *Indian Land Cessions in the United States.* Bureau of American Ethnology, 18th Annual Report, Part 2. (Washington, D.C.: GPO).

Servicios Geografico e Historico del Ejercito. 1949. Cartografia de Ultramar. Carpeta I. America en General, Madrid. 1953. Carpeta II. Estados Unidos y Canada, Toponimia de los Mapas que la Integran Relaciones de Ultramar, Madrid.

Solis de Meras, Gonzalo, 1967. *Pedro Menendez de Aviles,* Reprint of the Florida State Historical Society edition, Lyle N. McAlister, ed. (Gainesville: University of Florida Press).

Spoehr, Alexander, 1941a. Camp, Clan, and Kin Among the Cow Creek Seminole. *Anthropological Series, Field Museum of Natural History,* 33.

——————————————, 1941b. "Friends" Among the Seminole. *The Chronicle of Oklahoma* 19:252.

————————, 1942. Kinship System of the Seminole. *Anthropological Series*, Field Museum of Natural History, 33 (2): 31-113.

————————, 1944. The Florida Seminole Camp. *Anthropological Series*, Field Museum of Natural History 33 (3):117-150.

Sprague, John T., 1964. *The Origin, Progress, and Conclusion of the Florida War*, Reprint of the 1848 edition, John K. Mahon, ed. (Gainesville: University of Florida Press).

Sturtevant, William C., 1956. R. H. Pratt's Report on the Seminole in 1879. *Florida Anthropologist* 9:1-24.

————————, 1956. Osceola's Coats? *Florida Historical Quarterly* 34: 315-328.

————————, 1962. Spanish-Indian Relations in Southeastern North America. *Ethnohistory* 9:41-94.

Sunderman, J. F., ed., 1953. *Journey into Wilderness; an Army Surgeon's Account of Life in Camp and Field During Creek and Seminole Wars, 1836-1838* (Gainesville: University of Florida Press).

Swanton, John R., 1946. *The Indians of the Southeastern United States.* Bureau of American Ethnology, Bulletin 137 (Washington, D.C.: GPO).

Wheeler, Sir Mortimer, 1954. *Archaeology from the Earth* (Baltimore: Penguin Books).

Wright, J. Leitch, Jr., 1967. *William Augustus Bowles: Director General of the Creek Nation* (Athens: University of Georgia Press).

Zubillaga, Felix, 1946. Monumenta Antiquae Floridae (1566-1572), *Monumenta Historic Societatis, Iesu,* (Roma).

————————, 1941. La Florida La Mision Jesuitica (1566-1572) y La Colonization Espanola. Bibliotheca Instituti Historici S.I., Roma, Institutum Historicum S.I.

Part II

The Ante-Bellum Elite

F. N. BONEY

THE upper class whites of the ante-bellum South have been dissected and examined by a host of scholars, but they remain veiled by time and distorted by legend. This relatively small fraternity of the elite was composed of a complicated conglomerate of people bound together by blood and land, marriage and money, tradition and necessity, but the essence of this fluid class was the planter, and he too remains an elusive historical figure. He could be a dignified, slightly seedy Tidewater Virginian, proud of his ancient and honorable lineage (all two or three generations of it) and content to sell enough crops to meet normal expenses and enough surplus slaves to pay for a burst of grand living or an overdue debt. Or he could be a rough and ready pioneer on the rich, virgin land along the Mississippi River, living in a crude cabin in the midst of vast fields of cotton and large gangs of black workers. The vague term planter encompassed a bewildering array of actual people, but basically the planter was an agriculturist with much land and many slaves, say twenty or, better still, say a large number which included at least twenty able-bodied field hands (Stampp 1956: 28-31; Randall and Donald 1969: 39-41).[1]

There really was no such thing as an "average" planter, not within a culture which encouraged individualism and tolerated eccentricity, but most of these diverse fellows were much closer to the Mississippi hustler than the Virginia mandarin.[2] The planter of the Old South was fundamentally a businessman, an American capitalist investing his resources for a profit, a thoroughgoing materialist as attracted to the fast buck as any Yankee. Early writers usually placed the planter in a very unique, isolated compartment of American and even Southern life, bequeathing a blurred, distorted image to

76

the future, and ironically some modern scholarship is swinging back full cycle toward this old view, especially the ante-bellum view of the planter as a genteel, hospitable, impetuous pleasure seeker who was indifferent to money matters and often ineffectual in a crisis (Genovese 1965:13-36 and 1969; Weaver 1968; Randall and Donald 1969:44; Stampp 1956:43; Atherton 1949:7-8; Elkins 1963:27-80; Taylor 1961).

The planter belongs in the broad mainstream of ante-bellum American society. He cannot be shuttled off into some feudal or seigneurial or nonmaterialistic or precapitalistic world which is not only gone with the wind but never really existed in any meaningful manner. The white master of many black slaves was obviously different to some degree from other southerners and other Americans but not nearly different enough to be placed in a rigidly separate social and cultural compartment. Basically the planter was an agricultural entrepreneur, well within the general context of American capitalism.[3] The upper class Southerner was not nearly as different from other Americans, North and South, as he is often portrayed. He never was and still is not (Cash 1961:36-37, 41-43; Phillips 1964:165; Owsley 1969:34-37, Craven 1939:63-97; Boney 1969:372-74).

The planter's general attitude toward Indians and Negroes was not out of the mainstream of white American thought either. America was a white man's country, North and South, and neither reds nor blacks really "fitted in" properly. These people were too different, too untypical to fit into the kind of neat, tidy cultural package Americans have always sought but only recently come even close to attaining. The Indians inhabited large areas of the South, including farmlands; white planters and farmers wanted this land for their own agricultural enterprises. One way or another the Indian and his ways had to be removed from the path of the American juggernaut called progress. The Negro was a greater abomination, an even more inferior being fit only to hew wood and draw water for his betters under some sort of strict social control; the greater the percentage of blacks, the more severe the control. These sentiments were shared by "true" (that is, white) Americans of every class in all sections of the country (Litwack 1961; Hagan 1961; Jordan 1969: 414-15).

The concentration of black slave labor in the South and the tendency of the frontier to linger there too stimulated the development of more intense feelings within the general white American consensus, but, then as now, the Southerner was not beyond this consensus but only in the vocal forefront of it. White Southerners spoke out louder and clearer than most Americans when they discussed ethnic minorities, but basically they said what other Americans believed. They reflected—and still reflect—with considerable candor the passions and prejudices of the great American folk. Throughout our history the vocal white Southerner has unwittingly given the American people a free look into their own souls. No greater outrage can be committed than to make a whole tribe or folk see themselves accurately; men have been crucified or burned or gassed or shot for this sort of cultural treason. The Southern people have only suffered a kind of exile (Craven 1939:63-97; Zinn 1964:262-63; Boney 1966:246-47).[4]

The ante-bellum planter has been exiled or isolated the most, for his large, direct stake in slavery, his insatiable land-lust, and his relative articulateness made him the most visible element within Southern society. Poor whites were highly visible—travelers like Frederick Law Olmsted did not miss a one—but largely muted. The massive Southern middle class spoke out well enough but was either ignored—it did not exist so how could it speak?—or mistaken for the elite. Well qualified in some respects, the confident planter spoke out loud and clear on the Indian and Negro questions (Owsley 1969:30-32; Olmsted 1959; Eaton 1961:18-19).

Probably the Southern elite's most idealistic, thoughtful spokesman on these matters was Thomas Jefferson, as good a man and as fine a mentality as this class ever produced. In his classic *Notes on the State of Virginia*, written in the 1780s, Jefferson warned that in judging blacks, "The opinion that they are inferior in the faculties of reason and imagination, must be hazarded with great diffidence." (1964:138). Yet in this same work he did hazard this basic opinion openly, even relentlessly, not hesitating a few pages earlier to refer to "the real distinctions which nature has made" (1964:132) and to point out proofs that "their inferiority is not the effect merely of their condition of life" (1964:136).

To Jefferson black was ugly, an aesthetic error by nature. He felt that Negroes were excessively lustful and inadequately reflective. Jefferson was willing to concede that in memory blacks were equal to whites—an occasional divergence from the general consensus is to be expected of a radical like "Mad Tom"—but he had no real doubt of their inferior powers of reason: "I think one could scarcely be found capable of tracing and comprehending the investigations of Euclid" (1964:134).[5] He also thought that blacks had deficient imaginations which left them relatively barren in the fine arts (with the traditional exception of music). Basically Jefferson suspected —really believed—"that the blacks . . . are inferior to the whites in the endowments both of body and mind" (1964:138). Theoretically he favored emancipation of the slaves, but he insisted that it had to be accompanied by a policy of removal. White society had to be purged not only of slavery but also of black people. Thirty years after Jefferson's death, when a new political party emerged with the determination to keep the western territories free of slavery (and, to be truthful, of Negroes too), it was only appropriate that it should reach back, borrow the worn banners of the Jeffersonians, and call itself the Republican Party (Jefferson 1964:132-38; Jordan 1969:435-40; Litwack 1961:269-72).

The master of Monticello (and of more than 200 slaves) had a very different view of Indians. This picture is not clear and concise, for the red man in his pure form was always somewhat shadowy, even for a young man who grew up near the frontier. Completely unlike the black man, the Indian was a free creature usually beyond the white man's pale. To Jefferson, Indians were brave, virile, and attractive, not the equal of the whites in their current environment, but, unlike the blacks, capable of improvement and even equality with the whites under the proper circumstances. He marveled at their natural talents in art and oratory which proved "their reason and sentiment strong, their imagination glowing and elevated" (1964:135). Jefferson so admired the red man that he, like his early mentor Patrick Henry, even speculated on the happy prospect of intermarriage between reds and whites and the evolution of a splendid new kind of American. This was the very opposite of his attitude toward blacks, a people he was convinced could never be properly absorbed into the white majority (Jefferson 1964:88-94, 134-5; Jordan 1969:163, 177-81).

Jefferson's overall image of the Negro was fairly standard. This son of the Enlightenment was learned and eloquent, and the cutting edge of his criticisms was slightly blunted by idealism and humanitarianism, but, even so, basically he stated what most other white Americans thought and said much more crudely—the Negro was inferior, debased beyond redemption. Put in the common vernacular most of his basic attitude was acceptable even to "rednecks," "peckerwoods," and other exotic variations of the lowest classes of Southern whites. His view of the Indian was less typical. Whites generally rated Indians higher than Negroes, but Jefferson not only blunted his criticisms of red men but shifted to outright praise in many instances. The image of the Indian was always complex and contradictory, allowing for considerable divergency of opinion among whites. Perhaps Mother Virginia had mellowed more than most areas as the red menace faded to the west. Some "First Families of Virginia," ever conscious of blood lines in people and horses, were (and still are) proud of an Indian forebearer—always nobility like Pocahontas, of course, and not just any run-of-the-wilderness red. Or perhaps the "noble savage" image which was so powerful and persuasive in literary circles made Jefferson more sympathetic to Indians than his less intellectual contemporaries, which included most planters as well as the masses (Phillips 1964:151-65; Sheehan 1969:327-59).[6]

Whatever the reason, Jefferson's view of the Indian was too favorable for most Americans. More typical, although slightly to the hostile side of the mainstream this time, was writer-planter Joseph B. Cobb, a native of Oglethorpe County, Georgia, who migrated to Mississippi. He thought Indians were as degraded as black slaves and besides "noted for cowardice, and craft, and meanness of every description" (Cobb 1851:156-78). He detected no nobility or virtue at all, and in some respects he found blacks, especially native Africans, more interesting and admirable, the red man's superior in every way.[7] The Choctaw and Chickasaw, the tribes he knew best, were beneath contempt, that is, even worse than black slaves (Cobb 1851:176-78; Rogers 1969:131-46).

Certainly many planters, without agreeing with Jefferson, were considerably more lenient in their appraisals of Indians. Even an old Indian killer like Andrew Jackson occasionally showed some sympathy for the red man, but he was certainly no admirer of the Indian's "erratic" way of life or of red military power, and his official removal policy still speaks louder than an occasional moderate utterance (Prucha 1969:527-39).[8] Cobb and Jackson more accurately represented planter attitudes toward Indians than did Jefferson, but all three would have agreed with most Americans on the hopeless inferiority of blacks (Davis 1969:286). Reduced to the slogans so dear to our own culture, planters could have put it this way: Good Indian = Long-Gone Indian, Good Negro = Sambo Slave.

Planter attitudes toward reds and blacks were particularly important because this elite class exercised great power within the Old South, power out of all proportion to its meager numbers. Even after the triumph of Jacksonian Democracy—that is, equal rights for all adult white males—this elite still maintained great influence. The white masses were not overawed by the planters—they knew them too well for that—but they did often turn to their prosperous, prominent neighbors for guidance and leadership. Never in American history has one small aristocratic group exercised such disproportionate power for so long. And never in American history did such a leadership group fail so disastrously.

Relatively poised and polished on the surface but confused and contorted within, the planter elite encouraged the South to defy several significant trends in western civilization, trends which had gathered considerable momentum early in the onrushing nineteenth century. Tenaciously defending and expanding an economy based on large-scale, commercial agriculture which was in turn based on black slave labor, the elite championed a way of life which, while by no means isolated from the mainstream of western civilization, did, especially in regard to slavery, challenge some powerful new currents within that mainstream. The Southern white masses cannot escape much responsibility for this suicidal strategy, but their greatest blunder was to allow an entrenched elite too much influence. Or, to put it rather bluntly, too often the yeoman masses followed elite asses (Craven 1939:78-80, 89-91; Owsley 1969:39-41; Randall and Donald 1969:37-49; Craven 1953:252-65; Davidson 1961:68-75; Mannix and Cowley 1965:263-87; Freehling 1968:49-86; Eaton 1964:35).[9]

History is not entirely inevitable, men are not powerless ciphers, and leaders can influence events. Change, especially reform, always comes hard, but it is almost always possible. Decay and disaster were not predestined for the Old South, but the Southern elite, the traditional leadership cadre, could not or would not fashion the necessary reform. From the beginning when slavery evolved in seventeenth century Virginia, the planters (and would be planters) encouraged the expansion of this peculiar institution which was the foundation of their prosperity—or at least seemed to be. The traditional Christian opposition to enslaving fellow Christians faded rapidly as blacks were converted—as usual in such eyeball-to-eyeball confrontations between God and man, God blinked first. And very soon appeared the slave codes, Sambo Statutes which debased a whole race. Every colonial appeal for a cessation of the importation of slaves during hard times was balanced by pleas for more slaves when crop prices were good and land was plentiful (Davis 1969:136-44, 197-211, 244-54; Jordan 1969:71-82; Franklin 1963:70-3).

If Indians possessed such land, they were usually muscled aside, but occasionally they were more useful unmolested. Virginia and Carolina planters involved in the extensive fur trade found cooperation with certain tribes quite profitable. Especially in South Carolina white leadership was sometimes able to play the blacks and reds off against each other effectively. Some planters felt that nearby Indians intimidated and pacified restless blacks, but this was always an un-predictable policy. As Andrew Jackson said, Indians were "erratic." They were not always reliable allies in the onward and upward march of white civilization. After the long, bloody second Seminole War of 1835-1842, planters could never be sure that neighboring Indians would not absorb runaway blacks into their own orbit and enlist them as allies in resistance to white aggression. Certainly white troopers who had faced the fury of red and black Seminole warriors would have expressed considerable doubt about using red men to control black men for the benefit of white men (Porter 1964:427-40; Hagan 1961:76-7; Morton 1960 [1]:227-55; Willis 1963:157-76).

In the long, grim history of Southern slavery there was never a significant, meaningful movement to free the blacks in a single Southern state, and the planter class, so often portrayed as the spearhead of Southern enlightenment, certainly failed to lead wisely or really to lead at all in this sensitive area. Even in mellow old Virginia emancipation never made any significant progress, not before the Civil War nor before the abolition crusade nor even during the golden age of Jeffersonian liberalism. And aging Jefferson himself, in the twilight of a glorious career, with little to lose politically and everything to gain historically, avoided the hard but vital task. Like lesser planters, his whole life was inextricably entangled with slavery, and he was in some ways as trapped as his field hands. The closest Virginia ever came to serious action was the dramatic legislative session following Nat Turner's uprising, a "fire bell in the night" if there ever was one. However, even then the reformers failed as the planter elite lined up massively on the side of the status quo. The picture is no better in the rest of the upper South and much worse in the real "land of cotton." A few upper class South-erners—a James G. Birney in Alabama and Kentucky, a Grimké in South Carolina, a Clay (Cassius Marcellus or Henry) in Kentucky —did try for some reform, but, overall, the planters were no more interested in real reform than the white masses (Cohen 1969:503-26; Robert 1941; Eaton 1966:350; McColley 1964; Sellers 1960: 40-71).[10]

Worse yet, upper class Southerners spearheaded a counter crusade to convince the Southern people (perhaps themselves most of all) that slavery was a positive good. Novelist Nathaniel Beverley Tucker, politician John C. Calhoun, minister Leonidas Polk, professor Thomas R. Dew, agriculturist Edmund Ruffin, scientist Josiah Nott, and a host of other elitists proclaimed the glad tidings. Many of this same class also championed the final great crusade, political separation from a Union increasingly less friendly toward slavery. The Southern masses were not really tricked or conned; the Old South's last disastrous decisions were reasonably democratic; but certainly in the final crises the planter elite demonstrated insufficient vision and wisdom (Eaton 1966:344-51; Craven 1953:349-401; Catton 1961:130-215; Randall and Donald 1969:85-90 and 135-41).

Within the overall leadership failure of the planter elite, special attention should be paid to the total failure of their women. The aristocratic ladies of the Old South were a super elite, the very cream of what is still sometimes referred to as "pure white Southern womanhood". Seldom has a group been so honored in word and so ignored in deed. The planter's praise for his women—and indeed all Southern white women—was so overwhelming that it continues to bemuse many observers. Even a skeptic like W. J. Cash was misled by the rhetoric when he declared that the rebel army charged into battle convinced it was fighting wholly for HER (1961:89). Alas, for every such chivalrous cavalier there was probably at least one Johnny Reb who marched into combat in order to get that much farther away from a nagging wife and a half dozen bawling brats (Eaton 1966:396-407).

Still, Southern women, and especially Southern upper class ladies, did have superficial prestige and thus some influence. They were not in a position to gain special knowledge of the Indian, but they did suffer superior insights into the grim reality of slavery. The vulnerability of black women, the helplessness of black men, the power and passion of white men, the inevitable mulatto children, the plantation lady knew the whole story—and did nothing. They gossiped surely and occasionally confided to their diaries, but they *did* nothing until the Civil War finally came. Then these gentlewomen sent their men off to a slaughter which would leave many of them embittered widows and spinsters, old "aunties" passing their hatreds and frustrations on to new generations (Catton 1967:400-3; Thomas 1968:396-401; Chesnut 1961:2-43; Boney 1969:35-6, 48-9; Eaton 1965:87-89).

The Civil War marked the bloody end of the Old South, and it was altogether appropriate that an aristocrat, Jefferson Davis, should preside over this last, greatest debacle. No better symbol could be found for a lost cause than the distinguished planter from Mississippi. Intelligent and patriotic, experienced in war and politics, brave and determined, he was the best the Southern elite had to offer in 1861—and he was inadequate. He was too aloof and reserved to fire a people who needed passionate leadership. He was too conservative at a time when daring chances had to be taken. He was a bumbling bureaucrat who failed to properly mobilize the South's meager resources. Like his aristocratic field commander, Robert E. Lee, he was good enough to prolong a war which exterminated more than 600,000 young Americans, but he was not good enough to win it (Potter 1968:263-86; Wiley 1968:1-42).[11]

President Davis did realize quickly that the Southern army would be greatly outnumbered, and, drawing upon his experience with western Indians while Secretary of War in the 1850s, he tried hard to recruit Indian soldiers. Working primarily with former Southern tribes which still held some slaves, he negotiated nine separate treaties with Creek, Cherokee, Choctaw, Chickasaw, and Seminole groups which for once gained significant concessions. Like white Americans the Indians were divided, and neither North nor South used red troops extensively. At the battle of Pea Ridge as many as 3,500 red rebels fought, and a few collected a scalp or two, but the Confederates still did not win that rather important western clash (Eaton 1965:49; Hagan 1961:99-103).

Davis, like an earlier planter named Jefferson, saw a vast difference between red men and black men. He spared no effort to recruit a few Indians, but he adamantly refused to even consider recruiting soldiers from the immense Southern black manpower pool. Even the North with its vast white population began to use black troops by the middle of the war, and by 1865 the Union army had recruited almost 200,000 blacks, mostly ex-slaves, that is, Southerners. Only in the very last months of the war, when defeat was inevitable, did it finally dawn on Davis and Lee and the other Southern aristocrats who prided themselves on knowing the Negro that black troops could have saved the Confederacy.[12] The rebel leaders retained their racial misconceptions to the bitter end—and beyond (Cornish 1966; Roland 1962:183-85; Eaton 1965:265).

The upper class of the Old South misjudged and mistreated the Indian and the Negro, but so did the rest of white America. When confronted with the same racial challenge, white Americans of every class and every section react very similarly. Indeed the wounds of the Civil War were not truly healed until white America closed ranks to resume its aggression against the Indian and its degradation of the Negro. The planter elite was soon back on top again, and in cooperation with its new urban-business allies it continues to exercise powerful influence in what is now called the New South. Hopefully upper class Southerners are finally ready, willing, *and* able to give consistently enlightened leadership to a region once again in considerable turmoil. After three centuries, it's about time (Faulkner 1959:6-8; Woodward 1951:211-15; Buck 1937).

NOTES

1. In this paper the term planter is used to designate men who cultivated large areas of land with gangs of slave laborers. It is not used in the colonial sense to designate anyone who cultivated the land from humblest farmer to the haughtiest grandee.

2. Of course, there were many agricultural hustlers in Virginia and by the 1850s some mandarins in Mississippi. Everywhere in the Old South the hustler outnumbered the mandarin by a large majority.

3. Any attempt to examine and evaluate the economy of the Old South usually boils down to an attempt to define capitalism as opposed to other economic systems. This often leads to a great deal of defining and very little describing.

4. Whether non-Southern Americans really think Southern whites are all that different or whether they consciously refuse to admit their own Southernism is difficult to determine. In such matters the mind of the North is inscrutable.

5. Jefferson's rampant "radicalism" is further evidenced by his sympathy for thieving slaves whose very freedom had been stolen. He also conceded that blacks were "at least as brave, and more adventuresome" than whites, but he added that this was perhaps the result of lack of foresight (Jefferson 1964:133-34).

6. As Alexander Hamilton and recent scholars like William T. Hagan and Leonard W Levy have indicated, Saint Thomas was capable of duplicity on occasion. Under pressure he was willing to muscle the "noble savage" beyond the westward horizon.

7. Cobb had some interest in the culture and language of these native Africans, and, even more unusual, he had considerable respect for them. His description of the difference between these true Africans and native American slaves is an impressive illustration of the brutal, degrading effect of slavery on Negroes. The process Stanley M. Elkins calls infantilization is here documented by a Southerner who was staunchly defending the institution of slavery.

8. F. P. Prucha makes a good case for a more lenient evaluation of Jackson's Indian policies, but he puts a little too much stress on Jackson's words as opposed to his actions.

9. It is unwise to directly connect the rise of Jacksonian Democracy and the increase of racism in the United States (Davis 1969:286). The image of the wise, enlightened aristocrat restraining the reckless, racist masses is quite misleading—then or now.

10. A few maverick planters with liberal tendencies are often given much greater historical coverage than the overwhelming mass of conservative and even reactionary planters.

11. For a more sympathetic evaluation of Jefferson Davis see Frank E. Vandiver, *Their Tattered Flags: The Epic of the Confederacy* (New York and Evanston: Harper's Magazine Press, 1970).

12. In January 1864 Confederate General Patrick Cleburne suggested recruiting slaves into the rebel ranks, but the Confederate government rejected his controversial plan. Ten months later Cleburne was killed leading his troops in a headlong attack at Franklin, Tennessee.

REFERENCES

Atherton, Lewis E., 1949. *The Southern Country Store: 1800-1860* (Baton Rouge, Louisiana: Louisiana State University Press).

Boney, F. N., 1966. *John Letcher of Virginia: The Story of Virginia's Civil War Governor* (University, Alabama: University of Alabama Press).

——————, 1969. Look Away, Look Away: A Distant View of Dixie. *Georgia Review* 23:368-74.

Buck, Paul H., 1937. *The Road to Reunion: 1865-1900* (Boston: Little Brown).

Cash, W. J., 1961. *The Mind of the South* (New York: Vintage of Random House). First published in 1941.

Catton, Bruce, 1961. *The Coming Fury* (Garden City, New York: Doubleday & Co.).

Chesnut, Mary Boykin, 1961. *A Diary from Dixie* (Cambridge, Massachusetts: Sentry of Houghton Mifflin Company). First published in 1905.

Cobb, Joseph B., 1851. *Mississippi Scenes; Or, Sketches of Southern and Western Life and Adventure, Humorous, Satirical, and Descriptive, Including the Legend of Black Creek* (Philadelphia: A. Hart, Late Carey & Hart).

Cohen, William, 1969. Thomas Jefferson and the Problem of Slavery. *Journal of American History* 56:503-26.

Cornish, Dudley Taylor, 1966. *The Sable Arm: Negro Troops in the Union Army, 1861-1865* (New York: W. W. Norton & Company). First published in 1956.

Craven, Avery, 1939. *The Repressible Conflict: 1830-1861* (Baton Rouge: Louisiana State University Press).

——————, 1953. *The Growth of Southern Nationalism: 1848-1861* (Baton Rouge: Louisiana State University Press).

Davidson, Basil, 1961. *The African Slave Trade: Precolonial History: 1450-1850* (Boston: Atlantic Press of Little, Brown and Co.). Published in hardcover edition as *Black Mother*.

Davis, David Brion, 1969. *The Problem of Slavery in Western Culture* (Ithaca, New York: Cornell University Press). First published in 1966.

Eaton, Clement, 1961. *The Growth of Southern Civilization: 1790-1860* (New York: Harper & Bros.).

——————, 1964. *The Freedom-of-Thought Struggle in the Old South* (New York: Harper Torchbooks of Harper & Row).

——————, 1965. *A History of the Southern Confederacy* (New York: Free Press of Collier-Macmillan). First published in 1954.

——————, 1966. *A History of the Old South* (New York: Macmillan Co.).

Elkins, Stanley M., 1963. *Slavery: A Problem in American Institutional and Intellectual Life* (New York: Grosset & Dunlap). First published in 1959.

Faulkner, Harold U., 1959. *Politics, Reform and Expansion: 1890-1900* (New York: Harper and Bros.).

Franklin, John Hope, 1963. *From Slavery to Freedom: A History of American Negroes* (New York: Alfred A. Knopf).

Freehling, William W., 1968. *Prelude to Civil War: The Nullification Controversy in South Carolina: 1816-1836* (New York: Harper Torchbooks of Harper & Row). First published in 1965.

Genovese, Eugene D., 1965. *The Political Economy of Slavery: Studies in the Economy and Society of the Slave South* (New York: Pantheon Books).

——————, 1969. *The World the Slaveholders Made* (New York: Pantheon Books).

Hagan, William T., 1961. *American Indians* (Chicago: University of Chicago Press).

Jefferson, Thomas, 1964. *Notes on the State of Virginia* (New York: Harper Torchbooks of Harper & Row). First published in 1785.

Jordan, Winthrop D., 1969. *White Over Black: American Attitudes Toward the Negro: 1550-1812* (Baltimore: Penguin Books). First published in 1968.

Litwack, Leon F., 1961. *North of Slavery: The Negro in the Free States, 1790-1860* (Chicago: University of Chicago Press).

McColley, Robert, 1964. *Slavery and Jeffersonian Virginia* (Urbana, Illinois: University of Illinois Press).

Mannix, Daniel P. and Malcolm Cowley, 1965. *Black Cargoes: A History of the Atlantic Slave Trade: 1518-1865* (New York: Viking Press of Macmillan Co.). First published in 1962.

Morton, Richard L., 1960. *Colonial Virginia*, vol. 1 (Chapel Hill: University of North Carolina Press).

Olmsted, Frederick Law, 1959. *The Slave States* (New York: Capricorn Books).

Owsley, Harriet Chappell, ed., 1969. *The South: Old and New Frontiers: Selected Essays of Frank Lawrence Owsley* (Athens: University of Georgia Press).

Phillips, Ulrich Bennell, 1964. *The Course of the South to Secession* (New York: Hill and Wang). First published in 1939.

Porter, Kenneth W., 1964. Negroes and the Seminole War, 1835-1842. *Journal of Southern History* 30:427-40.

Potter, David M., 1968. *The South and the Sectional Conflict* (Baton Rouge: Louisiana State University Press).

Prucha, F. P., 1969. Andrew Jackson's Indian Policy: A Reassessment. *Journal of American History* 56:527-39.

Randall, J. G. and David Donald, 1969. *The Civil War and Reconstruction* (Lexington, Massachusetts: D. C. Heath and Co.).

Robert, Joseph Clark, 1941. *The Road from Monticello: A Study of the Virginia Slavery Debate of 1832* (Durham, North Carolina: Duke University Press).

Roland, Charles P., 1962. *The Confederacy* (Chicago: University of Chicago Press).

Rogers, Tommy W., 1969. Joseph B. Cobb: Antebellum Humorist and Critic. *Mississippi Quarterly* 22:131-46.

Sellers, Charles Grier, 1960. *The Southerner As American* (Chapel Hill: University of North Carolina Press).

Sheehan, Bernard W., 1969. Paradise and the Noble Savage in Jeffersonian Thought. *William and Mary Quarterly* 26:327-59.

Stampp, Kenneth M., 1956. *The Peculiar Institution: Slavery in the Ante-Bellum South* (New York: Alfred A. Knopf).

Taylor, William R., 1961. *Cavalier and Yankee: The Old South and American National Character* (New York: George Braziller, Inc.).

Thomas, Lately, 1968. *The First President Johnson: The Three Lives of the Seventeenth President of the United States of America* (New York: William Morrow & Co.).

Vandiver, Frank E., 1970. *Their Tattered Flags: The Epic of the Confederacy* (New York and Evanston: A Harper's Magazine Press Book).

Weaver, Richard, 1968. *The Southern Tradition at Bay: A History of Postbellum Thought* (New Rochelle, New York: Arlington House).

Wiley, Bell Irvin, 1968. *The Road to Appomattox* (New York: Atheneum).

Willis, William S., 1963. Divide and Rule: Red, White, and Black in the Southeast. *The Journal of Negro History* 48:157-76.

Woodward, C. Vann, 1951. *Reunion and Reaction: The Compromise of 1877 and the End of Reconstruction* (Boston: Little, Brown and Co.).

Zinn, Howard, 1964. *The Southern Mystique* (New York: Alfred A. Knopf).

The Non-Plantation Southern White in the 17th and 18th Centuries

Joseph L. Brent III

Broadly, I am here concerned with the conception of difference and the effect of its perception as dangerous. The equating of difference and danger seems to lie at the root of much social enmity. Specifically, I am concerned with how white Europeans, principally lower class Englishmen, reacted to the differences they perceived in the new world. In 1630, that remarkable migration to New England called the Puritan Exodus began. In 1636, Harvard was founded and a year later the Pequot tribe was utterly destroyed. Eleven years before the Exodus, black slaves were introduced into Jamestown and were put to work in the tobacco fields alongside the white contract labor of the time called indentured servants. Eleven years after it, the English philosopher, Thomas Hobbes, published *Leviathan*, his dark prescription for government. Hobbes was born in the year of the Armada, 1588, when as he put it, "my mother bore twins, myself and fear." His remark reflected accurately the temper of the times.

An important part of the transit of culture to North America, often developed differently than I have done here, was the framework of religious beliefs.[1] Of particular interest to me was its dualistic nature in which, especially in popular thought, a cosmic battle between God and Satan was mediated by Christ. The very vocabulary of Christianity exhibited a manichean order presided over by the princes of light and darkness. In the 17th century, the word "black" carried at least these connotations: soiled, dirty, having dark purposes, malignant, deadly, baneful, disastrous, sinister, dismal, gloomy, sad, and threatening. In the same period, "white" carried these, among others: morally or spiritually pure, stainless, spotless, innocent, free from malignity or evil intent (especially as opposed to something characterized as black), propitious, auspicious, and happy. The invisible

88

world to which these meanings referred was (and often is) believed real and powerful. In the animistic popular religious cosmology of the period, witches and saints, demons and angels were embodied in men, animals, plants, places, the wind, indeed in almost everything that could be hypostatized. The world was the battleground for enormous spiritual powers and the likelihood of suffering eternal pain in the fires of hell very great. In a common saying of the times, none had entered the gates of paradise for three hundred years.

This aspect of Christian belief was important for two reasons. First, it created a world in which conceivable alternatives for belief and action were radically limited by dialectical dualism, thus making confrontations more likely and heightening the violence of the times. Second, it provided a relatively complete system into which black Africans and their slavery could be fitted without challenge to Christendom and to the dreams of wealth and empire associated with it. To illustrate both points at once, I suggest this complex dichotomy from a slightly later period: white, godly, pure, clean, enlightened, reasonable, responsible, adult, agrarian, law-abiding, enterprising, and Southern; black, sinful, corrupt, dirty, ignorant, emotional, irresponsible, childish, urban, law-breaking, lazy, and Yankee.

The Indian, instead of being absorbed into the supernatural dialectic of protestant Christianity, was conceived as part of the natural world. As such, he was either romanticized as "the noble savage" or dehumanized by relegation to the status of beast. The first characterization was a luxury indulged by a few churchmen, frontiersmen, and enlightenment intellectuals. The second quickly became the belief of the great majority of white settlers and provided justification for the policies of Indian removals, perhaps better thought of as policies of elimination in the same sense that a dangerous animal pest is "removed." At any rate, for the European settlers, very few of whom had anthropological interests, Indian land became white land by virtue of desire alone. If the Indian chose to resist, he risked virtual extermination. One way of perceiving the distinction between red and black is to realize that while the Negro was a necessary part of the great North American drama of salvation, both sacred and secular, the Indian was not. While the black man became inhuman and demonic (in those fearful circumstances when it was impossible any longer to believe him childish), the red man became non-human—an animal. An exception to this dialectical distinction was that as the Negro and Indian intermixed, the former predominated and the red man blackened both literally and figuratively in white eyes.

The influence of Frederick Jackson Turner has obscured an important factor in early American settlement: the degree to which colonial life was an extension of the situation in England and western Europe generally. In the 17th century, England went through one of the most rapidly changing periods of its history—foreign war, regicide, civil war, imperial expansion, industrialization and generally a political, intellectual, religious, social, and economic revolution in which not the least important part was depopulation of the country-side and creation of urban slums. Especially in the Southern colonies, the perspective common among whites had its source in the attitudes brought from the English slums and jails. This slum population had lost whatever inclination it had to support the medieval values whose hierarchical order could find no place for them. In the English society which Hobbes describes as the *bellum omnia contra omnes*— a society in which wealth and position were increasingly up for grabs—the main chance was also increasingly the province of the commercial middle class, and not often available to the displaced yeomanry which had neither the skills nor capital for success. That the English leadership recognized the danger is obvious from the policy they established to siphon off the threat of revolution to the colonies, where frontier conditions would redirect the energies of sedition to more productive channels. The main mechanisms of that policy were transportation and indenture, and so effective were they that the majority of white settlers coming to the Southern colonies between first settlement and the Revolution came as trans-ported convicts or redemptioners. In this respect and in that of a county system of organization centered in the plantation, the South differed widely from the North, where free emigration and town government dominated the processes of development.

While life was uncertain throughout the colonies, the Southern ones, where only the plantation seemed fixed, produced an especially violent tenor of life. I shall take the Chesapeake region in the middle 17th century to illustrate the point, delineating a representa-tive composite county from court records and accounts.

The county court, a main focus of local life, is in session and is attended by at least half the population. On the docket are five murders, thirteen cases involving adultery or fornication, two cases of prostitution, one accusation of witchcraft, three charges against the sheriff for dereliction of duty, one charge of assault brought by the same sheriff against one of the men charging him with dereliction, five suits against citizens for aiding white runaways, four cases involving the status of blacks, and an indeterminate number of suits for slander and defamation, the hearings of which constitute among the most prized of colonial entertainments. As the cases proceed, only occasionally in closed session, since they deal with the lives of no more than one thousand adults over half a year, the passions of everyone are aroused in one way or another. A murder is committed that will come up at a future session. A dozen or more suits of slander have their origins in the testimony presented. Fights are numerous and the jury notoriously fickle to the delight of the citizens.

At the end of the session, only a few of the cases have been settled. In the five murders, only one man is convicted, but he is a stranger. Of the rest, two are acquitted and two plead benefit of clergy, show that they can read, and are released to a church jurisdiction which scarcely exists One of those so released murders twice again in the next few years and is released again in the same way both times before he is himself murdered. Of the thirteen cases involving adultery and fornication, only one is decided. It involves a servant girl who has produced a boy surprisingly like her master, but she is required to serve an extra year. For the rest, charges and counter-charges have cancelled each other out, leaving only the prurient residue of slander. The two prostitutes, one of whom is laughingly referred to as "the notorious fire-ship," are fined and released. The presumed witch is a senile crone who is stoned after titillating the assemblage with mumbled threats.

The sheriff, whose duty it is "to inquire by the Oathes of Good and Lawful Men . . . of all Manner of felonies, Witchcrafts, Enchantments, Sorceries, majick arts, Trespasses, forestallings, Ingrossings, and Extortions whatsoever and wheresoever done and perpetrated," appeals his fines and complains that he cannot do his duty when he is continually attacked by the citizenry and forcibly prevented from carrying out the laws. He carries a scar from his eye to the nape of his neck where a particularly outraged citizen, an ex-servant, has beaten him wickedly with a pronged tobacco drying stick and torn the scalp from his head to "the detriment of his dignity," as the sheriff puts it. The sheriff is of the gentry.

Two cases in which indentured servants are suing their masters for freedom have a deep interest for most of the crowd, since it is made up almost entirely of ex-servants. In one case the servant is freed and the two additional years she worked are paid for in tobacco. But in the other case, the master is wealthy and powerful and claims additional servitude owed him. Fear of the reaction of the crowd if the servant is not freed and fear of the master if she is lead the court to continue the case. The same ambivalence of feeling is evident in the five cases charging aid to runaways. On the well-founded assumption that the injuries will be settled out of court, all five cases are continued.

There is no doubt, however, in the minds of either the court or the citizens when the question of Negro status arises. Each case clarifies and reaffirms one or more aspects of the blacks' condition as slaves. In the first, the hereditary status of Negro slavery is confirmed, despite papers of indenture held by the black. In the second, killing of slaves as a result of severe punishment is adjudged no crime. A third establishes that the price of slaves killed by legal officers is to be paid to the owner from public money. The last levies heavy fines on owners for freeing slaves without paying their passage out of the country and, at the same time, sets the penalty for white marriage with black, mulatto, or Indian persons at banishment forever. The judge calls the children of such a union, "that abominable and spurious issue."

After about a week of such cases, the court, perhaps with a kind of reluctant anticipation, turns to the first of the cases involving slander. It concerns a planter who has been called publicly "a common hog stealer" and he has brought his tormentor to court. Everyone knows that the planter's hogs, which run wild as is the custom, have increased disproportionately. This planter, as everyone also knows, has only recently become a man of some substance, having started in the colonies as a transported convict. He is doing his awkward best to pass for "quality." Because his success is so recent, the planter has an advantage over his older neighbors in acquiring swine. Identification of these partly domesticated animals is by means of notches in the ears. By the mid-17th century, these patterns have become quite complex, so that later marks can often be superimposed upon earlier ones. It happens that the recent planter has settled on and expanded holdings within a few miles of his former master, a gentleman, who has a simple pattern of identification which is easily made into the mark of his former servant. Hence the accusation and the suit. The county is divided in its feelings. On the one hand, the citizenry has enjoyed the spectacle of a member of the gentry losing his stock. On the other, the ex-servant's presumption of gentility is deeply irritating. Since the amateur gentleman was not caught in the act, there is no way in which to determine evidence, and the case is dealt with socially, not legally. The court finally assesses a fine of a few shillings on the defendant, the gentleman, who is satisfied that everyone believes in the guilt of his ex-servant and who has, along with the spectators, enjoyed exhibiting the man's obvious pretensions. The *nouveau riche* considers himself exonerated and, along with the audience, has enjoyed winning a case against the gentry. Neither man could be aware that their children will intermarry, or that distant descendants will create organizations to celebrate these heroic beginnings.

The second such case is one in which Mary Dodd brings suit against Joan Nevill for calling her Captain Batten's whore. Goody Dodd and Goody Nevill are neighbors and have been feuding in and out of court for years. They have assaulted each other, cursed each other, accused each other of highly original sexual acts and are addicted, along with the county, to these court battles in which years of their lives are publicly relived. As the case proceeds, detailed accounts of conversations, daily actions, prejudices, love affairs, deaths, spells, indeed the whole plethora of personal relations, pours out as almost all concerned give accounts to the accompaniment of laughter, ribald commentary, fights, and indignation. Very few escape some sort of slanderous, vicious, or incidental involvement in the vital ordeal which ends simply because there is nothing left to say. Barring the death of one of the principals, the case will continue indefinitely. After perhaps a week of such cases, the session is ended with a satisfactory sense of catharsis.

While much of the common life of the county has its focus in the drama of the court, much of it also centers on the external world which threatens by its gloomy magnificence to swallow up the puny areas of European cultivation and settlement. The land is largely climax beech and oak forest, dark and inhabited sparsely by small Indian tribes whose trails interlace the wilderness. They are called "Doegs" and "Susquehanouggs", some are friendly, some not. To the whites there is little to choose: they all look the same, build the same bark structures and are different and dangerous. In the 1670s, a group of planters sits about drinking punch. Into the gathering run two men shouting that a planter has been found dying at his doorstep with a tomahawk in his skull. Still conscious when found, he muttered, "Doegs! Doegs!" and died. He lived on the site of a Doeg burial ground. The planters, quite drunk, excitedly organize a party and go off on foot down the Indian trail until they come to a fork. There the party divides, one taking each branch. After a few hundred yards, each party comes upon an Indian village. In one party a planter speaks a little of the language and calls for a *matchacomicha wheewhip*, a council. An Indian comes forward and identifies himself as the Doeg chief. He denies any knowledge of the planter's death, turns to walk back and is shot. In the ensuing battle, at least a dozen Indians are killed and no whites. The other party, having surrounded the other village, is debating its course of action when it hears the shots and immediately opens fire. Since the Indians have had no warning, half the settlement is slaughtered before an Indian is able to establish that he is a Susquehanna, a friend.

The planters then return to their punch drinking, taking with them a captive, the pubescent son of the Doeg chief. The boy is intended as a pet for one of the planters' wives, but retreats into a state of taciturn silence. It is decided that the boy is bewitched and he is baptized, whereupon he begins to feed and the incident is counted a minor miracle, forming the subject of numerous arguments about the possibility of Indian salvation which is generally denied. One of the planters had married the sister of the same boy in anticipation of a dowry of land. When that did not happen, the planter murdered his Indian "princess" and shortly married a striking young servant girl transported for harlotry. It is she to whom the boy is given as a gift. As an adolescent, the Indian slave escapes, taking with him a number of black slaves. His knowledge of white culture makes him a dangerous leader of Indian resistance and he is especially hated for his habit of taking black slaves as captives. In time, his descendants will be considered Negro.[2]

With these vignettes in mind, I shall suggest some hypotheses and conclusions. The South was profoundly rural well into the 20th century, a fact both obvious and important. Cities like Boston, or even towns like Fall River did not develop in the Southern colonies. What towns existed were either depots or political centers or both, but not lively, self-conscious institutions like the New England town. As the white South was intensely rural, it also became populist in temper, because of the manner in which the plantation and mobility became institutionalized. The early plantations were weak autocracies because escape was relatively easy. There were, at first, only two classes of whites, planters and servants, but as the servants were under indenture for specified short periods, almost immediately a third class, a fluid mass of freemen, came into being. For various reasons, important among them being the desire to achieve stability, the servant when freed was given something with which to begin. This expedient charity, called the custom of the country, and the easy availability of land made it likely that white freemen would quickly become independent. Rather than strike out on new paths, freemen usually imitated their former masters in trying to buy slaves and becoming planters. Everything pushed them in that direction, because as servants they learned to cultivate tobacco or some other cash crop, and because indenture forcibly gave them the model to copy which could provide entry into the elite.

In summary, Southern white colonial society may be thought of as an open system with built-in delays. Although opportunity was closed off temporarily at the bottom by indenture and by wealth and position at the top, the freeman was at worst independent and always potentially a planter and man of status. Many freemen succeeded spectacularly and others could imagine their sons' success. By 1700, in the more populous Southern colonies, at least three-quarters of the white population were freemen and the plantation was already the major institution, instead of being what the manor had been in England—a feared constraint upon liberty.

The explanation of the hegemony of the plantation lies in the way mobility for whites was established. So far as the servant was concerned, the element of delay imbedded in the social structure made transition from level to level quite smooth, while certainty of freedom and expectation of success prevented the appearance of any dangerously radical situation, so long as land was easily available. For the planters, the appearance of substantial freemen, despite reservations about the long-range effects, was taken as the appearance of allies in the hard struggle to maintain order and property in a time made chaotic by an uncontrolled increase in a free white population. And if the more successful freeman insisted upon being called a gentleman, it was practical to do so. It was even more useful to run him for the legislature, appoint him to the bench, or even give him a younger daughter as a wife and put him to work where his servant background could be used to good advantage. In a short time, processes like these produced a paternal planter oligarchy of thoroughly mixed origins, while they simultaneously augmented its power and weakened opposition. Thus, the plantation became the formative and dominant institution of Southern life.

Jefferson, in his theory of a "natural aristocracy" justified exactly this kind of mobility: a "natural" movement of rural freemen into accepted positions of governance. That Jefferson's view was an easy idealization is apparent on two grounds: the presence of black slaves and of an unexploited land which allowed men to bury their hostilities in a battle with abstract nature. In fact, Jefferson's idealized freeman inhabited a different world from the arcady he described. The egalitarianism Jefferson romanticized was in practice the harsh and egoistic sense of competitive equality which is a mark of a mass society. It often meant a violent refusal to admit that rank existed and depended ultimately upon an uneasy equilibrium in which every freeman proclaimed his independence and difference from every other, but denied the superiority of anyone over another. This fiction was more easily maintained because of the presence of black slaves.

Equality also meant swilling the voters with bumbo, a technique well employed by George Washington, who remained a failure in popular politics until he used it. In a district which cast no more than 355 votes, Washington provided the freeholders with forty gallons of rum punch, twenty-eight gallons of wine, twenty-six gallons of rum, forty-six gallons of beer, six gallons of madeira and three and one-half pints of brandy. Thereafter Washington remained securely in office until he went off to lead the armies of independence.

Yet if Jefferson's evaluation seems too sanguine by far, the mobility central to his thesis was obviously also central to the structure and stability of Southern society. The freeman considered the plantation ideal as the most important content of his attitudes about equality: it was the ultimate attainable realization of his individuality and, as such, dominated his aspirations with the dream of every man a king. And even when the ideal failed him, his whiteness provided him with a foundation for psychological equality; so that, even then, the plantation ideal continued to dominate Southern life. Thus, the presence of a caste of black slaves added to this sense of intense equality by establishing the mudsill beneath which no white could fall. In fact, the freeman was psychologically doubly protected against a fall in status. Being white he could fall neither to the animal condition of the Indian, nor to the demonically perceived condition of the black.

Another factor tended to increase the sense of equality among whites—the relative independence of the freeman. While this was a passive attitude, dependent in part upon the physical separation of small farms, it had the important effect of cushioning the results of decreasing mobility in the latter half of the 18th century.

Other than delays on mobility demanded by indenture and the planter oligarchy, only two obvious constraints existed, the resistance of the land itself and the refusal of the "animals vulgarly called Indians" to give it up without a struggle.[3] But these were both understood as abstract and impersonal forces which had the effect of translating the perception of human competition from one of men against each other to one of cooperation among men against natural forces. The consequence of this transformation was to make the South appear as a self-generating and self-perpetuating egalitarian society, a kind of classless heaven-on-earth—unless slavery were attacked or the Indian permitted to keep the land.

Although the dominance of the plantation was great, it was by no means complete. A potentially unstable situation always existed within the white South—a danger probably greater than the threat of slave revolts and surely of Indian uprisings. The source of this danger lay in the creation of a class of non-plantation whites—freemen who were simply farmers or workmen—that had no function deemed necessary, or even important, to the dominating plantation. Moreover, the non-plantation white, who made up the vast majority of the white population, was only recently removed from the conditions of English city or rural slums—or parallel circumstances—and his resentments had scarcely cooled. Indeed, Southern egalitarianism had its major origins in the attitudes of class antagonism developed in Europe. Especially in the South, where the absence of restraints fostered indulgence in dangerous forms of freedom, the single effective institution, the plantation, encouraged the development of an apparently unfettered individualism.

And yet, the freeman had no important relationship with the plantation except becoming a planter himself, and too few freemen became planters. The non-plantation white could provide occasional services for the plantation, but nothing it produced he bought except slaves and their price rose steeply. Thus, there was created a segregated class of whites. Furthermore, this white intermediate class was in an ambiguous and ambivalent position, because no institution developed simultaneously with the plantation which could effectively implement the goals and aspirations of freemen as such. The resulting condition is best described as a rural mass, or more simply, populist society. It was a society of discrete individuals, both competitive and passive, unorganized within any institutional structure, harshly egalitarian. Because its position was ambiguous, this populist society was ambivalent in its feelings about the oligarchy. If satisfied, it supported and accepted planter dominance. If dissatisfied, its populist fervor posed a continuing threat.

While this account of potential dissent holds likely for the majority of the non-plantation white population of the colonial South, it does not account for the second important source of dissent, whom I will call the yeomen, since they were opposed to slavery and committed to the ideal of the family farm. Before the Revolution, the upland, as distinct from the piedmont, South was scarcely settled, so that what became in time a distinct region did not yet exist. Instead, pockets of yeomanry existed here and there as relatively weak communities. As settlement moved inland past the fall-line into the piedmont, these pockets were enveloped by the plantation and generally fell under its influence. Even though in the lowlands, some isolated communities continued to remain as unreconstructed yeomanry into the present, the general pattern was one of slow digestion of these separate yeoman communities by the plantation from the coast to the mountains. The process resulted in a westward sprawling population of varied conviction, far more influenced by the plantation, but containing significant yeoman opposition which increased toward the West. By the mid-18th century, both sources coalesced to form that thrust of populist dissent which made the American Revolution as much a struggle of freemen against the oligarchy as a war for independence.

After the Revolution, this populist agitation was partially blunted by the successes of popular government under the Jacksonians during the 20s and 30s and by the enormous increase in the availability of land. But by the 50s the attack on slavery and the rapid decline in land suitable for plantation agriculture so threatened the nature of Southern white egalitarianism that the issue of race and the mudsill came to predominate to such a degree that the whole South increasingly fell into a rural form of totalitarian domocracy, where in part it remains today.

NOTES

1. For example: Winthrop D. Jordan, *White Over Black* (Chapel Hill: University of North Carolina Press, 1968) and Joel Kovel, *White Racism: A Psychohistory* (New York: Pantheon Books, 1970).

2. Principal sources include: *Archives of Maryland* (1883——), vols 51, 53, 54, 57; C. H. Brent, *The Descendants of Collo. Giles Brent, Capt. George Brent and Robert Brent, Gent.* (1946); and *The Journal of Nicolas Cresswell* (New York: Dial Press, 1924).

3. Hugh Henry Brackenridge, "The Animals, Vulgarly Called Indians." In *The Indian and the White Man*, Wilcomb E. Washburn, ed. (Garden City: Doubleday & Company, Inc., Anchor Books, 1964), pp. 111-117.

Divide and Rule: Red, White, and Black in the Southeast

WILLIAM S. WILLIS, JR.

NORTH of Mexico, the Colonial Southeast was the only place where Indians, Whites, and Negroes met in large numbers.[1] Little of the fascinating story of this contact has been told and some crucial parts may be beyond recall for lack of documents. The early attitude of Indians toward Negroes is obviously of great importance. To some extent, it has been dealt with, but conclusions have differed. Laurence Foster and James Johnston are certain that the early feeling of Indians was one of friendliness.[2] On the other hand, some students, mainly Southern historians, stress hostility.[3] As a matter of fact, a great deal of hostility seems to have existed in the eighteenth century. In 1752, the Catawba Indians showed great anger and bitter resentment when a Negro came among them as a trader.[4] Perhaps the Cherokee had the strongest color prejudice of all Indians. Even the Spaniards were not "White" enough for them. In 1793, Little Turkey, a prominent chief, declared that Spaniards were not "real white people, and what few I have seen of them looked like mulattoes, and I would never have anything to say to them."[5] According to John Brickell, an early eighteenth century reporter, Indians had a "natural aversion to the Blacks."[6] In 1763, George Milligen Johnston, a South Carolina physician, opined that this hostility was mutual and spoke of the "natural Dislike and Antipathy, that subsists between them [Negroes] and our *Indian* Neighbors."[7] But the Southern historians have not explained why Indians disliked Negroes. This paper examines this hostility, and that of Negroes to Indians. The story is the familiar

---

*Reprinted from *The Journal of Negro History*, Vol. XLVIII, No. 3 (July, 1963), pp. 157-176, with permission of the author and The Association for the Study of Negro Life and History, Inc. The paper is reprinted in the style in which it was originally published except that footnotes originally listed at the bottoms of pages are collected together and listed at the end.

99

one of divide and rule. Specifically, it will be shown that Whites will-fully helped create the antagonism between Indians and Negroes in order to preserve themselves and their privileges.

In the Colonial Southeast, Negro slavery and trade with Indians were more prominent in South Carolina than anywhere else. The province sanctioned slavery from its beginnings in 1670, but South Carolinians brought in few Negroes until the late 1690's. From that time, the steady increase in the number of Negro slaves correlates with the steadily increasing demand for labor. First, there was the expansion of rice production on slave-operated plantations. This occurred at about the same time, near the turn of the eighteenth century, that the general supply of slaves in the New World swelled. In the 1720's, the manufacture of pitch and tar, and in the 1740's the growth of indigo production added to the demand for slave labor. Meanwhile other events conspired to curtail other supplies of labor. Indian slavery dwindled and virtually disappeared after the Yamassee War of 1715-1717. This rebellion of tribes trading with the province produced a widespread notion that South Carolina was a dangerous place and few Whites entered for two decades after the fighting. The demand for Negroes grew in tandem with the mounting political power of the planters and the government was increasingly responsive to the latter's demands. By the beginning of the eighteenth century, Negroes outnumbered Whites and they increased their proportion of the population later in the century when various estimates put the ratio at two or three to one and even higher.[8]

Despite allegations about the submissiveness of Negroes and their acquiesence to slavery, eighteenth century Whites were afraid of their slaves. This fear grew as Negroes became more numerous. Whites especially dreaded slave insurrections; to South Carolinians, Negro rebels were an "intestine Enemy the most dreadful of Enemies."[9] The eighteenth century was punctuated by a steady succession of insurrectionary plots and actual insurrections. Indeed, the Charles Town government at times kept half of its soldiers in the capital. Negroes also struck back at their masters in other ways. They poisoned them, they set fires, and they committed suicide. They also employed subtle everyday resistances, such as, malingering and feigned stupidity. They also ran away. Some went for only short periods to nearby places; others went permanently to distant hiding places, to the mountains and swamps, to the Indian country, and to the Spanish in Florida. Running south to Florida became especially common after the Yamassee War when Spain encouraged more Negroes to come and offered them freedom. By the late 1720's, Negro subversion had become the main defense problem of South Carolina.[10]

Indians were also a big problem, and they were feared. The Colonial Southeast was an arena of an unremitting struggle for empire among Whites: English, French, Spaniards, and later Americans. Indian tribes were caught in the middle of this struggle; and Whites competed for their allegiance, for their trade and their warriors. Success in the empire struggle depended upon success in the Indian country. For a decade at least, the mere survival of South Carolina remained uncertain and the position of the province among Indians was precarious. But even before the eighteenth century, South Carolina had become much more secure and had constructed a remarkable system of Indian alliances. These alliances gave South Carolina sway over the majority of Indians in the South and forced the Spanish and French to keep retreating. Through its successes, South Carolina became confident, perhaps overconfident, of controlling Indians. Then came the Yamassee War. For a time South Carolinians were on the verge of being driven into the sea; however, in the end they had their victory. But with all the devastation, their province emerged from the war weakened and insecure, with Spain and France stronger than ever. The old confidence of managing Indians was gone, and gone for good. They now believed more than ever that Indians could never be really trusted. From now on, they and all Whites lived in dread of the next Indian uprising—an uprising that would be supported by enemy Whites.[11]

The picture in the Colonial Southeast was this: a frightened and dominant White minority faced two exploited colored majorities.[12] To meet the Negro danger, South Carolina devised a harsh slave code; the police control of slaves was comprehensive, specific, and brutal. To meet the Indian danger, the province had a system of trade regulation that was less brutal than the slave code but of approximately equal thoroughness. That Indian tribes were still independent and had some freedom of choice necessitated their being dealt with somewhat like equals. After the Yamassee War, the province played tribe off against tribe; indeed, village against village.[13] They also watched the munitions trade to prevent any stockpiling of arms.[14] In meeting each danger, South Carolinians were plagued by the discrepancy between what they willed and what they could actually do. This discrepancy became greater with time. It did not take much imagination on the part of the Whites to put the two dangers, Indians and Negro slaves, together. As early as 1712, Governor Alexander Spotswood, of Virginia, juxtaposed them.[15] In 1729, the French delayed sending an expedition against the Natchez Indians who had slaughtered French citizens because they feared that New Orleans without troops would be attacked by the Choctaw Indians, and Negroes in order to "free themselves from slavery, might join them."[16] This was the biggest fear of all. In 1775, John Stuart, British Superintendent of Southern Indian Affairs, explained that "nothing can be more alarming to Carolinians than the idea of an attack from Indians and Negroes."[17]

What did South Carolinians do about this nightmare? One answer was, keep Indians and Negroes apart—do not let them mix. In 1757, Captain Daniel Pepper, agent to the Creek Indians, stated that "intimacy" between Indians and Negroes should be avoided.[18] In 1767, Stuart expressed this idea again, perhaps even more strongly: "any Intercourse between Indians and Negroes in my opinion ought to be prevented as much as possible."[19] If this were done, Negroes could not establish personal relations with Indians and learn their languages. This would eliminate the dreaded coordinated blow by Indians and Negroes. But Whites also had other goals in mind. Whites believed that whenever Negro and Indian talked in private the talk was against them. The government believed that Negroes could spread discontent among the tribes and foil its schemes in the Indian country. In 1779, the British Indian Service stated that "Negroes infused many very bad notions into their [Indians] minds."[20] To do this, Negroes need not always lie; as servants, they were sometimes privy to important secrets. Moreover, the government *was* double-dealing with its Indian allies; for instance, stirring up trouble between Creeks and Cherokee. On the other hand, Indians could offer freedom to Negroes and tell them how to get to their villages.

To this end of keeping these colored peoples apart, South Carolinians tried to prevent Indians from coming into the province unless they were on official business. In 1742, a Committee on Indian Affairs warned against frequent visiting by Indians because of the hazard of their associating with slaves, "particularly in regard to their talking, and having too great Intercourse with our Slaves, at the out-plantations, where they camp."[21] Even when on official missions to Charles Town, chiefs were discouraged from bringing too many *aides-de-camp* and were hurried away as quickly as possible.[22] The Settlement Indians, those partially detribalized natives living within the province, presented a special problem. Here again the government opposed contact with Negroes; trading and intermarriage were frowned upon.[23] This determination to prevent Indian-Negro contacts within the White settlements was a main cause for curtailing the enslavement of Indians. Indian slaves got to know Negroes and, since they escaped easily into the hinterland, they might carry Negroes along with them. In 1729, Governor Etienne Perier, of Louisiana, explained that "Indian slaves being mixed with our negroes may induce them to desert."[24]

Keeping Negroes and Indians apart had another aim: keep Negroes out of the Indian country. Eighteenth century legislation consistently prohibited any Negro, slave or free, from going to any Indian tribe either as a trader in his own right or as a White trader's helper.[25] Violations of this prohibition almost always led to hasty action to remove these Negroes. Later in the eighteenth century when the westward movement was getting into high gear, opposition to Whites taking their slaves into Indian country became an important obstruction to White settlement of the interior.[26]

Fugitive Negroes among the Indians were the biggest headache. In 1767, Stuart declared that "to prevent the Indian Country [from] becoming an Asylum for Negroes is a Matter of the Utmost consequence to the prosperity of the provinces."[27] To keep slaves from escaping, South Carolina assigned patrols to watch the roads and countryside; to keep Indian raiding parties out of the province, the government built forts at key approaches and sent rangers out to ride along the frontiers. But Indians were excellent slave catchers. The Settlement Indians in particular were regularly employed to track down fugitive slaves; indeed, slave catching was so profitable to them that they readily agreed in 1727 to move their villages so that they could do a better job.[28] Whites went to great lengths to get their Negroes back. In negotiations, they pressed Indians about these fugitives.[29] They made threats. In 1773, David Taitt, Indian agent, threatened to cut off the Creek trade unless the Indians returned fugitive Negroes.[30] Most treaties stipulated that Indians surrender all Negroes and return all future runaways at an agreed price.[31] Moreover, traders were required to report all Negroes found among Indians and to hold them until they could be sent back to their masters.[32] On their tours of duty, Indian agents also watched for Negroes, and sometimes they made special trips into the Indian country to regain these fugitives.[33]

Keeping Negroes and Indians apart had still another aim: keep Negroes out of the swamps and the mountains. Negroes frequently escaped to these out of the way places. These fugitives, called Maroons, preferred the swamps, especially those in the direction of St. Augustine. Their preference for the southern swamps was dictated by the prospect of freedom among the Spanish in Florida. Meanwhile in these swamps, they could expect help from the Spanish and their Indians. Probably this explains why they went less often to the Southern Appalachians, northwest of Charles Town. But sometimes fugitive Negroes did try for these mountains; for instance, fifteen from Virginia did this in 1729. Large parts of these mountains were impregnable from the east; indeed, South Carolinians realized they could never annihilate the Cherokee in these mountains and they feared that Maroons might team up with these Indians, who were becoming less friendly to the English and more inclined to the French. If this occurred, the dispersed and almost defenseless White settlers on the Northwest frontier would be at the mercy of a truly formidable antagonist. On the other hand, if the Cherokee were driven from their villages, Maroons might occupy them and become prosperous and secure. These considerations weighed heavily with the Charles Town government, and they were important in leading this government to a policy of appeasing the Cherokee.[34]

Maroons were the most resourceful of all fugitives. They aimed at nothing less than setting up small self-sufficient societies in the most inhospitable places. They had to plan ahead, carefully and secretly. They knew a hard life of hard work and hard fighting awaited them. Those fifteen Virginia Maroons carried guns, ammunition, clothing, furniture, and implements into the mountains; before they were captured, they had started clearing land in order to farm. Once established in their fastnesses, Maroons then lived as banditti; they plundered White settlements, killing masters and rescuing slaves. In 1717, a band under the leadership of one Sebastian terrorized the southern parishes of South Carolina.[35] In the early 1770's, a frightened William Bartram, the noted naturalist, encountered a band of marauders north of Charles Town and later explained that "people [were] . . . frequently attacked, robbed, and sometimes murdered" by Negro bands in this region.[36] These Maroons were dangerous men and women, and they struck out against slavery. No threat, however, was greater than the possibility of their cooperating with hostile Indians and coordinating their attacks against White settlements. Top priority was given by Whites to the immediate destruction of the Maroons. This job was too important to be handled by a local community. Instead the government sent soldiers into the wilderness to eliminate them.[37] Indians were also called upon to help, and they were especially good at ferreting out Maroons from their lurking places.[38]

In addition to keeping Indians and Negroes apart, Whites pitted the colored groups against each other. In 1725, Richard Ludlam, a South Carolina minister, confessed that "we make use of a Wile

grounds were dangerous places; enemies were always lurking about. Hence, an Indian often lost time fighting, if he were lucky enough not to lose his life. In a word, Indians were usually short of goods and in debt. The reward for fugitive slaves was, therefore, something they could rarely afford to turn down. Moreover, the avariciousness of Indians was proverbial in the South.[51] But Indians knew what slavery was like among Whites. They saw its cruelty and brutality whenever they visited the White settlements. They also remembered that Whites had once enslaved Indians in large numbers and occasionally still did so. Indeed, the great fear of Indians was that Whites, and especially South Carolinians, would at sometime make slaves of all Indians in the South. This fear was in the background of all their dealings with Whites.[52] All of this worked in two contradictory ways on Indians. Self-interest made the Indian act as an enemy of Negro freedom; but human feelings made him guilty. Like other men in this ambivalence, he suppressed his guilt with a convenient hostility.

Since it was important that Negroes should fear and hate Indians, it is likely that Whites told their slaves many horror stories about Indians, especially those depicting the terrible things that Indians did to Negroes. Actually it was not difficult to portray Indians in a bad light. Indians did kill and they were cruel. Sometimes their raiding parties striking swiftly and with surprise killed Negroes alongside their White masters.[53] Indians also scalped and otherwise mutilated their victims regardless of race.[54] Besides, Indians were known in the early days to subject their male captives to prolonged and deadly tortures; now and then they did this even in the eighteenth century. In 1730, the French gave the Choctaw three Negroes who had helped the Natchez in 1729. The French expected the Choctaw to torture these Negroes; moreover, they hoped this would discourage Negroes from cooperating with Indians. The French were not disappointed. Father Petit, a Jesuit missionary, reported that these Negroes "have been burned alive with a degree of cruelty which has inspired all the Negroes with a new horror of the Savages, which will have a beneficial effect in securing the safety of the colony."[55] But atrocities were not the main thing. The main thing was that Indians often behaved as real enemies of Negro freedom. To a large extent, Whites encouraged Indians to act this way. As we shall see, this was partly done to make Negroes fear and hate Indians. Given this aim, we assume that Whites publicized these unfriendly acts of Indians among their slaves—and conveniently overlooked their own responsibility. We will now give attention to some situations in which Indians behaved as enemies of Negro freedom.

As we know, Whites employed Indians as slave catchers, and Indians were eager for these jobs. Moreover, Negroes knew that Indians, being expert woodsmen, were better slave catchers than White soldiers and patrols.[56] Negroes also realized that death sometimes awaited the unsuccessful runaway instead of a return to slavery. The Charles Town government executed leaders of fugitive slave parties and those slaves who ran away repeatedly. This government also instructed slave catchers to kill fugitive Negroes when they could not capture them; therefore, dead fugitives were paid for as well as live ones.[57] This encouraged Indians to be more bloodthirsty than White slave catchers: the labor of these fugitives was not going to benefit them. Besides, scalping was more profitable to them than to Whites: Indians could make one scalp look like two or more scalps. To prevent this cheating, the Charles Town government tried to buy only scalps with two ears.[58] Bloodthirstiness was a particular characteristic of Settlement Indians, for slave catching was almost the only opportunity of recapturing the excitement of their old culture. The enthusiasm and violence of Indian slave catchers, as well as the dread Negroes had for them, have been forcibly described by Brickell: "As soon as the Indians have Notice from the *Christians* of their [slaves] being there [in the woods], they disperse them; killing some, others flying for Mercy to the *Christians* . . . rather than fall into the others [Indians] Hands . . . [who] put them to death with the most exquisite Tortures they can invent, whenever they catch them."[59] It is not surprising that a Committee on Indian Affairs in 1727 instructed the Indian Commissioners to have "any Negroe or Negroes Corrected who shall threaten the [Settlement] Indians for Executing any Orders that the said Commissioners shall see fit to give the Indians."[60] Whites did not employ Indians as slave catchers only to recover valuable property and to punish offenders. They also employed them to make their slaves hate Indians. In 1776, some Maroons established themselves on Tybee Island; the Charles Town government secretly arranged for Creek slave catchers to kill these Maroons. Colonel Stephen Bull explained that this would "establish a hatred or aversion between Indians and Negroes."[61]

Indians also permitted and even helped Whites round up Negroes in and about the Indian villages.[62] These Negroes were then conveyed back to slavery. This was a hard blow. These runaways had eluded all the slave catchers and then experienced the intoxication of freedom among the Indians. Some of these runaways only lingered in these villages before moving on to Florida; other runaways settled down in these villages and started making some kind of life for themselves among the Indians. In either case, Indians betrayed them, blasting their hopes. Moreover, these Indians were betraying their own principles of hospitality and sanctuary for strangers—and these principles applied to fugitive Negroes.[63] It seems that Indians, in their greed for trade goods, sometimes betrayed the same fugitives twice. After returning Negroes and collecting their reward, Indians helped these fugitives to escape again before White agents delivered them to their masters. Then these Indians recaptured these fugitives and demanded another full reward from the agents.[64] In time, fugitive Negroes realized that they stayed in jeopardy while among Indians. In 1758, James Beamer, an old Cherokee trader, warned Governor Lyttleton to be discreet in sending for some runaways "for they are always on their Watch and the Least mistrust they have they Will fly Directly to the Woods."[65] In retrieving fugitive slaves from the Indian country, Whites again had the additional motive of making Negroes antagonistic to Indians. Indeed, this motive at times made Whites willingly forego repossessing their slaves. It seems that Whites were pleased when Indians scalped fugitive slaves who lived in Indian villages but would not peaceably surrender. This happened among the Creeks in 1768; Stuart then explained that "this cannot fail of having a very good Effect, by breaking that Intercourse between Negroes & Savages which might have been attended with very trouble-some consequences had it continued."[66]

Indians were *bona fide* slave traders. They stole Negroes from White slaveholders in order to sell them to other White slaveholders. Indians had been prepared for this Negro trade by the earlier trade in Indian slaves; for instance, they had learned that male captives were often too valuable to be done away with. Except for raids by Spanish Indians against South Carolina, Indians did not steal too many Negroes in the first half of the eighteenth century. About the only other Indians that regularly raided for Negro slaves were the Chick-asaw and other allied tribes of South Carolina living near the Missis-sippi River. These tribes raided French settlements in Louisiana and French convoys on the Great River. Negroes captured in these raids were sold to Charles Town traders who carried them to South Carolina.[67] This trade did not bring many slaves into the province; the French were always so short of Negroes. For the Negroes, this trade was a calamity. Their capture meant the substitution of one enslavement by a more severe one. Therefore, these Negroes must

have been bitter anti-Indian propagandists among the slaves of South
Carolina.

   After the mid-century, Indians began stealing and selling more
and more Negroes. In these years, White settlers increasingly en-
croached on Indian lands, coming in from almost all sides, and Indians
struck back. These years were years of almost continuous warfare
between Indians and Whites. Indians made a point of taking Negro
slaves from these settlers to discourage their rush into the interior. It
was also a fairly easy matter to steal Negroes from slaveholders in
transit and in newly established settlements. Moreover, the American
Revolution brought a new lawlessness to the South that lasted throughout the century. This meant that more Whites engaged in this Negro
trade: these Whites encouraged Indians to steal Negroes and even
stole Negroes themselves and disposed of them in the Indian country.
British officers during the Revolution had a big part in promoting
this Negro stealing: they got Indians, who sided with the British
cause, to rob rebel slaveholders. After the Revolution, many White
outlaws who were involved in this trade were British sympathizers.
In time, this trade became well organized. Negroes were stolen from
one part of the Indian frontier and carried into the Indian country
and there traded about among Indians, and between Indians and
Whites, until they ended up in slavery on another part of the Indian
frontier.[68]

   Indians had little trouble selling these Negroes. Whites in the
frontier settlements never had enough slaves. Moreover, law enforce-
ment was lax. Sometimes Indians sold nearly every Negro they had.
In 1784, Alexander McGillivray, the famous half-breed chief, reported
that the Creeks were "now pretty well drained of Negroes."[69] This
trade extended outside the South. The Cherokee sold Negroes north
of the Ohio River and Shawnee traders came from the North into
the Creek country to buy Negroes.[70] This trade even extended into
the West Indies. In 1783, McGillivray sent Negroes to Pensacola for
shipment to Jamaica.[71] It is clear that Indians were avid and heartless
slave traders. They looked upon these Negroes as nothing but chattel
property. In 1796, John Sevier, Governor of Tennessee and slave-
holder, reprimanded the Cherokee for trading Negroes to the Chickasaw for horses: he told them that "you know it is wrong to swop
people for horses, for negroes is not horses tho they are black."[72]
These were the people Foster and Johnston have made out to be
friends of Negroes. We can be sure that eighteenth century Negroes
felt differently. We can not say, however, that Whites deliberately
fostered this slave trade to create antagonism against Indians. But

we can be sure that Whites did not fail to remind Negroes that Indians were slave traders.

Finally, Whites employed Indians to help crush slave insurrections. In the Stono Rebellion of 1739, the most serious insurrection in South Carolina during the eighteenth century, about eighty Negro slaves killed more than thirty Whites. At the outset, the Charles Town government called upon Settlement Indians for help. These Indians pursued those slaves who eluded the militia at Stono; in a few weeks, they managed to capture some of these slaves and to kill a few others.[73] Indians also aided the province in suppressing slave insurrections in 1744 and 1765.[74] Slave insurrections in the eighteenth century were small-scale affairs; South Carolinians did not need many Indians to help them restore order in any particular one. What mattered most was speed in putting them down; otherwise, more timid Negroes might respond to the call of liberty and join the rebel slaves. Therefore, for this job the Charles Town government turned to Settlement Indians and Eastern Siouans. Although few in numbers, these Indians lived closer to White settlements and could be quickly mustered whenever needed.

The Charles Town government paid Indians high wages for helping suppress slave insurrections. In the Stono Rebellion, each Indian was given a coat, a flap, a pair of stockings, a hat, a gun, two pounds of powder, and eight pounds of bullets. The legislature, dominated by large slaveholders whose eyes were on the future, wanted to increase this payment. It declared that "Indians should be encouraged in such manner as to induce them always to offer their Service whenever this Government may have Occasion for them."[75] In 1774, the Natchez, now living as scattered Settlement Indians in South Carolina after their defeat by the French in 1729, informed Governor Glen that they wanted to be "together to be ready to assist the Government in case of any Insurrection, or Rebellion of the Negroes."[76] We can be certain that Negroes knew how eager Indians were to help keep them in slavery.

The Charles Town government did not wait for an uprising before calling on Indians. This government tried to anticipate trouble and then prevent it by using Indians to intimidate Negroes. On November 10, 1739, less than two months after Stono, the legislature ordered its Committee on Indian Affairs to cooperate with its special committee investigating this insurrection in "finding the most effectual means for preventing of such Dangers throughout the province." South Carolinians feared insurrections especially at Christmas, Negroes having so much more free time during these holidays.[77]

During the Christmas of 1716, the Charles Town government ordered Settlement Indians to move nearer White settlements to terrorize the slaves. Moreover, the government made a practice of locating Settlement Indians near places at which slaves might become troublesome. In the summer of 1716, it maintained the Wineau Indians around the Santee settlements "for keeping ye Negroes in awe."[78] But South Carolinians did not rely only on Settlement Indians to prevent insurrections. These tribes and even the Catawba were not large enough to intimidate all Negroes in the province; there were not enough Settlement Indians to station at every danger point. As we know, South Carolinians saw the danger of a big insurrection in every little one. For intimidating all slaves, South Carolina needed at least one big inland tribe. Therefore, the government turned to its most trusted ally and probably the tribe most hostile to Negroes: the Cherokee. In 1737, Lieutenant-Governor Thomas Broughton reported that he was sending for Cherokee warriors "to come down to the settlements to be an awe to the negroes."[79] Thus, a special effort was made after the Yamassee War to keep Negroes isolated from the Cherokee. In 1741, the legislature requested that Broughton purchase two Negro slaves owned by a Cherokee chief so that they could be shipped to the "West Indies or Northern Colonies to prevent any Detriment that they might do this Province by getting acquainted with the Cherokees."[80] It is clear that this intimidation by Indians helped prevent slave insurrections.

Conclusions

Hostility between Indians and Negroes in the Colonial Southeast was more pronounced than friendliness. Southern Whites were afraid of these two colored races, each of which outnumbered them. Whites were especially afraid that these two exploited races would combine against them. To prevent this combination, Whites deliberately maintained social distance between Indians and Negroes and created antagonism between them. To maintain this social distance, Whites segregated Indians and Negroes from each other. They did this by keeping Indians out of White settlements as much as possible and by trying to keep Negroes out of the Indian country and other out of the way places where these colored races might meet. To create antagonism, Whites deliberately played Indians and Negroes against each other. They pointed out to these races that each was the enemy of the other. To this end of mutual hostility, Whites also used Negroes as soldiers against Indians; on the other hand, they used Indians to catch runaway slaves and to suppress slave insurrections. In the eyes of Negroes, Indians were enemies of Negro freedom. At times, Whites encouraged Indians and Negroes to murder each other. In these ways, Whites created much of the hostility between Indians and Negroes in the eighteenth century.

NOTES

1. Gratitude is extended to Margaret Furcron, Brooklyn College, to Elliott P. Skinner, New York University, and especially to Morton H. Fried, Columbia University, for valuable suggestions, but any infelicities of style or errors of fact are the author's.

2. Laurence Foster, *Negro-Indian Relationships in the Southeast* (Philadelphia, 1935), p. 74; James H. Johnston, "Documentary Evidence of the Relations of Negroes and Indians," *Journal of Negro History*, XIV (January, 1929), 21-23.

3. W. J. Rivers, *A Sketch of the History of South Carolina* (Charleston, 1856), p. 48; W. C. Macleod, *The American Indian Frontier* (New York, 1928), p. 306; Chapman J. Milling, *Red Carolinians* (Chapel Hill, 1940), p. 63.

4. W. L. McDowell (ed.), *Documents relating to Indian Affairs, May 21, 1750-August 7, 1754* (Columbia, 1959), p. 201.

5. *American State Papers, Indian Affairs*, I, 461.

6. John Brickell, *The Natural History of North Carolina* (Dublin, 1737), p. 263.

7. Milling (ed.), *Colonial South Carolina: Two Contemporary Descriptions* (Columbia, 1951), p. 136.

8. David D. Wallace, *South Carolina: A Short History, 1520-1948* (Chapel Hill, 1951), *passim*; Verner W. Crane, *The Southern Frontier, 1670-1732* (Durham, 1928), *passim*.

9. J. H. Easterby (ed.), *Journals of the Commons House of Assembly, September 12, 1739-March 26, 1741* (Columbia, 1952), p. 97.

10. Herbert Aptheker, *American Negro Slave Revolts* (New York, 1943), *passim*; Alexander Garden to Secretary, October 31, 1759, Society for the Propagation of the Gospel in Foreign Parts MSS (later cited as SPG MSS), Series B, II, Pt. 1, 962 Library of Congress; Robert L. Meriwether, *The Expansion of South Carolina, 1729-1765* (Kingsport, 1940), p. 6.

11. Crane, *passim*.

12. Around 1750, Whites were estimated at 30-40,000; Indians, 60,000; Negroes, 70-90,000. Kenneth W. Porter, "Negroes on the Southern Frontier," *Journal of Negro History*, XXXIII (January, 1948), 53-54.

13. Commons House of Assembly to Francis Nicholson, February 3, 1721, Great Britain Public Record Office, Colonial Office (later cited as CO), 5/426, pp. 20-21, Library of Congress.

14. McDowell (ed.), *Journals of the Commissioners of the Indian Trade, September 20, 1710-August 29, 1718* (Columbia, 1955), p. 137.

15. *Colonial Records of North Carolina*, I, 886.

16. Reuben G. Thwaites (ed.), *Jesuit Relations* (Cleveland, 1900), LIX, 189.

17. *Colonial Records of North Carolina*, X, 118.

18. Pepper to Lyttelton, March 30, 1757, South Carolina Indian Book, February 21, 1757-March 6, 1760, p. 19, Library of Congress.

19. Stuart to Gage, November 27, 1767, Thomas Gage Papers, William L. Clements Library, Ann Arbor.

20. Report of Board of Commissioners, August 16, 1779, CO, 5/81, p. 451.

21. Report of Committee on Indian Affairs, May 27, 1742, CO, 5/443, p. 31.

22. McDowell, *Documents*, p. 109.

23. Report of Committee on Indian Affairs, February 29, 1727, CO, 5/430, p. 37.

24. Dunbar Rowland and A. G. Sanders (eds.), *Mississippi Provincial Archives, French Dominion, 1701-1729* (Jackson, 1929), I, 573. Later cited as *MPAFD*.

25. Crane, p. 203; John R. Alden, *John Stuart and the Southern Colonial Frontier, 1754-1775* (Ann Arbor, 1944), pp. 19, 342.

26. Stuart to Gage, March 19, 1765 and December 27, 1767, Gage Papers.

27. Stuart to Gage, September 26, 1767, *ibid.*

28. Report of Committee on Indian Affairs, February 29, 1727, CO, 5/430, p. 37.

29. Stuart to Gage, December 26, 1767, Gage Papers.

30. Taitt to Stuart, September 9, 1773, CO, 5/75, p. 23.

31. *Colonial Records of North Carolina*, III, 131-133; McDowell, *Documents*, p. 190.

32. Pepper, "Some Remarks on the Creek Nation, 1756," William H. Lyttelton Papers, William L. Clements Library.

33. Stuart to Gage, September 26, 1767, Gage Papers.

34. Alden, p. 108; John S. Bassett (ed.), *The Writings of William Byrd* (New York, 1901); pp. 391-392; *Great Britain . . . Calendar of State Papers, Colonial Series, America and the West Indies, 1728-1729* (later cited as *CSP, AWI*), pp. 414-415.

35. Wallace, *The History of South Carolina* (New York, 1934), I, 372.

36. Mark Van Doren (ed.), *The Travels of William Bartram* (New York, 1940), p. 371.

37. Peter Timothy to Lyttelton, November 13, 1759, Lyttelton Papers.

38. E. Merton Coulter (ed.), *The Journal of William Stephens, 1743-1745* (Athens, 1959), II, 245.

39. Ludlam to Secretary, March, 1725, SPG MSS, A, 19, p. 85.

40. Glen to Lyttelton, January 23, 1758, Lyttelton Papers.

41. R. W. Gibbes (ed.), *Documentary History of the American Revolution* (New York, 1855), I, 268-269; "Papers of the Second Council of Safety. . . ," *South Carolina Historical and Genealogical Magazine*, IV (July, 1903), 205-206.

42. Langdon Cheves (ed.), "Journal of the March of the Carolinians into the Cherokee Mountains, 1715-1716," *Year Book of the City of Charleston for 1894*, p. 344.

43. Crane, pp. 180-184, 193-194.

44. Samuel C. Williams (ed.), *Adair's History of the American Indians* (Johnson City, 1928), pp. 244-245.

45. Easterby, p. 64.

46. Crane, p. 183; Cheves, "Journal," p. 348.

47. B. F. French (ed.), *Historical Collections of Louisiana* (New York, 1853), V, 105, 111

48. Wallace, *South Carolina: Short History*, p. 185.

49. *MPAFD*, I, 64; French, pp. 99-101.

50. Stuart to Gage, August 31, 1771, Gage Papers.

51. McDowell, *Documents, passim.*

52. Edmund Atkin to Lyttelton, November 3, 1759, Lyttelton Papers.

53. George Gilmer, *Sketches of Some of the First Settlers of Upper Georgia* (Americus, 1926), p. 251.

54. *American State Papers*, Indian Affairs, I, 452.

55. Thwaites, LXVIII, 197-199.

56. Glen to Newcastle, April 14, 1748, CO, 5/389, p. 58.

57. Aptheker, "Maroons within the Present Limits of the United States," *Journal of Negro History*, XXIV (April 1939), 169.

58. Samuel Hazard (ed.), *Pennsylvania Archives, 1756-1760* (Philadelphia, 1853), III, 200; Easterby, p. 681.

59. Brickell, p. 273.

60. Report of Committee on Indian Affairs, February 29, 1727, CO, 5/430, p. 37.

61. Gibbes, p. 268-269; "Papers of the Second Council of Safety," pp. 205-206.

62. Stuart to Gage, December 26, 1767, Gage Papers.

63. Francis Baily, *Journal of a Tour in Unsettled Parts of North America in 1796 and 1797* (London, 1856), pp. 370-371.

64. Taitt to Stuart, July 13, 1777, CO, 5/79, p. 25.

65. Beamer to Lyttelton, May 20, 1758, Lyttelton Papers.

66. Stuart to Gage, July 2, 1768, Gage Papers.

67. *MPAFD*, III, 635.

68. Joseph B. Lockey (ed.), *East Florida, 1783-1785* (Berkeley, 1949), *passim;* John W. Caughey (ed.), *McGillivray of the Creeks* (Norman, 1938), *passim.*

69. *Ibid.,* p. 67.

70. "An Indian Talk," *American Historical Magazine, III* (January, 1898), 85; Adelaide L. Fries (ed.), *The Records of the Moravians in North Carolina* (Raleigh, 1941), V, 1985.

71. D. C. Corbitt (ed.), "Papers Relating to the Georgia-Florida Frontier, 1784-1800," *Georgia Historical Quarterly*, XXI (March, 1937), 75.

72. Williams (ed.), "Executive Journal of General John Sevier," *East Tennessee Historical Society's Publications,* I, (1929), 119.

73. Easterby, *passim.*

74. Milling, *Red Carolinians*, p. 229; Wallace, *South Carolina: Short History*, p. 185.

75. Easterby, pp. 65, 76-77.

76. South Carolina Council Journal, December 11, 1743-December 8, 1744, CO, 5/448, pp. 187-188.

77. Easterby, pp. 24, 69.

78. Wallace, *History of South Carolina*, I, 185; McDowell, *Journals*, p. 80.

79. Quoted in Wallace, *History of South Carolina*, I, 368.

80. Easterby (ed.), *Journals of the Commons House of Assembly, May 18, 1741-July 10, 1742* (Columbia, 1953), p. 45.

The Indian in the Old South

John H. Peterson, Jr.

Far too many studies of historic Southern Indians have erroneously assumed that they were socio-cultural isolates, existing outside a complex, stratified society that included several kinds of white and black people. It is my intention to show that this erroneous assumption has resulted from a failure to attempt to deal with the totality of human social relations in the Southeast as they changed through time.[1] Without some framework capable of including all major socio-cultural elements it is impossible to adequately describe or understand the position of the Indian in the Old South. I will suggest a conceptual framework which will permit the analysis of the total social relations in the Southeast through time and as a test case indicate how it is able to account for the historical experience of a single Southern Indian group, the Choctaws.

The description of the Southern Indian as a social isolate stems in large measure from the limitations associated with the term "Old South," which came into usage following Henry W. Grady's coinage of the term "New South" to indicate and emphasize the growing importance of manufacturing in the South in the 1880s. In opposition to this, the term "Old South" came to designate the earlier historical period in the southeastern United States.

Historians have debated the utility of the term "Old South" and its implication of discrete historical periods as opposed to a recognition of continuity and the evolutionary nature of change in Southern society (Cotterill 1964). This argument for continuity may have validity as it pertains to white Southerners, but there is no question of the drastic and sudden changes in the social position of non-whites, especially Indians, in Southern society.

A brief examination of historical titles dealing with the Old South indicates that this period is most frequently considered to begin with European settlement in the southeastern United States and to end with

116

the Civil War or Reconstruction, and that the geographic area covered under the term "Old South" only included territory under English or American control or occupation.[2] Indeed, the areas of the present southeastern United States which were not part of the Old South are often identified by the term "Old Southwest." The westward movement of the frontier thus represents the expansion of the Old South into the Old Southwest. The term "Old Southwest" is sometimes thought to be limited to that portion of the Southeast west of the original seaboard colonies. However, Henderson's (1920) title, *The Conquest of the Old Southwest: The Romantic Story of the Early Pioneers into Virginia, The Carolinas, Tennessee and Kentucky, 1740-1790*, clearly indicates that the Old Southwest began at the borders of the Old South.

In other words, the term "Old South" designates a recognizable period in the history of English-speaking immigrants and their descendants in southeastern North America beginning with settlement and lasting until the Civil War or shortly thereafter. As a historical period, the Old South has meaning only in terms of the activities and way of life of these immigrants and the society they established. It does not pertain to, in fact it excludes Southern Indians, their way of life, and their history. Historical scholarship on Negro life in the Old South has increased in recent years, but this literature is yet so small and information on non-whites in more general histories so slight that one is still justified in saying that the history of the Old South remains to this day a primarily white history.

The degree to which Southern Indians are excluded from histories of the Old South can be further demonstrated by examining histories and historiographical writing for information about Southern Indians. In many works one looks in vain for any mention of Indians (Dodd 1937; Hart 1910; Simkins 1948; Eaton 1949; Stephenson 1959). This may at times be justified in terms of the particular interest of an author, but it is hardly excusable in general works on the Old South where the geography is more often described than are the Indians. Where mention is made of the Southern Indians, it is often sandwiched between descriptions of geography and colonial settlement. Two examples of this approach are Cotterill's (1939) chapter on "The Oldest Inhabitants" and Betterworth's (1964) chapter on "The First Mississippians." Furthermore, the few accounts that do exist more nearly resemble static, ahistorical descriptions of the natural landscape than descriptions of historical events in the lives of human beings. The historians can scarcely be blamed for such static descriptions, since most of their material both summarizes and follows the form of standard ethnographic accounts by anthropologists. As a result, the Southern Indian in history has become like a part of the natural landscape, serving primarily as a setting for the territorial expansion and development of the Old South.

In many scholarly works there is one further subject or section that is often included before the history of the Old South can really begin, and this is a description of colonial rivalries and the struggle between France, Spain, and England for control of the Old Southwest. With the gradual demise of competing colonial powers, the emergence of the United States as a nation, and the final elimination of the Indians, the Old Southwest vanishes and the history of the Old South begins. In fact, some studies do not recognize the emergence of the South as a recognizable region until around 1820, after most of these events had occurred (Rankin 1965:3).

As a result, in most Southern histories the Indian is merely a kind of prologue, and the main portion of the history of the Old South begins only after his removal or destruction. Admittedly, Indians continued to occupy most of the Old Southwest after white settlements covered most of Virginia, North and South Carolina, and eastern Georgia, but in such cases would it be correct to say that the Indian inhabitants of the Old Southwest were part of the Old South? They were not within the geographic confines of the continuous territory occupied by English speaking settlers of European ancestry, nor were they for much of the period within the control of the government of these settlers. Certainly they were influenced by European contact, and one can talk about the relations between Indians and the inhabitants of the Old South, or one can describe scattered tribal remnants within the contiguous territory occupied by the holders of Old Southern culture. But the masses of Southern Indians could never be considered to be in the Old South. Only after the final massive Indian removal in the 1830s could the term "Old South" be applied to all the states in the Southeast.

Here we can see at least part of the reason for the false assumption that the Indians were a relatively isolated socio-cultural element existing outside a complex, stratified society known as the South. The problem lies not so much with the definition of "Indian," as it does with the use of the term "Old South" to identify primarily the post-settlement pre-Reconstruction period of the history of English-speaking people of European ancestry living in the Southeastern United States. The Indian was not thought to be part of the Old South simply because of the continuing description of the Old South as a society dominated by whites and composed exclusively of whites and Negroes.

The study of the Southern Indian as a social isolate can not be blamed entirely on historical research on the South. Students of Indian history have also failed to see a unified picture of the Southeast. Indian historians, like students of the Old South, frequently begin their books with a description of the Southern Indian in terms of "traditional culture" with detailed references to ethnographic works. They then generally proceed to write the history of a particular tribe. Where the study is of one of the five civilized tribes, the study usually follows the removal of the mass of tribal members to Oklahoma and continues their history there while ignoring the Indians who remained in the South (Debo 1934; McReynolds 1957; Woodward 1963). The students of Indian history are likely to describe in detail the relations of the Indians with non-Indians, and in fact the political relations between the Indians and the non-Indians constitute a large measure of their study. However, with their central focus on the Indian people, they do not describe the Indian *in* the Old South, and their relevant historical periods are not the same as those of the Southern historian with his interest in European immigrant society.

Like the students of the Old South, the beginning point for the Indian historian is initial white contact, but the removal west constitutes the basic end of a historical period for the Indian historian. The second period deals with the establishment of tribal government in Oklahoma. While the Indians in Oklahoma were significantly affected by the Civil War, this event was far less significant than the beginning of Oklahoma statehood and the ending of the Indian "nations." Since the recognized Indian nations were never an integral part of the Old South, the writers of these Indian histories largely ignore the Old South. Dealing with different people and recognizing different historical periods, the Indian historian has little or nothing to contribute to discussions about the Old South.

Not all historians of the Southern Indians have followed the subjects of their studies to Oklahoma. Some have dealt with groups who were never removed (Brown 1966), and others have dealt with those who were left behind (Bounds 1964). But in either case, the historian tends to place major emphasis on the period before the removal or destruction of the majority of the Indian group. Removal or destruction is the key turning point in the history of the individual Indian group, and by comparison the history of the remaining period is extremely brief and rarely deals in depth with the relations with non-Indians.

Finally, turning from the historian dealing with the Old South or with Indian history to the ethnographer focusing on the Indians themselves, we find preoccupation with a "traditional culture." The unfortunate consequence of this attention given to traditional culture and to survivals of traditional practices is that little attention is given to the history or events between the original documentary descriptions of the people and the ethnographer's later personal observations and research. Where the ethnographer has been primarily interested in the contemporary Indians rather than traditional culture, he has concentrated on various points of theoretical interest, such as acculturation, thereby substituting measurable social phenomena for chronological history.

At this point it should be clear that the position of the Indian in the Old South can be discussed only by changing the generally established meaning of the term Old South, or perhaps better by rejecting the term altogether as primarily applying to only one ethnic group. The studies of Indians by Indian historians and ethnographers offer us no satisfactory alternatives. Indian historians, like the Southern historians, use a point of view suitable to only one ethnic group, and ethnographers are too often prone to ignore history altogether or to focus on short historical periods.

I am therefore suggesting that the only way to avoid dealing with the Indian as a social isolate is to avoid following any one of these scholarly traditions, trying instead to merge or combine their approaches and strengths. This requires that we set as our goal the description of the position of the Indian in the totality of human social relations in southeastern North America from the time of white settlement to reconstruction. In order to do this, I will suggest a framework for describing the totality of human social relations in the Southeast between these two events and the position of the Indian in this totality.

Any statement of the position of the Indian in the Southeast in relation to non-Indians must incorporate a historical framework that is meaningful to both Indian and non-Indian experience. By combining the historical periods of the Southern and Indian historians, we find two established historical periods during the time span under consideration. As we have seen, a historical period that seems to have meaning for English-speaking European immigrants in the Southeast is the period from initial settlement to Reconstruction. For the Southern Indian, this same period seems better conceived as *two* historical periods, the first lasting from white settlement to the removal or destruction of the Indian group and the second being the history of those remaining behind after the mass removals or destruction. A combination of the two historical experiences of both groups involves a recognition that the period between white settlement and reconstruction comprises two historical periods divided by Indian removal or destruction.

This additional distinction is required only if we are interested in the relation of Indians to other inhabitants of the Southeast. Thus, the combined framework indicates changes in the total social relations of inhabitants of the Southeast, and not just changes within one group.

Given the three major turning points listed above, four major periods or phases can be identified in terms of the total human social relations in the Southeast. These periods, particularly the earlier ones, can be more correctly called phases since the key events took place only gradually, with large sections of the Southeast remaining unaffected by the changes for some time. These phases are:

Phase	*Event ending phase*
Traditional	White settlement
International	Destruction or removal of Indian groups
Slavery	Civil War and Reconstruction
Post-slavery	Civil rights movement

Prior to European discovery and settlement, social relations among the inhabitants of the Southeast were limited to traditional relations among Indian groups. Details of social relations existing among the different Indian groups at the time of white contact are far from completely understood and indeed probably will never be completely understood, although archaeological and ethnohistorical research is making some headway. White exploration and settlement introduced a new complex of ideas about inter-group relations based on Western European ideas about relations among nations. While traditional relations long continued to be the pattern among Indian groups remote from white settlement, the expansion of white settlement and the emerging competition between colonial powers gradually made the entire Southeast a battleground between Britain, France, and Spain. Each colonial power attempted to secure additional lands or favors from Indian groups adjacent to them. These Indian groups were most often accorded legal recognition as Indian "nations," equal or semi-equal allies of the particular colonial power. Their leaders were given European titles and often commissions within the military hierarchy of the colonial power. Gradually almost all Indian groups were brought into the spheres of influence of competing colonial powers.

The very concept of Indian "nation" seems related to this colonial rivalry. Possession of lands and a large number of warriors were the defining characteristic of an Indian nation for the colony of South Carolina in the eighteenth century (Hudson 1970:47). Loss of fighting men or land ended the existence of the nation. Even the Indian nations which continued to hold land and which had a considerable population were doomed when the period of colonial rivalry came to an end. With the rise of the new American nation and the defeat of its Colonial rivals, international relations in the Southeast came to an end. There was no longer any utility in the United States as a sovereign state recognizing individual Indian nations, nor were there international allies to whom the Indian nations could turn for assistance. Southern state governments were able to unilaterally terminate Indian sovereignty and force the Federal Government to adopt a removal policy. During the 1830s the bulk of Indians remaining in the Southeast were removed to Oklahoma, often with their tribal governments intact. This, however, was not the end of Indians in the Southeast, contrary to the impressions one would receive from the literature. Many small groups of Indians remained behind where they became what might be called an ethnic group within a single pluralistic society, rather than a nationality within an international society.

Even before the end of the international period in the Old South, whites and blacks were masters and slaves. It is certainly true that the mass of whites were never slave-owners, but most aspired to this position, especially in the newly opened Indian frontier lands, and it is equally true that almost all Negroes were slaves. The end of the international period had little effect on the relations between whites and Negroes within the Old South, but if our framework for analysis of social relations within the Southeast is to include all peoples, we must recognize that for the Indian the position of being a third ethnic group in a society based on rather clear-cut and mutually exclusive social relations between white and black was most difficult. The remaining Indians were not land-owners, as were most whites, nor were they slaves, as were most blacks. They were the people in between, belonging to neither of the two largest social groups in the Old South. As such, they had little choice but to retreat onto inaccessible or undesirable land where as squatters they maintained to some degree their traditional life, isolated from both whites and blacks.

This state of affairs continued for the end of the international period until the end of the slave period. Following the Civil War and

Reconstruction, Negro slaves were freed, and several variants of the share-cropping system arose to replace slavery. In the changing economic situation, even some whites became sharecroppers, and the idea of working on shares was not restricted to a single ethnic group, as was slave status. The basic change in agricultural work made it possible for Indians to begin to work as sharecroppers without accepting the slave status or demanding the status of free white landowners, which would have been necessary under the plantation system.

This, then, summarizes the basic framework for viewing Indian participation in the Old South. To glance forward a moment, one can observe that both Negroes and Indians emerged only gradually from sharecropping and marginal agricultural labor and began attempting to be true equals with whites, first in industrial jobs and more recently in politics and education. The impact of the Civil Rights movement in the South often benefitted Indians as much as Negroes. The growing consciousness of a separate identity as Southern Indians, the increasing power of tribal governments, and the formation of a United Southeastern Tribes all could be interpreted as signaling a fourth stage in Southern Indian history. To cite only one example, in 1968 the Mississippi Choctaws regained the right to administer justice to their own people on their own land, and a tribal court began operating for the first time in almost one hundred and forty years (Dean 1970).

Having presented a framework for analysis of the position of the Indian in the total social relations of the inhabitants of the Southeast, our final task will be to see how this framework throws light on the history of a particular tribe, the Mississippi Choctaws. The available literature on the Choctaws demonstrates the traditional historical approach to the Southern Indians discussed above. Traditional Choctaw culture and more recent survivals have been described by Swanton (1931). The best history of the Choctaw people virtually ignores the continued presence of Choctaws in Mississippi after removal, instead focusing on the Choctaw people in Oklahoma (Debo 1934). The most widely read general history of the state of Mississippi (Bettersworth 1964) has a chapter on the traditional Indian culture but virtually ignores the presence of Choctaws in Mississippi after removal. The only published work on the history of the Mississippi Choctaws (Bounds 1964) devotes 50 pages to traditional culture and early history but only 3 pages to history between removal and the establishment of the Choctaw Agency in 1918. In other words, the prevailing trends in studies of Southern Indians and Southern society has resulted in an almost total blank in the history of the Choctaws from the time of removal until relatively recent years.

In reading standard accounts, one gains the impression that there was little change in the condition of the Choctaws in Mississippi from the time of removal until recently. In the words of one author (Bounds 1964:51), "They were marking time in a 'no man's land'." My own research (Peterson 1970) has led me to the opposite conclusion. Far from marking time, a radical change in the position of the Choctaws in the local society occurred between the time of removal and the present day, and this change seems to have been part of a more general restructuring of human social relations throughout the Southeast. Moreover, this was only one of a series of such changes experienced by the Choctaws in social relations with other peoples. This can be seen by examining the Choctaws in the different phases of Southern Indian history that were identified above.

Although "traditional" Choctaw social and ceremonial life has been described in detail by Swanton, much of this information comes after the period of colonial rivalries was well established. We know virtually nothing about the relations between the Choctaws and their nearest neighbors, such as the Natchez to the West and the Chickasaw to the North, before the relations among these groups became dictated to a large degree by colonial rivalries. Moreover, the early maps of the area show numerous small "tribes" whose relationships with the Natchez, Chickasaw, and Choctaw remain unknown. In short, we are not even sure who was or was not a Choctaw, much less the relations between Choctaws and other groups before the Choctaws were identified as a nation by Europeans and began to be influenced by colonial rivalries. Colonial military operations and the inter-Indian warfare promoted by colonial powers quickly reduced the number of identifiable Indian nations in Mississippi to the Chickasaw, who allied with the English, and the Choctaw, who were allied with the French.

During this period of international rivalry the Choctaws rapidly adopted many of the traits of European settlers. In this regard they were exceeded in the Southeast only by the Cherokees. But the declining cultural differences between some members of the Choctaw "nation" and members of the American nation did not change the fact that to a large extent the Choctaws continued to control internal affairs within their borders, although they came increasingly under the political control of the United States.

The international period ended for the Choctaws when state jurisdiction was unilaterally extended over them, making it illegal for their tribal government to function and granting all Choctaws the status of Mississippi citizens, thereby making them subject to all state laws. The Choctaws were now *in* the Old South for the first time. The response of many of the Choctaws was to accept the necessity of removal to Oklahoma where they were told their existence as a nation would not be challenged.

Large numbers of Choctaws, however, initially preferred to accept their changed status and remain in their traditional homeland as citizens of the state of Mississippi, an option open to them under the terms of the removal treaty. The experiences of this group support the proposition that with the ending of their status as an Indian nation there was drastic change in the position of Indians in the Southeast. While slavery had existed in the Choctaw "nation," it had little effect on the majority of Choctaws; it was only with the extension of state laws over the Choctaws that social relations based on slavery had a major impact on the relations of Choctaws with non-Choctaws. The Choctaws remaining in Mississippi rapidly lost possession of their land. As a result, they were left free but landless in an agricultural society in which one social group was primarily composed of white landowners and a second social group was primarily composed of non-landowning Negro slaves.

Although the Choctaws, like other Southeastern Indians, had been forced into slavery during earlier times, the use of Indian slaves had largely died out by the late eighteenth century as the supply of Negro slaves increased and as slave owners found their working abilities to be more satisfactory (Lauber 1913). Whites who could afford to use extra agricultural labor bought Negro slaves. Poor white landowners could exchange agricultural labor with each other, but the only alternative to this was the use of slave labor; there was no generally established pattern of wage agricultural work. But even if whites had offered to use Choctaws in agricultural work, Choctaws could not have accepted such work without becoming slaves in their own eyes (Rouquette n.d.: 12-14).

As a result, there was no social role in agriculture in the Old South for a free, non-white, non-landowning Indian. The only solution for the Choctaws was to become squatters on marginal agricultural land, isolated from both Negroes and whites. The existence of large numbers of Indian and mixed-blood Indian populations along the eastern seaboard and the Southern Appalachians in isolated areas with marginal soil indicates that the Choctaw experience was far from unique and that this was probably the only manner in which the Indian could continue to exist in a society based on slavery. I would suggest that a detailed examination of the origin of isolated Indian settlements throughout the Southeast would indicate that many of them are the result of Indians remaining after the passing of the line of white settlements. Also one would expect that a study of "settlement" Indians in the colonial South (Hudson 1970:56) would demonstrate that they faced a problem similar to that of the Choctaws after 1830.

It seems probable that the Choctaws remaining in Mississippi after the period of Indian removal were more isolated from contact with whites than they had been prior to removal. The tribal government had allowed whites to move freely within Choctaw borders, and traders, government agents, and missionaries had sought them out. It was this intensive interaction within the borders of the Choctaw "nation" that resulted in the rapid rate of adoption of European practices. After they became citizens, however, the remaining Choctaws were a disinherited ethnic group rather than an influential "nation." Within Choctaw borders prior to removal a white man could aspire to be equal to a Choctaw. But within the borders of the Old South it was almost impossible for a Choctaw to aspire to be the equal of a white man. Yet there were those few who did, such as Greenwood LaFlore, the wealthy educated half-blood who prior to removal was one of the leaders of the Choctaw nation. He was influential in securing the execution of the removal treaty and was generously rewarded by the Federal Government with a gift of land in the Mississippi Delta. Here he became a wealthy and respected plantation owner and was elected to the Mississippi legislature. It is doubtful if a full-blood could have accomplished the same even if he had owned property and slaves. Certainly the equally prominent leader Moshulatubbee, a full-blood, was unable to do so. Thus, the wealthy land- and slave-owning half-breed could be accepted in white society in Mississippi after the removal of the Choctaw "nation." Other Choctaws had the choice of remaining in Mississippi as isolated squatters, following traditional subsistence agricultural practices, or of leaving for Oklahoma. In either case, they were separated from both Southern whites and Negroes.

The contention that the position of the Indians who remained after removal was determined in large part by the established social relationship between black and white under the plantation system can be verified in two ways. The change in the position of the Indians following the loss of their status as a "nation" has already been described. A second test can be provided by looking forward to the end of the plantation period and ascertaining the change in the posi-

confirmed the adequacy of the proposed framework, and, more important, indicated that the framework focused attention on important aspects of the Choctaw experience that had been ignored by research using alternative approaches. Although fragmentary, information on other Southern Indians indicates that their histories paralleled that of the Choctaws. This would suggest that fuller confirmation of the conceptual framework herein presented can be found in comparative research on the largely neglected post-removal history of the Southern Indians.

The importance of the conceptual frameworks representing the diverse historical experiences of separate ethnic or social groups in a complex society reaches beyond the subject of this paper. If the comparative research suggested above validates the conceptual framework suggested here, it will have demonstrated the necessity of a holistic approach to the historical study of complex societies. Otherwise, both descriptions and histories of individual social groups tend to be based on situations and events which have meaning primarily to one group. As a result we have a limited and biased understanding of total social relations as they have changed through time, and our history as it is written cannot avoid being ethnocentric.

NOTES

1. I am indebted to several individuals for the ideas expressed in this paper. Charles Hudson stimulated my interest in the problems of plural societies and their history as they applied to the Southern United States. His research on the Catawba (1970) was especially influential in establishing the difference between Indian "nations" and "settlement" Indians in the colonial South. J. C. Vinson and Joseph Parks instructed me in historical methodology and together with Hudson encouraged the questioning of both established facts and assumptions. Emmett York, Chairman of the Choctaw Tribal Council, patiently helped me to understand that a Southern Indian's view of Southern history is quite different from that of a Southern white. Finally, it was only through a reading of Southern Negro history, especially from Vernon Wharton (1965), that the full significance of post-removal Choctaw history began to occur to me. Although I am indebted to these men for the originality of their ideas, responsibility for the use or distortion of these ideas is truly mine.

2. A detailed examination of all the literature on the Old South is beyond the scope of this paper. Southern historiography is considered in detail in Link and Patrick (1965). Recent trends in Southern historical writing are described by Stephenson (1964). A sample of the interests of Southern historians can be seen in the collection of almost thirty years of presidential addresses of the Southern Historical Association edited by Tindall (1964). In addition, specific histories bearing the title Old South or including it as a major subsection include: Cotterill (1939); Dodd (1937); Eaton (1949, 1961); Phillips (1941); and Simkins (1948, 1967).

REFERENCES

Beckett, Charlie M., 1949. Choctaw Indians in Mississippi Since 1830. Unpublished M.A. thesis, Oklahoma A. and M.

Bettersworth, John K., 1964. *Mississippi Yesterday and Today* (Austin: Steck-Vaughn Co.).

Bounds, Thelma V., 1964. *Children of Nanih Waiya* (San Antonio: Naylor Co.).

Brown, Douglas Summers, 1966. *The Catawba Indians: The People of the River* (Columbia: University of South Carolina Press).

Cotterill, Robert S., 1939. *The Old South* (Glendale: The Arthur H. Clark Co.).

———————————————, 1964. The Old South to the New. In *The Pursuit of Southern History: Presidential Addresses of the Southern Historical Association 1935-1963*, George Brown Tindall, ed. (Baton Rouge: Louisiana State University Press).

Dean, S. B., 1970. Law and Order Among the First Mississippians. Mimeographed Report, Association on American Indian Affairs, Inc., Washington, D. C.

Debo, Angie, 1934. *The Rise and Fall of the Choctaw Republic* (Norman: University of Oklahoma Press).

Deweese, Orval H., 1957. The Mississippi Choctaws. Unpublished M.A. thesis, Mississippi State University.

Dodd, William E., 1937. *The Old South Struggles for Democracy* (New York: Macmillan Co.).

Eaton, Clement, 1949. *A History of the Old South* (New York: Macmillan Co.).

———————————————, 1961. *The Growth of Southern Civilization 1790-1860* (New York: Harper Bros.).

Farr, Eugene, 1948. Religious Assimilation: A Case Study of the Adoption of Christianity by the Choctaw Indians of Mississippi. Unpublished Ph.D. diss., New Orleans Baptist Theological Seminary.

Hart, Albert B., 1910. *The Southern South* (New York: D. Appleton and Co.).

Henderson, 1920. *The Conquest of the Old Southwest: The Romantic Story of the Early Pioneers into Virginia, the Carolinas, Tennessee and Kentucky, 1740-1790* (New York: Century Co.).

Hudson, Charles M., 1970. *The Catawba Nation* (Athens: University of Georgia Press).

Langford, Etha Myerl, 1953. A Study of the Educational Development of the Choctaw Indians of Mississippi. Unpublished M.A. thesis, Mississippi Southern College.

Lauber, Almon Wheeler, 1913. *Indian Slavery in Colonial Times Within the Present Limits of the United States* (New York: Longmans, Green and Co.).

Lindquist, G. E. E., 1923. *The Red Man in the United States* (New York: George H. Doran Co.).

Link, Arthur S. and Rembert W. Patrick, eds., 1965. *Writing Southern History: Essays in Historiography in Honor of Fletcher M. Green* (Baton Rouge: Louisiana State University).

McReynolds, Edwin C., 1957. *The Seminoles* (Norman: University of Oklahoma Press).

Peterson, John H. Jr., 1970. The Mississippi Band of Choctaw Indians: Their Recent History and Current Social Relations. Unpublished Ph.D. diss., University of Georgia.

Phillips, Ulrich B., 1941. *Life and Labor in the Old South* (Boston: Little, Brown and Co.).

Rankin, Hugh F., 1965. The Colonial South. In *Writing Southern History: Essays in Historiography in Honor of Fletcher M. Green*, Arthur S. Link and Rembert W. Patrick, eds. (Baton Rouge: Louisiana State University Press).

Rouquette, Dominique, n.d. The Choctaws. Unpublished Manuscript, Louisiana State Museum Library, New Orleans.

Simkins, Francis, 1948. *The South: New and Old* (New York: Alfred A. Knopf).

———————————, *A History of the South*, 3rd ed. (New York: Alfred A. Knopf, 1967).

Stephenson, Wendell H., 1959. *A Basic History of the Old South* (New York: Van Nostrand Co.).

———————————, 1964. *Southern History in the Making: Pioneer Historians of the South* (Baton Rouge: Louisiana State University Press).

Swanton, John, 1931. *Source Material for the Social and Ceremonial Life of the Choctaw Indians*, Bureau of American Ethnology Bulletin No. 103 (Washington, D. C.: GPO).

Tindall, George Brown, ed., 1964. *The Pursuit of Southern History: Presidential Addresses of the Southern Historical Association 1935-1963* (Baton Rouge: Louisiana State University Press).

Tolbert, Charles, 1958. A Sociological Study of the Choctaw Indians in Mississippi. Unpublished Ph.D. diss., Louisiana State University.

Wharton, Vernon Lane, 1965. *The Negro in Mississippi, 1865-1890* (New York: Harper and Row).

Woodward, Grace Steele, 1963. *The Cherokees* (Norman: University of Oklahoma Press).

Comments

CHARLES CROWE

EVEN a cursory glance at the history of relations between the white man and the Indian reveals a record of unmitigated disaster for the native peoples of North America. Four centuries of white imperialism makes a depressing tale of invasion, despoilation, massacre, treachery, and random violence of all kinds. Despite the challenging work of Alden Vaughan (Columbia) and the less persuasive efforts of Bernard Sheehan (Indiana), the historical record stands generally as Helen Hunt Jackson reported it more than eighty years ago in *A Century of Dishonor*. It is not surprising that nineteenth century pretensions, accusations, and international "peace" efforts by leaders of a nation which had nearly completed the extermination of the red man reminded Otto von Bismarck of a wealthy and reformed gangster's demand for the most rigid morality from his new, respectable neighbors. More recently an Asian diplomat told an American audience that while the Western World may not have invented genocide, Americans were the only people who commemorated genocide so persistently for generations in a children's game called "cowboys and Indians." An unusually ironic contrast can be seen if one compares the bloody reality of Indian-white relations with the schoolbook tales of Pocahontas and John Smith, Squanto and the Pilgrims, and William Penn's allegedly generous policy of peace and the righteous purchase of land.

A more accurate barometer of white opinion was the maxim "the only good Indian is a dead one," held by Andrew Jackson and millions of soldiers, frontiersmen, politicians, traders, and farmers who actively took part in the dispossession of the red man. One may note partial exceptions such as Benjamin Franklin, and one may appreciate in this symposium F. N. Boney's reminder that Jefferson expressed more generous attitudes toward the original inhabitants of the continent. Even so, Franklin lacked consistency, and Jefferson's warm words

134

of praise for Indians stand in vivid contrast to his failure to stop or to slow down the continuing white war of annihilation. A related failure and a similar contrast can be found in the enormous gap between Jefferson's largely private criticisms of slavery and his active support, as planter, politician, and president, of the "peculiar institution" during an era in which it expanded from the Atlantic seaboard to the Mississippi River and beyond.

The westward expansion of slavery and the dispossession of the Indian took place almost simultaneously. After tribal removal, could the remaining red men find a place in a society of white masters and black slaves? John H. Peterson, who offers a conceptual framework for all of Indian history from the arrival of Europeans to the present, pays particular attention to Indians left behind after the great migration to Oklahoma territory. Professor Peterson argues that these Indians constituted a significant part of the history of the old South rather than being merely "cultural isolates." Certainly Peterson provides important information and insights: the loss of Choctaw literacy can be seen as a sign of general cultural shock, and the tendency of Choctaws to follow the lead of black freedmen in establishing churches and schools surely gives us an important lead. For the most part, however, we are still left with the larger realities of white devastation. Twentieth century historians in ignoring the Indian enclaves of the Southeast reflect the scorn of their forbears who drove the red men from the land. After defeat and dispossession the Indian had no place in the white man's domain or in the histories he wrote. As Ambrose Bierce suggested in *The Devil's Dictionary*, "Aborigines, n. Persons of little worth found cumbering the soil of a newly discovered country. They soon cease to cumber; they fertilize."

To consider the black man as well as the Indian is to become aware of still larger historical ironies. The enslaved African paid an extraordinarily high blood price to the imperialist who often credited the *defeated* Indian with some virtues in a comparative rhetorical context which stripped the black man of the last vestiges of humanity. For example, it is worth noting that the Spanish priest Las Casas advocated for "humanitarian" reasons the enslavement of Africans to replace the perishing Indians as forced laborers. In United States history the expansion of American democracy almost inevitably meant the advance of white racism, and the conquest and removal of Indians made it possible for whites to find admirable qualities in the defeated foe which the African lacked. Indians may have been more feared and hated on a precarious frontier during a period of active warfare, but as the frontier moved West and most Indians were pushed beyond the Mississippi hatred of the red man diminished sharply. White hatred and scorn toward blacks existed even in the absence of danger and indeed infected areas entirely or nearly devoid of black inhabitants. The fact that fewer than a hundred scattered black persons lived in Oregon during the 1850s and had never been seen by most whites did not prevent the territorial legislature from expressing a rabid Negrophobia.

Why was the hostility and the contempt more pervasive and enduring toward the black man? For one thing it was more difficult to ignore the continuing presence of the black man in the life of the nation, in patterns of work and play, songs and stereotypes, and guilt and apprehensions. The defeated and largely displaced Indian could in a sense be "forgiven," but the preservation of dominant myths of liberty, equality, and American innocence required the continuing dehumanization of the black man. Americans could not forget the long centuries of war with the Indians for the land, and though the Indian had to bear the reputation of a barbarian stripped of the land he did not merit, few Americans wished to *denigrate* (the word itself tells us much) completely an old and persistent foe for fear of making their own fighting prowess inconsequential and their final victory unworthy. White America needed to remember Indian courage and to forget black resistance. It was less disturbing to think of Tecumseh than of Nat Turner, and it was best to forget that most Africans had been wrenched from their homelands in small groups and denied the historical experience of the Indians who struggled on native soil for the existence of their land and people.

The sources of cultural strength which enabled many West Africans to survive plantation slavery while Indians commonly perished in bondage were regarded by whites not as creditable but as further evidence of cowardice and a natural aptitude for slavery. Moreover, when the existence of rebels such as Nat Turner could not be denied, their rebellions were described as "senseless violence." In other cases, the historians and the myth-makers simply "forgot" that resistance and rebellion had taken place. The Seminole Wars of the 1830s and 1840s, which might well be called "the Negro and Seminole Wars," constituted the longest, bloodiest, and most expensive Indian wars the United States ever fought. These wars raised the specter of black-red military cooperation and aroused the most intense fears among pioneer slaveholders on exposed frontiers. It is interesting to note that the Florida wars provide one of the best instances of stubborn black resistance. When peace came to Florida, some blacks made an incredible "long trek" to northern Mexico where they waged guerilla warfare for many years against Texas planters who were so skeptical about black courage that they invented fanciful stories about refugee "Marmeluke" soldiers from the remote Ottoman Empire to explain the presence of the troublesome dark-skinned fighters.

Of white imperiousness and white contacts with red and black we know much, but of initial contacts between African and Indian we know very little. Black contacts with Seminoles appear to have been mutually sympathetic ones. However, tribes such as the Cherokees and the Creeks, either initially or in imitation of the whites, behaved in a condescending manner toward blacks. In any case the most important single fact is that whites were able to establish a multi-caste system in which they were dominant over red and black. The long-range thrust of white supremacy was to compel most Indian tribes to accept grudgingly the inevitable white dominion, while trying to establish for themselves a status superior to that of the blacks. In the minds of most whites the situation was quite simple— the red man had been banished to the far West or limited to a few unimportant Eastern conclaves, and where white, red, and black happened to live in physical proximity a triple caste system existed. Yet actual social situations contained many incongruities which official ideology did not allow for. Although whites almost always granted the superiority of Indians to blacks, they frequently attempted to force Indian children into black schools. In several Mississippi counties at the turn of the century, consciousness of status and color was so intense that the ruling elite maintained four separate school systems for whites, blacks, Indians, and recent Southern Italian immigrants. If some Indians learned condescension from whites, so did some blacks: Western Indians who attended Hampton Institute and lived in "the Indian dormitory" did not escape the stigma of being considered "savages," and black soldiers who fought in Indian wars toward the end of the nineteenth century often spoke scornfully of their red enemy.

Despite all of the group hostility, a significant number of liaisons existed among whites and blacks, whites and Indians, and Indians and blacks. The offspring of these "illegitimate" unions sometimes entered social groups from which they were excluded by the official definitions of the social system. Hundreds of thousands of people with both European and African ancestors ended by "passing" as white; some persons of largely African ancestry accepted an Indian identity; and scattered individuals with largely European or Indian forebears became "black." We can learn much about color attitudes from what several scholars call "tri-ethnic" communities of men and women with varying degrees of Indian, black, and European ancestors. Faced with the reality of white domination and rejection, these people of multiple origins tried, often successfully, to maintain a separate identity as well as a social status superior to that of the blacks. It should be noted, however, that in recent years at least a few of these communities have disintegrated, that most of them exist at a level of poverty below that of the majority of blacks, that black communities have become the most dynamic sources of social change, and that leadership roles in coalitions of the poor and the non-white have been assumed largely by blacks.

Several historical discussions of the tri-ethnic communities are misleading in the use of "mestizo" and "mulatto," terms which have so much meaning in Latin-American history. Despite the scattered use of terms such as "mulatto" and "mustee" in colonial times, the two terms had little legal or formal meaning north of Mexico in the nineteenth century. According to most American laws and all official creeds, men were implacably and unchangingly white, black, or red. By contrast, in the complex social hierarchies of most Latin national societies of the New World, many status levels existed, and the status of a particular individual was determined by wealth, education, ancestry, and political power as well as by color. Thus, unlike the United States, Brazil and Cuba allowed wealthy and powerful dark-skinned men to rise to very high positions.

The existence of American "tri-ethnic" communities sprang from the iron determination of whites to continue the debasement of blacks, as well as from the desperate striving of "mixed" communities to avoid at all costs the despised label of "Negro." The study of these communities tells us important things but we must remember that they were scattered and isolated enclaves, often unknown a few miles away from their location and lacking significant influence on the history of American society. Presumably an iron wall of total separation existed between white and black, and whites almost invariably tried to deny the obvious evidence of their senses by acting as if Americans came in only one of the two totally opposite and different colors. The inevitable confusion appeared, among other places and times, during the suppression of the Philippine insurrection when white soldiers commonly spoke of Philippinos as "niggers." Yet the same soldiers back in America would almost certainly have made a rigid distinction between "Indian" and "Negro." When lawyers tried to work with the problem, they sometimes said that a Negro was a person with one-quarter, one-eighth, one-sixteenth, one-thirty-second, or "any known trace" of African ancestry. White public opinion also granted the all-conquering nature of "Negro blood," often to the extent of asserting that "one drop" would over-whelm gallons of "European blood." Every village and county which contained both peoples had its secrets of black-white kinships, but whites continued to stress the terrible black "biological threat" to the white race. Presumably "race-mixing" and "mongrelization of the races," a fate worse than death, had never happened and should be prevented at any cost.

Yet the actual conduct of whites frequently conflicted with their own passionately expounded rhetoric. For example, the fact of race mixture was often acknowledged to demonstrate that any merit or ability displayed by a black person could be attributed to white ancestry. Before the Civil War many planters emancipated those slaves closest to their own color, and a much more common means of expressing color preference was to allow light-skinned slaves to escape the brutal conditions of field labor by becoming house servants. After Civil War and Reconstruction, access to better occupations such as barbering, farming, catering, and the skilled trades was given much more freely to black persons of "mixed" ancestry. Moreover, these economic patterns were reinforced in countless ways by a culture which made "black" synonymous with sin, death, dishonesty, treach-ery, and ugliness and associated "white" with God, heaven, angels, virtue, purity, morality, and beauty. Nevertheless the prosperous black who traded on a lighter skin color to the extent of forgetting his membership in a subordinate caste courted death. Favors promised by the white man to the more industrious and the "less offensive" often turned out to be the promises of, as the expression goes, Indian givers. Americans insisted both on keeping blacks in the one rank assigned to all persons with known African ancestors, and at the same time they acted in complete contradiction to this principle by making a number of color distinctions in daily life.

The common devotion of every social class in the dominant caste to capitalism and white supremacy becomes evident in Pro-fessor Boney's paper. Joseph L. Brent tends to support Boney's case as well as to give information about the insistent demands for both equality and higher status which helped to make white racism functional. Perhaps it will be best to clarify the point by making more explicit the nature of the clash between official ideology and conflicting social experiences. White Americans could have their cake and eat it too by preaching universal equality while simul-taneously reaping status gains from the maintenance of servile castes.

The American creed of "equality of opportunity" often seemed a mere euphemism for the frantic scramble for wealth, status, and power in which a few would gain a great deal of "equality," or to speak more plainly, ascendancy over others. These basic contradictions have made realistic assessments of American society hard to come by. Americans, seeing themselves as an innocent people, found it difficult to acknowledge the fact that the continent was gained by the near extermination of the Indian, the exploitation of poor whites and immigrants, and the oppression of black people. Because America is by definition the land of freedom and equality, the elaborate system of status and caste as well as the long history of imperialism and racial oppression must be denied. Recently, however, the emergence of oppressed minorities, particularly blacks, has thrust the nation toward a confrontation with its own history which must end in a restructuring of American society or in massive civil strife.

In the final analysis American history is a part of Western history, and racism must be traced to its European roots. The United States did develop a much more fanatical domestic version of white supremacy, but American racism can best be seen in the context of world history. For generations "civilized" Europeans expressed irritation over white American arrogance toward the black middle class: in 1850 Frederick Douglass could hope to gain the sympathetic ear of English aristocrats over indignities he suffered after his flight from slavery; in 1918 French army officers could express disgust over the determination of white Americans to treat black officers as subhuman; Richard Wright could realistically hope to find a life largely free of harrassment by fleeing to Paris in 1945; and even today black Mississippians can evoke concerned responses among millions of Europeans. Protestations of European "innocence," however, bear a strong resemblance to similar myths about innocent Americans. In the early years of the twentieth century it would have been easy to raise money for American lynch victims in Brussels but very difficult to get a hearing over the massacre of hundreds of thousands of people in the Belgian Congo. For centuries white European imperialists sacked the world and grew fat with arrogance at the expense of "the lesser breeds without." For many generations France, England, and other Western nations enjoyed a growing domestic equality and liberty, while the very same nations continued the colonial oppression of the Afro-Asian and Latin American peoples of the world. Today, thoughtful men know that the future must be different and that the system of Western exploitation of the world must be dismantled completely to make possible a humane existence for red, white, black, and yellow.

The Contributors

F. N. Boney is associate professor of history at the University of Georgia. He has published two books and 20 articles on various aspects of Southern history, and now he is investigating slavery in Virginia and Georgia in the late ante-bellum period.

Joseph L. Brent III is associate professor in the Department of History at Federal City College. His principal field of study is the history of ideas in the United States, and his main interest lies in the philosophy and methods of history. He has done work on Charles Pierce, the mind of the South, and Afro-American issues, among other topics. He has published on the South and is co-editor of *The Process of American History*.

Charles Crowe is associate professor of history at the University of Georgia and a member of the editorial board of *The Journal of Negro History*. The author of three books, he has done research on New England trancendentalism, American socialism, and more recently on black-white racial violence.

Louis De Vorsey, Jr. is acting head of the Department of Geography at the University of Georgia. His major research interests include the historical geography and historical cartography of the Southeast during the eighteenth and early nineteenth centuries.

Charles H. Fairbanks is chairman of the Department of Anthropology at the University of Florida. His primary interests are Southeastern archaeology, including colonial archaeology, cultural evolution, and revitalization movements in the Southeastern United States.

Mary R. Haas is professor of linguistics and program coordinator of the Survey of California and Other Indian Languages at the University of California, Berkeley. She has done field work on several Southeastern languages, particularly Tunica, Natchez, Creek, and Koasati, and also on the languages of Southeast Asia, especially Thai and Burmese. Her publications include articles on comparative (gene-

141

tic) and areal linguistics and on linguistic classificatory systems (e.g. noun classifiers and classificatory verbs). A recent book is *The Prehistory of Languages.*

David J. Hally is assistant professor of anthropology in the Department of Sociology and Anthropology at the University of Georgia. His topical interests include archaeological field methods and settlement archaeology. His area interest is the Southeastern United States.

Charles Hudson is associate professor of anthropology in the Department of Sociology and Anthropology at the University of Georgia. His main interests are in the Indians of the Southeastern United States and in folk belief systems.

John H. Peterson, Jr. is assistant professor in the Department of Sociology and Anthropology and assistant anthropologist in the Social Science Research Center at Mississippi State University. His theoretical interest in pluralism is reflected in his research in ethnohistory, contemporary community, minority relations, and applied anthropology in education and natural resource development. In addition to applied research, he has done field work among the Choctaw and among Negro and white Southerners.

William S. Pollitzer is associate professor of anatomy at the University of North Carolina at Chapel Hill. He also serves the Department of Anthropology, the Genetics Training Program, and the Carolina Population Center. His main research interests are in the application of genetic factors to the problems of physical anthropology. His field studies have included isolated populations of Negroes, Indians, and persons of mixed ancestry in the Southeastern United States.

William S. Willis, Jr. is an associate professor in the Department of Anthropology at Southern Methodist University and a research associate with the Smithsonian Institution. He is also a visiting associate professor in the Graduate Department of Anthropology at Columbia University. His main interests are in Black-Indian-White relations in Southeastern North America and in problems in the development of anthropology.

Index

phenomenon of power in nineteenth and first half of twentieth century, 220, 223–26; theories of human flexibility and plasticity, 220; three phases in development of corresponding to phases in development of American society, 219–27; vs. that of European countries with colonial territories, 269

American cemeteries: characterization as a garden, 427; emphasis on lineal kinship ties, 429

American colonial life, extension of the situation in England and western Europe, 544

American Ethnological Society, 215, 234

American ethnology, distinctive from that of other nations, 220

American Farmer, 342

American Indian: "noble savage" image, 534, 543

American Indian-African American admixture, in Old South, 491–92

American Indians: action programs, 222; antagonism toward blacks, 553–69; concept of "nation," 576; Houma of Southern Louisiana, 386–96; in the Old South, ix–x, 570–87; physical anthropology of, 485–97; pottery, 511, 512; removals, ix, 458, 543, 572, 576, 589; as slave traders, 563–64; treaties with confederacy, 538; white stereotype of, 462. *See also specific tribes*

American Journal of Physical Anthropology, 255

American society: movement toward reform, 221–23; periods of, 219

American structuralist school of linguistics, 275–76

"amoral familism," 376

analogy, 286

analytic judgments, 287

ancestral shrine, 122

ancient Egypt, "open" cities of, 122

Anglo-American welfare state, 413

Angola Farm, 509

anomie, 137

anthropological linguists, 8

anthropological research: community research, 441–42; field work, 61–62, 269; of one's own culture, 435–40;

pertaining to health and disease, 8–10; problem of acceptance by those being studied, 435–36; in the South, 440–43

anthropology: anti-urban ethos, 111, 135; approaches to culture and personality, 222; call for study of American culture, 434–43; commitment to the doctrine of cultural relativity, 286; conservatism, 14; contribution to understanding of modern, complex societies, 434–35; delineation of culture patterns of a group, 438; deterministic and materialistic, 281–84; dictum about studying cultures which are foreign to one's own, 229, 230; divergence from medicine, 94; duality, 286–87; empiricist dogma, 284; and epidemiology, 64–66; ever-widening scope of interest, 261; fragmentation, 261; general interests of as indicated by titles of books and monographs over time, 242–54; and geography, 466–67; holism and eclecticism, 291–92; holistic approach to the study of man, 292; humanism, 262; increasing preoccupation with psychology, organization, and structure, 243; medical, 651–68; in medical education, 10–12; of medicine vs. anthropology in medicine, 7; need to examine basic assumptions, 215; problem of generalizing, 438; and psychiatric views, synthesis of, 33–37; reliance upon functional "modes" of social and cultural analysis, 62; rural ethos, 134; school programs in, 207–8; as a science of culture, 246–48; as a science of ethnos, 244–46; as a science of man, 250–53, 262; as a science of society, 248–49; scientification of methodology, 262; sub-disciplines, 288–89; tendency to perpetuate traditional concerns in context of the city, 142; viewing of behavior in its cultural setting, 435; worldwide, evolutionary, and cross-cultural comparison, 113. *See also* American anthropology; social anthropology

anthropometric studies, of living Indians, 490

Apalachee, 511, 512
Apalachee mission, 512
Apalachicola settlement, 510
Appalachian culture: devastation of the
natural environment, 331; fatalism,
331, 337; illegal distilling, 360;
individualism, 334–35; "line" patterns
of settlement, 330; structural changes
as a result of coal mining, 329–41
a priori knowledge, denial of, 285–86
Arapata, Bolivia, 163–64
archaeology, 456; acceptance of the
concept of culture, 263–64; assumption
that all sciences operate in identical
fashion, 262; basic assumptions, 261–
66; commitment to the comparative
method, 263; and concept of diffusion,
263; of European-Indian contact in the
Southeast, 509–20; evolutionism, 262–
63; expanding interest in historical
archaeology, 261; historical, 261, 509;
interest in the diseases of
palaeoanthropic man, 8; new brand of
geographic determinism, 264–65; and
rise of modern, "industrial" cities, 127;
salvage, 111, 126; in the South, 458;
study of artifacts, 131; and urban
studies, 126–40
Arden, North Carolina, 401
Arensberg, Conrad M., viii, 111, 139, 203,
204, 206, 385, 435, 440
Armenia, 22
arrabal, 141
arthritis, 489
artifacts, 264
Ascension Parish, Louisiana, 386, 388,
392
asceticism, 413
Asia, distribution of swaddling in, 21
Assembly of God, 82n.9
assortative mating, 259
Atakapa, 499, 500, 501, 504
Atlas region, 168
aubia, 90, 91
Augusta Conference, 560
Australian kinship systems, 270
Australopithecines, 258
Avicenna, 21
Avoyel, 503, 504
Ayer, A. J., 287

Aymara, 160
Aymara peasants, distribution network,
161
Azande, 35

"bad blood" (venereal disease), folk
remedies for, 73–74
Baggett, Susan, 150n.7
Bailey, F. G., 165n.4
Bailey, Wilfrid, 464n.2
Banfield, Edward C., 120, 376
Banks, E. Pendleton, 217
barriadas, 141, 143
barrios, 130, 143
"barrow-coat," 22
Barton, Benjamin Smith, 499
Bartram, William, 480, 482, 558
Barzini, Luigi, 120
Basketmakers, 21, 487
Bass, W. M., 488, 489
Bastide, Roger, 188
Bataillon, Claude, 187
Bayou Goula site, 509, 514
Bayou Grand Caillou, 389
Beamer, James, 563
Beattie, John, 34, 36, 71, 80
Beers, Howard K., 330
behavioral scientists: and human biology,
257; in medical and public health
schools, 10–11
behaviorism, 276, 281–85
Bell, Daniel: on directed population
change, 137; *The End of Ideology: On the
Exhaustion of Political Ideas in the Fifties*,
224
belly ache theory, 98
Belo Horizonte, Brazil, 187
Bender, Ernest, 502
Benedict, Ruth, 237
Bengal, 117
Berg, Elliot J., 170
Berry, Brewton, 494
Bethlehem, Pennsylvania, archeological
excavation, 131
Betterworth, John K., 571
Bierce, Ambrose: *The Devil's Dictionary*,
589
Big Cypress, Florida, 492
Bihar, 117
Biloxi, 498, 499, 500

bio-anthropology, 525
biologism, 251
Birdsell, Joseph B.: *Races: A Study of the Problem of Race Formation in Man*, 256–57
Birney, James G., 536
birthmark, 75
birth practices and beliefs: afterbirth, 79; breast "risin's," 80, 82n.9; concerning conception, 73–74; concerning labor and delivery, 76–78; concerning sex of infant, 74–75; concerning unwanted pregnancy, 75; incorporation of father into the birth process, 77–78, 80; as indices of attitudes toward health and life, 70; "marking the baby," 75; period of separation from and re-entry into the group, 70; stillbirth, 78; "stopping blood," 78; umbilical cord used to prognosticate number of future deliveries, 78–79
biscateiro, 186–87
black divine healers. *See* healing meeting; "Saints" (black divine healers)
black pepper tea, 76
Bleibtreu, H. K., 257
blockade still, 361, 363
blood types, 490, 525
Bloomfield, 275, 503
blue-singers, 313
Boas, Franz, 221–22, 275, 485, 501
Bogotá, 187
Bohannan, Paul, 136, 137
Bolivia: abolishment of hacienda system, 160; official hierarchy prior to reform, 159; social revolution and agrarian reform of 1952–53, 159–60
Bolivian Highlands, 112; cantonship of extraordinary importance, 160; education as one of most important issues, 160–61; post reform counties, 159; regional peasant syndicate, 161; reorganization of counties, 112, 158–67
Bonar, William: "A Draught of the Creek Nation, 1757," 473, 474
bone identification, 257
Boney, F. N., 460, 462, 464n.2, 588
Bonilla, Frank, 148

Boulding, Kenneth, 114
"Boundary Line Between the Province of South Carolina and the Cherokee Indian Country, Marked Out in Presence of the Head Men of the Upper, Middle and Lower Cherokee Towns, Whose Hands and Seals are Affixed...," 476
Bowles, William Augusts, 525
Boyd, William: *Genetics and the Races of Man*, 256
brachycephalization, 490
Braidwood, Robert J., 128
Brasília, 148
Brass Ankles, 462
Brazil: biscateiro, 186–87; effects of urban industrialization, 186–87; inter-ethnic marriages in the middle and upper classes, 191
Brent, Joseph L., 460, 461, 462, 593
Brickell, John, 553, 562
Bridenbaugh, Carl, 405
British Indian Service, 556
British social anthropology, 249
Broom, Leonard, 464n.3
Brown, Charles, 403, 407
Brown, Davis, 401, 402, 403, 409
Brown, Edward, 403
Brown, Evan Javan Jr., 402, 409
Brown, James S.: *Beech Creek Studies*, 330
Brown, Javan, 401–2, 407, 408, 409
Brown, John Henry, 402
Brown, Louis, 401, 402, 403–4, 407, 409
Brown, Robert, 403
Brown Pottery, 401–4
Brukman, Jan, viii, 217
Bruner, Edward M., 180n.5
Brzezinski, Zbigniew, 139
buccal disorders, 99–100
Buchan, Alexander, 22
Buddhist "world-mountain," 119
Buechler, Hans C., viii, 112, 206
Buechler, Judith-Maria, 166n.8
Buenos Aires, 187
Bull, Stephen, 559, 562
Bunzel, Ruth, 121
burial mound construction, cessation of, 512
Burma, 33

bush medicine, 84, 88–90; relies primarily upon cause for identification and treatment, 90; results in high degree of patient understanding about why he is sick, 91; snake-bite, 90; vs. doctor medicine, 92

Butler, Mosette, 360, 366, 367

Byington, Cyrus A., 502

caboclos, 189

cachexia africana, 95

Cajans, 462

Cajun French, 389

Caldwell, Joseph R., 515

Calhoun, John C., 536

Cali, 187

callampa, 141

callejones, 141, 143

Calusa, 503, 510, 515, 527

Camdomblé, 189

Campbell, John C., 366

Cant, of Irish Travelers, 324–27; began as systematic modification of Irish Gaelic, 325; function in business dealings and situations of danger, 325–26; function of identifying its speakers as members of a particular group, 326; as jargon, 324; secret mode of communication, 325

cantón: formation, 158, 161; as a major intersection of a variety of sub-systems, 165; reorganization, 161–65, 166n.7; system before and after reform, 159–60

Capitalism Triumphant, 219

Capron, Louis, 526

Cariay, Costa Rica, 193

Carnap, Rudolf, 287, 293n.9

Carr, Arthur C., 33, 36

Cartago, Costa Rica, 193, 198

Carter, William E., 109, 110

"Cartographic Portraits," 469

Cash, W. J., 537

Cassel, John, 63

"castestreets," 117

Castillo de San marcos, 510

Catawba Indians: converts to Mormonism, 582; hostility toward blacks, 463, 553; "identity crisis," 582; Iswanid

variety, 487; language, 499; relationship to present-day populations and Indians of the past, 489, 492–93; Speck's work on, 458

categorization (classification), 286

Caudill, William, 7, 9

causality, 281, 282, 286

cause, in diagnostic systems, 84, 86, 87, 90

cavalo, 189

Cedar-Chopper, 343

census data, 135

Central America, large cities of, 187

Centralids, 487

cerumen (earwax), 490–91

Chafe, Wallace, 502

Champs Charles (Isle St. Jean Charles), 389, 395n.4

Changing Woman, 20

Chattahoochee River, 473

Chauga, 510

Chawasha Indians, 461

Cheever Meaders Pottery, 398–401

Cherokee Indians, 459, 498; adopted institution of black slavery, 461; blood type survey of, 491; compared to Seminoles, 492; Iroquois-speaking, 489; languages, 499; slave trade, 564; smallpox epidemic, 559; southernmost branch of the Iroquoian family, 500; strong color prejudice, 553

Cherokee sites, 510

cherry tree bark tea, 73

Chesapeake region, life in the middle 17th century, 544–48

Chichicastenango, 121

Chickasaw Indians, 510, 578

Chickasaw sites, 513

Chiggerville site, 486, 487

Childe, V. Gordon, 127–28

children, with pica, 96

Chile, 191

chiliastic sects, 422

Chinese Association (Asociación China), 197

Chinese city, 118

Chitimacha, 499, 500, 501, 504

Choctaw Agency, 577

Choctaw-Chickasaw, 499

Choctaw Indians, 498, 501, 510, 570;

adopted traits of European settlers, 578; churches, 581; dry type earwax, 491; effect of social relations based on slavery, 579; entry into agricultural system as sharecroppers, 581; language, 499; position of those who remained after removal determined by social relationship between black and white under the plantation system, 580–82; radical change of position in local society between time of removal and present day, 578; squatters on marginal agricultural land, 579–80; status of Mississippi citizens, subject to all state laws, 579; traditional historical approach to, 577–78

Chomsky, Noam, 276, 277, 290

Chote, 510, 514

Chouacha Indians, 560

Chua, 162

Chucuita, 121

Church of God, 82n.9

cities: administrative, 143; anthropology of, 141–57; of Central America, 187; differ markedly from civilization to civilization in history, 116–21; "empty," 120; general typology of African, 168; green cities, 118, 119, 120; Hellenistic, 118; industrial, 129–30, 139, 178, 204; institutional inventory of, 206; Latin American cities, 186–92; as link between rural areas and their people and the state, 135; medieval, 130, 173; modern, 127, 130, 131; Moslem, 118; nexus of interrelationships, 193; "open," of ancient Egypt, 122; palace, 116, 122–23; port, 116; preindustrial, 119–20, 139, 186, 204; pristine, 129–30, 204; problems, 138; royal/palace, of West Africa, 116, 122–23; transitional, 139; working definitions, 114

Civil Rights movement, benefit to Indians, 577

Clapperton, Hugh, 168

Clark, Colin, 137

Clarksville site, 488, 493

class, 128; importance of mass media in transition from ethnic subculture into a class culture, 191; more important than ethnicity in Latin American cities, 185, 187–88, 190–91; sociological approach to, 185; as subculture, 185

classical functionalists, 267–68

Classical Protestant Ethic Disease, 412, 413, 414–15

Clay, Henry (Cassius Marcellus), 536

Clay-Eater, 343

Cleburne, Patrick, 539n.12

Clements, Forrest E., 9

Cleveland, Georgia, 398

Clifton, James A., 141

closed-range laws, 348

"clusters," 238

coal, 131

coal mining: affect on non-miners, 334; appeals to action-seeking personalities, 368; changes in technology and increased interdependency, 335–36; changes in technology and increasing stability of employment, 336; changes in technology and unemployment, 335; creation of peasantry, 332–35; culture, 331–35; and "debt peonage," 332, 333; and emergence of urban patterns, 337–38; impact on traditional mountain subculture, 329–41; increase in community participation, 338; "independent" handloader, 336–37, 338; non-unionized miner, 337, 338; and occupational family types, 336; owners' paternalistic attitude toward miners, 334; replaced barter and exchange with wage system, 331–32; social class distinctions unknown to the mountain culture, 332; unionization, 334; unionized skilled mining, 336, 338

Cobb, Joseph B., 534, 539n.7

Coca-Cola, folk beliefs about, 76–77

Cochran, Gloria, 110

Coe, Joffre, 517n.3, 524

cognitive anthropology, 278

cognitive maps, 277–78

coking process, 131

Collins, Henry B. Jr., 487

Collomb, H., 31, 32, 33

colonial expansion and exploitation, 269

comitas, 381, 382
community, as a process, 139
community diagnosis laboratory, 64–65
community studies, 113, 118, 135, 141
company store, 332
comparative method, 263
Compi, 162
complimentary distribution, 274
componential hypothesis, 63, 68n.1
comprehension operator, 290
concubinage, 177
conformance model, 290
Congaree, 343
"conjure," 78
conquest states, 130
contagious magic, 77, 79
contextual theory, 290, 291
Continental European Gypsies, 320
contingent model, 290
contour plowing, 350
control, and libidinal fields of the ego, 37
conversion experience, 413, 415
Conzemius, Eduard, 88, 92
Coon, Carleton S.: *Races: A Study of the Problem of Race Formation in Man*, 256–57
Cooper, Marcia, 94
Coosa, 510, 516–17
Coosa River, 473
Copell Place, 487
Corpeno, Helen, 110
cortiços, 143
Costa Rica: Central Plateau (Meseta Central), 198; integration of the West Indians with Costa Rican institutions and culture patterns, 198; lowland development, 194–95; lowland esprit de corps in opposition to the highland population, 199; Revolution of 1948, 199; urbanization, 193–94; West Indian laborers, 195; whites as cultural brokers of the highland culture, 195. *See also* Puerto Limón, Costa Rica
Cotterill, Robert S., 525, 571
Cottier, J. W., 488
Coushatta Indians, 490
Cow Creek Indians, 492
Cracker, 343
cradle board: deformation of the skull induced by, 485; isometric exercise induced by, 24; use by Semitic speaking peoples, 20, 21; used by virtually all native peoples of North and South America, 20
craft specialists, 128
Crane, Verner W., 509
Creek Confederacy: Dallas focus, 488; language, 498, 499; legends indicating a western origin for Muskogean-speaking tribes, 515; map of heartland, 473–75; matrilineal organization, 511; movement into Florida, 492; political entity, 516; prehistory, 516; Swanton on, 459; *Talwa*, 517n.5; tolerance for escaped blacks, 463
Cressey, Paul F., 330, 337
Crocker, Eleanor, 431n.1
cross-cultural research, 205, 237
Crowe, Charles, ix
Cruz Loma, 163, 164, 166n.6
cult centers, 189
cultural anthropology, changing orientations, 267
cultural determinism, 265
cultural evolution, unilinear concepts of, 119
cultural heterogeneity, as a salient criterion of urbanness, 205
cultural plurality, 222
cultural relativity, 231, 232
"cultural turncoat," 174
culture: as an adaptive mechanism, 256, 258; blurring of frontiers between subjectivity and objectivity, 33; concepts of, 234–41, 246; cultural definitions, 237–38; importance to human biologists, 257–58; injection of non-random element into genetic processes, 259; linguistic definitions, 236–37; in modern geography, 466; in the partitive sense, 234–35, 237; as a powerful adaptive mechanism, 256; social definitions, 235–36; understanding of, 12
culture of poverty, 115, 137, 308
Cumming, William P., 468; *The Southeast in Early Maps*, 426, 475–78, 526
cuneiform tablets, 128

curandeiros, 186
Curitiba, 187, 188

Dahomey, 121, 122
Dallas focus, 488, 515
Dandler-Handhart, Jorge, 166n.7
Dania, 492
Dar-es-Salaam, 174
Darien Bluff site, 512, 514
Darlings Creek Peasant Settlements, St.
    Helena Parish, Louisiana, 342–51;
    basic notions of breeding both plants
    and animals, 349–50; churches, 345,
    347; communities, 347; courthouse-
    market town, 347–48; farmers as
    "mesotechnic" peasants, 350; food-
    and-feed (subsistence) complex, 349;
    hamlet leaders, 346–47; railroad towns,
    348; settlement, 347; system of crude
    mixed farming, 349; use of the land,
    348–50
Darwin, Charles, 244
dating, new methods of, 523
Davis, Allison, 228
Davis, Jefferson, 537–38
Davis, Kingsley, 116, 138
Davis Brown Pottery, 401
death, white Southern way of, 418–29;
    manner and time in which persons
    inside and outside the immediate
    family are notified, 423–24; presence
    of "loved ones," 421; spreading news
    of, 422–23. See also funeral practices,
    white Southern
debt peonage, 332, 333
defense mechanisms, 32
definitive movements, 171
DeJarnette, David, vii
delusional states, 32–33, 38
denial, 32, 33, 38
Dennis, Wayne, 23, 24
Densmore, Frances, 526
Department of Housing and Urban
    Development, 126
dermatoglyphics, genetics of, 491
de Soto, Hernando, 516
detribalization, 172–73, 175
Devereux, George, 11–12
De Vorsey, Louis, Jr., 457, 468, 522–23;
    The Indian Boundary in the Southern

Colonies, 1763–1775, 471
Dew, Thomas R., 536
Dewey, John, 221, 222
diagnostic systems: analysis of, 84;
    communications processes of, 65
dialectical dualism, 543
Dickens, R. S., 488
Diego factor, 491, 492
differential migration, 259
diffusion studies, 268
direct historical approach: application to
    specific ethnic groups, 516–17;
    application to specific known towns,
    524
direct observation, 435
dirt dauber nest tea, 76
"dirt-eating," 95. See also pica
disease diagnosis: among the Subanun, 62;
    and evidence, 84, 86, 87, 89, 90; socio-
    cultural identity as a significant
    dimension in, 84
distribution studies, 268
divide and rule, ix
Dixon, Roland B., 500
Dockstader, Frederick J.: The American
    Indian in Graduate Studies, 523
"doctor medicine," 84
dogpwe militiamen, 121, 122
Dohrenwend, Bruce P., 50
Dollard, John, 228
Dorsey, James Owen, 500
Dorseys (potters), 399
Douglass, Frederick, 594
Dravidian, 117
Dubos, René, 92
duck nest furnace, 362
Duke University Center for Southern
    Studies, 442
Dulac, 389, 393, 395n.4
Dulac-Grand Caillou community, 319,
    387, 389, 393
DuLarge, 395n.4
Duncan, Ronald J., 435, 438–39
Durand, Loyal Jr., 360, 367
Durkheim, Emile, 109, 289, 429
du Toit, Brian M., 112, 204, 206

ecological factors, cultural response to,
    128
economics, 113

Eddington, Sir Arthur, 281
Eddy, Elizabeth M., viii, 110
Edmonson, Munro S., 217
education, as rite of passage, 379–80
efficient cause, 84
Eggan, Fred, 62, 435, 437, 464n.3
ego defense mechanisms, 38
ego functioning, and belief in witchcraft, 30
ego-structure, weak, 32, 33
Eisenhower, Dwight D., 219
eliciting heuristic, 274
Elkins, Stanley M., 539n.7
emergency treatment of traumatic injury, 88
"empty cities," 120
England, bomb-damage archeology, 131
English Gypsies, 320
environment, destruction of, 132
environmental physiologists, 257
epidemiology and anthropology, 8, 64–66
Epstein, A. L., 175, 176
Erasmus, Charles, 64
Eridu, 129
Eskimo, 258
Essene, Frank, 261
ethnic club, 190
ethnic endogamy, 190
ethnicity, 172; class more important than ethnicity in Latin American cities, 185, 187–88, 190–91; study of, 244–46
ethnographers: alienation from own culture, 271–72; effect of own culture upon culture under investigation, 270; preoccupation with traditional Indian culture, 574; reasons given for research and of other cultures, 271
ethnographic materials, formal analysis of vs. the generating of, 273–74
ethnography: of communication, 65; history of, 270; language as the source of primary data as well as the data itself, 274; national schools of, 269–70; and new approaches to the study of man, 267
ethnohistorical data, 516
ethnohistorical medicine, 63
ethnologic record, 274
ethnology, 132, 244; American, distinctive from that of other nations, 220

ethnos, 244, 245
etiology, cultural factors in, 65
European-Indian acculturation, in the Southeast, 516, 517
European-Indian contact in Southeast, archaeology of, 509–20
Evans, E. Estyn, 342
Evan's Pottery, 402
Evans-Pritchard, E. E., 31, 32, 34, 35, 36
Eva Site, 486
Everglades, 492
evidence: in diagnostic system of sukya, 89; used to diagnose medical conditions, 84, 86, 87, 90
evil eye, 186
evolution, 256, 258, 281
evolutionary theorists, 220, 245
exact sciences, 127
experimentation, 381, 382

"face" jugs, 400, 408
"factories in the fields," 123
factory complexes, 131
factual sciences, 293n.10
Fairbanks, Charles H., vii, ix, 111, 204, 207, 464n.3, 511, 514
"faith healing" religious sects, 82n.9
Fallers, L. A., 169
Farganis, James, 224
Fatherland Incised, 513
Fatherland site, 509, 514
favelas: boundary conditions that delimit, 144; direct and indirect institutional effects on, 144; of São Paulo compared to Rio, 141; studies of, 143
Federal Bureau of Public Roads, 126
federal capitals, 116
Feldman, A. S., 172
fevers, 87
fictive kinship, 334
Field, J. J., 34
field work: among African Americans, reasons for absence of, 229–32; constraints on in cities, 145–46; empiricist dogma, 284; incompatibility with research predilection of the epidemiologist, 61–62; methodological error of studying a single example or very few examples of, 146; rise of, 270
field work, urban: comparative or

genetics, 8
genocide, 588
genotypes, 258
Gentian Violet, 87
geographical misconception, 469
Geographical Review, 360
geographic determinism, 264–65
geography, 113, 456; and anthropology, 466–67
geophagy. *See* pica
Georgia-Creek Indian Boundary Line, 475
Georgia Piedmont, 482
The Georgia Review, 368n.1
Gesellschaft, 245
gestation, folk beliefs, 74–75
Ghana, 34
ghetto life, social process of, 379
Gilbert, William, 464n.3
Gillin, John P., 101n.2, 434, 441, 442
Glades pottery complex, 515
Glass, Bentley, 491
Glass, Y., 172
Glen, James, 559
Glick, Leonard B., 84
glottochronology, 521
Gluckman, Max, 175, 179, 435, 437
Goffman, Erving, 379
Goggin, John M., 464n.3, 511, 512–13, 514, 527
Goldrich, Daniel, 148
gonorrhea, 88
Goodenough, Ward, 274, 275
"good ol' boy" ethic, 415
Goodrich, Carter, 335
Gordon, John, 436
Gottman, Jean, 115
Grady, Henry W., 570
Grand Caillou-Dulac Community, 393; Bayou Grand Caillou, 389; map of, 387
Grand Village of the Natchez, 509
Gray, Lewis Cecil, 343
Gray, Robert F., 34
Greeks, swaddling beliefs, 21, 22, 25
Greenberg, Joseph, 292n.5
green cities, 118, 119, 120
Greene, Patrick, 322
Greene County, Georgia: aboriginal forest

cover, 475–82; location maps showing study area, 481
Greensburg, Louisiana, 347
Grigra, 503, 504
Grimkés, 536
group life, necessary suppression of aggression within, 35
Guale, 510, 511, 513
Guatemala, 32
Gulf languages, 502
Gulf type, 486, 487
Gulick, John, vii, 112, 464n.3
Gullah Coast Renegade, technology of, 370–77
Gulliver, Philip H., 170
gun flints, 511
Gunter, Edmund, 478
Gunter's chain, 478
Gutkind, Peter C. W., 172
gypsies, in American South, 320–28

Haag, William, vii, viii, 217
Haas, Mary R., 457, 501, 521, 524
haciendas, 159
Hackenberg, Robert A., 238
Hagan, William T., 539n.6
Halbwachs, Maurice, 185
Hale, Horatio, 500
Haliwa, 494
Hallowell, A. Irving, 29
hallucinations, 32
Hally, David, 458, 464n.2, 523–24
Halpern, Joel, 123
Hamilton, Alexander, 539n.6
hamlets, 119
Hampton Institute, 591
handloading, 335
haptoglobins, 490
Harappan civilization, 116
Haring, Douglas G., 292n.3
Harper, Francis: "Naturalists' Edition" of the *Travels of William Bartram*, 526
Harper, Jared, 320, 435, 436, 441
Harris, Marvin, 116, 118
Harris, Zellig, 276, 502
Haufendorf settlement, 117
Hauser, Philip M., 137
Haynes Bluff, 509
healing meeting: encourages rational

methods to attain one's goal, 308, 315, 317, 318; healing, 313–14; testimony, 312–13, 315–16. *See also* "Saints" (black divine healers)

healing systems, social organization of, 65

health/health personnel, 9, 10

Health Opinion Survey (HOS), 46–47

heavy-industry towns, 143

Hegel, Georg Wilhelm Friedrich, 292

Hellenistic cities, 118

Hellman, E., 172

hemoglobins, 490

Henderson, Archibald: *The Conquest of the Old Southwest: The Romantic Story of the Early Pioneers into Virginia, The Carolinas, Tennessee and Kentucky, 1740–1790*, 571

Henry, Patrick, 533

Henshaw blood type, 491

Heredia, Costa Rica, 198

Hero Twins, 20

Herskovits Melville, 230; *The Myth of the Negro Past*, 228, 229

Hertz, Robert, 74

Hertzberg, H. T. E., 487

Hewes, Gordon W., 70

Higham, John, 224

Hill, Carole, x

Hill, Samuel S. Jr., 412, 413, 416

Hill, W. C. Osman, 489

Hill-Billy, 343

Hinkle, Lawrence E., 64

hippies, 378–85; alienation, 379; "elders," 384; individuals who consciously seek alternatives to the larger society, 380; peculiarly American phenomenon, 379; period of cultural distortion in the revitalization process structure, 383–84; secondary rite of passage out of institutionalized educational system, 380; social processes of ghetto life, 376–83

historical archaeology, 261, 509

historical cartography, 468–70

historical geography, ties with both anthropology and history, 467–68

historical linguistics, 268

historical particularism, 221

historic urban sites, destruction of, 126

history, 113

history of architecture, 113

Hitchiti, 499, 501, 510

Hiwassee Island, 488

Hobbes, Thomas, 542, 544

Hobsbawm, E. J., 120

Hodges, 436

Hoffmann, Hans, 238, 239n.4

Hofstadter, Richard, 220

Hohokam settlements, 132

Hokan-Siouan, 500, 502, 505

holism and eclecticism, 291–92

hominid ecology, 258

homozygosity, 259

Honigmann, John, vii, 110

honorary pallbearers, 428

Hopewell, Pennsylvania, archeological excavation of, 131

Hopi children, swaddling, 24

hospitals, elements of that serve to interpret and define the nature of dying, 420

Houma (city), 388

Houma Indians, 386–96; adoption of rural Cajun French ways, 390; became part of a larger socio-cultural unit, 389; dialect, 388; extended family, 390–91; forced to move into swamp country, 388; future of, 394–95; general poverty level, 391; historical setting, 386; kinship ties, 394; lack of tribal or intra-group unity, 389; loss of land rights with discovery of oil and natural gas, 388; as middleman in a three-tiered hierarchy between whites and African Americans, 389; some degree of African American ancestry, 390; stages of cultural change, 392–94

Hrdlicka, Alex, 485–86; "Indians of the Gulf States, 486

Hudson, Charles, vii, 6, 307, 320, 368n.1, 431n.1; on cradleboard and swaddling, 24; on evolutionary spread of yaws and syphilis, 63; on illness and dying in Southern Christian belief, 430; research on Catawba, 582, 585n.1

Hudson, Joyce Rockwood, 216

Hulse, Frederick, 488, 489

human biology: and anthropology, 254;

appearance as an identifiable discipline, 255–60; collaboration between students of biology and those of behavior, 257; focus on human variation, 255–56; proliferation of courses in colleges and universities, 257

Human Biology, 255

human crowding, 115

human geneticists, 257

human mobility, types of, 169–71

"human nature," study of, 250–53

Hume, David, 281, 287

Hundt, Magnus: *Anthropologium de hominis dignitate*, 243

Hunter blood type, 491

Hutchinson, H. W., 111, 206

"hydraulic" cultures, 204

Hymes, Dell, 236, 239n.2

"Hymn to Delian Apollo," 21

hypertension, 87

hypokalemia, 95

hysterectomy, 73

Iemanja, 189

illness, cultural background of, 9

Imperial Forbidden city, 118

inbreeding, 259

incorporation, third stage of the rite of passage, 379, 380, 382–83

indentured servants, 544, 545–46

India: commonality of form between village and city, 117; problems of crowding, 115

Indian Claims Commission studies, 527

Indian-European acculturation, 524

Indian Knoll, 488, 489, 493

Indian Knoll people, 486, 487

Indian Latin America, pre-Spanish city form, 120–21

Indian removals, 458, 543, 572, 576, 589

induction, 286

industrial archeology, 131

industrial city, 129–30, 139, 178, 204

industrial commitment, 172

industrial revolution, 123

Indus Valley, 116

inference, 282, 286

infield-outfield system, 348

infra-human primates, 257–58

Institute of Research in Social Science, University of North Carolina, 441

instrumental cause, 84

inter-ethnic marriages, in the middle and upper classes of Southern Brazil, 191

international medicine, 8

Interstate Highway Program, 126

interstitial populations, 187

interviewing, 321

in vitro studies, 435

in vivo studies, 435, 438, 439–40

Iraq, garya or madina, 205

Irene, Georgia, 488, 489, 493

Irish Potato Famine, 322

Irish Travelers, 320; business practices, 325–26; history, 321–22; known as "tinkers" in Ireland, 322; mule trading, 321, 322, 323; new itinerant occupational specialties, 323; as painters, 323; rapid change through education and media contact, 323–24; role in the economic and social history of the rural South, 321; as rug peddlers, 323; uxorilocal residence after marriage, 322. *See also* Cant, of Irish Travelers

Iroquois, 220, 504

isometric exercise, 24

Iswanid variety, 487

Italy, 22

Ithiel de Sola Pool, 224–25

Jackson, Andrew, 534, 536, 588

Jackson, Helen Hunt: *A Century of Dishonor*, 588

Jacksonian Democracy, 534, 539n.9

Jacquel, G., 30–31

Jake's Bottoms (urban milltown), 353–59

Jamaican Independence Day, 199–200

James, William, 293n.7, 294n.15

Jank'o Amaya, Bolivia, 161–63, 164

Jefferson, Thomas, 499; attitudes toward blacks, 532–33, 539n.5; attitudes toward Indians, 462, 533–34; avoidance of slavery issue, 536, 588–89; *Notes on the State of Virginia*, 532; theory of a "natural aristocracy," 549–50

Jennings, Jesse D., 510, 513, 514

Jesuit mission field, Florida, 526
jiggering, 402
Johnston, Francis, viii
Johnston, George Milligen, 553
Johnston, James H., 553, 564
Jones, Ernest, 30
"jugtowns," 406
justice, theme of, viii

Kampala, 177
Kano, 168–69
Kant, Immanuel, distinction between
    analytic and synthetic knowledge, 287
Kaolin, 95
Kardiner, Abraham, 231, 245
Kasita, 510, 514
Kaukira, 85
Kay, Paul, 274
Keil, Charles, 310, 313
Keith, Minor C., 194
Kelly, Art, vii
Kennedy, John G., 29
Kentucky, eastern, 330, 331
Kephart, Horace: *Our Southern Highland-*
    ers, 360, 366
Kerr Reservoir Basin, 488
Keyauwee, 487
Kimball, Solon T., vii, 110, 118, 123, 139,
    385, 442
King, Arden, vii, 215, 217
King, Martin Luther Jr., 309
kinship semantics, 275
kinship studies, 113, 249
kinship system, 279, 423
Klemm ??: *Culturwissenschaft*, 246
Kluckhohn, Clyde, 23, 29–30, 36, 38, 229,
    234, 237
Kneberg, M., 486, 488
Koasati, 500, 501
Koger's Island people, 486, 487
Koroa, 503, 504
Kovit, Leonard, 431n.1
Kreig, Margaret B., 76
Kroeber, Alfred L., 236, 237, 457, 463,
    500, 501
Krogman, W. M., 490
Kudzu, 398
Kupferer, Harriet, 464n.3

labor migration, 170, 179n.3

LaFlore, Greenwood, 580
La Fontaine, Jean, 34
Lamar influence, 493
land rotation, 349
language isolates, 500, 501, 504
languages: and cultural theory, 246;
    distinction between ethics and emics
    of, 274; natural, 284; private and
    public, 291; as the source of primary
    data and data itself in ethnography,
    274; spoken by Southern Indians, 457;
    structure, 158; superstock, 500, 501,
    502, 503, 505
Lantis, Margaret, 437
La Paz migrant organizations, 160
Lapps, 22
lasa, 91
lasa diseases, 90
Las Casas, 589
"latifundista," 138
Latin America, "hot" and "cold" dietary
    categories, 63
Latin American cities: class more
    important than ethnicity, 185, 190–91;
    class segregation in suburban develop-
    ments, 187–88; disintegration of
    traditional urban structure, 187, 191;
    effects of industrialization, 186; ethnic
    clubs of European and Asian immi-
    grants, 190; ethnic ghetto as a
    transitional rather than a permanent
    phenomenon, 186; subcultures, 185;
    transformation of formerly isolated
    folk communities into residential or
    industrial suburbs, 188; urban classes
    and acculturation in, 185–92
Lattakia, Syria, 143
Laufer, Berthold, 94, 95
Laughlin, W. S., 257
Laurens, Henry, 559
"law of contact," 71
"law of similarity," 71
Lawson, John, 485
Leach, Edmund, 215
lead-poisoning, 95
Lee, Robert E., 414, 538
Leeds, Anthony, 111, 112, 141, 203, 204,
    206, 207
Leibniz, Gottfried Wilhelm, 287
Leighton, Alexander, 64; *My Name is*

Legion, 66
Lenape (Delawares), 485
Lenapids, 488
Lenneberg, Eric H., 286
Léons, Madeline B., 163
Leroy (French physician), 22
Lessa, William A., 71
Lévi-Strauss, Claude, 118, 237, 246, 274, 279, 289
Levy, David M., 23
Levy, Leonard W., 539n.6
Levy-Bruhl, Lucien, 431
Lewa, 92
Lewis, Oscar, 149; community study approach, 141; Culture of Poverty, 137, 308; new approaches to ethnography, 357–58; restudy of Tepoztlan, 62; work in New York City, 207
Lewis, T. M. N., 486, 488
Liberal Reform, 219, 222
Liberian tribal peoples, 34
Liebow, Elliot, 207, 310, 357, 443n.5
Lima, 187
liminality, 379, 380, 381–82
Limón Province, 198, 201n.2
Lindquist, G. E. E., 583
linguistic prehistory, reconstruction of protolanguages, 502–3
linguistics: American structuralist school, 275–76; and anthropology, 274–80, 456; classification problems, 502; of Southeastern Indians, 498–508
Lipton, Earle L., 24
Little, Kenneth, 176, 177
Little Brown Jug, 403
Little Turkey, 553
Lloyd, P. C., 179n.4
location, outcome of econological competition for a scarce commodity, 185
Lommel, Andreas, 271
long-distance trade, 127–28
Lopes, Juarez R. Brandão, 186
loquacious facts, doctrine of, 284–85
"losing the hounds," 370–77
Lounsbury, F. G., 274, 275, 503
Low Bush Myrtle (*Myrica cerefera*), 76
Lower Bayou Lafourche, 395n.4
Lower Creek, 516
Lower Pointe au Chien, 395n.4

Ludlam, Richard, 558
Ludwig, Arnold, 30
lumbar arthritis, 489
Lumbee, 462, 494
Lyttelton, William, 559

Machiavellian politics, 224, 225
Macon Plateau, 515
Macon Trading Post, 514
Macumba, 189
magic: contagious, 77, 79; definition and function, 71; provides way of coping with situations of misfortune or danger, 80
majolica, 511
Malabar Coast, 120
malacia, 94, 97
malaria, 85, 91
Malaya, "hot" and "cold" dietary categories, 63
Malinowski, Bronislaw, 175, 270; "extensionist" hypothesis, 279
malnutrition, 86
malocculusion, 489
Malone, Henry T., 525
malpractice suits, 8
"the Man," 372
mandarinate, 120
mandarin empire, 123
Mandelbaum, David G., 438
Mangin, William, 141
Manucy, Albert C., 514
mapping, 206
maps, early, 522; examples of use, 470–84; mixture of fact and fiction, 468–69; as source of reconstruction of Southern Indian landscapes, 466–84
"Margids," 486
marginal populations, 187
Maroons, 557–58, 562
Marris, Peter, 177
Martin anthropometry, 257
Martinet, André, model of phonological change, 158, 165n.1
Marxists, 289
mash "recipe," 362
Mason, Carole I., 511
mass media, effect on transition of ethnic subculture into a class culture, 188, 191

Matina Valley, 193
Maupied, François-Louis-Michel: *Prodrome d'ethnographie*, 244
Mauriceau, Francois, 21
Mayer, Philip: *Townsmen or Tribesmen*, 173, 179n.1
mayordomos, 163
mazeway reformulation, 383–84
McCurdy, R. Layton, 12
McGavran, Edward G., 64
McGillivrary, Alexander, 564
McLeod, Norma, 230
McLuhan, Marshall, 225
McReynolds, Edwin C., 527
Mead, Margaret, 14, 228, 231, 436, 438
Meaders, Cheever, 399, 400, 409
Meaders, Lanier, 399–401, 406, 408, 409
Meaders Pottery, 398–401, 408
mechanical discovery procedure, 274
"mechanical models," for variable cultural phenomena, 118
mechanistic interpretations, of biologic functioning, 75
medical anthropologists: at the bottom of the status hierarchy in a medical setting, 13; goal of as a teacher in schools of medicine and public health, 11; limited contacts with other social scientists, 13; philosophical isolation from the medical faculty, 12; problems and prospects, 12–15; reluctance to assume a dependent role in the medical setting, 14; types of courses offered, 11
medical anthropology, vii, 7, 94, 95, 651–68
medical anthropology students: cross-departmental exposure, 66–67; human ecology course, 67; participation in psychiatric and medical clinics, 67; training in ethnohistorical materials, 63
medical economics, 8
medical sociologists, 9
medical students, resistance to materials involving anthropology and behavioral sciences, 13
medical technology, 8
medicine: changes and trends in, 7–8; in contemporary western society, 9;

depersonalization of, 8
medicine bundles, 526
medieval city, 130
megalopolis, 131, 137, 138
Mehta, J. D., 489
Melungeons, 462, 494
mental hospitals. in the South, 412
Mercier, Paul, 267
Merton, Robert K., 14
Meso-American Indian theories, 270
Mesopotamia, genesis of urbanism, 127, 128–29
"mestizo," 494
metalanguage, 273, 275, 278, 279
metaphor, 286
Metzger, Duane, 274
Mexican peasant society, 331
Mexico, genesis of urbanism, 128–29
Mexico City, 187
Miccosukee, Lake, 492
Micronesia, problems of crowding, 115
Middle Ages: cities, 130; notion that an infant would become deformed if it were not swaddled, 21; pica distinguished from "malacia," 94; slave-based system replaced by new sources of energy, 130
migration: and culture change, 515; labor, 170, 179n.3; oscillatory, 171; seasonal, 170; and urban settlement patterns, 186; vs. immigration, to a city, 172; vs. mobility, 169–70
Mikesell, Marvin: "Geographic Perspectives In Anthropology," 466, 467
military-industrial complex, 219–20
Miller, G. A., 290
Miller, Walter, 230
millet, 118
Mills, C. Wright, 225
milpa, 119
Miner, Horace, 205; *Timbuctoo*, 119
Miramar Club, 195
miscarriage, 76
Miskito Indians, Kaukira, Honduras, 84–85
Mississippian culture, 490, 515
Mississippi Choctaws. *See* Choctaw Indians
Mississippi (state), four separate school

systems for whites, blacks, Indians, and Southern Italian immigrants, 591
Mitchell, J. C., 173, 175, 176
mixed-bloods, 462, 491
Mle14, 514
Mle 90, 514
Model Cities Program, 126
modern city, 130
modernity, and urban concept, 123
Moerman, Michael, 238
Mohenjo-daro, 116, 117
Mooney, James, 458
moonshining, 370; folklore of, 360; in the Georgia Mountains, 360–69; popularity of, 366; stimulated by economic pressures, 366; technology of, 361–65; thrill factor, 367–68
Moore, Clarence B., 485
Moore, John Hebron, 343
Moore, W. A., 172
Morant, G. M., 486
Moravian Church Clinic, Kaukira, Honduras, 85–88
Moravian Church Mission, 84
Moravian Mission, 85
Morel, J., 30–31
Morgan, Lewis Henry: *Ancient Society*, 127; definition of cultural evolution, 263–64; *Systems of Consanguinity and Affinity*, 220
Morland, J. Kenneth, ix
Mormons, 493
Morrell, L. Ross, 514
Moslem cities, 118
"moundbuilder," 458
Mound Key, 510
Moundville, 515
mountain culture. *See* Appalachian culture
Mount Meru, 119
mourning, 424, 429–30
Mühlmann, Wilhelm, 269
multiple disease causation, 8
multiple stress in disease, 9
Mumford, Lewis, 122, 129, 135
Munda, 117
Murdock, George Peter, 238, 249; Human Relations Area File, 115
Murphy, Emmett J., 441
Muscovy, 120

Muskogean languages, 388, 501
Muskogean people, 490, 493, 504, 522
Muskogee, 499
mutual aid societies, 176

Naroll, Raoul, 236
Natchez, 499, 500, 501, 504, 510, 513
Natchez Incised, 513
Natchez-Muskogean, 502
Natchez pottery, 513
Nationalist Party (Kuo Ming Tang), 200
National Park Service, 131
National Register of Historic Sites, 126
Native Americans. *See* American Indians
natural languages, semantics of, 284
natural resources, devastation of, 137
Navaho: cradle board customs, 20, 23, 24; sings, 121; witchcraft, 30
Nayar Kingdoms, 120
Ndola, 169
Near Eastern Urban Revolution, 127
necessity and contingency, 287
negros velhos, 189
neighborhoods, 119
Neitzel, Robert S., 514
Nelms, Annelle, 216
Neumann, Georg, 487, 488, 489
New Choctaw communities, 582
Newcommen engine, 131
New Deal, 221
New Echota, 510
"new ethnography," 238, 267, 270, 273–80; defined, 273, 279–80; four principles related to linguistics, 274–75; question of descriptive adequacy, 278; role of linguist paradigm in, viii
Newman, M. T., 486, 489, 490
"new realism," 224
"New South," 570
New York City garbage collectors, 123
Nicklas, T. Dale, 502
Nigeria, 168, 170
Nile-Delta, 168
"noble savage," 534, 543
nodal centering of functions, 116
non-plantation Southern white, in 17th and 18th centuries, ix, 542–52
Norris Basin, 486, 489
North Carolina, map of geographic areas

and sample counties in public health nurse study, 60

North Carolina Medical Anthropology Program: challenge of epidemiology, 61–64

Nott, Josiah, 536

noumenal order, 287

nucleated settlement, of the Near East, 117, 118

núcleo escolar, 160–61, 162, 163, 164

nutmeg, 75–76

Nuyake, 511

Oakboro, 308

obsessive-compulsive scheduling, 415

Occaneechi, 488, 489, 493

Ocmulgee Fields culture, 511

Ocmulgee Old Fields, 523

Ocoee, 510

Oconee, 492

Ofo, 498, 499, 504

Ogeechee River, 475

oikoumene, 129

Okeechobee, Lake, 492

Okuli, 89

"old ethnography": characterized by continuous expansion of consciousness of man, 267–72; striving for total explanations for cultural behavior, 267–68

Old Maya Empire, 132

"Old South," 570–71. *See also* South, Colonial; Southern whites, of antebellum period

Old Southwest, 571, 572

Old Yedo (Tokyo), 120

Olien, Michael D., vii, 112, 203, 206, 464n.2

olive jars, 511

Olmsted, Frederick Law, 532

Olsen, Stanley J., 511

"one drop" rule, 593

oral fixation, 97

oral tradition, form of communication becomes almost an end in itself, 376–77

organizing vs. displaying knowledge and beliefs, 278–79

Oriental Despotism, 128

Orissa, 117

Osborne, R. H., 257

Osceola's coats, 527

oscillatory migration, 171

osteitis, 489

osteoporosis, 489

Oswald, Felix L., 22

Overhill Cherokee, 510

Owens, Bob, 400, 402

Owsley, Frank L., 343

Padilla, Elena, 141

palace cities, 116, 122–23

Palachacolas, 510

paleopathology, 8

Pallas, Peter Simon: *Vocabularia Comparativa*, 498

pallbearers, 428

palm prints, 491

Panama City, 187

Parkin, David J., 177

Parks, Joseph, 585n.1

participant-observation: among gypsy culture, 321; in one's own culture, 306, 435–36; in remote societies, 437; in urban research, 206

Patch, Richard, 141

patent medicines, 71, 72

pathology, 489

Patrick, Ralph, 5

"patrimonial bureaucracy," 122

patron-client relationship, 334

Paul, Benjamin D., 11, 32

Peachtree site, 488, 489

Peacock, James, 431n.1

Pea Ridge, Battle of, 538

Pearsall, Marion: *Little Smoky Ridge*, 330

Pearson's Coefficient of Racial Likeness, 486

"The Peasant and His Wife," 342

peasants: defined, 343–45; inherent powerlessness, 333–34, 339; land-use pattern, 348; structural relationships to a larger society, 331, 332; term not considered applicable to citizens of the United States, 342

Pease, Andrew, 148

Pecan Island, Louisiana, 487

PeeDee culture, 493

Price, E. T., 494
Prickly Ash *(Xanthoxylum clava-herculis)*, 73
primates, evolution of behavioral responses to environmental changes, 258
prime movers, 129, 130
primitive medicine in nonliterate societies, 9
pristine cities: differences from industrial city, 129–30, 204; Near Eastern, 130
private languages, 291
process, 84, 86, 87, 90
projection: as major defense mechanism, 32, 33; witchcraft as one mechanism of, 38
prophet, 384
Protestant Christianity, view of Indians and slavery, 543
Protestant Ethic: terrifying distance between God and man, 412. *See also* Classical Protestant Ethic; Southern Protestant Ethic
Prothero, R. M., 171
Proto-Algonkian, 521
Proto-Iroquoian, 503
protolanguage, reconstruction of, 502–3
Proto-Siouan, 503
Proto-Tunican, 504
Prucha, F. P., 539n.8
psychiatry, and behavioral science, 10
psychological syndrome theory, 442
psychology, and anthropology, 252
psychosomatic medicine, 8, 9
ptyalism, 100
public health nurses: mental health complaints faced, 44–45; mental health training, 44, 51; mental health work, 42–43; patient characteristics, 48, 53; patient HOS scores by gender, race, region, income, and education, 48–50, 54; Questionnaire IV to assess patients' health, 56–59; response to mental health problems, 45–46; study of, 43–44
public languages, 291
public power, nature of, 220
public works, 127, 128
pueblos, 121
Puerto Limón, Costa Rica, 112; Africans, 196–97; banana exporting port, 194; Chinese, 197; Costa Rica's major port, 195; intra-community relations, 195–98, 200; middle class whites, 196; migration to United States as temporary stop-gap to conditions of unemployment, 200; network of relations different from those found in other Costa Rican cities, 194–200; upper class whites, 195–96; urban-international relations, 199–200; urban-national relations, 198–99, 200; urban-rural relations, 198, 200
Puntarenas, 194
Puritan Exodus, 542

Queens Delight *(Stillingia sylvatica)*, 73
Querétaro, Mexico, 200
Quimby, George I., 514

Races: A Study of the Problem of Race Formation in Man (Coon, Garn, and Birdsell), 256–57
raciology, 244
racism: studies of normative theory of, 442; traced to its European roots, 594
radical empiricism, 276
Raine, James, 367
Rainwater, Lee, 231
ramage type social-political organization, 527
rancherias, 119
ranchos, 143
Rand, Earl, 502
Raper, Arthur F., 343
rationalism vs. empiricism, 287
rationality, and successful adjustment to modernized society, 317
Reader, D. H., 172, 174
Reader's Digest, 379
reality sense, and reality testing, disorder between, 33, 34, 36
Redbones, 462
Redfield, Robert, 134, 137, 200
Red-Neck, 343
Red Oak *(Quercus Falcata)* bark tea, 76
reducciones, 121
Reedy River, 475
reference group theory, 179
referential theory, 290

regression, 38
Reid, Ira, 343
religion, and magic, 71, 82n.9
religious beliefs, and black slavery, 542–43
removal. *See* Indian removals
representational art, 128
"rerun" still, 361
revitalization, 383–84
Reyburn, W. D., 502
Ribeiro, Darcy, 226
Richardson, Miles, vii, 215, 230
Richmond, Julius B., 24
Ricketts Mound, 487
Rife, David C., 491
Rio de Janeiro: disintegration of tradi-
    tional urban structure, 187; favelas of
    compared to those of São Paulo, 145,
    146–48, 151n.2
Ristow, Walter W., 468
rites, classification of, 75
rites of passage, 379–82, 424
Rivers, W. H. R., 9
Roanoke River sites, 489
Robert Owens Pottery, 398
role theory, 179
Romany Gypsy groups, in the rural South,
    327
Romany language, 327
Roosevelt, Theodore, 221
Rosen, George, 64
Rotberg, Robert I., 174
Rouse, Irving, 262
Rousseas, Stephen, 224
Rousseau, Jean Jacques: *Emile*, 22–24;
    three main objections to swaddling,
    23–24
"routine-seekers," 367–68
royal/palace city, of West Africa, 116,
    122–23
Ruffin, Edmund, 536
rural institutions, as prototypes for the
    formation of new associations and
    institutions in urban situation, 176
rural micro-fields, 177, 178, 179
rural movements, thaumaturgic, 188
rural-urban networks and hierarchies, 112
Russia: cradle board beliefs, 24; swad-
    dling, 22

"Sabine," 386

sacred and profane, dichotomy of, 74
sacy, 186
Safety Harbor ceramic complex, 510, 515
St. Augustine, Florida, 513
St. Helena Baptist Church, 345
St. Helena Parish, Louisiana, 345, 348
St. Hoyme, L. E., 488, 489
"Saints" (black divine healers): disagree-
    ment with violence as a means to an
    end, 309; education and occupations,
    309; increasing dependence on their
    surrounding society, 317–18; lack of
    political action, 309–12; menial or
    manual labor, 309; participation in
    formalized churches, 310; relationships
    between the sexes, 310–11; sociocul-
    tural situation, 308–9
Salisbury, 176
Saltzman projector, 482
Salvador, 187
salvage archaeology, 111, 126
sampling techniques, 135
Sanders, William T., 129
Sand-Hiller, 343
Sandner, Gerhard, 187
San Francisco de Oconee, 510, 512
San José, Costa Rica, 187, 194, 198
San Luis, 510
San Marcos series pottery, 513
Santals, 117
Santa Rosa Pensacola, 514
Santiago, Chile, 187, 188
Santo Domingo de Talaje, 512
São José, Porto Alegre, intermarriage of
    German-Brazilians, 190–91
São Paulo: *banlieue*, 188; cult centers, 189;
    favelas of compared with those or Rio,
    146–48, 151n.2; interstitial popula-
    tions, 187; suburban development,
    188; underemployment, 186–87
Sapir, Edward: on culture, 235, 237;
    superstock languages, 500, 501, 502,
    503, 505
Saponi, 492
Sauer, Carl O., 457, 467
Saunders, Lyle, 70
Savannah River, 475
Savery, Samuel, map of the Georgia-
    Creek boundary of 1768, 475, 477
saw mill ledgers, 482

scapegoat theory, 442

science: classification of, 287; conception of, 278

science of "man," 243

scientific education, 222

Scottish Gypsies, 320

Scott Miller site, 512, 514

scrip, 332, 333

seasonal migration, Africa, 170

Second Natchez War, 560

Second Seminole War, 461, 463, 526, 536

self-treatment practices, 72

semantic markers, 274, 275

Seminário Interuniversitário, 150n.10

Seminole, 510; arrival in Florida, 513; earwax, 490–91; gradual accretion, 492; kinship, 526; language, 499; music, 526; of Oklahoma, 490; patchwork men's clothing, 527; physical measurements and blood studies, 492; tolerance of escaped blacks, 463

Seminole Wars, 590

sense experience: doctrine of, 285–86; factors that cause doubt of, 33–34

sentence frame technique, 274–75

separation, 379, 380

Settlement Indians, 556, 557, 562, 565, 566

Sevier, John, 564

sex act, folk beliefs focused on, 73

share-cropping system, 577, 581

Sheehan, Bernard, 588

Shell Mound, 487, 488

Shell Mound Indians, 489

Shell Mounds, 486

Shelta, 326

Shine Mound Site, 488

shrine centers, 120

sickle cell anemia, correlation with malaria and the development of agriculture, 8

Siebert, Frank T., Jr., 501–2, 503, 521

Sigmon, B. A., 489

Sind, 117

Siouan people, 489, 492, 499, 504

sisin, 89

site reports, 514

"Six Nations," 499

Sjoberg, Gideon, 136; on anti-urban tendencies of sociologists, 136; *The Preindustrial City*, 119–20, 186, 204; preliminary typology of cities, 139

Skârland, Ivar, 486

skeletal studies, 485

Skelton, R. A., 468

skin rashes, 87

"skipped intermediaries," 293n.7

slash-and-burn land management, 349

slave codes, 535, 555

slavery: among Cherokee Indians, 461; championed by Southern planter elite, 535; and Choctaw Indians, 579; Jefferson's avoidance of issue, 536, 588–89; and planter class, 535, 536; Protestant Christian view of, 543; religious beliefs and, 542–43; superior insights of Southern women into the reality of, 537

slaves, African American: among Houma peoples, 388; contacts with Seminoles, 591; insurrections, 461, 554, 565–66; introduced into Jamestown, 542; stripped of the last vestiges of humanity, 589

slave trade, 121–23, 563–64

slip-casting, 402

smaya kaikaya, 92

Smith, Hale, vii, 514

Smith, Samuel Stanhope, 256, 259

snake bites, 90

Snow, Charles E., 486, 487, 489

social ambiguity: contribution to perceptual ambiguity, 34–36; due to concealed frustrations, 35

social anthropology: on the aboriginal peoples of the South, 458; avoidance of blacks in the South, 459; British, 249; dependency links to medical sociology, 9; and urban studies, 134–40

social class. *See* class

Social Darwinism, 219, 220–21, 221

social engineering, 222

social medicine, 9

social scientists, role in medical setting, 10

society: anthropology as science of, 248–49; concept of, 246, 248

sociology, 113, 248

618

sociology of religion, 249
socio-psychological transition, to the
    urban life, 172
sorcery accusations, as entirely post hoc
    constructions, 36
South: Christian belief about illness and
    dying, 430; complexity of regional
    subculture, 306; dearth of middle class
    craftsmen, 405–6; destruction of
    archaeological sites in, 458; folk beliefs
    and practices concerning birth, 71–82;
    "gypsy" research in, 320–28; linguistic
    diversity, 457–58; mythology of
    egalitarianism, ix; as a region in
    transition, 397; structural amnesia,
    462, 463; way of death, 418–29
South, Colonial: ideological superstruc-
    ture of social system, 461–64; Indian
    in, 570–87; physical anthropology of
    Indians of, 485–97; several distinct
    social and cultural sections, 459–60.
    See also Southern whites, of ante-
    bellum period
South, Stanley, 262
South Carolina: black subversion as main
    defense problem of, 555; demand for
    slave labor, 554; employment of
    Indians as slave catchers, 560–61, 562;
    harsh slave code, 555; pitting of
    Indians and blacks against one another,
    556–62, 566; policy of appeasing
    Cherokee, 558; system of Indian
    alliances, 555; use of black slaves as
    soldiers against Indians, 560
Southeast Asia, lack of usable information
    on urbanism, 129
Southeastern Archaeological Conference,
    viii
The Southeastern Geographer, 468–70
The Southeast In Early Maps (Cumming),
    468–70
Southern Anthropological Society: annual
    publication of Proceedings, 5; first
    proceedings, vii–viii; goals of Proceed-
    ings, 5–6; origins, 5; second annual
    meeting, 5
Southern Frontier, 509
Southern Highlander, 343. See also
    Appalachian culture

Southern Indian Boundary Line, 470–84,
    522; barrier beyond which white
    settlement was not allowed to extend,
    472; on the eve of the American
    Revolution, 471
Southern Indians: aboriginal sites, 509–
    10; archaeology of European contact,
    509–20; early maps as a source in
    reconstruction of landscapes, 466–84;
    erroneous assumption of socio-cultural
    isolation, 572–73, 583–84; European
    acculturation, 516, 517; excluded from
    histories of the Old South, 571–72;
    four major historical periods, 575–77,
    584; linguistics, 498–508; post-
    reconstruction religious developments
    among, 582–83; United Southeastern
    Tribes, 577
Southern mystique, 460
Southern peasant, 343
Southern pottery tradition, 397–411, 513,
    515; aboriginal, 511, 512; change in,
    408–10; during the Civil War, 406;
    dynastic regeneration, 408; Georgian
    "wagoners," 399; institutionalized
    identities peculiar to their own region
    from a very early time, 406; isolated
    shops with local markets, 407; lack of
    formal training, 407; low social
    position, 407; male potters, 406;
    utilitarian products, 408
Southern Protestant Ethic Disease, 412–
    17; ascetic prohibitions as absolute
    laws, 413; conversion hysteria, 413,
    415; fears derived from an authoritar-
    ian father, 415; guilt or shame from
    one or more discrete and traumatic
    lapses, 414; tendency toward violence,
    416
Southern Sociological Society, 5
Southern whites, of ante-bellum period,
    530–52; attitudes brought from
    English slums and jails, 544; crusade of
    planter elite to convince Southern
    people that slavery was a positive good,
    536; facing two exploited colored
    majorities, 555; fear of slaves, 461,
    554–55; non-plantation, ix, 542–52;
    relations with Indians, 460–61, 553;

technetronic society, 139
temple cities, 116
"temporary urbanization," 179n.3
Teotihuacan, 129, 193
Terrebonne Parish, Louisiana, 388
terreiros, 189
Territorial Papers (Carter), 526
territorial states, 128
thaumaturgic rural movements, 188
thermoluminescence, 523
Thompson, Edgar, 431n.1
Thompson, Sister, 308, 309, 310
thrill seeking behavior, 367–68
Thurnblad, Robert J., 12
Tierra del Fuego, 258
Timbuctoo, Mali, 205
Timucua, 499, 500, 504, 511, 512, 515
Tiou, 503, 504
Tocobago, 510
Tohopcka, 511
Tolliferro site, 488, 493
Tolman, Edward C., 283
Tonga, 177, 179n.2
tool inventory, aboriginal, 512
toothache, 90
Town Creek, 489
Towne, Charles, 510
trade, long-distance, 127–28
"Trail of Tears," 492
transcultural psychiatry, 30, 32
transformational grammar, role of
    universals in, 292n.5
transformationalists, 279
transitional city, 139
transitional sector, between city and
    countryside, 187
translation, complications of, 443n.3
transportation, 544
Transvaal complex, 168
"treed," 372
tribalism: six indices of, 172; in the urban
    context, 173–77
tribal social field, linking a rural micro-
    field with an urban micro-field, 178
tribute, 127
"tri-ethnic" communities, 592
Trigger, Bruce G., 517n.6
Trinidad Pampa, 164
Tschopik, Harry, 121

tuberculosis, 87
Tucker, Nathaniel Beverley, 536
tumors, 87
Tunica, 498, 499, 500, 501, 504, 510
Tunican, 500, 502
turcos, 190
Turner, Frederick Jackson, 544
Turner, Nat, 461, 536, 590
Turner, Victor W., 221, 380, 382, 383
Tutelo people, 489, 492, 493, 499, 500
"T.V." medicine, 72
Tybee Island, 562
Tyler, Stephen, 215, 278
Tylor, Edward B., 127, 263–64
typologies: "original sin" of physical
    anthropology, 256; urban, 204

ultimate cause, 84
Umbanda, 189, 191
underemployment, 186–87
Underhill Cherokee, 510
United Fruit Company, 194, 195, 196,
    197, 198, 200
United Southeastern Tribes, 577
United States Information Agency, 200
universal ethnography, 279
universal grammar, 279
Universal Negro Improvement Associa-
    tion (U.N.I.A.), 196, 197
universals, 286
University of North Carolina Medical
    Anthropology program, 66–67
untadukya, 89
Upland South Culture, 345
Upper Creek, 516
Upper Creek town, 511
Ur, 129
urban African population, hypothetical
    continuum of commitment to urban
    life, 174–75
urban anthropology, viii, 111–12; in
    crosscultural perspective, 113–24;
    defined, 206; failure to address
    methodological and theoretical issues,
    142–43; general outlook, 203–5; need
    to elicit native definitions of the city,
    205; need to focus on mobility, 170;
    "relevance" problem, 207–8; research
    strategies, 205–6; tendency to resort to

typologies with evolutionary implications, 204; tendency to treat urban
areas as if all were basically the same,
200; two major approaches to, 158
"urban ethos," 119
urbanism: destruction of environment,
127; problems of, 137; viewed in its
wider cultural context, 158
urbanization: as concentration and
scientific rationalism, 137; two basic
criteria, 171
urban laborer vs. urban resident, 169
urban micro-field: communication with
rural micro-field, 177; differences from
relations and institutions in rural
micro-field, 179
urban middle class, value orientation,
337–38
urban milltown, 353–59
"urban phenomenon," 158
urban political science, ethnocentrism,
203
"urban society," 114, 203
urban sociology, ethnocentrism, 203
urban studies: applied nature of, 136;
archeological contribution to, 126–40;
and social anthropology, 134–40
urban subcultural types, 136, 138
"urban tribalism," 172
U.S. Armed Forces Radio Station, 200
uterus, referred sensation, 98
Uwhaarrie ceramic traits, 493

Valentine, Charles, 228
"Valorware," 403
Van Gennep, Arnold, 70, 75, 424
Van Velsen, J., 177, 179n.2
Vaughan, Alden, 588
Veblen, Thorstein, 221
vecindades, 141, 143
Vedic therapy, in India, 63
venereal disease ("bad blood"), folk
remedies for, 73–74
Verrazano, Giovanni da, 469
vertebrate evolution, 258
Vidich, Art, 439
Viet Nam, 224
"village-city network," 180n.5
village therapy, in India, 63

Villa Nueva de la Boca del Monte, 194
Vinson, J. C., 585n.1
Virginia, 330; coal mining, 331; Southwest
triangle, 329
Virginia Snake plant (*Aristolochia serpen-
taria*), 73
Voget, Fred W., 267
Vogt, Evon Z., 71
Voice of America, 200
voluntary health insurance programs, 7
von Bismarck, Otto, 588
von Bonin, G., 486

Wagley, Charles, 118
Wagner, Günter, 501
Walcolids, 487, 488, 489, 490
Walker, Deward E., Jr., 29
Wallace, Anthony F. C., 378, 383, 384
Warner, W. Lloyd: *The Family of God*,
432n.2
Washburn, Sherwood L.: "*The New
Physical Anthropology*," 8, 257
Washington, George, 550
waterpower, 129, 130
Watson, J. B., 23
Watson, W., 171
Wauchope, Robert, vii
weak ego-structure, 32, 33
Weaver, Herbert, 343
Weaver, Thomas, 5, 6
Webb, Malcolm, vii
Webb, W. S., 487
Weber, Max, 120, 122, 412, 413
Webster, Thomas G., 10–11
Weisman, Avery D., 36
welfare state, 413
Weller, Jack: *Yesterday's People*, 330, 368
Wells, H. G., 223
Werner, Fred, 384
West, David, 502
West Africa: royal or palace city, 116,
122–23; urban conglomerate, 168;
voluntary associations, 176
West African kingdoms: ancestral shrine,
121–22; form of the city, 121–23
West Virginia, 330
Wharton, Vernon, 585n.1
Wheeler, Mortimer, 524
White, Leslie, 434

Whiteford, Andrew H., 146, 200
Whitehead, Alfred North, 292
White southerners. *See* Southern whites, of ante-bellum period
Whyte, William Foote, 443n.5
Willems, Emilio, 112, 206, 207
Willey, Gordon R., 128
Willis, William, 459, 461
Wilson, G., 179n.3
Wind and Water Revolution, 130
windmills, 130
Wineau Indians, 566
Winston, Sanford, 360, 366, 367
Winter, E. H., 34
Wintrob, R., 31–32, 34
Wirth, Louis, 134, 137
Wissler, Clark, 440
witchcraft beliefs: in Africans' relationship to the environment, 31; anthropological view, 29–30; association with paranoidal systems, 31; emotionally ameliorative, 29–30; and feelings of suspicion, fear, and hatred, 34–35; function in the maintenance of the personality system, 37–38; and guilt associated with forbidden incestuous wishes, 30; psychiatric view, 30–33; six main functions, 29
witches, 186
Wittfogel, Karl A.: "hydraulic empires," 120; model of cultural response to ecological factors, 128
Wittgenstein, Ludwig, 291
Witthoft, John, 511
Wittkower, E. D., 31–32, 32, 34

Wiyot, 502
Woccon, 499
Wolf, Eric R., viii, 217; *Anthropology*, 261; *Peasants*, 331, 342, 349, 350
Wolfe, Tom, 415
Wolff, Hans, 502, 503
women: African American, and pica, 96, 97–98; elite, of the Old South, 537; and geophagy, 96
Woodland site, 487
World Health Organization, 85
worms, 86
Worsley, Peter, 226
Wright, Richard, 594
Wright site, 487
Writi, 92
writing, and urban revolution, 127

Xangô, 189
Xhosa, in East London, 179n.1

Yadkin, 489, 493
Yankee Peddler, 321
Yap, P. M., 32
yaws-syphillis-endemic-syphillis, 63
Yemasee (language), 503
Yemassee War, 492, 554, 555, 560
yeomen, 551–52
York, Emmett, 585n.1
Yuchi, 492, 499, 500, 501, 504
yumu, 90, 91
Yurok, 502

Zambian mining centers, 173–74
Zona Bananera, Puerto Limón, 196